PAOLO UCCELLO

FRANCO and STEFANO BORSI

PAOLO UCCELLO

TRANSLATED BY ELFREDA POWELL

HARRY N. ABRAMS, INC., PUBLISHERS

LIBRARY OF CONGRESS CATALOGING-IN-PUBLICATION DATA

Borsi, Franco.
[Paolo Uccello. English]
Paolo Uccello / Franco and Stefano Borsi.
p. cm.
Includes bibliographical references and index.
ISBN 0-8109-3919-3
1. Uccello, Paolo, 1397–1475—Catalogues raisonnés. 2. Uccello, Paolo, 1397–1475—Criticism and interpretation. I. Borsi, Stefano. II. Title.
ND623.U4A4 1993
759.5—dc20 93-39788

Published in 1994 by Harry N. Abrams, Incorporated, New York
A Times Mirror Company

Printed and bound in Italy

CONTENTS

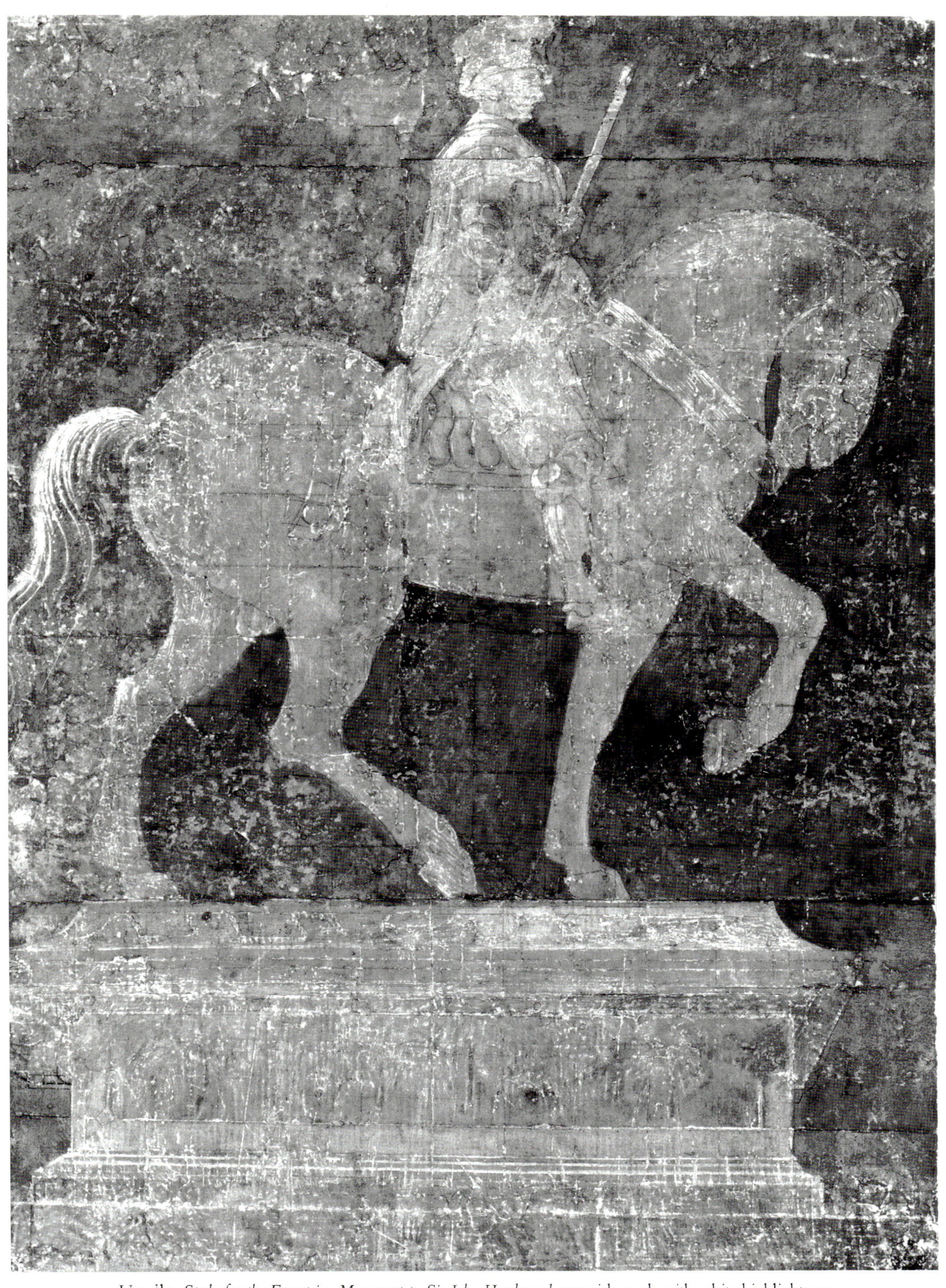

Uccello, *Study for the Equestrian Monument to Sir John Hawkwood*, greenish wash with white highlights on a purple background, 45 × 32 cm. Florence, Uffizi, Gabinetto dei Disegni, cat. fig. no. 31. This is one of the earliest examples of a drawing made on squared paper for transfer.

INTRODUCTION

The disturbing charm of the work of Paolo Uccello derives from his allegiance to Gothic Europe and his marginal position in Florence, the city which historians from the Renaissance onwards have seen as the centre from which a new language was disseminated. To that language Uccello remained alien, although probably not inflexibly opposed. It is no accident that Alberti does not include him in his list of artists in *De Pictura* (see p. 108) – a group of strong, contrasting personalities, united by a common historical role and more especially by belonging to the same generation.[1]

Paolo Uccello was born at the turn of the century, in 1397, twenty years after Brunelleschi. It was therefore natural that he should aspire to something other than the harsh, aggressive, popular realism of Masaccio and Donatello, and also natural that, in his conversion to the Classical ideal, he should interpret Classicism in his own way, more Romanesque than Roman, with original and inimitable results.

Historical syntheses have always sought to establish the existence of a deep conflict between Gothic and Renaissance: the very rivalries, the wars between Florence and Siena (or Florence and Milan), have been interpreted as reflecting the contrast in character between the Sienese, who remained faithful to a courtly, pleasant and rather lifeless Gothic, and the Florentines, who were bourgeois, realistic, commercial and austere. Uccello remains impossible to integrate, incomprehensible and inexplicable in this schematic dialectic.

Although the originality of his work has been recognized for a long time, and in astonishingly similar terms (Vasari as usual occupying a key position), Uccello has always been credited with a sort of split personality: a distinction is continually made between the intellectual and the artist. The originality of his scientific investigations into geometry and perspective has been acknowledged, and so too have his verve and the magical immediacy of his figurative '*imagerie*'. In the former, he extended the exploration of perspective begun by Brunelleschi, and achieved a new concept of space; while the latter derived from the traditional tendency of Gothic to escape from realism into the fantastic. Gothic and Renaissance are terms that are irremediably opposed and consequently, in Uccello's work, impossible to reconcile, in spite of his great blend of qualities as man, intellectual and artist.

Uccello himself has lent force to this interpretation, with the discrepancies between documents and commissions, his absences from Florence, his declaration to the

Cadastre that reads like a lament on poverty and old age,[2] with the eye-witness accounts that describe him as a secretive, introverted personality, a sort of foreshadowing of Leonardo's *solitudo*, an incomprehensible and uncomprehended protagonist in the attempt at a synthesis between art and science. For Vasari he was '*di sofistico ingegno dotato*' – gifted with subtle genius. If we consider what he meant by *sofistico*, we see that there is a negative tone to Vasari's judgment, an implication of intellectualism closed in upon itself, whereas Vasari, in his pragmatic way, prefers an 'opulent and serene' style, a felicitous creativity which Picasso encapsulated in his 'I do not search, I find' – rather than investigation or research. Here lies the explanation of that famous reproach made (according to Vasari) by Donatello to his friend Uccello, of 'forsaking certainty in favour of uncertainty': of deserting the certainties of realism and Albertian classicism, with the parallel between the Ancients and the Moderns which Alberti had been the first to establish, and instead committing himself to a process of renewal of tradition from the inside, heedless of its dogmatic rules, and, *de facto*, lacking any certainty.

This crippling thesis of the split between intellectual and artist continues even when, beginning with Cavalcaselle, we begin to understand that research into perspective does not conflict with pictorial representation, that science is not an obstacle to art. The charge of ambiguity persists in a subtler, less overt form until the 1930s with Lionello Venturi, Marangoni and Schlosser, and still persists today under Panofsky's influence, which emphasizes the symbolic value of perspective and evolves theories on styles from it (Francastel, White, Parronchi, Gioseffi). Experts have also 'dissected' Uccello, hoping – as with other leading Renaissance writers and artists – to go beyond schematic positions and clichés, to more thorough, philological studies, centred on his writings and his work. And there, with his gaps, his contradictions, his 'variousness' ('*vario*' Landino called him), Uccello offers fertile ground for controversies on attributions and unanswered questions in a catalogue which, it must be said, presents few certainties.

But whatever partial results can be gleaned and whatever stimulating interpretations can be made, there can be no synthetic judgment, no resolution to Uccello's historical position. This is even more the case for the *en artiste* interpretations proposed in the 1920s and 1930s by critics like Carrà or Soupault who attempted to use the reading keys of the avant-garde to interpret the past, and took as criteria – as they had for Giotto and Piero della Francesca – the '*valori plastici*' (plastic values), considered in isolation, of the 'style of the subject' (the iconology) and historico-documentary elements. *See note 112*

But even here the opposition between Gothic and Renaissance lingers, bypassed but not overcome, since one and the other of these two worlds, these two languages, possess their own very definite values – not without flagrant, blatant contradictions, such as Gothic realism or the fantastic imagery of the Renaissance. And there, at the centre, is Uccello, issuing contradictory signals which cause art historians to prune their catalogue vigorously and ask the same questions over and over again, to which stylistic analogies are only an inadequate answer. Uccello poses even stranger questions concerning dating: he challenges the apparently logical statement that, while it did not happen all at once, the humanist language of the Renaissance succeeded Gothic. To the idea of 'Gothic first', forced into crisis by the novelties of Renaissance perspective, he issues a firm denial with his own sequence of 'Gothic after'. Defeatist, appealing for sympathy, cheating on his tax, in that pitiful declaration to the Cadastre which bears no relationship to his actual circumstances, shifty when it comes to problems of his time, Uccello was brought by the length of his years to 'shut up shop' in the middle of the era of Lorenzo the Magnificent. By 1475 this had already undergone a year of austerity, even though its cultural trend towards 'Antiquity' – based on Alberti's theories – was not yet fully defined.

For this crippling historical concept to be overcome – and that is the purpose of this book – we must adopt a different approach to Uccello. We must study him from oblique angles. We must put his exploratory work back into its proper context, in a Florence that will appear quite different from the trite triumphalist cliché of a totally dominant Renaissance. This means 're-reading' Florence, viewing it as a coherent whole, with its urban fabric, its active building projects, its great architectonic and figurative themes. This is the Florence of 1403 – when Uccello was six years old – of which Leonardo Bruni wrote, in his *Laudatio* dedicated to the city, 'We see Florence so spotless and so neat that nowhere else can one find such a clean place.'[3] A little further on he added: 'But I return to the private citizens' houses which are conceived and constructed with much charm, beauty and nobility, and with singular magnificence. What finer or more delectable thing can there be than to see these palace portals, these halls and ceilings, these loggias, these dining-rooms, and diverse portraits? What more splendid than to see their great capacity for housing a huge number of people, the balconies, the arches, the vaults, the roof-timbers and richly ornamented roofs above? And that in many cases there are rooms for summer which are separate from rooms for winter? And with all this, the most beautiful chambers and sumptuous furnishings, gold, silver, elaborate fabrics, draperies and other fine embellishments of diverse and precious materials and of different colours.'[4]

noi veggiamo Firenze sì monda et tersa che in niuno altro luogo si trova cosa più netta . . . Ma io ritorno alle case de' particolari cittadini, le quali a delicie, a grande bellezza, a honore et a singulare magnificencia construtte ordinate et edificate sono. Qual chosa più bella o più dilettevole puote essere, che vedere l'entrate de' palazzi, le sale et solaii, le logie, le sale a mangiare, et diversi ritratti? quanto bella chosa è vedere la grandezza delle dette chose capace di molte genti, le balchonate, li archi et le volte et le travature, et i tetti sopra modo richi et ornati? et, quello che in molte chase si trova, le stanzie de la state spartite da quelle del verno? Et con questo, le bellissime camere, e' ricchi fornimenti, oro, argento, veste lavorate, drapparie et altri ornamenti di diverse et preciose materie et di varii colori?

In Florence at this time Gothic and Renaissance styles coexisted, as much in the typology of the houses as in the formal language of the churches and even in the

uno alto et nobilissimo palazzo, di grandissima bellezza et di fabricha meravigliosa, il quale nel primo aspetto agevilmente dichiara a che fine elli è edificato

Palazzo Vecchio – 'a tall and very noble palace, of very great beauty and marvellous construction, that clearly shows the purpose for which it has been built, from the very first glance'.[5] Gothic and Renaissance coexisted in orderly transitions, with an obvious coherence in the sense of space and a continuity in the manner of building, for which Brunelleschi, through his training, innovations and aspirations, became the prototypical figure. This coexistence continued right through to Lorenzo the Magnificent's era. During Piero the Gouty's time in office there is evidence of it in the Palazzo Medici chapel, in Benozzo Gozzoli's famous cavalcade in the *Adoration of the Magi*, a typical Late Gothic narrative. Later, young Lorenzo and his brother would take part in tournaments and write poems about hunting, in a quasi-historical concern to maintain the ideal of Chivalry. We must also look at the context of an aggressive, pragmatic merchant oligarchy, competing in international markets and European finance, but also tempered with Neo-Platonism and a love of Petrarch, and with esoteric anxieties and aspirations at this time of renewed interest in religious faith. Florence then was simultaneously élitist and popular, sombre and joyful, idealistic and small-minded, cultured and artisan. In so complex a reality, the picture of Uccello, which until now has been contradictory and strange, fits harmoniously into that expression of artistic and cultural pluralism that sprang from a vitality that would be difficult to conceive were we to insist on conventional ideological and aesthetic parameters.

With the Brancacci chapel recently restored, Masaccio can no longer be seen as the sombre, severe precursor of the Novecento[6] of Sironi and Rosai; his painting now appears closer to the bright, graceful work of Masolino. A further, contrasting example can be seen in Brunelleschi and Donatello, travelling together to Rome, then clashing violently with each other in the Old Sacristy of San Lorenzo, their respective approaches to Classicism revealing them to be diametrically opposed. Take yet another example: Michelozzo, described in a contemporary chronicle[7] as 'an all-round architect' ('*architettore di tutto*'), an expressive phrase that signified his willingness, his efficiency, an ability to conform to his patrons' wishes, yet with a certain clear-cut austerity that allowed room for his virtuosity in stonework, so characteristic of the ornament of Quattrocento Florence. Predominating in this mid-century period of painting was a tempered realism, a manner of telling stories that vividly documented contemporary life, and expressed the Florentines' satisfaction at being what they were: inheritors of and successors to a serene magnificence and wisdom and harmoniously exercised political power, which we see echoed in Alberti's golden rules of economy.[8]

This was the Florence in which Uccello lived and worked. We could say he occupied a central position, in the right place at the right time. He began his career polishing and cleaning Ghiberti's first doors, in the company of the most subtle mind, the most refined interpreter of that period of equilibrium between Gothic and Renaissance, a learned man, an enthusiast of geometry and perspective. From him, Uccello surely inherited the demon of research. 'I have always sought to understand the early processes,' Ghiberti wrote, 'how nature proceeds in itself, and in what manner I can approach it myself, how the species appear to the eye, how the virtue of vision comes into being and how the act of vision works, and how the theory of the art of statuary and painting should be practised'.[9] These are many of the themes to be found in Uccello's painting, though none of his theories was ever written down. It was not by chance that his studio was in Piazza San Giovanni, in the very hub of the city, close to the great building site of Santa Maria del Fiore. Here he worked on several occasions, each very important, whether it was on the monument to *Sir John Hawkwood*, or the stained-glass windows for the oculi of the cupola, at the very moment the great architectural epoch came into being, an event that would assure Florence a supremacy more lasting than any military victory.

sempre i primi processi ho cercato di investigare in che modo la natura proceda in essa e in che modo io mi possa appressare ad essa, come le spezie venghino all'occhio e quanto la virtù visiva adopera e come le cose visuali vanno e come la teorica dell'arte statuaria e della pittura si dovesse condurre.

Ill. pp. 168, 204, 205
Ill. p. 238

In 1436 Uccello could also be found in Santa Maria Novella, which is marked by the persistence of Gothic, and by the first manifestations of humanism, from the stay of Eugenius IV, the first humanist pope, to the construction of Alberti's façade. Uccello could also be found in the cathedral at Prato, where Michelozzo and Donatello collaborated. And with his *Battles* he was present in the great hall on the ground floor of the Medici palace, where Lorenzo the Magnificent governed and entertained. As a background to this cultivated princely figure, he painted glorious episodes in the war against the Visconti, using the chivalrous imagery of weapons and armour. In Lorenzo's own words, 'to copy and do as the other jousters sumptuously assembled on the Piazza di Santa Croce at great expense, where it seems to me close on ten thousand florins *di suggello* were spent, and although I am not very courageous when it comes to weapons and blows, I was given the highest distinction: that is to say a helmet embellished in silver, with the crest in the form of the god Mars.'[10]

Ill. p. 207ff.

Per seguire e far come gli altri giostrai in su la piazza di Santa Croce con grande spesa e gran sunto, nella quale trovo si spese circa fiorini diecimila di suggello, e benché d'armi e di colpi non fossi molto strenuo, mi fu giudicato il primo onore, cioè un elmetto fornito d'ariento con un Marte per cimiero.

Starting from a few firmly established reference points, when confronted with a catalogue subject to many interpretations and questions, we can discern to what point all the themes, lay and religious, abstract and naturalistic, epic and domestic, were subjected by Uccello to rigorous and original selectivity, which sometimes ran counter to the current mode, and nearly always had a polemical element in their connection with the world asserting itself around him. There remains at least one spectacular trace of this polemical element in the Signoria's refusal of his first version of *Sir John Hawkwood*. That he had to take it back may perhaps have been because the vertical foreshortening of horse and knight from bottom to top would not harmonize well with a large epic haut-relief made for orthogonal viewing; or it may have been that he had to abandon the abstract geometry of curves, so visible in the preparatory drawing, in favour of a more naturalistic style. Whether it was its pretensions to realism in the perspective construction, or, quite the opposite, its tendency to abstraction that may have displeased his patrons, from the very beginning of his public commissions, Uccello was opposed to the *communis opinio* that public patrons were naturally obliged to express. Such a polemical position, which can be found in all the themes Uccello embarked upon – a realistic treatment of nature, allegiance to Gothic traditions, to themes of architecture and the countryside, to the narration of 'stories' and even the vexed question of perspective, central to his endless explorations (which are perhaps overemphasized) – now needs to be considered in a meticulous and more closely argued manner by using a new approach that encompasses as yet unresolved philological questions.

CHRONOLOGY

* History and politics
** Architecture
*** Painting and sculpture
Life of Uccello

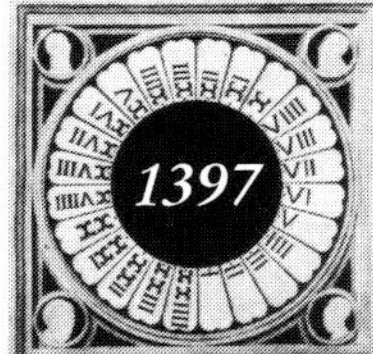

* The Florentine Republic routs the troops of Galeazzo Visconti, Duke of Milan, at Governolo. With the support of the humanist Coluccio Salutati, Chancellor since 1375, the first chair in Greek is founded at Florence and given to the scholar Manuel Cristoloras.
** To commemorate the victory over Milan, a decision is made to build the church of Sant'Agostino in Oltrarno, begun only in 1434, to the design of Filippo Brunelleschi, and dedicated to the Holy Spirit.
*** Lorenzo Monaco has been registered for a year as a member of the Guild of Saint Luke (the painters' guild in Florence) under the name of Piero di Giovanni.

Birth of Uccello (according to most of his declarations to the Cadastre), son of a barber-surgeon from Pratovecchio in Casentino (a citizen of Florence since 1373) and of Antonia di Giovanni Castello del Beccuto (married in 1387), who belonged to a well-to-do Florentine family from the parish of Santa Maria Maggiore.

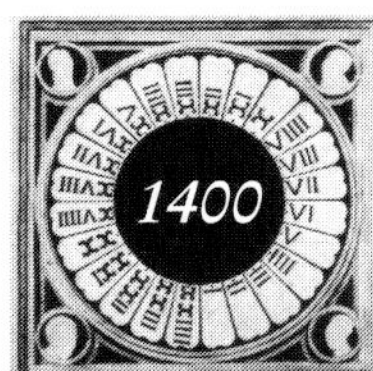

* The war with Milan continues. Outbreak of the plague in Florence.
** Fortifications are built around Florence at Signa and Castellina. Consolidation work is carried out at the Baptistery. Building of the chancel of San Pancrazio. The Ardinghelli family finance work on the façade of Santa Maria del Carmine.
*** Birth of Luca della Robbia and Antonio Averlino, who achieved fame under the name of Filarete. *Madonna of Humility* by Lorenzo Monaco (Moscow, Pushkin Museum); triptych of San Giusto at Montalbino by Cenni di Francesco di Ser Cenni; triptych of San Francesco at Arezzo by Niccolò di Pietro Gerini (Florence, Uffizi).

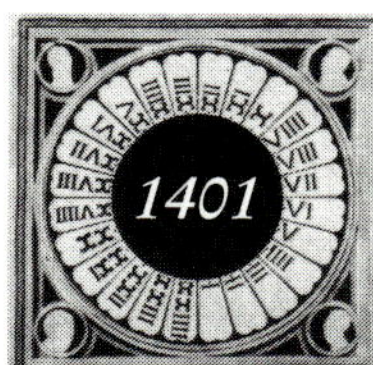

* Many of the Florentine nobility are condemned to exile: among them almost the entire Alberti family.
** The Arte della Lana (one of the richest and most influential guilds in Florence) launches a competition for the north door of the Baptistery, in which (according to Ghiberti) the following take part: Niccolò d'Arezzo, Niccolò di Pietro Lamberti, Simone da Colle, Filippo Brunelleschi, Jacopo della Quercia, Francesco di Valdambrino and Ghiberti himself, who wins.
*** Gherardo Starnina is in Spain. Birth of Masaccio. *Coronation of the Virgin* by Spinello Aretino (Florence, Accademia); Ambrogio di Baldese, a disciple of Orcagna, decorates Orsanmichele with frescoes.

* Leonardo Bruni writes his panegyric on the town of Florence (*Laudatio Florentinae Urbis*).
** Orsanmichele (begun in 1336) is completed; so is the Hospital of San Matteo (begun in 1388). Birth of Leon Battista Alberti in Genoa.
*** On his return from Spain, Starnina paints frescoes in the Chapel of Saint Jerome in the Carmine. Two important works by Lorenzo Monaco: *Man of Sorrows* (Florence, Accademia) and the Empoli triptych (Museo della Collegiata di Sant'Andrea). Ghiberti is working on his reliefs for the north doors of the Baptistery, in accordance with an agreement reached in 1403. Among his collaborators is 'Maso di Cristofano', probably Masolino.

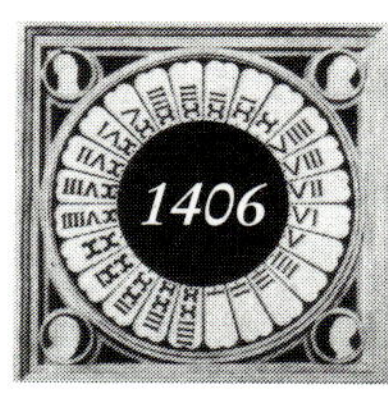

* Death of Coluccio Salutati. Florence succeeds in conquering Pisa.
** Work in full progress to complete the transepts and apse of the Duomo.
*** Donatello carves the 'Profetino' for the Porta della Mandorla of the Duomo. Birth of Filippo Lippi and Giovanni di Ser Giovanni, known as Lo Scheggia, brother of Masaccio. Statue of *Saint Luke* by Niccolò di Pietro Lamberti for the Magistrates' niche at Orsanmichele.

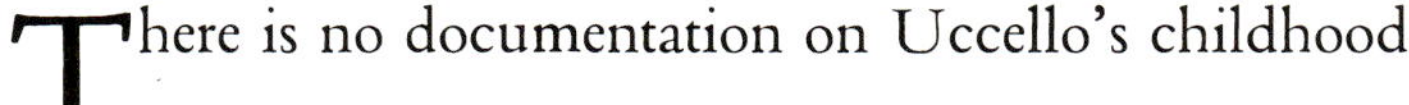

There is no documentation on Uccello's childhood.

* Ladislas, King of Naples and pretender to the throne of Hungary, sets out to conquer vast territories in Italy, occupies Rome, Perugia, and other cities belonging to the States of the Church.
** Building of the sacristy of San Pancrazio.
*** Donatello's marble *David* for Santa Maria del Fiore. Mariotto di Nardo,

Nardo di Cione's son-in-law, signs and dates the *Coronation of the Virgin* (London, National Gallery). Jacopo della Quercia begins the Fonte Gaia.

After the second agreement with Ghiberti for the north doors (1407), Uccello's name appears among those working with him. His youthfulness explains the modest remuneration for his first efforts: 'Paolo di Dono, workshop *garzone*, at 5 florins per annum, then at 7 florins. He had in total 20.10 florins.' He is thus employed in the most important studio in Florence while work is being done on the doors (not delivered and hung until 19 April 1424). At the studio, he mixes with Donatello, Masolino, Giovanni di Francesco – (perhaps Il Toscani) and probably Dello Delli.

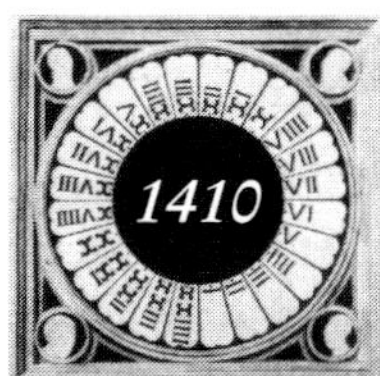

* Leonardo Bruni is elected Chancellor. Cortona is captured.
** After the completion of the north transept of the Duomo, work begins on the octagonal drum, to the design of Giovanni di Lapo Ghini.
*** Giovanni del Biondo's *Coronation of the Virgin* (Chantilly, Musée Condé). Frescoes by Cenni di Francesco in the Oratory of the Croce di Giorno in San Francesco at Volterra. Death of Spinello Aretino. Lorenzo Monaco's triptych for the Palazzo Davanzati, Florence.

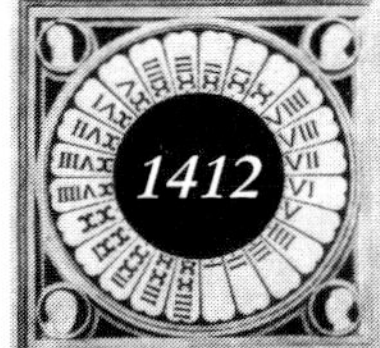

* Filippo Maria Visconti becomes Duke of Milan. War between Florence and King Ladislas of Naples, who, having surrendered Cortona to the Florentines, tries to recapture it.
** Repairs to the crypt of San Miniato al Monte. The Duomo changes its name from Santa Reparata to Santa Maria del Fiore.
*** Polyptych of San Lorenzo in Collina at Mezzomonte (Pozzolatico, Florence) by Lorenzo di Niccolò. Lorenzo Monaco's *Madonna of Humility* (Pisa, Museo Nazionale). Ghiberti supplies cartoons for the windows of Santa Maria del Fiore.

According to a recent suggestion (J. Beck 1980, p. 837), Uccello's decisive years of apprenticeship with Ghiberti occurred between 1412 and 1416. Uccello appears first as an assistant, aged about ten (fourteen at most), then at a more elevated level, as is indicated by his higher salary. The last mention in Ghiberti's accounts shows Uccello receiving 25 florins per annum: 'Paolo di Dono at 25 florins a year. He received in total 31.1.7 florins' – a sign of a substantial change in status.

* Sudden death of Ladislas of Naples at the height of his expansionist phase in northern Italy and his conflict with Florence. The Council of Constance deposes three anti-popes, re-establishing the *status quo* of 1378.
** Niccolò di Pietro Lamberti at work on the west doors of Orsanmichele.
*** Nanni di Banco completes the *Four Crowned Saints* for the Masons' and Carpenters' niche at Orsanmichele and begins the reliefs for the Porta della Mandorla of the Duomo. Lorenzo Monaco is painting the high altar of Santa Maria degli Angeli (*Coronation of the Virgin*, Florence, Uffizi).

In all probability Uccello becomes a member of the Guild of Saint Luke; the date, which is illegible in the document, is often interpreted as 1424 (D. Colnaghi 1928, p. 264), which is much too late. By the time he reaches his majority, he is an independent master, as is evidenced in the markedly higher salary Ghiberti pays him.

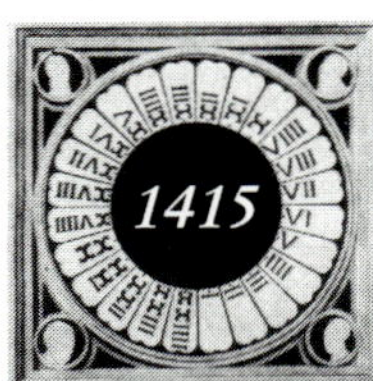

* Peace between Florence and Naples. The Medici family, from Cafaggiolo, begin their rise.
** The niche of the Arte di Calimala (Guild of Finishers and Dyers of Imported Fabrics) at Orsanmichele is created in late Gothic style.
*** Niccolò di Pietro Lamberti leaves for Venice. Presumed date of the birth of Piero della Francesca. The Office of Works (Opera) of the Duomo commissions statues of prophets for the campanile of Santa Maria del Fiore. Francesco d'Antonio signs and dates the Cambridge triptych (Fitzwilliam Museum). Probable date of the death of Niccolò di Pietro Gerini, formerly associated with Spinello Aretino.

While he is working in Ghiberti's studio, Uccello becomes a member of the rich and powerful Arte dei Medici e Speziali (Guild of Doctors and Apothecaries), to which all the great Florentine painters from Giotto onwards belonged; he features in it from 15 October 1415.[11]

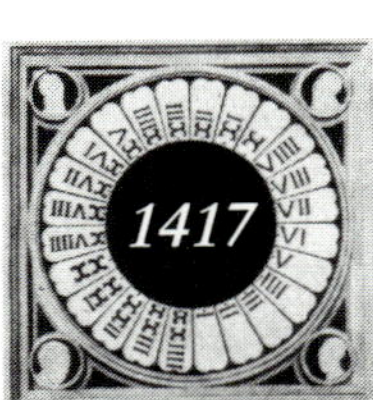

* The Great Schism comes to an end in November: the Roman Martin V Colonna is elected pope.
** Building of altars and chapels at San Pancrazio.
*** Donatello finishes *Saint George* for the Armourers' niche at Orsanmichele (Florence, Bargello); he applies his new principles of perspective in the predella. Masaccio arrives in Florence from Valdarno.

Uccello probably left Ghiberti's studio in 1416. The separation seems to have taken place without any heartbreak and with Ghiberti's agreement. In this initial obscure period of the artist's career, no work can be attributed to him with certainty. He is living in Florence in the parish of Santa Maria Nepoticosa, in the Corso degli Adimari (or dei Dipintori),[12] not far from Bicci di Lorenzo's renowned studio. The attribution to Uccello of the Lippi e Macia chapel frescoes (see cat. p. 341), for which eighteenth-century sources give the date 1416,[13] is probably to be rejected. We can only note its strict observance of Ghibertian principles if we compare it with Ghiberti's windows for the façade of the Duomo.[14]

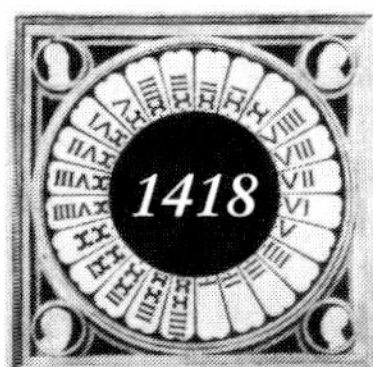

* Council of Constance ends. Hussite heresy condemned.
** The Arte di Calimala, which is financing the building of the Duomo, organizes a competition for the cupola, which Brunelleschi wins. The building of San Lorenzo begins. Works at Santa Trinita are financed by Palla di Nofri Strozzi, who had commissioned Ghiberti's reliefs for the north doors of the Baptistery at the time of the first agreement. Work begins on rebuilding Sant'Egidio, attached to the hospital of Santa Maria Nuova.
*** The Bankers' Guild commission the statue of *Saint Matthew* from Ghiberti for their niche at Orsanmichele. The young Fra Angelico makes his début as an illuminator in the circle of Lorenzo Monaco.

In this period, perhaps at the instigation of Ghiberti (with whom he seems to have kept in contact, and with whom he shares the Hispanicist and 'international' leanings made fashionable again in Florence by Starnina), Uccello embarks on several educational trips. These are not documented but, as can be deduced from stylistic signs, they must have been to Pisa (to see the Camposanto frescoes) and, probably at a later date, to Siena.

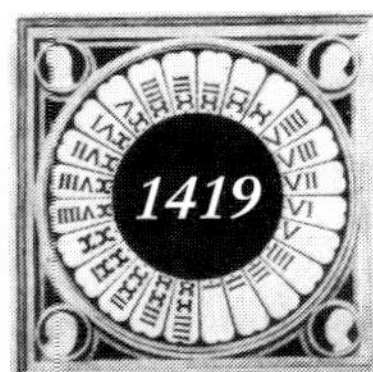

* The Anti-Pope John XXIII (Baldassare Cossa), whom Pope Martin V had made a cardinal, dies in Florence. He is buried in San Giovanni (the Baptistery).
** Construction of the Spedale degli Innocenti (the Foundling Hospital), financed by the Guild of Silk Merchants (Arte della Seta), begins. Programme of works at the convent of S. Maria Novella associated with the residence there of Martin V, with the participation of Ghiberti and the painter Giuliano d'Arrigo, known as Pesello. Sant'Egidio is consecrated.

*** Death of Pietro Nelli. Triptych of the Master of 1419 (Cleveland Museum of Art).

Uccello may have made his first visit to Siena, where he could have met Giovanni di Paolo and Sassetta, and studied the works of Ambrogio Lorenzetti, whom Ghiberti admired more than any other artist of the past.[15]

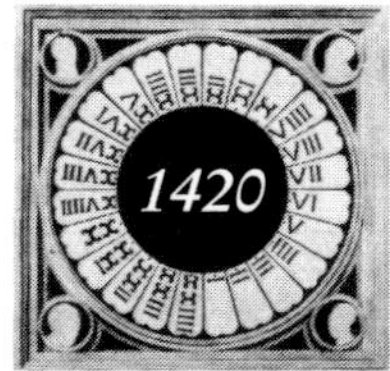

* Agreement with the Duke of Milan on reciprocal spheres of influence: Florence would control Tuscany and Romagna, while Visconti would control Lombardy and Genoa. Martin V makes his entry into Rome.
** Work on the cupola of the Duomo begins, directed by Brunelleschi, Ghiberti and Battista d'Antonio. Santa Maria Novella is consecrated.
*** Arcangelo di Cola da Camerino arrives in Florence. Birth of Bertoldo di Giovanni and of Benozzo Gozzoli. Donatello sculpts the *Marzocco* (the rampant lion symbolic of the city). *Coronation of the Virgin and Saints*, triptych signed and dated by Rossello di Jacopo Franchi (Florence, Accademia). The Bartolini Salimbeni chapel at Santa Trinita cannot yet be used for liturgical functions, probably because Lorenzo Monaco is working on its decoration.

In this period no work can be attributed to Uccello with certainty: only the Oxford *Annunciation*[16] and the lunette formerly above the door of the del Beccuto house (see cat. no. 1) – can be confidently associated with him between 1416 and 1420. These are obscure years, clouded by difficulties in finding a niche professionally in a city where very varied trends came into conflict at the beginning of the 1420s.[17]

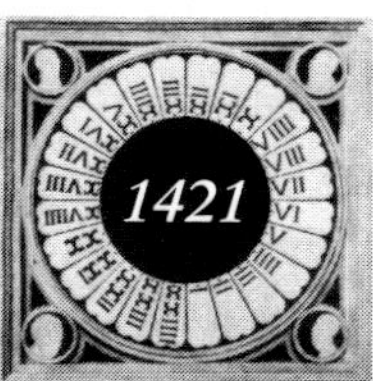

* Florence recaptures Livorno. Following Florentine military successes, Leonardo Bruni writes *De Militia*, in which he compares Greek, Roman and Florentine military institutions. Giovanni di Bicci de' Medici, born in 1366, is elected Gonfalonier of Justice.
** Work begins on the building of the Old Sacristy of San Lorenzo. The church of San Niccolò in Oltrarno is completed on the site of a Romanesque church. The apse of the Duomo is completed.
*** Premature death of Nanni di Banco. Birth of Andrea del Castagno. Mariotto di Nardo dates and signs the triptych of the parish church of San Leolino at Panzano. Bartolomeo di Fruosino illuminates the choral book of Sant'Egidio (Florence, Museo di San Marco).

Little definite information about Uccello until 1425.

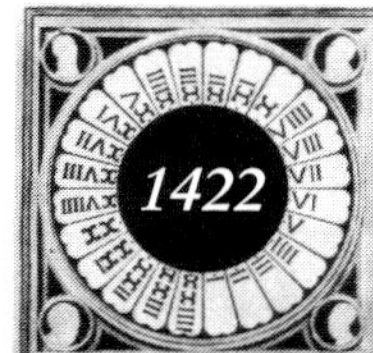

* There are an estimated seventy-two money changers in the Mercato Vecchio, a sign of the economy's growing prosperity. Hostility increases towards the Duke of Milan, who has taken possession of Brescia and Genoa, conceding Sarzana and other lands under Florentine influence to the Doge of Genoa, Tommaso di Campofregoso, on the basis of agreements made in 1420.
** The Carmine is consecrated.
*** Triptych of San Giovenale at Cascia near Reggello, the first dated and signed work by Masaccio (formerly in San Lorenzo, Florence). Arcangelo di Cola da Camerino leaves Florence as Gentile da Fabriano arrives. Birth of Benedetto da Maiano.

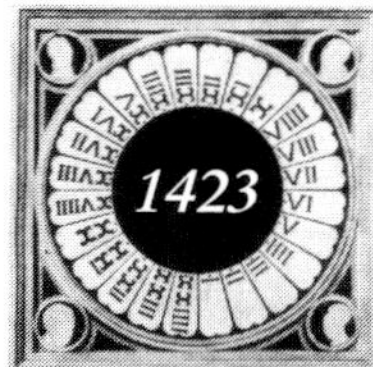

* Preparations for war with Filippo Maria Visconti: the Dieci di Balìa (a special magistrature responsible for military campaigns) are elected; new taxes are created, troops enlisted.
** A fire destroys the convent of Santa Croce; Brunelleschi, Michelozzo and Bernardo Rossellino are assigned the task of its reconstruction. Work on the Strozzi Chapel at Santa Trinita is completed.
*** Gentile da Fabriano's *Adoration of the Magi* for the Strozzi chapel in Santa Trinita (Florence, Uffizi), a masterpiece of International Gothic in Florence. Masolino's *Madonna of Humility* (Bremen, Kunsthalle). Triptych by the Portuguese artist Alvaro Pirez at Volterra (Pinacoteca Comunale). Donatello embarks on his five *Prophets* for the campanile of the Duomo, and the *Saint Louis of Toulouse* for Orsanmichele (Florence, Museo di Santa Croce).

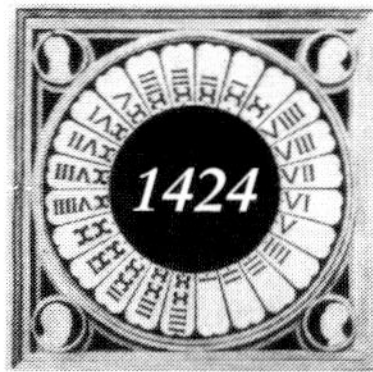

* Major defeat of the Florentines at Zagonara (28 July). Milanese troops enter Tuscany.
** The construction of the Foundling Hospital reaches the level of the architrave. Gilding and hanging of the north doors of the Baptistery. Brunelleschi is consulted on the cathedral at Prato.
*** Masolino begins the frescoes in the Brancacci chapel at Santa Maria del Carmine and in Santo Stefano at Empoli. Masaccio paints the *Sagrà* frescoes in the cloister of the Carmine. End of Andrea di Giusto's apprenticeship in Bicci di Lorenzo's studio. Ghiberti is entrusted with the 'Doors of Paradise' for the

Baptistery (finished in 1452). Michelozzo and Donatello begin the monument to John XXIII in the Baptistery. Ghiberti supplies the bronze reliefs for the font in Siena cathedral. Dello Delli, having finished work on the lunette of the portal of Sant'Egidio, is exiled from Florence and goes to Siena. Giovanni del Ponte is imprisoned for eight months for insolvency. The retable in Sant'Ambrogio, a collaboration between Masolino and Masaccio, is probably begun (Florence, Uffizi). At the end of the year, Ghiberti goes to Venice.

It is probable, but not certain, that Uccello was involved as early as 1424–5 in the decoration of the first bay of the Chiostro Verde at Santa Maria Novella, with *Stories from Genesis*. He embarks upon an adventure that will take him away from Florence for the next five, decisive years: following the death of the last local specialist, the Venetian Senate decides to approach a Florentine master to complete the mosaics of San Marco. Times are propitious: the two towns, linked by their common opposition to the Visconti of Milan, are on good terms. Uccello is unexpectedly chosen. He may possibly already have had some experience in this area, with the restoration of the Baptistery mosaics. This choice is probably due to the good offices of Ghiberti himself, who is in Venice during the winter of 1424–5.

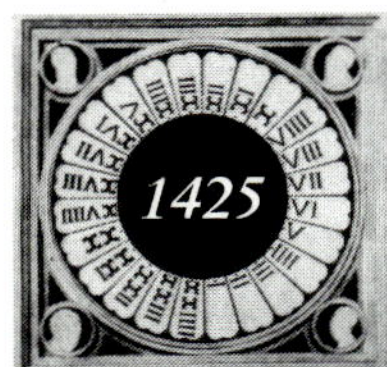

* Florence and Venice unite against Milan. Rinaldo degli Albizzi proposes a fairer allocation of taxes.
** Work on the Foundling Hospital slows down.
*** Having finished the polyptych for the Quaratesi chapel at San Niccolò Oltrarno (Florence, Uffizi), Gentile da Fabriano goes to Siena where he embarks on the polyptych for the Notaries' Guild. Donatello finishes the *Habakkuk* for the Office of Works of the Duomo and becomes an associate of Michelozzo. Masolino leaves for Hungary. Probable death of Lorenzo Monaco (or later, at the beginning of 1426). Birth of Alesso Baldovinetti. Contract with Ghiberti (2 January) for the Doors of Paradise.

The young Uccello goes to Venice, after making a will in favour of the hospital of Santa Maria Nuova.[18] The journey promises to be fraught with uncertainty because of the war with Milan. Uccello stays in Venice from 1425 to 1430. Of the work he carries out during this period, there is mention of a *Saint Peter Blessing* in mosaic (now lost) at the top left corner of the façade of the basilica of San Marco, done in 1425, perhaps as a sample to demonstrate his ability (see cat. p. 288).

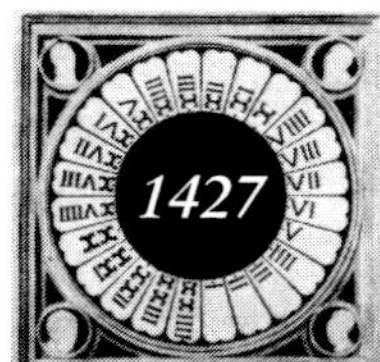

* In Florence the Cadastre tax collection is instituted, initiated by Giovanni di Bicci de' Medici, whereby ten citizens in each district assess the tax that each inhabitant must pay according to his capital.
** At the Foundling Hospital, where work has begun on the infirmary and the women's refectory, Francesco della Luna is re-elected to the Office of Works of the Duomo; Brunelleschi's name has not appeared for almost a year.
*** Masolino returns to Florence. Luca della Robbia becomes a member of the Arte della Lana (Wool Manufacturers' Guild). Deaths of Gentile da Fabriano and Lorenzo di Bicci.

Uccello is still in Venice and it is a relation (possibly Deo di Deo del Beccuto) who makes his declaration to the Cadastre by proxy: 'He left more than two years ago by the grace of God and is now in Venice.'[19]

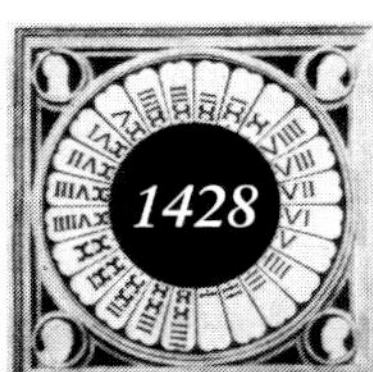

* Peace with Milan. Death of Giovanni di Bicci de' Medici. His son Cosimo (born in 1389) takes over the running of the family's affairs.
** The Old Sacristy of San Lorenzo is completed. Brunelleschi begins work on the design for Santo Spirito, which will be a long time in building.
*** Death of Masaccio. Birth of Giovanni di Francesco del Cervelliera. Masolino goes to Rome. Michelozzo signs the contract for the external pulpit of Prato cathedral in his and Donatello's names.

There is no information on Uccello's stay in Venice.

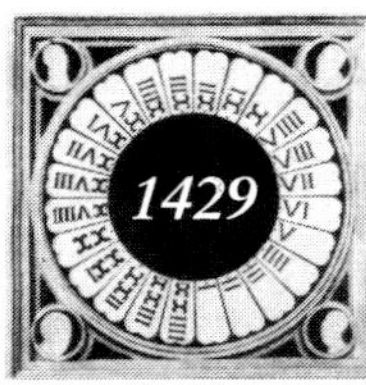

* Paolo Guinigi, *Signore* of Lucca, allied to the Visconti, maintains an ambiguous political posture towards Florence. Capture of Volterra. The campaign against Lucca begins in November, sustained by the Medici and Rinaldo degli Albizzi. On 10 December, the Dieci di Balìa are nominated to manage the war.
** Brunelleschi, Ghiberti and Battista d'Antonio are asked for a plan to complete the renovation of the Duomo, which will ultimately be Brunelleschi's sole responsibility. The decorative scheme for thirty-two windows for the apse of the Duomo begins.
*** Death of Ambrogio di Baldese. Birth of Mino da Fiesole. Giovanni dal Ponte takes on Smeraldo di Giovanni as a partner to fresco the Chapel of the

Crucifix at Santa Trinita. Francesco d'Antonio paints the organ case at Orsanmichele and possibly (the date is not very legible) the *Madonna della Cintola* in the parish church of Santi Vito e Modesto at Loppiano near Incisa Valdarno (Florence).

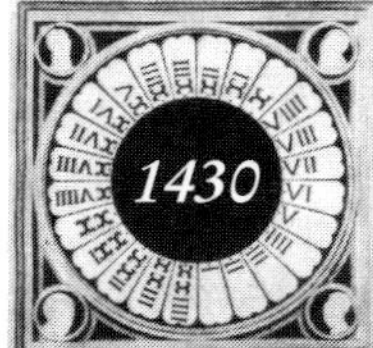

* War between Florence and Milan and attempt to lay siege to Lucca, in which Brunelleschi takes part.
** Brunelleschi perfects a system of chains intended to reinforce the Gothic vaulting of the nave in the Duomo. Francesco della Luna departs from Brunelleschi's design for the Foundling Hospital. Building begins on the Pazzi chapel in the cloister of Santa Croce.
*** Death of Giovanni Toscani. Bicci di Lorenzo paints the fresco of the *Virgin and Child with Saints* of the Porta San Giorgio in Florence. Donatello leaves for Rome. Completion of the font of Siena cathedral.

From the little evidence we possess, it seems that this is Uccello's last year in Venice. It is perhaps possible to see a link between his work in Venice this year and a second trip to Venice by Ghiberti (G. Fiocco, *Dedalo*, 1927–8, p. 346; R. Krautheimer 1956, p. 5).

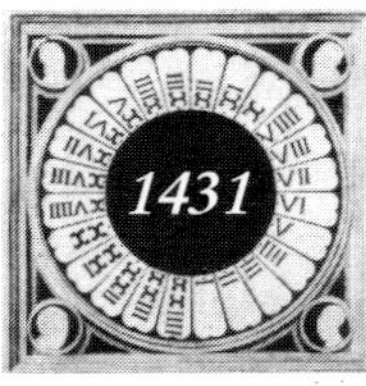

* The Venetian Eugenius IV is elected pope. The war against Lucca continues without success. The Duke of Milan sends the *condottiere* Niccolò Piccinino to Tuscany. The Florentines enlist Micheletto Attendolo da Cotignola.
** The Benedictine convent of the Badia at Florence is being remodelled: the two-storeyed Chiostro degli Aranci is built.
*** Luca della Robbia begins the *Cantoria* (choir gallery) for the Duomo. *Coronation of the Virgin* by Mariotto di Nardo (Florence, Acton Collection). Masolino finishes the frescoes at San Clemente in Rome.

Uccello returns to Florence at the end of 1430 or the beginning of 1431. On 31 January he presents his declaration to the Cadastre in person, mentioning several possessions and giving his age as thirty-three.

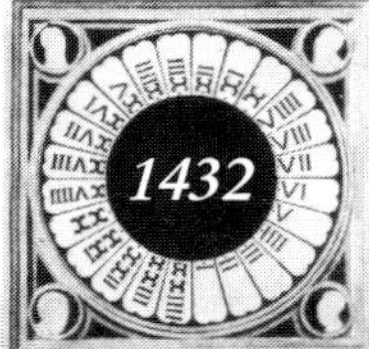

* Death of Niccolò da Uzzano. In June the troops of the Sienese and Visconti, led by Bernardino Ubaldini della Ciarda, are attacked by the Florentine troops of Niccolò Mauruzi da Tolentino: this is the battle of San Romano, of which the outcome is uncertain, but which Leonardo Bruni will greet as the triumph of Florentine republican virtues. The decisive element will be the intervention of Micheletto Attendolo da Cotignola, whom the Milanese had underestimated because his contract (*condotta*) had formally expired. The two winning *condottieri* are allied to the Medici, now openly ambitious politically.

** A plan for the lantern of the cupola of the Duomo is commissioned from Brunelleschi.

*** Birth of Giuliano da Maiano. Filippo Lippi's frescoes at the Carmine (partially preserved) are thought to date from this year: these constitute his first known work. The competition for the reliquary shrine of Saint Zenobius at Santa Maria del Fiore is won by Ghiberti. Masolino has finished the Palazzo Orsini cycle at Montegiordano in Rome, and paints a fresco in the church of San Fortunato in Todi.

Immediately after his return to Florence, Uccello must have sought an important commission from the Office of Works of the Duomo, who write on 23 March to Pietro Beccanugi, '*oratore communis florentie*' (Florentine ambassador) in Venice, for information on Uccello's work as a '*magistro musayci*' – a master of mosaics. It is an important document: not only does it give proof of Uccello's Venetian work, but it also shows that that work was little known in Florence. The letter tries in particular to obtain information that would determine the financial value of his work, with a view to a commission (of which nothing would come at the time). Uccello is probably being backed by Ghiberti for work on the interior decoration of the Duomo. The Office of Works is indeed also seeking information on the cost and availability of Venetian glass (see below, under 1443). No works of Uccello can be dated or documented securely to this period: possibilities are the Melbourne *Saint George* and Karlsruhe *Adoration*, and the lost fresco of the *Four Elements* on the vault of the Peruzzi loggia, which derives in part from Masolino's in the Orsini Palace in Rome.

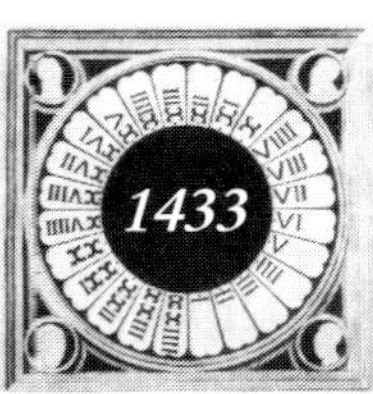

* Peace treaty of Ferrara between Milan and Florence (and Venice). In September a group of Florentine aristocrats, led by Rinaldo degli Albizzi, succeed in exiling the Medici for a period of ten years: Cosimo is imprisoned, then exiled to Padua. Birth of Marsilio Ficino.

** Decision taken to have stained-glass windows in the eight oculi of the drum

of the Duomo; Brunelleschi is in favour. The Camaldolites buy the land on which the church of Santa Maria degli Angeli will be built. Rossellino is working at the Oratorio della Misericordia at Arezzo.
*** Fra Angelico's first dated work, the *Tabernacle of the Linaioli* (Linen Weavers' Guild). The frame is based on a design by Ghiberti. Last documentary reference to Francesco d'Antonio. In November Donatello, who had returned from Rome, signs a contract for the second *Cantoria* of the Duomo (Della Robbia is working on the first). Domenico di Bartolo signs and dates the *Madonna of Humility* (Siena, Pinacoteca). The Office of Works of the Duomo commissions the first stained-glass window for the drum from Ghiberti.

On 31 May, in a declaration to the Cadastre, Uccello gives his address as a rented house in Campo Corbolini in Florence. Among the works that can be placed in this period (probably before 1434) are three Franciscan Stories on the inside of the façade of Santa Trinita, an important enterprise which is not documented but is remarkable because it is the only one, apart from the scenes in the Chiostro Verde, to be mentioned by Antonio Manetti.[21]

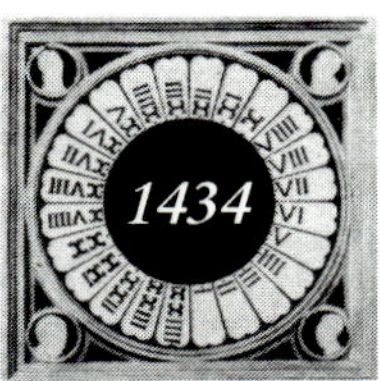

* In September the sentence of exile passed on the Medici is revoked. Cosimo returns to Florence and with popular support exiles his principal political adversaries: the Albizzi, Palla Strozzi, Felice Brancacci, the Ardinghelli and the Peruzzi. Uprising against the Pope in Rome: Eugenius IV stays in Florence, at Santa Maria Novella, until 1436. There are also uprisings in Bologna, supported by the Duke of Milan. Florence and Venice send troops, led by Gattamelata and Tolentino who are beaten by the Visconti's *condottiere*, Niccolò Piccinino, at Imola (on 28 August). The *condottiere* Francesco Sforza is elected as Gonfalonier of the Church in March; in November the Pope, in Florence, renews his agreements with Francesco Sforza.
** Private chapels are being built along the nave of San Lorenzo. Brunelleschi draws up plans for the Rotonda of Santa Maria degli Angeli. Maso di Bartolomeo collaborates with Donatello and Michelozzo in work on the pulpit at Prato.
*** Filippo Lippi is in Padua. Bicci di Lorenzo, *Visitation* (Velletri, Museo Capitolare). Alvaro Pirez, *Madonna and Child* (Brunswick, Herzog Anton Ulrich Museum). Cosimo de' Medici commissions Donatello to execute the

stucco decoration of the Old Sacristy of San Lorenzo. Andrea di Lazzaro Cavalcanti, known as Il Buggiano, works on the tomb of Giovanni de' Medici and his wife, destined for San Lorenzo.

Uccello's professional life, not documented until now, is going well enough: on 21 April with his first earnings he buys a house in Via della Scala. Among the probable works of this period are the Benedictine Stories in the cloister of Santa Maria degli Angeli (now lost), which showed 'great *disegno* and many felicities'.[22] The cycle falls within the context of works promoted by the Father General of the Order of Camaldolites, the humanist Ambrogio Traversari, probably between 1434 and 1437, when Brunelleschi abandoned work on the Rotunda of Santa Maria degli Angeli and echoes of Uccello's paintings can be found in the frescoes of the Chiostro degli Aranci at the Badia, attributed to the Portuguese Giovanni di Consalvo (1436–9). It is more difficult to establish the chronology of Uccello's frescoes at the Lelmo hospital, which are the first works mentioned by Vasari.[23] It must be emphasized that during these years (from about 1431) the provost of the hospital was Girolamo Traversari, Ambrogio's brother, from which one might assume that these two commissions from Camaldolite sources came close together. But we must not rule out the possibility that the house was purchased with the first payments for the Prato frescoes. Here, Uccello once more takes up the question of 'attitudes', already raised by Starnina in the Carmine (see Vasari[24]). The purchase of property forms part of his declaration to the Cadastre in 1442.[25] The following year, Andrea di Giusto is at Prato, continuing the cycle begun by Uccello (see cat. no. 10). Furthermore, in 1435 the death of Niccolò da Tolentino and his solemn funeral may have persuaded Cosimo to commission a work to commemorate his victory at San Romano. It is here suggested (see cat. no. 14) that this project was intended for the earlier house of the Medici and not for the palace designed by Michelozzo.

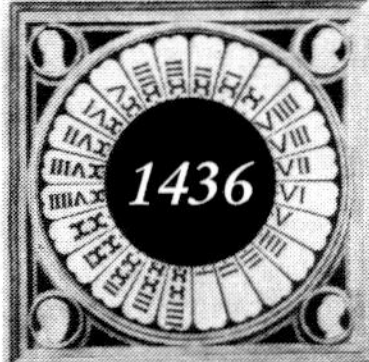

* In April Eugenius IV goes to Bologna. In May Genoa, where there had been an uprising against the Visconti in 1435, becomes Florence's ally. In October Niccolò Piccinino's mercenaries reach Lucca where they threaten Florentine territory. The Pope attempts mediation. In a state of uncertainty, Florence confronts the enemy troops without formally declaring war.

** The masonry of the cupola of the Duomo is complete; it is solemnly consecrated on 25 March by Eugenius IV.

*** Leon Battista Alberti, *De Pictura*. Fra Angelico, *Lamentation over the Body* *of the Dead Christ*, also known as the *Deposition* (Florence, Museo di San Marco). Fresco of the *Virgin with Six Saints* by Paolo Schiavo in San Miniato al Monte. Triptych by Andrea di Giusto in Sant'Andrea at Ripalta (Figline Valdarno, Florence).

By now Uccello had almost certainly finished the fresco in Santa Maria (later San Martino) alla Scala, which is remarkable for its perspective with two vanishing points, which may have been inspired by the oblique perspective of Brunelleschi's second experimental panel.[26] The monument to the *condottiere* Sir John Hawkwood in the cathedral marks the point at which Uccello becomes totally at ease with the climate of humanism in Florence. The *Hawkwood* confirms Uccello as a 'public' painter: after Masaccio's *Trinity* it is the most deliberate expression, on a monumental scale, of the new developments in perspective. It is hardly surprising that Albertini in 1510 referred to 'the terre-verte horse by the hand of Masaccio': the error in attribution is significant.[27] It is the first signed, dated and documented work by Uccello. He is asked to repaint; but the fact that the Office of Works of the Duomo chose him for this second version and undertook to pay for both rules out the suggestion that he was held at fault.

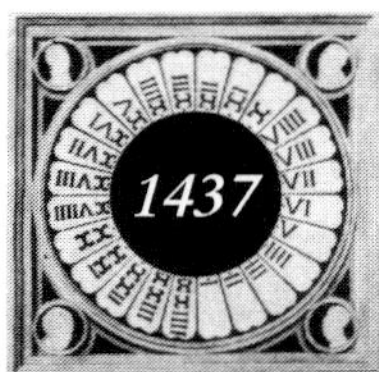

* The Council for reconcilation between the Eastern Orthodox and Roman Catholic Churches is transferred from Basel to Ferrara. In February, Florentine troops led by Francesco Sforza oblige the Visconti troops led by Piccinino to abandon the siege of Barga. The Venetian troops of Giovan Francesco Gonzaga attack in Lombardy, thus forcing the Duke of Milan to recall Piccinino's militia. Gonzaga goes over from Venice to the service of Visconti. Florentine military pressure against Lucca.

** Work begins on the Dominican convent of San Marco, financed by Cosimo de' Medici. Work on the Rotunda of Santa Maria degli Angeli is abandoned for lack of funds. The first stained glass is put in place in one of the oculi of the Duomo: the *Coronation of the Virgin*, the cartoon for which was drawn by Donatello.

*** Death of Giovanni dal Ponte. Filippo Lippi's first dated work: the *Virgin and Child* of Corneto-Tarquinia (Rome, Galleria Nazionale d'Arte Antica), painted for Giovanni Vitelleschi, Bishop of Florence. Andrea di Giusto's triptych, *Madonna del Sacro Cingolo* (Florence, Accademia), with echoes of Fra Angelico and of Uccello's cycle at Prato.

The date 1437 incised on the *Adoration* in San Martino Maggiore at Bologna is the *terminus ante quem* for this important fresco. The facts are not documented; the commission may be due to the presence in the city of Eugenius IV, who had came there from Florence. While apparently later than the *Hawkwood*, the fresco returns to earlier stylistic characteristics.

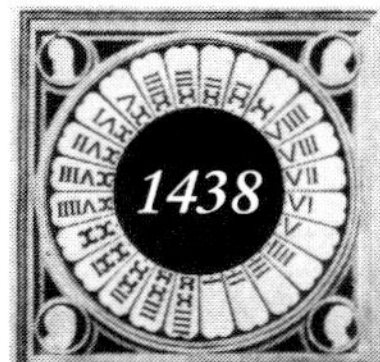

* The Emperor of Constantinople, John Paleologus, arrives in Ferrara accompanied by Joseph, Patriarch of Constantinople. In April Cosimo is in Venice trying to persuade the Doge to renew the agreement with Francesco Sforza. Peace between Florence and Lucca.
** The first architectural alterations at the Santissima Annunziata. At the Duomo, Luca della Robbia's *Cantoria* is finished.
*** Filippo Lippi paints the Barbadori altarpiece (Paris, Louvre). Domenico Veneziano must have known of this commission: he writes to Piero, Cosimo de' Medici's son, from Perugia to try to obtain a commission for a religious work. Death of Jacopo della Quercia. Work completed on the pulpit for Prato cathedral. Fra Angelico is in Cortona.

During this period Uccello finishes the Jacquemart-André *Saint George* (Paris) and the Medici *Battles*.

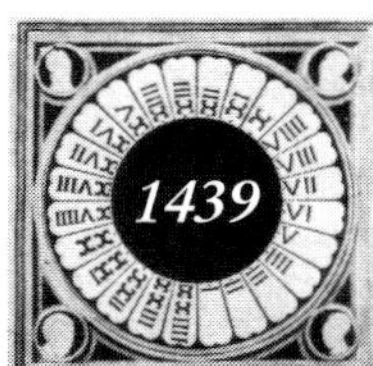

* The Council moves from Ferrara to Florence: in July, publication of the declaration of ecclesiastical reconciliation. Piccinino and Gonzaga, in the pay of the Duke of Milan, advance on Venice. In September, Venetian naval defeat on Lake Garda. In November, the Venetian army defeats Visconti's troops under Piccinino near Pescara.
** The Signoria decide to use some of the revenues from the salt tax to finance the construction of Santo Spirito. At San Marco the first phase of work is completed.
*** Domenico Veneziano begins the frescoes at Sant'Egidio assisted by the young Piero della Francesca. Birth of Cosimo Rosselli. Rossello di Jacopo Franchi, *Coronation of the Virgin* (Siena, Pinacoteca). Lorenzo di Pietro, known as Il Vecchietto, is documented as being present in the city: he has returned after collaborating with Masaccio at Castiglione Olona.

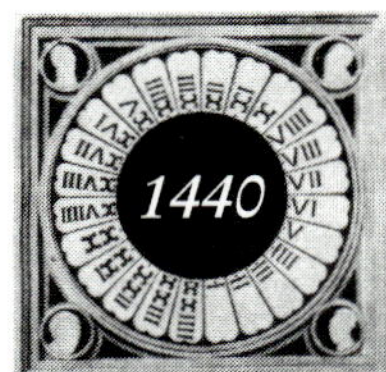

* At Anghiari, important Florentine victory over Milanese troops and exiles of the Albizzi faction which reinforces Cosimo de' Medici's position. Gattamelata, the Venetian *condottiere*, suffers a stroke.
** Antonio Manetti is working on the wooden cupboards (*armari*) in the Sacristy of the Mass at Santa Maria del Fiore, where Andrea di Lazzaro Cavalcanti, known as Il Buggiano, is finishing a marble lavabo. Maso di Bartolomeo is working at Prato.
*** Andrea del Castagno paints the fresco of the *Hanged Men* at the Bargello (now lost), which depicts the exiled Florentine leaders defeated at Anghiari. Bicci di Lorenzo, *Annunciation* at Sant'Arcangelo di Legnaia. Death of Masolino.

The third panel of the *Battle at San Romano* (Paris, Louvre) probably dates from this time. The four *Battles* (now lost) painted by Uccello in the Bartolini house in Valfonda, described by Vasari and crudely restored in the sixteenth century by Giuliano Bugiardini (see cat. no. 18), certainly postdate the victory at Anghiari.

* New Florentine victory at Montaperti, and peace treaty of Cavriana between the Duke of Milan and the anti-Visconti league to which Florence belongs, thanks to Francesco Sforza's mediation. Marriage of the latter with Bianca Maria Visconti, who brings the town of Cremona with her as a dowry.
** Cosimo de' Medici undertakes the cost of building San Lorenzo, for which the plans are revised. Brunelleschi stops working there.
*** Presumed date of Fra Angelico's retable in San Marco.

No definite facts about Uccello, who now seems very interested in Donatello's work. Proof of this phase is the Dublin *Madonna and Child*, which must date from the years 1440–42.

* In Naples, Alfonso of Aragon deposes René of Anjou, supported by Florence. Cosimo de' Medici reforms taxes, replacing the Cadastre by the *Arbitrio*, based on the revenues of the richest merchant class. In July, René of Anjou goes to Florence, and in the autumn to Marseille.
** Consecration of the Dominican convent of San Marco. Antonio di Betto begins his long career on the building site of San Lorenzo. A decision is made to continue glazing the oculi in the Duomo.

*** Fra Angelico paints his *Crucifixion* in the chapterhouse of San Marco. Andrea del Castagno is working in Venice. Birth of Benedetto da Maiano. Lorenzo Ghiberti delivers the shrine of St Zenobius for the Duomo, commissioned ten years before.

New declaration to the Cadastre (*Arbitrio*), by Uccello, which mentions the acquisition of a house in Via della Scala, in the parish of Santa Lucia d'Ognissanti. He says he is forty years old. He also declares a property at San Stefano a Ugnano, near Settimo (not far from Ghiberti's mansion), and mentions he is renting a studio in Via delle Terme, near Brunelleschi's Palazzo di Parte Guelfa.

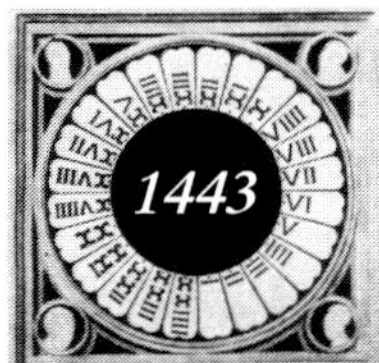

* Florence clashes with Alfonso of Aragon over the throne of Naples. In June, Annibale Bentivoglio drives out Piccinino, the Visconti *condottiere*, and re-establishes his family's sovereignty in Bologna. Florence is in league with Venice and Milan against Naples.

** Foundation of the monastery of Santa Monaca. Ghiberti provides three cartoons for the windows of the drum of the Duomo. At the Santissima Annunziata, special wooden tablets are installed in the nave in order to exhibit the numerous votive images in wax. Work begins on the marble pulpit at Santa Maria Novella, ordered by the Rucellai family and commissioned from Buggiano.

*** Buggiano's tabernacle of the Holy Sacrament in the Duomo. Donatello leaves for Padua. Stained-glass windows in the oculi of the Duomo from cartoons by Ghiberti: *Ascension, Agony in the Garden* and *Presentation in the Temple*. Domenico Veneziano and Bicci di Lorenzo are working on the frescoes at Sant'Egidio, while Piero della Francesca has already returned to Sansepolcro. Fra Angelico is bursar ('*sindicho*') of the convent of San Marco; the high altar of the church is consecrated by Eugenius IV on the feast of the Epiphany.

Uccello provides cartoons for stained glass in three oculi of the Duomo. The decision to have stained glass goes back to 1433, after Florence had asked Venice for information on the cost of glass and on Uccello's salary: '*et an de vitreis potest haberi et reperiri et cuius pretii sunt*'.[28] Afterwards the work advanced slowly (only one window was finished, in 1437, from a cartoon by Donatello) until January 1443 when a committee, of which Brunelleschi and Ghiberti were members, voted by a large majority to continue the cycle. Uccello provided cartoons for the *Nativity*, the *Ascension* (actually the *Resurrection*) and the *Annunciation*, removed in 1828 (see cat. under no. 20). The *Nativity*, now much restored, was made by the glazier Angelo Lippi, but Uccello was asked for another cartoon for the glazier Carlo Zati, as if the Office of Works of the Duomo wanted to guard against possible defections of rare and expensive master glaziers. The fact that his work was 'translatable' led to Uccello obtaining other commissions and having a long collaboration with the master Bernardo di Francesco who, from 1439, became the official supplier and chief restorer of windows in the service of the Duomo, a solid monopoly which lasted many years. The cartoon of the *Ascension* was paid for on 2 May and Uccello received 40 *lire* for the *Nativity* on 5 November.

At the same time, the Office of Works commissioned him to paint a clock face in fresco on the inner wall of the façade. The heads, in accentuated perspective, highlighted like 'fencers' (in Filarete's phrase) in bronze in the manner of Donatello, possibly depict the Evangelists; they were interpreted as Prophets in a replica by Giovanni di Francesco framing a *Virgin* (formerly in the Kaiser Friedrich Museum in Berlin).[29] A first version of Uccello's fresco is completed on 22 February and the finishing touches paid for on 2 April: '*pro dorando stellam oriuoli et pro dorando una pallam in punta razi, et pro remuneratione sui laboris in mictendo d'azuro campum ubi manet stella*'; the clock hand was in the form of a comet, as in the *Nativity*, and was modelled on that when it was restored in 1969.

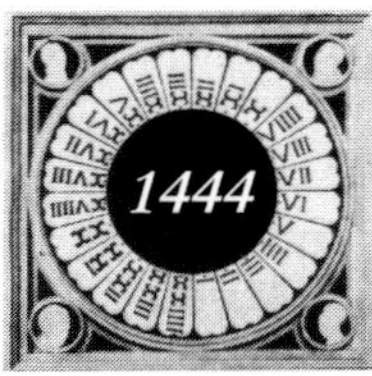

* Cosimo de' Medici persuades the Florentines to form a special council (Balia) with extraordinary powers. Death of Leonardo Bruni; the post of Chancellor of the Republic falls to the humanist Carlo Marsuppini, who is allied to the Medici.

** Work begins on the construction of the Palazzo Medici in Via Larga, to a design by Michelozzo. Work also begins on the apse of the Santissima Annunziata, again to a plan by Michelozzo. Consecration of Santa Croce, of which the façade is still unfinished. Foundation-laying ceremony at Santo Spirito.

*** Bernardo Rossellino begins the monument to Leonardo Bruni at Santa Croce, Parri Spinelli's *Crucifixion* at the convent school of Santa Caterina at Arezzo. Andrea del Castagno has returned to Florence where he becomes a member of the Guild of Doctors and Apothecaries; he is paid for a cartoon intended for one of the oculi of the Duomo.

Further documented payments to Uccello for the stained glass of the oculi: on 7 January '*pro suo labore in pingendo unum oculum factum per dictum Bernardum*' (i.e., the *Resurrection* executed by Bernardo di Francesco)[30] and on 18 February '*pro solutione unius designe facti in quo est ymago Anuntiationis virginis Mariae*'.[31]

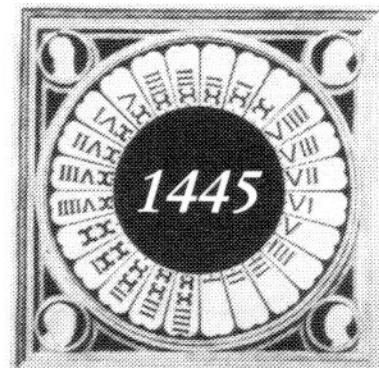

* Florence and Venice support Federico da Montefeltro of Urbino against Sigismondo Malatesta of Rimini, who is supported by Milan and Naples. Riots in Romagna and in the Marche. At Bologna, Annibale Bentivoglio, *Signore* of the city, is assassinated.
** Cosimo de' Medici finances the construction of the novitiate of Santa Croce, probably to a design by Michelozzo. Luca della Robbia begins work on the bronze doors of the sacristy of the Duomo.
*** *Sacra Conversazione* by Domenico Veneziano for Santa Lucia de' Magnoli (Florence, Uffizi). Having finished the decoration of the convent of San Marco, Fra Angelico goes to Rome. Birth of Sandro Filipepi, better known as Botticelli. On 25 February, the last stained-glass window is put in place in the oculi of the Duomo. This is the *Presentation in the Temple*, from a cartoon by Ghiberti.

On 28 January Uccello is paid by the Office of Works of the Duomo '*pro ristoro et additione quod fit sibi pro suo labore picture duorum oculorum*', – for retouching and 'restoring' two cartoons for the oculi of the Duomo. The payment is made before Ghiberti begins the last window. According to Vasari, Uccello was summoned to Padua by Donatello. Even if the reasons for the journey are unknown, we can guess a connection with Donatello's designs for the equestrian monument to Gattamelata. Who could be more familiar with the *quadratura* of a horse than the author of the *Hawkwood*? In Padua, Uccello paints the *Giants* in the Casa Vitaliani (see cat. no. 22) with a rapid, economical technique, in terre-verte; he is paid one ducat per figure. The same technique is used in the Chiostro Verde and probably in the cloister of Santa Maria degli Angeli. Uccello does not stay in Padua as long as Donatello, and his friend does not seem to have included him in his Paduan enterprises.

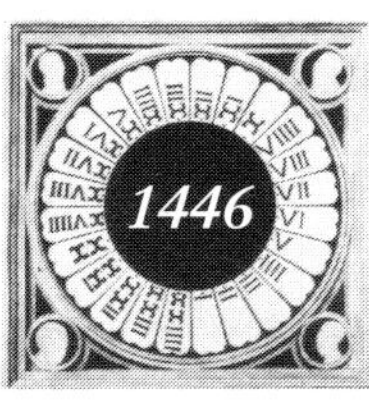

* In September, the Florentine militia (with Micheletto Attendolo da Cotignola at their head) and the Venetians defeat Visconti's troops, led by Francesco Piccinino, son of Niccolò, near Castelmaggiore.
** First phase in the construction of the Palazzo Rucellai, to the design of Alberti. An Office of Works is created at the Palazzo Vecchio to supervise the

modernization and restoration of the building. Columns are supplied for the nave of San Lorenzo, up to the level of the transept.
*** Death of Brunelleschi and of the painter Giuliano d'Arrigo, known as Pesello. Dello Delli returns from Spain. Il Buggiano makes a bust of Brunelleschi which will be placed in Santa Maria del Fiore.

Back in Florence, Uccello presents his Cadastre declaration,[32] giving a different date of birth, 1396; his financial situation is stable.

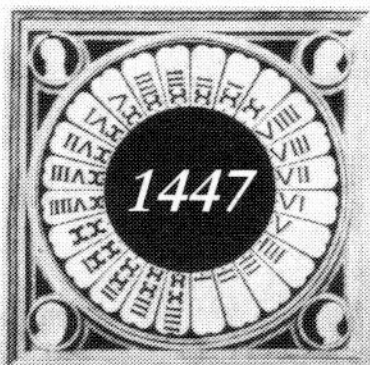

* Death of Eugenius IV. The humanist Niccolò Parentucelli from Sarzana is elected pope. He takes the name Nicholas V and chooses Cosimo de' Medici as banker to the Church. Federico da Montefeltro, Count of Urbino is captain of war in Florence's pay. Death of Florence's implacable enemy, Filippo Maria Visconti. In the autumn, Florentine troops block those of Alfonso of Aragon, King of Naples, who was preparing an expedition into Tuscany.
** Piero de' Medici (Piero the Gouty), Cosimo's son, finances the construction of the shrine of the Crucifix in San Miniato, attributed to Michelozzo and Rossellino and with ceramic decoration by Luca della Robbia. Work finishes on the cloister of San Miniato. Antonio Manetti presents a plan for the modernization of the Santissima Annunziata. At San Lorenzo, the chapels are vaulted and columns erected in the nave.
*** Ghiberti begins his compilation of the *Commentari*. Giovanni di Domenico da Gaiuole begins work on the canons' library at the Duomo. Andrea del Castagno and Paolo Schiavo are painting frescoes in Sant'Apollonia. Fra Angelico and Gozzoli are painting the chapel of San Brizio in Siena cathedral, finished by Signorelli at the end of the century.

Probable date of the *Stories of Noah* in the fourth bay of the Chiostro Verde of Santa Maria Novella. Building work on the cloister of San Miniato is completed, a providing a *terminus post quem* for Uccello's frescoes in the upper cloister, the most significant work of his long relationship with the Olivetan convent. These scenes of hermits and Benedictines, a new step in his elaboration of perspective, belong to a cycle of which little is known: no patrons, no chronology, no collaborators or iconological programme (see cat. no. 24). The cycle occupies him for at least a decade, on and off – a fact which is confirmed by the clear disparity in styles between the two walls of the cloister.

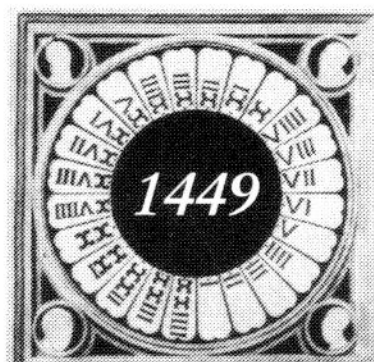

* Birth of Lorenzo de' Medici, Piero the Gouty's son. Agreement between Venice and Milan. Cosimo de' Medici lends support to Francesco's Sforza's aspirations to the Duchy of Milan.
** Construction work begins on the great cloister of Santa Croce. The roof of the Carmine church is repaired. Maso di Bartolomeo begins compiling his second *Notebook* or *Book of Memories*. Work on the nave of San Lorenzo continues.
*** Andrea del Castagno begins the *Assumption* of San Miniato fra le Torri (Berlin, Staatliche Museen). Birth of Domenico Bigordi, known as Ghirlandaio. Giovanni di Francesco has restored a panel by Giotto on behalf of Filippo Lippi (before 1450) and will subsequently take him to court.

During these years which are perhaps the least documented of his entire career, but which were in all probability creative, Uccello is likely to have done a great deal for private patrons, producing works now either lost or unidentified: he is mentioned in Giovanni Rucellai's notes (compiled *c.* 1471, relating to the works in the Palazzo Rucellai),[33] seemingly with reference to 'small items' (see p. 251).

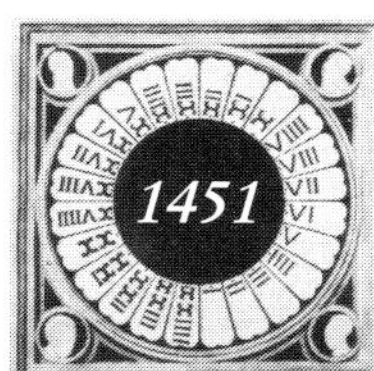

* Francesco Sforza has been in power in Milan for a year, with Florence's support. In the spring, Venice and Alfonso of Aragon form a league, to which the republic of Siena also allies itself. Difficult attempt on the part of Cosimo de' Medici to settle the disagreement with Venice.
** Work on the church of the Santissima Annunziata (doorway of the small Cloister of the Vows). Maso di Bartolomeo and other Tuscan masters are working on the façade of San Domenico at Urbino.
*** Andrea del Castagno is painting a fresco at Sant'Egidio. Piero della Francesca is working in the Tempio Malatestiano at Rimini.

In 1450 (though the date is uncertain and could be as late as 1453), Uccello is paid for a tabernacle at San Giovanni, perhaps a *Crucifixion* or a *Lamentation*; it is not known whether this was ever finished.[34] In 1451, Uccello is painting a panel (now lost or unidentified) for the merchants Jacopo and Giovanni di Orsino Landredini, and he gives an estimate for a tabernacle painted by Stefano d'Antonio in Santa Maria at Montici.[35]

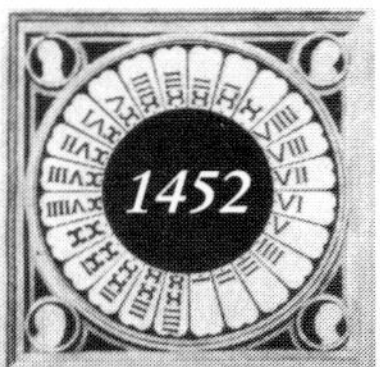

* The Emperor Frederick III stays in Florence before going on to Rome. A French embassy arrives, to reaffirm traditional ties between the Signoria and France. Birth in Ferrara of Girolamo Savonarola. War breaks out in the summer: Venice and the Marquis of Monferrato attack Milan, while the King of Naples attacks Florence. Alfonso of Aragon's army, reinforced by Sienese troops, is led by Federico da Montefeltro of Urbino.
** Antonio Manetti is in charge of the work at the Duomo. Ghiberti delivers his Doors of Paradise. Work on decoration of the interior of San Lorenzo.
*** Fra Angelico declines the offer to decorate the chancel of Prato cathedral with frescoes; the Office of Works then calls on Filippo Lippi. Death of Bicci di Lorenzo; Piero della Francesca takes over the fresco cycle in San Francesco at Arezzo. Birth of Leonardo da Vinci. Benozzo Gozzoli decorates the church of San Francesco at Montefalco with frescoes.

The predella of the Oratory of Avane (Florence, Museo di San Marco) dates from this year: the attribution to Uccello has sometimes been rejected (see cat. no. 26), and the main panel, perhaps an *Annunciation*, disappeared in the nineteenth century. We do not know who commissioned this work (the inscription is barely legible); it may originally have been commissioned for an urban setting, like the early triptych by Masaccio later rediscovered at San Giovenale at Cascia near Reggello.[36] Also in this year, Uccello marries a much younger woman, Tommasa di Benedetto Malifici, aged about nineteen. They will have two children – Donato, born in 1453, and Antonia, born in 1456, both of whom will gravitate towards their father's trade.

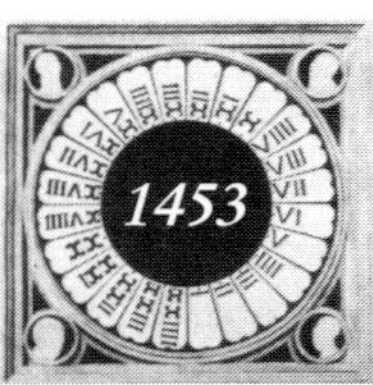

* Capture of Constantinople by the Turks. Death of the Chancellor Marsuppini. His place is taken by the humanist Poggio Bracciolini, who is a great admirer of Classical texts. Birth of Giuliano de' Medici, Lorenzo the Magnificent's brother. In Tuscany, the Sforza troops join forces with the Florentines against Alfonso of Aragon's army.
** Work on enlarging the Hospital of San Paolo, perhaps directed by Michelozzo. The plan for renovating the Palazzo Vecchio, also probably by Michelozzo, is approved.
*** The monument to Carlo Marsuppini at Santa Croce is commissioned from Desiderio da Settignano. Donatello returns to Florence. Andrea del Castagno interrupts his work at Sant'Egidio. Benozzo Gozzoli begins his cycle of frescoes in Santa Rosa at Viterbo.

On 30 June, Uccello is paid for a picture (now lost) of the Blessed Andrea Corsini for the library of Santa Maria del Fiore.[37] Neither the medium nor the support is known.[37] Since July 1448 the library has occupied the chapel of San Pietro in Ciel d'Oro; the cabinet maker Gaiuole is at work there from 1447 to 1454. The probable patron was the provost Giovanni Spinellini (G. Richa, 1754–59, VI, p. 91). Birth of Uccello's first child, to whom he gives the Christian name of his friend Donatello.

In this period and for some time later, Uccello figures among the *capitani* of the Guild of Saint Luke, a sign of long service in the Florentine guild of painters.

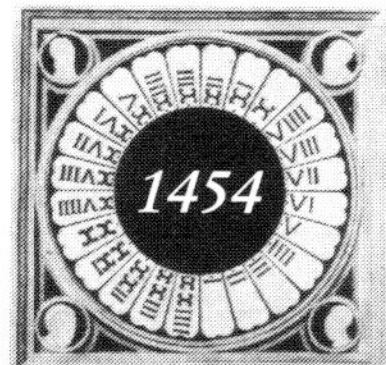

* Peace treaty of Lodi between Milan (and Florence) and Venice (and Naples) which determines borders between the two states. Subsequently Florence, Venice and Milan work towards improving the treaty to extend it to twenty-five years. Birth of Agnolo Poliziano, who will be a famous man of letters during Lorenzo the Magnificent's rule.
** Michelozzo's intervention in the courtyard of the Palazzo Vecchio. Work on the Palazzo Medici and San Lorenzo continues.
*** Giovanni di Francesco's frontal for San Biagio at Petriolo. Alesso Baldovinetti colours a picture by Andrea del Castagno for the Gonzagas of Mantua. In Perugia, the contract commissioning Bonfigli to paint the frescoes for the Priors' chapel makes provision for the work to be estimated by Filippo Lippi, Fra Angelico or Domenico Veneziano.

On 31 October Uccello begins painting a *Crucifixion* in the refectory of San Miniato al Monte. His assistant is Antonio di Papi, who will later work in the chapel of the Cardinal of Portugal. This is one of the few established facts concerning Uccello's long association with San Miniato. Vasari's anecdote about the miserly abbot who frightened the painter off after stuffing him with cheese till he could no longer stand the sight of it is probably true: we can see veiled suggestions of prolonged, difficult relations with the Brothers, his flight and his return some time later, and a hint that he might have finished the cycle grudgingly (the frescoes on the second wall of the cloister are in fact simplified and lack any complex perspectival construction). There may also be a grain of truth in Vasari's colourful tale, which describes Uccello's fear of cabinet makers, after the cheese diet imposed by the Olivetans: cabinet makers use a great deal of cheese in their glues and mastics, a fact confirmed by documents on the marquetry furniture in the Sacristy.[38–39]

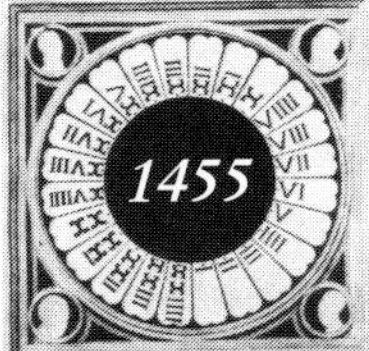

* Death of Nicholas V. Callistus III Borgia is elected pope. Poggio Bracciolini writes the *Historia fiorentina* in the style of Livy. Alfonso of Aragon belatedly ratifies the treaty of Lodi.
** Work continues on the façade of the Palazzo Rucellai. Estimates for Michelozzo's work on the Santissima Annunziata are in hand.
*** Death of Ghiberti and of Fra Angelico. Donatello's modern statue of *Saint Mary Magdalen*. Pesellino is commissioned to paint the retable for the church of the Trinity at Pistoia, finished by Filippo Lippi (London, National Gallery).

Uccello, with Antonio di Papi, is paid for the decoration of the refectory at San Miniato del Monte.

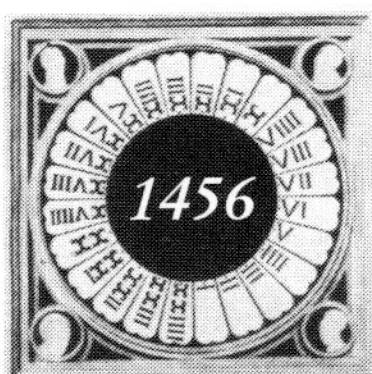

* Alfonso of Aragon declares war on Genoa, and pushes the militia led by Jacopo Piccinino against that of Sigismondo Pandolfo Malatesta of Rimini.
** Cosimo de' Medici has work done on the interior of the Badia at Fiesole.
*** Andrea del Castagno paints in fresco the equestian monument of Niccolò da Tolentino in the Duomo. Giovanni da Piamonte, one of Piero della Francesca's collaborators, signs the retable of Santa Maria delle Grazie at Città di Castello.

Uccello supplies two cartoons to the master glazier Bernardo di Francesco. Birth of Uccello's daughter, Antonia, who will become a Carmelite nun and, as is believed by some sources, a painter.

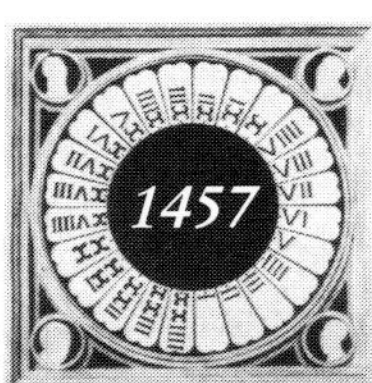

* Plague epidemic in Florence. Genoa, under threat from Alfonso of Aragon, looks to Charles VII of France for support.
** Restoration of the library of San Marco, to Michelozzo's original design. Litigation between Giovanni di Domenico da Gaiuole and Antonio Manetti about work at San Lorenzo.
*** Deaths of Andrea del Castagno, Francesco Pesellino and Mariotto di Cristofano. Birth of Filippino Lippi. Donatello goes to Siena. Antonio Rossellino makes the tomb of Neri Capponi in Santo Spirito. Luca della Robbia finishes the tomb of Bishop Federighi at San Pancrazio (later moved to Santa Trinita).

In order to escape the plague, Uccello probably takes refuge on his estate at San Stefano a Ugnano.

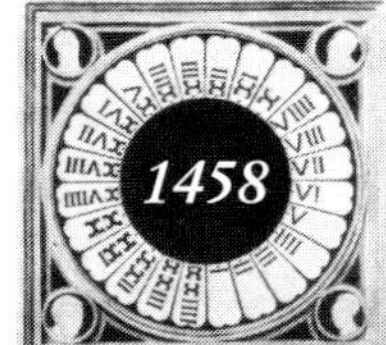

* Death of Pope Callistus III. Enea Silvio Piccolomini, a humanist scholar from Corsignano near Siena, succeeds him, under the name of Pius II. Death of Alfonso of Aragon; his son Ferdinand becomes King of Naples. Cosimo de' Medici has the Consiglio dei Cento (Council of a Hundred) ratified. New urban Cadastre.
** Decision to enlarge the Palazzo Rucellai. The façade of Santa Maria Novella is under construction, to Alberti's design.
*** The lunette of *God the Father* in the portico of the Foundling Hospital is commissioned from Giovanni di Francesco. In October Benozzo Gozzoli is once more in Rome.

In his declaration to the Cadastre for this year, Uccello reveals a certain affluence, with no significant changes since his previous declaration. While his standard of living is not that of Ghiberti or Luca della Robbia, he has no immediate financial worries. He declares that he is sixty-two years old. Among new developments are a slight enlargement of his estate at San Stefano a Ugnano and, under persons for whom he is responsible, his daughter Antonia, aged one year and four months.

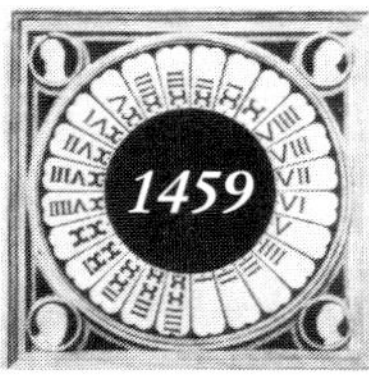

* Death of Poggio Bracciolini. Cosimo founds the Platonic Academy. Luca Pitti instigates a constitutional reform: in January, the Priors of Liberty are created to replace those of the Arts.
** Antonio Manetti takes over direction of the works at Santo Spirito. The Pazzi chapel in the cloister of Santa Croce is almost finished: the date appears in the crown of the cupola.
*** Benozzo Gozzoli begins the frescoes in the chapel of the Palazzo Medici, paid for by Piero de' Medici. Death of Giovanni di Francesco. Piero della Francesca is in Rome. Antonio del Pollaiuolo finishes the Reliquary of the Cross for Santa Maria del Fiore.

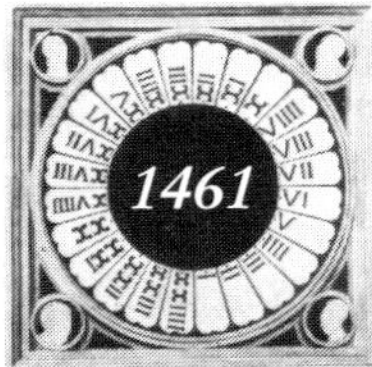

* Piero de' Medici is Gonfalonier of Justice.
** Construction of the great cloister of the Cistercian abbey of San Salvatore at Settimo. The cloister and refectory of the Badia at Fiesole are finished. Consecration of San Lorenzo. Building starts on the palace of Luca Pitti.
*** Donatello is working on the bronze *Judith* which will be installed in the

Piazza della Signoria. Death of Domenico Veneziano. At Sant'Egidio, Alesso Baldovinetti finishes Domenico Veneziano's *Marriage of the Virgin* and paints *Saints* in fresco on the wall of the choir.

No documented data on Uccello. Among works we can associate with this period are the London *Saint George* and the *Life of the Holy Fathers* (Florence, Accademia), perhaps painted for the convent of Franciscan Tertiaries of Santi Girolamo Francesco alla Costa in Florence.

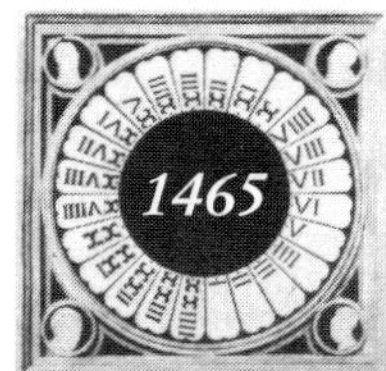

* Since the death of Cosimo de' Medici in August 1464, power is in the hands of his son Piero the Gouty. Louis XI, King of France, lends support to Francesco Sforza's designs on Genoa; in exchange the Duke of Milan supports him against the Dukes of Berry and Bourbon and against Charles the Bold. Ferdinand of Naples rids himself of the *condottiere* Francesco Piccinino, after arresting him by treachery.
** Giuliano da Sangallo dates his famous book of drawings now in the Vatican Library (ms. Barb. lat. 4424). Antonio Rossellino is on the point of finishing the tomb of the Cardinal of Portugal at San Miniato al Monte.
*** Presumed date of the diptych of the counts of Urbino by Piero della Francesca (Florence, Uffizi) and of the *Madonna and Child* by Andrea del Verrocchio (Berlin, Staatliche Museen).

Uccello paints a *Saint George* for the Florentine merchant Lorenzo di Matteo Morelli.[40] This is neither the London nor the Paris work, but a lost work, perhaps similar to the *Study of a Knight* in the Uffizi. In the same year (though the documents are now lost),[41] it seems that he had his first contacts with the Company of the Corpus Domini, one of the richest and most influential confraternities in Urbino; he receives a payment of 59 *bolognini*, for reasons now unknown (perhaps for a processional banner painted with a chalice in perspective?). In this period, Urbino greatly admired Tuscan culture, and Florentine culture in particular. Tuscany is described as 'the fountain of architects' in the famous 'licence' given to Laurana in 1468 by Count Federico for the construction of the ducal palace.[42] Examples of artists who worked in the city are the mysterious architect referred to as 'Pippo Fiorentino', Maso di Bartolomeo, Pasquino di Montepulciano and Luca della Robbia; the masters working in the Studiolo (after Uccello's departure) were Florentine; the local artists were mostly trained in Florence in the studio of Filippo Lippi; Federico treasured the parade helmet by Pollaiuolo which Florence awarded him after his achievement at Volterra in 1472.

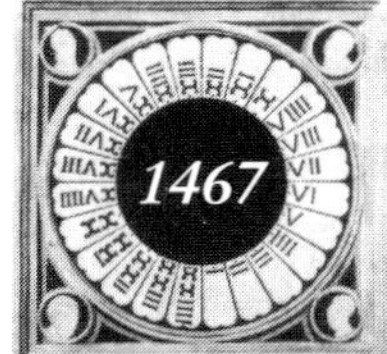

* Galeazzo Maria Sforza has been Duke of Milan for a year, since Francesco Sforza's death. In the Apennines, Venice and Ferrara attack territory belonging to Florence, which is allied to Milan and Naples. The captain of the allied army is Federico da Montefeltro of Urbino.
** Giovanni di Domenico da Gaiuole is working on the choir stalls of San Miniato al Monte. Work on San Felice in Piazza is commissioned by Mariotto Lippi, who will be Gonfalonier of Justice in 1468. Luciano Laurana arrives in Urbino from Pesaro.
*** Frescoes in the shrine of the Holy Sepulchre in the Rucellai chapel in San Pancrazio, attributed to Giovanni di Piamonte. In Urbino, Fra Carnevale is paid for the retable of Santa Maria della Bella (now lost). Candelabra by Andrea del Verrocchio (Amsterdam, Rijksmuseum) for Sala dell'Udienza in the Palazzo Vecchio.

From 10 August onwards, Uccello receives several payments from the Company of the Corpus Domini. Donato, his son, is assisting him. We do not know what the payments are for, but relations with the powerful lay confraternity seem to go beyond the provision of the retable for the Oratory of the Corpus Domini, which was abandoned for reasons unknown. Uccello was certainly unsympathetic to the 'Albertian' principles of the Montefeltro court, and produced only the predella of *The Miracle of the Profaned Host*. The retable itself, after long delays, was finally painted by a foreigner, Justus van Ghent: *The Communion of the Apostles* was executed *c.* 1473 and paid for in 1474.[43] The final payment to Uccello registered at Urbino dates from 31 October 1468 and has no direct connection with the predella. Also 1468, Uccello pays a special tax ('*ventina*') of 9 *soldi* and 4 *denari* in Florence: it is therefore possible that he interrupted his stay in Urbino to return to Florence at least once.

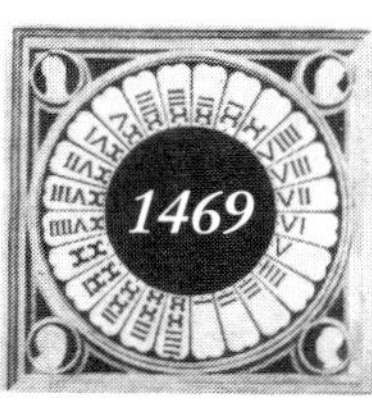

* In February, joust in Piazza Santa Croce, in which the young Lorenzo de' Medici takes part; he marries Clarice Orsini di Monterotondo, niece of Cardinal Napoleone Orsini. In December Piero de' Medici dies, leaving power to his son Lorenzo.
** Work on enlarging the convent of the Carmine. Interior decoration work is decided on at the Palazzo Vecchio.

*** In October, Filippo Lippi dies at Spoleto. Piero della Francesca receives the final payment for the polyptych of Sant'Agostino at Sansepolcro. In January, Benozzo Gozzoli is commissioned to execute frescoes in the Camposanto at Pisa. Verrocchio is commissioned to do the tomb of Piero and Giovanni de' Medici for the Old Sacristy in San Lorenzo.

On 8 April Giovanni Santi is paid for having housed and accompanied Piero della Francesca 'to see the panel to be executed for the Confraternity' (of the Corpus Domini in Urbino): Uccello must have disengaged himself by then. Piero was to decline the offer. Piero's and Uccello's positions on the perspectival treatment of space are among the most different that could be found in Italy. On 8 August, Uccello makes a declaration of income to the Cadastre which has excited speculation ever since.[2]

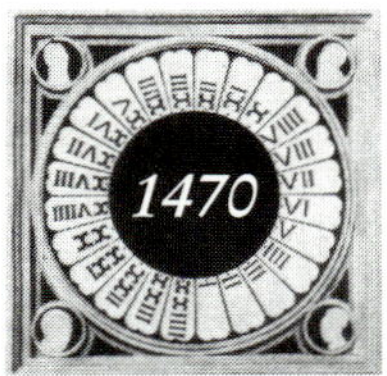

* The Florentine exile Bernardo Nardi with a few soldiers occupies the fortress and the Palazzo Pubblico at Prato, inciting the town to revolt against Florence. Popular riots at Prato and Pistoia.
** The façade of Santa Maria Novella is finished. After a serious fire, it is decided to complete the work on Santo Spirito. Benedetto da Maiano builds a wall in the Palazzo Vecchio, creating the Sala dei Gigli and the Sala dell'Udienza.
*** A retable for Sant'Ambrogio is commissioned from Alesso Baldovinetti, which will be finished three years later. Probable date of the *Baptism of Christ* for San Salvi by Verrocchio with the collaboration of the young Leonardo (Florence, Uffizi). First public commission for Botticelli: *Fortitude*, for the series of *Virtues* for the Tribunale della Mercanzia (Florence, Uffizi).

Despite the self-pity shown in his declaration to the Cadastre of 1469, we have to believe that Uccello's activities bear no relation to his despair. Among the known works, the remarkable *Hunt* at Oxford (Ashmolean), his best preserved work, probably belongs to this period, immediately after his time in Urbino; it is painted with an extreme sureness of touch, great inventive felicity and great intellectual refinement. The bouncing rhythms and the piercing notes of the scarlet clothes are spread through the depths of a moonlit forest, and the shadows created by the trees seem to form a kind of distant counterpoint to the vast southern sunlit open spaces of Piero della Francesca.

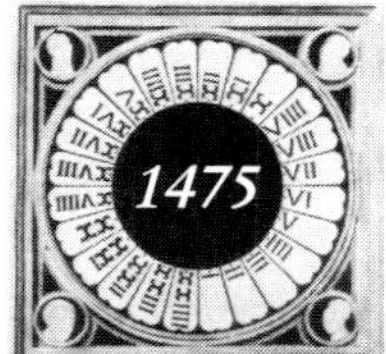

* In January, a great joust in honour of Simonetta Vespucci, Giuliano de' Medici's mistress. Savonarola enters the Dominican order.
** Restoration campaign at the convent of the Certosa del Galluzzo.
*** Birth at Caprese of Michelangelo Buonarroti. Botticelli's *Adoration of the Magi* for the Del Lama chapel at Santa Maria Novella (Florence, Uffizi). Giuliano da Maiano, Francesco di Giovanni (known as Francione) and Giovanni di Domenico da Gaiuole are paid for a major job of woodwork in the Palazzo Vecchio.

A note of 25 August of the preceding year, 1474, records that the cabinet maker Domenico del Tasso owed Uccello money for two paintings;[44] it is impossible to identify them or to know whether they were '*lettucci*' or '*spalliere*'[45] or perspectives in marquetry. That is the last known record of payment in Uccello's long professional life. On 11 November 1475 he makes his will, and on 12 December he is buried at Santo Spirito, in the family vault he had chosen in 1425 at the time of his departure for Venice. The declaration to the Cadastre of 1480 by his son Donato confirms that the master left his family comfortably off. His estate near Settimo had received several additions, the house remained his property, and he was even able to restore to his forty-one-year-old wife her dowry of two hundred gold florins. In 1491 his daughter Antonia, painter and nun, died; she represents perhaps the last trace of her father and master's unrivalled style. Donato, a faceless painter with no known works, died in 1497. For a long time he retained the bulk of his father's drawings, if we are to believe Vasari who succeeded in acquiring some.[46] According to the Anonimo Magliabechiano (see note 70), the elderly Uccello '*morse allo Spedale*' – died in the Hospital.

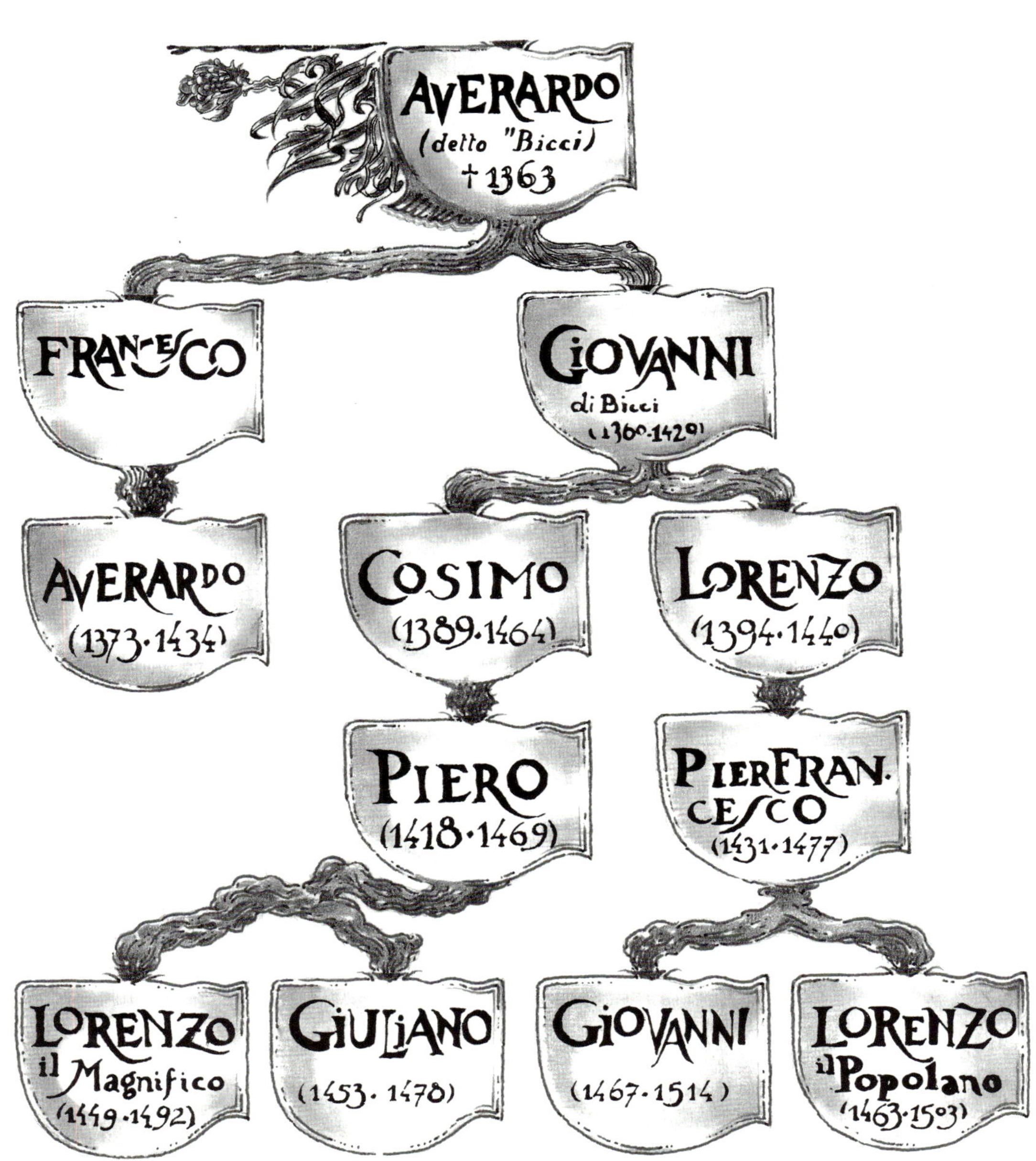

AVERARDO
(detto "Bicci)
† 1363
FRANCESCO
GIOVANNI
di Bicci
(1360-1429)
AVERARDO
(1373-1434)
COSIMO
(1389-1464)
LORENZO
(1394-1440)
PIERO
(1418-1469)
PIERFRANCESCO
(1431-1477)
LORENZO
il Magnifico
(1449-1492)
GIULIANO
(1453-1478)
GIOVANNI
(1467-1514)
LORENZO
il Popolano
(1463-1503)

Chapter One

FLORENCE

1397–1475

Portrait of a City

Explaining a personality as strange and complex as Uccello's is made even more difficult by the constraints of monograph writing. The monograph is like a halftone which has been trimmed all round its edges in order to focus attention on it, but in the process, stuck artificially on a white page, it has become divorced from its context. Such is the disciplinary perspective of art history, in which pride of place is given to a study of the works, and which more often than not encourages us to forget the context, neglect the artist's involvement in his milieu and his cultural ties, the entire way of life within which the man and the artist develop. And so, when we try to extrapolate from the huge bibliography on Uccello, we notice that all the monographs tend to be compiled along the same lines, and in spite of the authors' quality as writers, their intuition and insight, the figure who emerges from their work is conventionalized, repetitive, and to a large extent incomprehensible. However, if pretensions to 'total history' are beyond our reach, some effort can still be made to restore the context, reduce the margin of incomprehension, and recreate – through induction at least – the climate and atmosphere in which the man and artist moved, worked and reacted to the voices of his time. There can be no question of taking such an enterprise to an absolute extreme: that would be beyond the scope of a monograph – not to mention the obvious difficulties involved. Nevertheless, we have attempted an experiment here with a dual purpose: to offer the reader precise information, the essential points of a historical resumé and perspective, and to suggest some ideas to the specialist that may, in their disarming simplicity, provide some new and perhaps enriching reflections.

If we take as reference points the documented parameters of Uccello's life with dates at either end, and if we consider the social, civil and artistic history of Florence – the city at the very centre of his existence – we can see that the complexity of the subject calls for synthesis. In the course of these eighty or so years, after decades of revolt by the Ciompi, we can witness the transformations in the Florentine Republic that paved the way for a 'return to order', before the first Medici came to power; finally, after

Cosimo the Elder's splendour and Piero the Gouty's troubled times, there is the spectacle of 'a city with more problems than certainties'[47] In Lorenzo the Magnificent's era.

Uccello's birth coincided with the Republic's victory over Galeazzo Visconti's Milanese troops near Governolo, at the confluence of the Po and Mincio. By the time he died in December 1475, the climate of opposition to Lorenzo that would erupt in the Pazzi conspiracy was already perceptible: two months earlier, Lorenzo himself wrote in a letter to Galeazzo Maria Sforza, Duke of Milan: 'I never cease trying to understand what foundation the message brought by your emissary, Messer Filippo, had, and in fact I find everything emanating from the same source, that is, from those Pazzi, my kinsfolk, who, contrary to their obligations – and because they rely on the king's and the Duke of Urbino's prestige – strive to do me as much harm as possible in the way they behave, for perhaps your Excellency may know that they are treated in our city in the same way that they are treated in our own house, a fact they take too much for granted.'[48]

Continuamente cerco de intendere che fondamente hanno le parole che furono riferite a messer Filippo suo oratore e in effetto trovo tutto uscire da una medesima fonte, cioè da questi Pazzi miei parenti, i quali per loro natura e per essere messi su dalla maestà del re e dal duca di Urbino, tentano di farmi quello male che è loro possibile contro ogni debito, perché, come forse è informata la vostra eccellenza, quella conditione che hanno nella nostra città hanno tutto da casa nostra contro alla quale sono troppo ingrati.

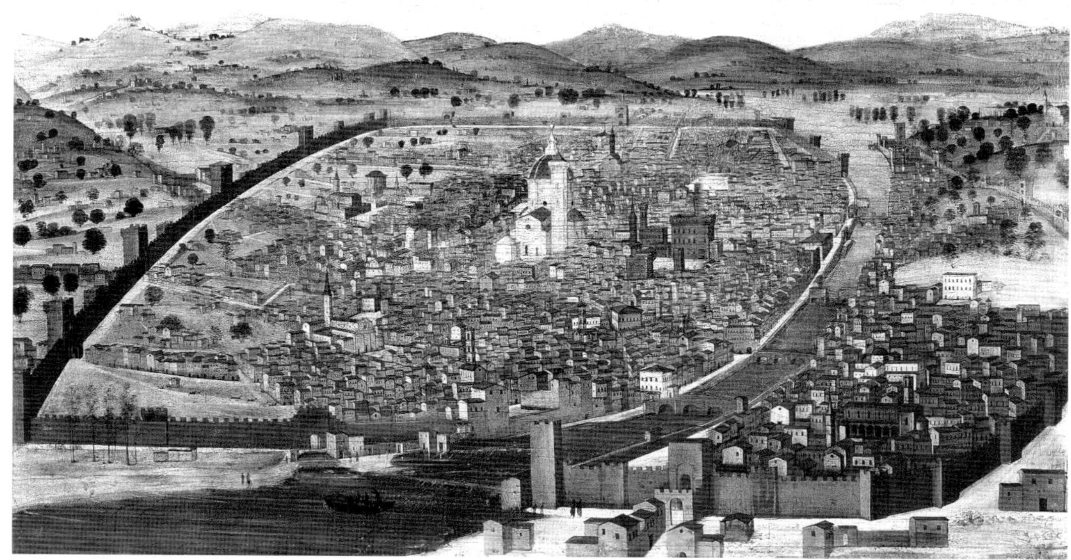

Anon. Florentine, *c.* 1490 (formerly attributed to Francesco Rosselli), *View of Florence*, tempera on wood. London, H. Bier Collection.

Uccello grew up in an atmosphere of restored Republican harmony when the city-state sparkled in all its magnificence. 'It is truly during those years that one saw all the power of our city when she was united,' Guicciardini wrote in his *Storie fiorentine*, 'for they endured twelve years of war against Gian Galeazzo with infinite expense for the Italian and foreign armies, on several occasions they summoned the Duke of Bavaria,

E veramente in quegli anni si dimostrò quanta fussi la potentia della città nostra quando era unita, perché sopportorno 12 anni la guerra di Gian

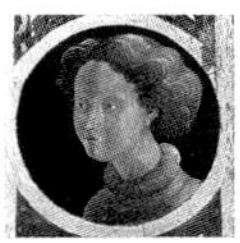

Galeazzo con spesa infinita di eserciti italiani ed esterni che feciono passare in Italia diverse volte uno duca di Baviera, uno conte d'Aurmignacca con 15.000 cavalli, uno imperatore Ruberto; ed appena sendo usciti di questa guerra, credendosi che la città fussi esausta, e per carestia di denaro e per riposarsi qualche tempo, fecero l'impresa di Pisa nella quale nella compera e nell'espugnazione spesono una somma infinita di danari. Ebbono dipoi la guerra con Ladislao re di Napoli, e difesonsi francamente; anzi ne acquistorono Cortona, in ricompenso però di buona somma di danari; comperorono Castrocaro, e finalmente ebbono tanti successi nelle città che si conservò libera, unita e governata da uomini dabbene, e buoni e valenti e fuora che si difesono dai nemici potentissimi e ampliorono assai lo imperio che meritamente si dice che quello è stato il più savio, il più glorioso e il più felice governo che mai per alcun tempo abbia avuto la città nostra.

the Count of Armagnac with 15,000 horse, and the Emperor Ruberto to Italy, and hardly had they emerged from this war – although one would think that the city would have been exhausted, both for want of money and the need to have some period of respite – than they embarked on the enterprise at Pisa, spending infinite sums of money on its purchase, and its assault and capture. Afterwards there was the war against Ladislas, King of Naples, and they defended themselves valiantly; so much so that in exchange for a goodly sum of money they acquired Cortona; they bought Castrocaro and in the end they achieved so many victories in different towns that Florence remained free, united and governed by honest, good, valiant men. Not only did she defend herself against very powerful enemies, but she enlarged her domain, to the extent that it could quite justly be said that this government was the wisest, the most glorious and the happiest that our city had ever had throughout its history.'[49]

This was also the Florence of Leonardo Bruni's *Laudatio Florentinae Urbis*, dated between 1401 and 1404, an imitation of Aristides' eulogy of Athens. It began by praising the layout of the city, its geographical organization, architecture, lands and agriculture. Unique champion of the city-state, and resisting the hegemonic designs of others, predestined through its historical tradition and geographical location to safeguard Italy's stability and the principles of the 'civil republics': such was the Florence in which Bruni highlighted the citizens' role in the state, as in the tradition of

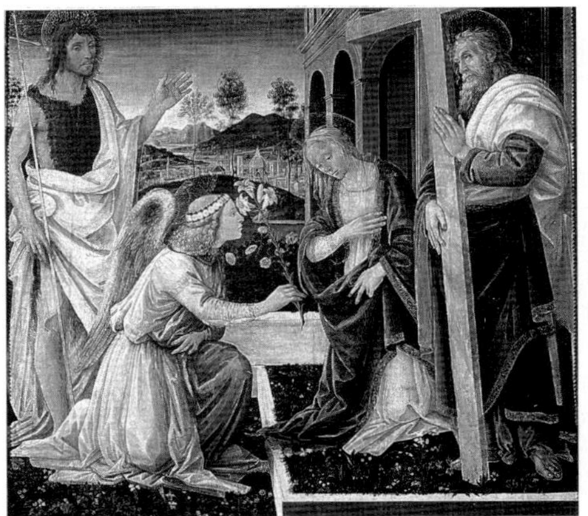

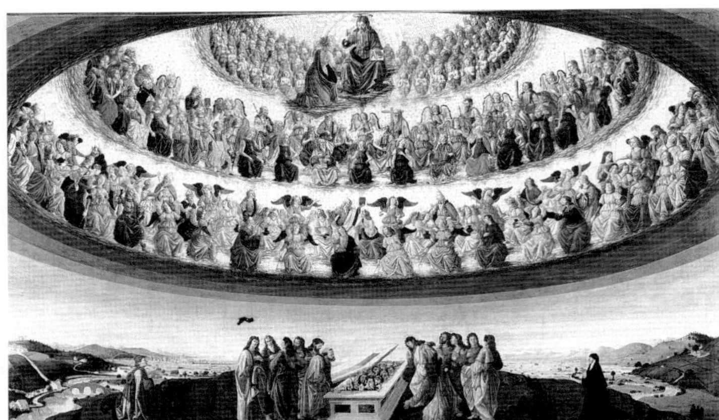

Left: Filippino Lippi, *The Annunciation*, *c.* 1483–5, tempera on wood, 114 × 122 cm. Naples, Museo di Capodimonte.

Right: Francesco Botticini, *The Assumption*, *c.* 1475, tempera on wood, 228.5 × 377 cm. London, National Gallery.

the Greek *polis*. He described the city as an ideal place, built to a rational plan 'in a geometrical perspective that encapsulates and defines its historic role'.[50]

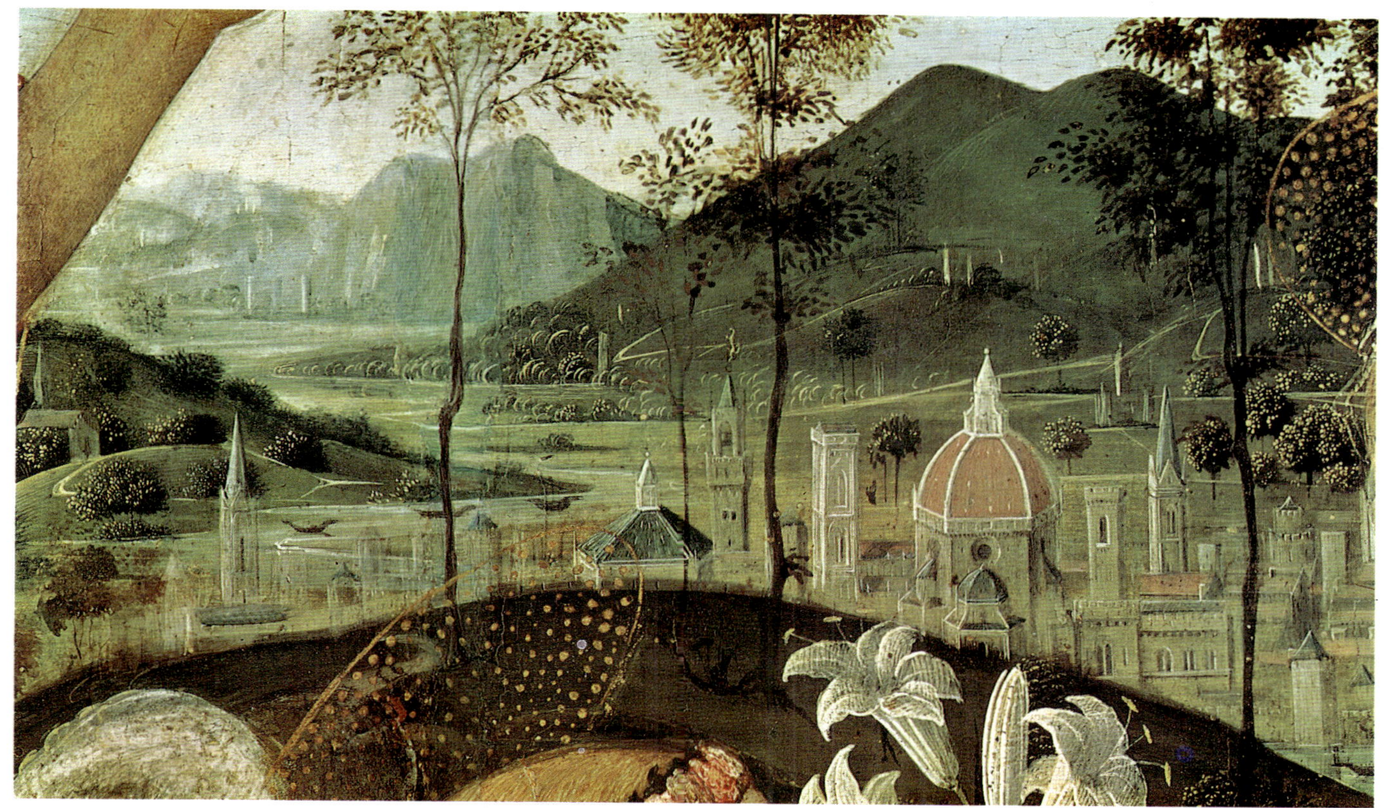

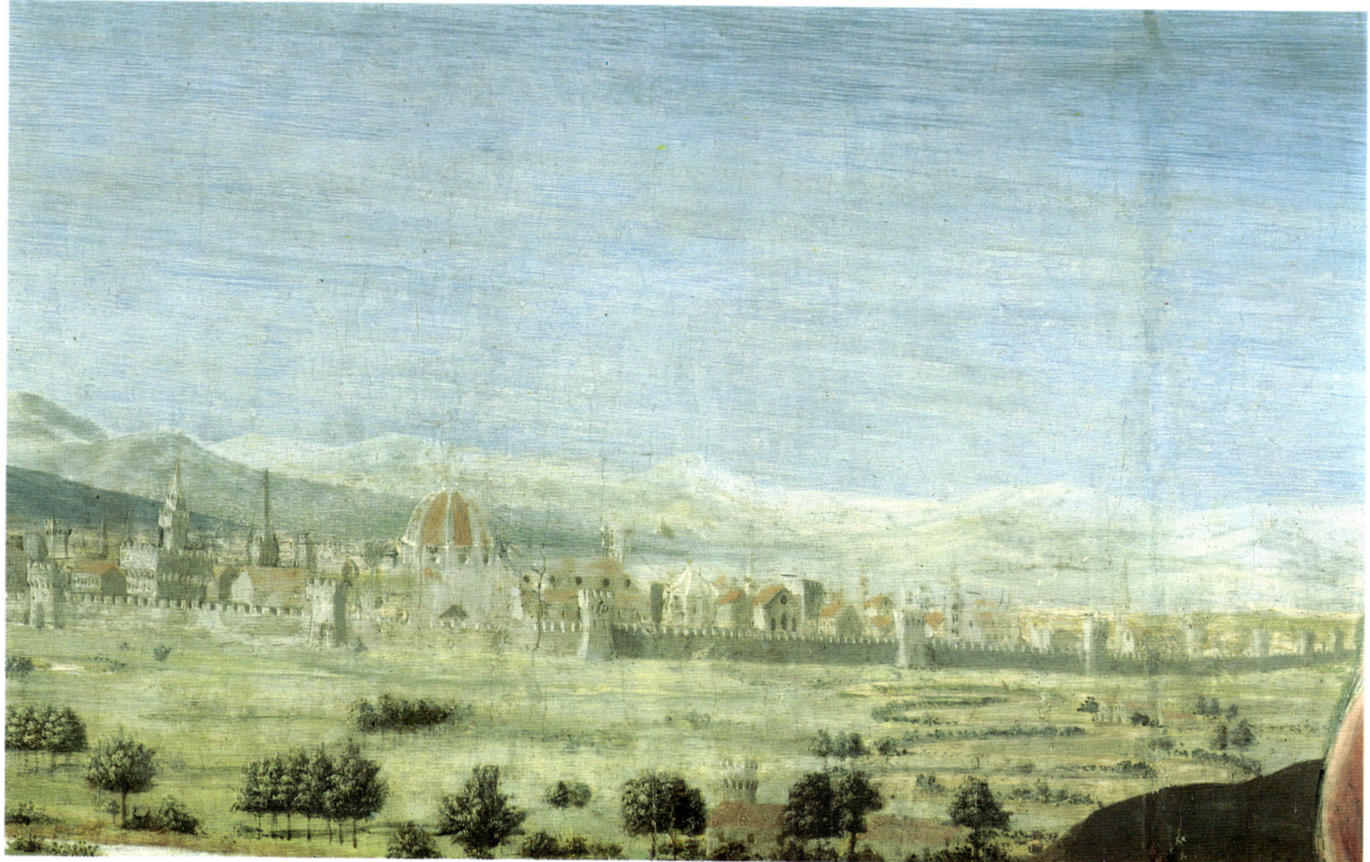

Details of the paintings opposite, showing views of Florence with the dome of Santa Maria del Fiore, 'so vast, so high in the sky, that it could shelter all the peoples of Tuscany in its shade' (Alberti).

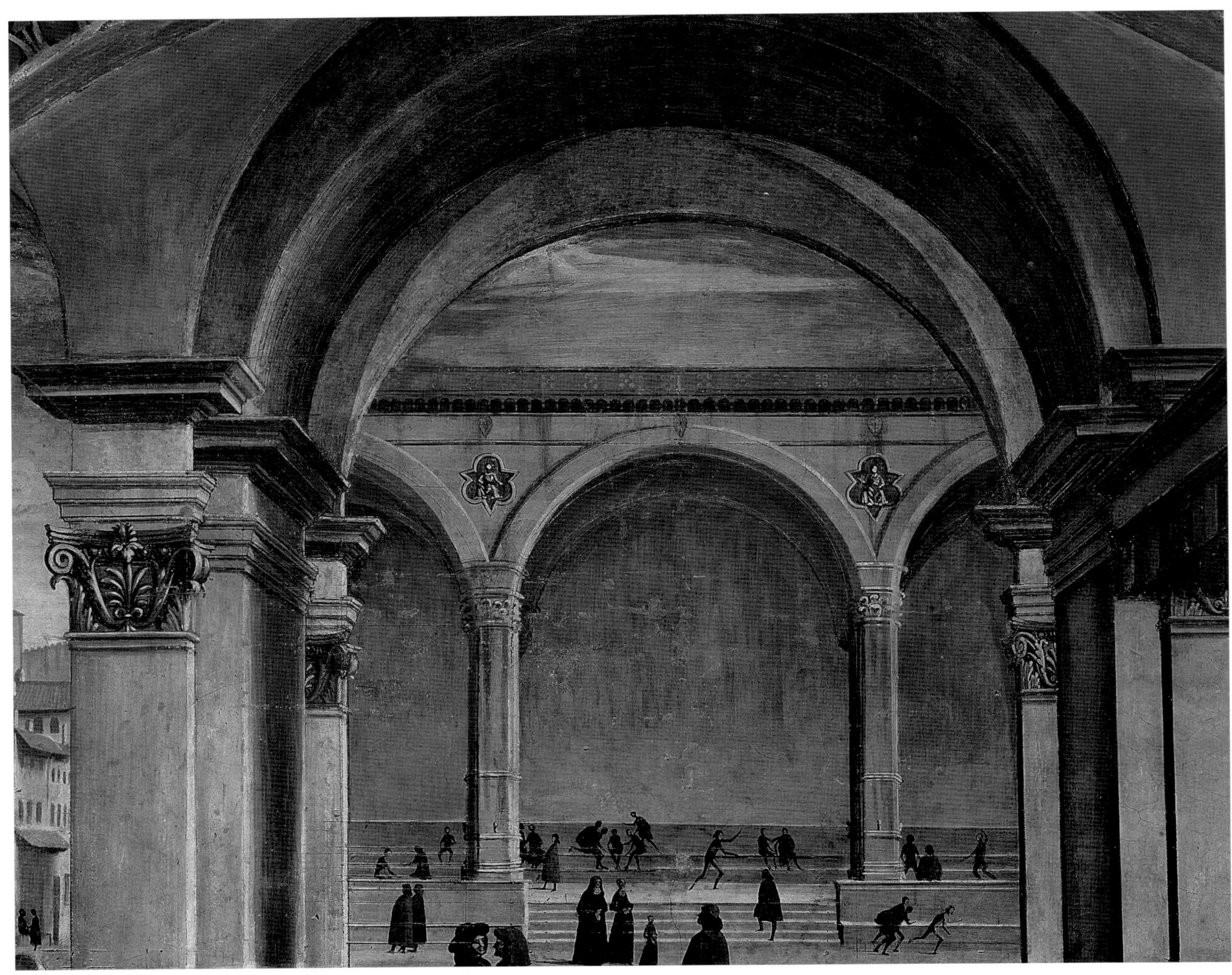

Domenico Ghirlandaio, *Confirmation of the Franciscan Rule by Pope Honorius III*, detail showing the Loggia dei Lanzi.

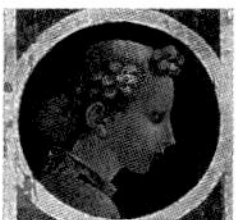

Inside Florence, at the point where all the main streets converge, was the Palazzo Vecchio where, in this society ruled by the divine norm of the law, the assembly of state magistrates upheld the traditional virtues of Republican Rome, of which Florence claimed to be successor.

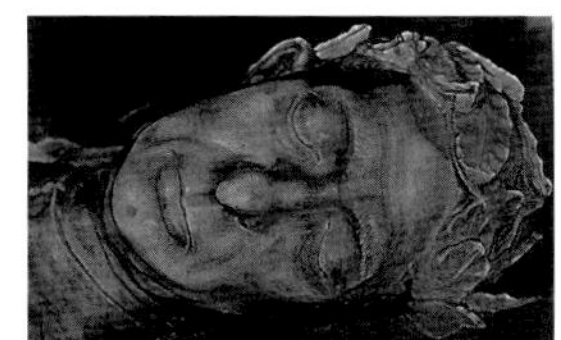

Bernardo Rossellino, detail of the tomb of Leonardo Bruni, after 1444, marble, complete work 6.10 × 2.16 m. Florence, Santa Croce.

In his exaltation of *libertas republicae* Bruni contrasted the personal, Caesar-like monarchical power idealized by the humanists of the north with his apologia for the hardworking prudent city, the small state: Florence's victory in recent wars was but the result of a long ideological apprenticeship founded on a natural vocation for freedom. And his eulogy of the city ended with praise for its citizens: '*non mura sed mentes*' (not walls but minds), in Isidore of Seville's phrase; not urban *physis* but the organization of society. 'Certainly in this city there are very great minds and whatever they undertake turns out to be for the common good,' Bruni wrote;[51] and he added, 'and what can I say of the gentle fluency of their conversation, of the elegance and politeness of their fine wit? In these respects this city without a doubt surpasses all others, and it is considered that she alone, in Italy, uses the purest and most polished language'.[52] The *Laudatio* ended with an invocation to the *Santissima Madre* 'for whom so great and magnificent a temple of pure polished marble has been built',[53] to protect them.

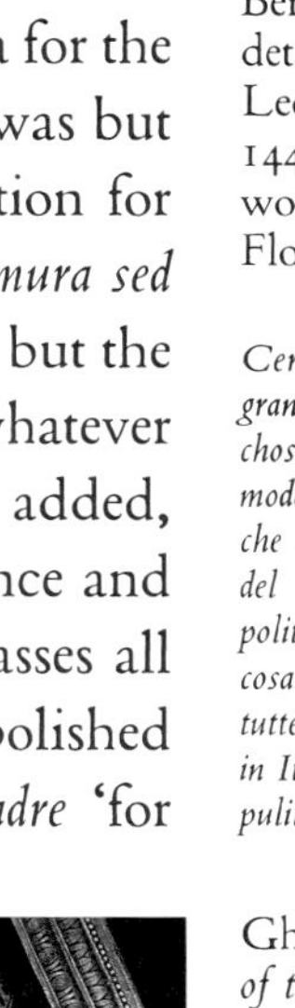

Certamente in questa città sono grandissimi ingegni et qualunque chosa intraprendeno avvantaggiono il modo di tutti gli altri huomini . . . et che dirò io della dolcezza et suavità del parlare e della aleganza et politezza de'bei motti. Nella quale cosa senza contrasto alcuno avanza tutte l'altre, però che questa solo città in Italia e stimata usare purissimo et pulitissimo parlare

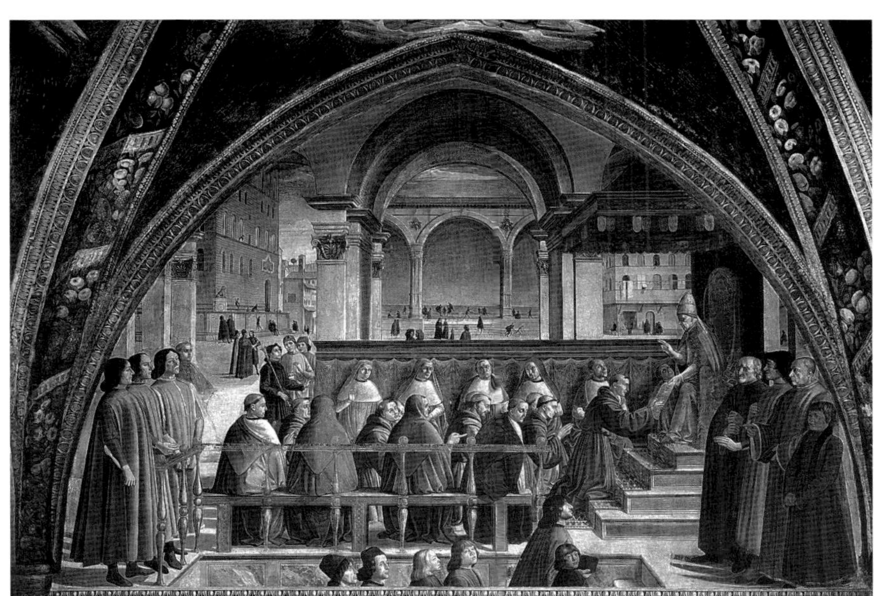

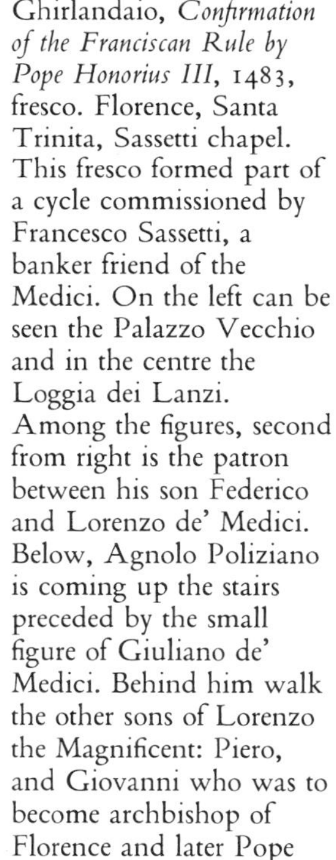

Ghirlandaio, *Confirmation of the Franciscan Rule by Pope Honorius III*, 1483, fresco. Florence, Santa Trinita, Sassetti chapel. This fresco formed part of a cycle commissioned by Francesco Sassetti, a banker friend of the Medici. On the left can be seen the Palazzo Vecchio and in the centre the Loggia dei Lanzi. Among the figures, second from right is the patron between his son Federico and Lorenzo de' Medici. Below, Agnolo Poliziano is coming up the stairs preceded by the small figure of Giuliano de' Medici. Behind him walk the other sons of Lorenzo the Magnificent: Piero, and Giovanni who was to become archbishop of Florence and later Pope Leo X.

In 1396, a year before Uccello was born, the Signoria and the Commune passed a resolution empowering the Masters of Works of the cathedral (*Operai del Duomo*) to repatriate the ashes of a number of famous Florentines: Accursio,[54] Dante, Petrarch

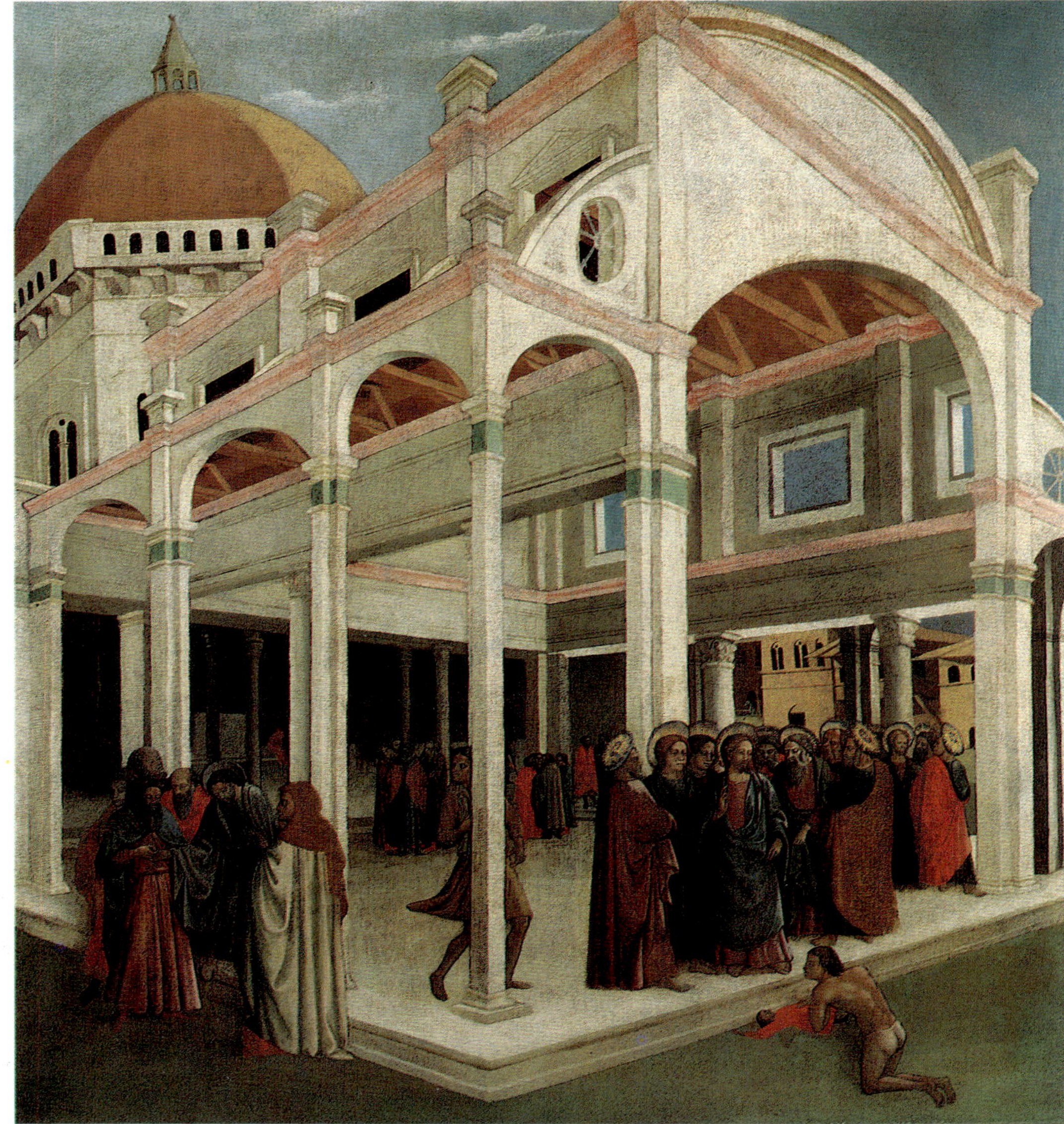

Attributed to Andrea di Giusto (after Masaccio?), *The Exorcism of a Man Possessed*, c. 1424–6, tempera on wood transferred to canvas, 115 × 106 cm. Philadelphia Museum of Art. The rendering of space is inspired by Masaccio's recent frescoes in the Carmine church. The temple is reminiscent of the Duomo in Florence, with a cupola very much in Brunelleschi's style.

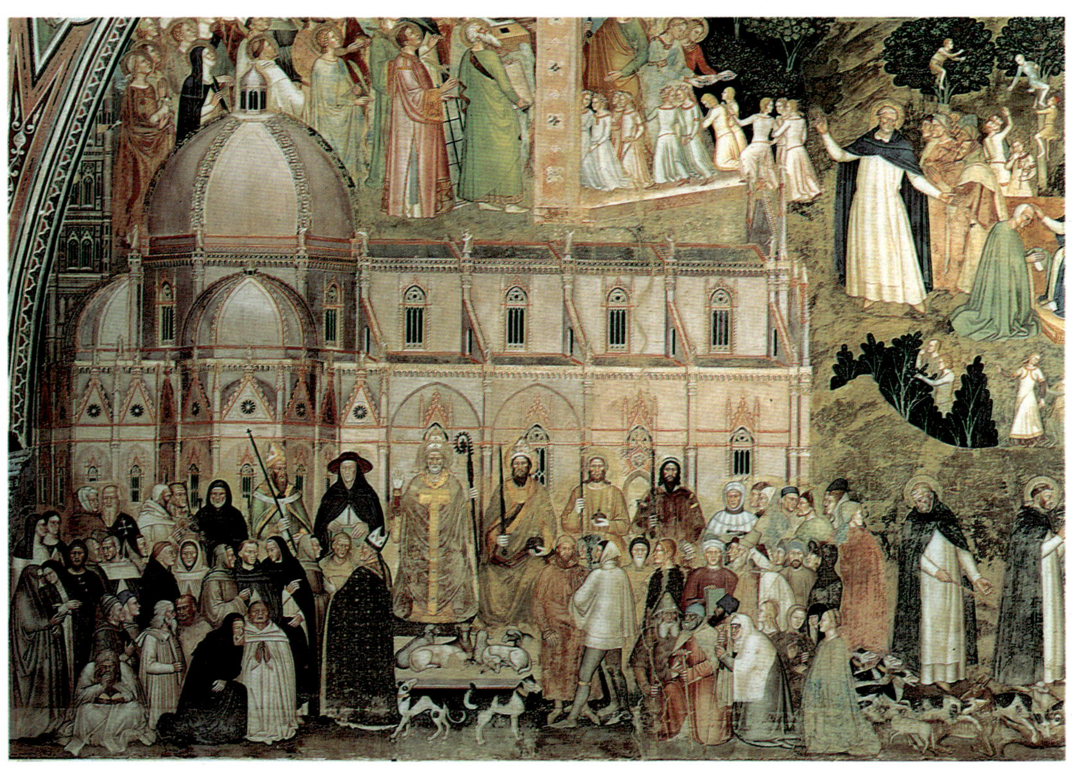

Andrea da Firenze (di Bonaiuto), *The Road to Salvation* (detail), *c.* 1365–7, fresco. Florence, Santa Maria Novella, Spanish chapel. The church depicted is modelled on the fourteenth-century design for Santa Maria del Fiore, which already anticipated an octagonal cupola.

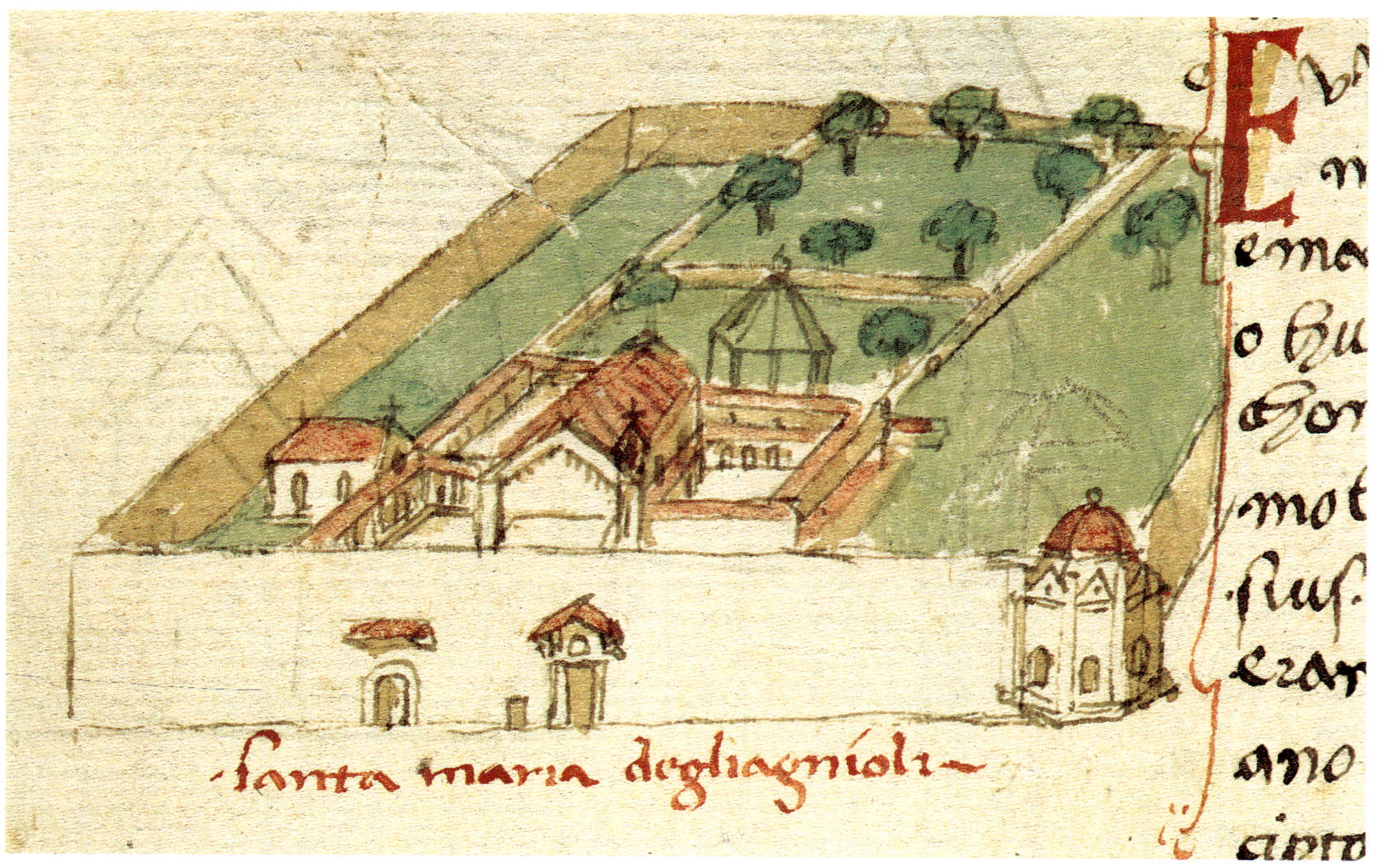

Santa Maria degli Angeli, San Tommaso and the *Mercato Vecchio*, and Santa Maria del Fiore: three illustrations from the *Codex Rustici*. Florence, Biblioteca del Seminario Archivescovile di Cestello. This manuscript is an illustrated guide to Florence. It was compiled by the Florentine merchant Marco di Bartolomeo Rustici, probably *c.* 1447.

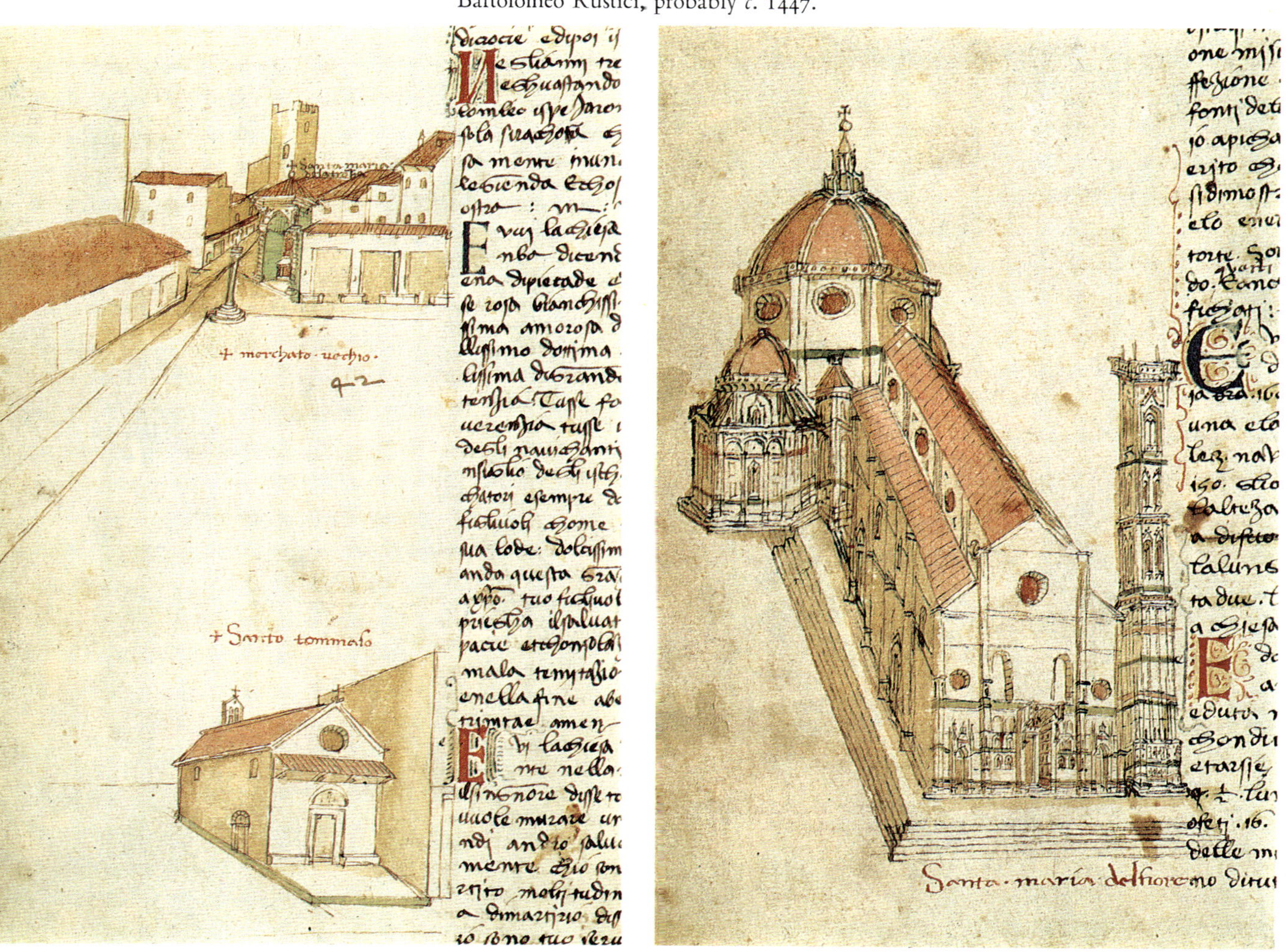

Florence, façade of the Palazzo Davanzati, *c.* 1330–60. Although heavily restored, it retains the typical appearance of a fourteenth-century Florentine nobleman's house, with its rustication and shops on the ground floor.

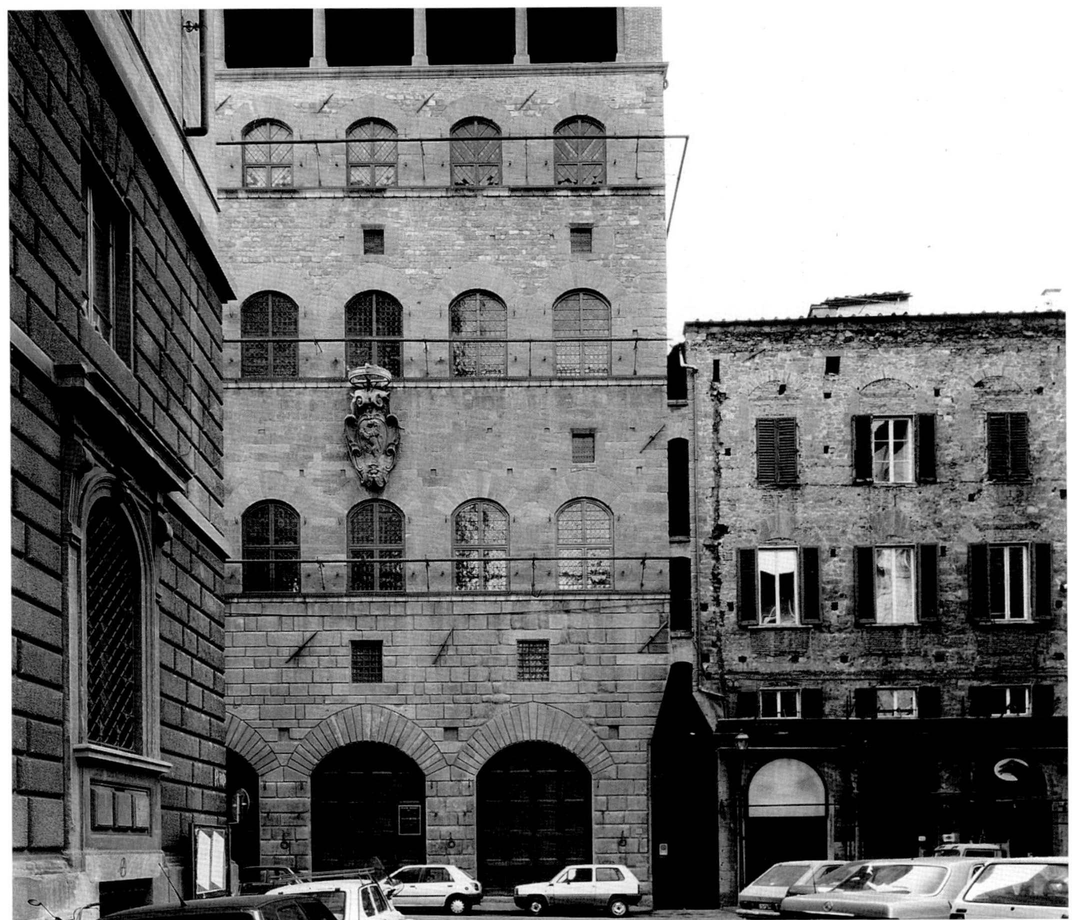

Florence, Piazza del Duomo. In 1389 a decision was made to build a great 'commercial centre' all around the apse of the Duomo. This is an important example of urban planning in the merchant city at the time of Leonardo Bruni: its projection into the fabric of the town even modified the cathedral's shape.

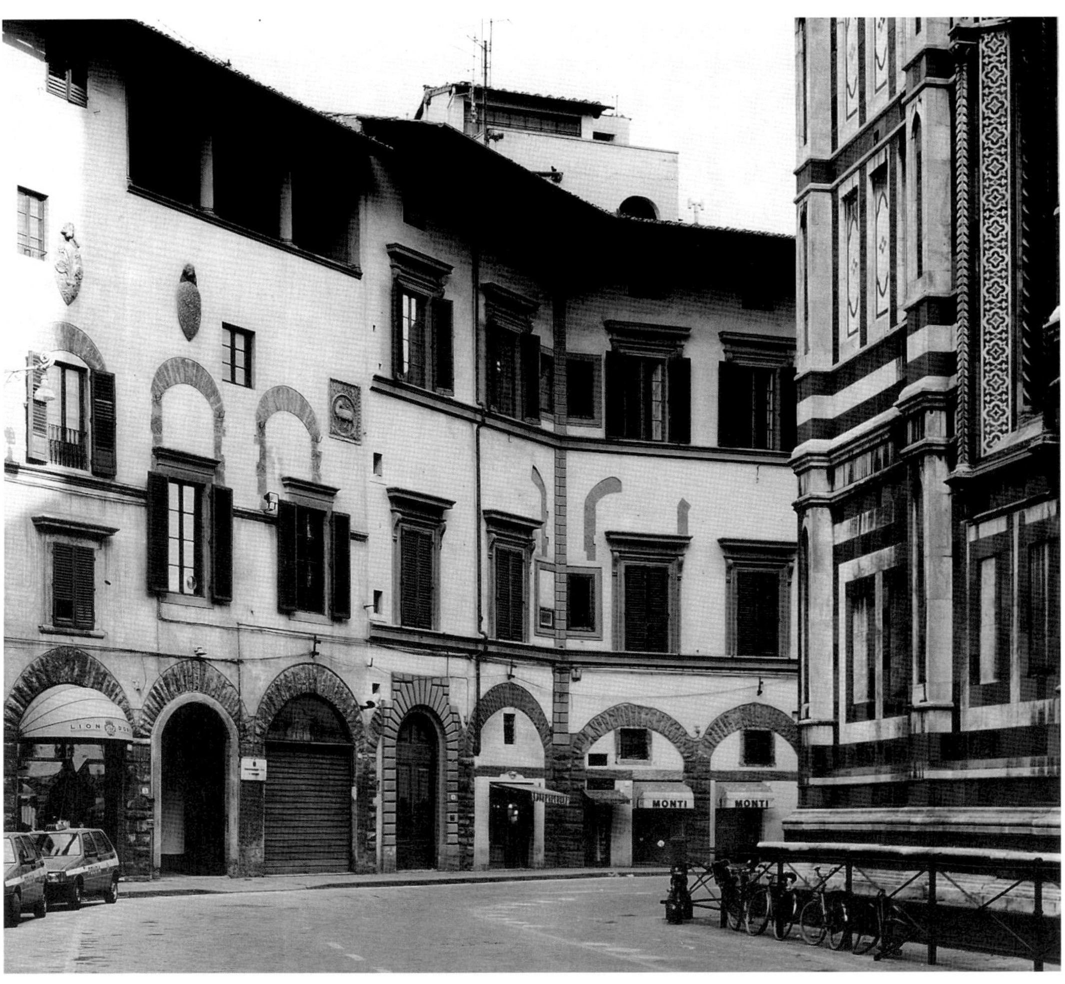

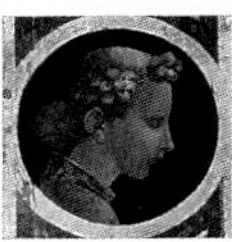

and Boccaccio. They planned to honour each by building a magnificent tomb inside the cathedral, decorated with sculptures and marbles. The fortunes of the Republic became identified with the Duomo building site, so creating a close relationship between the government of the city and the greatest architects and artists of Santa Maria del Fiore. Uccello was involved in this from an early age, and in the creation of important works of art there.

Uccello therefore took part in a great slice of Florence's history over a period of almost eighty years, not just political history, but also artistic and architectural history and in the great transition from Gothic to Renaissance. Here these two terms are not to be understood as having the general conceptual framework we normally associate with them, but a more particular, specific one. It is at this moment that we can see a fundamental continuity between a rich, delicate Gothic on the one hand, one which developed in the closing years of the Trecento and can be seen in the spatial harmony of the Loggia dei Priori (Loggia dei Lanzi) – not to mention the austere native Gothic of Santa Trinita which is not without its unpretentious eccentricities – and on the other hand, the new humanist language that arose from independent designs and developed into a Classical style based on Roman Classicism. In this Florence, civil architecture was evolving a geometric rational pattern of building, decorated with rustication, and wide open at ground level with great, low-arched vaults that anticipate nineteenth-century warehouses. Linked to this typology was the enormous process of urbanism around the new cathedral's apse: in an extroverted mood, the octagonal drum's large oculi on each of its sides (which formed the basis of the cupola and dictated its shape) looked out over the city.

In the Corso, the ancient Florentine *decumanus*, Brunelleschi was also playing a role in this new civil architecture, as the house of Apollonio Lapi[55] shows in its clear arrangement and symmetrical layout. No one has yet made a systematic study of this effervescence of Late Gothic which forms a large part of the precious fabric of the old centre of Florence, and whose solidity and resistance to fire constitute an exceptional phenomenon in Europe, paralleled only in other merchant cities such as Ghent.

If we take into account the architectonic language of the most 'committed' building work, it is at once obvious that in Florence Gothic was rethought and
Ill. p. 56 restructured in an original way. Andrea Orcagna's Tabernacle in Orsanmichele,
Ill. p. 113 surmounted by a cupola; the broad rhythm of the pillars in the nave of the new cathedral; Arnolfo di Cambio in the Palazzo Vecchio and at Santa Croce; the project for a gigantic cupola at Santa Maria del Fiore: all these were moving in the same direction: towards spatial synthesis instead of fragmentation, unity instead of multiplicity, calculated numbers instead of endless repetition, rational overall

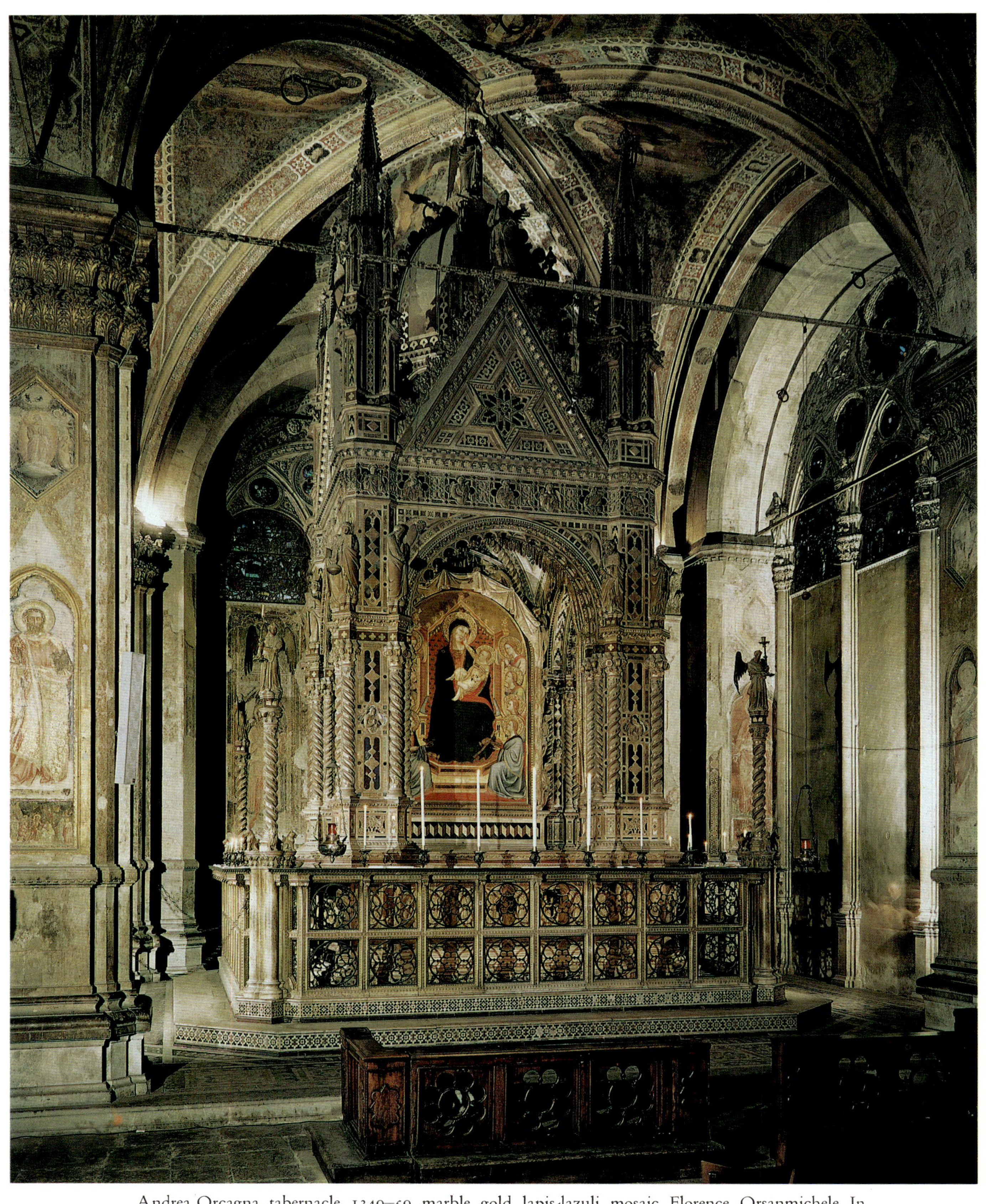

Andrea Orcagna, tabernacle, 1349–59, marble, gold, lapis-lazuli, mosaic, Florence, Orsanmichele. In this granary-chapel, Orcagna – who was also an important architect – adopted the cupola form to cap his tabernacle, which was to provide a source or a precedent for Brunelleschi.

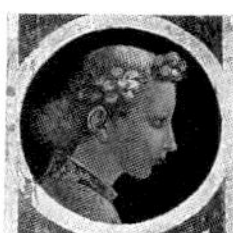

planning instead of the tradition of repetitious juxtapositions which was customarily practised on Gothic building sites. This Florentine way of being Gothic – which is so equivocal that it is sometimes interpreted as anti-Gothic and subjected to facile games such as reading characteristics into it that anticipate the Renaissance – concerns architecture, painting and sculpture simultaneously, with traditional Gothic aspects more marked in the figurative arts than in architecture, where the Gothic accent is attenuated by the austerity of the decoration. This tradition combines both respect for models and a calm disregard for them, and is found equally among the great masters and among minor artists. Personalities are distinguished within the general confines of an austere realism surrounding the 'narrative' and, despite all its diversity, giving works of art an indisputable unity, that smallest common denominator which is '*florentinitas*'.

Down the years, from the moment the branches of a burgeoning Renaissance language come to be grafted on to the stock of this tradition, from their first greening to their maturity, and until the moment they are finally marked by the most sophisticated intellectuality, Uccello was to be there, immersed in the most varied of contexts and apparently unperturbed, as if his intake was being filtered through his own introversion. He seems a stranger in the world around him, like a survivor from a bygone age. His distant attitude, his reclusive manner when faced with the wealth and complexity of cultural, artistic and social events, says much about his personality and stature. We might think that his plan was to create a disturbing universe exclusively through his painting, sidestepping all doctrinal and theoretical constraints and without always having to defer to a powerful family of patrons or bow to pressure from associations like the guilds. He built up, from work to work, a vigorous, subtle argument in defence of this personal universe, which would be categorized neither as 'Gothic' nor 'Renaissance', but which integrated all the spatial and expressive values of both these styles.

Given that he knew Ghiberti from childhood and during his crucial years of training, there is little doubt that Uccello had witnessed the 'competition' between Ghiberti and Brunelleschi – their collaboration was characterized by their conflicting styles – in the great saga of the cathedral's cupola, even though he was in Venice between 1425 and 1430, probably on Ghiberti's advice. Historical tradition tends to emphasize Brunelleschi's argumentative, polemical, bantering side, but more recent studies[56] have thrown new light on the positive aspects of his collaboration with Ghiberti, even if it did finish in a great quarrel over the cupola's lantern. Argument and conflict evidently sprang from differences in character between the two men: Brunelleschi, a pragmatic scientific mind, a man *senza lettere* but with a gift for

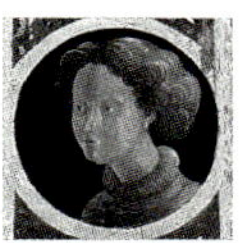

mechanics and subtle speculation, individualistic, caustic, disinclined to reveal the secrets of his art, having like Taccola[56a] that same Gothic mental watchfulness; Ghiberti, sociable, at ease in his dealings with his patrons, a pliable doctrinarian, a talent scout and the leader of a school organized around the forge in his workshop.

Uccello was doubtless there while Brunelleschi's plans were being realized, which, had they been carried to full term, would have marked the overall appearance of Florence with the master's *lucida ratio*, as much through his invention of architectonic types as through the creation of landmarks in the city or through innovation in stylistic characteristics. This grand design was to be completely disrupted, first by the war with Milan and its economic consequences, then by Brunelleschi's own death in 1446. The following ten years were to be blemished by the quarrel over the '*modo di Filippo*': the interpretation of Brunelleschi's heritage, a quarrel that set minor figures at loggerheads in noisy intrigues which were very Florentine in their ambitions, and which vindicated Brunelleschi's teaching without really having understood it, reducing his grand visions to a level of trivial workaday questions.

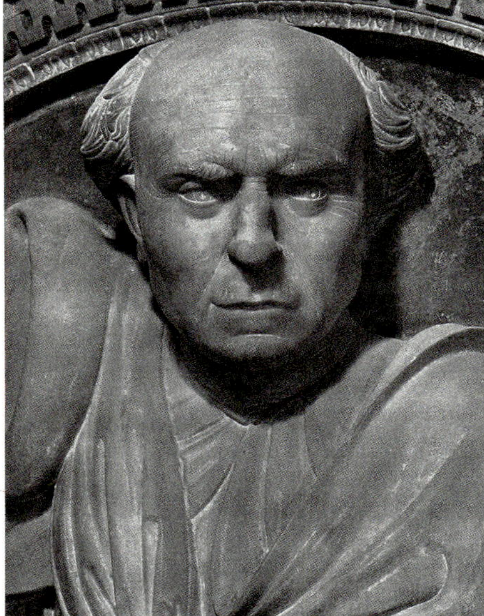

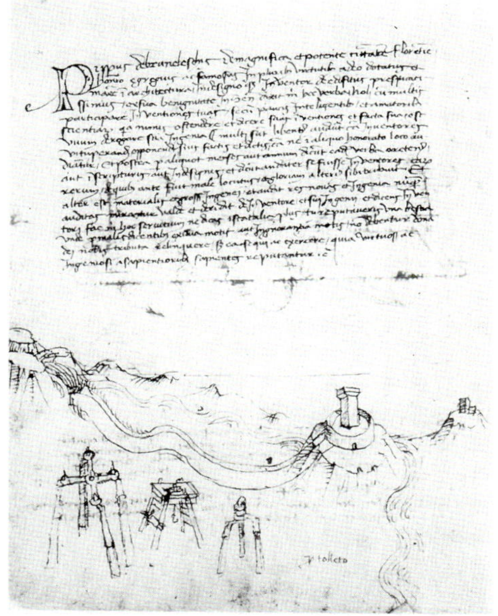

Left: Andrea di Lazzaro Cavalcanti (Il Buggiano), bust of Brunelleschi, detail, 1446–8, marble. Florence, Santa Maria del Fiore.

Right: Mariano di Jacopo (Il Taccola), manuscript relating his discussion with Brunelleschi at Siena. Munich, Bayerische Staatsbibliothek, ms. lat. 197, fol. 107–8v.

Meanwhile Leon Battista Alberti's new language must have appeared, from as early on as *De Pictura*, as the expression of this now maturing, solidly established humanism that was to grow into something didactic and doctrinaire in his *De Architectura*, where the new Vitruvius set out both old and modern values in an attempt to remedy the ills of the world and to found a new social order.

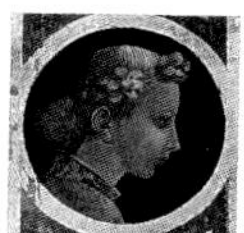

Ill. pp. 60, 61, 109

And yet in the three works he produced in Florence under the Rucellai's patronage – the palace, the chapel of San Pancrazio and the façade of Santa Maria Novella – Alberti, who was of good Florentine stock himself but who had trained in exile in Padua, took into account the city's tradition as regards proportions, materials and two-colour work. He relied on a continuity between Roman, Gothic and Renaissance which was to distort both the network of proportions and the architectonic structure set out by Classical antiquity.

At the centre, midway between the original humanism of Brunelleschi and Alberti's orthodoxy, and not so far removed from the ordinary artisan class of the *Quattrocentisti*, was Michelozzo, empirical, pragmatic, '*architettore et scultore di tutto*' according to Benedetto Dei's *Memorie* and according to the same source, in conflict with Brunelleschi, '*re del mondo*': a striking eye-witness view of the profound difference between a reductive attitude, one which could assimilate, was compliant and commercial, and an intellectual intransigence tailormade to appeal to and be welcomed by Alberti. Bright surfaces, snow-white lime-washed masonry, a simultaneous balance between naïveté and complexity, an ability to work stone

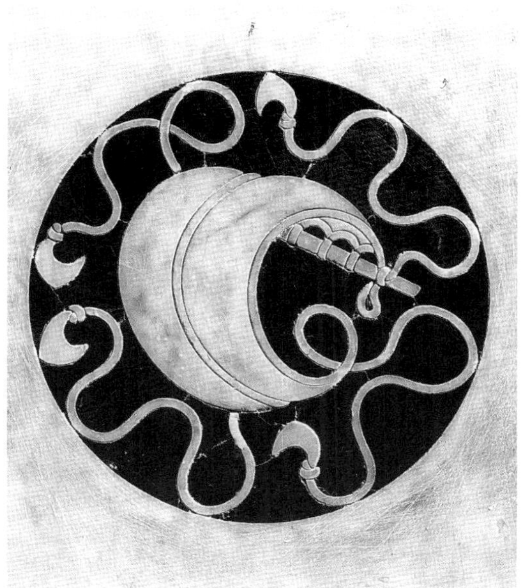

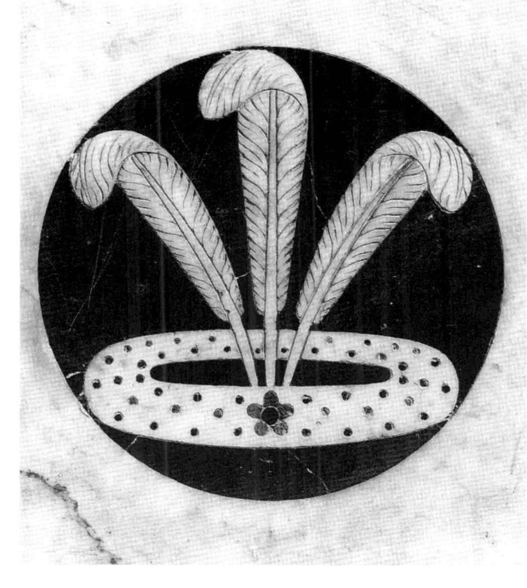

Leon Battista Alberti, details of the shrine of the Holy Sepulchre, with the heraldic emblems of the Rucellai family. Florence, San Pancrazio, Rucellai chapel.

which almost anticipated prefabricated mass production: such were Michelozzo's characteristics, in his haste to build under Medici patronage, thanks to that bank account with God that Cosimo, father of the state, had opened.

Recent studies by the Florentine school of architectural history have restored, bit by broken bit – and ever more clearly since the sixth centenary celebrations of

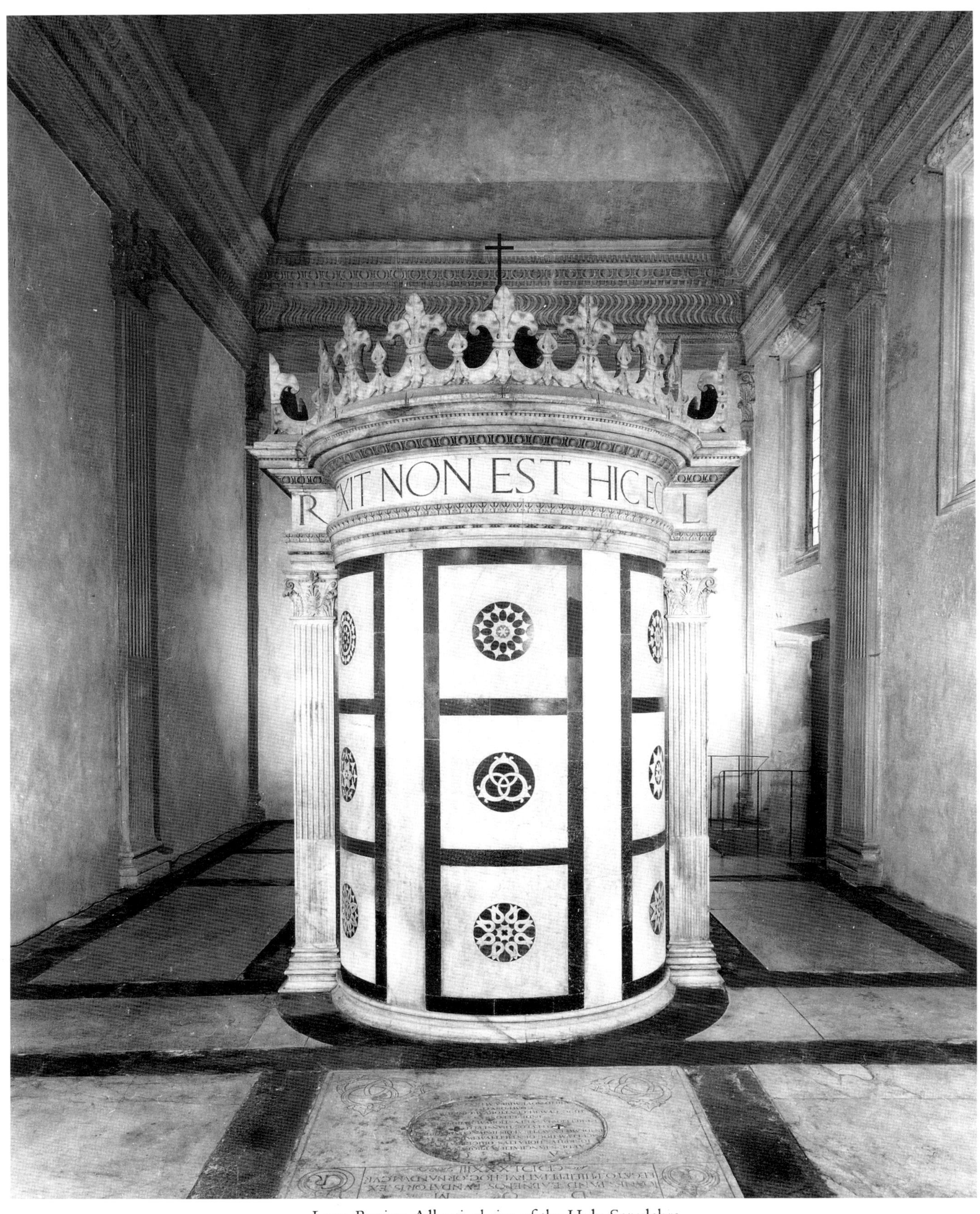

Leon Battista Alberti, shrine of the Holy Sepulchre,
Florence, San Pancrazio, Rucellai chapel.

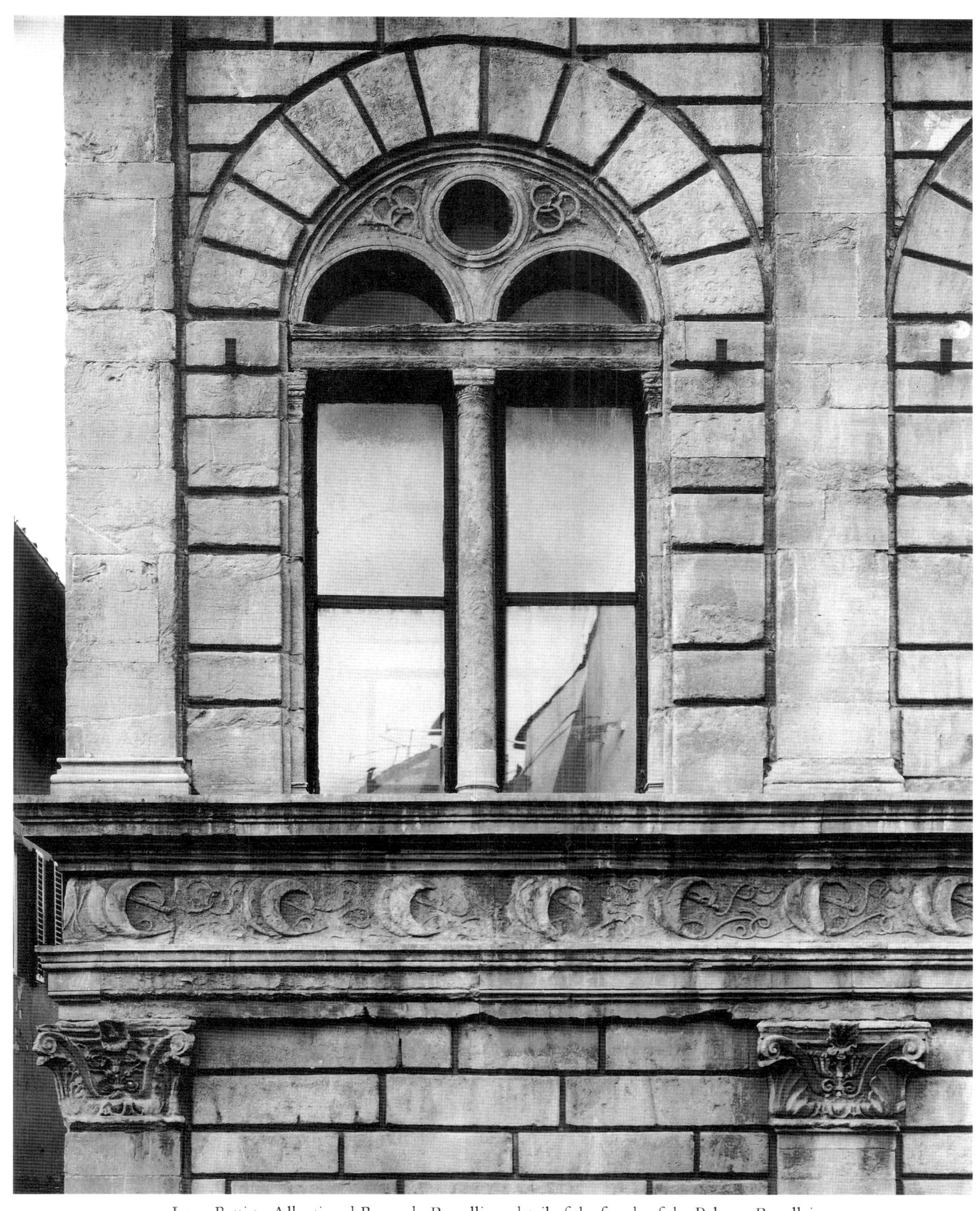

Leon Battista Alberti and Bernardo Rossellino, detail of the façade of the Palazzo Rucellai, Florence, showing the family emblem of a sail.

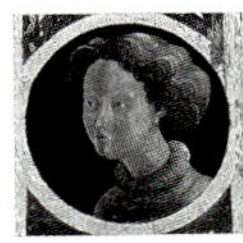

Brunelleschi's birth – the face of an 'alternative humanism' which can be identified in painting as it can in architecture, and which goes hand in hand with the concept of a Renaissance that abandons the usual historiographic schemata. It was in this particular Renaissance that Uccello participated, with his way of abstracting – as in a process of filtering or decanting – the visual expectations of his era, the culture of perspective, and the imagery, and at the same time rejecting those elements that had become most tainted with naturalism, aspects relating to the narrative and the chronicle. He found a kind of refuge in the enchanted palace of his images, where a return to courtly ritual was much more compelling than the urgency of the narrative.

His most significant success was to install the *Battles* in Lorenzo's apartments, at a time of subtle, intellectualized ambiguity that combined Neo-Platonism and religious piety, Petrarchism and popular poetry, extreme refinement and the practice of indulgences, epicurism and spirituality, social activity and solitude, ego-worship and a sense of statesmanship, tilting matches, cavalcades, tournaments and deep anxieties.

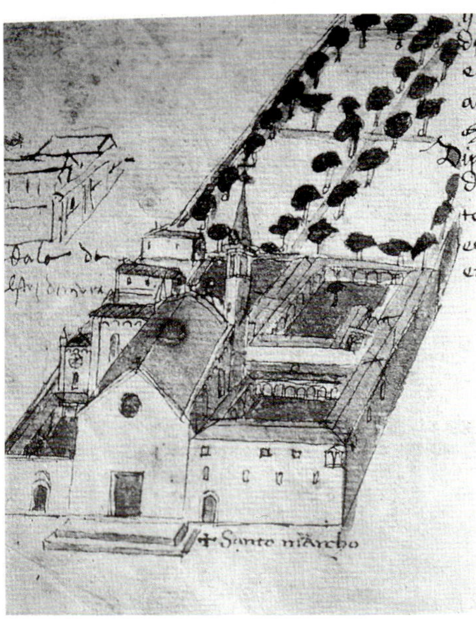

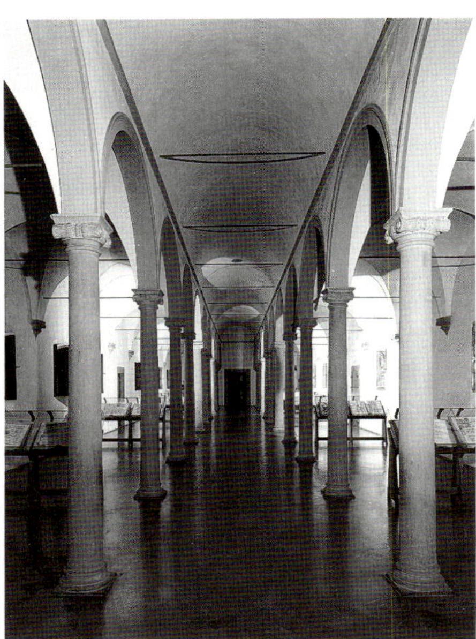

Left: the convent of San Marco depicted in the *Codex Rustici.* Florence, Biblioteca del Seminario Arcivescovile di Cestello.

Right: Michelozzo, library of the convent of San Marco.

At many levels, these are the themes that predominate in work common to genius or artisan, artist or stonecutter (a survival of Gothic in the new language – if we acknowledge certain special part-Florentine, part-Tuscan elements in this Gothic), and they predominate as much in the historical vocabulary as in the techniques used on the building sites. The novelty was in the reference to Antiquity; but this was an

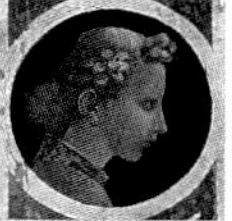

improbable invented, dreamed antiquity that lay outside any reference to the sources of Classical antiquity, a culture of images which rebounds from Fra Angelico's predellas or Gozzoli's frescoes, a culture common to sculptors, painters and architects, which had no need of theoretical support and formed its models from its own practical experiences.

In contrast to that culture, and totally absorbed in his *trattato*, Alberti refused any contact with building sites, any contamination from empiricism. Thus, in decisive mode he forged ahead, along new paths, to the mature world of the Renaissance. Alberti's advance would not make complete sense until later, when the need for models and solid references, for anchor-points and theoretical bases would be truly felt. Florence had not yet reached that stage; the most authentic spirit of the Renaissance during Uccello's lifetime is encapsulated in his own pictures. If by Renaissance we mean Classicism or a return to Antiquity, we must not forget that we see them through the filter of Neo-Classicism, and, before that, the Roman sixteenth century. The very relative character of the Classical code and the eclecticism of the sources of Roman Antiquity have little in common with the received idea of a

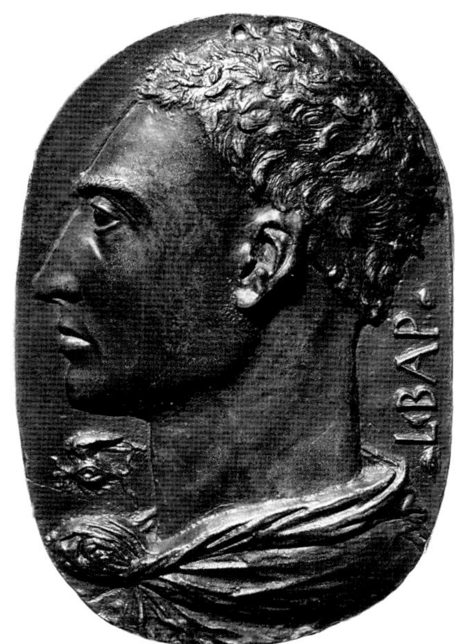

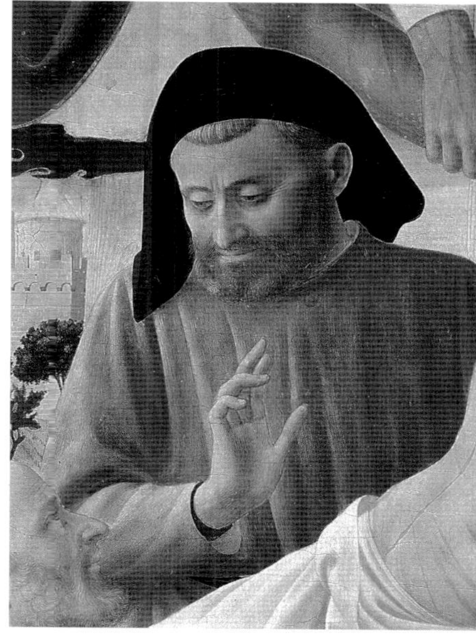

Left: Leon Battista Alberti, *Self-portrait.* Paris, Bibliothèque Nationale, Cabinet des Médailles.

Right: Fra Angelico, *Deposition*, detail (presumed portrait of Michelozzo), *c.* 1440, tempera on wood. Florence, convent of San Marco.

Renaissance that is homogeneous in style and in its system of codified signs. For this reason, the slogan-makers have invented a Brunelleschi who is anti-Classical, as though in opposition to some non-existent Academy. As for the '*crassa Minerva*', as Alberti would have said (or as we would say today in some anti-historical oversimplification), they reap their harvest among these signs, seeking to trace the

... alla quale si grande et magnifico tempio di puro et polito marmo in questa città si edifica

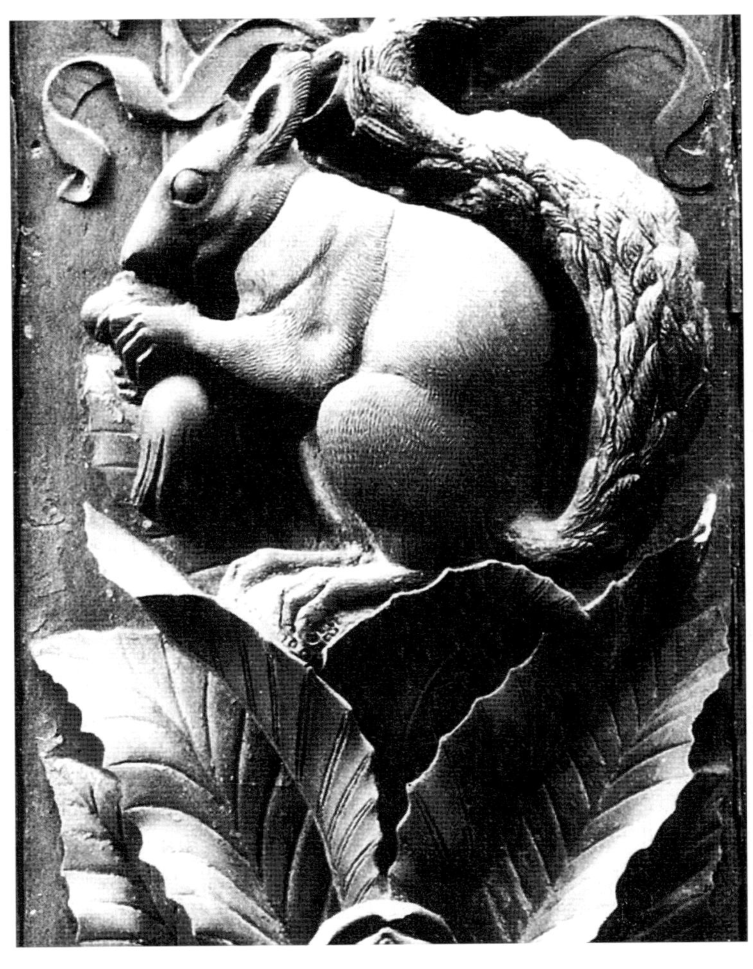
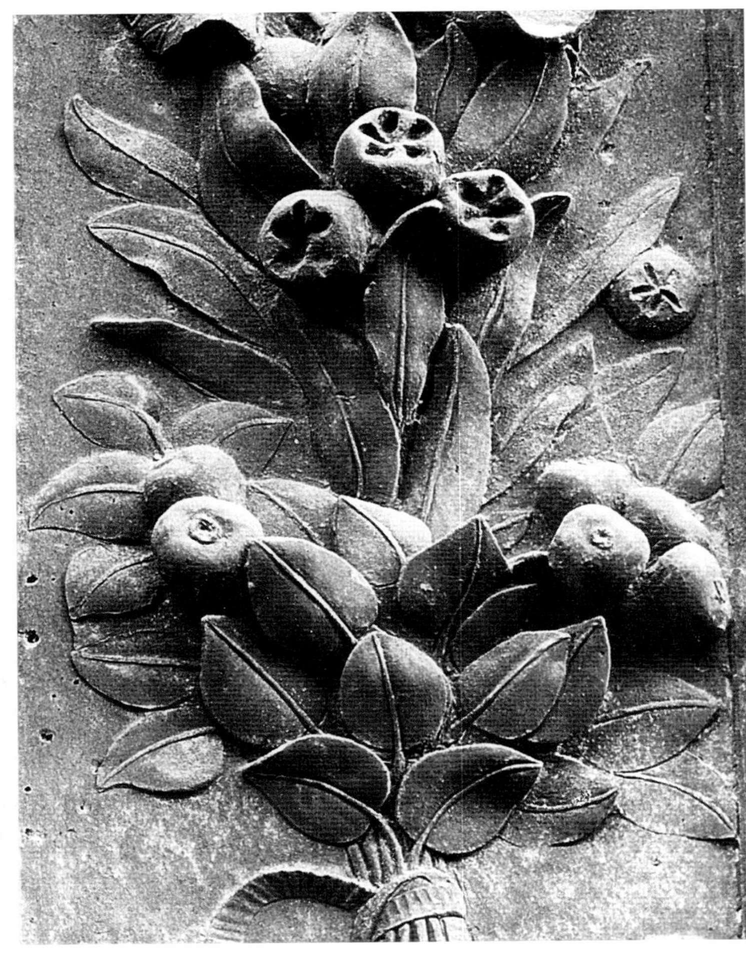
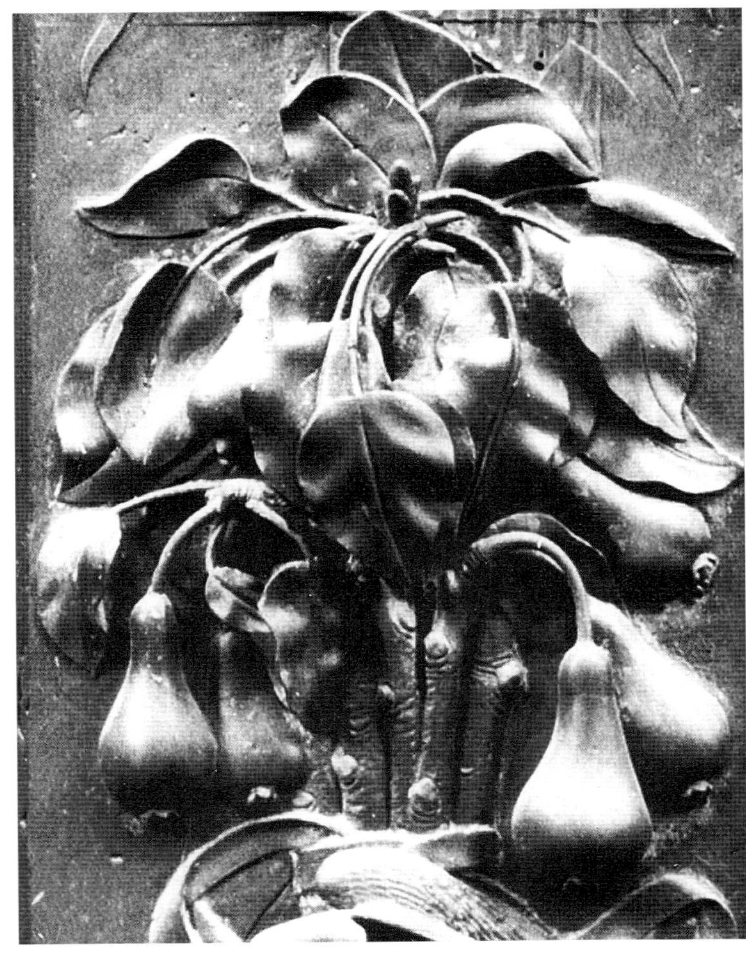
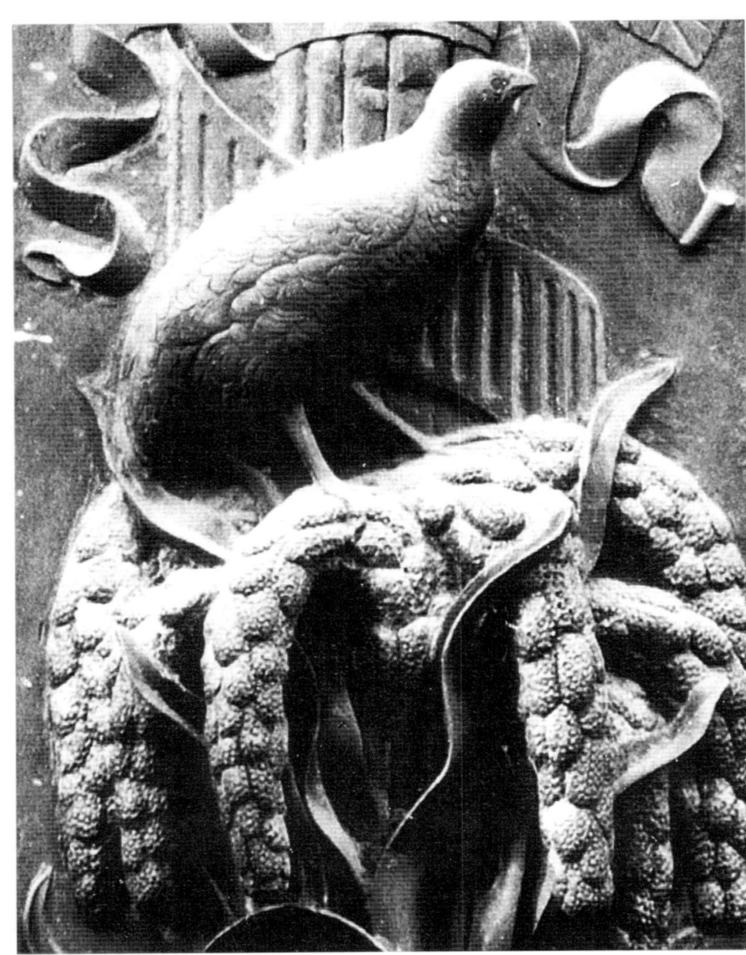

limits of a phenomenon which is basically evident in the profound otherness of Florence in relation to Rome. In fact, in spite of tangential points such as Donatello and Brunelleschi's trip to Rome, jubilees, the fact that Tuscan workmen and masters were working on the building site of the papal seat, all the catalogue of morphology in Renaissance Florence sprang from native matrixes. We do not have to look as far as the equivocal use of Romanesque instead of Roman for definitive evidence of this uninterrupted tradition. In the architectural orders, in their eidetic function, their proportions, the finesse of their craftsmanship, in the floral decorations, in the exuberance of frondescent candelabras, or in the opulence of the entablatures, everything is redolent of a native sense of the fantastic. For Ghiberti – with his quotations from Pliny and Vitruvius – as for Pisano, Antiquity was only a necessary reagent and not a categorical imperative.

Such then was the city where Uccello's life evolved, a life whose trajectory touched upon every aspect of Florentine complexity. He witnessed everything, but he was a witness who knew how to maintain his solitary, polemical role and who, in the course of his geometrical calculations and in his recourse to traditional forms, brought together all the visual enticements of his age, all the exigencies of science and all the transgressions.

Facing page: Lorenzo Ghiberti, details of the north doors and the Doors of Paradise. Florence, Baptistery.

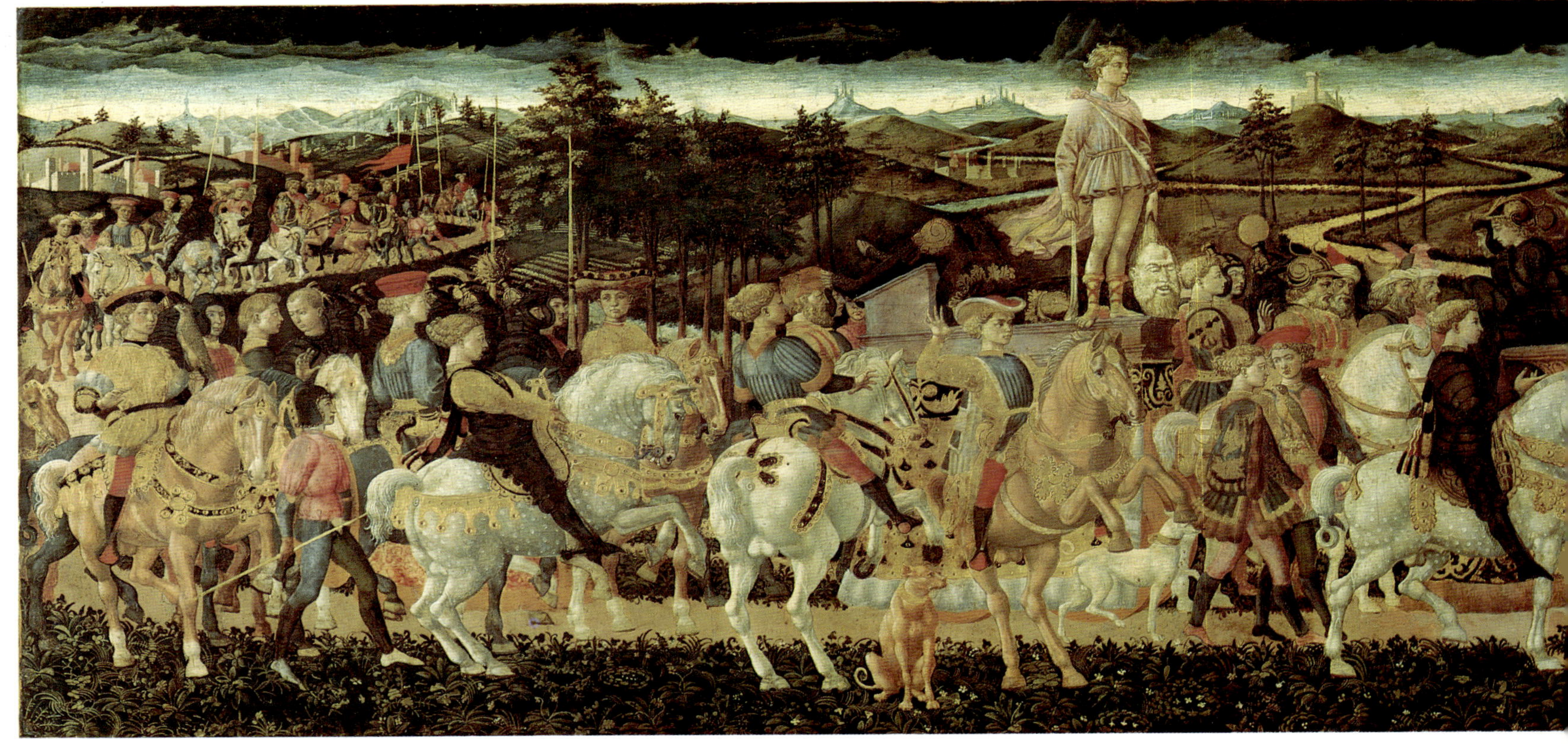

Francesco Pesellino, *The Triumph of David*, *c.* 1440–50, tempera on wood, 43.2 × 177.8 cm. London, private collection, on loan to the National Gallery.

Francesco Pesellino, *David and Goliath*, *c.* 1440–50, tempera on wood, 43.2 × 177.8 cm. London, private collection, on loan to the National Gallery.

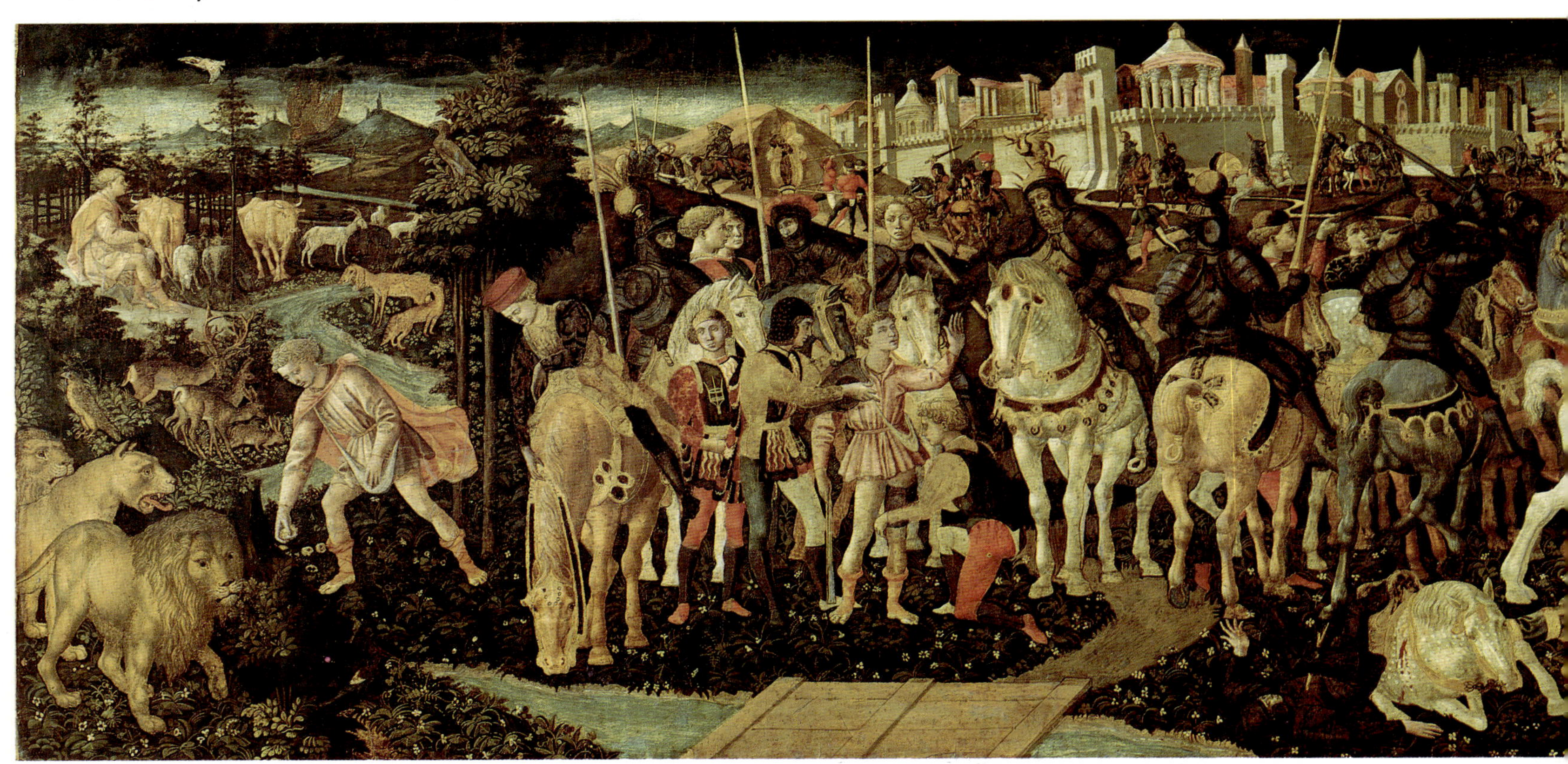

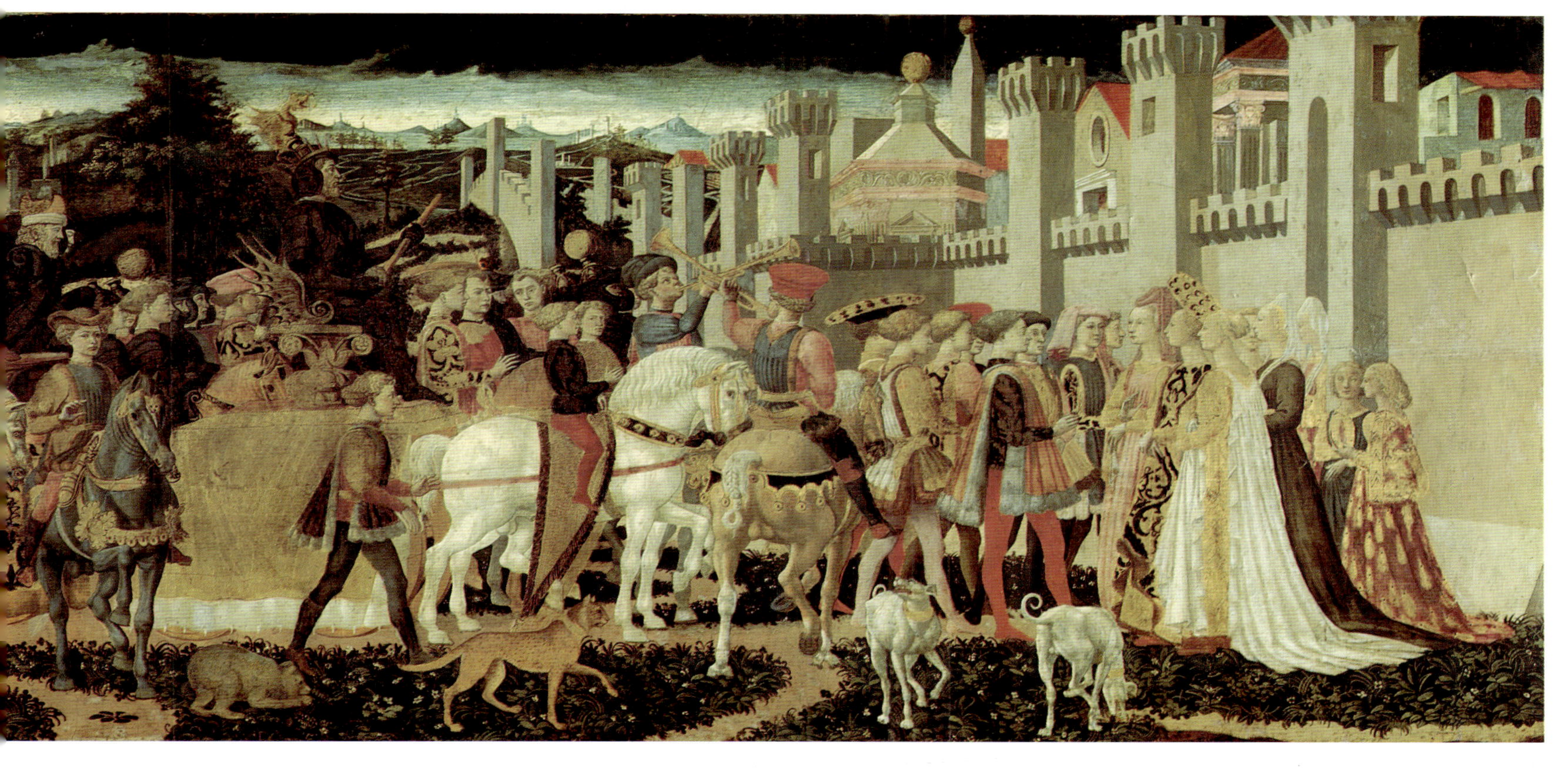

Chapter Two

ART IN FLORENCE
at the time of Uccello

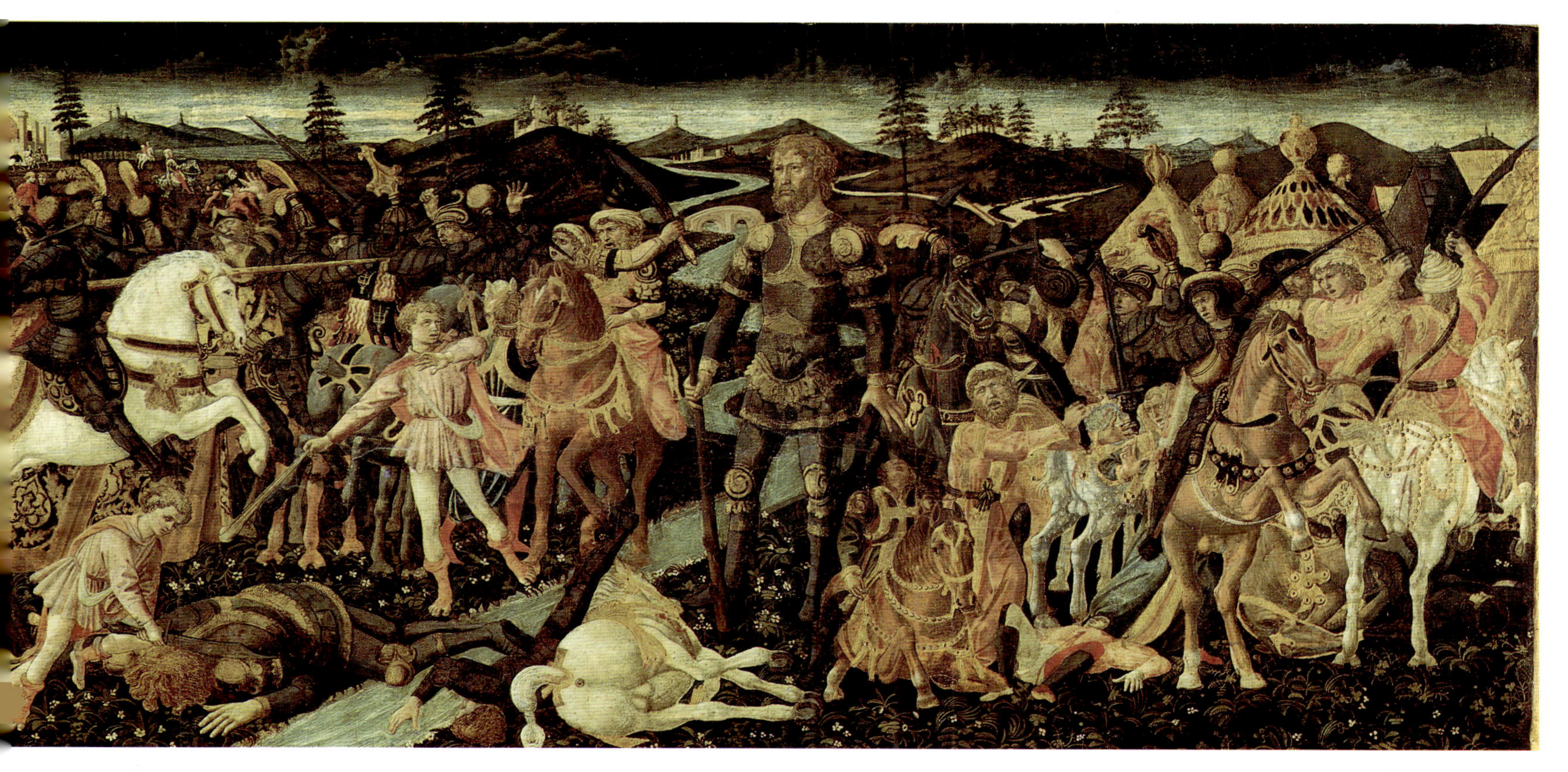

THE BEGINNINGS OF A CENTURY

To understand where Uccello's paintings came from, we must delve into a little-known period in Florence's history, namely the first and especially the second decades of the Quattrocento. Florence was then a complex, diversified milieu characterized – not always consciously – by the unequivocal caesura between the new attractions of humanism and solid tradition inherited from the rich, extraordinary era of the Trecento. In painting, this tradition was represented, in a great variety of degrees, by a generation who followed Gaddi, the Orcagnas and Spinello Aretino. But in the field of 'modern' figurative art, sculpture – the 'Antique' theme of statuary – was the preferred medium. It was the well-known competition of 1401 for the bronze doors of the Baptistery that opened the new century – according to a view so deeply entrenched that it could well serve as a chapter heading for a textbook. Just ten

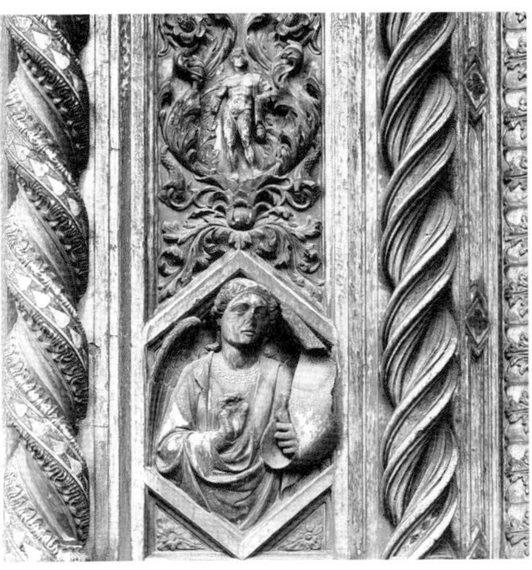

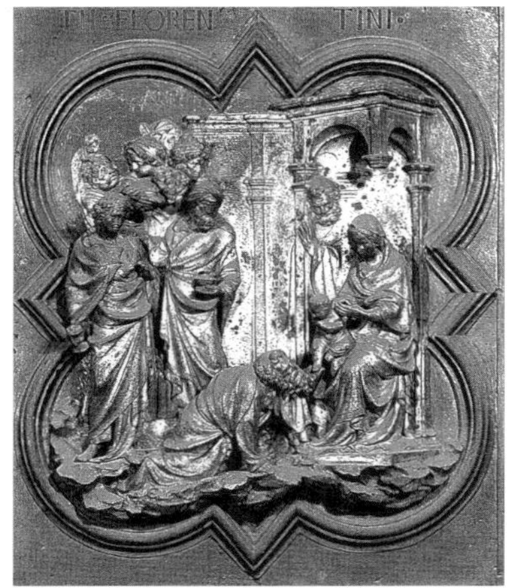

Left: Porta della Mandorla, detail of upright, *c.* 1391. Florence, Santa Maria del Fiore.

Right: Lorenzo Ghiberti, north doors, detail, *The Adoration of the Magi.* Florence, Baptistery.

years before, the sculpted decoration of the Porta della Mandorla, at Santa Maria del Fiore, had illustrated the continuance of late Trecento figurative art beyond its time. And it was to be a sculptor, Donatello, who – even before Masaccio – would first (*c.* 1417–22) translate Brunelleschi's theories on perspective into pictorial form, in his predella of *Saint George and the Dragon* in almost flat relief.

In contrast to this indisputable dynamism, painting in Florence for the first twenty years of the century might appear stagnant, backward and somewhat leaden. However, close examination reveals that it was not lacking in innovation and exploratory approaches, and in contacts in a variety of directions, all bearing the germs of future developments. Everything was evolving in a complex dialectic between, on the one hand, a tendency for art to withdraw into its shell (the 'return to Giotto' approach promoted by the active, versatile Agnolo Gaddi) and, on the other hand, the tight network of connections throughout the Tuscan region – notably with the Sienese world – relationships that political conflicts do not appear to have hampered (nor would they suffer from Florence and Siena's continuing hostilities when Uccello became a mature artist) – and finally the international open-mindedness of Late Gothic, oriented first towards Lombardy, then Bologna and Spain (and Valencia in particular). These many different trends were what most characterized the end of the Trecento at the time of Uccello's birth,[57] and were orchestrated first by a group composed of Orcagna's successors and disciples, and then by Agnolo Gaddi, whose studio was no less flourishing and indeed very well organized.

Neither delicate painters like the Master of the Straus *Madonna*, nor good elegant *Ill. p. 70* calligraphers versed in the problems of space like the Master of 1419, pleasant

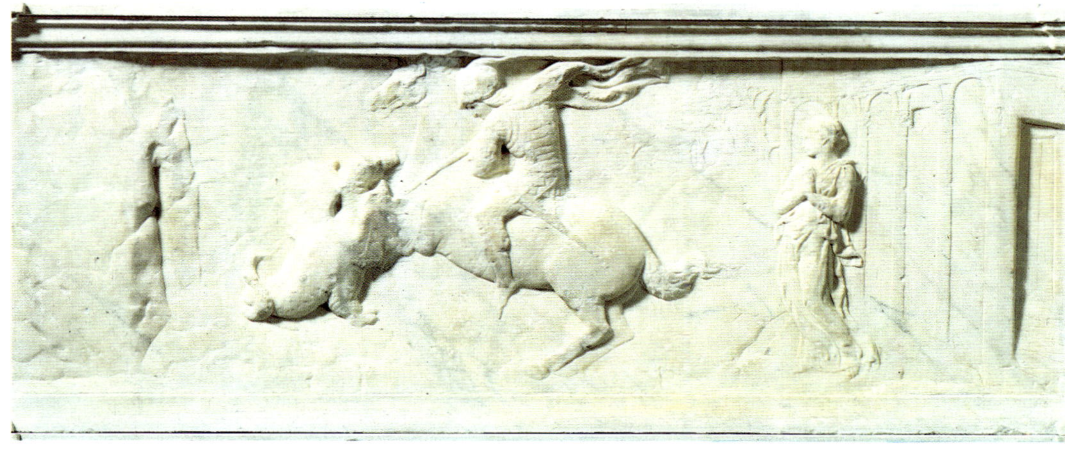

Donatello, *Saint George and the Dragon*, *c.* 1417–22, predella of the *Saint George* niche at Orsanmichele, marble, 39 × 120 cm. Florence, Bargello.

narrative history painters like Giovanni del Biondo, nor popular chroniclers like Francesco di ser Cenni could be said to have been the young Uccello's references. He much preferred the clever, mannered Gherardo Starnina, proselytizing an open-mindedness towards Europe and specially Spain. He was indeed a master of the first order, whose importance, since his famous cycle in the Carmine (1404) disappeared,

STARNINA

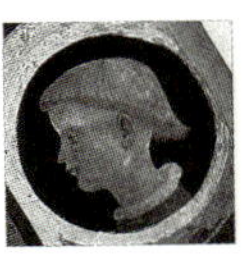

can be glimpsed in the few panels and precious fragments of frescoes that remain. Starnina, Masolino's immediate predecessor, also had a certain ascendancy over Lorenzo Ghiberti, who undoubtedly also practised the art of painting.[58] In Florence, Starnina championed International Late Gothic, focusing his refinements in monumental compositions with fluid, rounded linear rhythms, coupled with an extremely delicate colouration and a powerful expression of 'attitudes'. All this is highlighted most thoroughly by Vasari who praised 'the abundance of ideas in the attitudes of his figures' and recalled the enormous success of the *Stories of Saint Jerome* in the Carmine 'owing to the verve with which he was able to render feelings and attitudes that none of his predecessors had ever expressed'.[59] After many years Starnina still had his emulators, as is evidenced in the detail recollected by Vasari of the master whipping a young pupil (cycle of *Saint Jerome*), which was used again in Benozzo Gozzoli's cycle at San Gimignano. Starnina's influence explains why certain stylistic characteristics survived and recurred in paintings by Lorenzo Monaco, Ghiberti, Masolino and the young Uccello. It was in this context, in this

per avere egli espresso vivamente molti affetti e attitudini non state messe in opera fino allora dai pittori stati innanzi a lui.

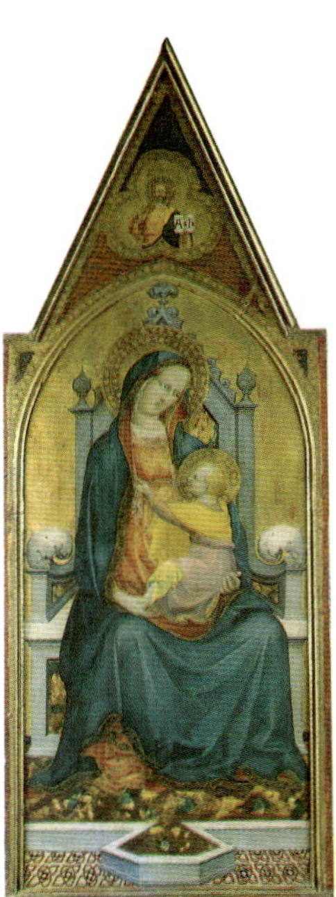

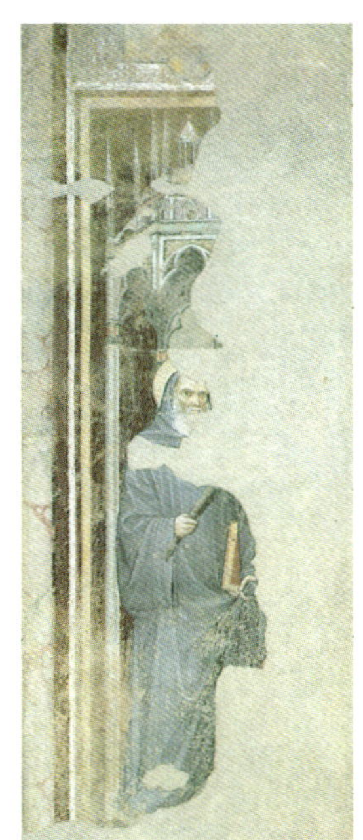

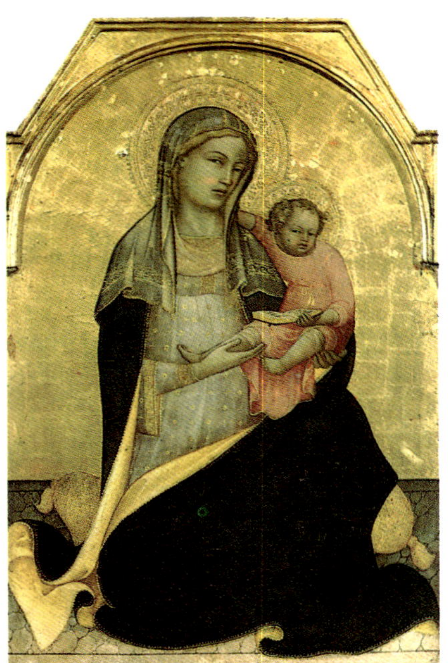

Left: Master of 1419, *Madonna and Child*, tempera on wood, 196.2 × 68.2 cm. Cleveland Museum of Art.

Centre: Gherardo Starnina, *Saint Benedict*, *c.* 1404, fresco. Florence, Santa Maria del Carmine.

Right: Lorenzo Monaco, *Maestà* (*Madonna Enthroned*), 1404, central panel of a triptych, tempera on wood, complete work 157 × 197 cm. Empoli, Museo della Collegiata di Sant'Andrea.

choice of a 'modern' style, that, at the heart of the best local Late Gothic trends, Uccello found himself in Ghiberti's workshop on the eve of the agreement of 1407 for the north door of the Baptistery.[60]

GENTILE DA FABRIANO

During the years he was in close contact with Ghiberti, Uccello developed an enthusiasm for Gentile da Fabriano who was collaborating with Ghiberti on the

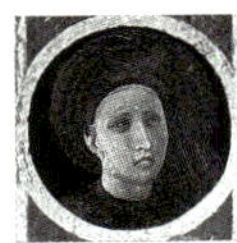

Strozzi commission at Santa Trinita. Gentile da Fabriano was one of the most outstanding personalities of the early 1420s but he was not the only one, and for a while he shared his laurels with his elder, Giovanni Toscani, the painter of coffers and decorator of chests. Toscani, who had probably also worked in Ghiberti's studio, achieved that same seductive universe of Gentile[61] in his *The Adoration of the Magi* (Private Italian Collection). Gentile painted important pictures in Florence,
Ill. pp. 71, 72 especially *The Adoration of the Magi* for Palla Strozzi, intended for the altar of the Sacristy in Santa Trinita (1422–3). Meanwhile, in Ghiberti's studio as it worked on the Baptistery doors, Masolino da Panicale was becoming established, almost at middle age (he was born in 1383), championing the new delicate style of painting that had originated with Starnina. In 1404, Starnina had converted the austere Camaldolite, Lorenzo Monaco, to Gothic elegance, as can be seen in Lorenzo's triptych for the Collegiata at Empoli and his triptych of Monteoliveto, 1407–10; and the Prague *Agony in the Garden*, 1408. In Lorenzo's work, we find plenty of motifs that Uccello would cherish throughout his own explorations in painting: there are

LORENZO MONACO

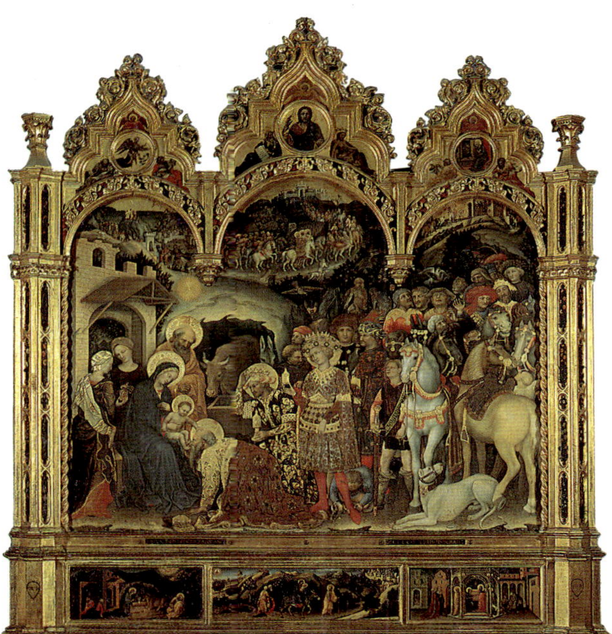

Gentile da Fabriano, *The Adoration of the Magi*, 1423, tempera on wood, 300 × 282 cm. Florence, Uffizi.

visionary landscapes, forests by night, hailstorms and tempests, even diamond-sharp scenery. All these motifs were developed in abundance in Lorenzo's monumental
Ill. pp. 72, 73 retable for Santa Maria degli Angeli (Florence, Uffizi) dating from February 1414–1413 in the Florentine calendar. (New Year's Day was 25 March, so for the first three months of the year there is a discrepancy between their calendar and ours.) Although

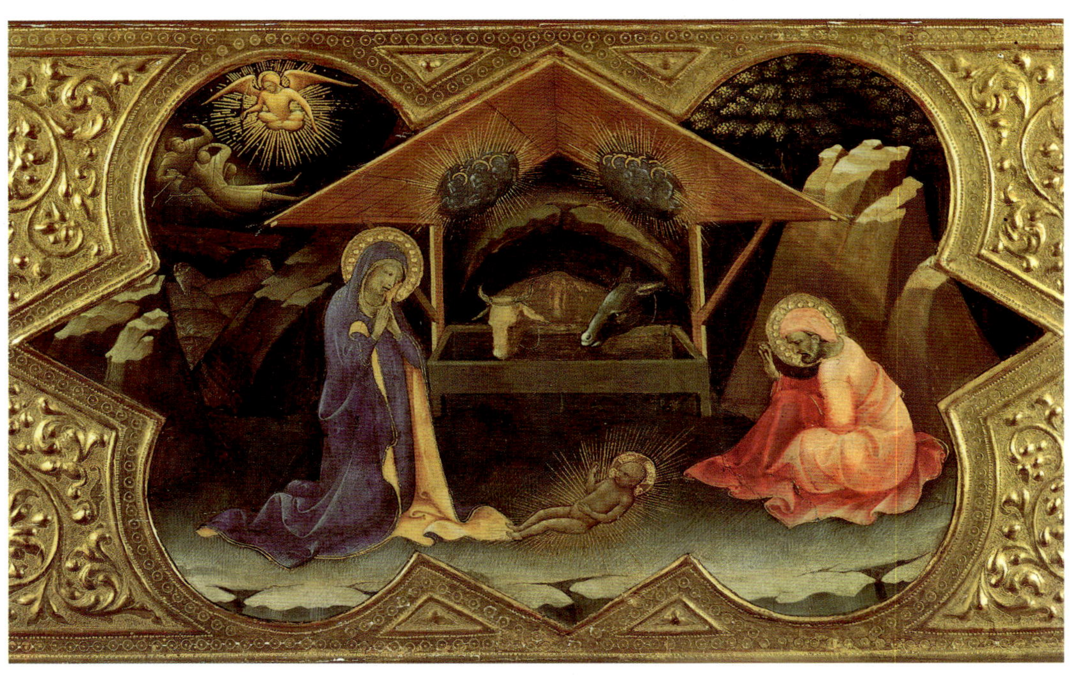

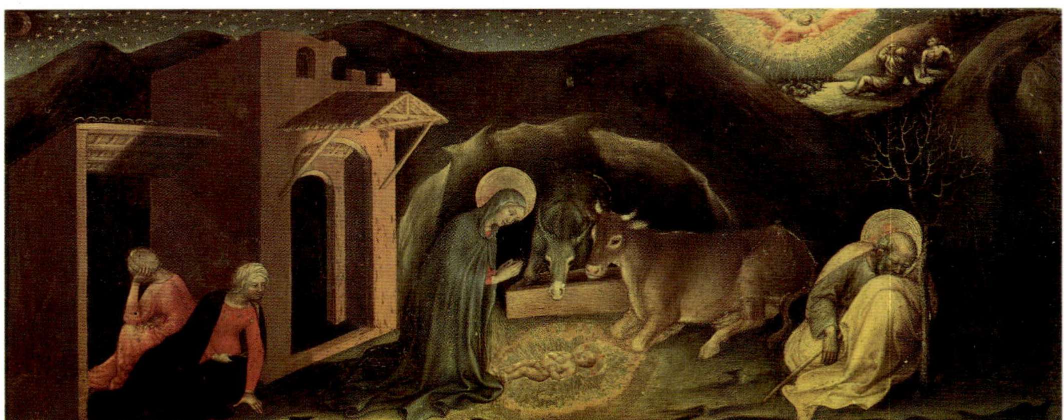

Above: Lorenzo Monaco, *Nativity*, detail of predella of the *Coronation of the Virgin* (*see facing page*).

Below: Gentile da Fabriano, *Nativity*, detail of predella of the *Adoration of the Magi* (*see preceding page*).

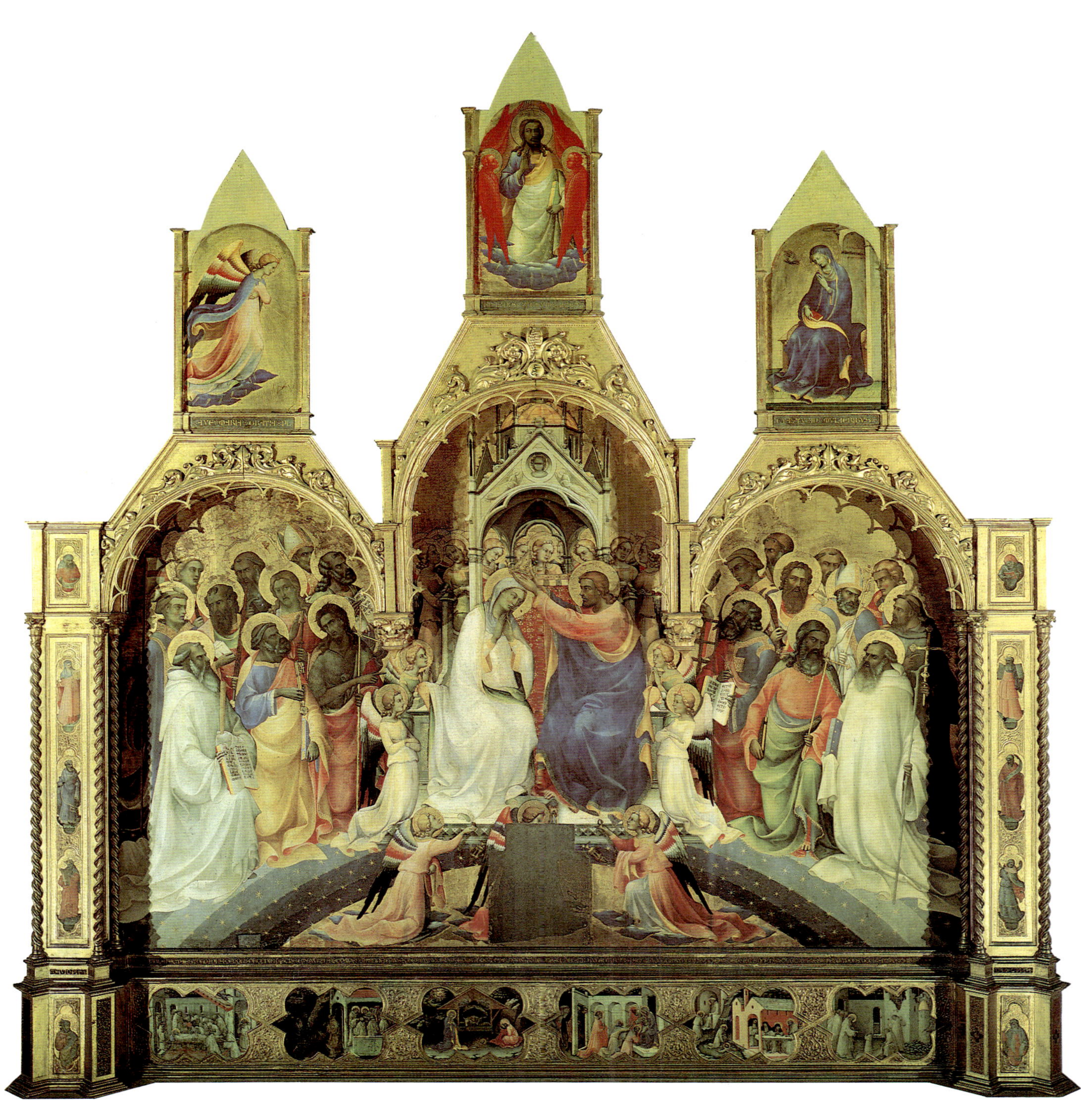

Lorenzo Monaco, *The Coronation of the Virgin*, tempera on wood, 450 × 350 cm.
Florence, Uffizi (formerly in Santa Maria degli Angeli).

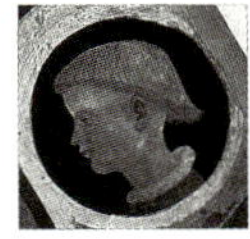

this was painted for a convent, Uccello would certainly have had the opportunity to study it in great detail later – after 1431 – when he gained admittance into the circle of Camaldolite patrons.

The beginning of the 1420s witnessed the arrival in Florence of the cool colourist, Cola da Camerino (between 1420 and 1422) and, as we have seen, Gentile da Fabriano who came from Venice, perhaps accompanied by two young pupils, Domenico Veneziano and Jacopo Bellini, whose careers are known after they became acquainted with Tuscan art. Masolino and Masaccio's débuts also date from this period, and they certainly left their mark on Bicci di Lorenzo's conservative studio, as can be seen in his polyptych at Empoli.[62] Uccello who was living near Bicci's studio in the Corso degli Adimari (or dei Dipintori) at this time would not be sidetracked by it. Gentile's da Fabriano's impact is particularly apparent: he exerted great influence through his *Adoration of the Magi* on young Florentine artists such as Giovanni Toscani, Masolino, Giovanni di ser Giovanni (Masaccio's brother known as Lo Scheggia and a pupil of Bicci di Lorenzo), and Mariotto di Cristofano (who

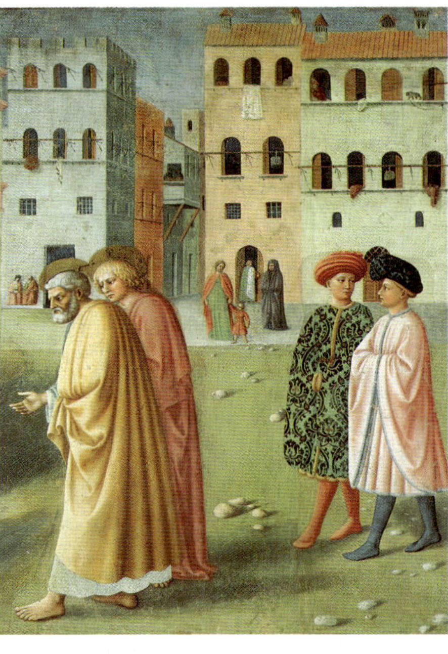

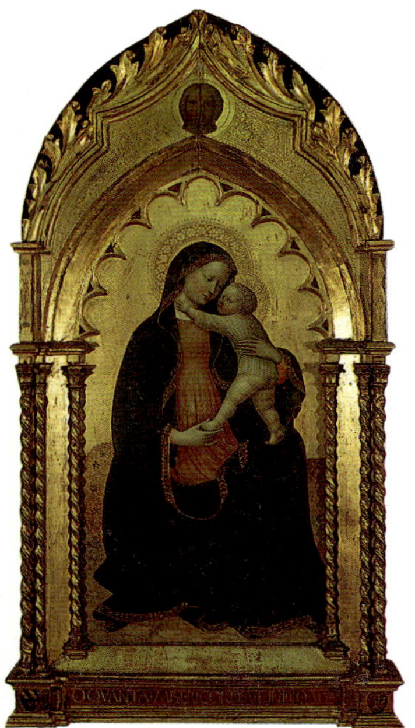

Left: Masolino da Panicale, *Saint Peter Healing the Sick*, *c.* 1425, detail, fresco. Florence, Santa Maria del Carmine, Brancacci chapel.

Right: Masolino da Panicale, *Madonna and Child*, *c.* 1423, tempera on wood, 96 × 52 cm. Bremen, Kunsthalle.

married Masaccio's half-sister). His impact – clearly shown in Uccello's *Battles* or Domenico Veneziano's tondo of *The Adoration of the Magi* – was to last until Gozzoli's late revival in the Palazzo Medici some twenty years later. Gentile, who was a subject of study at Santa Trinita – where Lorenzo Monaco was also decorating two chapels – left for Siena *c.* June 1425, having given Florence another painting, the

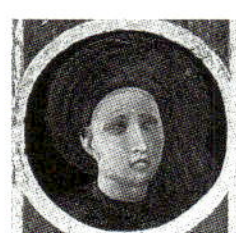

Quaratesi polyptych, which is of a very high level. And, from Siena, came Giovanni di Paolo in order to study the *Adoration* at Santa Trinita. Around 1424 Ghiberti was working in Siena on the baptismal fonts in the cathedral, and it was to Siena that Dello Delli fled, when his father was accused of treason and the whole family was forced into exile. Uccello's friendship with Ghiberti and Delli, his interest in Gentile and in Jacopo della Quercia (whose work he found again in Bologna) could explain his probable journey to Siena in 1424–5. This is not documented, but the hypothesis is based on his stylistic borrowings from Giovanni di Paolo, Sassetta and in some small measure from Domenico di Bartolo.

MASACCIO

Meanwhile, in Florence events were moving apace. After painting his first known work, his triptych for San Giovenale (1422), Masaccio moved on to more important commissions: the *Sagrà* in monochrome (now lost) in the cloister of the Carmine, the retable for Sant'Ambrogio with Masolino (Uffizi), the polyptych at Pisa (1426) and the frescoes for the Brancacci chapel. Masolino, who had registered with the Guild of Doctors and Apothecaries in 1423, was painting the Bremen *Madonna* (Kunsthalle).

Ill. pp. 74, 77

Ill. p. 74

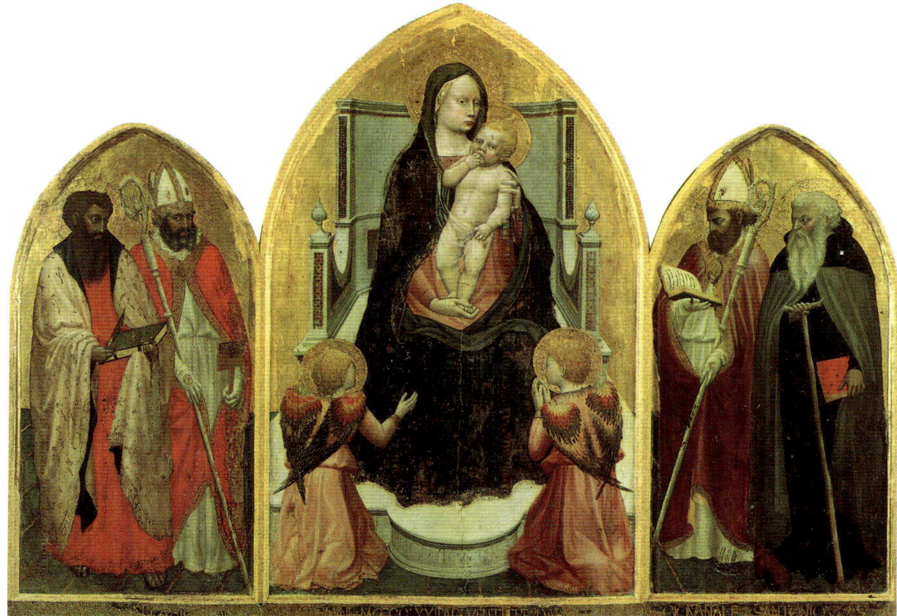

Masaccio, *San Giovenale Triptych*, 1422, tempera on wood, 108 × 153 cm. San Giovenale di Cascia di Reggello, church of San Pietro.

In 1424, he began the frescoes for the Brancacci chapel on his own, then finished the cycle at Empoli in November 1424. Masolino took his young associate to work with him on the scaffolding in the Brancacci chapel, then, at the height of his fame, accepted Filippo Scolari's invitation to go to Hungary.

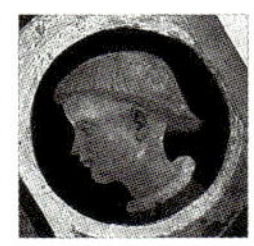

Among the young painters to emerge at the end of 1425 was the Dominican Fra Angelico (Guido di Pietro) who had already been working in Florence in 1417 when Masaccio arrived, and who painted the triptych of San Pietro Martire shortly after 1425, followed by the retable for San Domenico at Fiesole. It was at this moment, just as the tide of new experiences and enticements was mounting, that Uccello, almost in reverse of Gentile da Fabriano's footsteps, left for Venice. Venice was undergoing a change, as the cultural atmosphere and figurative arts of the period show: it was beginning to distance itself from the traditional Byzantine-Aegian axis, and instead draw closer to Italy. The 'quest for *terra firma*' became apparent as much in its receptivity to International Gothic as in its contacts with Tuscan innovators such as Michelozzo, Donatello, Uccello and Andrea del Castagno. When Uccello arrived in 1425, Venice had become *the* important centre for International Gothic, and an unrivalled market for glass, lacquerware, silks and precious pigments. Uccello would have been able to admire the sculptures of the Dalle Masegne brothers (the iconostasis of San Marco, the balcony of the Council Chamber in the ducal

VENICE

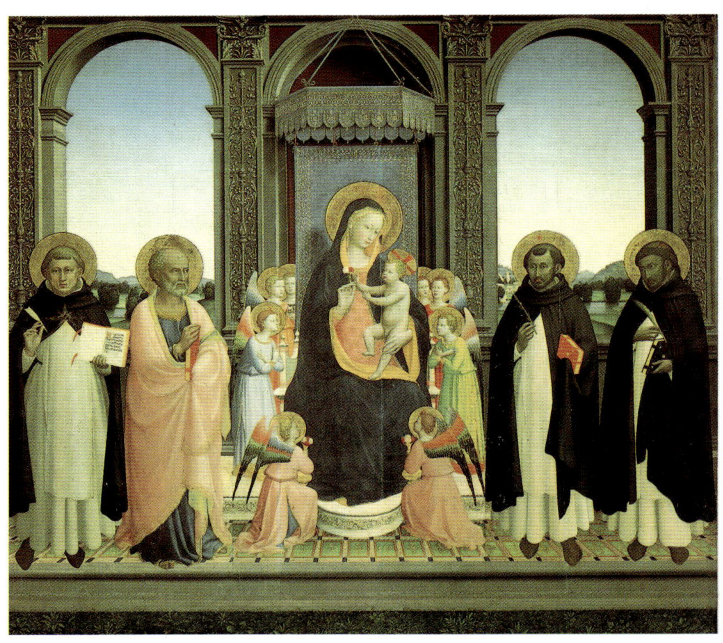

Fra Angelico, San Domenico Altarpiece, *Madonna with Angels and Saints*, Fiesole, San Domenico. Conceived as a triptych, the work was changed into an altarpiece in 1501 by Lorenzo di Credi.

palace), the flamboyant architecture of the Lombard Matteo Raverti, precious painted panels by Michele Giambono, Niccolò di Pietro Gerini and Jacobello del Fiore, and marvellous frescoes by Gentile da Fabriano (painted after 1408) and Pisanello (painted after 1417) in the ducal palace, not to mention the work of Tuscan sculptors such as the monument to Tommaso Mocenigo (1423) at Santi Giovanni e

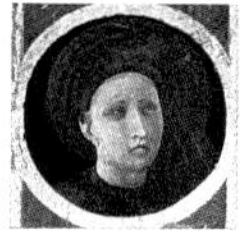

Paolo. It was no accident that Uccello's long Venetian visit took place between two of Ghiberti's trips to the lagoon, one during the winter of 1424–5 and the other, whose date is less certain, in 1430 (Krautheimer). Uccello's absence was to be heavy with consequences, at a time when the debate on painting in Florence was fuelled by Masaccio's accomplishment. Uccello was not among the first of its 'dumbstruck' viewers (Longhi) when the scaffolding in the Brancacci chapel was dismantled and the *Trinity* revealed, nor did he have immediate sight of works of art whose atmospheric sensitivity would herald the future, like Masaccio's *Annunciation* (now lost) in San Niccolò Oltrarno.

FRA ANGELICO AND FILIPPO LIPPI

In 1425 (or later in 1426), Lorenzo Monaco died, followed in 1427 by Gentile da Fabriano, in 1428 by Masaccio and in 1430 by Giovanni Toscani, Masolino left Florence for good. A new generation who would be dominated by Fra Angelico and Filippo Lippi came to the fore. Lippi, who was born in 1406, was greatly influenced by Masaccio at the beginning of his career, displaying a complete 'Masaccism' that verged at times on the vernacular. His first works date from *c.* 1430. Paintings such as the *Trivulzio Madonna* (formerly in Florence, in the Rinuccini chapel at the Carmine), the *Madonna with Angels and Saints* of Venice (Cini Collection) and *Madonna Enthroned with Angels and Saints* of the Collegiata at Empoli, and especially the fragments of frescoes in the cloister of the Carmine, next to Masaccio's *Sagrà*, were produced by an artist working energetically towards a revival of Florentine pictorial

Ill. p. 78

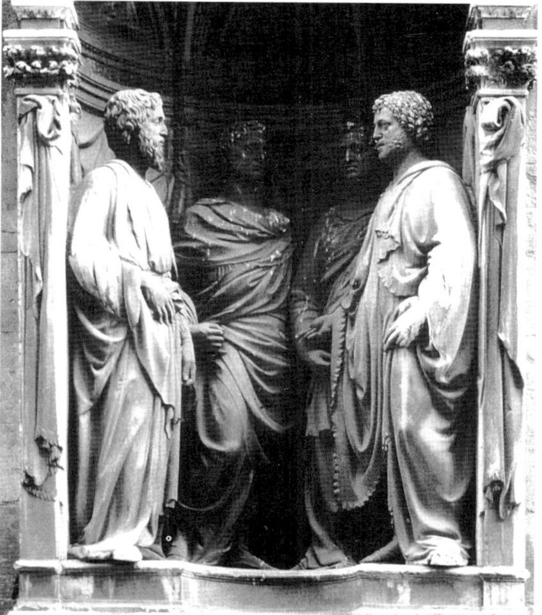

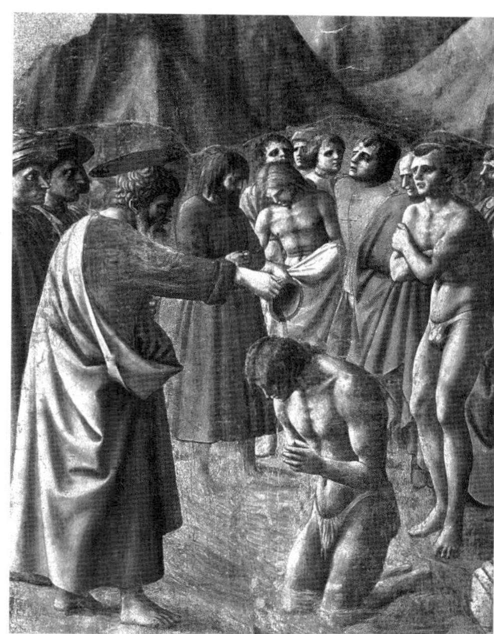

Left: Nanni di Banco, *Four Crowned Saints*, 1410–12, marble. Florence, Orsanmichele.

Right: Masaccio, *Baptism of the Neophytes*, detail, fresco. Florence, Santa Maria del Carmine, Brancacci chapel.

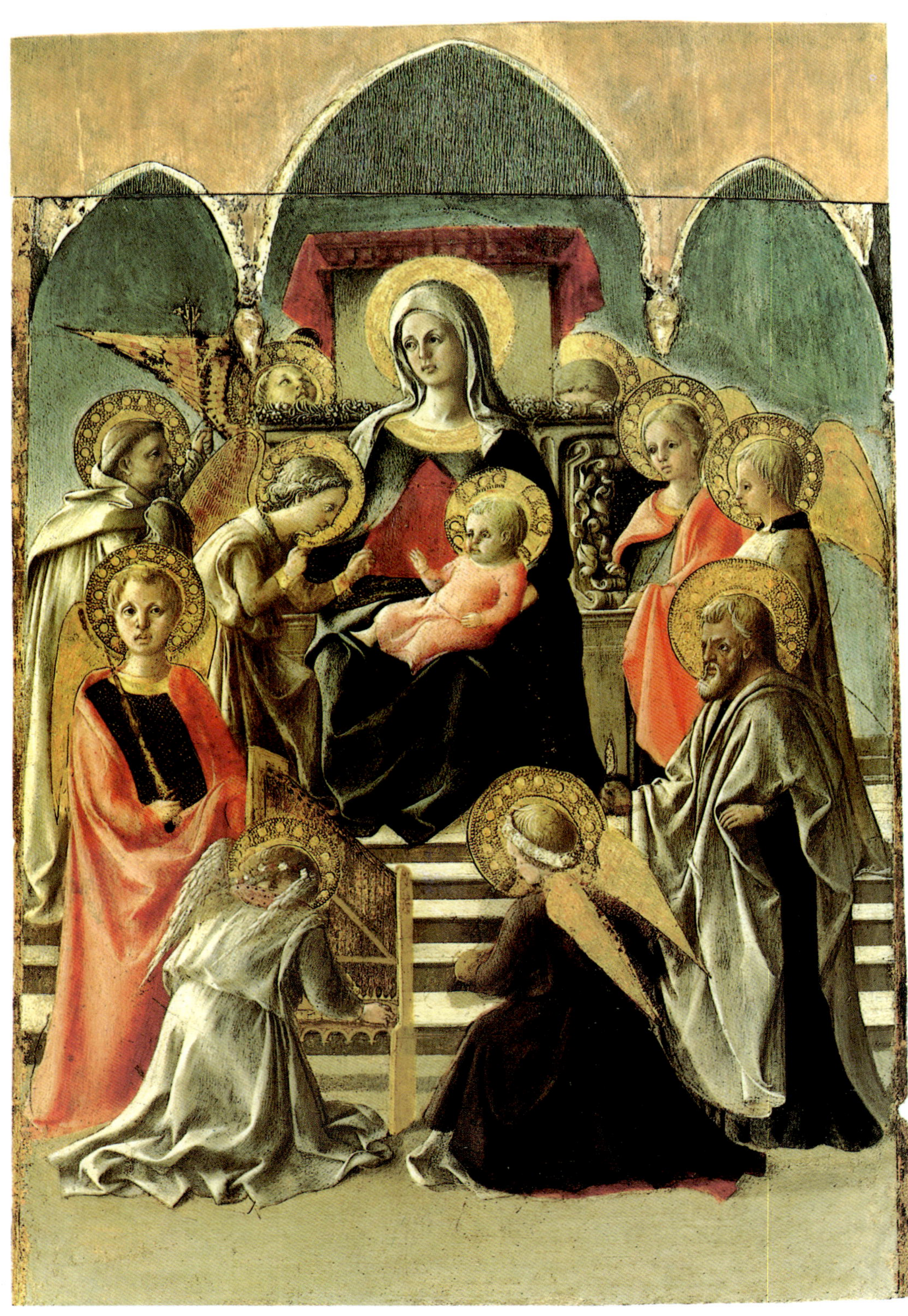

Filippo Lippi, *Madonna Enthroned with Angels and Saints*, *c.* 1430–33, tempera on wood, 43.7 × 34.3 cm. Empoli, Museo della Collegiata di Sant'Andrea.

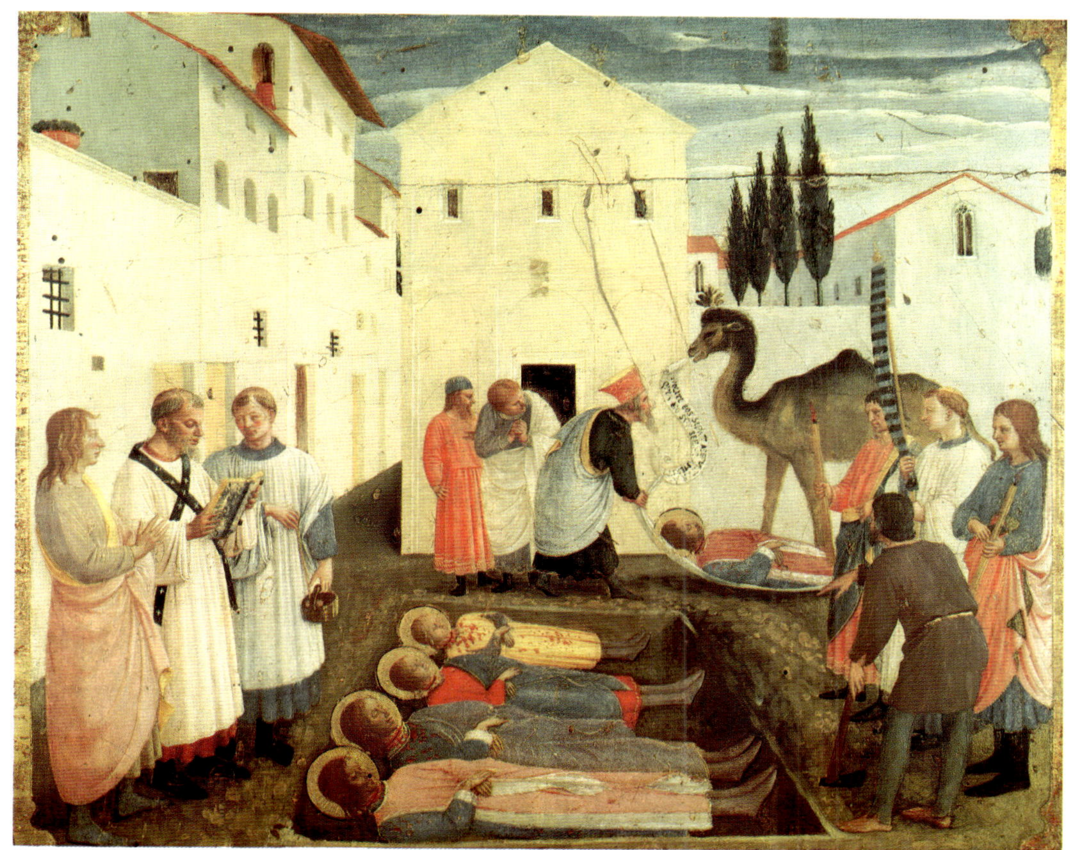

Fra Angelico, *The Burial of Saints Cosmas and Damian*, *c.* 1438–40, tempera on wood, 37 × 46 cm. Florence, Museo di San Marco.

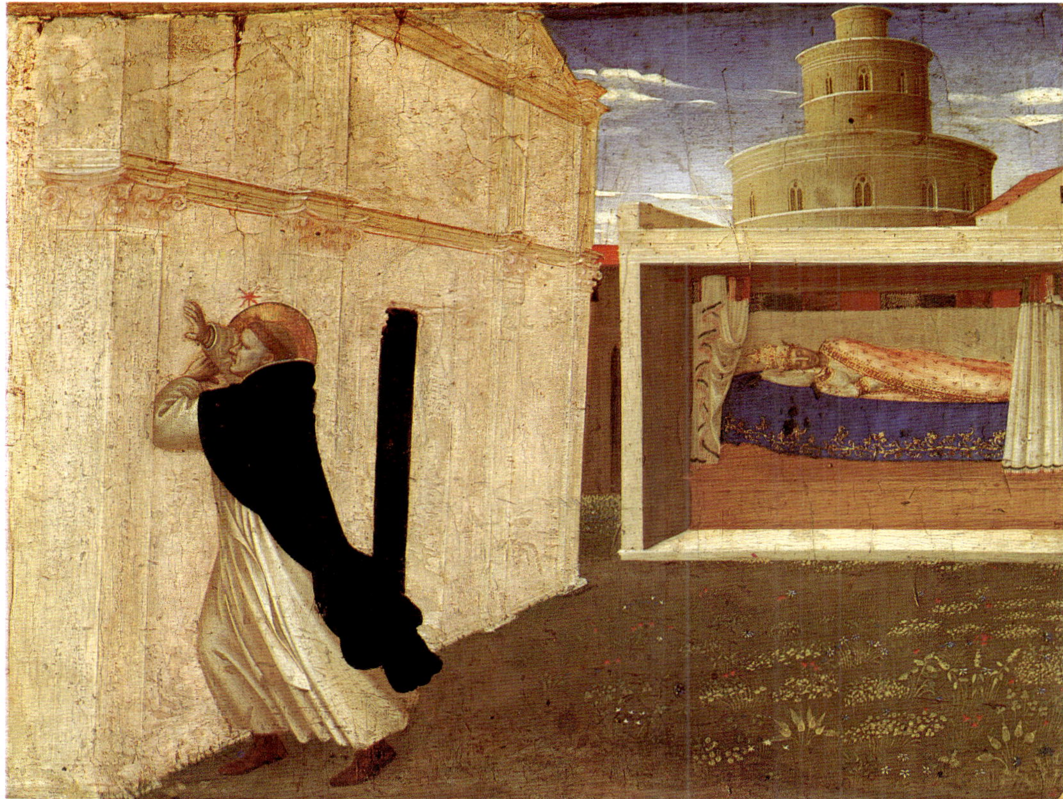

Fra Angelico, *The Dream of Innocent III*, predella of the *Coronation of the Virgin*, *c.* 1434, tempera on wood. Paris, Louvre.

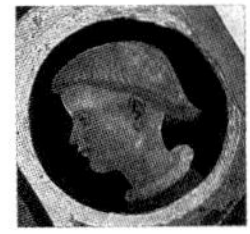

art. All these paintings were done under the aegis of the Carmelites. Lippi entered their order as a young man in 1421 and became a formidable competitor in the domain of sacred painting. In 1437 Lippi's famous *Tarquinia Madonna* of Corneto, commissioned by Giovanni Vitelleschi, Archbishop of Florence, also raised the issue of Flemish-style pictorial representation, of which his knowledge was unprecedented in Italian painting.

Meanwhile, Fra Angelico was painting *The Last Judgment* in Santa Maria degli Angeli, presenting himself as heir to Lorenzo Monaco, among patrons whom Uccello also shared. To confirm his succession, Fra Angelico completed Lorenzo Monaco's retable at Santa Trinita for Palla Strozzi. Shortly after he had finished the panel for Santa Maria degli Angeli which, significantly, adhered closely to the new ideas on perspective and space, Fra Angelico painted the retable of the Linaioli Tabernacle (1433, his first dated work), whose rich frame was based on a design by Ghiberti; the *Coronation of the Virgin* (Paris, Louvre) for San Domenico in Fiesole; and the similarly named picture in the Uffizi for the hospital of Santa Maria Nuova in Florence. All these were important works of art, ranking him at the top among the 'modern' painters, and likely to exert a certain amount of influence on Uccello (see his *Nun-Saint*, formerly in the Contini-Bonacossi Collection, and the Quarate predella).

Running parallel with this were less committed endeavours, like Paolo Schiavo's *Madonna and Six Saints* at San Miniato, which like the *Sir John Hawkwood* dated from 1436 (shortly afterwards Schiavo would be with Masolino at Castiglione Olona), or truly determined attempts to return to Gothic, such as Giovanni del Ponte's frescoes at Santa Trinita (Crucifix chapel, 1429–30; Scali chapel, 1434–5), or Bonaiuto di Giovanni's, Bicci di Lorenzo's and Stefano d'Antonio's frescoes in the same church (Compagni chapel), completed in 1434. Uccello was near at hand on a number of these occasions: Bicci di Lorenzo and Stefano d'Antonio painted a monochrome fresco of *The Last Supper* at the hospital of Lelmo when he too was working there – perhaps for the same patrons. Uccello also did frescoes of three Franciscan stories at Santa Trinita, a setting noted for its Gothic style and for its paintings by Gentile da Fabriano and Lorenzo Monaco.

BRUNELLESCHI'S PERSPECTIVE PANELS

It is widely thought, and also confirmed by a reference by Antonio Manetti, Brunelleschi's biographer, that Uccello participated in Brunelleschi's famous experiments in perspective[26] and took a stand on the subject. Brunelleschi's second panel is generally dated at *c.* 1435. It is easy to imagine the interest he would have aroused in Uccello. But the paintings known to us date from this period are proof of a pictorial freedom which far exceeds 'mathematical' limitations. The panels placed

Ill. pp. 142, 143

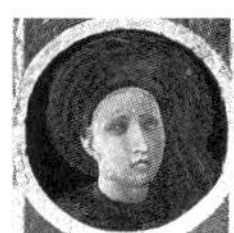

objects in space with a great stress on 'comparisons', according to a method that Argan[63] has compared to Nicholas of Cusa's reflections, but the sky is present only in the reflections of real clouds in a metal mirror. Lippi did not depict the sky because it did not occupy a measurable 'physical' space, it defied geometrical construction. Uccello rode into battle on his skies, sometimes anticipating results achieved in the Cinquecento, and at the same time recapturing the morning light of those vast spaces found in Fra Angelico's work and learning from Domenico Veneziano's use of 'atmosphere'. Alberti, engaged in 1435–6 in writing *De Pictura*, which owed much to Lippi's experiments, thought that painting should only show what is visible and not the 'things unseen' of Cennino Cennini, who was expressing Late Gothic notions. The sensitivity with which Uccello viewed the modern experiments was deeply rooted in Gothico-Aristotelian ideas, and his conception of what was visible was perhaps the most far-reaching of the period.

The frescoes at Prato can be dated to *c.* 1435, and have echoes in Andrea di Giusto's work (he was at Prato from 1435 onwards painting a polyptych, which

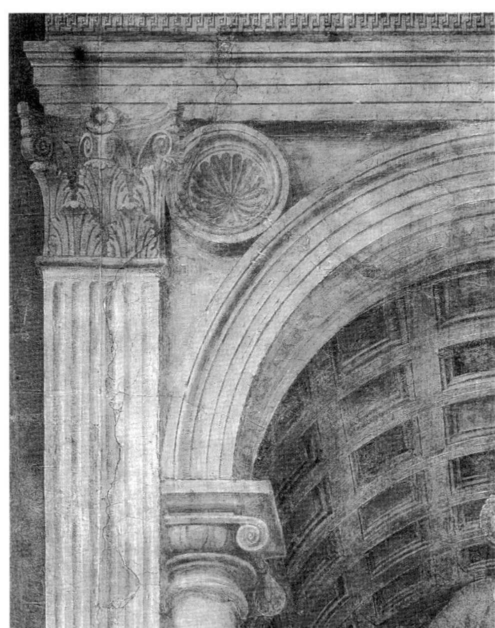

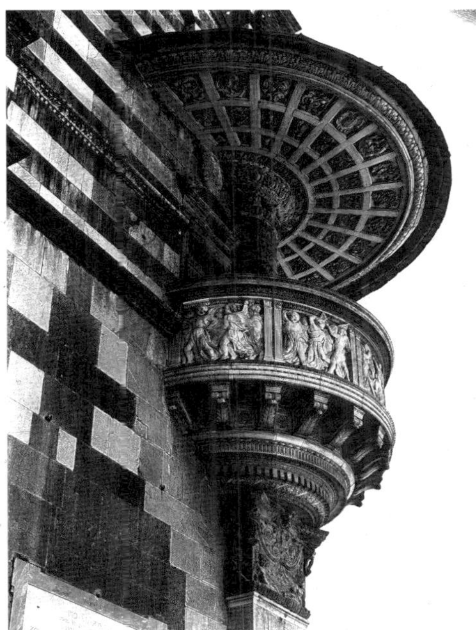

Left: Masaccio, *Trinity*, *c.* 1426–7, detail of the architecture (for the complete painting, see p. 144). Florence, Santa Maria Novella.

Right: Donatello and Michelozzo, external pulpit of Prato cathedral, *c.* 1428–35.

shows that he began to follow Fra Angelico's style after Masaccio died). This same Andrea di Giusto, one of Bicci di Lorenzo's numerous pupils, took over Uccello's cycle at Prato. The cycle, which is redolent with badly synthesized and conflicting forces,[64] coincides with an important moment on the cathedral site at Prato: renovations and the creation of a decorative setting for the important relic of the Sacro

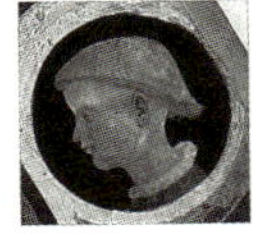

Cingolo (the girdle of the Virgin, supposed to have been given by her to Saint Thomas at the time of her Assumption) were in full swing and Brunelleschi was frequently consulted. In 1428 Donatello and Michelozzo were asked to carry out the work on the outside pulpit, where it was intended to display the relic. Work extended over a long period and from 1434 it was directed by Maso di Bartolomeo, who was responsible for the pulpit on the inside wall of the façade and after 1438 for the bronze grill in the Sacro Cingolo chapel.

Ill. p. 81

During these years the pictorial debate raged on about the interpretation of space; Uccello immersed himself in it, applying the 'sophisticated and subtle' mind Vasari recognized in him. Brunelleschi 'published' his second panel, showing the angular perspective of the Palazzo Vecchio, Alberti wrote *De Pictura* dedicated to Brunelleschi, Ghiberti his *Commentario Terzo* and Manetti his treatise on perspective (both *c.* 1435). Toscanelli returned to Florence after his studies in optics and philosophy at the Studio in Padua. Uccello was among those masters who had most work, and not solely because of the *Hawkwood* which in 1436 was the only work

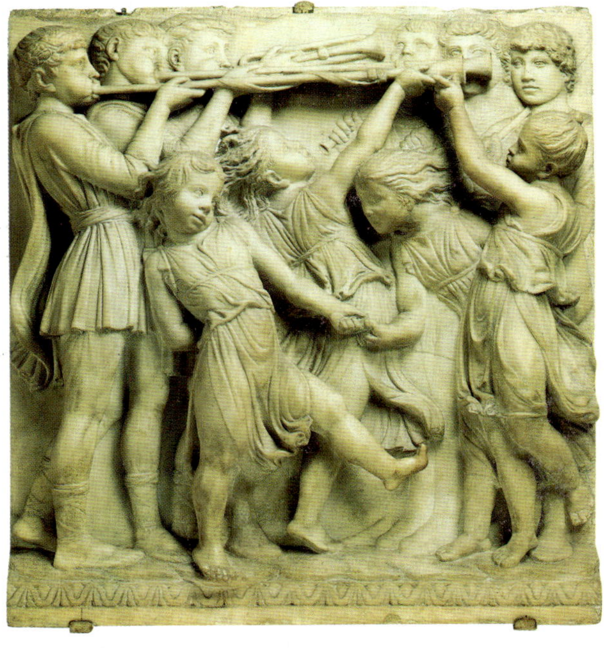

Luca della Robbia, *Cantoria*, 1423–8, detail, marble, complete work 328 × 560 cm., Florence, Museo dell'Opera del Duomo. The young trumpet-players are echoed in Uccello's *Battles*.

worthy of comparison with Masaccio's revolutionary *Trinity*, painted around ten years earlier.[65]

Ill. pp. 81, 144

At this critical juncture, Uccello made a significant choice that would distance him as much from the Brunelleschi-Masaccio axis as from Alberti's new theories, and Fra Angelico's religious preoccupations which, however, he much admired.

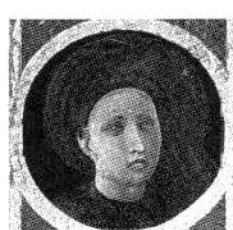

Even if he had sloughed off Ghibertian influence, it is not surprising that his sympathies still lay with his old master, a man who was a 'complete' artist and the most renowned in the city. This was the year the Duomo was consecrated and the year the cupola was completed, while Donatello and Luca della Robbia were working together on the important enterprise of the *Cantorie*, and Ghiberti was directing all the work on the decoration of the interior. Until recent times an important artistic venture, contemporary with the *Hawkwood*, has been neglected, because of its very poor state of conservation: this comprises the frescoes for the apse of Santa Maria del Fiore, painted between 1436 and 1440 by Rossello di Jacopo Franchi, Lippo d'Andrea, Bicci di Lorenzo and Giovanni del Ponte. It is strange but significant that after the vision of the future launched by Uccello's *Hawkwood*, and while the protracted history of the stained-glass windows for the oculi of the cupola's drum was still in train, the Office of Works should have offered this opportunity to painters who epitomized Gothic conservatism at its purest. We can detect the long hand of Ghiberti and his preferences here: the fact that Uccello did not participate in this group effort undoubtedly signifies that he had reached a state of artistic autonomy. Obviously he could not take part in this Late Gothic group and it was probably his awareness of this state of affairs that made him decide to go to Bologna.

GOTHIC'S DYING FLAMES: BOLOGNA

Fortuitously, fragments of Uccello's *Adoration of the Child* (or *Nativity*, or rather *Adoration of the Magi*) have been recovered at San Martino Maggiore in Bologna; these reveal him to be still under the spell of Lorenzo Monaco's fantastic nocturnal world and attracted to painting that had come from the north, as if he were aware of locally current trends. Bologna was in fact one of the great centres of Italian Late Gothic: Uccello would have been able to admire Giovanni da Modena's frescoes in the Bolognini chapel at San Petronio there. As Longhi has pointed out, Uccello's visit to Bologna (which can be placed around 1437, by a date incised in the top layer of the fresco[66]) was not without its repercussions, but it took place too early to have been properly understood in this ultra-Gothic climate.

In the 1430s Cosimo chose Uccello to commemorate Niccolò da Tolentino, through the series of *Battles*. The reasons for this choice are clear: after Cosimo's early problems with Brunelleschi, he sifted through the more docile of the artists who had worked with Ghiberti. But in the course of the second half of the 1430s, the real innovation in painting, in Florence, was the arrival – from Perugia – of Domenico Veneziano, whose first visit was probably around 1435. He was the only artist of sufficient stature to rival Uccello as successor to the great Gentile da Fabriano. In his mysterious past (in Venice?) he had come to know Van Eyck's school of painting. From Perugia, where he appears to have been extremely well-informed on Florentine

DOMENICO VENEZIANO

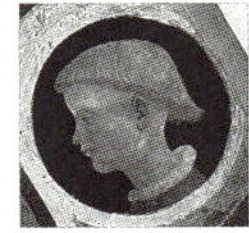

affairs, he applied in 1438 for a prestigious sacred commission, addressing himself to Piero de' Medici who was in Ferrara for the Council.[67] A year later Domenico was on the scaffolding in the choir of Sant'Egidio working on the Marian cycle commissioned by the Portinari, who were connected to the Medici. The young Piero della Francesca was with him, but there was soon to be a parting of the ways: Domenico, an anxious, refined man, never completed the cycle; and Piero left Florence, which had proved singularly unresponsive to him, and went home to Sansepolcro.

At the beginning of the 1440s a movement towards narrative and naturalistic painting became apparent, a trend Uccello had difficulty in following and Piero della Francesca totally rejected, which would explain why he left the field free. Domenico Veneziano catalyzed the whole movement towards 'atmosphere' and colour, of which we can find scattered traces in Florentine painting at that time. Among those who were rapidly won over to this movement, the Master of the Chiostro degli Aranci at the Badia (often identified as the Portuguese Giovanni di Gonsalvo) in the

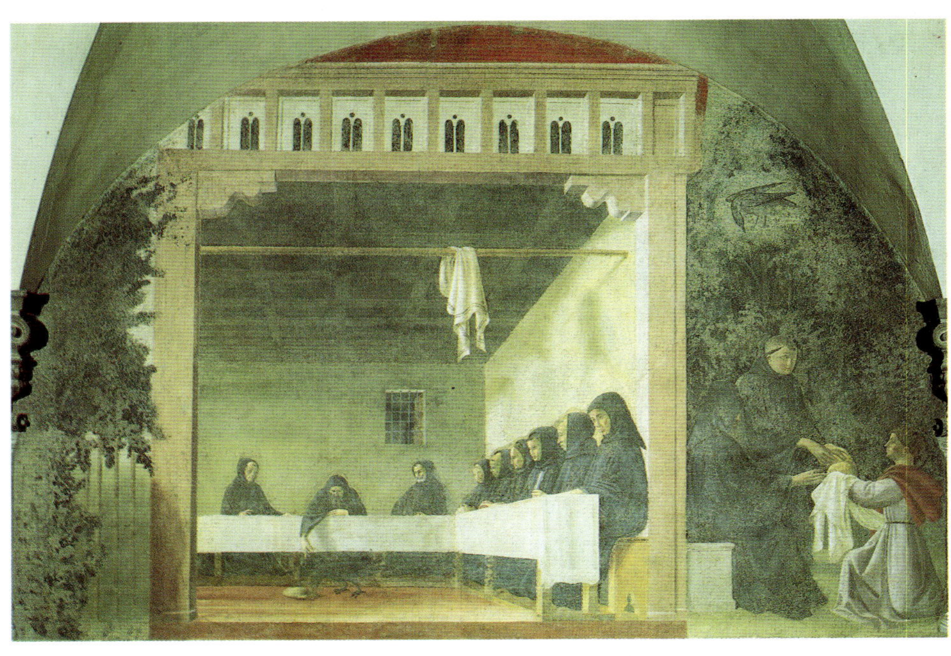

Master of the Chiostro degli Aranci, *Scene from the Life of Saint Benedict*, c. 1436–9: *Saint Benedict Orders the Crow to Take the Poisoned Bread Away*, fresco, 218 × 306 cm. Florence, Badia. This is the most important episode in the great Benedictine cycle in which the artist developed elements taken from Uccello (Santa Maria degli Angeli cycle, now lost), while drawing inspiration from Fra Angelico's clarity of space and colour.

Benedictine cycle (1436–9) revealed an equal acquaintanceship with Uccello and especially Fra Angelico. Other young Florentine painters, like the sensitive, delicate Pratovecchio Master or the 'Lippian' Master of the Castello *Nativity* quite openly displayed their debt to Domenico Veneziano. After abandoning the frescoes at Sant'Egidio, Domenico left yet another work of very high quality in the admirable

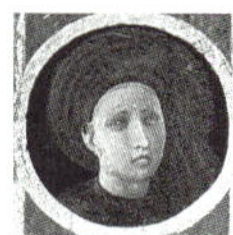

retable of Santa Lucia de' Magnoli (*c.* 1444–5), an exemplary fusion of delicate atmospheric colouring and an Albertian construction of space.

AN ARTISTIC EFFERVESCENCE

But an overall view of Florence at that time reveals an immense richness. In 1440, the young Andrea del Castagno was commissioned to portray the *Hanged Men* at the Bargello (now lost). Giovanni di Francesco, who had registered with the Guild of Doctors and Apothecaries in 1442, painted first under Uccello's influence before moving on to Domenico Veneziano. One of his masterpieces, the Cavalcanti predella, is placed next to Domenico's *Saint John the Baptist and Saint Francis* in Santa Croce. Fra Carnevale, from Urbino, was working in Florence at Filippo Lippi's studio in 1445–6. Fra Angelico was summoned to Rome in 1447 by Pope Eugenius IV and called back again by his successor Nicholas V (1447–55). Francesco Pesellino painted the *Triumphs* (Boston, Isabella Stewart Gardner Museum) towards 1447. Paolo Schiavo and Andrea del Castagno were working at Sant'Apollonia almost simultaneously, and the Pratovecchio Master painted the *Three Archangels* (Berlin-Dahlem, Staatliche Museen) *c.* 1446. Lippi was getting into his stride with

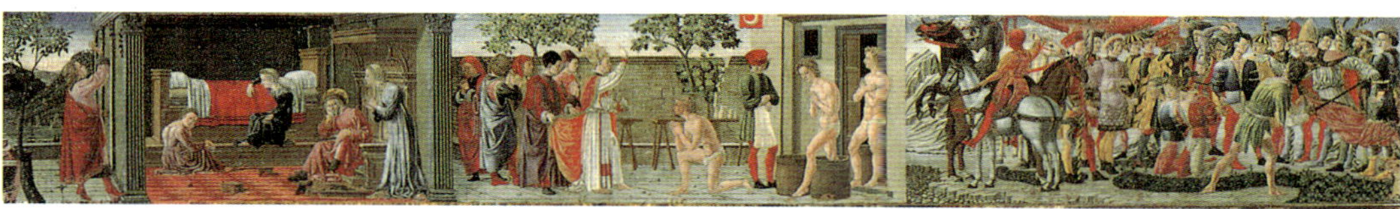

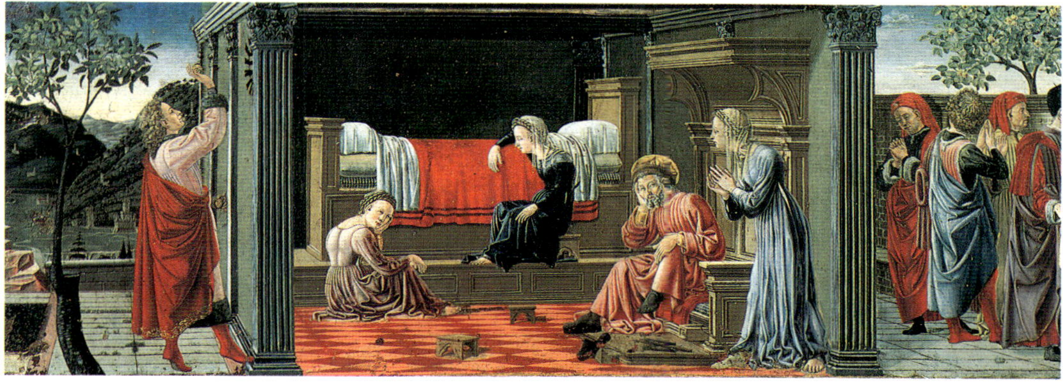

Giovanni di Francesco, Cavalcanti predella, *c.* 1452–9, tempera on wood, complete work 23 × 158 cm. and detail (*Saint Nicholas of Bari Provides a Dowry for Three Poor Young Girls*). Florence, Casa Buonarroti. This work was at Santa Croce, below Donatello's *Annunciation*, itself framed by saints painted in fresco by Domenico Veneziano.

important commissions, among them the *Madonna and Saints* for the noviciate of Santa Croce, paid for by the Medici (the predella was painted by Pesellino *c.* 1450–52) and *The Coronation of the Virgin* for the high altar of Sant'Ambrogio, finished around 1447 (both now in the Uffizi). At the time Fra Angelico left for Rome – after the young Piero's return home – we can discern two great trends in Florentine art: at the head of

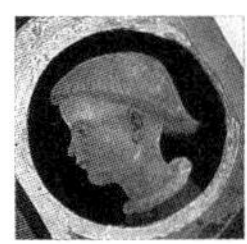

one was Domenico Veneziano; at the head of the other, now in the ascendant, was Filippo Lippi. While remaining wildly individualist, Uccello appears to have been closer to the group who drew inspiration from Domenico's experience. As time passed he continued to oppose the mounting tide of 'Lippism', without sharing the Albertian concept of space that Domenico had captured in mid-flight and made his own when he was working on the Sant'Egidio cycle.

DONATELLO, PADUA

During this period Ghiberti – who, along with Donatello, continued to be a model for painters – finished the reliquary of Saint Zenobius (1442) for the Duomo, echoes of which can be found in Uccello's Jacquemart-André *Saint George* (Paris). *Ill p. 257* Shortly afterwards, just when Uccello was studying his work with growing interest, Donatello left for Padua. Uccello followed him, perhaps in so doing betraying a deep anxiety or an early symptom of intolerance towards his Florentine milieu. It was at this moment that Brunelleschi died, leaving behind a difficult legacy. Now that painting was moving in directions he found alien, Donatello remained in the Veneto. As far as religious commissions went, the artist who commanded the field was Filippo Lippi. Uccello rejected his facile naturalism and popular sentimentality although there were moments when their styles were tangential, (and there are even curious echoes of Uccello in Lippi's late work) arising from their common reference to Donatello. It was a momentary reference for Uccello as can be seen at the end of the

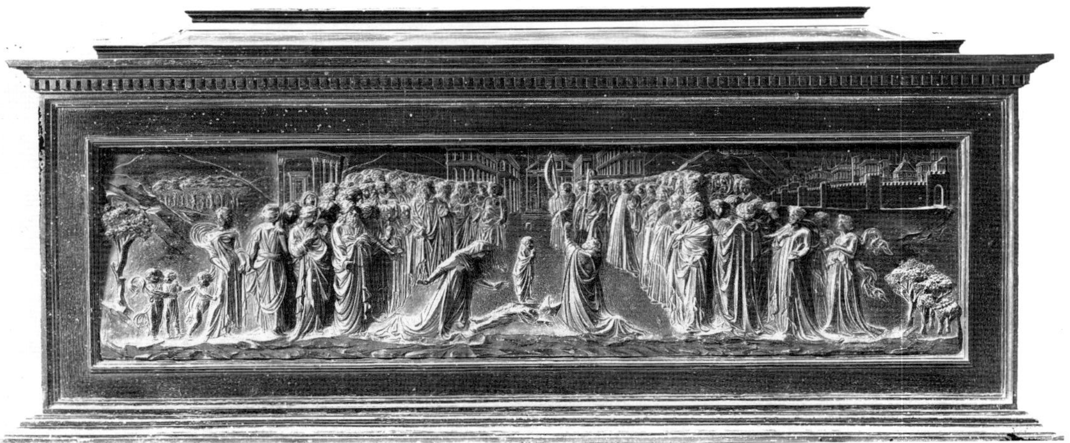

Lorenzo Ghiberti, reliquary shrine of Saint Zenobius, completed in 1442, bronze, 41 × 160 cm. Florence, Santa Maria del Fiore.

decade, for example, in the Dublin *Madonna and Child* of *c.* 1437–40 (National Gallery of Ireland). *Ill. p. 237* This *Madonna* seems to have shown the Carmelite painter his future course – as he emerged from the influence of 'Masaccism' in its most complete form – and revealed the influence that Uccello exerted: an influence critics have had difficulty in recognizing, preferring the romantic image of a solitary old man.

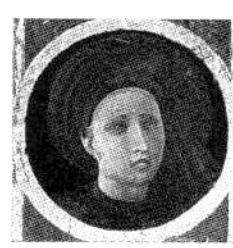

The rapprochement with Donatello and his exchanges with him mark this anti-conformist phase of Uccello's. But the role of leader seems to have weighed heavily on him and his friendship with Donatello coincided with a period when his hand appeared less free and successful. Testifying to this difficult association are the
Ill. pp. 118–19 metallic, haggard *Evangelists* (1423) around the clock face in the Duomo which are reminiscent of Donatello's *Prophets* on the campanile of Santa Maria del Fiore, the reliefs in the Old Sacristy of San Lorenzo and the pulpit at Prato. But Uccello and Donatello had different horizons. Their aspirations diverged; their rapprochement could not be a lasting one, and we can believe Vasari when he recalls the sculptor's
Cat. no. 31 criticisms of Uccello *à propos* the fresco of *Saint Thomas* in the Mercato Vecchio. As far as Donatello was concerned, his interest in perspective waned after his adherence
Ill. p. 88 to Albertian theory had reached its highest level in *The Feast of Herod* (Lille, Musée des Beaux-Arts, Wicar Collection *c.* 1435–6): for him space had only an auxiliary role in relation to figures.

Donatello may have asked the illustrious *quadraturista* of the *Hawkwood* to come to Padua (if Vasari is to be believed), because he himself was grappling with a similar problem in his project for the equestrian monument in bronze to the *condottiere* Gattamelata. He does not appear to have included Uccello in any later enterprise, and Uccello must have had to earn his living in Padua with the *Giants* (now lost) for Casa Vitaliani. This was a cycle of monochrome murals, painted in tempera, in

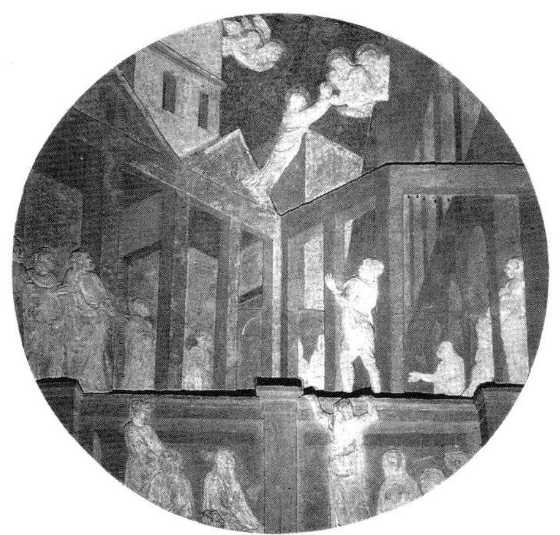

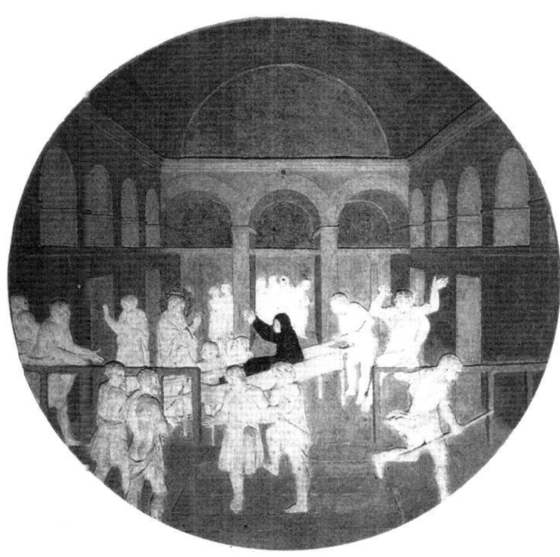

Donatello, painted stucco in the Old Sacristy of San Lorenzo, 1434–43, 215 cm. in diameter.
Left: The Ascension of Saint John the Evangelist.
Right: The Resurrection of Drusiana.

which he used the Late Gothic and humanist theme of *Famous Men*, already used on the façade of the town hall, to which the pediment inside the small Vitaliani palace explicitly referred. The choice of theme was consistent with its setting: Padua was Livy's city, humanist *numen* of History, and a place where Petrarch had played an active role.

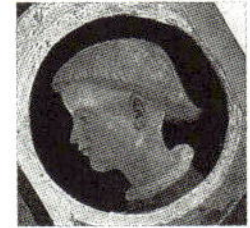

When Uccello arrived, Padua was still one of the great Gothic centres of the Po region. It could remember Giotto; Altichiero and the Bolognesi had left their mark there; Guariento had worked there; Giusto de' Menabuoi had brought Florentine influences there, and, *c.* 1400, Cennino Cennini had been there: gradually the town had come under Venice's influence and had adopted that city's choice of International Gothic. Between 1400 and 1445, painting in Padua presented a varied and fragmented panorama: Stefano da Zevio was working there until 1421; in 1420, Niccolò Miretto and his collaborators embarked on an astrological cycle there; Gentile da Fabriano stayed there, Michele Giambono left important works there such as the polyptych (now lost) in the church of San Michele; the Venetian Giovanni Storlato decorated San Giustina chapter-house (1436), while in the 1440s the Murano school was active there (Antonio Vivarini's polyptychs in San Francesco and Praglia): they would give the decoration of the Ovetari chapel in the Eremitani its final touches. Francesco dei Franceschi's polyptych of Saint Peter (dated 1447)

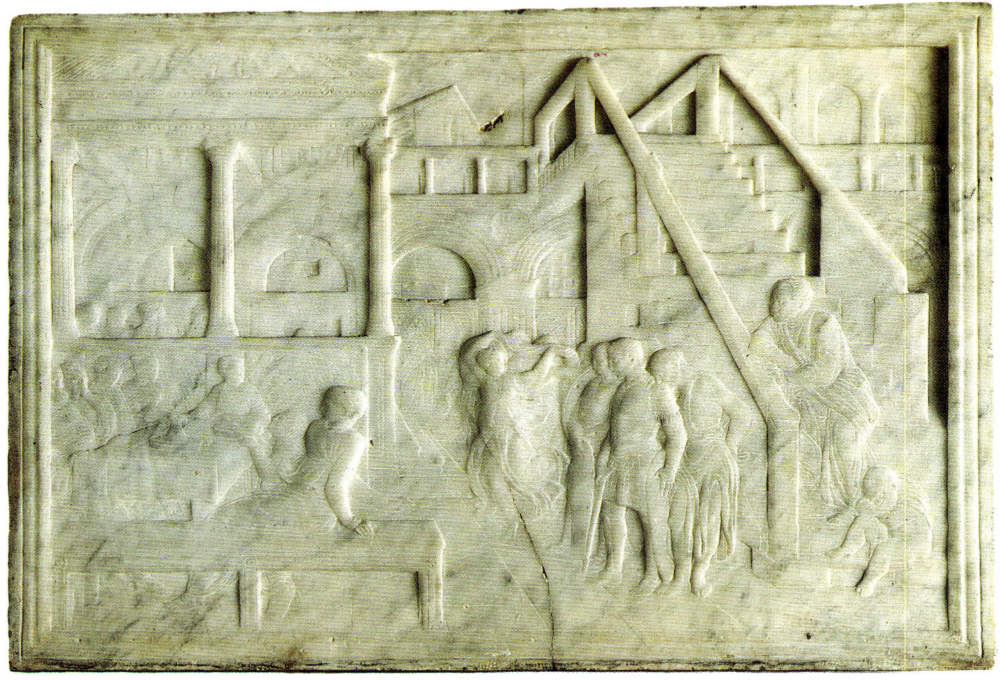

Donatello, *The Feast of Herod*, *c.* 1435–6, marble, 50 × 71.5 cm. Lille, Musée des Beaux-Arts. This work marks the point where Donatello adhered most closely to Alberti's theory of perspective, shown in the minute gradation of planes, in very low relief.

shows how well Giambono's and Vivarini's Venetian teaching had been assimilated, while in the 1430s, Francesco Squarcione's work enhanced local Late Gothic with the rich culture of Antiquity of Urbino's humanist circles (Mantegna would be a pupil of his).

Uccello's lost decorative ensemble was probably a continuation of what he had

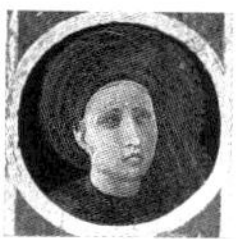

produced in Florence on the clock, elaborating certain problems relating to perspective, the relationship between the size of the giants and the *trompe-l'oeil* architecture and its monumental quality, which would certainly have appealed to Andrea Mantegna, Niccolò Pizzolo and other young 'moderns' at work in a church near the Eremitani. But questions arise on the real significance of Uccello's work in this context which was so deeply imprinted with International Gothic.[68] Relations with Donatello, engaged in groundwork for his great masterpiece of drama and perspective for the altar of Sant'Antonio, appeared to be flagging, while Uccello's confidence in his own theories was growing. Vasari's anecdote about the fresco in the Mercato Vecchio in Florence shows the rift between Uccello's interests as a painter and Donatello's preoccupations as a sculptor. It was at this time (*c.* 1455) that Donatello created his *Mary Magdalen* in wood and his bronze of *Saint John the Baptist* in Siena (1457); he had become the sculptor of suffering humanity, light years from virtuous humanism, self-aware and self-confident in his monument to *Gattamelata*. This was a Donatello who avoided public commissions, willing even to go to Siena 'to live or die' and preparing to translate his dramatic vision into the two pulpits at San Lorenzo.

END OF AN ERA

But the 1450s also saw the completion of Ghiberti's Doors of Paradise (commissioned in 1425 and delivered in 1452). It also saw Benozzo Gozzoli embarking on his painting career in Umbria, already heavily influenced by Fra Angelico. It was a time when Giovanni di Francesco had freed himself of his debt to Uccello and was asserting his own style; and when Domenico Veneziano handed over the reins to Andrea del Castagno at Sant' Egidio (1451). In 1452, Filippo Lippi was summoned to Prato to replace Fra Angelico; Lippi would become indispensable at the cathedral there as the great bourgeois illustrator of the *Saint Stephen and Saint John the Baptist* cycle. Also in 1452, Bicci de Lorenzo died at Arezzo – his work at San Francesco was taken over by Piero della Francesca. Dello Delli had returned from Spain in 1446 and was mentioned among other living artists by Filarete in his treatise *c.* 1464–5, but we know nothing of his later working life. In the early 1450s, too, Rossello di Jacopo Franchi and Ventura di Moro were painting the *Stories of Saint Peter Martyr* at the oratory of Bigallo. Rossello went on to paint in an old-fashioned, mannered Gothic style (*Staggia Madonna*) and he died in 1456. One of the last works, a *Madonna and Saints*, by Mariotto di Cristofano, dates from 1453 (he died in 1457, probably from the plague). Among the 'minor masters' – painters of chests, coffers, furniture decoration – Masaccio's brother (Lo Scheggia) signed *The Martyrdom of Saint Laurence* in 1457 in the oratory of the same name at San Giovanni in Vallarno (his long career ended in 1486). The fantastic narrative painter Apollonio di

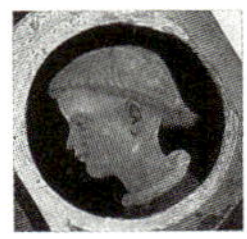

Giovanni, who disappeared from view in 1465 and who was associated with Marco del Buono Giamberti in a famous and very active studio from 1445 onwards, produced a painting that owed much to Uccello's, Dello's and Pesellino's experimentation. He decorated the Rucellai loggia (1451). The work on the plate cupboard of the Santissima Annunziata must also be placed at around this time (from 1449). This was a mature work by Fra Angelico, on which the young Alesso Baldovinetti collaborated, perhaps more than is generally admitted. In 1454, Baldovinetti worked with Andrea del Castagno on *The Last Judgment* (now lost) commissioned by the Marquis of Mantua, a reliable indication of a new orientation in his interests.

At the turn of the new decade, the course of Florentine painting was well-defined and ever more distant from Uccello's explorative work: it is perhaps no accident that, except for the much debated, mannered and almost ruined predella of Avane of 1452, Uccello's catalogue from this moment on becomes sparse, problematic and inconsistent. Filippo Lippi was very much in fashion at this time, which we can no longer claim for Uccello. Lippi was in favour with the Medici patrons: *c.* 1457, Giovanni di Cosimo commissioned him to paint a precious triptych which he wished to give to Alfonso of Aragon, King of Naples. In 1492, a '*tondo grande*' of Lippi's was inventoried in the '*camera di Lorenzo*' – so not far from Uccello's *Battles*. Lippi's eloquent narrative style bears important echoes of Uccello: these can be seen

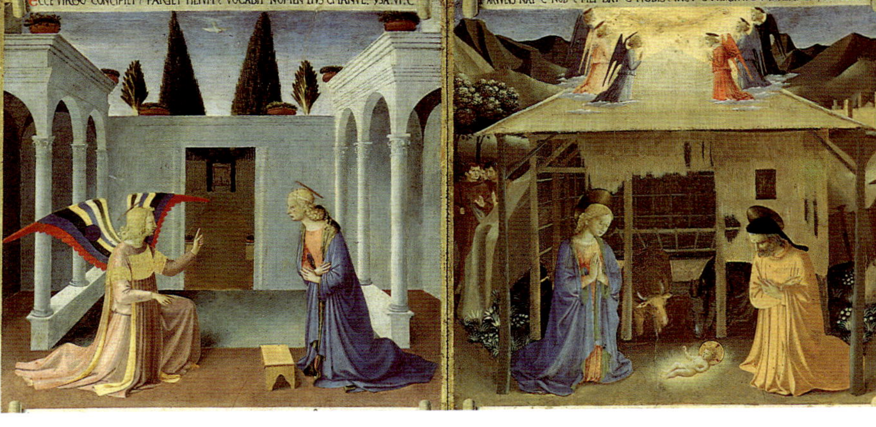

Fra Angelico, two scenes from the plate cupboard of the church of Santissima Annunziata, *c.* 1449–50, tempera on wood, each scene 39 × 39 cm. Florence, convent of San Marco. *Left: The Annunciation. Right: The Adoration of the Child.*

in his *Obsequies of Saint Jerome* in Prato cathedral, which reflects Uccello's cycle at Santa Maria degli Angeli and Starnina's at the Carmine (according to Vasari) and in his extraordinary *Adoration of the Child* in the Uffizi, painted *c.* 1455 for the hospital of Annalena, where Uccello had painted two pictures in fresco (Vasari), not identified in the sources. This *Adoration* – which has been described as a 'quasi-return

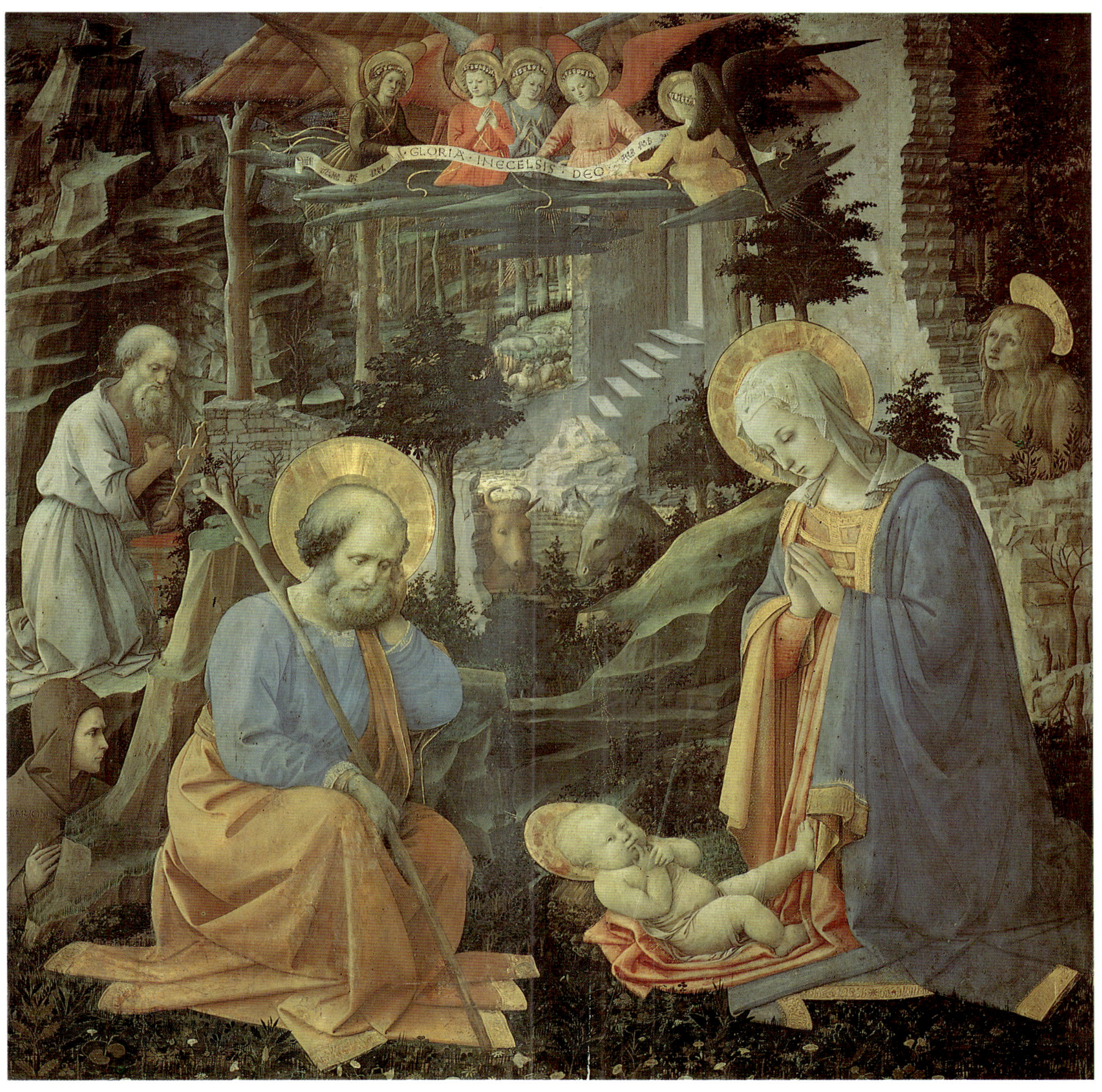

Filippo Lippi, *The Adoration of the Child*, *c.* 1455, tempera on wood, 137 × 134 cm. Florence, Uffizi. This panel, painted for the Annalena convent in Florence – where Uccello had also worked – mixes elements from Donatello and Uccello in a deliberately archaizing manner.

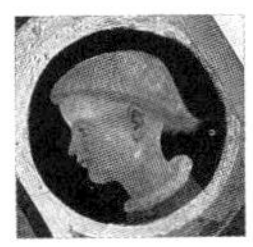

to Gothic' and as having 'distorted perspective'[69] – with its small animals, its forest in the background and its dislocated perspectival construction, was a deliberate reference to Uccello's earlier experiments. Perhaps it was a special request from the patrons who had steered the 'capricious' painter-monk – whose painting was usually the antithesis of Uccello's – fairly overtly towards mystery and nostalgia.

ANDREA DEL CASTAGNO

In 1456, another important event marked even more obviously the distance between Uccello's chosen path and the direction contemporary painting was taking. It was at this date that Andrea del Castagno painted the fresco in memory of Niccolò da Tolentino (who had died in 1435) in Santa Maria del Fiore, after the project, for political reasons, had been prudently shelved for many years. This was the *analogon* of the *Hawkwood* painted twenty years earlier, from which he must have been explicitly instructed by the Office of Works to draw his inspiration. The juxtaposition of these highlights the changes during twenty extraordinary years in which Uccello was an attentive witness and undisputed protagonist, in spite of his progressive withdrawal. Almost nothing of the *Hawkwood* survives in the *Tolentino*. Andrea del Castagno had

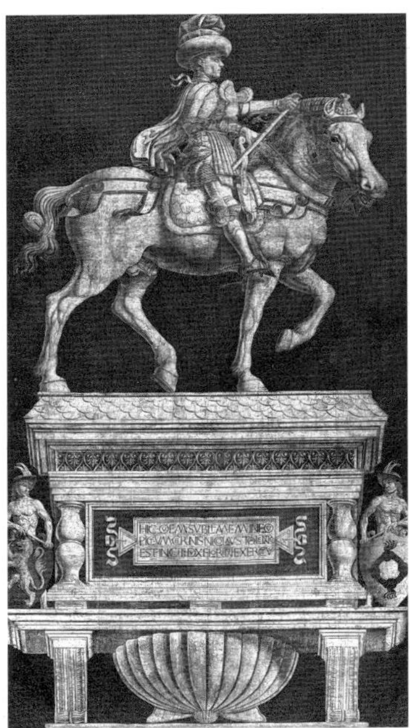

Andrea del Castagno, *Equestrian Monument to Niccolò da Tolentino*, 1456, fresco, 833 × 512 cm. Florence, Santa Maria del Fiore.

pursued his career ardently and impetuously, and had an undisputed influence on masters as assured as Giovanni di Francesco and Domenico Veneziano himself. Castagno had created fundamental works, ranging from the *Famous Men* of Legnaia (1450–51) to the frescoes of Sant'Egidio (1451–3) and the *Tolentino*. The *Assumption* of San Miniato fra le Torri (Berlin-Dahlem, Staatliche Museen) was a late work by

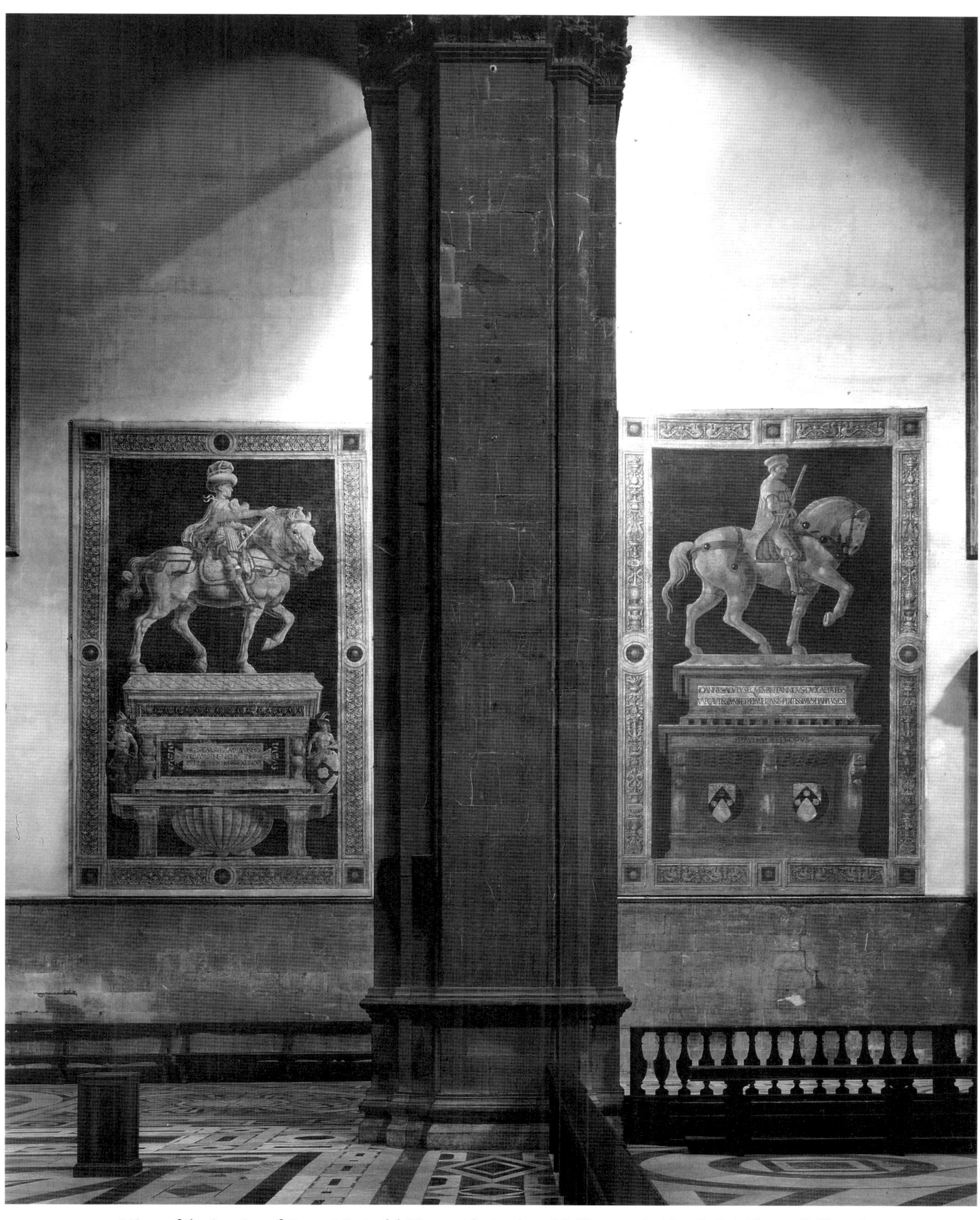

View of the interior of Santa Maria del Fiore with Andrea del Castagno's *Niccolò da Tolentino* (left) and Uccello's *Sir John Hawkwood*. The frescoes are now lower than they were originally. The *Hawkwood*, which was detached in the nineteenth century, was, until its modern restoration, on the inside wall of the façade.

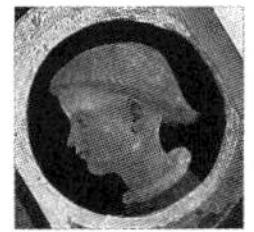

Castagno, who died prematurely in August 1457 from the plague which was currently devastating Florence (Francesco Pesellino had also died from it in July). While Castagno influenced Giovanni di Francesco, he was himself inspired by the late work of Domenico Veneziano, who, in his turn, in his *Two Saints* painted in fresco in Santa Croce towards the middle of the 1450s, was clearly paying homage to Castagno.

Very little remains of Domenico's work from the 1450s, which indicates a probable lessening of interest in him. As far as he was concerned (he died in 1461, and therefore could not have been assassinated by his pupil Castagno as local tradition repeated by Vasari claimed), Florence had taken a different course. Among the many artists promoting this new wave was the Pratovecchio Master who painted his great eponymous masterpiece, the *Assumption* at Pratovecchio in Casentino (*c.* 1455), while the Cavalcanti predella (Florence, Casa Buonarroti), a masterpiece by the mature Giovanni di Francesco (died 1459), can be dated after 1452.

Ill. p. 95
Ill. p. 85

It was during this period that Uccello's *Battles* were taken down and remounted on the '*spalliera*' in the great chamber on the ground floor of Michelozzo's new palace, its precious décor glittering with lacquer and silver. They were now in a strictly private domain, which was not what Cosimo had intended when he commissioned them to celebrate – through those two captains, the House of Medici's allies – his own elevation to head of Florentine public affairs. As Leonardo Bruni's Florence became that of Agnolo Poliziano, the 'Rout of San Romano' became 'paintings of jousting in the Palazzo Medici in Via Larghi', in the words of the Anonimo Magliabechiano.[70] But this significant reuse apart (which nonetheless indicates a lasting interest in the work) the Medici patrons' cultural orientations (Gozzoli, Filippo Lippi, Pollaiuolo) had changed: they were no longer directly inspired by Cosimo but by his sons.[71]

See note 45

During this period Benozzo Gozzoli's career was progressing outside Florence: he had already collaborated with Fra Angelico at the convent of San Marco (around 1442–3), with Ghiberti in 1445 and with Fra Angelico again in Rome and Orvieto (1447–9). In 1450, he was painting at San Fortunato near Montefalco, launching a career in Umbria that would culminate in the San Francesco frescoes at Montefalco (1452) and the retable at La Sapienza Nuova in Perugia of 1456 (Perugia, Galleria Nazionale dell'Umbria). In 1459 he returned to Florence for an important commission from Cosimo's son, Piero, for the frescoes in the Palazzo Medici chapel.

GOZZOLI, POLLAIUOLO, BALDOVINETTI

That same year, the completion of the *Reliquary of the Cross* for the Duomo's Office of Works marked Antonio del Pollaiuolo's official début as one of the most representative of the new generation of artists. These were the young men who,

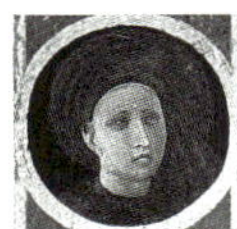

alongside the famous Filippo Lippi, catalyzed the new Medici patrons' tastes. While Gozzoli was painting the palace chapel, Filippo Lippi provided the altar retable and the young Pollaiuolo painted *The Labours of Hercules* for the 'great chamber' (1460). In this decade work was still being done by different masters of Fra Angelico's school, such as Fra Zanobi Strozzi (the illuminated choral books for Cosimo de' Medici date from 1453; the three antiphonaries in the Biblioteca Laurenziana, on which he worked with Francesco d'Antonio, are from 1471) and Domenico de Michelino (his *Dante* in Santa Maria del Fiore, for which Baldovinetti had initially been contacted, dates from 1465), and Pesellino himself, whose only documented work is the 1455 *Trinity* of Pistoia (London, National Gallery), completed after his death by Lippi's omnivorous studio at Prato. The year 1452 saw the beginnings of Neri di Bicci's rich career: he had inherited his father's – Bicci di Lorenzo's – studio (Spini chapel at Santa Trinita); initially he was equally influenced by Fra Angelico, Domenico Veneziano and Lippi. His best known work, *San Giovanni Gualberto and the Vallombrosan Saints*, dates back to 1435. (This was formerly at San Pancrazio and is

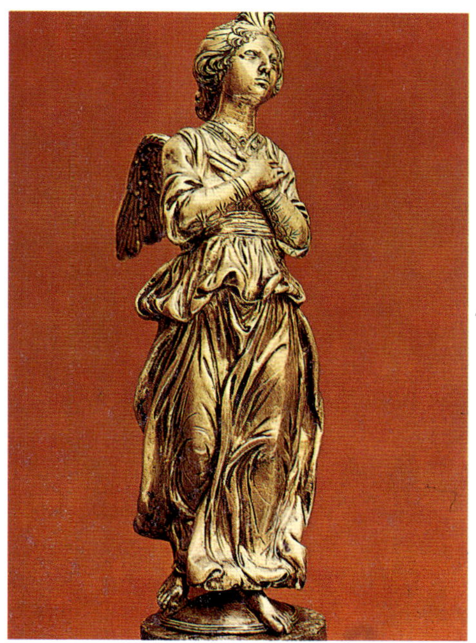

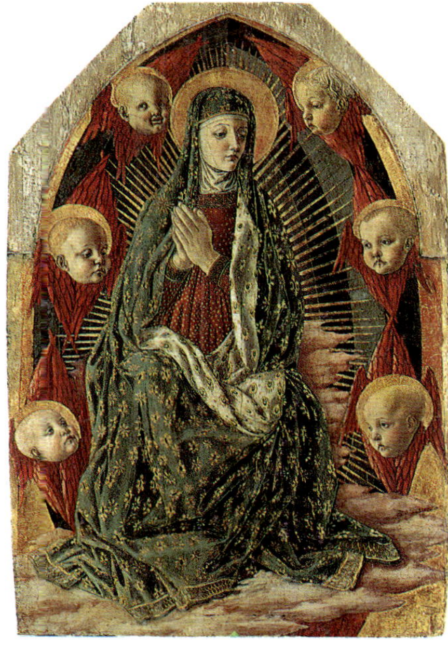

Left: Antonio del Pollaiuolo, *Madonna of the Annunciation*, *c.* 1459. detail of the reliquary of the Cross. Florence, Museo dell'Opera del Duomo.

Right: Pratovecchio Master, *The Assumption*, *c.* 1455, tempera on wood, 85.5 × 59.5 cm. Central panel of a polyptych, Pratovecchio, convent of San Giovanni Evangelista.

now in the Compagni chapel at Santa Trinita.) In the 1450s Pesellino, rather than the eclectic Neri, entered Lippi's circle, with Jacopo d'Antonio, Lorenzo del Pratese and Zanobi di Meliore who ultimately joined Fra Angelico's already imposing group of disciples, a group strengthened by the remarkable, enigmatic personalities of Fra Diamante and Fra Carnevale, a painter from the Marche.

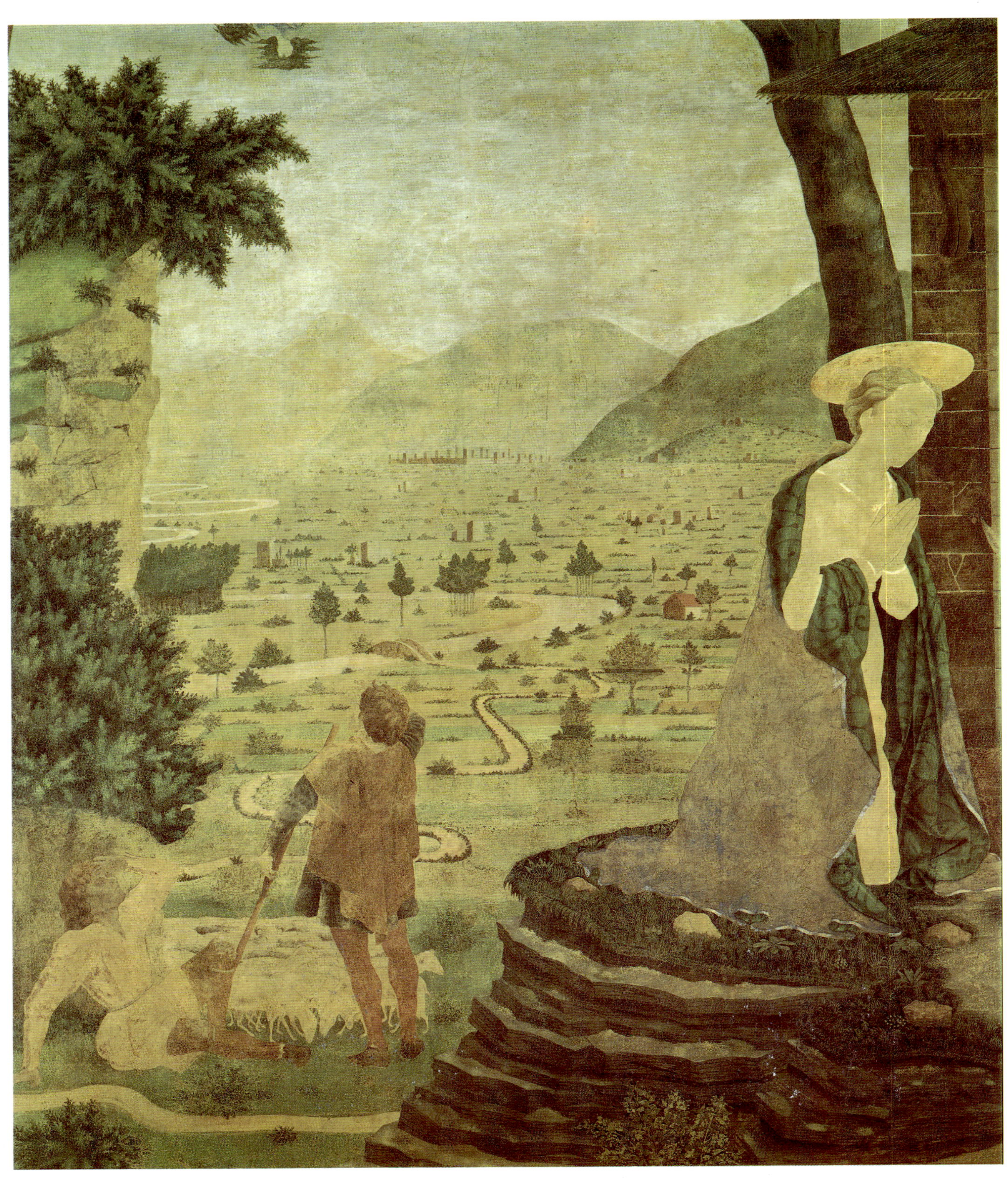

Alesso Baldovinetti, *The Nativity*, detail.

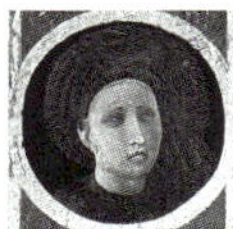

While Filippo Lippi's fame reached its zenith with the retable for the Palazzo Medici and his work for Prato, once the plate cupboard was finished at the Santissima Annunziata, the young Baldovinetti re-embarked on the cycle of the Virgin at Sant'Egidio in 1461, after a long interlude. He may well have begun his career there in the shadow of Domenico Veneziano at the beginning of the 1440s. From 1460 to 1462 he painted *The Nativity* in fresco (with large parts of it left 'dry') in a small cloister of Santissima Annunziata. Of all Florentine work, this *Nativity* comes closest to Piero della Francesca in its feeling of amplified space. Baldovinetti, who experimented greatly in technique – after Uccello and before Leonardo – and practised the 'applied arts' a good deal, (glass, mosaics, enamel, cartoons for marquetry, fabrics) was an artist whose wide range of interests reminds us of Uccello's work. Also at this time the marquetry decoration for the Sacristy of the Mass at the Duomo, which Giuliano da Maiano (1463) had been asked to do, was being finished (1463): this was an important enterprise, the apotheosis of the science of

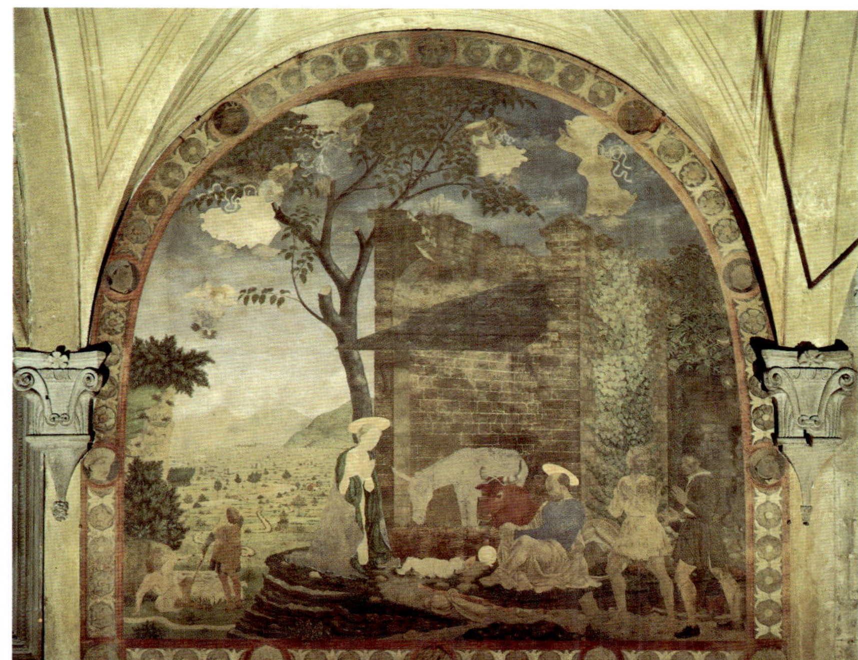

Alesso Baldovinetti, *The Nativity*, 1460–62, fresco. Florence, Santissima Annunziata, Cloister of the Vows.

perspective. Baldovinetti was among those who provided cartoons, along with Maso Finiguerra, a painter-goldsmith-engraver whose style resembled Lippi's and of whom all mention ceases from as early as 1464. Elsewhere, Baldovinetti was decorating the Cardinal of Portugal's chapel in fresco from 1466 at San Miniato al Monte, where the retable was supplied by Pollaiuolo. Scarcely twenty years after

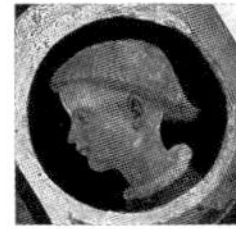

Uccello's cycle in the cloister, with its unrealistic red-green architecture and supernatural colours, Baldovinetti's work, commissioned by the same Olivetan patron, demonstrates the rift in taste that had developed between then and the period when Uccello could have been considered as the greatest interpreter of cloister cycles in Florence.

Style apart, Baldovinetti was Uccello's successor through his interest in experiment that led him to develop certain techniques like mosaics or stained glass right through to old age. Baldovinetti ultimately took over Uccello's role: he became restorer of mosaics at the Baptistery and San Miniato al Monte, and between 1490 and 1500 he was principal supplier of cartoons for stained-glass windows. While Baldovinetti was busy decorating the Cardinal of Portugal's chapel, Gozzoli was embarking on his 'provincial' career. From 1464 to 1467 he worked in San Gimignano, in 1466–7 at Certaldo and in 1467 at Castelfiorentino, after which he went to Pisa for a prestigious commission: that of the great Old Testament cycle in the Camposanto (1467–9 to 1485) where echoes of Uccello's scenes in the Chiostro Verde can be found. Gozzoli's frescoes at San Gimignano resound with echoes of Uccello's frescoes (now lost) in Santa Trinita or at Santa Maria degli Angeli. It is strange that after his Medici cycle, Gozzoli had to try his luck outside Florence, but the city's artistic climate had taken a particular turn. On reflection, it is no accident that at the very moment Gozzoli was working in Pisa, the elderly Uccello was seeking pastures new in Urbino. The coincidence in timing is, on the contrary, worth noting, since it also includes Lippi's late cycle at Spoleto cathedral (where Fra Filippo died in 1469); this was the outcome of a shrewd policy of exporting Florentine culture, conducted by the Medici.

For Uccello, the 1460s was a decade of progressive isolation, of increasingly recherché exercises in perspective, of sublime craftsmanship in small-format paintings for private clients, sometimes revealed by sources, but with an inexorable indeterminacy. From now on we regard him as a survivor of his generation. Brunelleschi was long dead, Ghiberti died in 1455, as did Fra Angelico, Castagno and Pesellino in 1457, Giovanni di Francesco in 1459, Domenico Veneziano in 1461 and his friend Donatello in 1466. Uccello was probably much admired for his craftsmanship and dexterity and for his 'difficult and impossible' (Vasari) artistic problems based on perspective. But essentially he was misunderstood and he became ever more isolated. In order to live he was obliged to provide cartoons for glass artists, engravers, marquetry and cabinet makers; nevertheless he still found the courage to travel. In spite of his age, he faced the difficult crossing of the Apennines to travel to

URBINO

Urbino, perhaps drawn by the rumour that Florentine art was welcomed in that city.

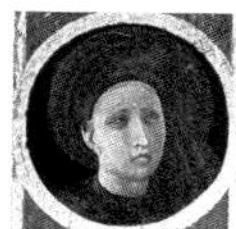

In Urbino (as yet without the status of a duchy) Florentine painting had become fashionable, including its superabundance of 'Lippism'. The town had been an important centre for International Gothic, with frescoes by the Salimbeni brothers at the oratory of San Giovanni (1416); Ottaviano Nelli da Gubbio had stayed there on several occasions (from 1417 to 1420 and from 1427 to 1435), while the humanist Bartolomeo Facio has mentioned that there was a panel by Van Eyck at Ottaviano Ubaldini's house.

Since Count Federico had been educated in Venice under the humanist Vittorino da Feltre, Urbino became one of the main centres of the Renaissance, one of the capitals of the world, and the ducal palace became the precious casket for this open culture. It had grown from what had originally been a Trecento core, on to which was added a complex series of buildings. In 1465 they were still working on the Count's bridal apartments – known as La Jole – under instructions from a number of Tuscan master architects, including Maso di Bartolomeo and Pasquino di Montepulciano. Later, on his return from Mantua where he had been studying Alberti's work, the Dalmatian architect Luciano Laurana managed – not without some difficulty – to be appointed supervisor of the building work and in 1468 Count Federico issued him with his famous 'patent'. In 1472, for mysterious reasons, Laurana abandoned his work and settled first in Naples, then in Pesaro, where he died in 1479. Uccello found an extremely unsettled situation in Urbino, where he had made connections back in 1465. He remained there from 1467 to 1469, bringing an original but eccentric contribution to a city which was stimulating and full of different experiences. It seems he worked only for the company of Corpus Domini, and not only as a painter. We may wonder what the worthy members of this lay fraternity would have made of his tormented intellectual researches. It is difficult to explain how such a prolonged stay could have produced only one painting, albeit a *Ill. pp. 261ff.* masterpiece like *The Miracle of the Profaned Host*. His presence passed almost unnoticed, as it had in Venice, Bologna and Padua, where he is known only for single works: a lost mosaic, a fragment of fresco, lost tempera murals, an unfinished retable.

Urbino, on the other hand, was an important commission, if we consider the company's role in the city's economic and social life. It was a propitious time for Florentine art. Count Federico described Tuscany as the 'fount of architects' in the licence he issued Laurana; he was a collector of Vespasiano da Bisticci's illuminated manuscripts, he was enthusiastic about the parade helmet Lorenzo sent him after Volterra had been captured (1472) and he summoned Pontelli and other Florentine artists to decorate the famous *Studiolo*. All the same, Uccello did not obtain any

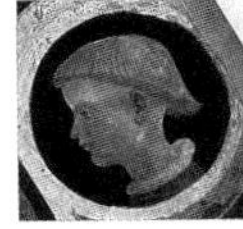

commission direct from the count (who became duke in 1474), whose tastes seemed to favour the Pollaiuolo brothers, as is shown in the portraits of his daughters, dispersed in numerous museums and sometimes (see catalogue) attributed to Uccello. The predella at Urbino would certainly have awakened a lively interest, but in spite of some sporadic references to Uccello in Giovanni Boccati's work[72] – a cultivated and receptive artist – Uccello had obviously not found fertile ground for his 'difficult' essays in perspective. Alberti's version of perspective which was about to establish itself in Urbino was incompatible with the disarticulation of space and perspective (Leonardo would call it 'composed') to be found in Uccello's predella. Piero della Francesca realized this: asked in April 1469 to paint the retable of Corpus Domini, the day after Uccello's disengagement, he responded with an abrupt refusal. If we recall the close links between Uccello's vision and Urbino's figurative culture – even in future developments up until the time of Raphael – Piero's refusal voiced the first official repudiation, which is echoed again at the beginning of Vasari's biography.

In Urbino, as in Florence, certain tendencies – even though in quite another direction – became more definite, which marginalized Uccello and his unsettling *quaestiones* of representation. We do not know if Uccello left behind his drawings for the retable, which could have influenced the Flemish painter Justus van Ghent, who was summoned to tackle monumental Italian space for the first time. Nor do we know if Uccello worked on anything else in Urbino: the attempt to attribute to him the *Famous Men* in the ducal palace (before 1467) seems unconvincing.[73]

The artist who ruled at court was Piero della Francesca, probably already in Urbino after his stay in Rimini (1451), and certainly there before the spring of 1469 when he was the erudite Giovanni Santi's guest to discuss the retable for the Corpus Domini. His *Flagellation* was greatly appreciated at court. The great ducal commissions date throughout the 1470s: the *Madonna* for the church of San Bernardino, now in the Brera; the Senigallia *Madonna*; a double portrait of Federico and Battista Sforza; and his only recorded presence puts him there after Uccello had left. We do not know what contact there may have been between the two artists in Urbino.

Uccello returned to Florence at a time when there was a close contest between Pollaiuolo and Botticelli for the *Virtues* for the Tribunale della Mercanzia, and *Ill. p. 101* simultaneously Alesso Baldovinetti's first attempt at the *Miracle of the Holy Sacrament* at Sant'Ambrogio (whose theme was similar to Uccello's predella in Urbino). In no way did the elderly Uccello appear overwhelmed by the despondency he cleverly feigned in his declaration to the Cadastre of 1469: quite the reverse – he remained active. It was not a question of him having to work through lack of funds:

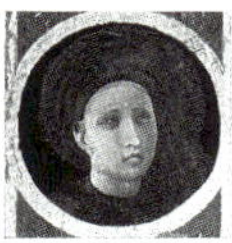

he was well off in a material sense. He owned a house and a property outside the town, he had a daughter who was a nun and a wife whose dowry he would return when he died.

THE END

Ill. pp. 270ff. His final years are surrounded in mystery but we can date the splendid *Hunt* at Oxford to around 1470. This masterpiece may perhaps have passed unnoticed at the time, but it is poles apart from what contemporary decorators of chests were producing. The only artist who even approached him was Botticelli in his panels of the *Story of Nastagio degli Onesti*, now in the Prado. And something of Urbino's climate of mathematics and perspective comes through in the ordered architectonic scansion of the 'regularly' spaced trees. At Lorenzo de' Medici's accession, Uccello produced a painting unrivalled in its evocative freshness. The pack of greyhounds – which bound away through the rigorous perspective of the wood towards a horizon that through the action of time on the pigments is now even darker than it was – is probably Uccello's last work. It is an emblematic painting in the race towards the gathering shadows of Florentine culture at the century's end that Uccello would not

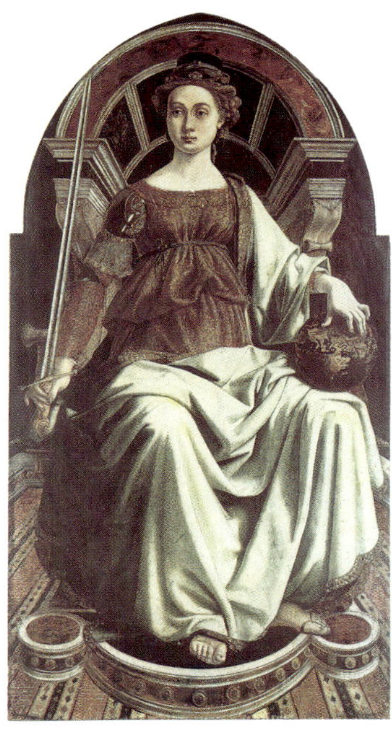

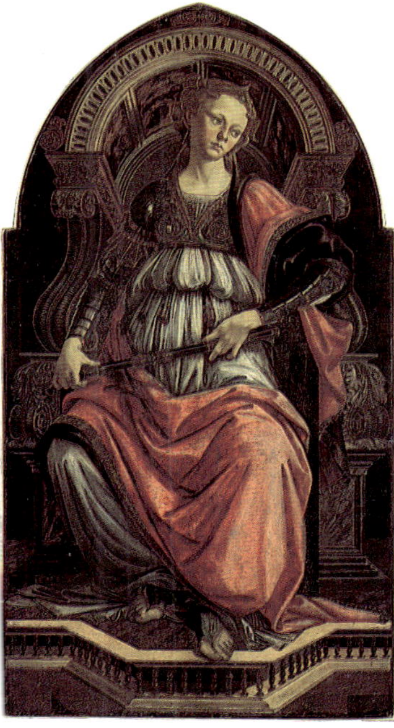

Two *Virtues* for the Tribunale della Mercanzia.
Left: Piero del Pollaiuolo, *Justice*, 1469, tempera on wood, 167 × 88 cm. Florence, Uffizi.
Right: Sandro Botticelli, *Fortitude*, 1470, tempera on wood, 167 × 88 cm. Florence, Uffizi.
The series had been commissioned from Pollaiuolo and it was Tommaso Soderini, elected consul in 1470, who arranged that the last panel should be given to his friend Botticelli.

live to see – Uccello who had been born into a world that still held in living memory the illustrious Giotto and sinister recollections of the great plague epidemics of the Trecento. It had been an heroic period for Florence, of which Uccello was an extraordinary witness and a passionate interpreter during his long life, his paintbrush always at hand. If he was not 'solitary, bizarre, melancholy and poor', as Vasari

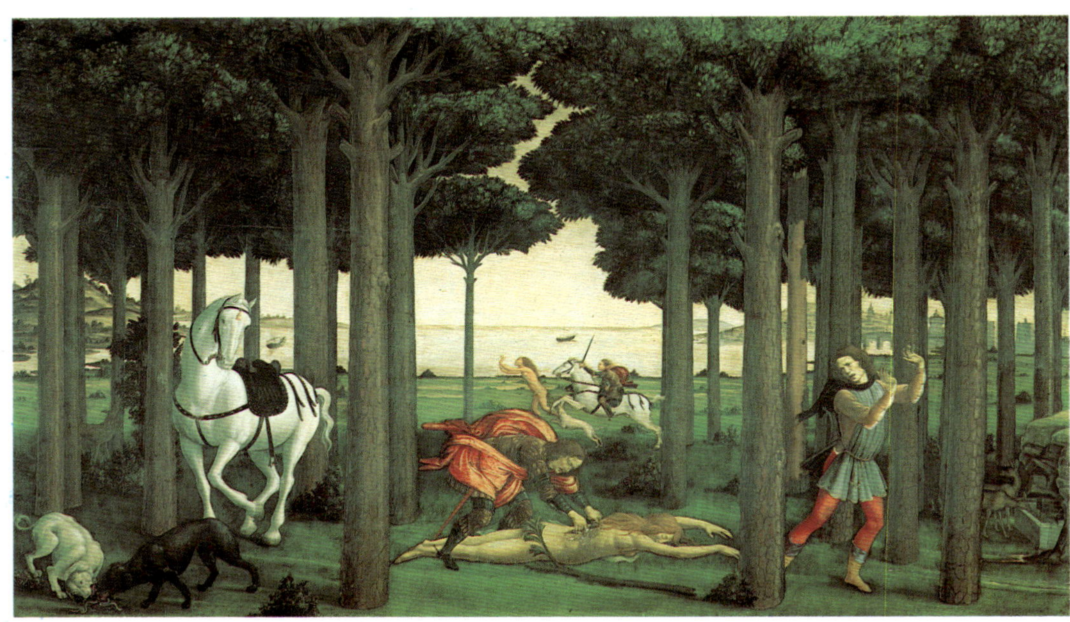

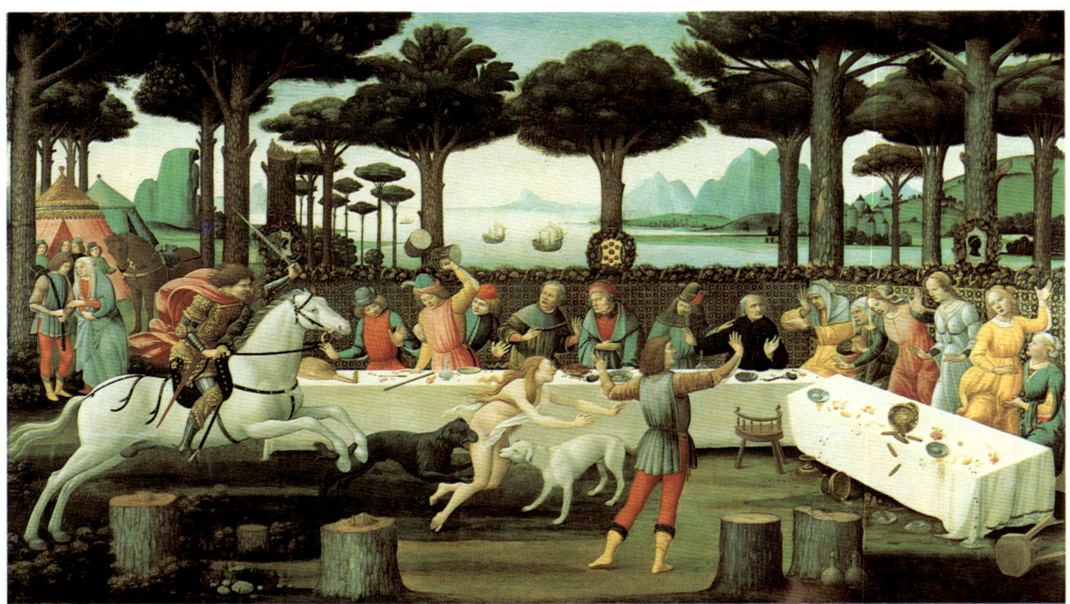

Sandro Botticelli, *Story of Nastasio degli Onesti*, 1483, tempera on wood, first panel 82 × 138 cm, second panel 84 × 142 cm. Madrid, Prado.

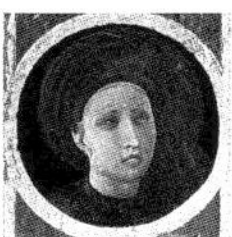

would have us believe, he was certainly a rather isolated figure, burdened by his intellectual explorations and generally misunderstood. The city was preparing to honour a new generation: Botticelli, Ghirlandaio, Rosselli, Perugino, Filippino Lippi, Pollaiuolo. The long history of Uccello, often misjudged but never surpassed, drew to its close. And in the fateful year of 1492, Lorenzo the Magnificent died in front of Uccello's *Battles* commissioned by his grandfather Cosimo: it was truly the beginning of a new epoch.

Overleaf: Uccello, *Scenes of Monastic Life*, detail of fresco on the east wall of the upper cloister. Florence, San Miniato al Monte.

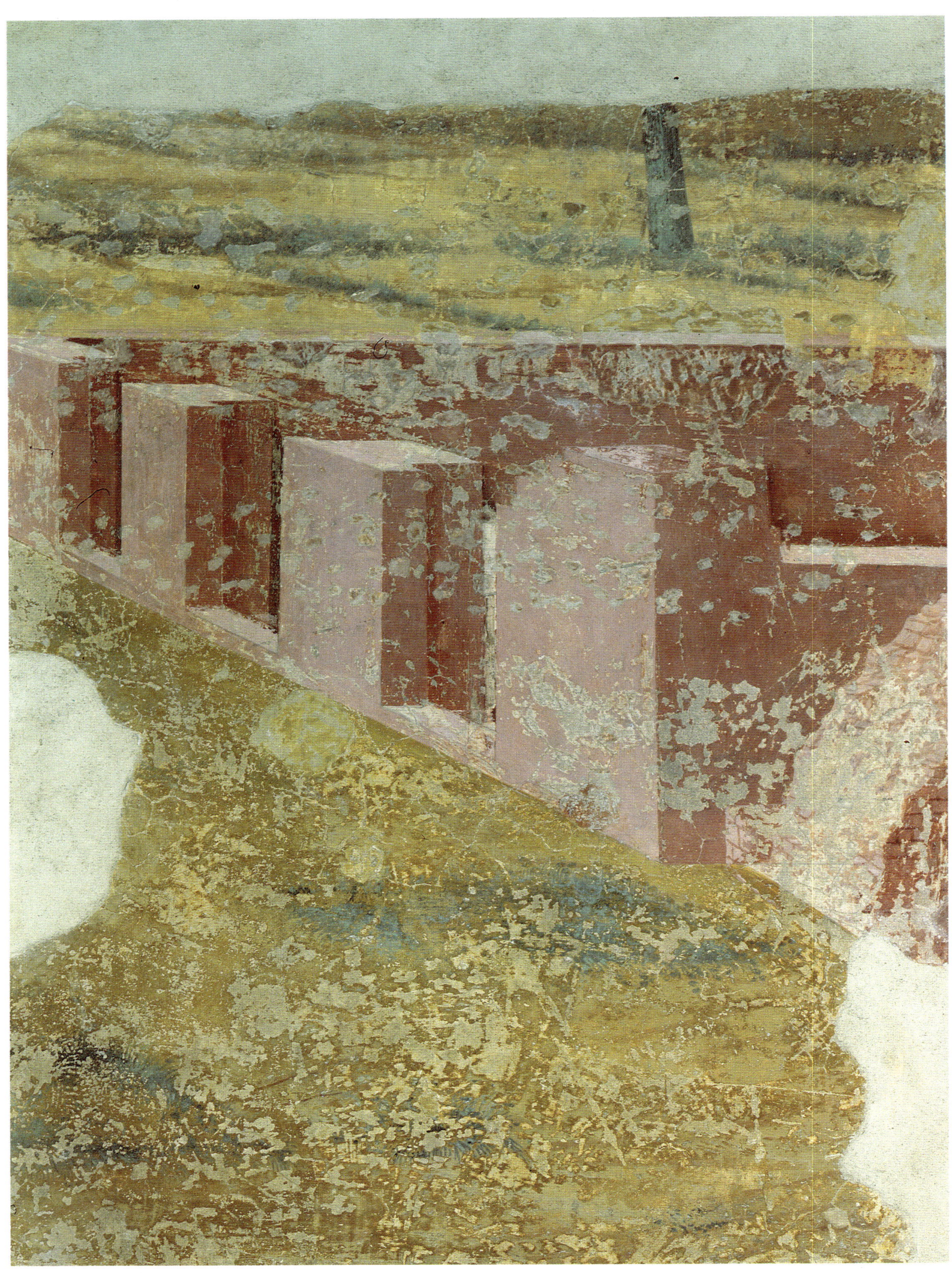

Chapter Three

PLACES ASSOCIATED WITH UCCELLO

SANTA MARIA NOVELLA

A few notes should be enough to give an impression of the significant role Santa Maria Novella has played in Florentine history. From the end of the thirteenth century onwards, the Dominican convent was an important study centre for Thomist doctrine. Dante was among its pupils, in his quest for places where 'philosophy is truthfully demonstrated'. And in the field of preaching, Santa Maria Novella was famous as a source of *lingua volgare*, modern Italian.

Jacopo Passavanti, author of the *Specchio di vera penitenza* (Mirror of True Penitence), a practical treatise on preaching, which is also one of the most sparkling texts in Italian Trecento literature, was a prior here in the mid-fourteenth century: his

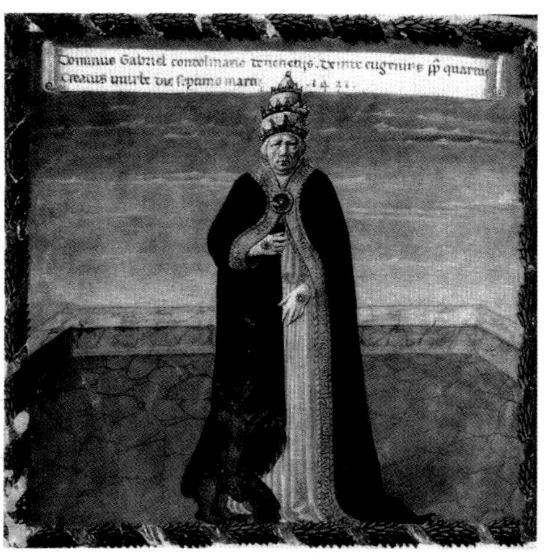

Attributed to Benozzo Gozzoli, *Pope Eugenius IV*. London, British Library, Harley ms. 1340.

treatise is basically a collection of sermons for the year 1354. Leonardo Dati, Superior General of the Dominicans, and one of the participants in the Council of Constance, died here in 1425, probably just at the time when Uccello began painting the Chiostro Verde. The library and the pharmacy were – and would remain for centuries – two key centres of humanist and scientific culture.

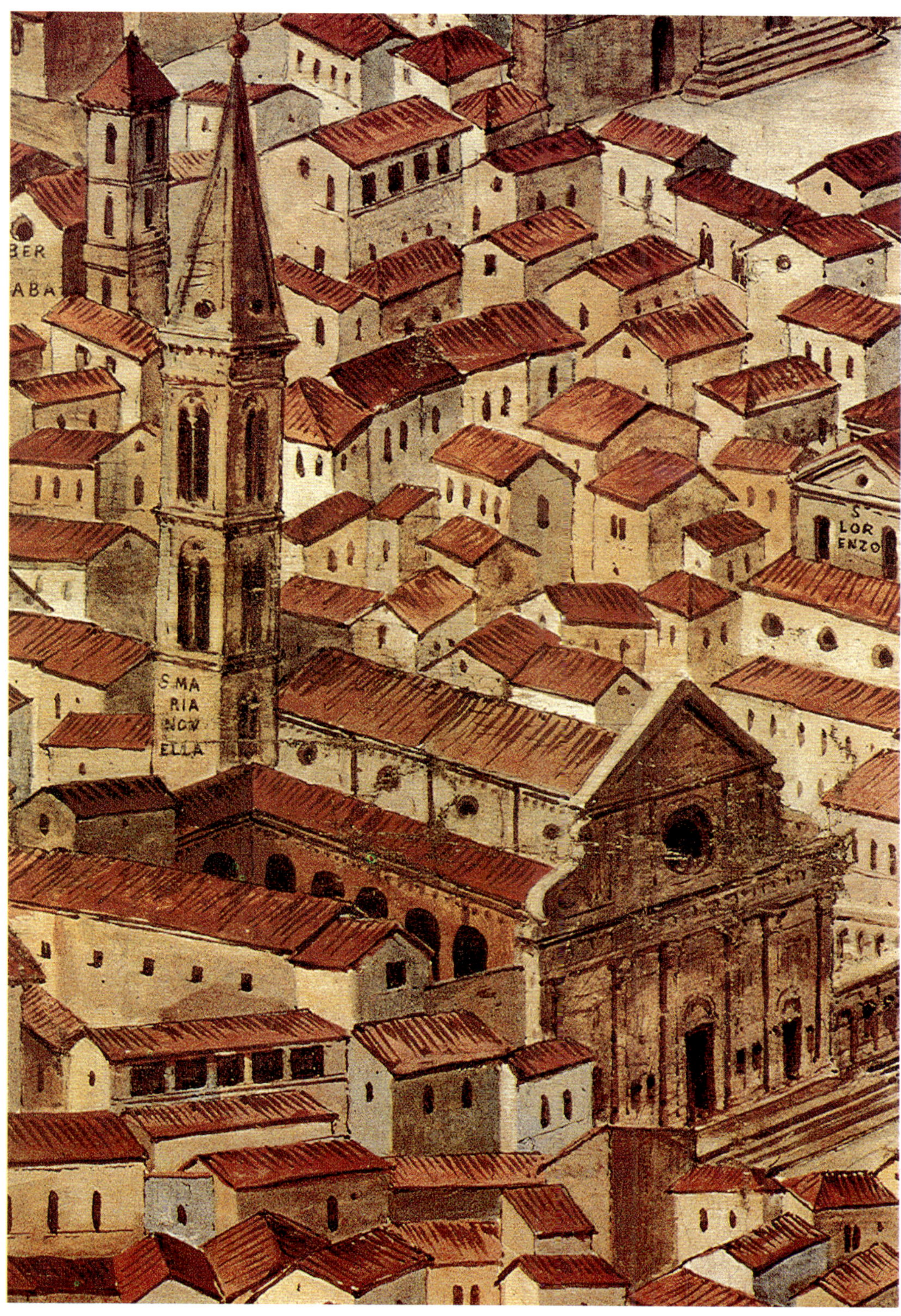

Santa Maria Novella, from the view of Florence known as the *Pianta della Catena* (Chain Map) after its frame. The woodcut view is attributed to Francesco Rosselli and dated 1472. This version was coloured at a later date. Florence, Museo Storico Topografico 'Firenze com'era'.

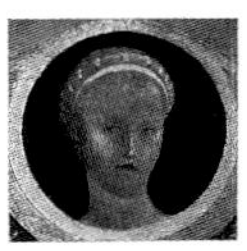

At the beginning of the Quattrocento, in 1418–19, Martin V, who had been elected pope at Constance, lived here as a sign of homage, in an apartment just off the great cloister. Eugenius IV, elected pope in the Dominican convent of Santa Maria sopra Minerva in Rome, also stayed twice at Santa Maria Novella: in 1434–6 after the troubles in Rome, and in 1439–43 for the Ecumenical Council between the Roman and Orthodox churches which had been transferred from Ferrara to Florence: just in the interval between Uccello's two campaigns in the Chiostro Verde: the *Stories from Genesis* (1424–5) and the *Stories of Noah* (1446–7). Alberti was also in Florence at this time, at the Papal Court, where he was writing *De Pictura*, his treatise on painting – first in Latin, then in Italian. In his dedication to Brunelleschi, he omitted Uccello from his list of great modern artists: 'But after I came back here to this most beautiful of cities from the long exile in which we Alberti have grown old, I recognized in many, but above all in you, Filippo, and in our great friend Donato the sculptor and in those others, Nencio and Luca and Masaccio, a genius for every laudable enterprise, in no way inferior to any of the ancients who gained fame in these arts.'[74] Uccello's absence from this list confirms his *goticitas*, not to mention his allegiance to another school, that of Ghiberti, – whose *Commentario Terzo* would be supplanted by the clarity and systematic arrangement of thought in *De Pictura*.

Ma poi che io da lungo exilio in quale siamo noi Alberti invecchiati qui fui in questa nostra sopra l'altre ornatissima patria riducto, chompresi in molti ma prima in te Filippo et in quel nostro amicissimo Donato sculptore, et in quegli altri Nencio et Luca et Masaccio essere a ogni lodata cosa ingegno da non postporli a qual si sia stato antico e famoso in queste arti.

The convent was one of the greatest architectural achievements of the thirteenth century, when the city had been completely involved in enlarging the old cathedral of Santa Reparata, and building the Palazzo della Signoria (Palazzo Vecchio), the convent of Santa Maria degli Angeli, and Santa Croce: in fact, all the important centres where autonomy of language and urbanity were in evidence as symbols of the pride taken in Florence's leading role. Even here, in Santa Maria Novella, secular values were combined with religious masterpieces in a world at its apogee. The church was consecrated only in 1420; as for the Chiostro Verde, whose low, rounded arches reverberated with local Gothic, a plan for its decoration had been devised as far back as 1348, at the time of Turino Baldesi's[75] legacy: in his will he had entrusted Jacopo Passavanti as his legal executor, with responsibility for having the church decorated with the Story of the Old Testament. But it was the erudite preacher himself who had decided that the *Stories from Genesis* – which at the time was the first figurative cycle in the city (Ghiberti's Doors of Paradise were undertaken only after 1425) – would be shown on the mute walls of the cloister, which would take its name from the predominant colour used in painting the scenes.

If in his sermons Passavanti used the rhythm and realism of the vulgar tongue, here in this silent sermon, whose purpose was to use pictures to encourage the brothers' meditation, another language had to be used: *aliter clericis aliter laicis est praedicandum*. It

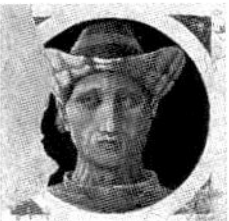

had to be the equivalent in pictures of a learned language, a grammar, a discussion of erudite matters; it was a narrative programme, crowded with suggestivity but also apposite, a noble, abstract pictorial language where the enticements of the real world were filtered through a stylized treatment: basically a 'Gothic' language. The frescoes themselves were to be painted in terre-verte, almost as though other colours might convey the noise of the outside world and the temptations of the visible, which here would be transmuted into a stylized grandeur, almost like a bronze relief.

The basic idea was to establish a parallel between the Dominican order, fulfilling pilgrim-like its priestly and apostolic mission of bearing witness to Christ and his Church on earth, and the people of Israel, making their pilgrimage towards the Promised Land. The story of Genesis was the premise needed to illustrate Salvation, whose path was traced by the Dominican order and by the two saints, illuminated one and the other by the inspiration of the Holy Spirit. This was the iconographical theme of the frescoes in the chapter-house decorated by Andrea di Bonaiuto (Andrea da Firenze) and known as the Spanish chapel. There was therefore a reversal in the

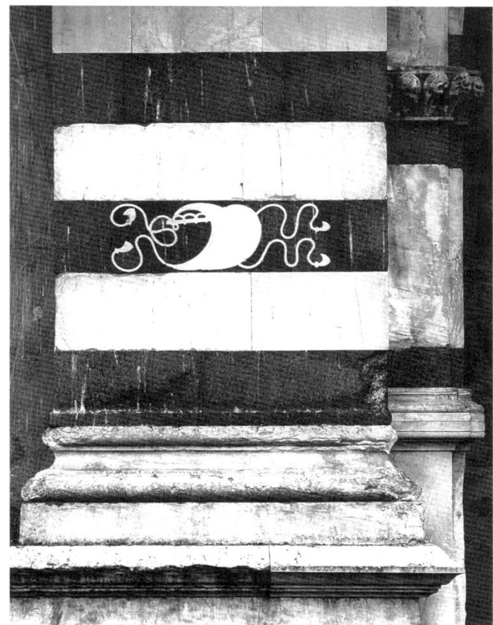

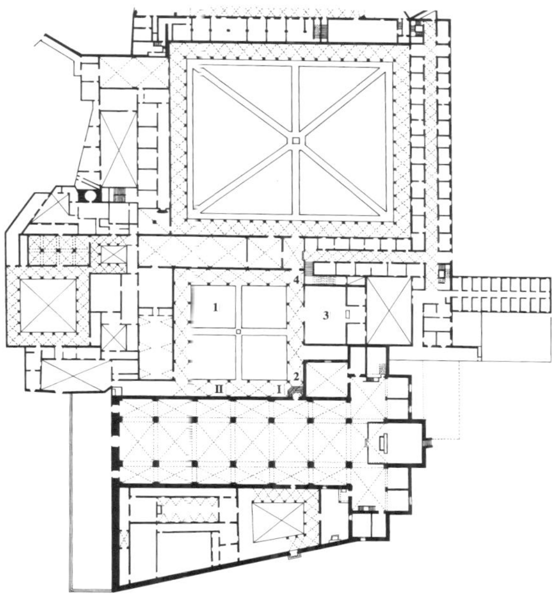

Left: Santa Maria Novella, detail of Alberti's façade showing the sail, emblem of the Rucellai family.

Right: plan of the convent. (1) the Chiostro Verde, next to the church; (2) passage from the church to the cloister; (3) the Spanish chapel (chapter-house); I and II indicate Uccello's frescoes.

time sequence between the prologue in the Chiostro Verde, painted many decades later in the Quattrocento, and the conclusion, painted by Andrea from 1365 onwards, a few years before Passavanti died. So the task of following his programme through was disrupted by two factors: both the passage of time and the artists' personalities.

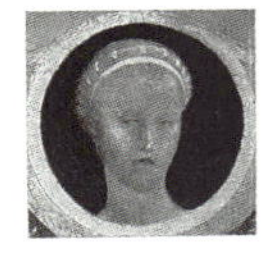

With his first lunette Uccello introduced more lively complementary colours into the monochrome terre-verte: wine reds in the skies, the hot earth colours of burnt Siena and Pozzuoli, which later in the *Stories of Noah* would double in intensity. We can see an allusion to Antiquity in this cave-like red and in the increasingly resolute use of perspective – perspective that Ghiberti's *Commentario Primo* attributed to Apelles and that had a connotation of nobility and Antiquity. 'Wishing to demonstrate the nobility of the art of painting and how much he excelled therein, Apelles laid down his brush and compiled a discourse on perspective as a part of the art of painting.'[76]

Ill. p. 180

Ill. p. 183

Volendo mostrare Apelle la nobiltà dell'arte della pittura e quanto egli era egregio in essa, tolse il pennello e compose una conclusione in prospettiva appartenente all'arte della pittura.

Such then was Uccello's first authenticated cycle, which showed two phases of development in his personality and reflected the intellectual concerns of his era, like an

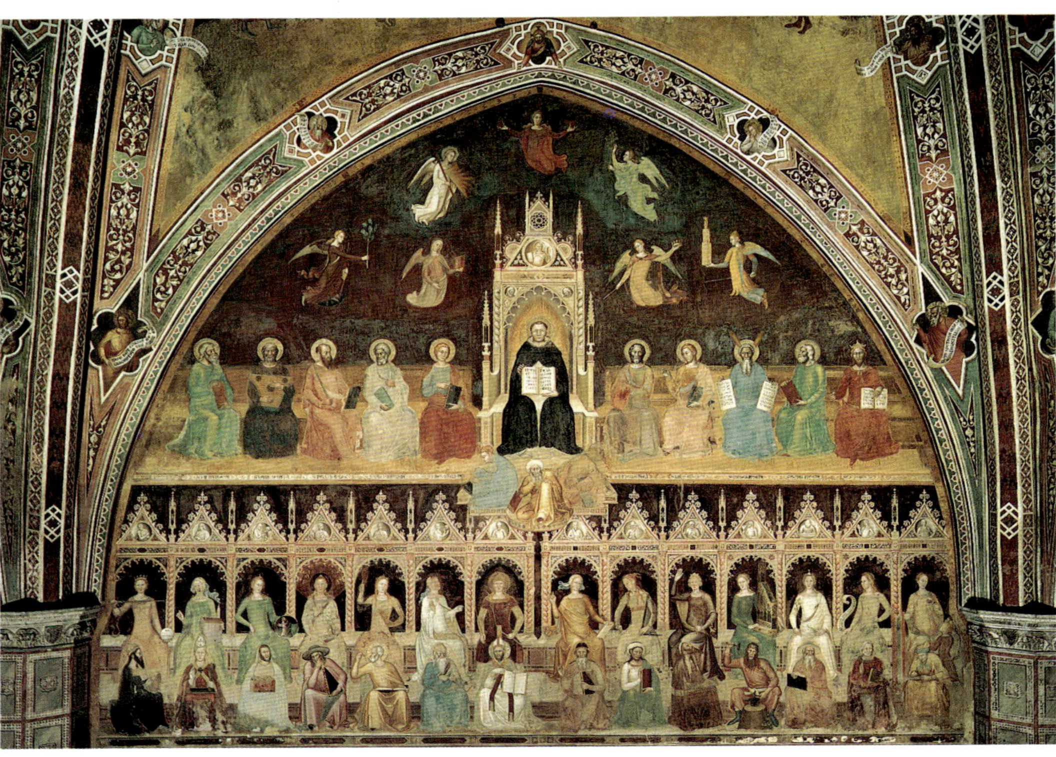

Andrea da Firenze, *The Teaching of Saint Thomas Aquinas*, *c.* 1365–7, fresco. Florence, Santa Maria Novella, Spanish chapel.

equivalent piece to Ghiberti's two sets of doors. One thing is certain: a painter who was not yet thirty had been entrusted with a difficult theme in a place was a focal point of Florence's cultural life.

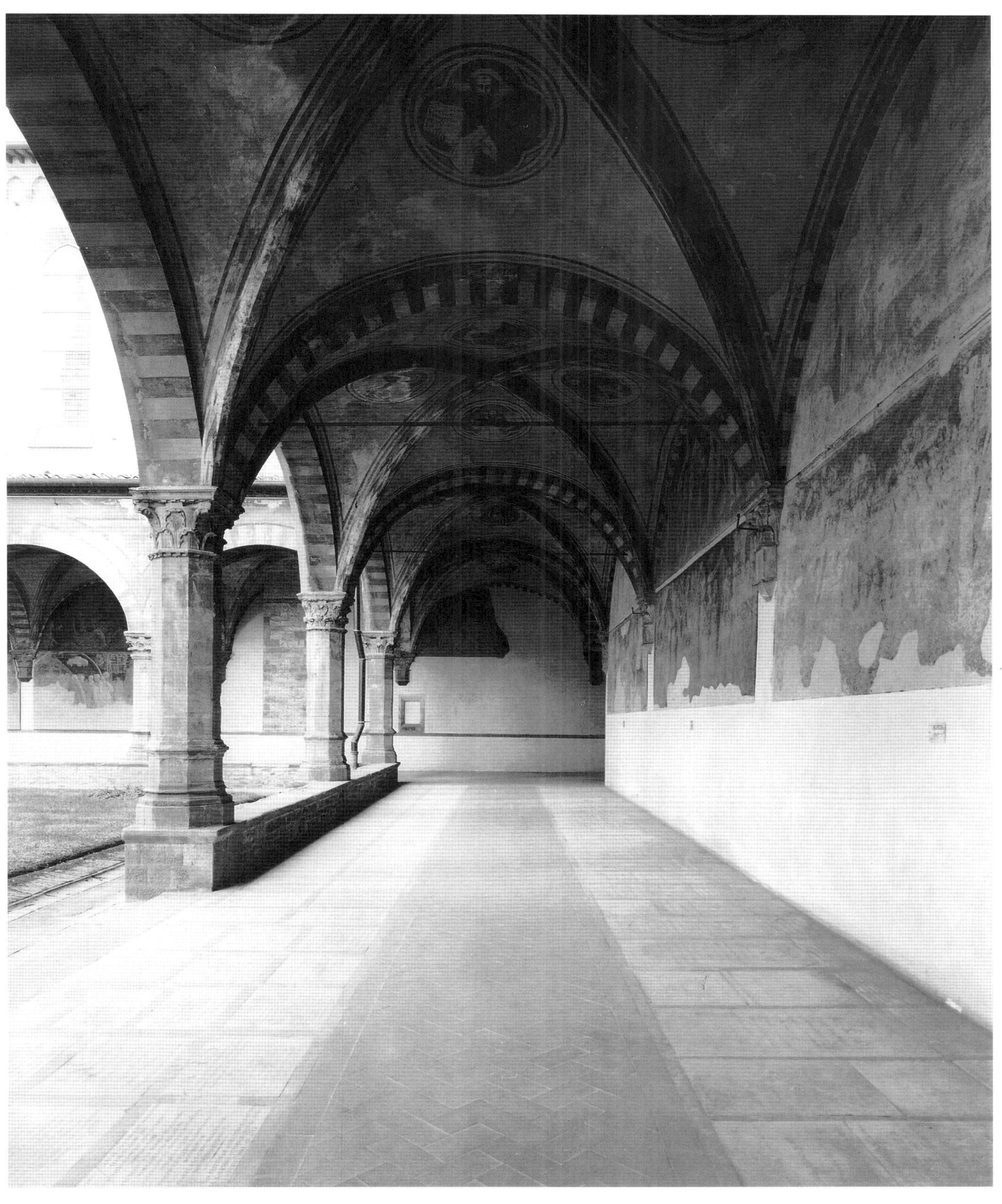

Santa Maria Novella, the Chiostro Verde.

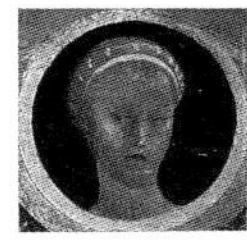

THE CATHEDRAL

It is a phenomenon common to all European cities that the cathedral forms a focal point for work, cultural endeavour and achievement, and progress. In Florence, from Arnolfo di Cambio's time to Brunelleschi's, Santa Maria del Fiore was to become a symbol both of a people's genius and their rational, austere character. It is a place ill-adapted to prayer (a feeling still widespread today), and in spite of furnishings and fittings accumulated over the centuries, it remains a bare, monochrome space on two registers: there is the roomy, luminous Gothic of the interior; and there is the haughty and sombre Romanticism of its façade, a nineteenth-century creation. It was here, between 1420 and 1436 – the years of his apprenticeship with Ghiberti, his journey to Venice and his first appearance as a painter at Santa Maria Novella – that Uccello watched the great architectural adventure of the cupola. This symbolized Florence's primacy and inspired Alberti to dedicate *De Pictura* to Brunelleschi, with that famous, but always moving phrase: 'a structure so vast, so high in the sky, that it could shelter all the peoples of Tuscany in its shade'.

Florence's cathedral resembled those of other northern countries in having no decoration or painted representation other than its stained-glass windows, which could only show limited episodes. For the rest, the sculptures were economically replaced by monochrome paintings or were limited to the medallions of famous tombs. Uccello, who now had the terre-verte paintings of Santa Maria Novella to his credit, was working on the great Duomo site on two important commissions: the equestrian monument in memory of Sir John Hawkwood, and the clock, to which must also be added the cartoons for the stained-glass windows of the oculi of the cupola. In fact, he achieved as much as a painter could there, for, to make amends for the enormous expenditure on the building, they merely scratched away at the interior decoration (Brunelleschi's wooden choir is typical of this parsimoniousness); painting was reduced to a very subsidiary role, but that was as much because of their taste for austerity as to economy in time and money.

Ill. p. 205
Ill. pp. 115, 118, 119

Sir John Hawkwood, who was known in Florence as Giovanni Acuto, was an Englishman who had participated along with his company in the Hundred Years' war. He had moved to Italy and served both Pisa and Milan until 1377, when for almost twenty years he was commander-in-chief to the Republic of Florence's troops, where he exercised an important political influence. Uccello's commission was therefore the most official that an artist could receive at that period, as much for the site in which it would be placed as in the person it would represent. Uccello's idea for the monument had an epic, *goticitas* orientation, with the foreshortening of the plinth and

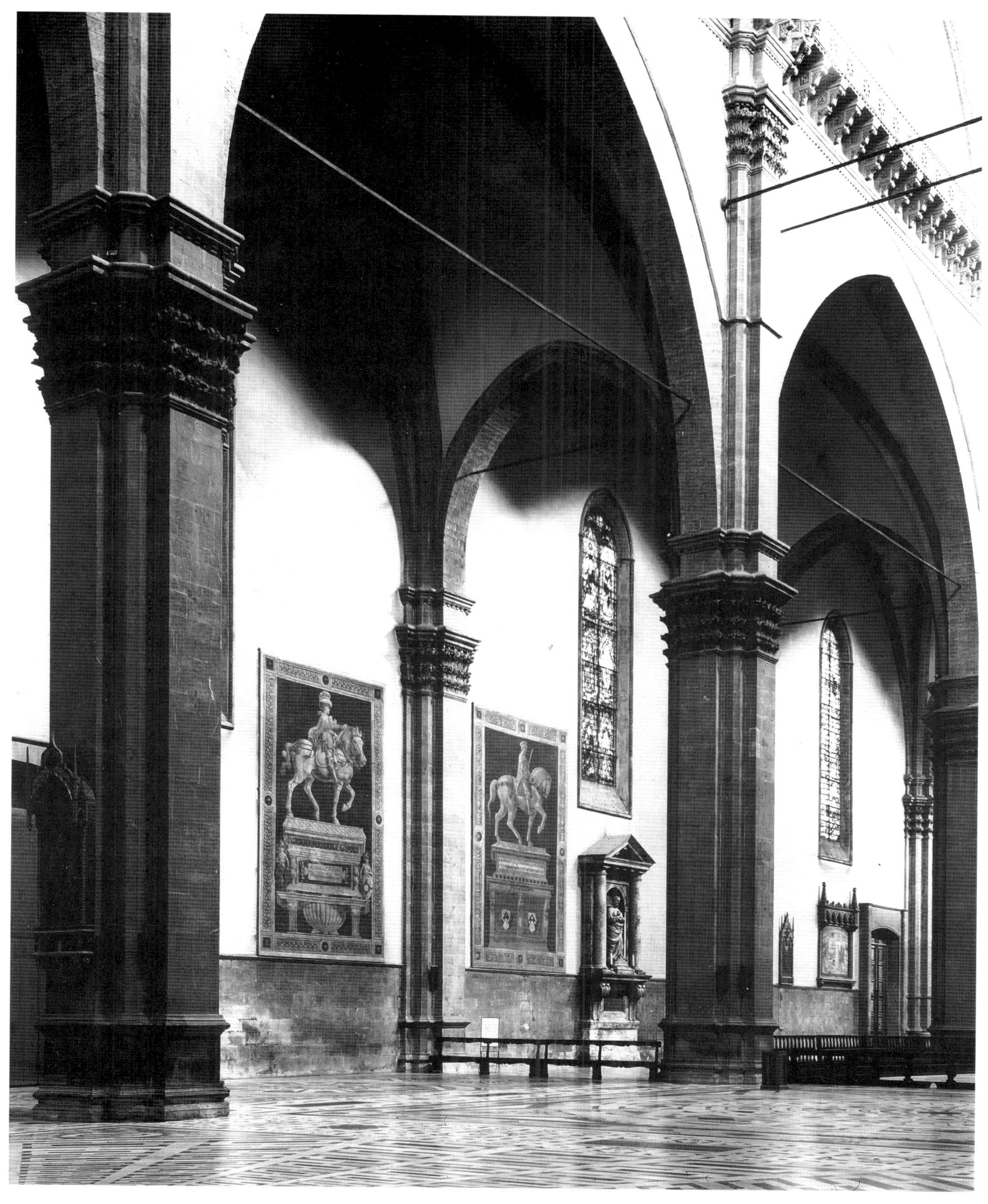

View of the interior of Santa Maria del Fiore
with frescoes by Andrea del Castagno and Uccello.

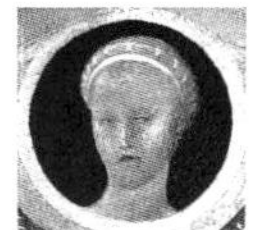

the noble, geometric stylization of horse and armoured figure. The *trompe-l'oeil* framework would later be decorated in the symmetric rhythms and scansions of a more fully blown Renaissance style, while preserving a robust solidity, without conceding to the elegance that can be found, for example, in Santa Maria Novella's façade. We shall not discuss the patrons' refusal of the work here, nor the decision of the cathedral's chapter to allow Uccello to do the fresco again. The monument's essential purpose was to glorify a famous personality, through geometricized stylistic elements which determined the way the hero was presented, and through the horse's gait which harked back to the horses of San Marco in Venice and gave the effigy nobility and an aura of Antiquity. The very character, the complexion of the animal, a true, heavy war horse, like something out of Pisanello, was the extreme opposite of the lithe, harmoniously designed horse of an almost Leonardoesque dynamism which Alberti described in his text of *De Equo Animante*, dedicated to Lionello d'Este on the occasion of the competition for the equestrian monument to Niccolò III d'Este in Ferrara, the *Arco del Cavallo*. Uccello thus perpetuated the idea of the horse as a war

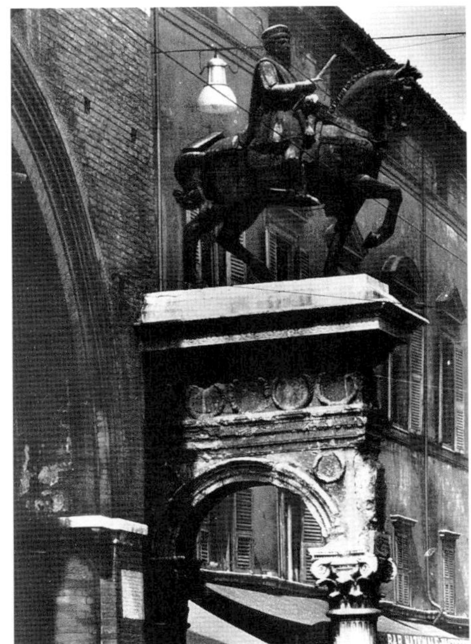

Niccolò Baroncelli da Firenze, *Equestrian Monument to Niccolò III d'Este*, Ferrara. The design of this 'Arco del Cavallo', based on the triumphal arches of Antiquity, is attributed to Leon Battista Alberti who inspired Duke Lionello d'Este's project.

machine, typical of the medieval universe, whose place would be usurped by the light, swift, dynamic cavalry used in raids and reconnaissance operations so characteristic of Renaissance warfare.

As for the cathedral clock, which was finished in 1443, this was a commission of remarkable austerity, which had only light gilding on the hand and on the small orb

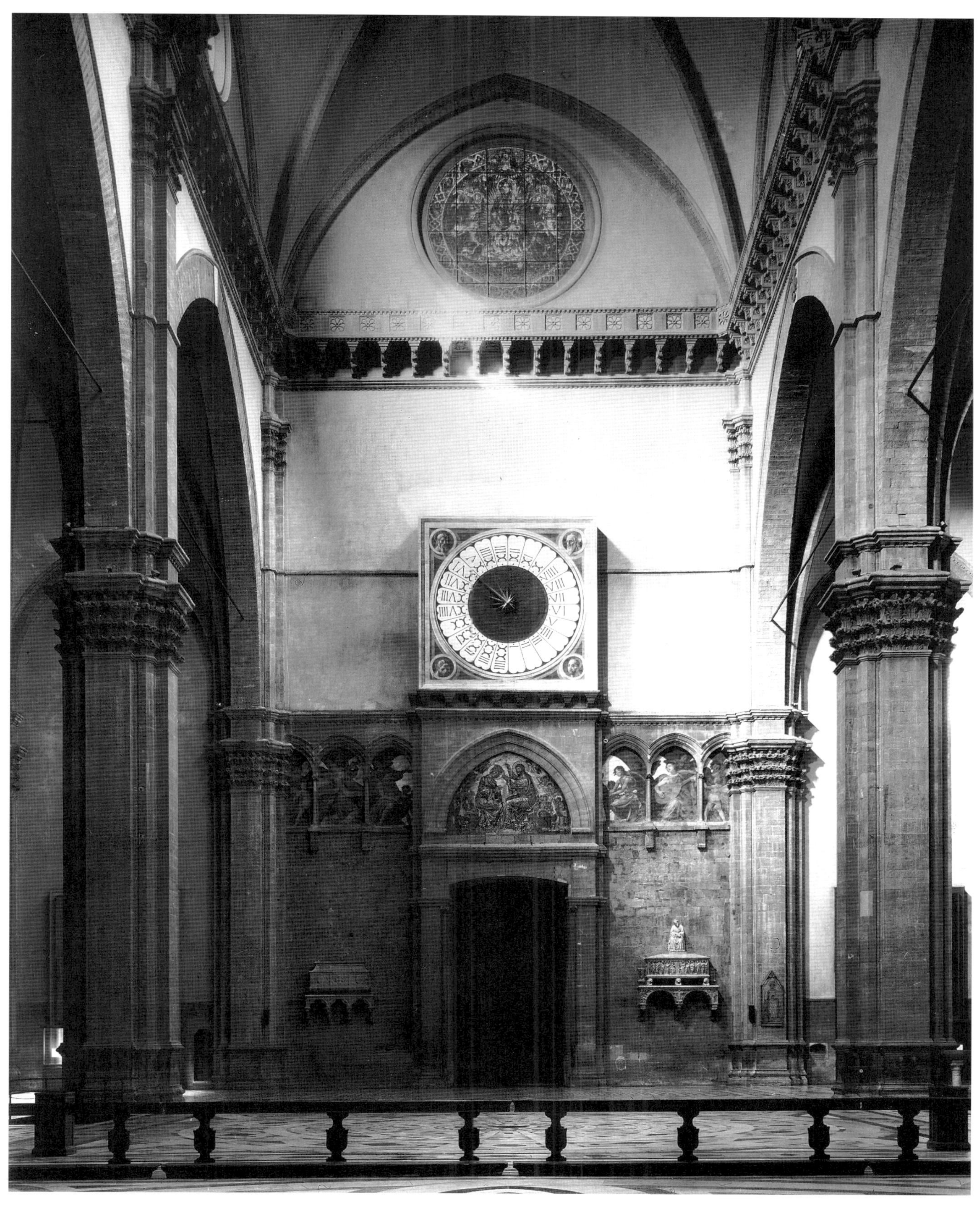

The clock on the inner face of the façade wall of Santa Maria del Fiore, Florence (see pp. 118–19).

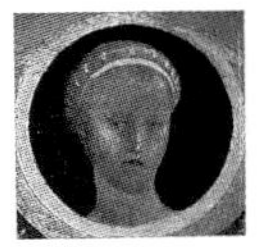

at its tip. Other than the document of 2 April 1433 relating to the payment, we know of this through its similarity to the detail of the comet in the stained-glass window of the *Nativity*, designed by Uccello himself for one of the oculi in the cupola (in the recent restoration of the clock this detail in the window was used as a reference). *Ill. p. 238*

We might have expected to see a transparent oculus rather than a clock above the projection of the central doorway on the inside of the façade. It therefore offers a different solution from the traditional rose window so characteristic of European Gothic cathedrals. In fact, in Santa Maria del Fiore an oculus would have been superfluous as a source of light, for its central nave was already lit by numerous windows. Being able to manage without a further window at this spot, the Florentines therefore installed an instrument for measuring time, which, in all cathedrals, symbolizes the confrontation with eternity and punctually spells out the hours of earthly day. The Florence clock has no astrological references or scientific complexities: it is essentially a mechanism. The numbers on its face are positioned in

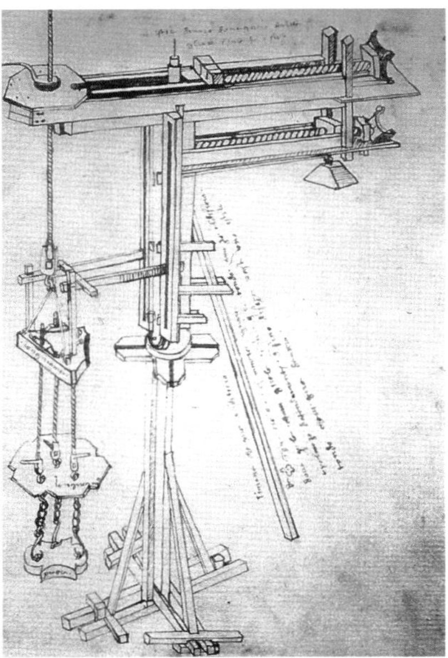

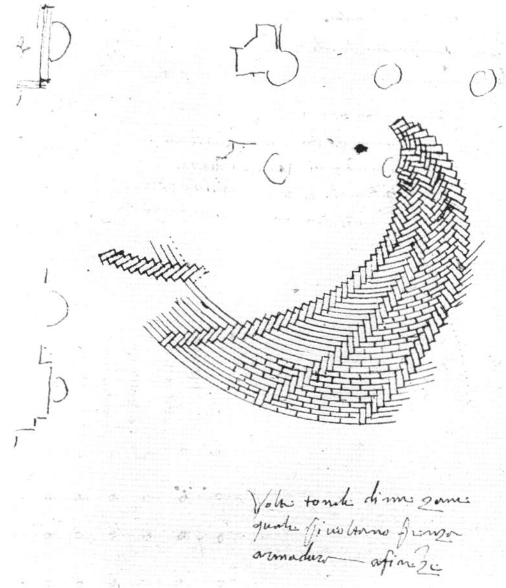

Left: Buonaccorso Ghiberti, machine for lifting weights, page from a notebook of drawings. Buonaccorso, Lorenzo Ghiberti's nephew, drew several of the machines used by Brunelleschi on the cupola of the Duomo.

Right: Antonio da Sangallo the Younger (?), drawing showing the technique of herringbone bricklaying for a circular vault to be erected without the use of scaffolding. Florence, Uffizi, Gabinetto dei Disegni.

an anti-clockwise direction and the outside edge of its sections are like twin petals, giving the whole the appearance of a large daisy.

The anti-clockwise direction derives from the sundial whose natural function the clock imitated. To Brunelleschi, great 'mechanic' of the cupola, his biographer Manetti attributed a passion for clocks: 'And since, in the past, he delighted in

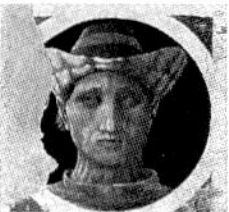

making clocks and alarms, in which were found varied and diverse "loads" (*mole*), and a varied multitude of appliances, of which he had learnt everything or most of everyting'.[77] 'Load' here means the system of gears on the machines for lifting weights used on the cupola building site. There are many references to them in the notebook of Buonacorso Ghiberti, (Lorenzo's nephew), whose foundry provided the bronze pieces and gears.

Ed essendosi dilettato nel passato e fatto alcuno oriolo e destatoio dove sono varie e diverse generazioni di mole, e da varie moltitudini di ingegni moltiplicate che tutte o la maggiore parte aveva vedute.

Even if it cannot be shown that Brunelleschi conceived the cathedral clock, there are affinities between Brunelleschi, Buonacorso and Uccello. Uccello was given exclusive responsibility for the graphic make-up of an essential theme, the circle inscribed within a square, a problem similar to those he had encountered in Venice as a mosaicist and that he resolved by letting the geometry dictate the lettering. Recent restorations have brought to light the authentic version, which is certainly not obviously clear. Complementary to the flatness of the clock-face design is the thickness of the oculi, in which the heads of the prophets or Evangelists appear, as though at a window, thus giving the expanse of the clock the value of a 'spatial box'. This is justified in view of its cumbersome mechanism and the projection of the doorway below, and also by the fine abstract effect of the play of metallic haloes on the intrados of the oculi.

Ill. pp. 118–19

In 1433, when a problem arose in closing the oculi of the cupola with wooden panels because of wind, cold and hazards connected with the site, there was a similar problem with the window situated above the chapel of Saint Zenobius, which was visible from the main entrance and nave. They turned to Venice for information: 'on a certain Paoli di Dono, of Florence, master of mosaics, if he had worked well on the said figure, and what, in the town of Venice, is his reputation and his price'.[78]

de quondam Paolo Doni de Florentia magistri mosayci utrum bene laborabit prefatam figuram et cuius est in civitate venezianorum extimationis et pretii.

Uccello's candidacy, probably proposed by Ghiberti, was based on a certain affinity between the art of mosaics and that of the stained-glass window, which obliged artists to draw cartoons, to serve as a staging point between designs and realization: so there had to be a certain stylized simplification in the background and in the chiaroscuro. The artist's main task was to supervise those who were making the piece, who, far from always being docile, faithful interpreters, would often prove their independence they had achieved through professional experience (of which there was a chronic dearth in Florence), so much so that making stained-glass windows required unrelenting research into stained-glass artists, glass blowers, glass makers and others. The first oculus saw a contest between Ghiberti's and Donatello's cartoons on the theme of the *Coronation of the Virgin*, a contest Donatello won. In 1439 it was established that the master in charge of the stained glass would be Bernardo di Francesco, at whose premises, twenty years later, when he had his workshop in

Ill. p. 120

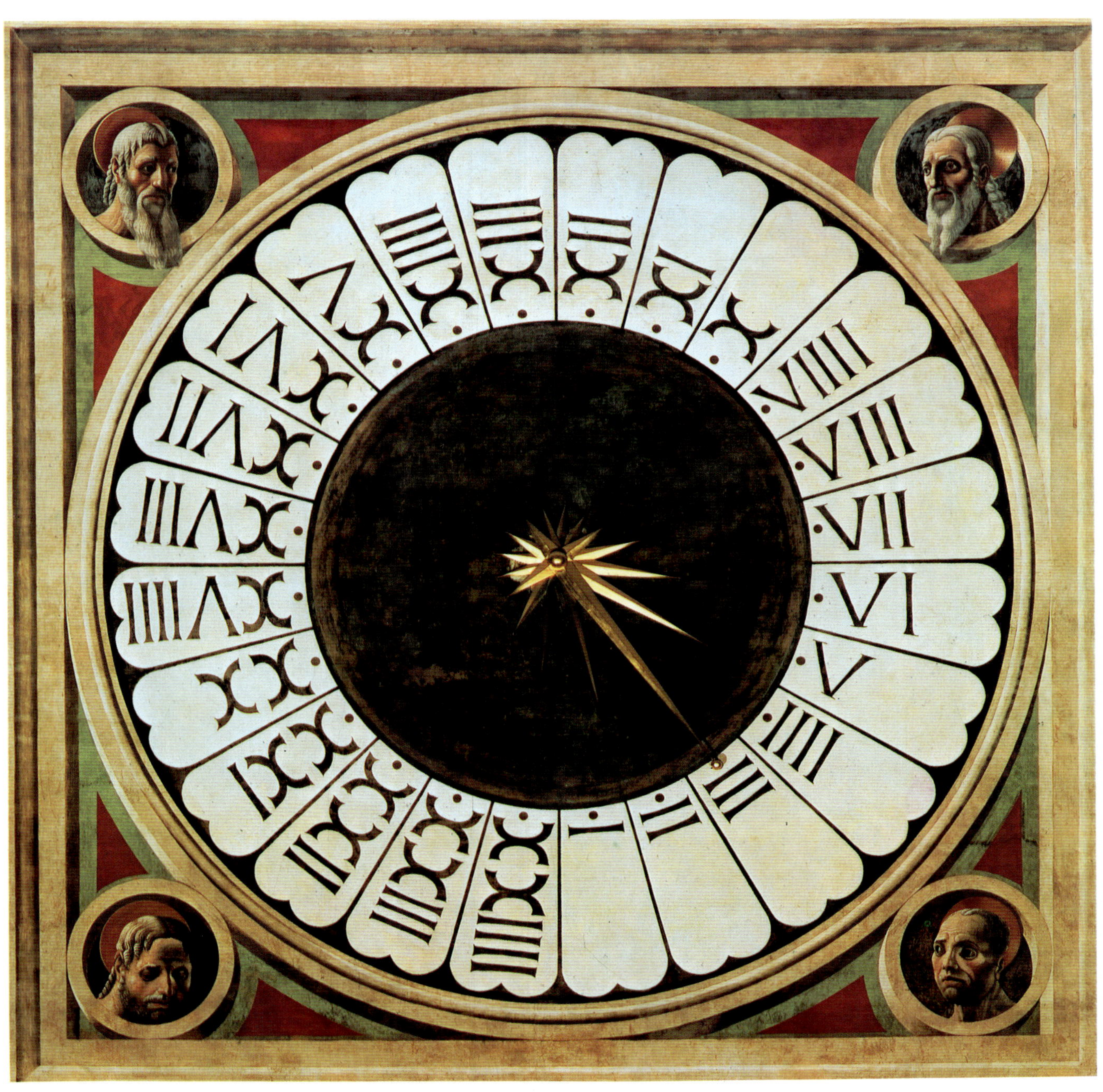

Uccello, clock face, 1443, fresco, 460 × 460 cm.
Florence, Santa Maria del Fiore.

Facing page: Heads of the four Evangelists.

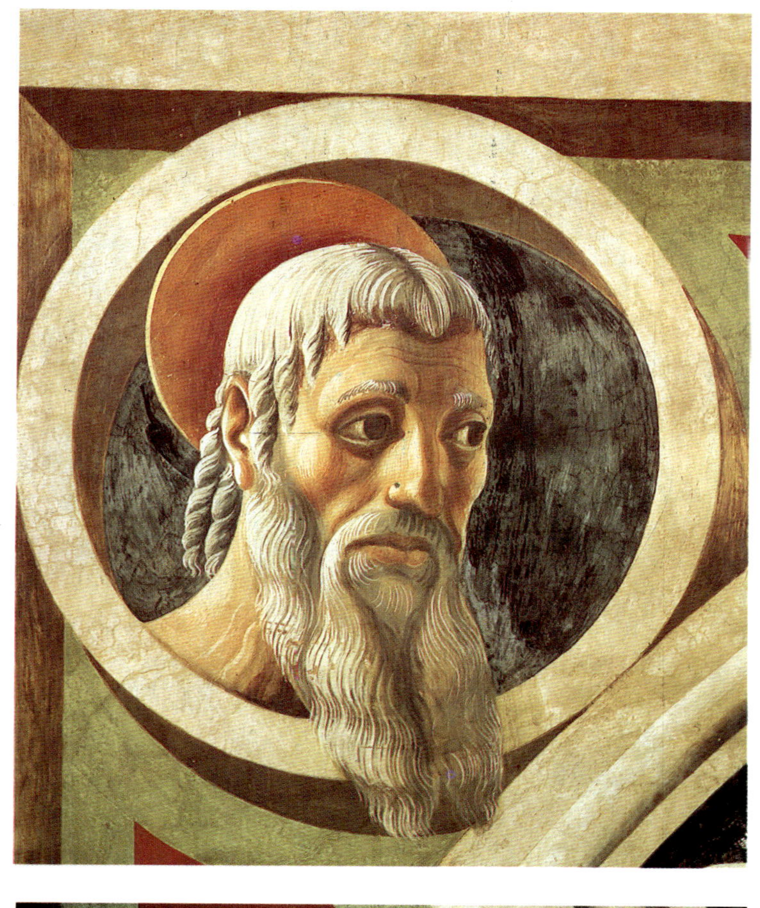
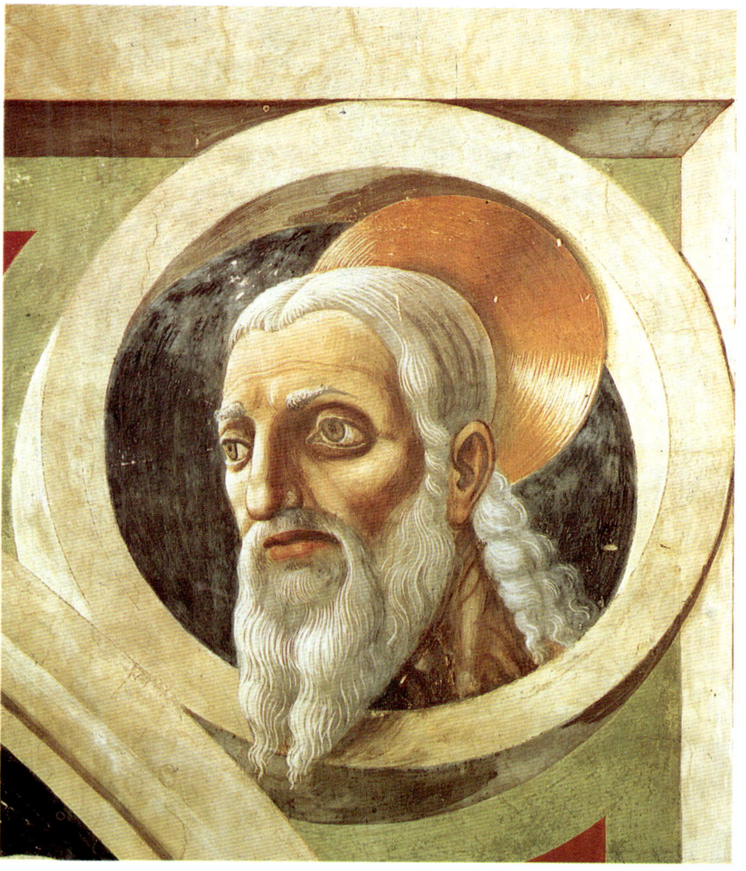
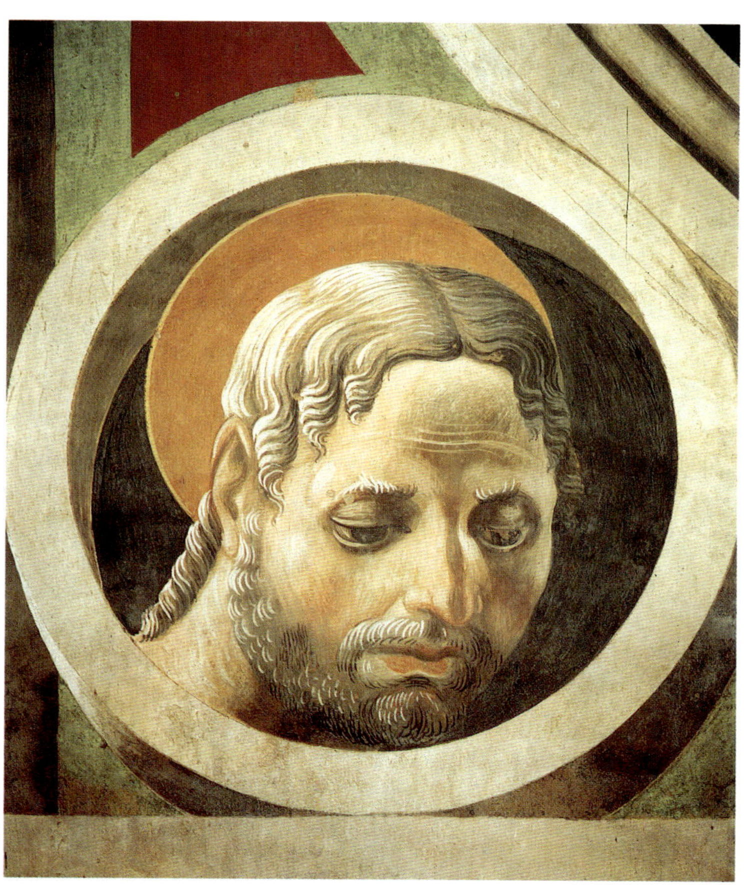
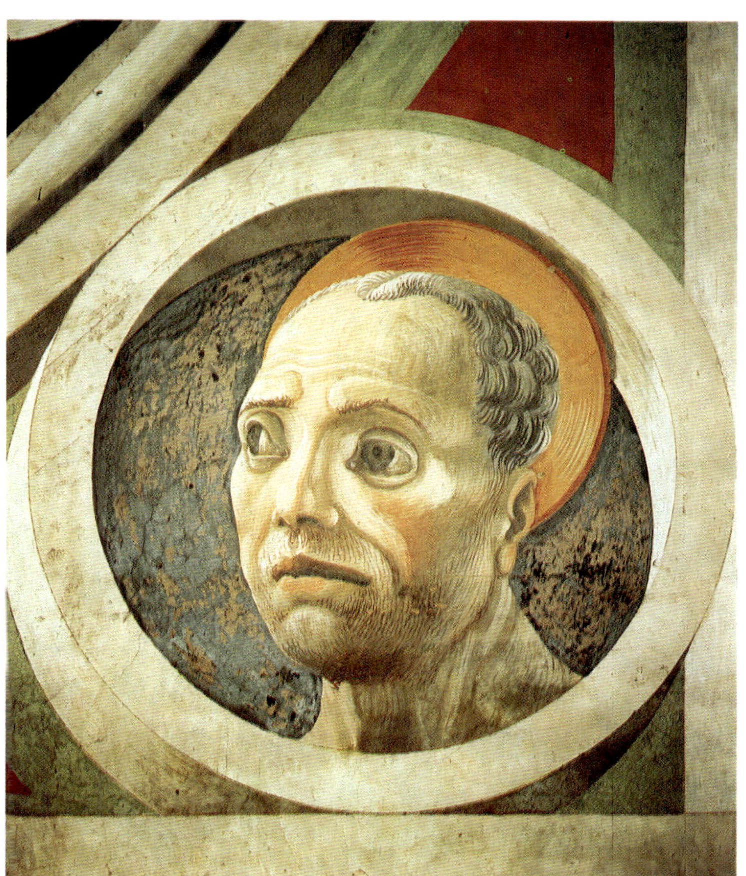

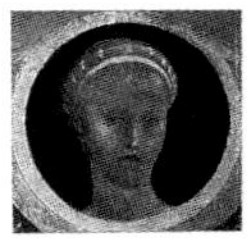

Piazza San Giovanni, Uccello would rent a place where he 'took refuge to paint'; proof among others of his involvement in stained glass.

In 1442 a meeting was held to decide whether or not the large oculi in the cupola should have stained glass. Taking part, other than the council of the Office of Works, were Francesco della Luna, Ghiberti, Brunelleschi and Battista d' Antonio.[79] Two questions were posed: first 'whether clear or coloured glass seemed more suitable and appropriate to them for the oculi (*occhi*) of the gallery, for there were different opinions on this matter' and second, 'if for the cupboards in the second sacristy, wood, marble, bronze, marquetry or another material should be chosen'.[80] The prevailing opinion was in favour of decorating the *occhi* with coloured figures, but there was a characteristic difference of opinion between Brunelleschi, who expressed himself in a stylized manner: 'As for the windows he is of the view that they would be richer with figures: and such is his view,' and Ghiberti who expressed his opinion more articulately: 'As for the first part of the windows he proposed that there should be as many coloured as clear, which would give more light, look richer and decorative as well.'[81] The difference lay in the fact that Ghiberti was preoccupied with the luminosity of the stained glass, while Brunelleschi was not. He would have liked the cupola dark, although in 1433 he had been ordered to get sixteen stone oculi made

voler sapere quale pare loro più idoneo e confacenti gli occhi della tribuna chiari o coloriti; perché ce n'è più pareri intorno.

se gli armadi della seconda sagrestia di materia o di marmi o di bronzi o di tarsia come gli altri o di altra materia

Alla parte degli occhi disse gli pare sia più ricco di figure: e così pare

Alla prima parte degli occhi disse d'ochi colorati e tanti chiari che daranno lume abbastanza e saranno più ricchi e più ad ornezza.

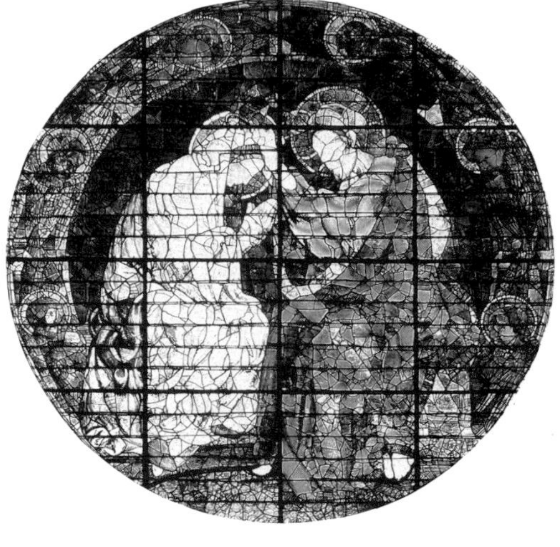

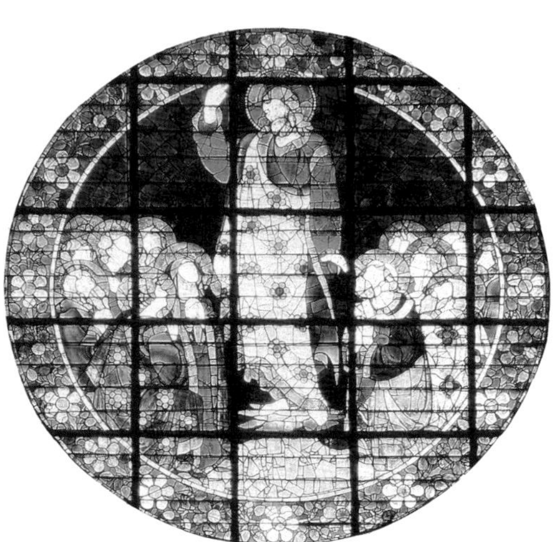

Two stained-glass windows in the drum of the cupola of Santa Maria del Fiore. *Left:* Donatello, *The Coronation of the Virgin*. *Right:* Lorenzo Ghiberti, *The Ascension*.

'*sedecim oculus de macigno pro cupola magna*'.[82] He had quite simply done nothing about it, and later, in completely contrary manner, he reduced the opening for the lantern at the apex of the vaulting, and consequently the amount of light that could enter. Whence Gherardo da Prato's[83] accusation – as someone who was always critical of Brunelleschi – that Brunelleschi wanted to keep the cupola not only dark but '*oscura e*

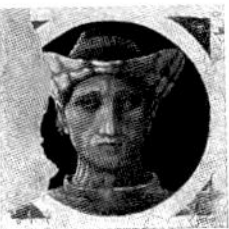

tenebrosa'. This judgment mattered little to Brunelleschi, since his precise intention was to give the great dome a mysterious, protective shadowiness pierced only by a few rays of sunshine, thus imbuing it with an almost mystical atmosphere. Later, in his theoretical treatises, Alberti certainly recollected the characteristics of Florence's cathedral when he advised that the nave be not too dark, but that a solemn atmosphere around the altar was preferable to an elegant one.[84]

Ill. p. 238 Uccello was asked to make two stained-glass windows, almost at the same time as the clock. In the *Resurrection* he included his cherished *mazzocchi*, almost like a coded language, and the foreshortened tomb, and he favoured Ghiberti's idea of the greatest amount of transparency by spreading broad areas of light symmetrically around the resurrected Christ. The other stained-glass window of *The Nativity* shows a perspective viewed from above, with figures as though crushed in space, with stronger colouring, which seems more rooted in traditional Gothic design.

Ghiberti became deeply involved in this programme. 'In the gallery,' he wrote in his *Commentario Secondo*, 'there are three *occhi* drawn by my hand: in one, Christ is seen ascending into the Heavens, in another praying in the garden, and in the third, being borne into the temple' and he concluded: 'There are few things of importance in our city that have not been designed and organized by me.'[85] And in keeping with what he said, his cartoons present a fragmented and almost constant light, a sagacious balance between the centre and edges and a homogenous distribution of chiaroscuro. As usual, there is a kind of happiness in his creativity, while Uccello, in his dolorous quest, is totally involved in each work as if it were always the first time, and as if all the problems of 'seeing' and 'representing' were continually posed afresh. Uccello's

Nella tribuna sono tre occhi disegnati di mia mano: nell'uno è come Cristo ne va in cielo, nell'altro quando adora nell'orto, il terzo quando è portato nel tempio . . . Poche cose si sono fatte di importanza nella nostra terra che non siano state disegnate e ordinate di mia mano.

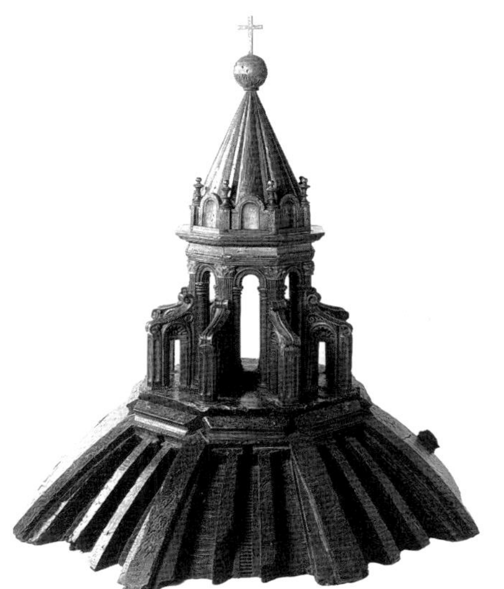

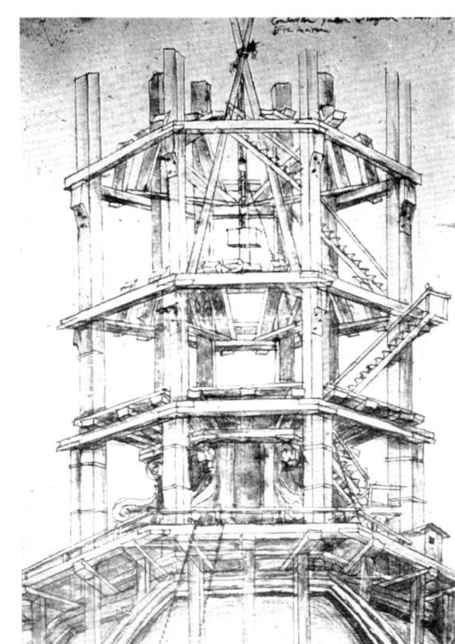

Work on the lantern saw a confrontation between Brunelleschi and Ghiberti, and dragged on for a long time. The young Lorenzo the Magnificent was a member of the commission that appointed Verrocchio to make the orb in gilded bronze.

Left: Filippo Brunelleschi, wooden model for the lantern of the cupola of Santa Maria del Fiore. Florence, Museo dell'Opera del Duomo.

Right: Gherardo Mechini (?), drawing for scaffolding on the lantern of Santa Maria del Fiore. Florence, Uffizi, Gabinetto dei Disegni.

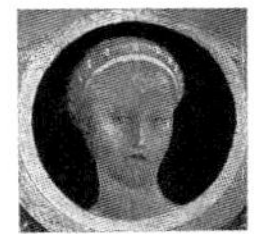

contribution to the Duomo's figurative decoration has a kind of lucid coherence and lies midway between Ghiberti and Brunelleschi. And between those two 'cross-currents', he somehow found a space for introversion and intimacy, in contrast to these two extrovert personalities, one mocking, the other grandiloquent, but both ringleaders, agitators of factions that sustained each in his own role.

Passeri arguti empian gli archi e gli sproni / incominciati di ser Brunellesco. / Cantavan laggiù donne e garzoni / c'era tanto sussurro e tanto fresco / intorno a te Santa Maria del Fiore! / E Paulo si scordò S. Francesco, / e fu tentato e mormorò nel cuore.

Yet, in his solitude, in what was perhaps stubborn isolation, Uccello, the cultivated obstinate artist, reached a poetic dimension that is echoed – in spite of an inappropriate reference to Franciscanism – in Giovanni Pascoli's poem that, at the beginning of the twentieth century, grasped the sense of his presence in the cathedral site. 'Under the arches and spurs/ That Ser Brunellesco began/ And where the air thronged with the sharp cries of sparrows/ Apprentices and girls sang/ And the air was filled with murmurings and was so cool/ around you, Santa Maria del Fiore/ And Paulo forgot San Francesco and was tempted/ And murmured in his heart.'[86]

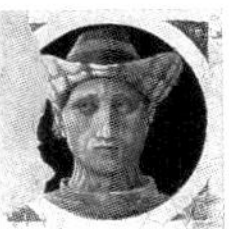

THE CLOISTER OF SAN MINIATO AL MONTE

A prime example of Romanesque architecture, the basilica of San Miniato al Monte is one of Florence's major sites. To Quattrocento eyes, it must have seemed vital proof of a continuing tradition rather than a revival – with its full-arched arcades, its composite columns and the subtle pilaster strips in the superior order of the façade and apse, and its polylobed columns and pillars in the nave, models which appeared to be perfect as they were, as much in their harmonious proportions as in the morphology of the moulding in discreet chiaroscuro, which so closely echoed the taste of the period.

Throughout the Trecento, the convent annexed to the basilica had had the privilege of being a sort of bishop's villa for the encumbents of the diocese of Florence. It was only towards the end of the century, in 1373, that the whole building was given over to the Olivetans. It then became a proper convent and was developed fully in the first half of the Quattrocento. The convent building was organized around a cloister

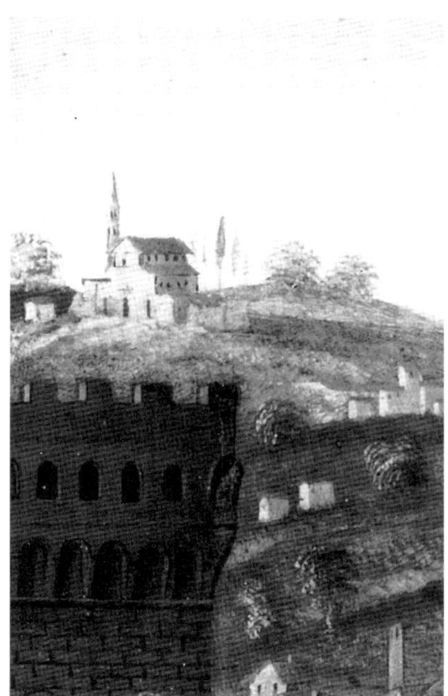

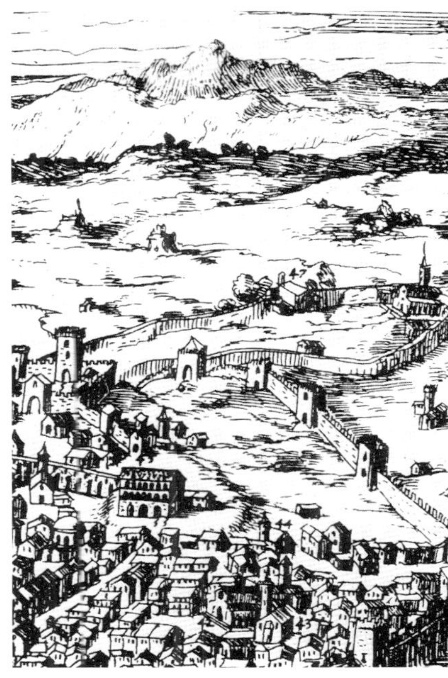

Left: Unknown Florentine painter (school of Perugino), *The Execution of Savonarola*, *c.* 1500, tempera on wood, detail showing San Miniato al Monte. Florence, Museo di San Marco (for the whole painting, see p. 143).

Right: Giulio Ballino, detail of a bird's-eye view of Florence, 1569. Rome, Biblioteca Alessandrina. San Miniato al Monte is on the extreme right.

begun in 1389: its lower level was composed of robust convex arcades resting on great
Ill. p. 125 massive stone pillars, while in the upper level, small, fine columns of grey stone supported a sloping wooden roof *ad impluvium* on the inside. In 1426, the building of the wing containing the chapter-house and dormitory began, followed in 1443 by the east wing, which backed on to the Trecento sacristy and housed the refectory and

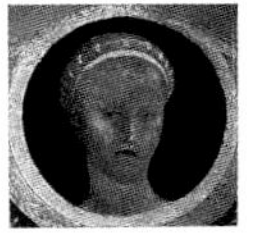

rooms to lodge the poor. The opposite wing was the bishop's palace, while the final, narrow wing was a simple portico to the outside.

The work was done by some of the most important workshops in Florence in the first half of the century, such as Rossellino's, who also built the Cardinal of Portugal's chapel in the church. There were other teams as well, linked with Michelozzo's workshop and those of less important masters, who can be found again on the San Lorenzo worksite.[87] It was a case of major architecture achieved with limited means, as instanced in the fact that in spite of the Arte di Calimala's support, the brothers were obliged to sell one of their estates in order to pay one of the entrepreneurs, Betto di Geri (who had done most of the work). In the artistic and technical fields, Florentine *botteghe* (workshops) had sprung up around Rossellino's and Michelozzo's 'enterprises' and they worked in complementary and coordinated fashion, principally in stone, joining forces when the occasion demanded or when speed was of the essence. Here then is proof, among other things, of the osmosis that existed between great personalities and anonymous artisans, who formed the connective tissue of

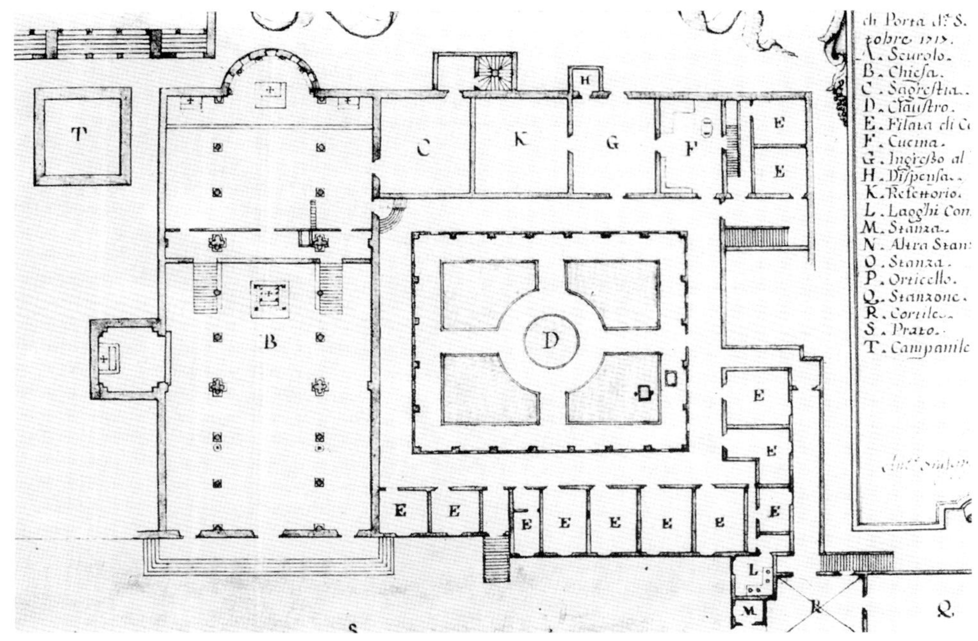

Plan of the convent of San Miniato, from the *Libro di piante e disegni*, 1718. Florence, Biblioteca di San Miniato al Monte. In the cloister (D) Uccello painted the walls to the east (top) and south (right).

architectonic production and urban building in the Quattrocento, and who represented a precise, serene, domestic language. It was in this ambience that Uccello, accompanied by an assistant, Antonio di Papi, began work in 1455.[88] His cycle of frescoes (which also had sections painted in oil colours, which explains the poor state of conservation) remained hidden under a layer of plaster until it was discovered in *Ill. pp. 198ff.*

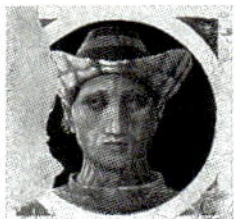

1925. It raised a host of questions which – despite restoration work and a number of interventions that increased the amount recovered – remained unanswered.

First, the problem of attribution, his assistants and the identification of themes and subjects: all these make this cycle one of the most singular, most 'arcane' (to coin Luciano Berti's phrase) of all early Renaissance Florentine painting. The fragments are also difficult to decipher. And yet in these fragments we can clearly discern a new phase in Uccello's experimentation, pioneering an unheard-of chromatic freedom which earned him Vasari's reservations: 'because he made the fields blue, the town a red colour and the different buildings whatever colour took his fancy' – and the Anonimo Magliabechiano's total condemnation: 'He also painted in the cloister at San Miniato al Monte, from top to bottom, all around the entrance, but these are things that are not highly valued.'[89]

perché fece i campi azzuri, le città di colore rosso e gli edifici variati secondo che gli parve

Dipinse anchora nel chiostro di San Miniato al Monte di sopra intorno et di sotto come s'entra dentro, ma sono cose non molto tenute in pregio.

Not having to endure the demands of a powerful patron, as in Santa Maria Novella, nor the hierarchy of the cathedral site where he constantly had to refer matters to Ghiberti in person, here in the tranquillity of the Olivetans' cloister, Uccello felt

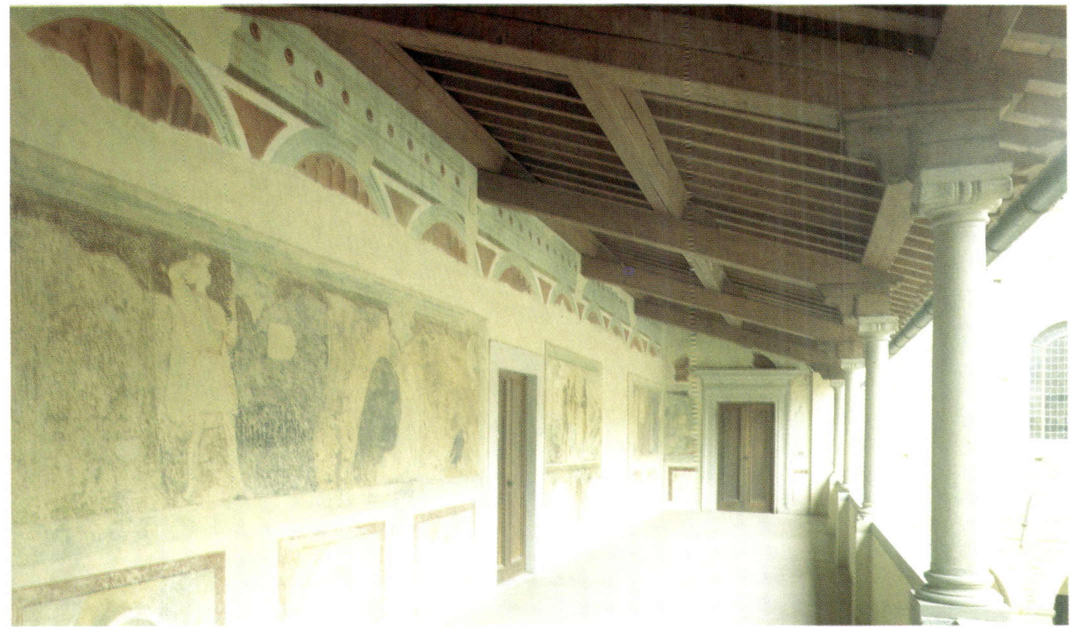

Scenes of Monastic Life, frescoes on the south wall and south-west corner of the upper cloister of San Miniato al Monte.

freer. Here he tackled the foundations of geometrical vision, the connection between colour and reality, violating the laws of mimesis and venturing down the path of surrealism.

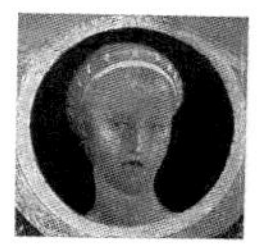

THE PALAZZO MEDICI

When Cosimo de' Medici was arrested in the Palazzo Vecchio, imprisoned in a room known as the '*barberia*' and condemned to a year's internment in Padua, three people were immediately informed: his brother Lorenzo who was at Mugello, his cousin Averardo in Pisa, and, according to Cosimo's own memoirs 'the news was transmitted to Niccolò da Tolentino, captain of war in the commune, who was my great friend'.[90] Following this, Tolentino, 'having heard this at eight, came that morning with all his company, to the *lastra* with the intention of freeing me. But this captain – and Lorenzo likewise – were advised to undertake nothing, so as not to endanger me – which is what they did: and although this advice came from relatives and friends with the best of intentions, it was not good advice; for had they acted, I would have been freed and the person who had instigated this plot would have been defeated.'[91]

così fu fatto intendere a Niccolò da Tolentino, capitano di guerra del commune che era molto mio amico . . . sentito il caso addì 8 venne la mattina con tutta la compagnia alla Lastra e con animo di fare novità nella terra perché io fossi lasciato. Ma fu confortato il capitano, e così Lorenzo, a non fare novità che potea essere cagione di farmi fare novità nella persona e così fecero; e benchè chi consigliò questo, fussino parenti e amici a buon fine, non fù buono consiglio; perché se si fossino fatti innanzi ero libero e chi era stato cagione di questo restava disfatto. . . . Infine vedendo non riusciva loro il pensiero di farci fallire, cioè da Bernardo Guadagni offertogli da due persone danari cioè, dal Capitano della guerra fiorini cinquecento e dallo Spedalingo di Santa Maria Nuova fiorini cinquecento, i quali ebbe contati, e Mariotto Baldovinetti per mezzo di Baccio d'Antonio di Baccio fiorini ottocento, addì 3 ottobre; la notte mi trassero di Palazzo e menormi fuori dalla Porta San Gallo. . . . "Ebbero poco animo; che se avessero voluto denari, li avrebbero avuti dieci mila o più per uscire di pericolo.

When subsequently the Balía[92] directed that Cosimo's punishment be extended to ten years, in spite of pleas from the ambassadors of Venice and Ferrara, his only method of obtaining his freedom was through payment of a fine, which seemed a rather corrupt way of doing things. 'Finally, seeing that they would never succeed in making me bankrupt,' Cosimo continued, 'when Bernardo Guadagni received an offer of money from two sources, that is to say five hundred florins from the Captain of War and five hundred florins from the Spedalingo of Santa Maria Nuova, after counting it and after receiving another eight hundred from Mariotto Baldovinetti through the intermediary of Baccio d'Antonio di Baccio, that night, on 3 October, they made me leave the Palace, and took me outside the Porta San Gallo.' And Cosimo added contemptuously: 'They had little courage, for if they had wanted money, they could have had ten thousand florins and even more to protect me from danger.'[93]

This episode is crucial in regard to Cosimo's later orientations. Michelozzo, who accompanied him into exile in Venice, would be his architect; he built the palace Cosimo refused to Brunelleschi in his desire for prudence, for cautious government and avoidance of risks, that Cosimo had learnt through experience. And it was to Niccolò da Tolentino that he would dedicate Uccello's *Battles*, where the encounter at San Romano would be elevated to a key episode in the republic's history, a thousand leagues from historical reality. For the battle of San Romano had no definite outcome; in fact the result may not even have been in the Florentines' favour.

Cosimo commissioned the *Battles* before Michelozzo's palace was even built. *Ill. p. 214* They were intended to decorate a room, which is now impossible to identify, in the

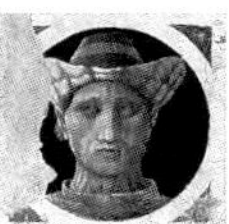

'*casa vecchia*', a group of three houses running almost parallel to Via Larga in the direction of San Marco, which had been their family home since Giovanni di Bicci's time. In the Cadastre of 1427, it was declared as 'the palace with the two houses beside it, one in the direction of San Giovanni, the other in the direction of San Marco, which is let.' But between 1446 and 1457, the three houses were joined together 'and converted with our living quarters above'.[94] It was undoubtedly a richly decorated house with paintings and beautiful furniture. Vasari reported that 'In Siena, in the Spedale della Scala and in Florence, in the *case vecchie* belonging to the Medici, there were some very famous paintings. They were the work of Barna, a Sienese, who did them in 1381. And since Barna was not only a good draughtsman, but also the first to depict animals as well, as can be seen in a drawing of his, full of wild beasts from different regions, which is in our book, he merits being highly praised and having his name honoured by artists.'[95]

il palazo con le due case accanto, una verso San Giovanni e l'altra verso San Marco, tenuta in affitto . . . e murate chola nostra habitatione di sopra

fece in Siena nello Spedale della Scala alcune pitture e così in Fiorenza nelle case vecchie de' Medici alcune altre che gli diedero nome assai. Furono l'opera del Barna, senese, nel 1381. E perché oltre a quello che s'è detto disegnò il Barna assai comodamente fu il primo che cominciasse a ritrarre bene gli animali come fa fede una carta di sua mano che è nel nostro libro tutta piena di fiere di diverse ragioni; egli merita di essere sommamente lodato e che il suo nome sia onorato dagli artefici.

Of Dello Delli, Uccello's associate in the Chiostro Verde, Vasari recorded that 'for Giovanni de' Medici in particular [he] painted the entire decoration of a room, whose originality was recognized and it was considered most beautiful of its kind.'[96] Later, he noted with regard to the *cassoni*, painted chests, that 'they are painted in this way, and not only chests, but *lettucci*, *spalliere*, frames and other ornamentation which, at that period were magnificent; and there must have been an infinite number of them in the city. For many years, the most excellent painters worked at this type of thing, without any sense of shame, unlike the artists of today who make a fuss about painting and gilding such works. That has been true right up till now: in Lorenzo the Magnificent's rooms, there were, among other things, chests, *spalliere* and frames, painted by artists who were not plebeian nonentities, but on the contrary excellent painters, [and they painted] all the tournaments, hunts, fêtes and other spectacles of their times, with judgment, marvellous imagination and skill. All that can be seen not only in the palace but in the Medici's *case vecchie*, and in all the noblest houses in Florence, which still have some left. And in certain of them, magnificent and most praiseworthy old customs have been kept and these things have not been swept aside to make way for modern decoration and usage.'[97] Vasari also noted: 'After Giovanni di Bicci de' Medici had seen how well [Lorenzo di Bicci] painted he had him paint all those famous men that one can still see quite well preserved today in the hall of the Medici's *casa vecchia* [later given to Lorenzo, Cosimo the Elder's brother, when the *Palazzo grande* was built]'.[98] According to Milanesi, Lorenzo di Bicci's *Uomini famosi* disappeared when the palace was rebuilt in the nineteenth century.

dipinse particolarmente a Giovanni de' Medici tutto il fornimento di una camera; che fu tenuta cosa veramente rara e in quel genere bellissima . . . si dipignevano in cotal maniera e non solamente i cassoni ma i lettucci, le spalliere, le cornici che recignevano intorno e altri così fatti ornamenti da camera che in quei tempi magnificamente vi si usavano come infiniti per tutta la città se ne possono vedere. E per molti anni fu di sorte questa cosa in uso che i più eccellenti pittori in cosifatti lavori si esercitavano senza vergognarsi come oggi molti farebbero di dipingere e mettere d'oro simili cose. E che poi sia vero si è veduto in sino ai giorni nostri: oltre molti altri alcuni cassoni, spalliere e cornici nelle camere del Magnifico Lorenzo vecchio de' Medici nei quali era dipinto di mano di pittori, non mica plebei, ma eccellenti maestri tutte le giostre, torneamenti, cacce, feste e altri spettacoli fatti nei tempi suoi con giudizio, con invenzione e con arte meravigliosa. Nelle quali cose se ne veggiono non solo nel palazzo e nelle case vecchie de' Medici ma in tutte le più nobili case di Firenze ancora alcune relique. E ci sono alcuni che attenendosi a quelle usanze vecchie magnifiche veramente e orrevolissime, non hanno siffatte cose levate per dar luogo agli ornamenti e usanze moderne.

Giovanni di Bicci de' Medici, veduta la buona maniera sua [di Lorenzo di Bicci] gli fece dipigner nella sala della casa vecchia de' Medici (che poi restò a Lorenzo, fratello carnale di Cosimo il Vecchio, murato che fu il palazzo grande) tutti quegli uomini famosi che ancora oggi, assai ben conservati, vi si veggiono.

So Uccello's *Battles* had as their background the courtly, refined, decorative atmosphere that expressed Cosimo the Elder's and his family's world. On the surface

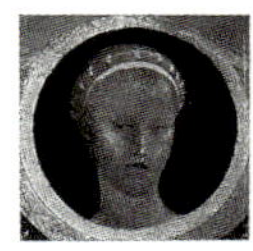

it appeared discreet, but its interior revealed artistic and cultural ambitions that were in keeping with the family's standing, wealth and role in the city.

The architecture of the new palace at the corner of Via Larga marked a qualitative leap. Its prestige at that time can be clearly glimpsed in Filarete's laudatory description, when writing of Cosimo the Elder: 'I will now speak of the palaces and houses he had had built, in and outside Florence: [in particular] his noble palace, which does honour not only to the quarter where it was built, but to the entire city. Those who have seen it know this to be true: one does not have to tell them what it is like, but I will give some details for those who have not seen it.'[99] And later: 'the main door which is on the Via Larga side is impressive. After passing through this, one reaches a portico that continues all the way round, in a square cloister, with rooms off it, and with a passage under a loggia which leads to a garden; and if that is not grand enough, the entire building is so noble that it demands the visitor's admiration.'[100]

Ora diremo dei palazzi e case che lui ha fatte fabbricare nella città di Firenze e ancora di fuora di Firenze; il suo degno palazzo, nonché la contrada o dove egli è edificato ma tutta la città rende onore: se sia vero, chi l'ha veduto il sa; non per questo gli è mestiere di narrar l'essere suo ma per quegli che non l'hanno veduto alcune particolarità d'esse diremo. [...] La parte verso via Larga è la porta maestra la quale è degna. Entrato dentro per essa porta si va sotto un portico il quale circonda intorno e fa un chiostro quadro sul quale sono camere e uno andito che va sotto una loggia che risponde su uno orto; benché non troppo grande sia ma si è degno che a chi v'entra dà ammirazione.

Such formal constraint within the Medici palace was required that it became something of a contest, in which, according to the *Libro di Antonio Billi*'s[101] testimony

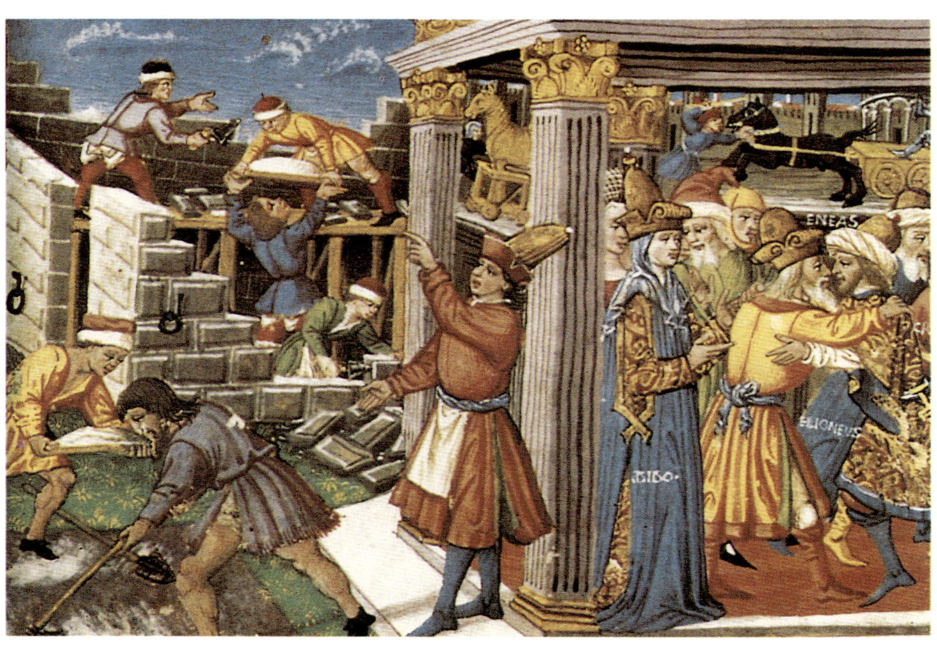

Attributed to Apollonio di Giovanni, *The Building of the Palazzo Medici*, c. 1460, miniature from *Virgilii Opera*. Florence, Biblioteca Riccardiana, ms. 492. The 'modern' building under construction on the left is clearly inspired by Michelozzo's palace.

Brunelleschi played the losing role. By siting the palace on the axis of San Lorenzo, an aggressive, monopolistic connection with the city was established, turning it into a sort of annexe to the palace, a kind of palatine chapel. All this ran counter to the Medici's discreet politics and their practice of unobtrusive government. The antagonism between Michelozzo and Brunelleschi subsequently flared up elsewhere,

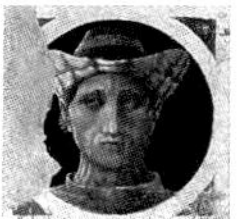

even giving rise recently to a reattribution of the building to Brunelleschi: this was founded on a lack of documentation about Michelozzo, who was never explicitly mentioned in the building-site records.[102] However, this is not the place to enter into an architechtonic reading of the palace on Via Larga. We shall simply note that the interior had a quite different character from the *casa vecchia*'s, and was noted for the snowy whiteness of its limewashed vaulting and architectonic purity. Even the ornamentation, described yet again by Filarete, had nothing in common with the décor of the *casa vecchia*, which was rather more similar, for example, to the Palazzo Davanzati.[103] *Ill. p. 54*

The Medici inventory of 1492 showed that Uccello's *Battles* were located in a room known as 'Lorenzo's room', on the ground floor next to the garden: there were 'six framed paintings, embellished with gold, above the said *spalliera* and the *lettuccio* forty-two *braccia* long and three and a half *braccia* high, three on the rout of San Romano, one battle with dragons and lions, one on the story of Paris, by Paolo Uccello's hand, and one by Francesco di Pesello's hand, which showed a hunt.'[104]

sei quadri corniciati atorno et messi d'oro sopra la detta spalliera e sopra al lettuccio di braccia 42 lunghi et alti braccia 3 e 1/2 dipinti coi tre della rotta di San Romano e uno di battaglie et draghi et lioni e uno della storia di Paris di mano di Paghofo Ucello et uno di mano di Francesco di Pesello entrovi una chaccia

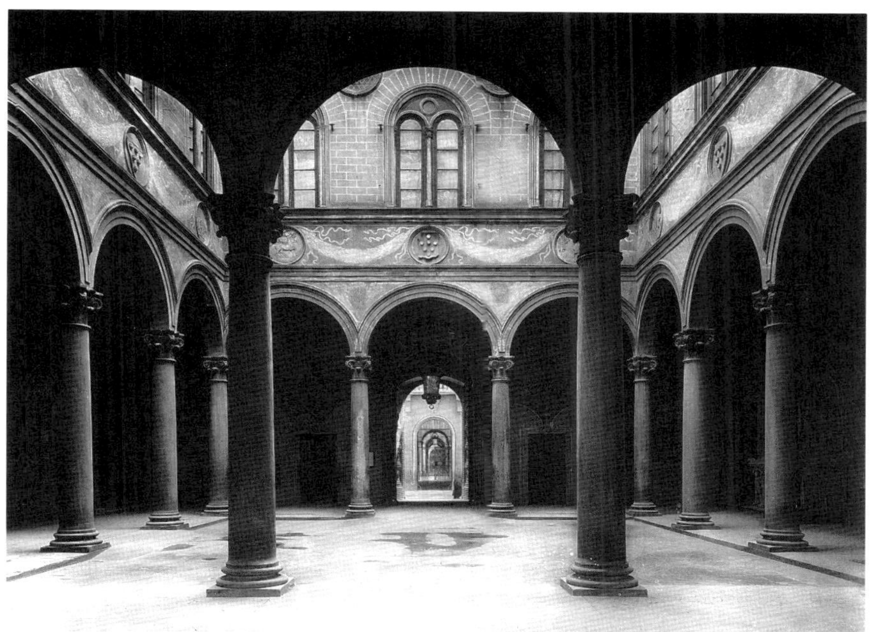

Inner courtyard of the Palazzo Medici.

We can therefore conclude that Uccello's paintings were originally made for a smaller room in the *casa vecchia* than the one in the new palace where they were transferred, along with other old masters. When work on the new residence was finished, the battle of San Romano had been history for twenty years. In the new high-ceilinged room on the ground floor ('*chamera grande terrena*') Uccello's *Battles*, which

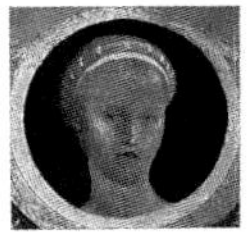

had originally hung on two walls at right angles, must have occupied the whole of the later wall.[105] These paintings, which had been cut down in order to fit their new position, were proof of the war with the Visconti, which had cost Florence so much effort. To mark the radical change of direction in his foreign policy, Lorenzo hung in his audience room portraits of Federico da Montefeltro and Galeazzo Maria Sforza, symbols of the alliance with Milan which had become an essential feature of his new politics.

Hereafter, as long as Lorenzo the Magnificent ruled, Uccello's *Battles* would be seen as a positive excuse for chivalrous pursuits, for the jousting and tournaments that Lorenzo took part in, more than as a pictorial testimony to historical events. Its similarity to Pesellino[106] from the viewpoints of form and style must have given the cycle which comprised paintings both on canvas and wood, hung closely together, a certain unity.

We have no documentation on Uccello's participation in the transfer and modification of his work. We can imagine that he stayed outside the palace in Via Larga, and that faced with Lorenzo's cultural tastes and his idea of a Classical architecture – for which Giuliano da Sangallo would be the archaeological expert and ideal interpreter – and with the influence of Alberti's ideas, Uccello's world, so subtly transposed through poetry, and sufficiently alien to classical Antiquity and its signs, now appeared merely as a survivor from a bygone age.

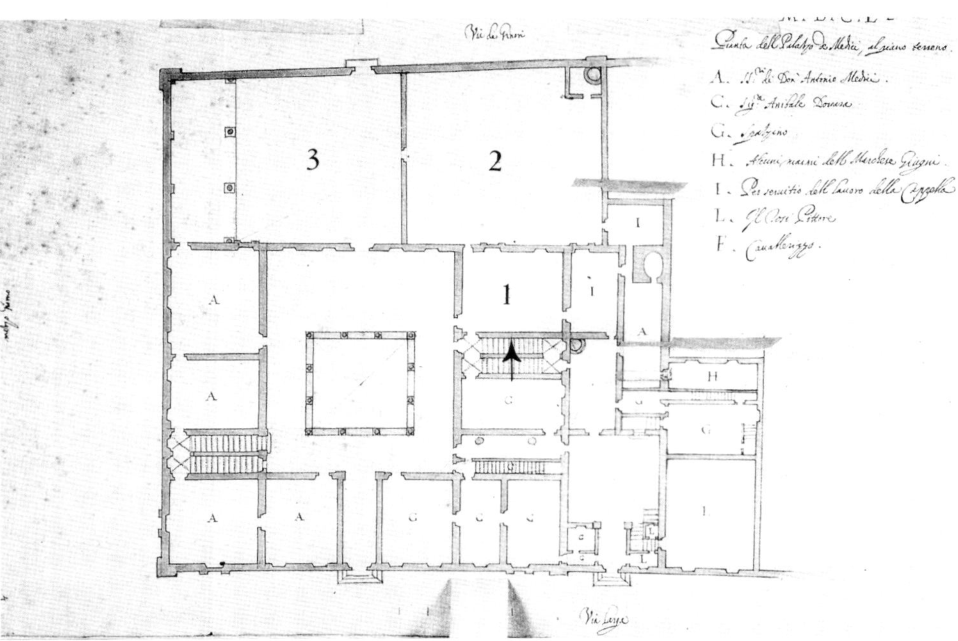

Seventeenth-century plan of the ground floor of the Palazzo Medici. (1) Lorenzo's bedchamber, containing the *battles* (→). (2) Private garden. (3) Garden with door to street.

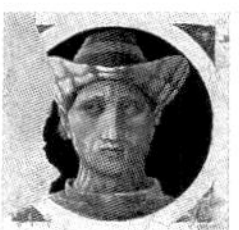

PLACES WHERE UCCELLO LIVED: HOUSE AND STUDIO

At the risk of turning this into a dry documentary, it might be useful to look at Uccello's day-to-day life, follow his itineraries and imagine the fabric of the city as he would have seen it.

He made his first definite appearance in the records in 1433: he was thirty-six and living in lodgings in Campo Corbolini. The house belonged to Chiara di Iacopo da Pistoia, to whom he paid a rent of nine florins a year. The church of San Iacopo in Campo Corbolini was among the oldest in the city. It had been built in the eleventh century by the Alerti family, on Via Faenza which ran from San Lorenzo out into the countryside. Later, Porta San Giovanni was built there and today this runs parallel to the Santa Maria Novella railway station. But Uccello also declared a property in the *popolo* (rural parish) of Santo Stefano a Ugnano, which had already been mentioned in a document of 1430, drawn up by Deo di Deo del Beccuto, when Uccello was in Venice. This was a piece of land near San Frediano a Settimo (so called because it was seven [*sette*] miles from Florence), on the Arno plain, on the left bank, site of the ancient Cistercian abbey of San Salvatore a Settimo; Ghiberti also owned a mansion ('*casa da signore*') in the same region. Today it stands in ruins, in a shameful state of neglect, in the middle of an agricultural development. Could this have been pure coincidence, or was it further evidence of the master-apprentice relationship?

By 1442 Uccello was no longer living in rented accommodation. He declared a house 'as my dwelling' ('*per mio habitare*') in the Santa Lucia d'Ognissanti quarter in Via della Scala, which he had purchased for a hundred florins in 1434. So he now possessed two properties one of them that at Santo Stefano a Ugnano, with a house and one labourer. His lifestyle was certainly very comfortable and he had substantial savings, amounting to almost two hundred florins. His studio was in Via delle Terme, a narrow medieval alley inside the first city wall, not far from Piazza della Signoria. It was quite big, consisting of rooms let by two different landlords and very cheap – six florins a year.

In 1458, in connection with money owed him by Bernardo di Francesco and company 'who make stained-glass windows', Uccello mentioned his rented place in Piazza San Giovanni 'where I take refuge to paint'. The stained-glass workshop must have been near the cathedral site, to make transportation easier. It was a retreat more than a studio, an entrenched camp, giving Uccello closer contact with the men carrying out the work, and expressed significantly in 'I take refuge' ('*mi reparo*').

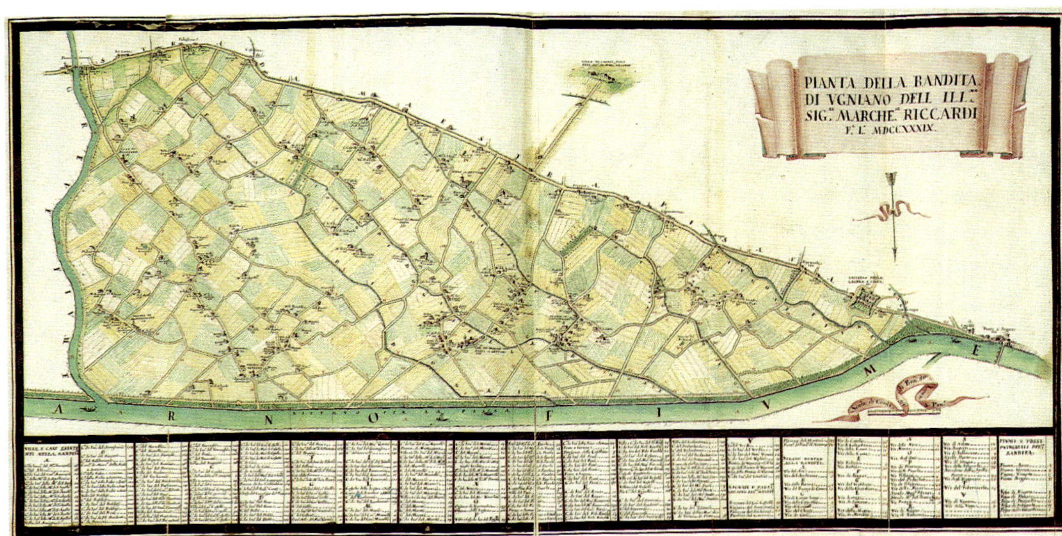

Map of the area of Ugnano and Settimo. Florence, Archivio di Stato, Fondo Riccardi, j. 819. Among the country houses on this vast hunting preserve of the Riccardi family (who subsequently bought the Palazzo Medici) is that of Uccello, which had passed at the beginning of the sixteenth century to Donato di Pero Baldovinetti.

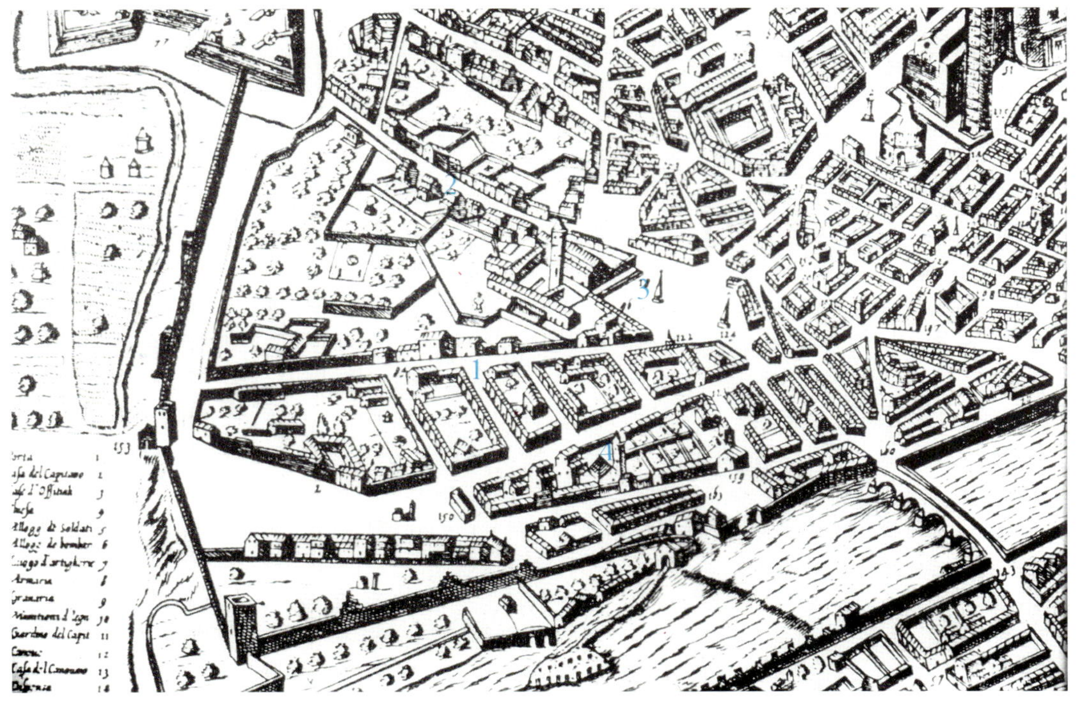

Matteo Florimi, detail of a map of Florence, 1600. (1) Via della Scala. (2) Via di Valfonda. (3) Santa Maria Novella and the Chiostro Verde. (4) Santa Lucia di Ognissanti.

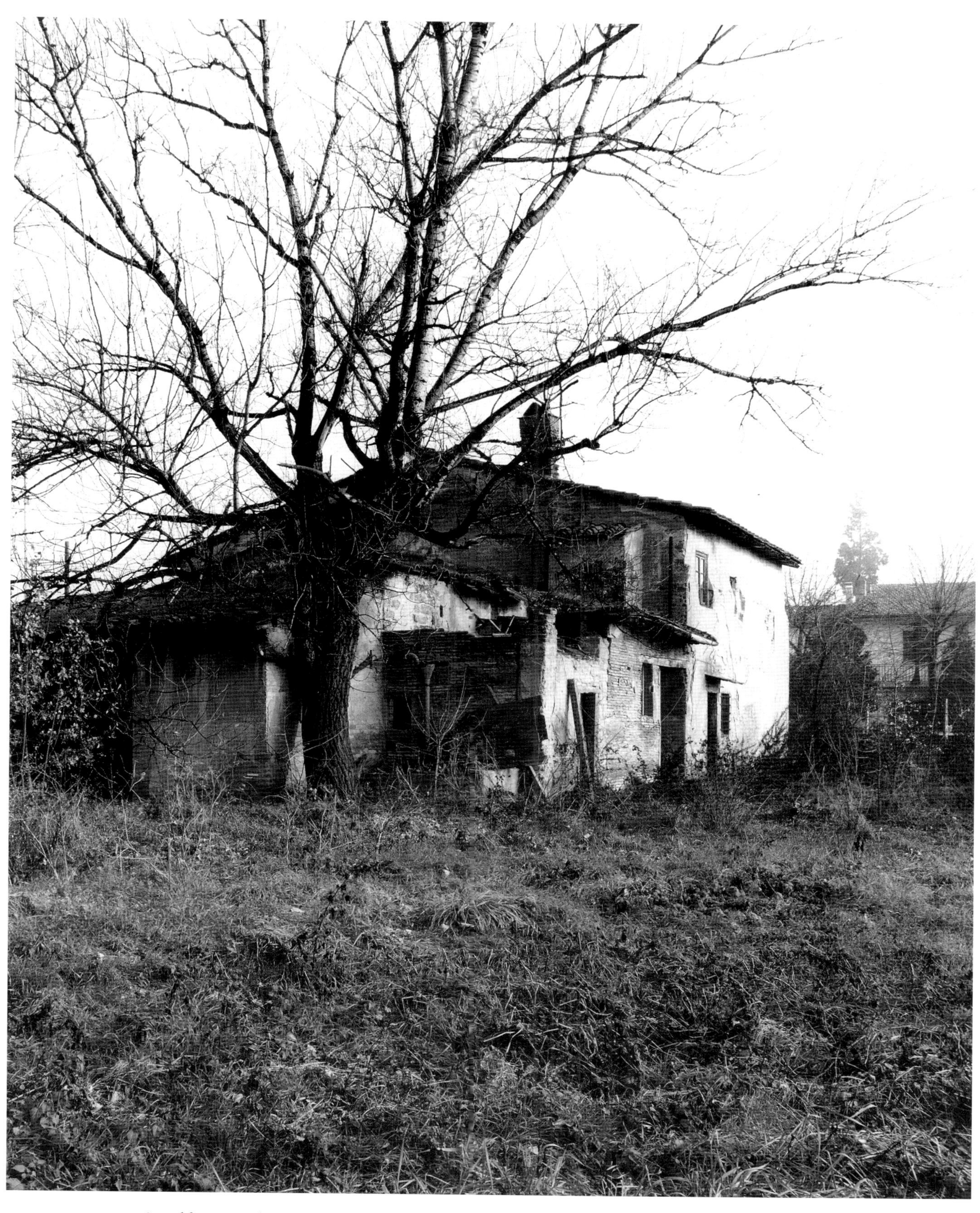

An old country house at Santo Stefano a Ugrano. This was probably Uccello's house, but precise identification is difficult because of damage to this area during the Second World War.

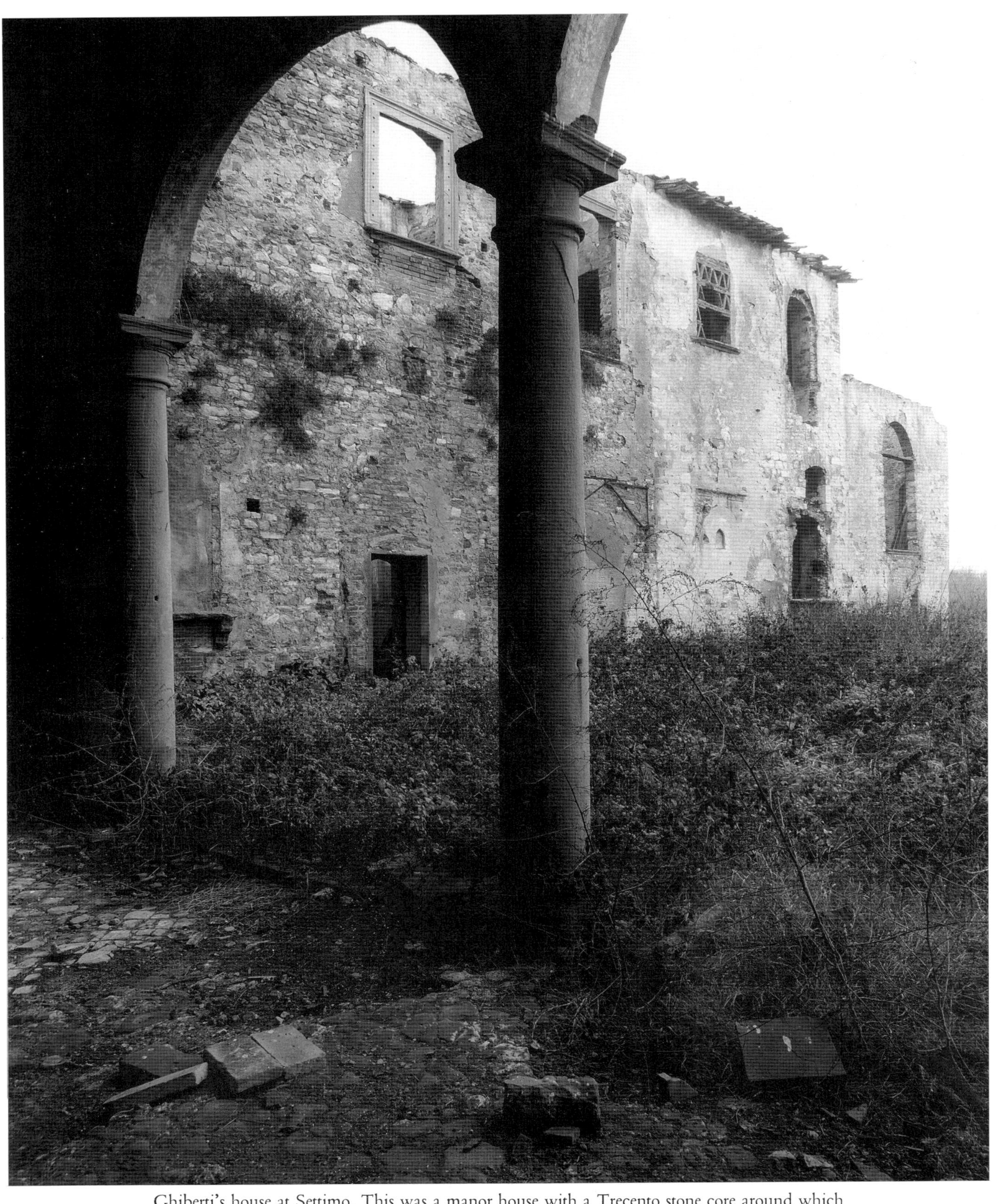

Ghiberti's house at Settimo. This was a manor house with a Trecento stone core around which extensions have been added over the centuries (such as the portico, of the sixteenth century). The house contained a complete laboratory and equipment for metal-casting. It is now a shell.

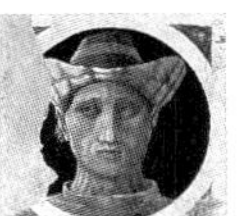

He was still living in the house on Via della Scala in 1469 but it seems that progress had been made on his country house, which was now defined as 'a master's house with labourer'. Since 1457 the amount of land seems to have increased to '52 bushels [i.e. area of land required to sow a bushel of grain], part ploughed, part vineyard'. Besides himself, now aged seventy-three, his family consisted of his wife Tommasa who was thirty-six, and a son of sixteen. There is no mention of Antonia who was sixteen months old in 1458. Uccello therefore had his first child at the age of fifty-six, with a wife of nineteen, and had given his son the first name of Donato, perhaps in Donatello's honour. But now, he concluded, 'I am old and without resources, I can no longer work and my wife is ill.'[107]

casa da oste e da lavoratore

staiora 52 di terra, parte lavoratia e parte vignatia e pergolata

truovomi vecchio e senza inviamento e no mi posso asercitare, e la dona inferma.

The sentence, which he may have dreamed up with the sole intention of paying less tax (since in the meantime he had acquired more land – he had bought another parcel of thirteen bushels) has given rise to the image of a lonely, introverted old man, unable to work and generally misunderstood, a state in which he would long remain until his death in December 1475. He was buried at Santo Spirito – as had been his express

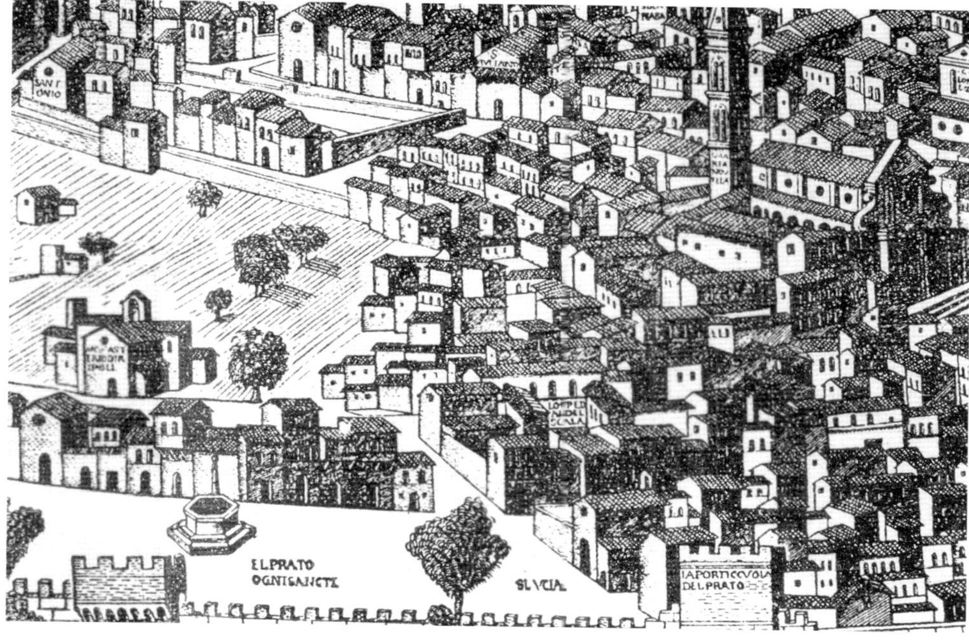

Detail of the view of Florence, known as the *Pianta della Catena*, 1472. Berlin, Staatliche Museen, Kupferstichkabinett. This shows the church of Santa Lucia di Ognissanti and, near Santa Maria Novella, the Via della Scala where Uccello bought his house in 1434.

wish in his first will, drawn up before he left for Venice – in the family tomb, which has now disappeared. The church was still being built at that time, and the master responsible for the sculpture was Salvi d'Andrea.[108] Appropriately, that December, six columns, furnished by Simone del Caprino, had just been added, more than twenty years after the first five commissioned by Brunelleschi.[109]

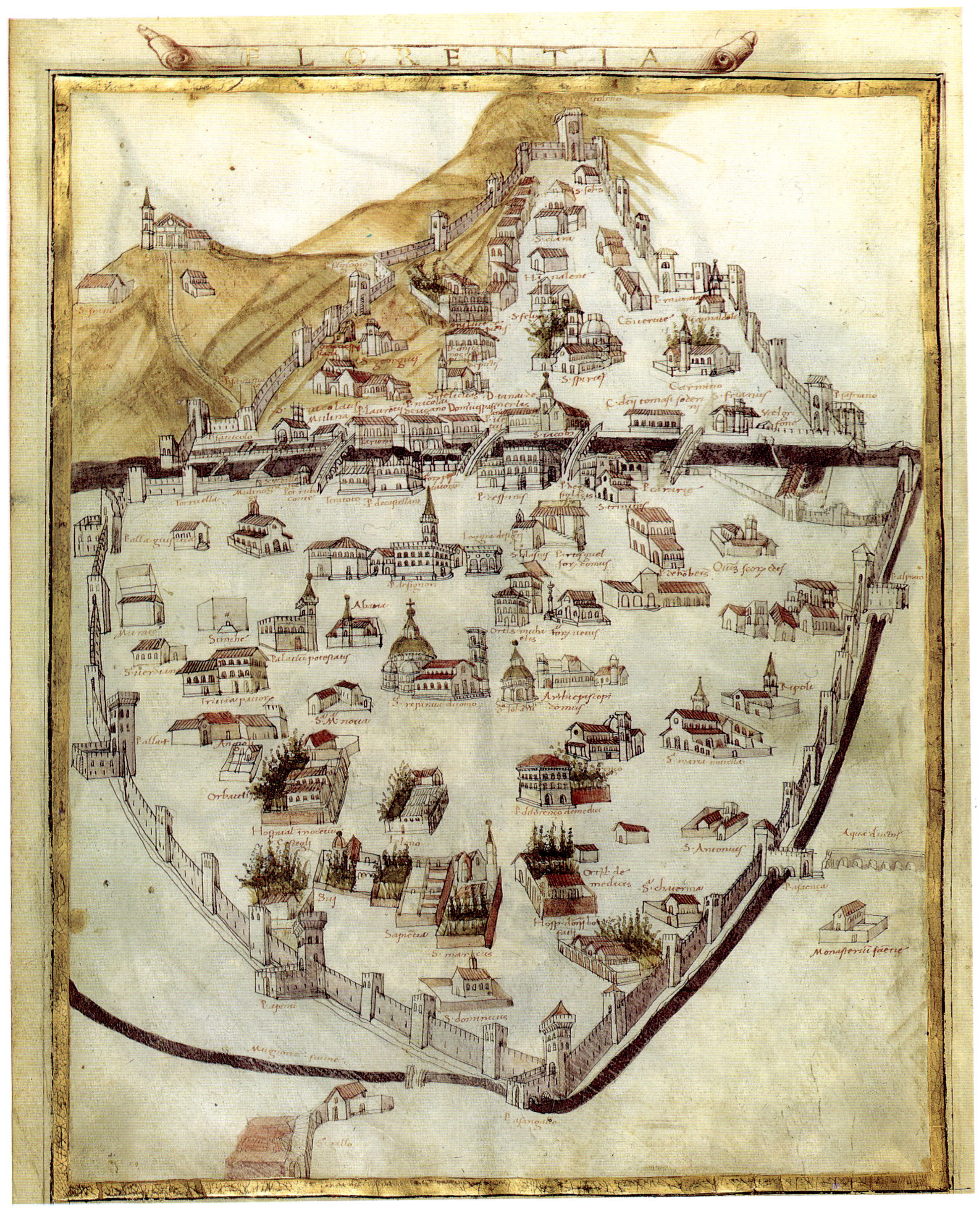

Studio of Piero del Massaio, *View of Florence*, *c.* 1472. Paris, Bibliothèque Nationale, ms. lat. 4802, fol. 132v.

These then were the places where Uccello lived and worked. He seems to have lived mostly around Santa Maria Novella, while his studio was closer to the centre, between Dante's Florence and the cathedral site. He had a feudal sense of landed property and, with his love of the countryside – that fertile plain beside the river, its air 'thick with mist' (as Ghiberti described it in his *Commentario*) – he modestly and prudently increased his territory. So, now, he could look out over his vineyard and contemplate the rows of vines in perspective, like the trellis in the *Stories of Noah*.

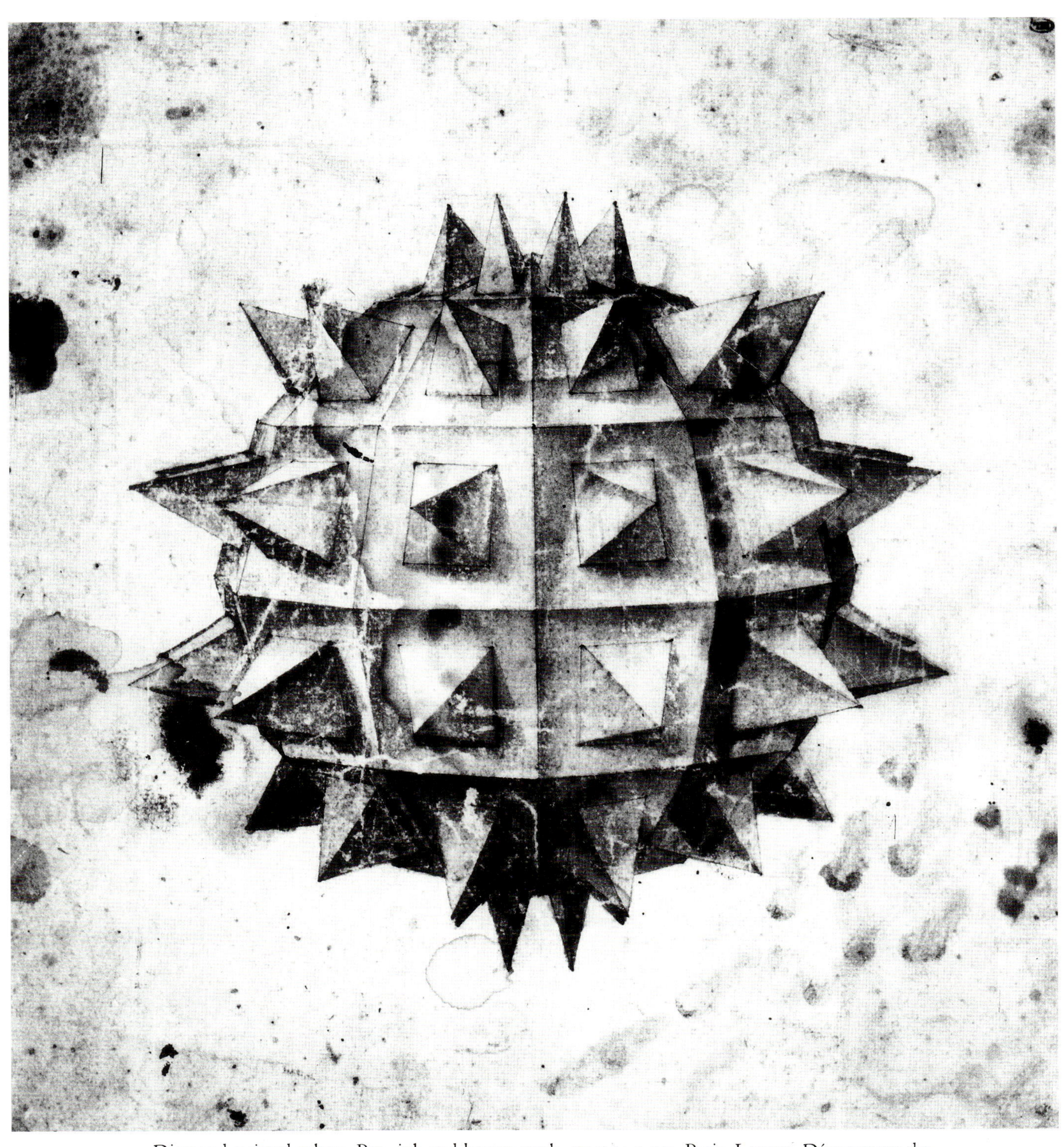

Diamond-pointed sphere. Pen, ink and brown wash, 27 × 24.5 cm. Paris, Louvre, Département des Arts Graphiques. A typical example of Uccello's experimentation with perspective, even if his authorship of the drawing is not completely proven.

Chapter Four

'LA DOLCE PROSPETTIVA'

The question of perspective has had a crucial effect on Uccello's fortune among the critics and in any analysis of his personality. Right from the beginning he was identified by his views on perspective, his eccentricities highlighted, his lonely position explained. Anecdotes about them abounded, including one which claimed that at night he remained deaf to his young wife's overtures. Following his contemporaries' accounts, reservations arose about his perspective, reservations that have changed down the centuries into scathing critical judgments: 'perspective – his pet hobby horse' wrote Lionello Venturi;[110] 'a semi-artist', J. von Schlosser commented.[111] Then came the twentieth-century avant-garde interpretations, which – enthusiastic to a man – turned Uccello into a forerunner of Cubism, or even better a precursor of the '*Valori Plastici*'.[112] There is a plethora of historical and critical literature by specialists and men of culture who would have liked perspective turned into a restricted zone, a privileged area of culture, where artistic research has to contend not only with questions of symbolism but also with highly significant scientific and philosophical problems. For these critics, Uccello is seen to be favoured with direct knowledge of the sources, of a methodology and body of theoretical knowledge which enlarge his intellectual stature beyond his due.[113]

'When she called him to bed, he replied: "Oh how sweetly appealing this perspective is."' (Vasari, *Life of Paolo Uccello*)

In the argument about perspective, the subtlety of the participants is such that it might discourage any attempt to read the personal and unpublished sources. We shall content ourselves by saying that, with all due respect to so much effort, it is better to put such excesses of theory and undemonstrable hypotheses aside, and stick to a more modest reading of the works themselves and what they contain. In so doing, we can discard the negative judgments found in the older sources, such as the passage in Manetti's biography of Brunelleschi, which gives Uccello only a passing mention: 'Then there was Paolo Uccello and other painters who wanted to emulate and imitate him [Brunelleschi]; I have seen more than one of them but none ever matched up to him.'[114] Here we can deduce the opposition, the distance separating Uccello from Brunelleschi, from his inventions and method. As for Vasari's lively descriptions and

Fucci poi Pagolo Uccello ed altri pittori, che lo vollono contrafare ed imitare; che n'ho veduti più d'uno, e non è stato bene come quello.

picturesque anecdotes, two negative factors and one positive one must be taken into account. First, perspective was no longer a central issue in Vasari's world, in his philosophical construction of space: it was just one among a number of elements, an accessory in a painter's academic training. Second, in his conception of the *maniera moderna*, founded on the primacy of the Florentine Renaissance, there was scarcely any tolerance for Gothic culture, nor in particular for Ghiberti. Vasari even went so far as to state that Ghiberti had written 'a work in vulgar tongue, in which he deals with many things but in such a manner that very little profit can be drawn from it'. On the patchwork of ancient texts that made up the *Commentario Terzo*, he added a precise, severe criticism: since in the sixteenth century the notion of plagiarism had not yet been defined 'I cannot remain silent on the fact that these show the book to have been created by others.'[115]

un'opera in volgare nella quale trattò di molte cose, ma siffattamente che poco costrutto se ne cava . . . né tacerò che egli mostra il libro essere stato fatto da altri.

On the positive side, we must emphasize just how much Uccello's personality must still have made its presence felt and disturbingly so, almost a century after his death, to have given rise to Vasari's portrait, which was to be a definitive one for all his

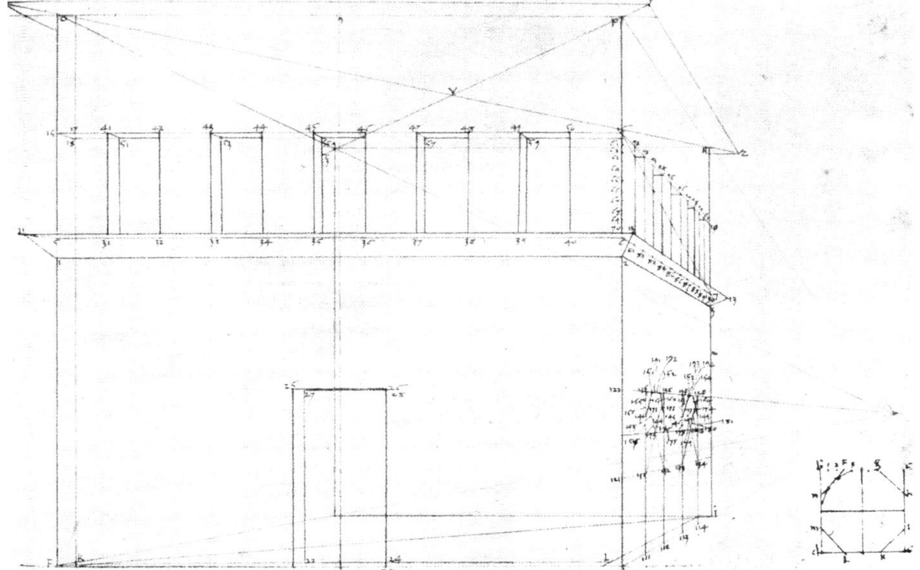

Piero della Francesca, *De Prospectiva Pingendi*, figure XLI.

future historiography. Such has often been the case with artists about whom Vasari wrote, in spite of all the inaccuracies for which he has been blamed; on the other hand, those he ignored have had a hard time making a place for themselves in art history.[116] His criticism of perspective aside, the attention Vasari paid Uccello demonstrates how the oral tradition, the strength of public opinion, had turned him

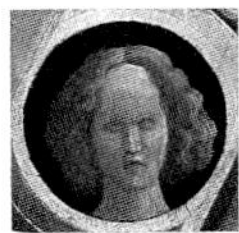

into a crucial figure, and that his research, even if it were not crowned with great success, and even if he did not have devotees or imitators or followers, had an important role alongside the dominant Brunelleschi-Alberti-Piero della Francesca camp.

Brunelleschi, with his two famous panels – one of the Baptistery of San Giovanni, seen from the front, from the cathedral door, and the other of the Palazzo Vecchio, seen from a diagonal viewpoint where the Via del Calzaioli opens on to the Piazza della Signoria – was providing examples of the two basic types of perspectival vision: vision with a central viewpoint, and vision with two vanishing points.[117] The first panel was not only a representation, but a means of verifying the correspondence between image and reality: the system in fact allowed the observer to see either the Baptistery through a hole made in the painted panel, in the spot corresponding to the viewpoint, or its painted representation, reflected in a mirror. In this representation, a polished metallic surface, like a mirror, took the place of the sky and reflected real clouds: as a trick, an amusing gimmick to increase verisimilitude. With this Brunelleschi's 'mechanical' genius had conceived a scenic contrivance more than a painter's tool, a piece of persuasive equipment that would give the method all its

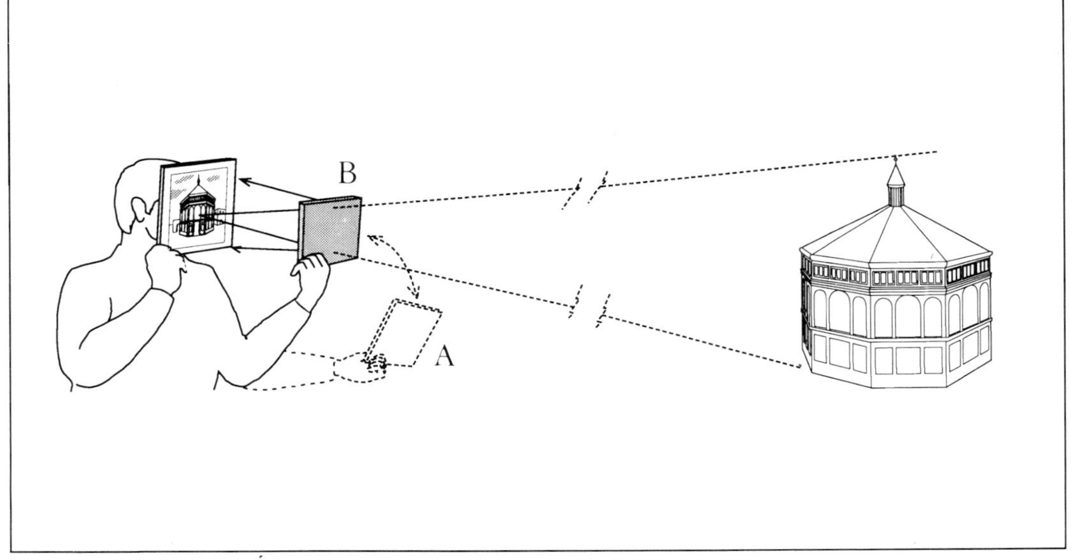

Brunelleschi's experiment with his panel painting of the Baptistery. The observer holds the painting in one hand and looks out through a hole in it. In the other hand he holds a mirror. With the mirror down (A) he looks directly at the Baptistery; with the mirror up (B) he sees a reflection of his painting of the building.

credibility when applying it to the more frequent situation of angular or oblique vision demonstrated in the second panel.

We know how much this half speculative technico-scientific invention, half conjuror's trick was to contribute – if we acknowledge Brunelleschi's assistance in the architectural perspective of Masaccio's *Trinity* at Santa Maria Novella – in the *Ill. p. 144*

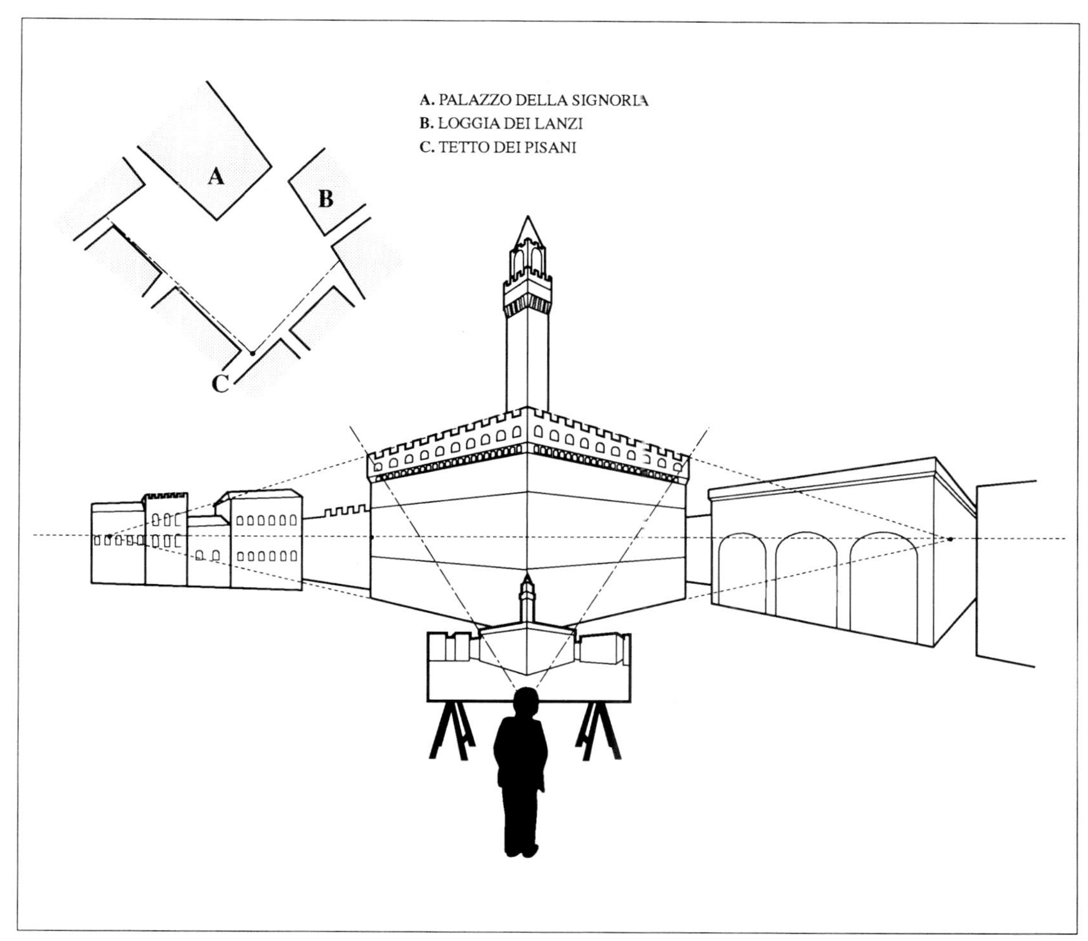

Brunelleschi's second panel, with the Palazzo Vecchio seen from the Via dei Calzaioli (formerly Corso de' Dipintori).

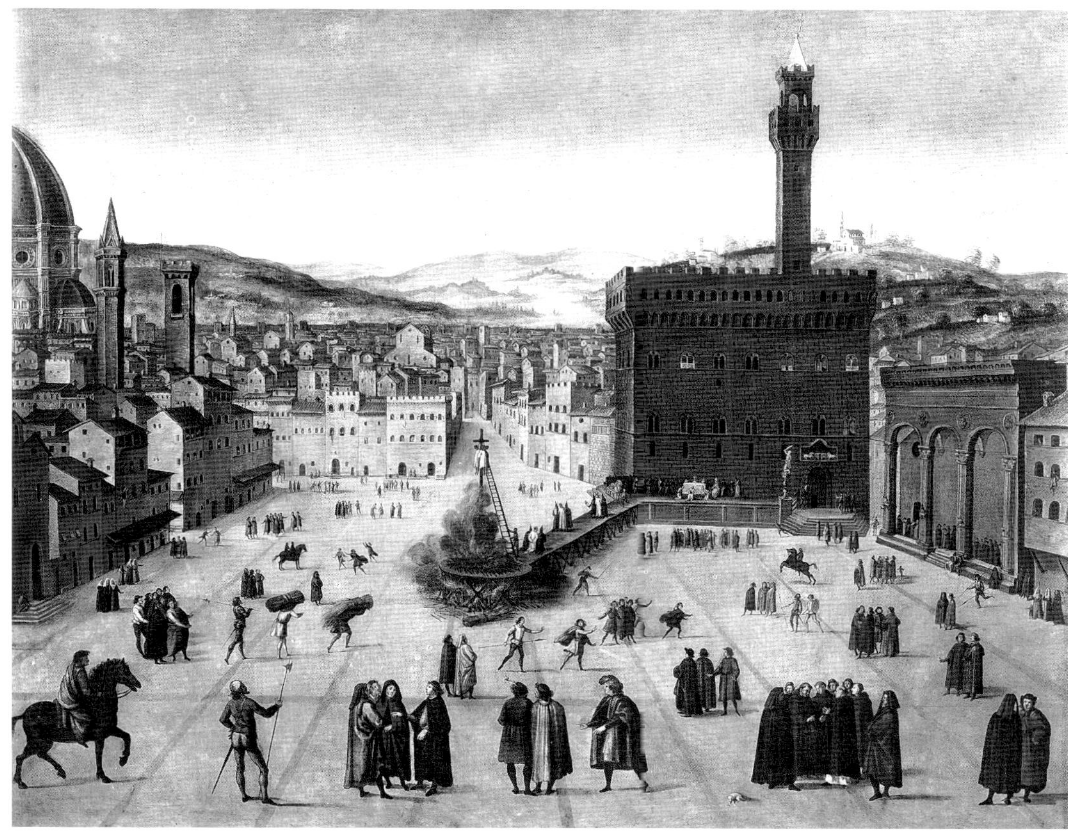

Unknown Florentine painter (school of Perugino), *The Execution of Savonarola*, c. 1500. Florence, Museo di San Marco.

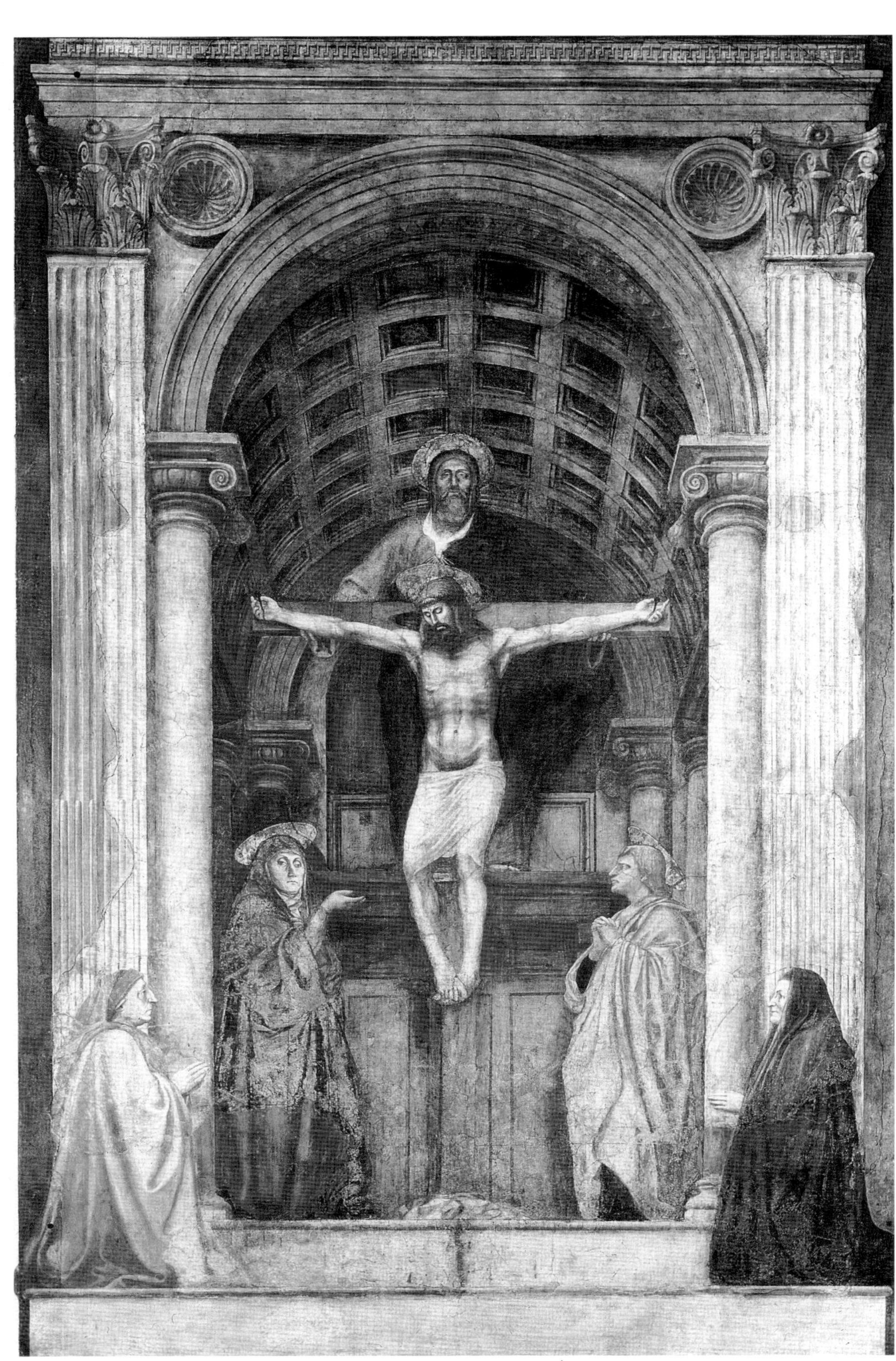

Masaccio, *Trinity*,
c. 1426–7, fresco,
667 × 317 cm. Florence,
Santa Maria Novella.

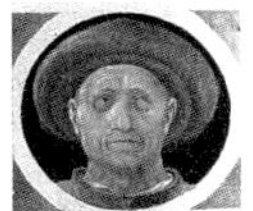

creation of Masaccio's spatial clarity and resolute realism. The two men were united by a mutual understanding and by common research, as Vasari was to point out in his *Vite*: 'He [Brunelleschi] deserves to be praised as much as if he had invented it himself.'

Merita esser commendato come se ne fusse stato inventore.

When Alberti came to express the theory of perspective in *De Pictura*, he made him make a qualitative leap. From the chronicle – Manetti's 'reported pieces' in his biography of Brunelleschi – and from 'mechanical' exploration, we pass to the system, the treatise where the handling of perspective and its principles of application had its value demonstrated through geometry and took on the cogency of a theorem. At the same time, Alberti defined the practical and operative limitations of perspective. We can see a sort of cultural atmosphere being designed, one that was well-demarcated when compared to the medieval tradition which included perspective in a general mass of optic problems, that also had metaphysical implications. If Alberti posed the problem in a less pragmatic, limiting way, if he gave depth to his theme, it is elsewhere: the small treatise on perspective published in

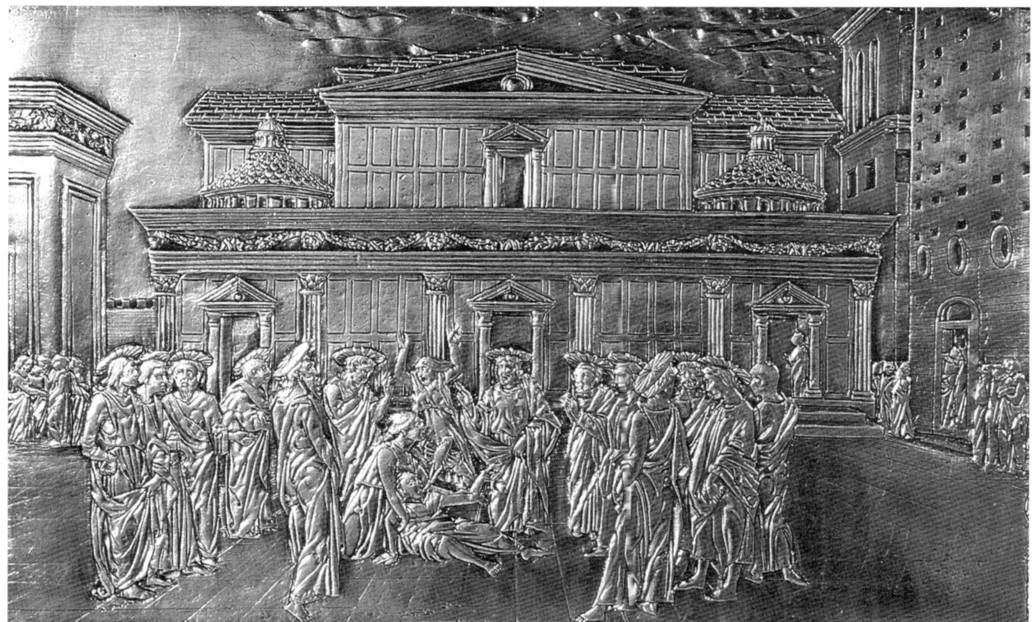

Attributed to Filippo Brunelleschi, *Christ Healing the Man Possessed by a Demon*, book cover, gilded silver and enamel. Paris, Louvre, Cabinet des Médailles.

the Bonucci edition[118] has been dropped from his works, though we may question the wisdom of this omission, given the very 'Albertian' tone of the dialogue.

In this context it might seem appropriate to seek a compromise with the opposing thesis proposed by Ghiberti: it was certainly confused, obscure, tortuous and full of repetitions but it had at base another inspiration: he had rediscovered the medieval

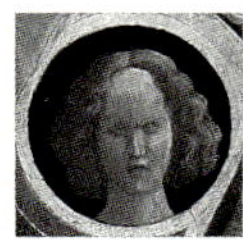

sources and once more proposed the need for general optics. Ghiberti's argument with Brunelleschi was fundamental, and though it was occasionally painful and punctuated by defeat, it was none the less an essential constant in his existence. Even in his almost threatening way of announcing his project: 'We shall produce a treatise on architecture,' he revealed a reaction against Brunelleschi's pragmatism and empiricism, a return to a broader cultural dimension, the authority of tradition, a serious, speculative substratum. In the face of Brunelleschi's method and the support given him by the young Alberti, Ghiberti's need for a different system, a broader manner of viewing the same subject of perspective was strengthened. His relationship with Brunelleschi explains, among other things, his activity as a writer beginning only after 1447, when he could rely on the resounding success he had achieved with the Doors of Paradise. Not to mention the obvious, acerbic polemical points in a text he would have preferred to have remained unruffled: 'In order that no doubt exist on what is to follow, we must therefore consider the composition of the eye, without which we can understand nothing of the way we see; some would say more about it, some less, and on certain issues they differ among themselves, while authors who write on perspective pay little attention to the composition of the eye.' There is another passage in which Ghiberti highlighted both the complexity of the subject and the disagreement among the sources, but clearly emphasized that 'authors who write about perspective' neglect the physiology of vision. And later: 'and yet something more must be said which is not found in writings on perspective; even if it is too hard to try to demonstrate the things I am trying to clarify'.[119]

Acciocché niuna dubitatione occorra nelle che seguitano, è da considerare, adunque, la composizione dell'occhio, però che sanza questo non si può sapere nulla del modo del vedere, ma certi autori dicono più, certi meno, in alcune cose hanno diversità tra loro, però che gli autori della prospettiva si passano più generalmente cioè delle composizioni dell'occhio.

Et però è necessario dire alcuna cosa più non si truova secondo e prospettivi, benché sia troppo malagevole a volere certificare queste cose et io cerco di chiarirle.

Ghiberti's system encompassed the anatomy and physiology of the eye, the theory of light, the geometry of optics, the theory of mirrors, and finally human anatomy and the theory of canonic proportions as applied to the human form from the time of Vitruvius' *homo ad circulum*: an exhaustive, cogent project which sought to make so difficult a subject more accessible. The *incipit* in the form of a dialogue, with vocatives – '*singularissimo*', '*nobilissimo*', '*dottissimo*' (most learned) – is addressed to a hypothetical interviewer who never asks any questions himself. This reinforces the didactic aim of the work and makes the subject matter easier to absorb, in the manner of the Master's 'school-workshop'. What is more, if what Maltese says is true, that 'Ghiberti [had] dictated his thoughts to someone, for certain distortions of words seem due to a poor phonetic transcription. For example, the name Alhazen[120] is transcribed with a surprising variety of spellings: Alfanten, Alfacen, Alfacenne, Alacom, Alacen, Allacen. This can only be explained by badly codified phonetic transcriptions. In other passages one has the impression of a simultaneous translation where the phrase is apparently correct, but the content incomprehensible. In fact the

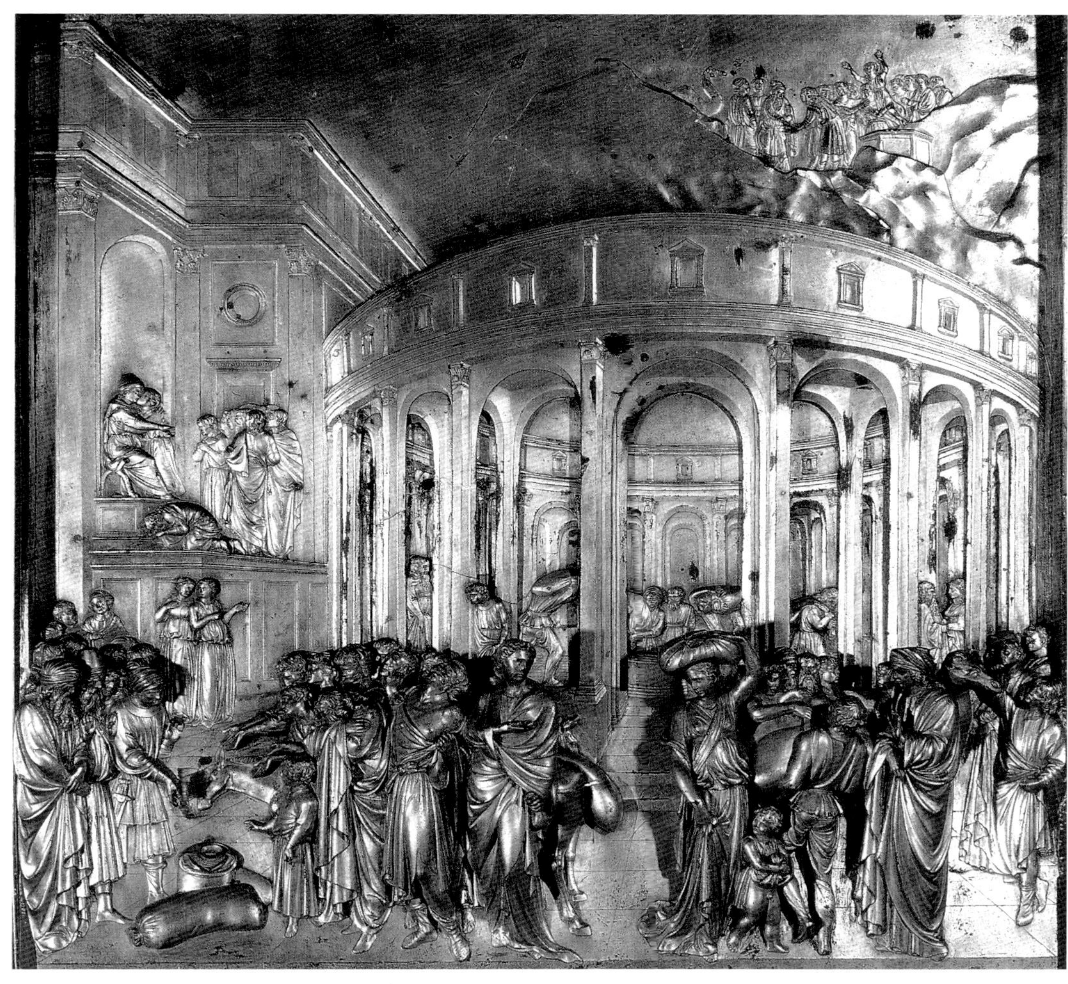

Lorenzo Ghiberti, two scenes from the Doors of Paradise of the Baptistery, 1429–52, bronze, each 79.5 × 79.5 cm.
Above: Story of Joseph.
Below: Story of Isaac.

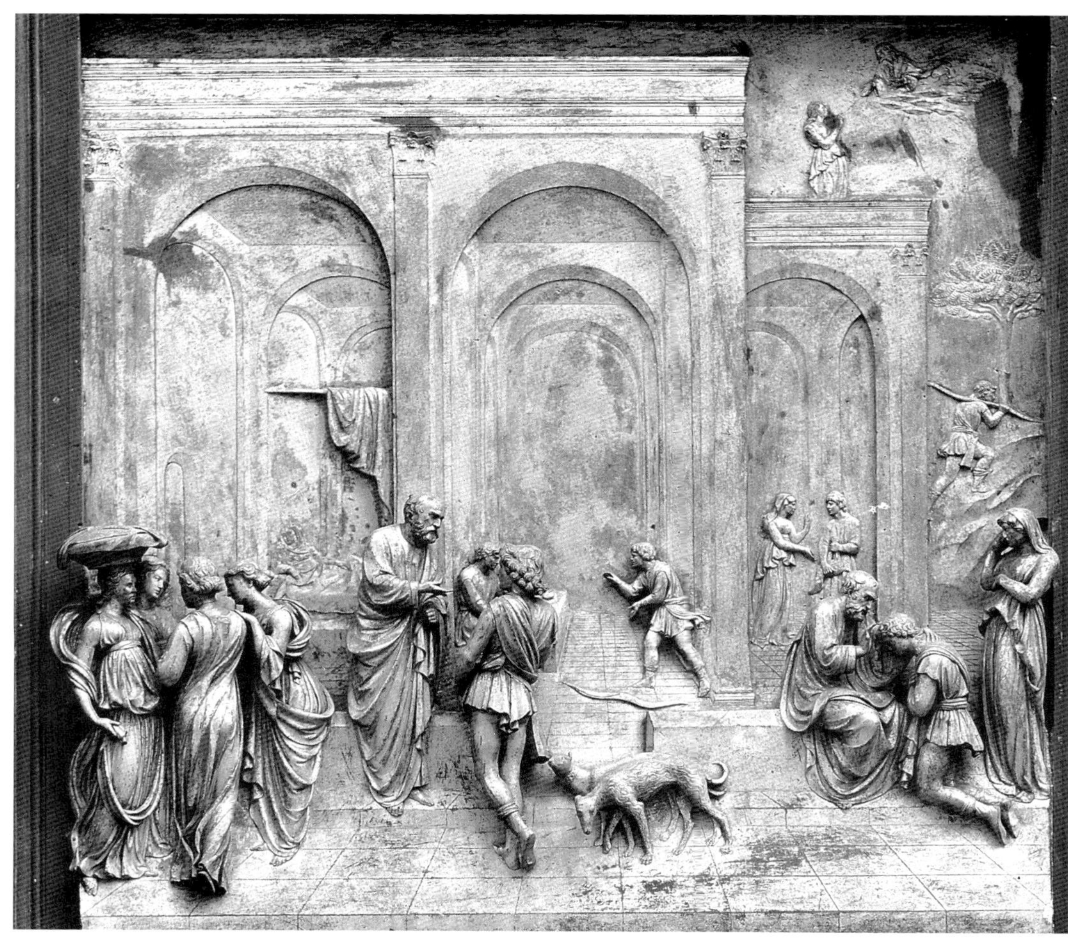

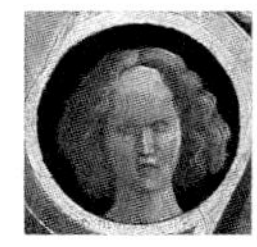

text is only clear where Ghiberti's direct personal real-life experience is present and alive.'[121] It is quite possible that Uccello would have been one of the questioners in such dialogues and that he participated in these theoretical discussions. It was certainly at Ghiberti's workshop that he began to grasp the whole complexity of the phenomenon of vision, to which he attempted to give his own personal solution. Ghiberti, on the other hand, was always careful to rely on the authority of ancient texts. Faced with modernity and innovation, he sought out the continuity and authority of tradition and stated: 'But in order not to repeat in a superficial and superfluous manner the principles which are basic to every opinion, I will deal with the composition of the eye, taking particular account of the opinions of three authors, that is to say, Avicenna, in his books, Alfacen, in the first book of his perspective, and Constantine in the first book on the eye, for these authors suffice and treat the matters that interest us with more authority.'[122] 'In this context of a new cultural situation', retrieval of a 'medieval and even more ancient pre-medieval type' of scientific culture 'contains a polemical gesture.'[123] Ghiberti himself tells us in the same passage that he is dealing with a controversial subject, full of contradictions, when he adds: 'However, we cannot follow the teachings of all three, for sometimes they contradict each other because of the bad translation.'[124]

Ma accioch'io non triti superficialmente, superfluamente i principi di tutti gli oppinioni, io tratterò la composizione dell'occhio spechialmente secondo tre oppinioni di autori, cioè Avicenna, nei libri suoi, et Alfacen pel primo libro della sua prospectiva, Constantino nel primo dell'occhio, però che questi autori bastano et più certamente tractano quelle cose che noi vogliamo.

Non di meno noi possiamo seguire le parole di ciascuno, però che alcuna volta si contraddicono per la cattiva traslazione

G. Federici Vescovini has clearly shown that the transcription of Alhazen's texts

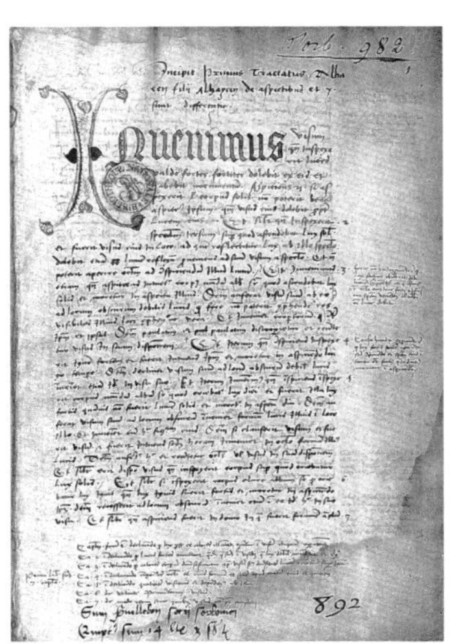

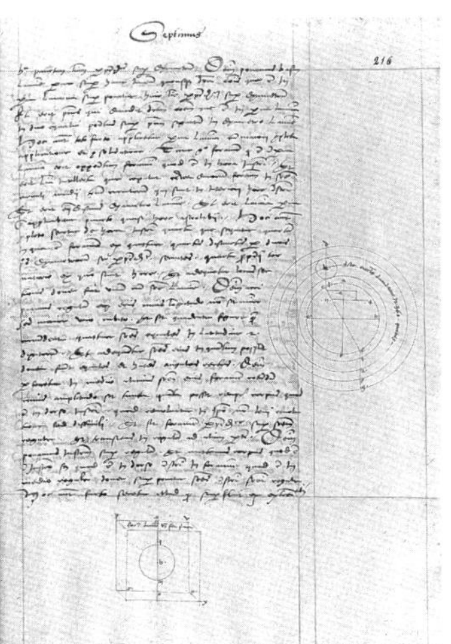

Alhazen, two pages from the manuscript of *De Aspectibus in Opticae*. Paris, Bibliothèque Nationale, ms. lat. 16199.

is almost literal.[125] But what matters are not questions of philology or plagiarism, but that Ghiberti should have chosen Alhazen as a source rather than Witelus.[126] Now that the theme of perspective had become the matter of the moment, he became devoted to a text from which he could draw a 'naturalistic' (what we would call 'physiological') explanation of the mechanism of sight, which took account of

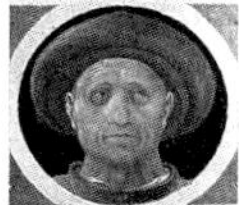

binocular vision and which allowed the existence of a margin of fantasy, as opposed to Brunelleschi's geometric planning. 'In the first aspect of vision, the one . . . which manifestly deals only with visual things through intuition and vision, without one being sure of the reality of the result, the form is called fantastic, sometimes linked with prior knowledge, and such vision is a result of fantasy and visible foresight, it does not follow appearance and is not guided by it'.[127]

Nel primo aspetto della visione, la quale per intuizione e per la visione, comprende l'intenzione manifestamente per la cosa visa solamente e non si certifica per questo così fatto effetto, la forma è chiamata fantastica, alcuna volta a cognizione precedente, e tale visione e secondo fantasia e visione precedente e visibili, il quale il viso non cognosce appresso all'aspetto e con questo non ne harà guidato essa.

Here the link with Uccello's experience can certainly be found: in his way of allowing an ambiguity to hover over the innermost optical, cognitive mechanism of vision, an ambiguity between the certainty of sensations and the certainty of intuition – that is to say between the domain of recognition through difference/resemblance and that of visual memory.

I do not propose here to give a detailed definition of the links between Ghiberti and his sources, which in any case have been amply studied by Vescovini, Parronchi and others, and which would leave less space for our subject. Nevertheless they do highlight two useful points, which help in understanding Uccello's position: first, his taste for Classical Antiquity, which is not a *rediscovery* as envisaged by the humanists or by Alberti, but which is perceived as a continuous present, linked with the human condition and the general process of knowledge; second, the plural approaches to the phenomenon of vision, which integrate all the values of the Gothic world and which make Renaissance perspective – well-established though it may have been – a special case, even a limiting device. Parronchi has rightly observed that 'In Paolo Uccello's works, the objects, rendered according to axonometric projections and centred on vanishing points which are always varied, seem to indicate what in Witelus's perspective appears to us as the fundamental principle in the understanding of the problem of space in this proposition: that two parallel lines to not meet in infinity. Brunelleschi, running counter to the theory of optics, decided to make these two parallel lines meet at one point: it was his way of giving vision a unified, instantaneous character. In a more subtle way, Uccello seems, on the contrary, to admit multiple vanishing points in a single work, which implies a more complex space, and not just successive moments of observation.'[128]

If we stick to the evidence provided in his work – whatever the lacunae and uncertainties regarding attribution and dating – Uccello's research into perspective aligns with Ghiberti's system, which allows for experimentation and fantasy, 'matter and reasoning,'[129] – whatever likelihood there was of Uccello's access to the sources, or hypothetical help from Fra Alessio Strozzi di Ubaldini, at the convent of Santa Maria Novella, to whom Brunelleschi and Ghiberti would have recourse for work on the cupola.[130]

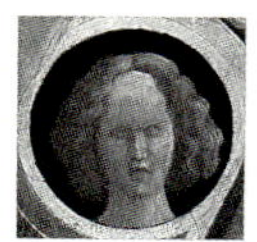

What then are the fragments from Ghiberti's optico-perspectival system that find practical application in Uccello's work? If we accept the (somewhat unlikely) hypothesis that he participated in the architecture of the *Story of the Virgin* in the Cappella dei Mascoli in San Marco in Venice, there is an immediate correspondence with the problems that Brunelleschi's two panels posed. Perspective is central in *The Visitation* where the skyline is placed exactly in the centre of the vault so that, as in the situation of a mosaic on a concave surface, the vertical lines are bent. Ensuing from this is an ambiguity in the foreshortening of the view from the top downwards (*di sopra in giù*) in relation to the paving and lower porticos, and in the view from below upwards (*di sotto in su*) on the twin-arched windows, central arcade and overhanging tympani. In *The Birth of the Virgin*, on the other hand, the perspective has two vanishing points, where the '*quadro*' coincides with the small columns at the corners, an indirect way of applying the proposition found in Brunelleschi's second panel.

As for the *Stories from Genesis* with the *Creation of Adam* and the *Creation of the Animals*, the convergence of the two-colour paving stones of the base line of the lunette into a unique central vanishing point provides a modern counterpoint – even if it is on *Ill. pp. 151, 180*

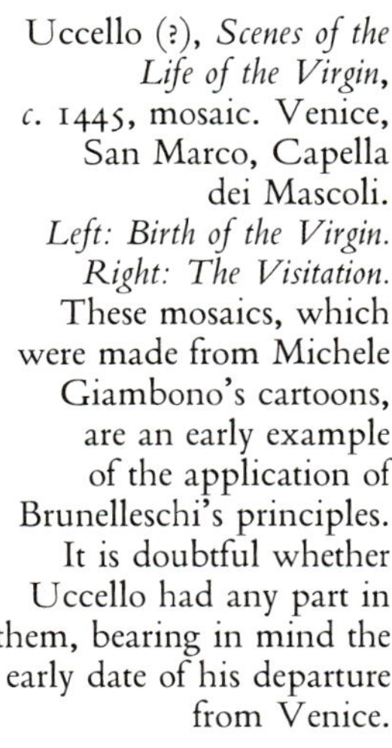

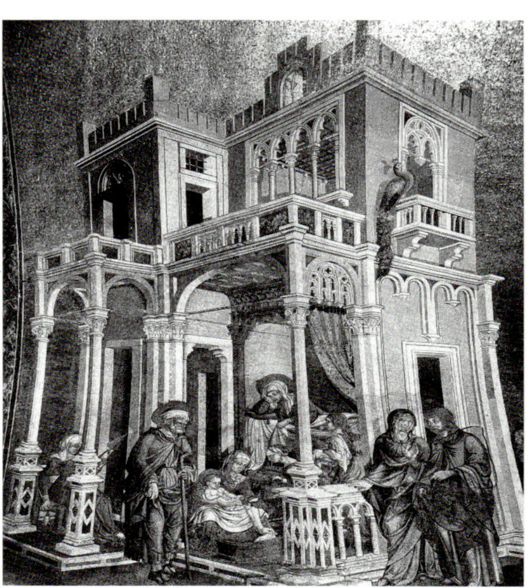

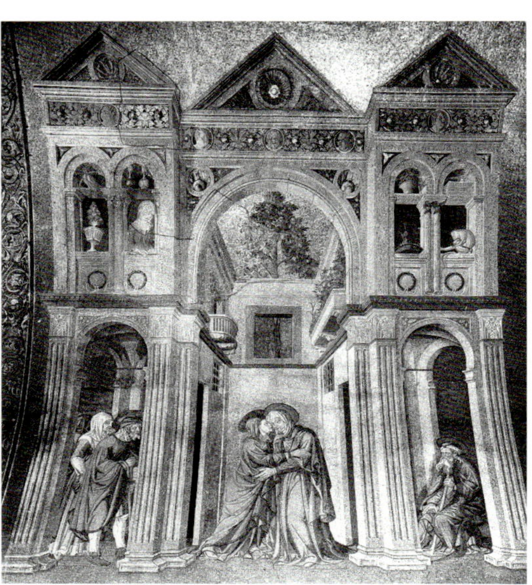

Uccello (?), *Scenes of the Life of the Virgin*, *c.* 1445, mosaic. Venice, San Marco, Capella dei Mascoli. *Left: Birth of the Virgin. Right: The Visitation.* These mosaics, which were made from Michele Giambono's cartoons, are an early example of the application of Brunelleschi's principles. It is doubtful whether Uccello had any part in them, bearing in mind the early date of his departure from Venice.

the margin of the story – to the ancient traditional character of the composition. It gives a unity to the two separate episodes, by individualizing an axis marked by the split in the rock, with a reference point formed by the extreme edge of God the Father's garment on the left and the tree trunk in the centre which corresponds to the observer's viewpoint. There is a sort of ambiguity here between the two focal points –

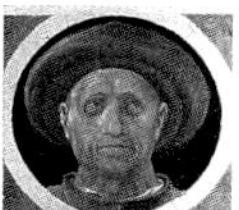

each of the two episodes is depicted in its own valley – and the convergence, occurring in the spaces of the big valley which forms the background of the painting, a convergence which is made towards the one vanishing point, indicated by the two-colour paved floor.

Ill. pp. 152, 168, 205

In the *Hawkwood* the ambiguity is in the vertical plane. Two different viewpoints are present in the same fresco: one for the projection of the horse and rider, which is almost orthogonal, the other for the architecture of the plinth and tomb, made to be seen from below according to a perspective whose '*quadro*' is made up from the cornice high up above the signature and by the extreme edge of the fresco on the left. These two elements determine the siting of the observer's viewpoint on the left, in keeping with the distribution of highlights on the fresco, which itself follows the natural lighting in this part of the nave. Thus we have a sort of balance on the horizontal axis – corresponding to the edge of the plane on which the horse's shoes are resting – which divides the fresco exactly into two squares. The moulding on the embouchure of the tomb lid, which is like a kind of negative imprint of great horseshoes, is there as a form of plastic mediation, a softening of the confrontation between the naturalistic

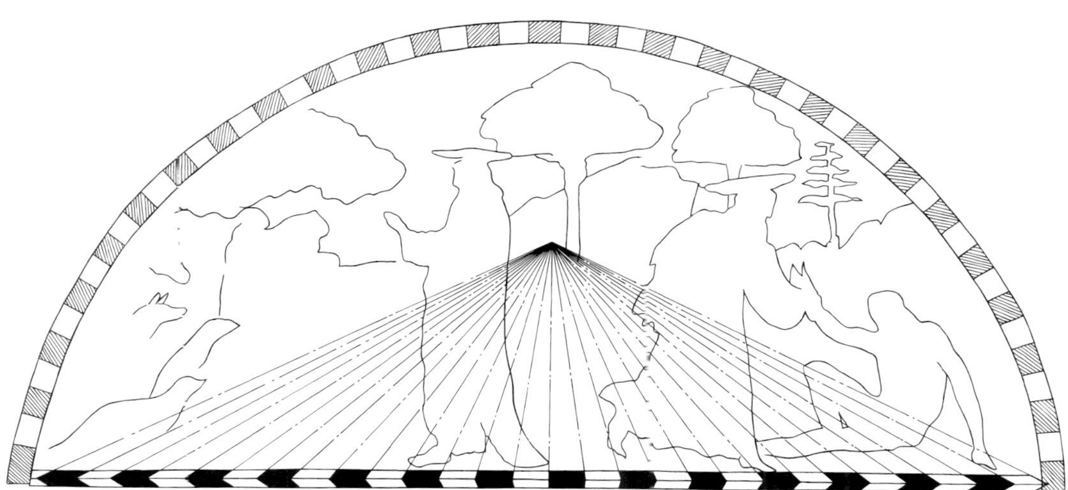

Reconstruction of the perspective used in the *Creation of the Animals and Creation of Adam*. The two-colour border below follows the rules of perspective, as if the upper border of the lunette had been projected downward (after Sindona-Rossi).

forms of horse and rider – themselves largely geometrized and stylized – and the light of this architectural concavity which would otherwise have been too emphatic and too hard. This refinement, this formal nuance, is in the exact spot where the two structures are separated by a kind of geometric hinge which emphasizes the existence of the two different viewpoints: one from a distance, almost from infinity, allowing us

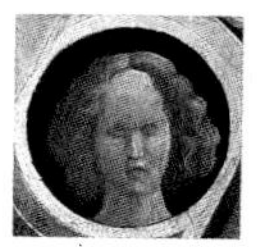

theoretically to look at the horse and rider from high up, and one from close up for the supporting architecture, where the painter tries to give the impression of a relief standing out from the wall: for it is truly not a matter here of a portrait but of a painted representation of a monument, sculpted in stone, marble and bronze.

The ambiguity can be seen again in the *Stories of Noah* where two vanishing points do not coincide on the horizon, and where the two sides of the ark can be seen to be arranged in an *almost* parallel way in the plan of the representation, when in fact they diverge and are not parallel. This ensemble can be explained by the non-parallel positioning of the arks on the horizontal plane, as much as by parallels which do not *Ill. pp. 153, 183*

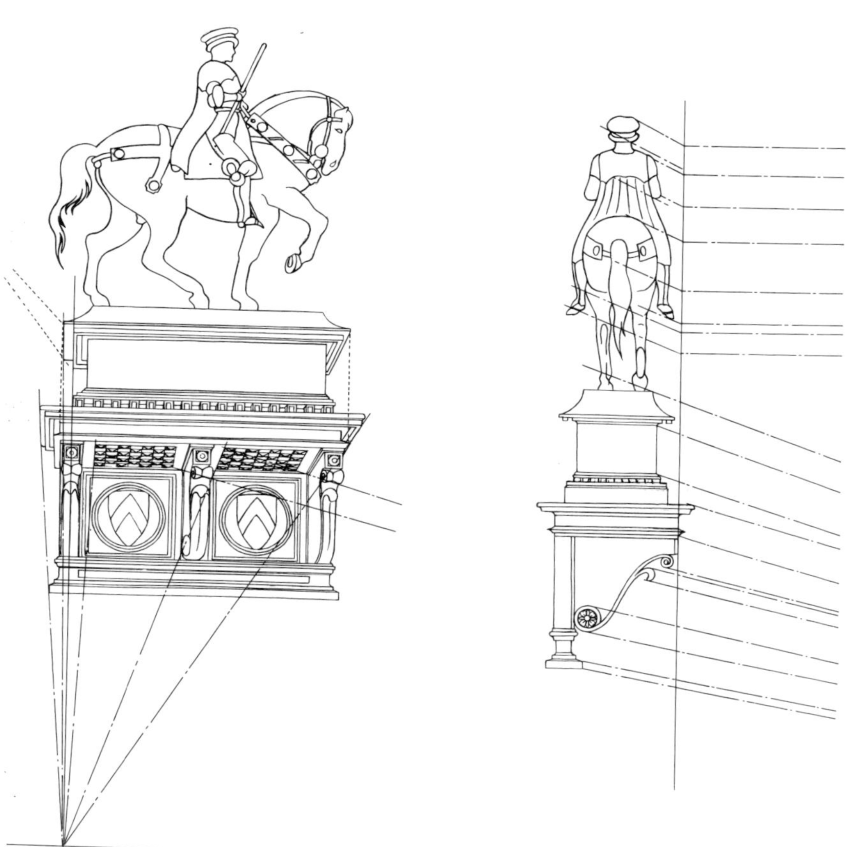

Reconstruction of the perspective used in the *Equestrian Monument to Sir John Hawkwood* (after Sindona-Rossi).

meet in infinity (Witelus). There is a further ambiguity that derives from the superimposition of the two scenes: that of the upper one, observed from an elevated viewpoint and consequently not natural, and the lower one from a viewpoint sited on a quite low skyline, which justifies the *sotto in su* of the trellis and cabin. Verisimilitude, realism might rather have suggested the opposite: the upper scene seen

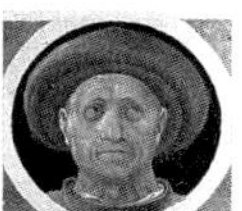

from below and the lower one from above. All this is even truer where in contrast to the cathedral nave, the space of the cloister – i.e. its width – forces the observer to see the fresco from close up.

Ill. pp. 214ff. In the *Battles*, Uccello bases a system of perspective on the ground, an ideal chessboard formed from the debris of lances, which serves as a reference for the dynamic forces at play: the rotation of lances which, as they are engaged in the action, progressively pass from vertical to horizontal at the centre of the encounter. There is ambiguity between the representation of space and the representation of the event which occupies the space and which in a certain sense modifies and deforms it. The

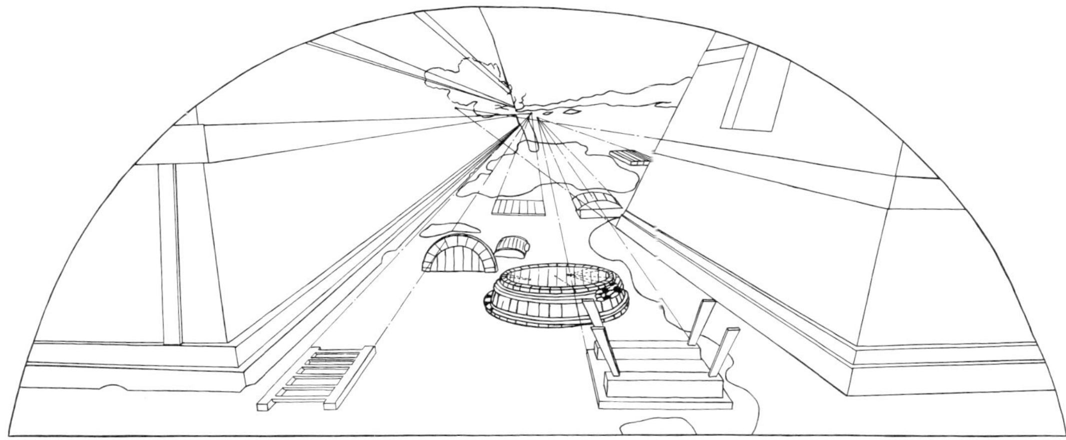

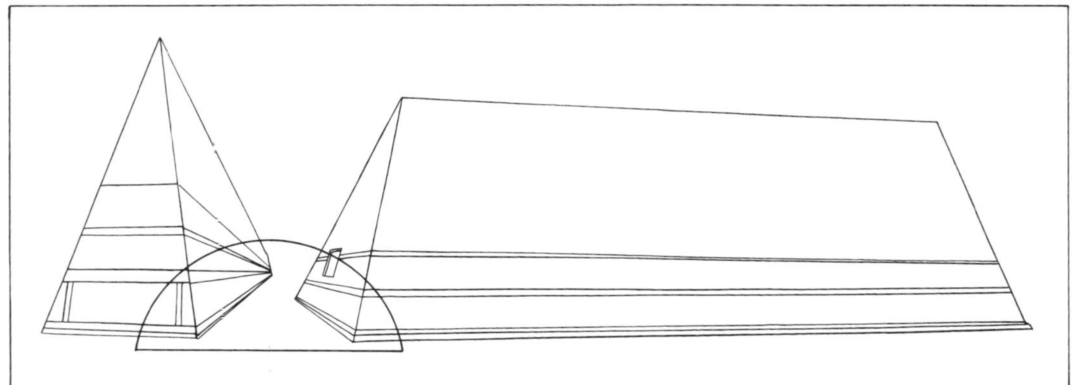

Reconstruction of the perspective used in *The Flood and the Retreat of the Waters*. The two stories, which are combined in one lunette, have vanishing points which almost coincide, but are nevertheless distinct. Two different sides of the Ark are depicted. The drawing below shows the dimensions of the Ark in relation to the total picture area (after Marin).

Ill. pp. 154–5 same separation is found in the famous sinopia of *The Adoration of the Child* in San Martino alla Scala: here it seems certain that Uccello had begun by representing space with three vanishing points, one exactly on the axis of the lunette, the two others on the sides, placed in such a way that all the lines to vanishing points are situated just inside the frame of the painting at the edge of the foreground, below. But he has not

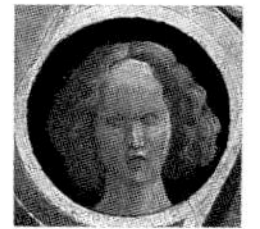

made use (or only in a very limited way) of the system of a central vanishing point, whose space is occupied by the cabin – 'the downstroke of the axis' of Brunelleschian memory. So he promoted the possibilities offered by diagonal vanishing points: as double vanishing points escaping in depth at the sides, and bifocalization of space. The principle is the same as in the *Battles*: the isotropic, geometric, intuitively accessible representation of space is one thing; the other is the event that partly occupies this space, and which can be understood more immediately, in a situation of anisotropic relativity, through its relationship with its environment.

We can conclude from this brief excursion through Uccello's main works, that he was elaborating a perspective founded on binocular vision, involving a phenomenology which could not be reduced to the simplification of a single viewpoint – that of a camera, as found in the Brunelleschi-Alberti system – but which, in contrast, integrated the possibility of an oblique, not perpendicular vision, which varied according to eye movement, the observer's movements, and his automatic or voluntary adjustments. This physiological complexity left the artist the most complete freedom and allowed him to determine effectively the degree of the observer's involvement, the *Einfühlung*, the emotional and psychological participation. From

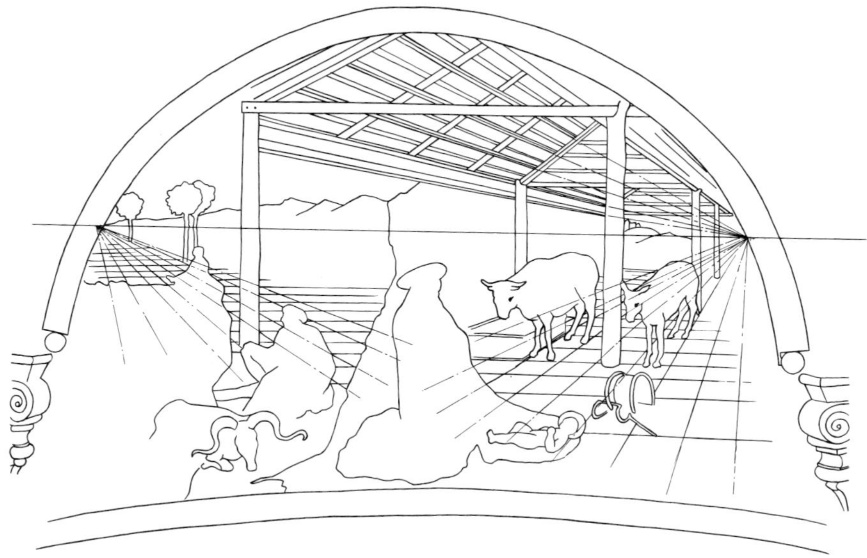

Reconstruction of the perspective of *The Adoration of the Child* in the Hospital of San Martino alla Scala. The construction uses two vanishing prints on the same horizon line.

this came a sense of marvel, astonishment and bewitchment, where reality and representation were no longer separate, for, from the very beginning of pictorial language, there has been no reality without representation, nor representation without reality.

But all this is only one aspect of vision: we must add the phenomena related to light

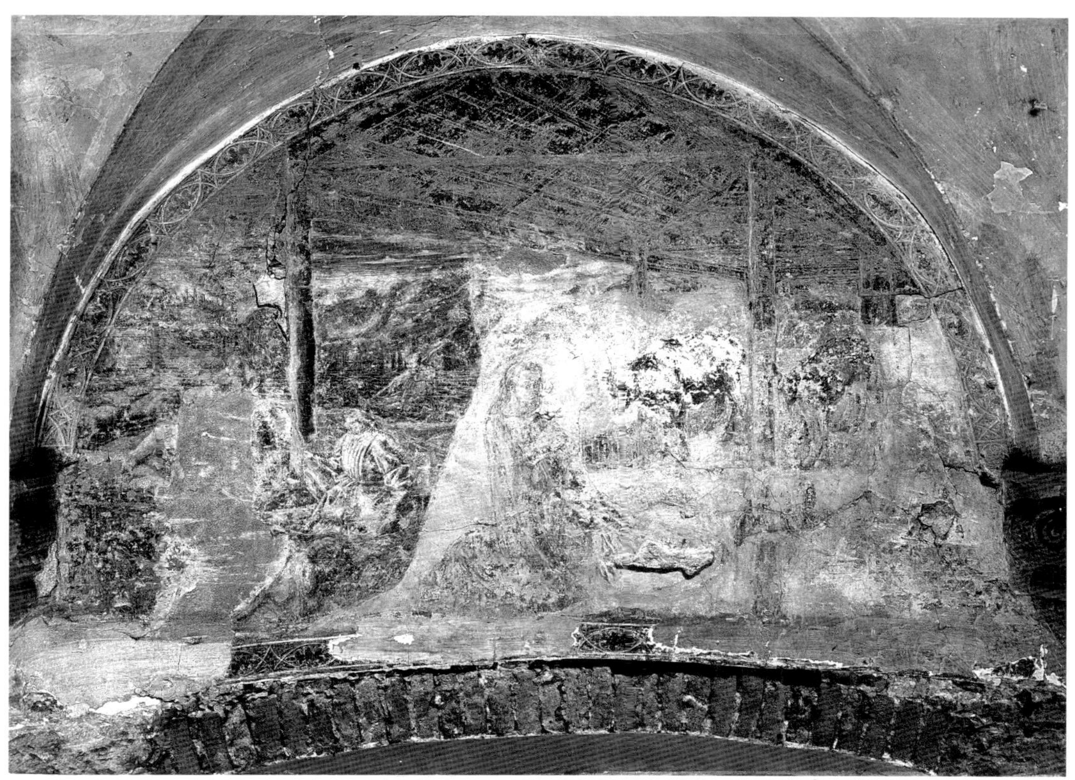

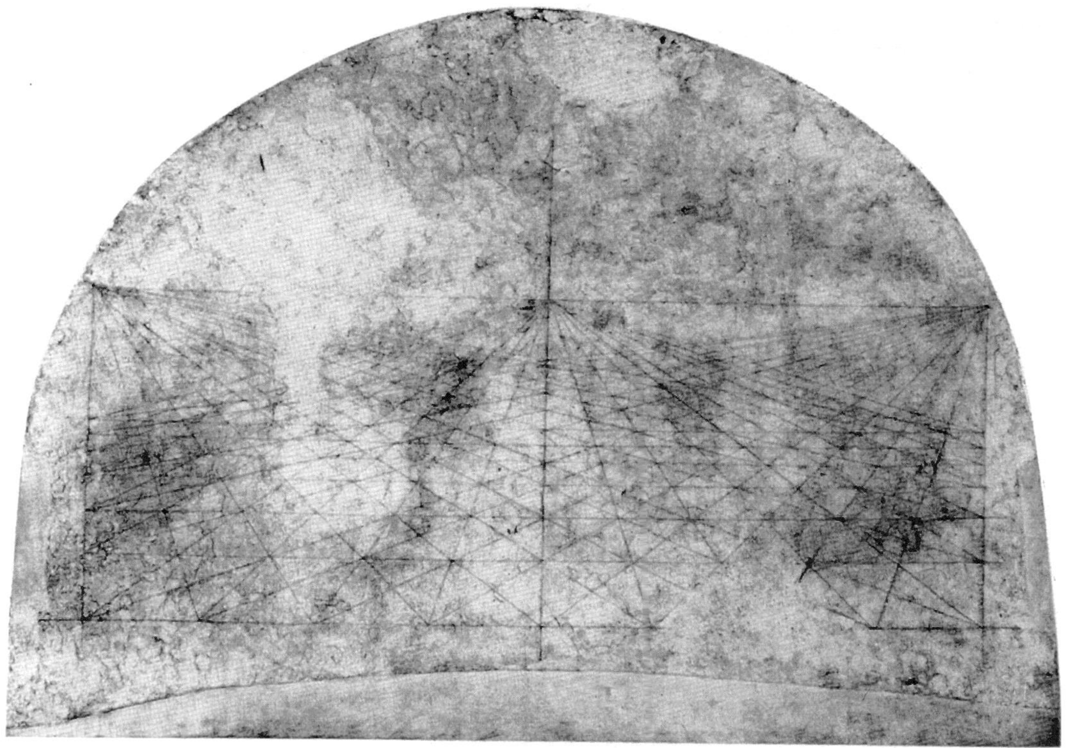

Uccello, *The Adoration of the Child*, 1435–7, fresco, 140 × 215 cm. Florence, Uffizi, reserve collection (formerly at San Martino alla Scala).
Above: the now almost indecipherable painting.
Below: the sinopia showing the perspective system with two vanishing points.

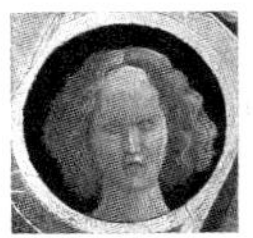

Adunque non sente il colore in quanto colore, né ancora luce . . . se non poi che è apparito dalla luce e dal colore . . . ma niuna cosa può esser colorato o luminosa se non la densa

Ciascuna visione di cuadunque per la comprensione della quantità della distanza, si piglia alla quantità dei corpi intragiacenti, verbigrazia, la nuvola in piena terra si vede congiunta al cielo, nella terra montuosa si vede prossima alla terra in però che in alcun luogo non oltrepassano l'altezza dei monti. La certezza, dunque, della distanza dei nuvoli, s'accagiona per l'apprensione della cosa intragiacente, che, se i corpi intragiacenti non sono mal confusi, non potrà certificare l'apprensione e la quantità di questa distanza più che non sia la distanza dal mezzo, non ne attinge il vedere a piena distinzione dei corpi remoti intergiacenti, per la debolezza delle specie visibili e per la distanza.

and colour: 'The eye cannot see colour just as colour, nor light as light . . . but only both together,' Ghiberti wrote;[131] 'But nothing can be coloured or luminous without having density.'[132] If it is true that 'all vision, as far as measuring the amount of distance is concerned, is measured by the amount of interposed bodies (*corpi intragiacenti*'); for example, if we are on the plain, the clouds seem to be part of the sky, while if we are in the mountains, we see them close to the earth, for in no place do they exceed the height of the mountains. Confirmation of the distance of the clouds is therefore generated through the perception of bodies which are situated between the clouds themselves and the observer, so much so that if the bodies are not distinct enough, perception will not be assured,'[133] this could serve as a very apt commentary on the London *Saint George and the Dragon*. Here the 'interposed bodies' are the fields and their network of plots painted in perspective, and the clouds composed at first of diffused light round the mountain tops, then stratus clouds which grow closer and closer together in the limpid sky. Behind the knight, the miasmas of the bog, gusts of wind and the dragon's putrid exhalations, which have been translated into ominous signs and stylized elements, form a furrow, like a trail produced by the dynamic acceleration that propels the knight forward towards the observer, on the diagonal line of the action – as opposed to the fields which regress in perspective and were put there as spatial reference points, as *corpi intragiacenti*. Using stylized and stylizing signs is a way of broaching the problems of aerial vision – the way the 'diaphanous forms' of air, water, crystal and mirrors modify the transmission of light. Uccello heralds a total, casuistic, mysterious sense of marvel that can be found later in Leonardo da Vinci's explorative work, but here Uccello does it in a number of ways. It makes us think of the browned metal and silver in the *Battles*, the convex mirror studs on the harness in the *Hawkwood*, the metallic, reflective haloes that reveal his way of delving into the kaleidoscope of reality in order to recompose fragmentary elements of it according to Witelus's twenty-one *intentiones*: 'distance, dimension, situation, corporeality, form, continuity, separation, division, number, movement, repose, roughness, smoothness, transparency, opacity, shade, darkness, beauty, deformity, similarity and difference'.[134] The twenty-one *intentiones* could be modified by eight phenomena: 'light, colour, distance, situation, dimension, solidity, transparency, time'.[135] Uccello's research was therefore in two registers: one into the infinite complexity of combinations of the visible and the other into transcending the geometrical construction of space.

Ill. pp. 157, 257

Distanza, dimensione, sito, corporeità, figura, continuità, separazione, divisione, numero, moto, quiete, asperità, liscezza, diafanità, densità, ombra, oscurità, bellezza, deformità, somiglianza e differenza.

Luce, colore, distanza, sito, dimensione, solidità, diafanità, tempo.

However, there was a key to resolving this ambiguity of reality, an element of certainty in the configuration, a symbolic object in which the absolute and the contingent met, in which the whirlpool created by the relativity of vision was steadied

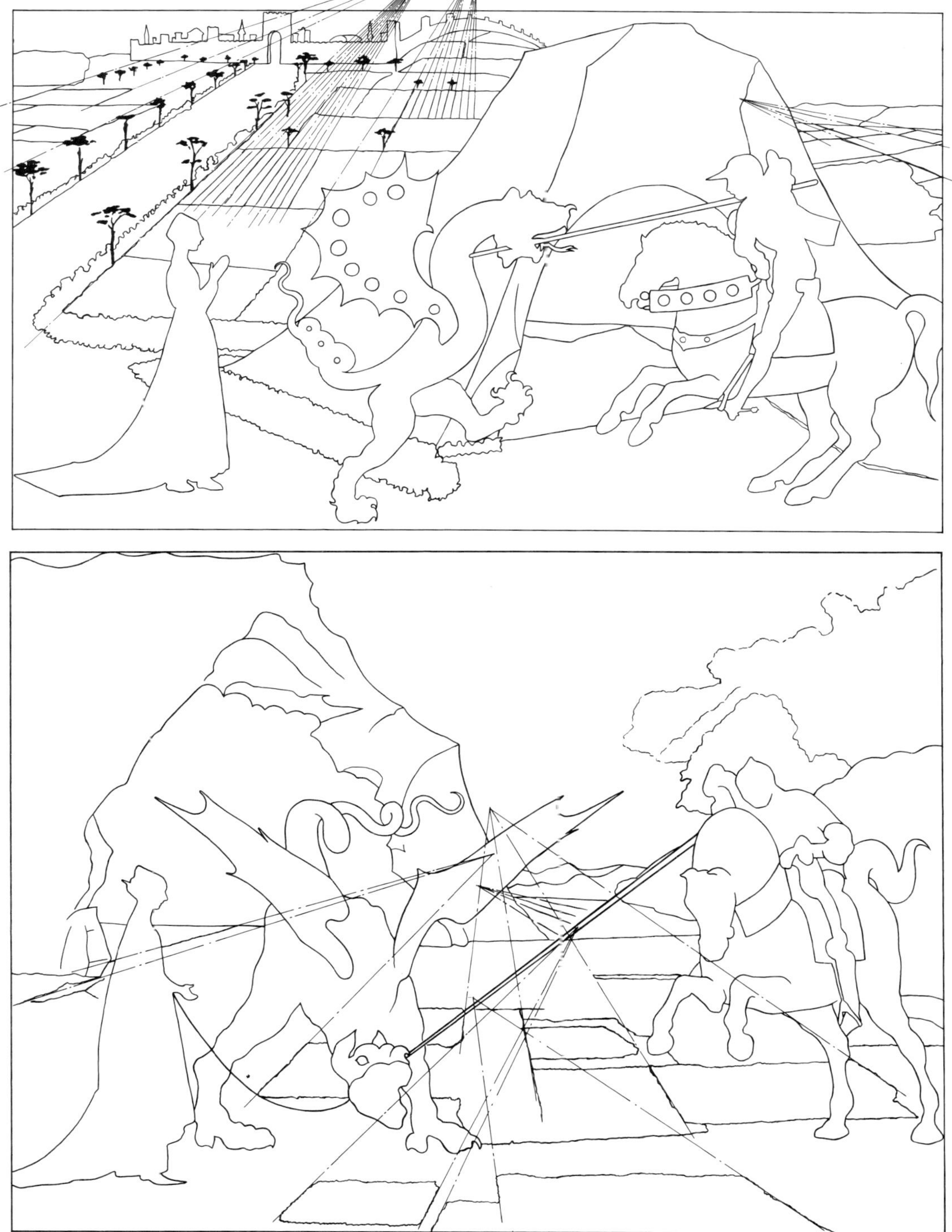

Reconstruction of the perspective used in the two *Saint George and the Dragon* paintings, in Paris (*above*) and London (*below*). In both cases it appears that the perspectival construction is not based on a single vanishing point (after Sindona-Rossi).

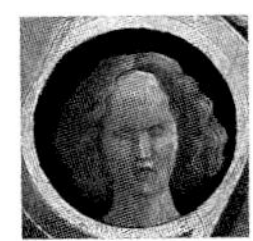

and stopped: this was the circle, a favoured, absolute, geometric figure, which assumed within it the idea of the cosmos, Aristotelian perfection of nature and also, *ad circini centrum*, Renaissance anthropocentric centrality, the basis of human proportion rediscovered in Vitruvius and reintroduced by Ghiberti. Uccello's register favoured the circle and its derivatives: the barrel, the chalice, the curl, the eye, the halo and finally the *mazzocchio*, a symbolic form, an emblematic cipher, a metaphysical pretext which almost became his signature. But with Uccello, we must distinguish between the circle as a regulating outline (the theme of Parronchi's numerous hypotheses in his graphic layouts of Uccello's compositions), and the circle as a favoured object of representation. Here we have two clearly distinct sets of data: the first relates to the domain of *a posteriori*, ever-suggestive but ever-arbitrary hypotheses; the second to the artist's objective reality and is justified by its internal coherence.

Ill. pp. 161, 162

Beyond geometric and philosophical speculations, we must also take into account a certain artisan enthusiasm – typical of Gothic artists, and particularly Ghiberti – that delighted in patiently and logically overcoming difficulties of representation and resolving delicate technical problems. For that, the method of representing the circle through an approximation of points is an essential tool: manifest proof of this can be seen in some 2,000 points of intersection in what is a relatively small drawing (34 × 24 cm) of a *Study for a Chalice* in the Uffizi.

The *mazzocchio* is the geometric representation of headgear in circular form (*a circine*), which Uccello sometimes depicted realistically (as in the *Stories of Noah* and the *Battles*, for example), but now combined with a foreshortened geometric solid and with fluid twisted drapery, the '*torculo*', as Piero della Francesca called it.[136] In the *Flood*, Uccello features two *mazzocchi*, drawn geometrically, using the system of constructing a circle through points: the *mazzocchio* is shown as a polyhedron with multiple facets, alternating in black and white like a chequerboard. Parronchi sees this as a desire to 'indicate the same effect as when two solid bodies are seen from a distance, the one being a truly angular solid and the other a solid which appears angular through colouring that simulates multiple facets. A principle expressed by Alhazen (I, III, theorem 59), for whom a body having a multifaceted geometric shape appears spherical when seen from far off, while if black lines are drawn on it, it appears to be subdivided into facets by the stripes.'[137] Even if it is difficult to accept Parronchi's analysis entirely, because of the state of the fresco and its successive restorations, the important point is that here Uccello was experimenting with the relationship between form and colour. The linear grid of the construction using points on the spherical bodies, of which the Uffizi drawing is a good example, represents an important preparatory phase, which could subsequently be modified

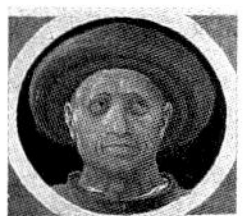

through the use of colour: the Louvre *mazzocchio*, which is monochrome, or almost, is, all things considered, coherent and has the effect of continuity, which is what the system of using points was seeking to obtain. On the other hand, the black and white chequerboards give a different effect, which derives from the different perceptions of an identical surface, depending on whether the colour is light or dark. This is an experiment on the relationship between form and colour (to which light must be added), very much in Ghiberti's domain, that goes beyond simple perspective and touches upon the psychology of vision. The recurrence of these elements – the barrel five times, the *mazzocchio* even more – the crystalline geometry of the drawings, and the obsession with the chalice represent both a metaphysical quest and a theoretical stance. They impressed 20th-century writers and did much for Uccello's intriguing, 'modern' reputation, which is incompatible with a coherent historical interpretation. 'He is seen first and foremost as an *authority on contraposition in the figurative field*, in the *mazzocchio*, where it actually becomes his signature, outside any iconographic interpretation.'[138] But in the face of all these geometric counterpoints, Uccello's work itself (when we think of the *Hawkwood* and the *Battles* especially), forms a geometric

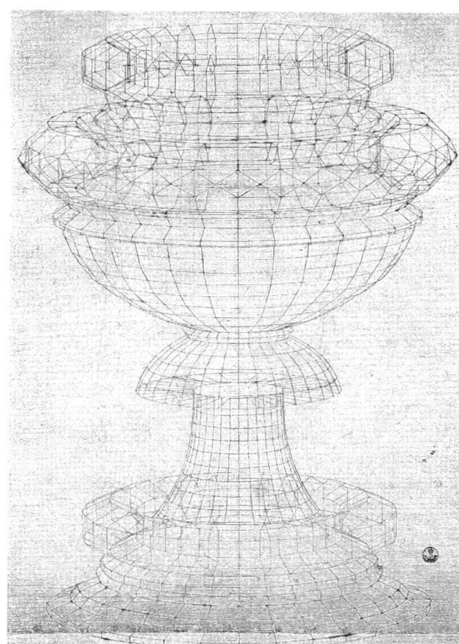

Uccello, *Perspective Study of a Vase*, pen and ink on white paper, 29 × 24.5 cm. Florence, Uffizi, Gabinetto dei Disegni.

'otherness'. We must not dwell too much on this 'stylistic' companion piece to the 'speculative-abstract' cliché in Vasari's biography, for we would then risk giving Uccello what is now considered an old-fashioned Cubist interpretation. On the other hand, by insisting too much on perspective and on the sources – as Parronchi and Gioseffi have – the risk, in spite of several enjoyable pieces of writing and many

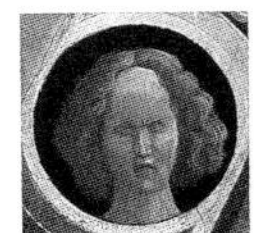

intelligent hypotheses, is to end up with an Uccello who appears to be a synthesis of Arab science and theology, as well as being a protagonist in the Renaissance renewal of Florence from Cosimo the Elder to Lorenzo the Magnificent; a personality of such intellectual stature that he becomes barely plausible. A more modest interpretation of this theme of perspective leads an analysis and critical appreciation of his work back to that dreamy disposition, that magical realism deeply rooted in Gothic tradition, whose full vitality, in his tenacious and perhaps discreetly polemical fashion, Uccello tried to show, as well as the richness of its nuances, its inexhaustible narrative potential and powers of persuasion.

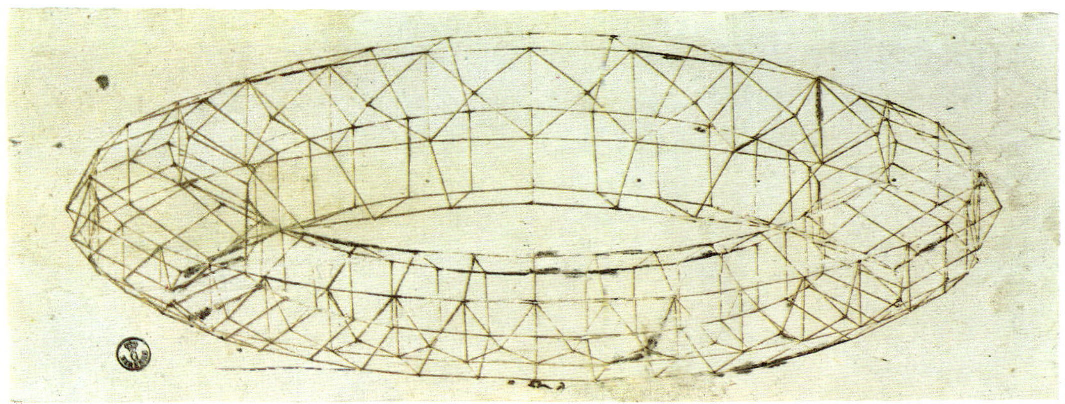

Pen on white paper, 10 × 27 cm. Florence, Uffizi, Gabinetto dei Disegni.

Three drawings of *mazzocchi*, probably by Uccello.

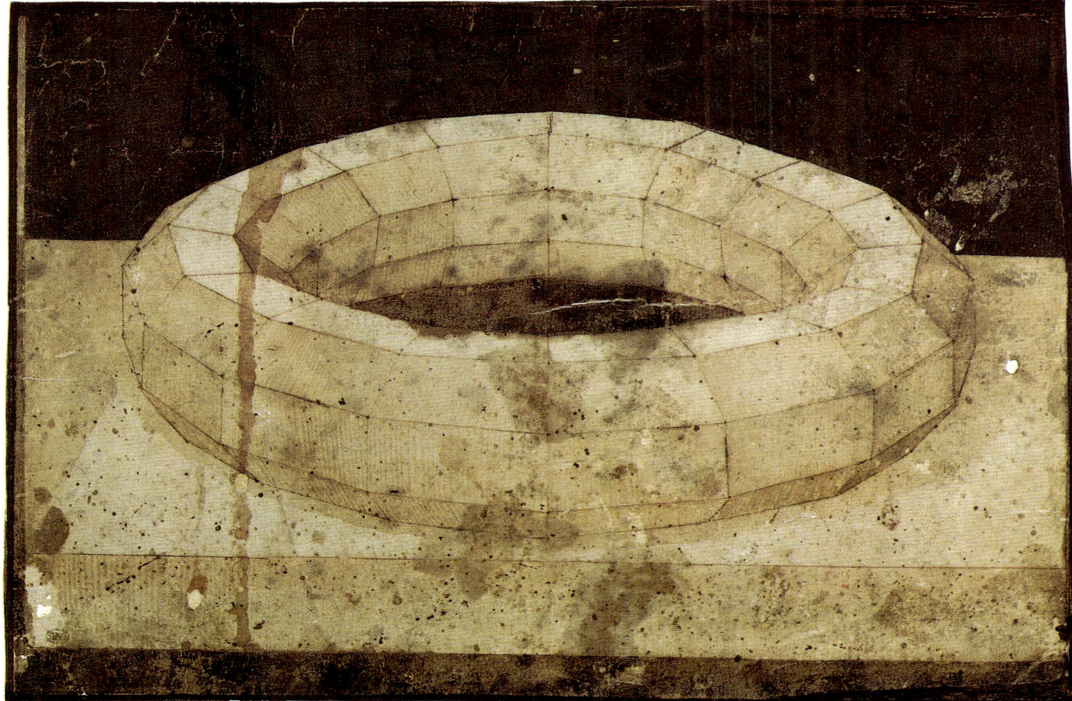

Pen and brown ink, brown and black wash, 16 × 23.3 cm. Paris, Louvre, Département des Arts Graphiques.

Pen on white paper, 9 × 24 cm. Florence, Uffizi, Gabinetto dei Disegni.

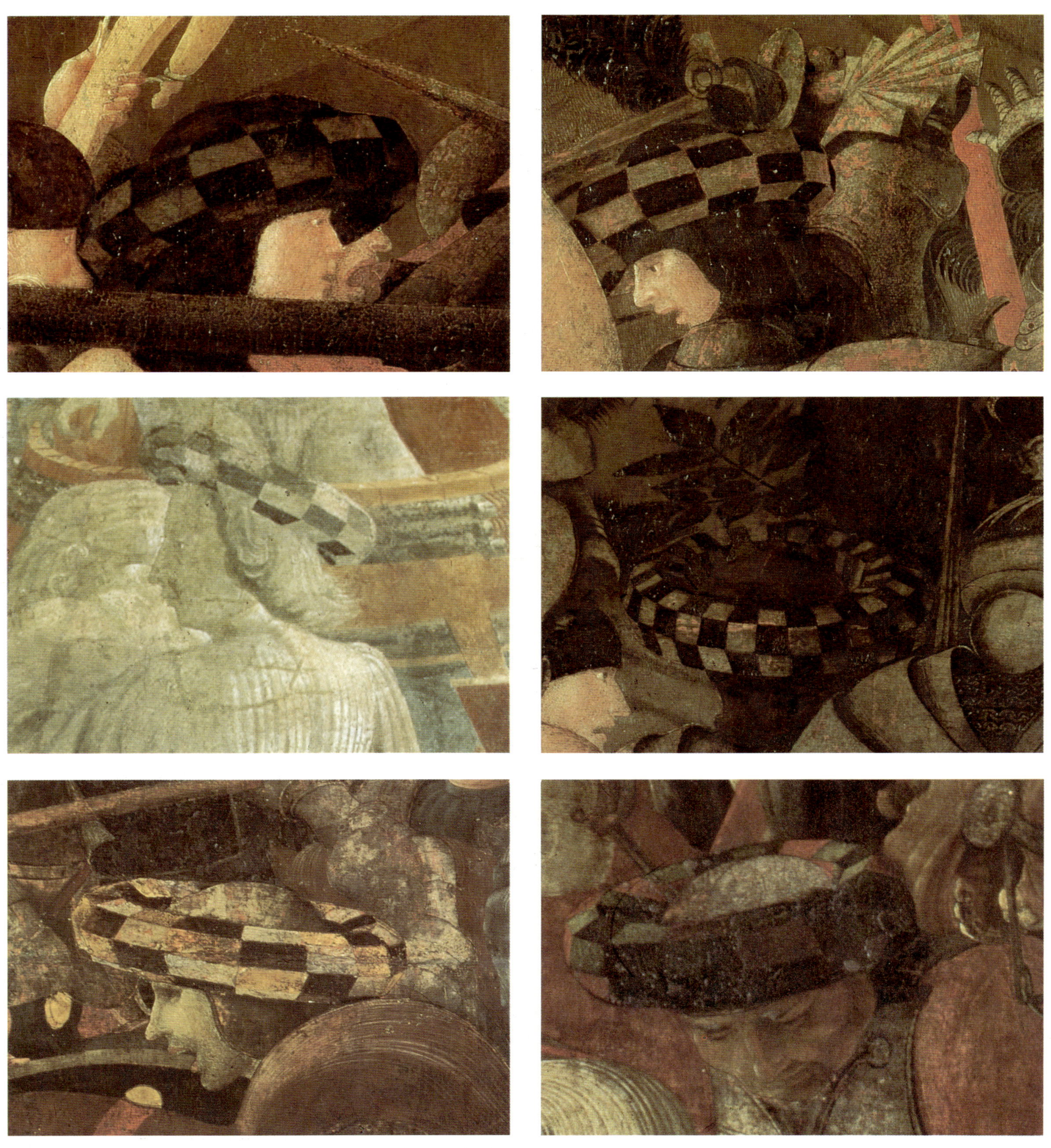

Details of the *Battle of San Romano* and of the *Flood* (middle row, left), showing various types of *mazzocchi*.

A NOTE ON THE ARCHITECTURE IN THE PAINTINGS

The architecture depicted in Uccello's work does not have the calibre of proper design, nor could it be said to belong to the culture of architecture. In the short time it took to paint, it does not add to the architectonic debate of its own times – which left its mark on a number of paintings of architecture of the period, from Masaccio's *Trinity* to Raphael's *School of Athens* (to quote only the most famous of examples) in a well-documented historical succession, on which studies abound.

Uccello uses his architecture as essential reference points as he plots the spatial surroundings for the enactment of his 'stories': it is not used paradigmatically, even in the domain of perspective. It simply occupies the spaces that are traditional to Tuscan Gothic painting, repeating its styles and discreet presence. But even in this role, that can in no way be separated from its pictorial context, Uccello cannot help but let his predilictions show, by presenting themes of his own times and adding his own contribution to a more general design. It is a contribution to that alternative city, which has no place in the history of architecture that derives from real works and authors or has distinctive stylistic characteristics: a city of whitewashed walls, severe ashlar-work and without any great formal refinements, but, instead, has a distant, serene objectivity; it is a city that reflects the true urban fabric of Quattrocento Florence or its Trecento tradition documented poetically by non-architect painters: by Uccello himself, or Fra Angelico, or Filippo Lippi.

In this vision an equal place is given to landscape, the figurative synthesis of which shows no concern for the temptations of realism or heroic accents, but simply the rustic reality of the hilly Tuscan countryside, a humanized, agricultural landscape, where towns are still enclosed within the shells of crenellated walls, where the very rocks seem more homely and are stone grottoes or caves rather than monuments to the unknown, cues for natural rustication rather than the mysterious mineral structures which were found later in Leonardo.

Ill. pp. 164–5
Acting as link between town and country is a completely rustic architecture, of huts and trellises, of frail farm sheds, which stem directly from his experience as a
Ill. pp. 132–3
small landowner on the Badia a Settimo plain, with its vegetable gardens, wheat fields and vineyards.

If we are looking for architecture in its true sense, we shall find in the Prato
Ill. pp. 190ff.
cathedral *Stories* in particular a purified, subtle but no less significant echo of the period. In *The Disputation of Saint Stephen*, the central perspective of the temple with its cupola sets out all the problems on which Uccello appears to have been informed:

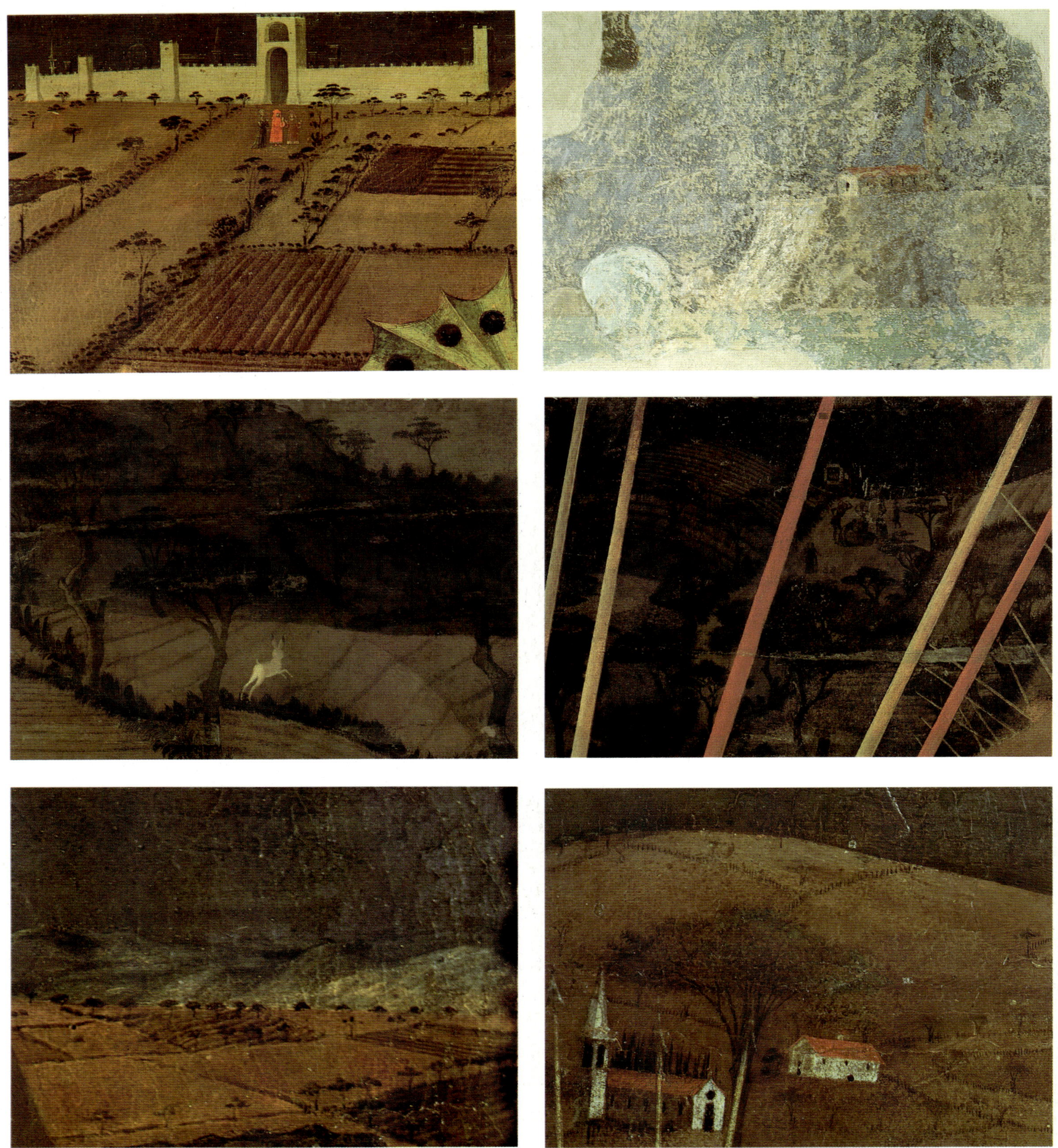

Details showing 'architectonic landscapes'. *This page, top left and bottom left:* from *Saint George and the Dragon* (Paris); *top right:* fresco in San Miniato (east wall); *centre row:* from *The Battle of San Romano* (Florence); *bottom right:* from *The Miracle of the Profaned Host* (scene of the execution of the Jew's family).

Facing page: from the *Thebaïd.*

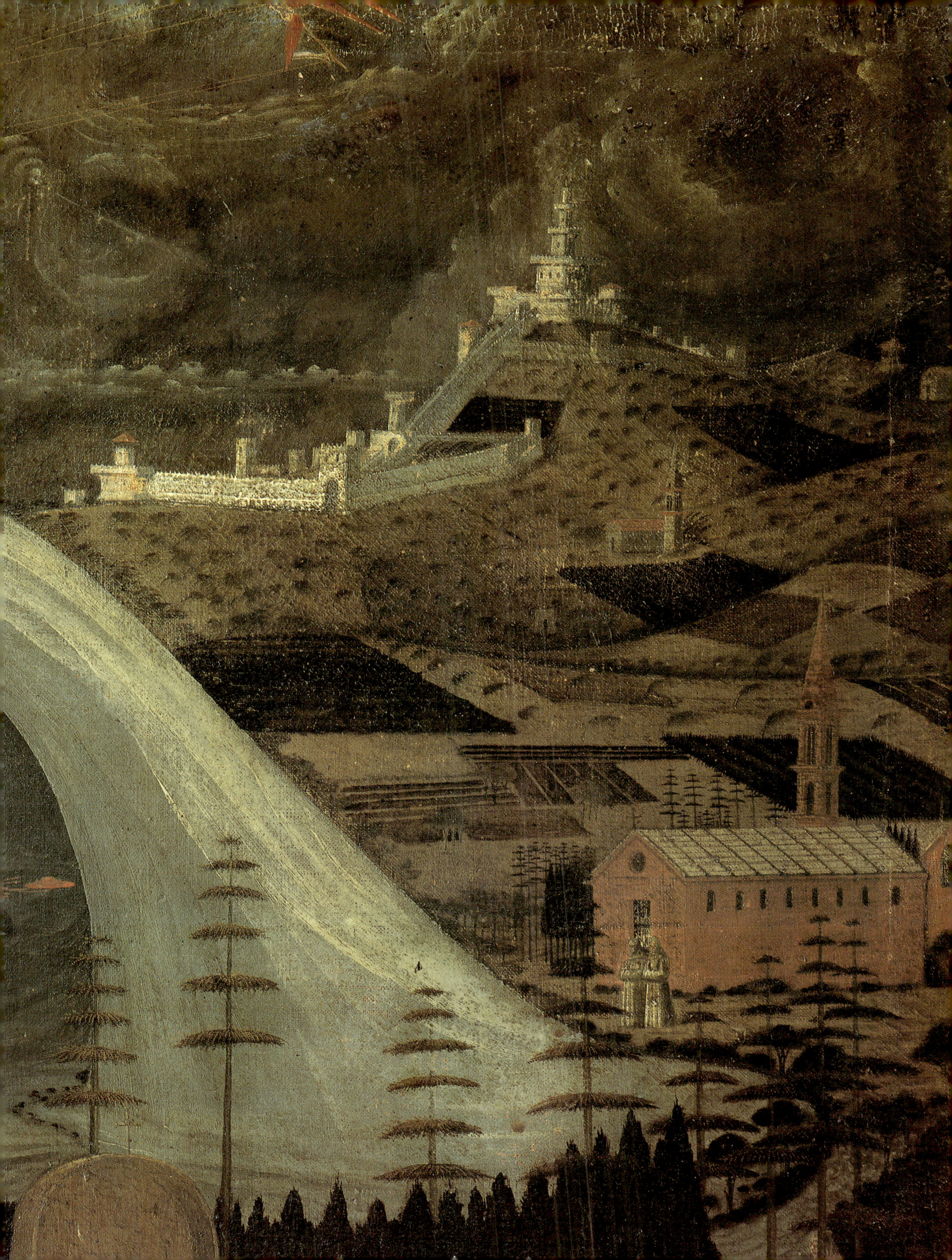

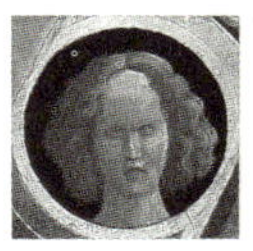

the question of the octagonal drum, the problem of the buttresses, the atypical interpretation of the pinnacles with their large vase-shaped finials, the cupola with its pyramidal lantern, which also has buttresses. The interpretation is rooted in fantasy, but in it are all the architectural problems that were current in his day, from Santa Maria del Fiore to San Lorenzo's apse. In the town that forms the background to *The Stoning of Saint Stephen* (if we agree with the attribution to Uccello), there is an explicit reference to Brunelleschi's Old Sacristy, and in *The Birth of the Virgin* a reference to the marble and wrought-iron balustrade surrounding Orcagna's Orsanmichele Tabernacle. And, finally, on a more general level, in *The Presentation of the Virgin* there is a reference to Florentine rustication and to other formulae found in Tuscan fourteenth- and fifteenth-century civil architecture: the infrequent windows, the silhouette of the moulding strongly emphasized in chiaroscuro, the simplicity of the door frame. There are very Florentine themes and Uccello offers a chromatically enriched version of them, bearing in mind the uniform colour of the stonework in Florence. He also accentuates the geometric ashlar-work, enlarging the bands between the stones, which in turn take on the appearance of blunt diamonds: a formalist accentuation that hardly reflects Florentine reality. But the basic element remains the temple and Uccello's idea for the middle ground: its shape is a sort of mixtilinear oval. It is difficult to know whether this results from joining the points of a circle seen in perspective, or whether it is really a figure constructed from straight lines joined by curves, as the base and second step seem to indicate. The step on which the

Ill. p. 56

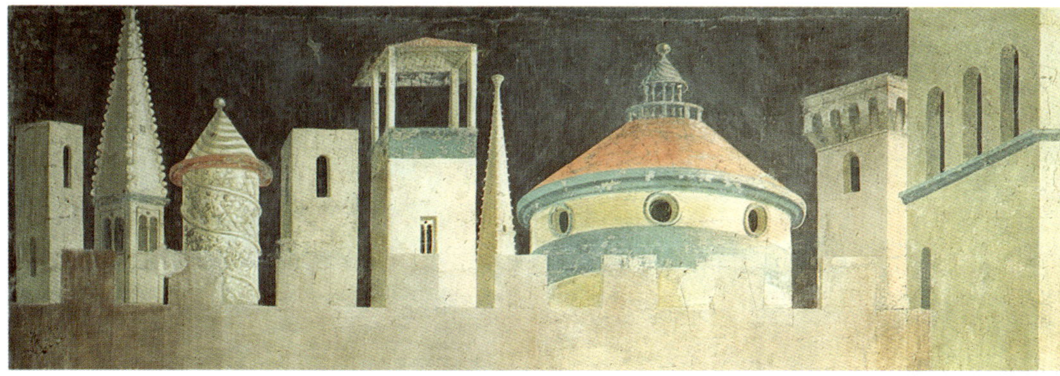

The Stoning of Saint Stephen: detail of the architecture which shows, along with Classical and Gothic echoes, an obvious reference to Brunelleschi's Old Sacristy of San Lorenzo.

small twisted columns of the building rest is smaller than the other three, which in turn rise from a square base, towards which the perspective of the flight of stairs in the foreground advances. This is a compromise between the converging perspective of the parallelepiped and that absolute perspective with no vanishing point which characterizes the elements in the circular plane.

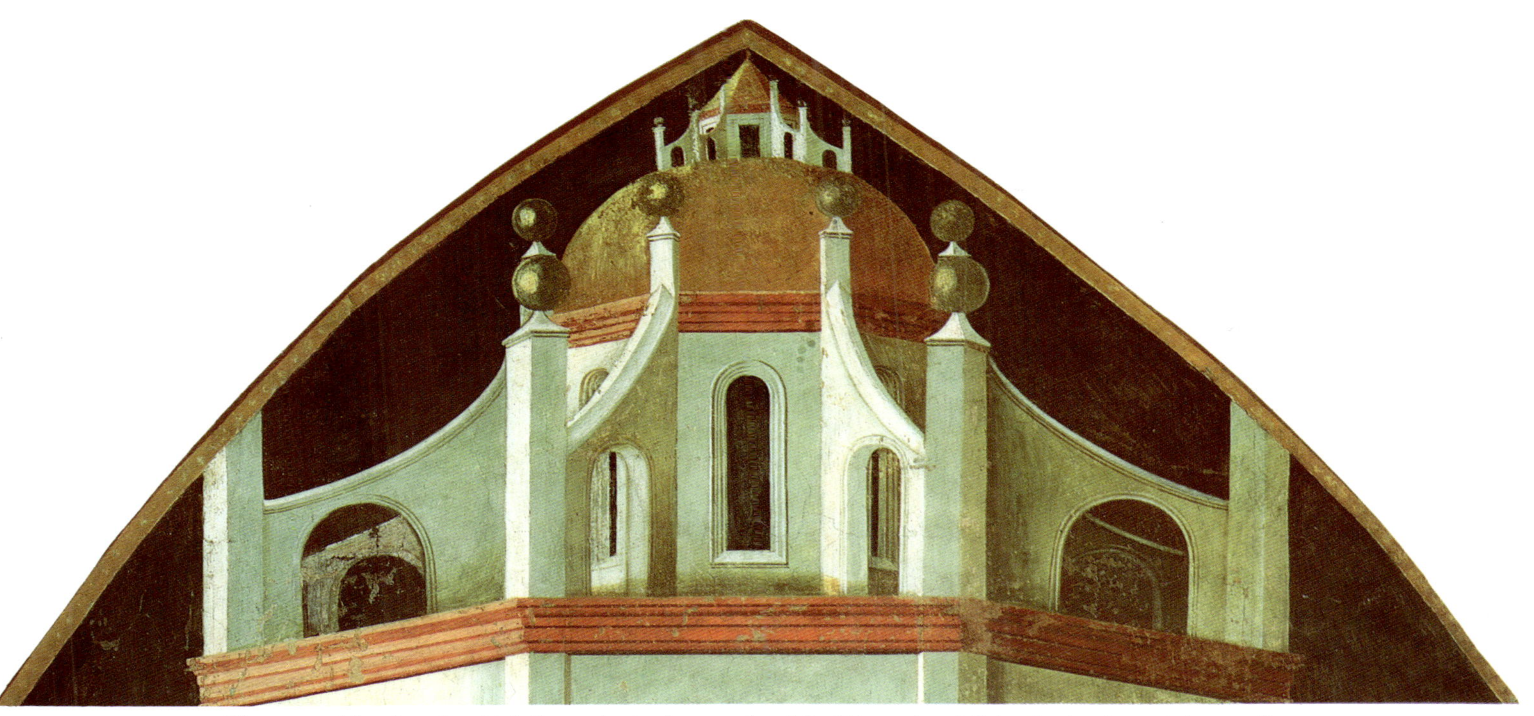

The apse of the church which forms the background to *The Disputation of Saint Stephen* is reminiscent of Santa Maria del Fiore, with accentuated Gothic flying buttresses. The design is repeated as a crown to the building, almost as if it were Uccello's contribution to the argument over the lantern (*see p. 121*).

The extraordinary circular temple in the *Presentation of the Virgin*. On the left, a strange 'modern' palace acts as a frame to a fine landscape with a fortified town in the background.

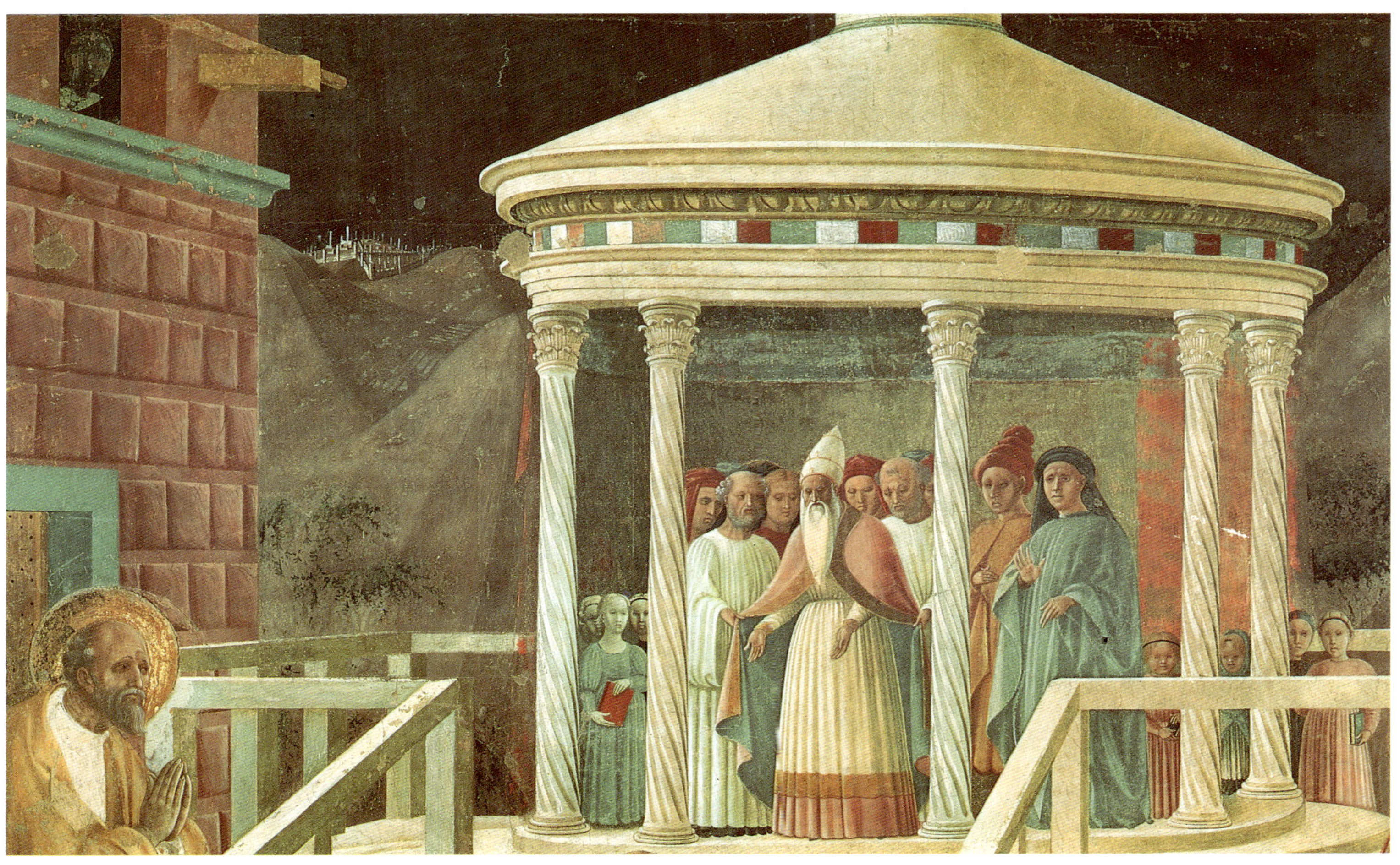

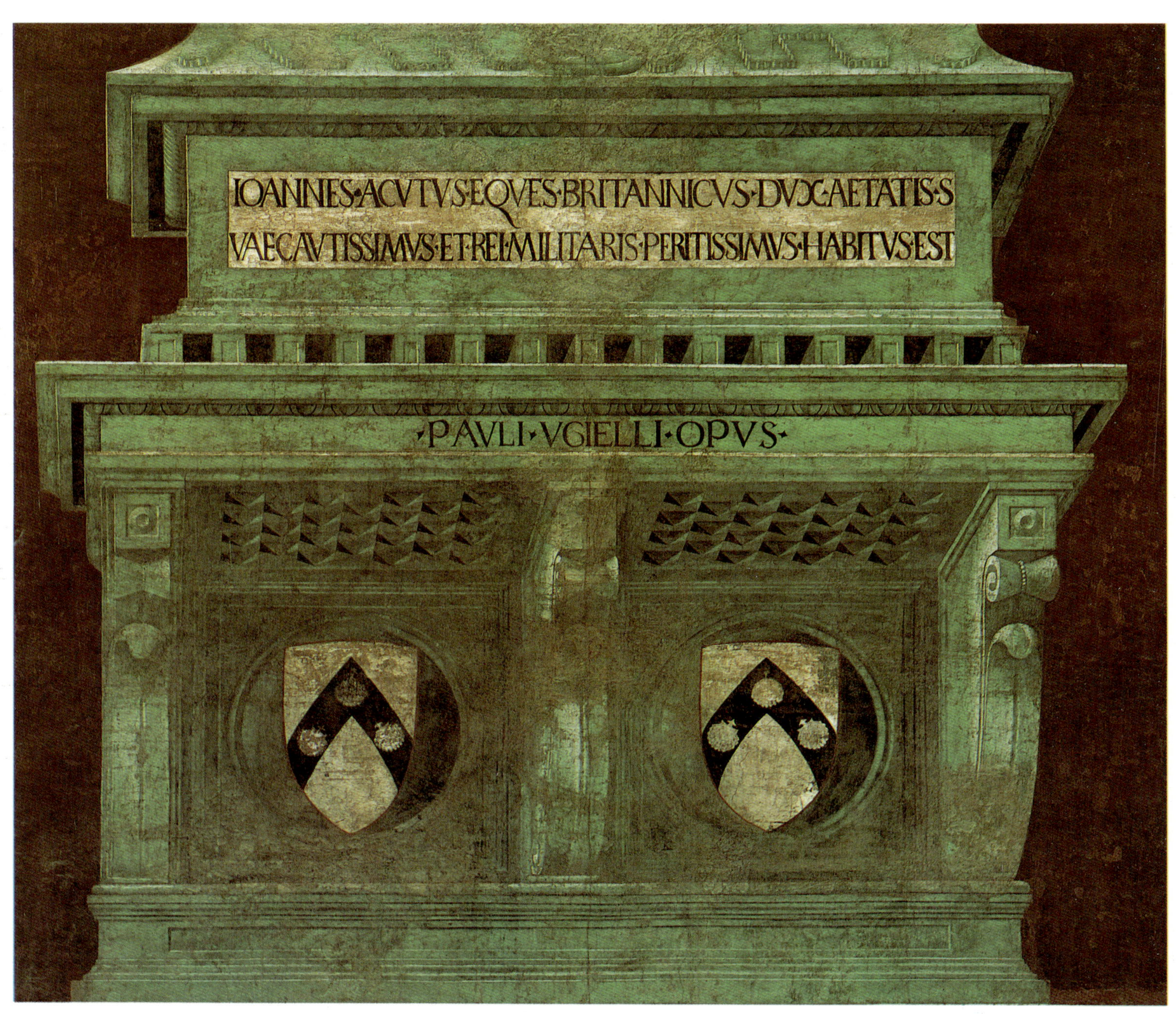

The architectural base of the *Monument to Sir John Hawkwood.*

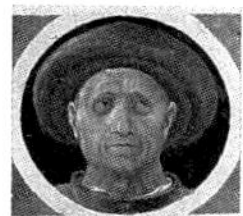

This is how Uccello conceived a classical, delicate architecture, in which he has rethought the morphological elements in his own special way. An example is the capitals and the moulding of the architrave – without any reference to the orders and canonic proportions – and above all the white, red and green polychrome frieze which almost has the intensity of majolica. It is unparalleled in Florentine architecture, even if the white-red-green of the marble is in chromatic harmony with the marquetry of the cathedral's marble ornamentation and Giotto's campanile. Uccello returned to this particular theme of the polychrome border in the *Birth of the Virgin*, where he imitated marquetry to give the illusion of a zigzag indentation, to harmonize with the Gothic fragmentation of all the elements in the painting, where a smooth border would have seemed out of place.

The architecture of the *Hawkwood* plinth, all too readily identified with Gothic because of the great stylized leaves of the consoles, is in reality Uccello's response to the new humanist language: a response based on a network of proportions using the square as a base, on the sober, firm sectioning of the moulding. The position of the decorated torus of *ovuli* just below the dripstone is interesting, a theme freely inspired by Classical architecture that we also find in the Prato *tempietto*. There is also the lettering, in Roman capitals; this is closely packed because of the number of letters, and invigorated by the thin upstrokes. The wavy tail of the letter Q is of special note: an extraordinary linking element between two rows of letters, which stretches over almost the whole of the white interspace.

Precisely because it is painted, the architecture is particularly subject to problems of representation and direction of vision: such it seems is Uccello's message. More generally (and here it is a pity not to have Ghiberti's promised treatise), he introduces an architectural conception linked to Vitruvius' *temperaturae*, a conception in which optical corrections and the relativity of vision determine perception and representation.

In Uccello's repertory of architectural forms and among his distinguishing marks is the shell-shaped niche which can be seen in the cloister at San Miniato, in *The Blessed Jacopone da Todi*, as well as in two of the six scenes of the Urbino predella, and finally in the Dublin *Madonna*. The common characteristic is a fleshy plasticity, an extension of the concentric flutes, which are closer to the artisan forms of the Quattrocento or Michelozzo than the linear subtleties of Gothic. Uccello also always arranges the shell's centre to coincide with the back of the niche, so the surrounding arch cuts the flutes at their maximum point of development, thus forming a series of indented arcatures. The shape of the flutes and their convergence reinforce the effect of depth that perspective confers on the niche.

Ill. p. 170

Ill. pp. 237, 260

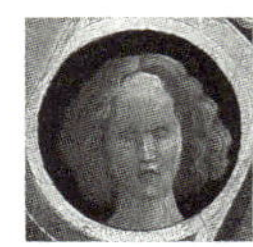

Ill. p. 262

Finally, a few words about the interiors. In the Urbino predella, the perspective box provides a real balance between ceilings and floors, the horizon line being situated in the middle. The single vanishing point remains inside the painting, whose scenes are articulated separately, using the rhythm of the double square. The ceilings are made up of close, parallel beams, forming a dense whole, with no border or decoration, in a style which is more Venetian than Florentine. Once again the floor has the chequerboard motif of black and white squares which serve to place objects and people in spatial depth with some precision: this was an essential reference to the '*costruzione legittima*' of perspective.

Architectonic notations are reduced to essentials: fireplaces, architraves, cornices surmounting simple doors with studded panels, the interior is conceived as a bare space, where elements of furniture are functional compositions and autonomous volumometers, like the bench-counter-library in the first episode. But in the second episode, Uccello introduces a light segmentation in the walls, using bands, stripes and door frames. The whole ensemble makes us look at these walls for themselves: each surface is placed in its setting with solids and empty spaces, as the essence of a form, as a group of tenuous signs.

From these few insights into salient features, we can conclude that Uccello did not forgo his personal vision in his architectural themes any more than he did his way of doing things – his *modo* – elsewhere, which always remained different from the *modo di Filippo* with which he was familiar enough to have witnessed the quarrel for his succession. His divergences on perspective can be found again in the field of

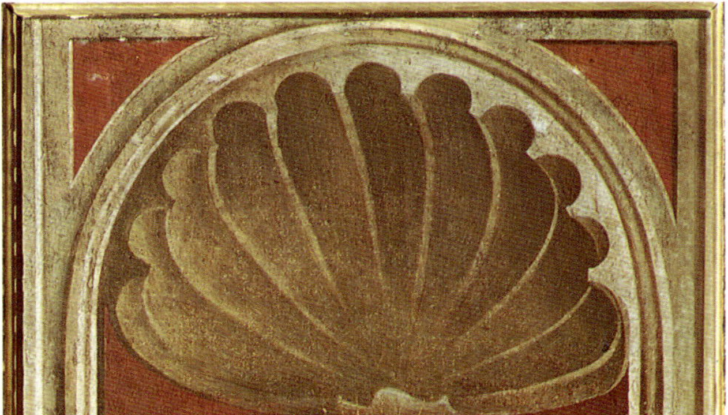

The shell niche of the *Blessed Jacopone da Todi.*

architecture where he avoided any recourse to the architectonic trademarks of Brunelleschi's teaching, but nevertheless proposed modern solutions, avoiding Gothic references, that were too marked, and traditionalism. Here, yet again, is proof of his attitude which was at once polemical and modest, and of his poetic manner. This was in clear antithesis to that 'Renaissance style' which leant so heavily on

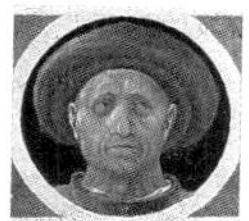

historical traditions, and in which today it is still difficult to distinguish the parallel presence of a subtler alternative humanism, that is in no way inferior to that humanism whose easy rhetoric all too speedily created the 'victorious' style.

The epitaph on the *Monument to Sir John Hawkwood.*

IOANNES·ACVTVS·EQVES·BRITANNICVS·DVX·AETATIS·S
VAE·CAVTISSIMVS·ET·REI·MILITARIS·PERITISSIMVS·HABITVS·EST

A NOTE ON THE SINOPIAS

Cat. p. 341

There is nothing in the Lippi e Macia chapel sinopias that makes them particularly different from work that was being done at the end of the Trecento, so there is little to lend support to an attribution to Uccello. With their numerous modifications, changes in iconography of the saints and spatial adjustments, they suggest 'youthful inexperience', in Procacci's view, who assigned them to Uccello's early years. The

Stemming from 'sinoper' or 'sinopia', an ochre red pigment, sinopia has come to mean a preparatory drawing, made on the second layer of fresco (*arriccio*), before the final layer (*intonaco*). It can be seen when the fresco is detached from a wall.

sinopias in the Chiostro Verde reveal an obvious qualitative leap. While it is sad that the ones for the *Stories of Noah* have been lost, we still have the *Genesis* sinopias as proof of a vigorous personality, whose efforts to perfect the delineation of the picture must have provided a model for other painters working in the cloister (who were quick to abandon this dynamic approach to space, and used the sinopias in a completely traditional manner). The *Genesis* sinopias are therefore unique. The drawing is confident, rapid and fluid, and the deployment of space becomes the predominant interest. The quality of finish is more elaborate: in the scenes of the lower part there is a marked difference between the sinopias and the more 'courtly', more traditional tone of the painting itself. The remarkable degree of finish in the sinopias of the first bay was due not only to a need to provide a model for the cycle, but also to the very nature of the technique adopted: it was not just a matter of a final layer (*intonaco*) as in a true fresco (*buon fresco*), but rather of a somewhat hybrid mural painted in tempera, with passages painted *a secco* which were probably much more significant than they now appear. Here we have a rapid, economical technique, in which the preparation has more 'finish' and the execution far less freedom, perhaps because there is a thinner covering layer.

At Prato, Uccello adopted the traditional technique of the fresco. In the basic cycle, he was more interested in exploring spatial problems and connections between figures than their linear definition. Here, there is a great freedom in the final execution when compared to the sinopia, with additions or omissions of figures on quite a large scale.

The sinopias of the *Virtues* on the vaulting focus and balance the relationship between mandorla and figures. Those of *The Disputation of Saint Stephen* show a figure kneeling at the saint's feet, an eye-catching, centre-stage witness of the efficacy of his inspired sermon. Why Uccello omitted this figure (which is reminiscent of those in the Bologna *Adoration of the Magi* was undoubtedly less to do with symmetry than the fact that the effects of the preaching were already explicit in the gestures, the 'attitudes'. This freedom of the sinopia is not particularly surprising. As he moved from the intermediate layer of fresco (*arriccio*) to the final layer (*intonaco*), Uccello used both cartoons with *spolvero* and scaled drawings on gridded paper. This process, which he *See note p. 291* clearly perfected at Prato, is borne out by the lack of precision in other sinopie in the cycle, such as those of the *Saints* on the intrados where Uccello limited himself to indicating the relationship between the figure and the niche it occupied.

A complete application of this technique can be found in the sinopia at San Martino alla Scala (now barely decipherable), where Uccello, exclusively, laid out the bifocal construction of the perspective. The figures, hut and landscape all result *Ill. p. 154*

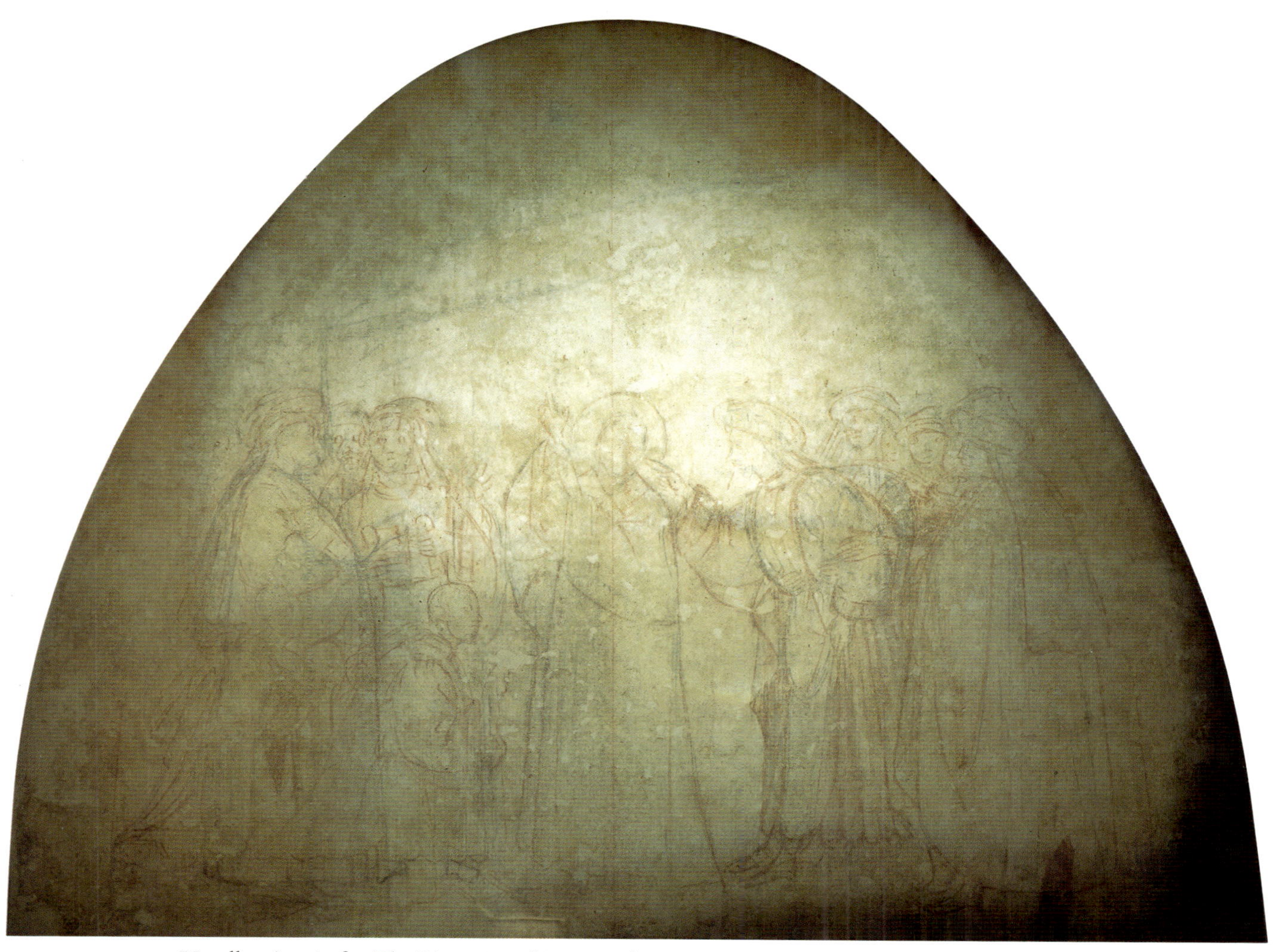

Uccello, sinopia for *The Disputation of Saint Stephen*. Prato, Museo della Pittura Murale. The final lunette (see p. 190) is very different from this sinopia, particularly in its omission of the kneeling figure.

Uccello, sinopia for the fifth scene of the *Scenes of Monastic Life*, east wall, San Miniato al Monte cloister. The sinopia determined the relationships between figures and extended space, and provided outlines for the complex perspectival construction.

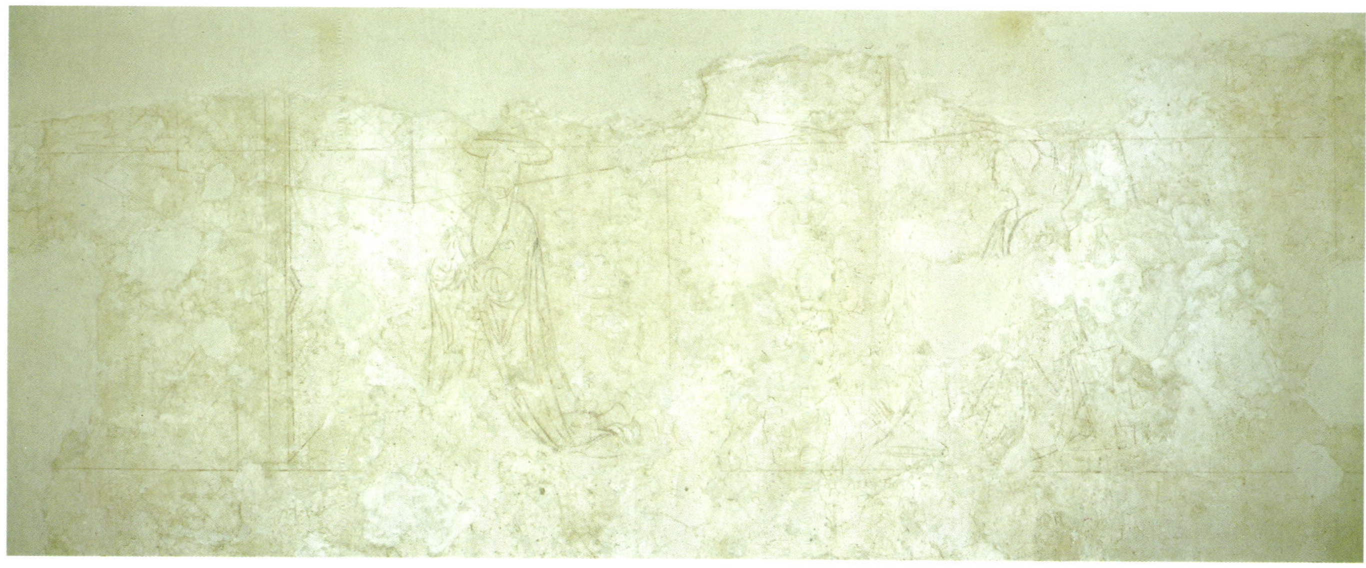

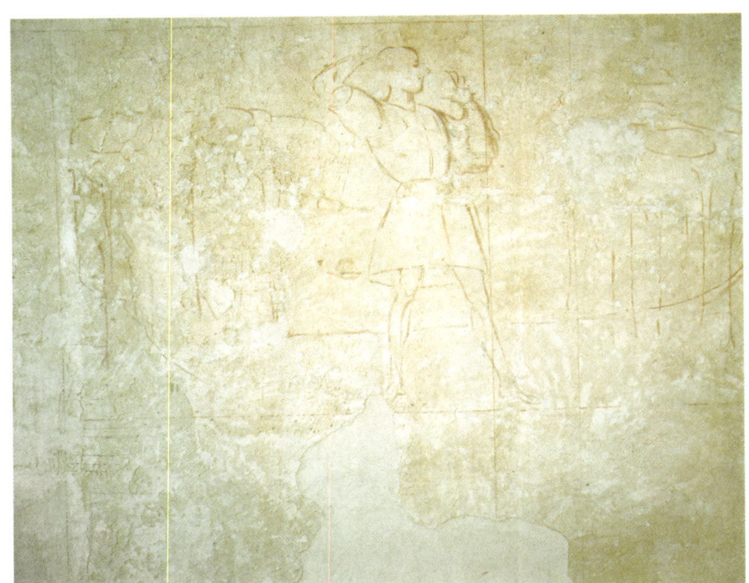
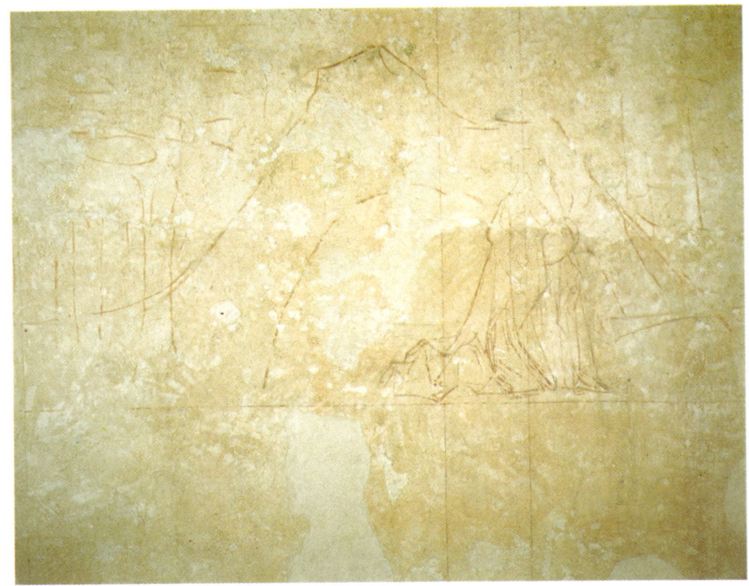

Uccello, sinopias for the first scene of the *Scenes of Monastic Life*, south wall, San Miniato al Monte cloister. On this side of the cloister the interest in depth and the complexity of the perspective are less marked, while the monumentality of the figures has increased.

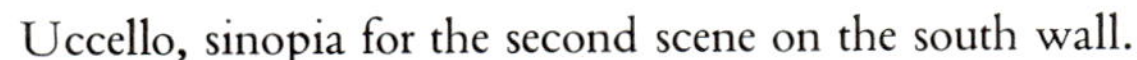
Uccello, sinopia for the second scene on the south wall.

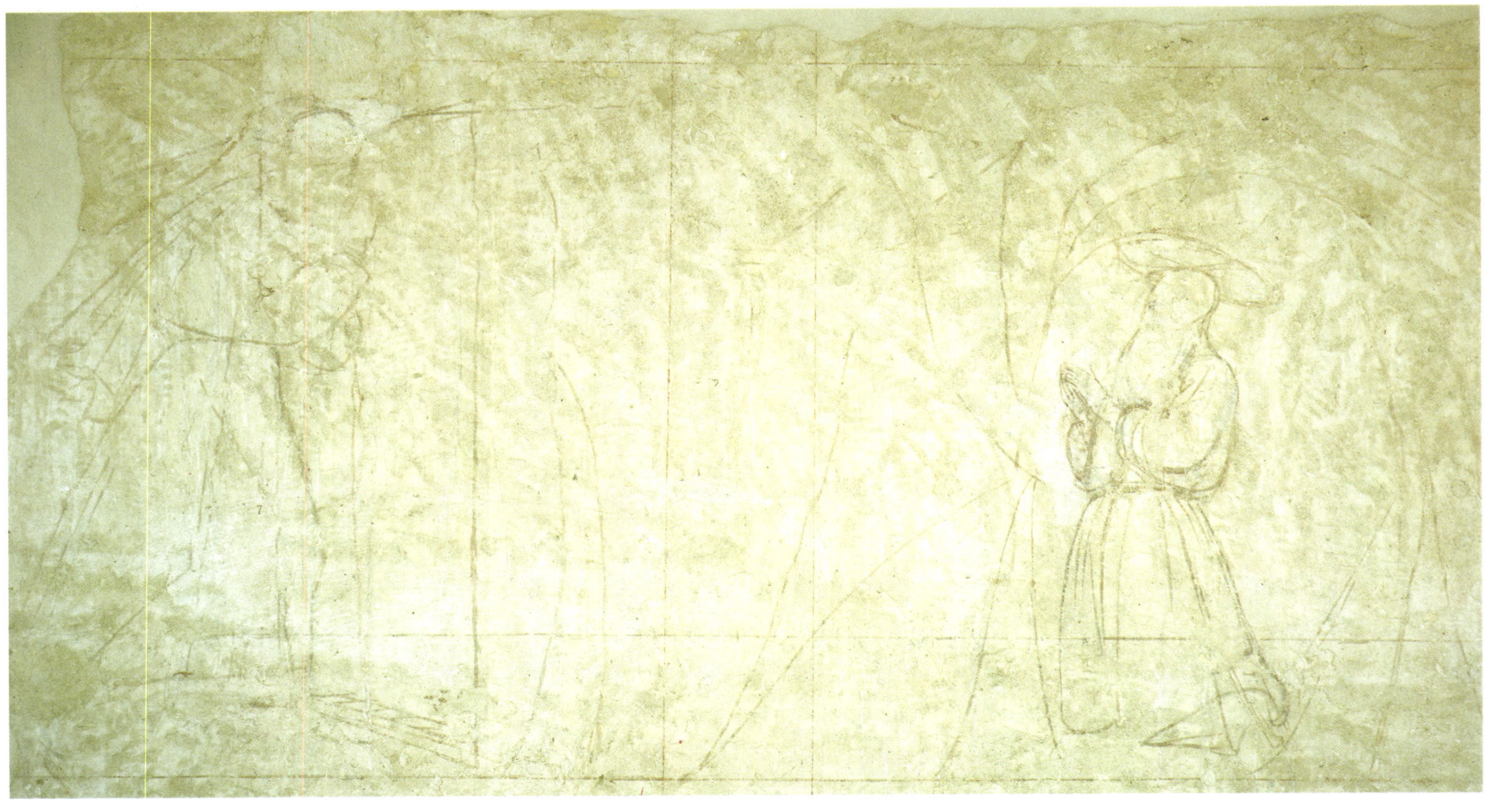

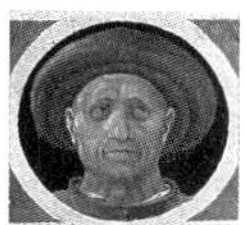

from free invention, on the perspectival framework laid down on the *arriccio*. But this is a single example and we are aware of the experimental and innovatory nature of the painting. This method would be abandoned: the Oxford *Hunt*, although painted on a panel, shows a system of perspective which has been finely engraved on the final layer, using drawings which have been perforated for *spolvero*. Here Uccello probably resorted to clay figures for his studies in perspective; in any case the work shows few modifications.

The important sinopias at San Miniato reveal a moment of reconciliation between tradition and innovation. The graphic synthesis of the sinopias has a great bearing on the decipherability of the cycle, in the fresco's present state of conservation. Had Vasari known of it, he would undoubtedly have praised the '*gran disegno*' and would have qualified his criticisms of their strange colouring. The sinopia on the east side reveals the full extent of spatial tension and the dense monumentality of the figures. The confident drawing binds together the complex perspectival constructions, the less frequent spaces and the distances indicated in minute detail. It needs only a few drawn lines to link actors and space effectively and to calibrate the less frequent 'spatial boxes': here we have a moment of complex intellectual research that was not repeated later on the south wall. Was this because he had to hurry to finish, to dwindling inspiration when he returned to the work (Vasari), or to a growing reliance on less reliable help? The space changes into rocky caverns or shadowy woods: in the first scene on the south wall the sinopia establishes the depth of spacing between the treetrunks and the foreshortening of the leafy tree tops (as in the Oxford *Hunt*). Uccello's great reliance on assistants, which can be glimpsed in the second wall, and is practically total in the sketching-out of the west wall, suggests that the elderly master was distancing himself from the cumbersome technique of fresco. Vasari had already said as much when he pointed out, albeit rather vaguely, that his first works 'were painted in fresco' and that the later 'small items' (*cose piccole*) – easel paintings, small-format works – were done with great care in his own house after he had abandoned his workshop, as his final declaration to the Cadastre would seem to confirm.

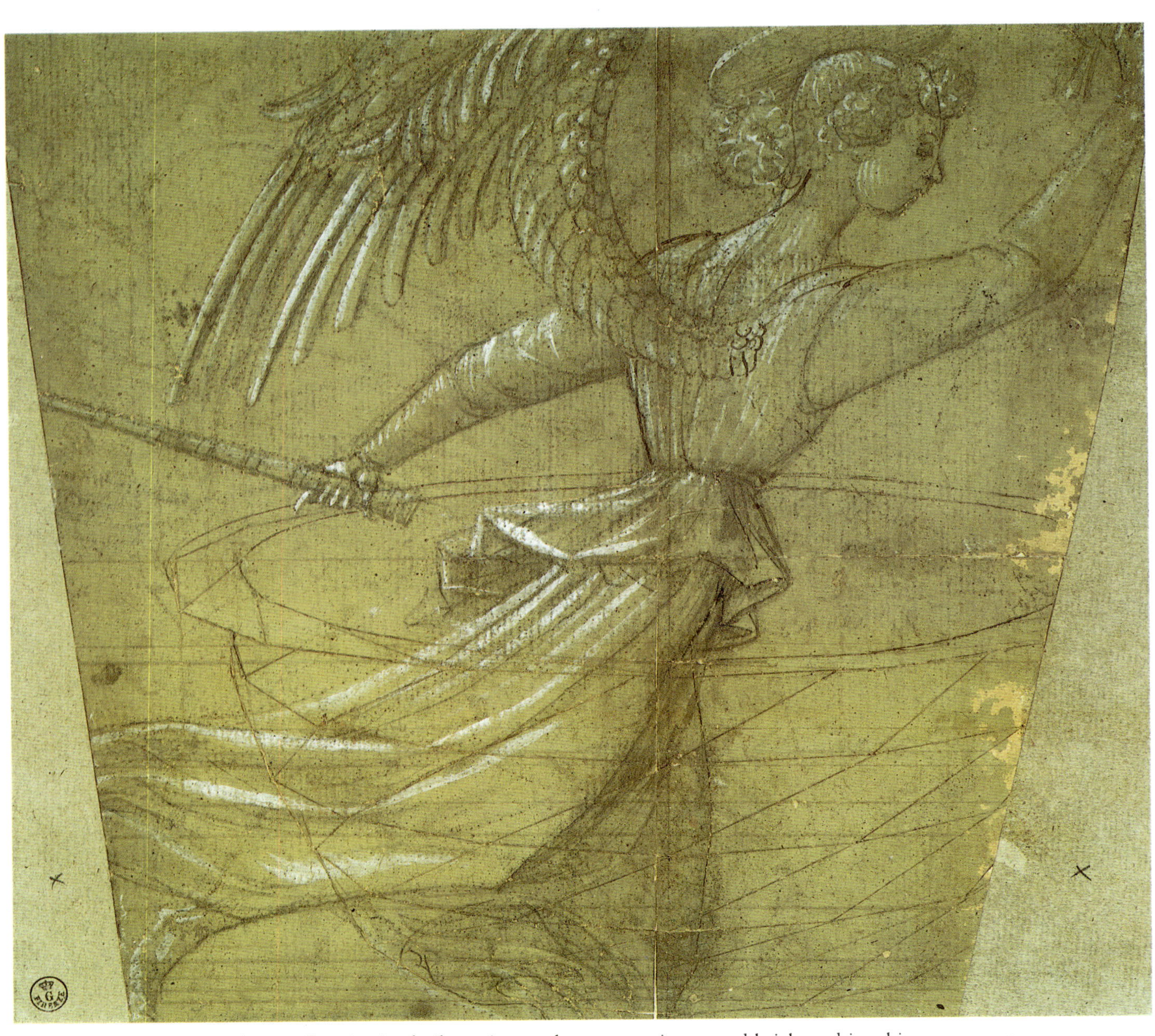

Paolo Uccello, *An Angel*, silverpoint, partly gone over in pen and heightened in white on pale yellow paper, 26 × 24 cm. Florence, Uffizi, Gabinetto dei Disegni, no. 1302. Agreement is not unanimous on the attribution of this drawing which is stylistically close to Uccello's last period. The angel, similar to those in the Urbino predella, holds an unsheathed sword – making this possibly a study for an *Expulsion*. The outlines are pierced with small holes for transfer on to the panel, using the *spolvero* technique (see note, p. 291).

Chapter Five

UCCELLO'S IMPRINT IN HIS WORKS

I THE GREAT CYCLES

THE CHIOSTRO VERDE

When Uccello embarked on the frescoes in the Chiostro Verde, he had to accept a plan that followed the iconological programme his patrons wanted. He therefore found himself with an overall layout that had been imposed by his superiors, in which each bay was divided into a lunette for the upper part – which was twice as wide as high, and which extended up to the slightly depressed vault – and a rectangle below, almost similar to a double square in its proportions (in practice this meant that the format tended towards the horizontal). The compact nature of the programme dictated that each bay be divided into four 'scenes', a formula used by Ghiberti; however, in comparison with Ghiberti's freedom of composition and elegant structure, Uccello remained anchored to a simpler, more synthetic design which had its derivations in the Trecento.

Cat. nos. 4, 23

We can see an essential characteristic of his narrative style taking shape in these paintings. Sometimes his division into scenes was dominated by a central episode which gave the whole painting its sense of unity; at other times the stories had a duality in their composition by having two focal points in the spaces shown. This in essence corresponded to the two types of perspective codified in Brunelleschi's panels: the first was centralized perspective with the concentration of space around a centre represented by a single vanishing point; the second, bifocal perspective, with two vanishing points and an angle, with a ridge separating the two diverging spaces where each of the episodes took place. The *Stories from Genesis*, painted first, belong to this second type. To help unify the bifocal composition, Uccello drew a sort of border, made up of bicolour, black and white, rectangular sections in perspective that had a single vanishing point in the centre of the lunette. This was an extension of the decorative motif painted on the ribs of the cloister (which disappeared during restoration work in the nineteenth century). A central mass of rock acted as a spur separating the two stories. These were developed inside a space which was not in the picture plane but rather within a sphere of which the lunette was the outside surface,

Ill. p. 151

Facing page, above: detail of *The Creation of the Animals*; *below:* detail of *The Fall.*

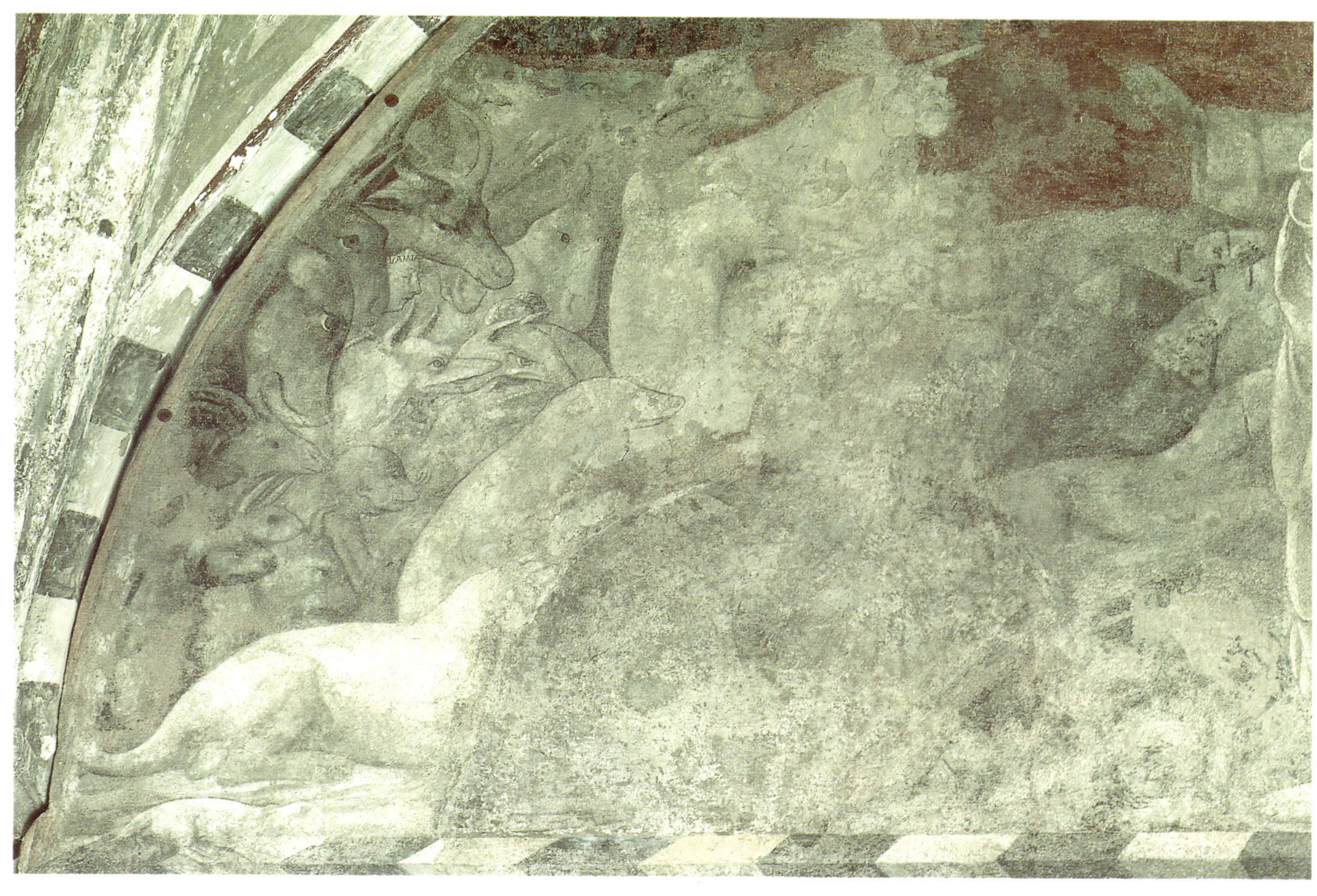

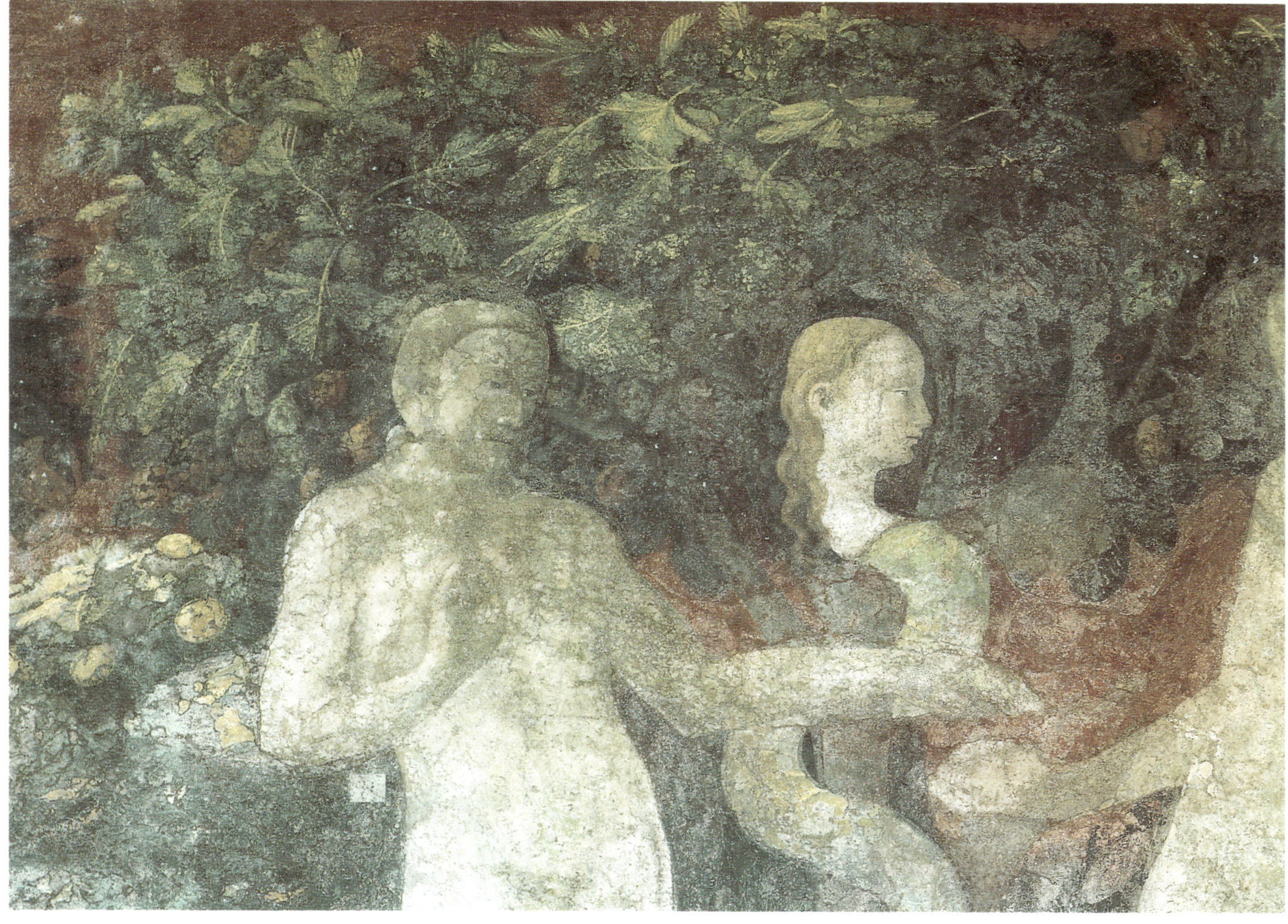

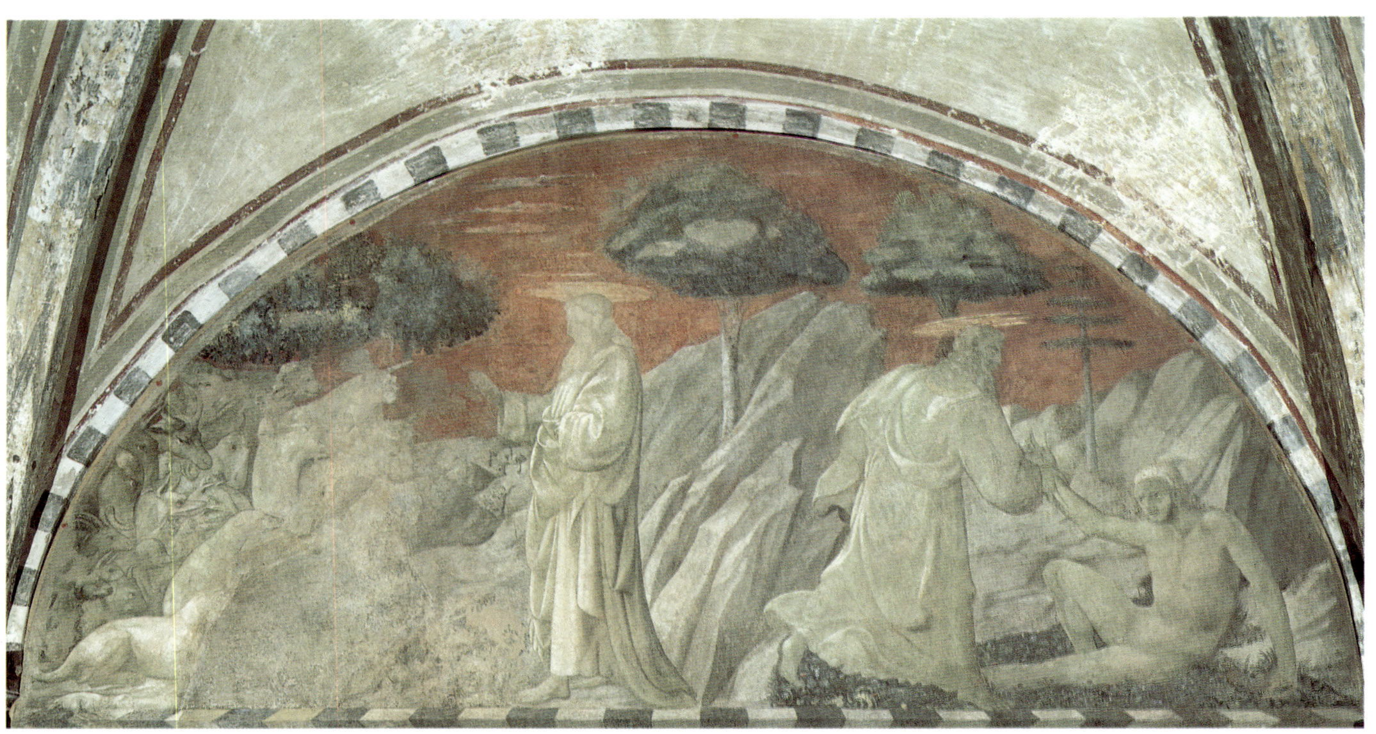

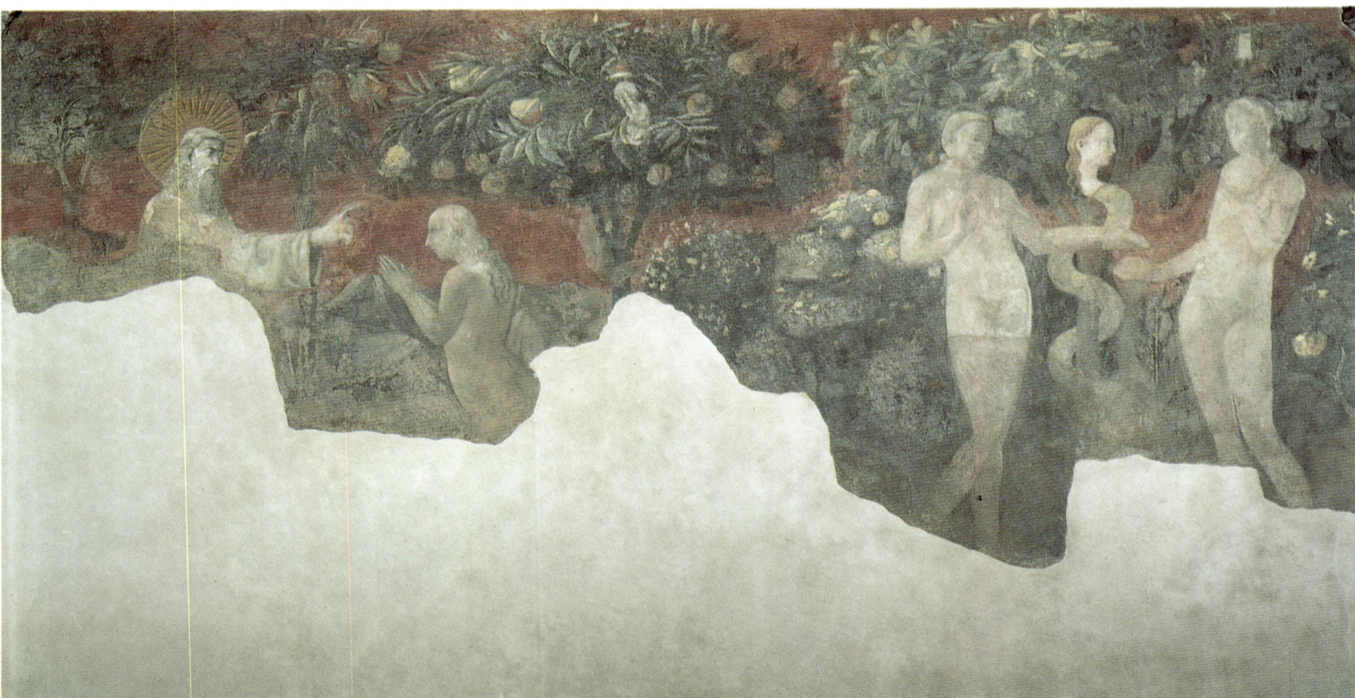

Uccello, *Stories from Genesis. Above: Creation of the Animals and Creation of Adam; below: Creation of Eve and Fall*, *c.* 1424–5, mural in tempera transferred to canvas, upper part 210 × 452 cm, lower part 244 × 478 cm. Florence, Santa Maria Novella, Chiostro Verde.

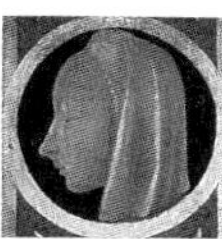

with the painting like a 'skin', the picture mysteriously unfolding as though inside a kind of crystal ball. We can see an obvious – if embryonic – preoccupation with optics and perspective within the narrative layout, which mixed traditional and modern (Ghiberti, Masolino). In the later *Stories of Noah*, a more organic consciousness of space and perspective renders the unifying role of the border between the two superimposed registers completely superfluous: here the upper part of the bicoloured border of the lunette is rotated towards the spectator, almost like an optical game with one of the cloister's architectonic elements.

The noble colour of terre-verte was intended to imitate bronze high relief (and, therefore, indirectly remind the viewer of the authority of Antiquity). However, there are subtle but precise chromatic nuances that distinguish the more luxuriant greens of the trees from those earthier ones for rock, and the statue-coloured greens of the figures whose vigorous relief derives from sculpture (almost in anticipation of Donatello). In the sky, which is treated in a complementary clay-like colour, we can see a naturalistic element of wind-driven clouds, which in their graduated planes belong completely to Renaissance perspective. Masolino had already experimented with this innovation and seems to have invented it – indeed, the first two bays of the Chiostro Verde reveal a deferential attentiveness to his work. The lower scenes in the first bay, the *Creation of Eve* and *Fall* are also conceived dualistically (within the unity of the wall's rectangular field), but with the unifying background of the garden, which forms a kind of decorative ground, almost a tapestry, without any particular accentuation of perspective. Throughout this work, there is a striking experimentation with colour, as much in the 'Pompeian' colour of the cloudless sky against which the trees stand like cut-outs, as in the differentiation of the clouds. The range of colour extends from the pale yellow of the serpent-*lamìa*'s hair to the luxuriant reds and pinks of the fruit on the trees; the terre-verte's austerity is softened by a subtle chromatism which is more effective in its discreet use than dazzling colours would have been. Through this abundance of colour Uccello complies with the need to imitate nature (Ghiberti: 'Stories from the Old Testament, in which I have forced myself, by every means, to observe and imitate nature to my best ability', *Commentario Secondo*).[139]

istorie del testamento vecchio, nelle quale mi ingegnai con ogni misura osservare in esse cercare imitare la natura quanto a me fosse possibile

There is another element which has a bearing on Uccello's sense of space: in the upper lunette, God the Father's halo is like a plate seen in perspective, and it has an intense metallic luminosity: this is a sort of Albertian 'definition' of space that is not visible elsewhere in the rest of the cloister paintings, and it has a disconcerting novelty. The rendering of the figures is founded on a kind of individual experimentation, with each case being treated separately: while the picture of Adam seated is inspired by Ghiberti's version of Classical art. God the Father, who is giving him the gift of life,

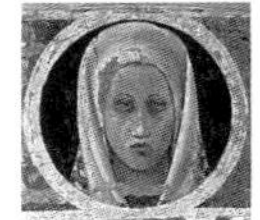

has such a dynamic quality that he almost becomes a structural element of space. In the *Creation of the Animals*, the draped clothes of the figure on the left have a calm, majestic Gothic rhythm, and the bestiary wavers between naturalistic touches of an almost ironic tenderness and references to medieval iconography. In the left-hand corner, the chameleon, painted with a realism that draws the perspectival border into the painting, is walking on black and white paving-stones in a bizarre *trompe-l'oeil*: this is a detail that reveals the artist's anti-conformity and is like a signature. Similarly, in the *Fall* Uccello wavers between forms derived from Classical art and naturalistic touches, particularly in the image of the serpent, as if evil belonged to the real world and Classicism practised a kind of protective exorcism through the dignity of its forms.

The fourth panel is again divided into four scenes: the *Flood* and *Retreat of the Waters* in the lunette, and *Noah's Sacrifice* and the *Drunkenness of Noah* below. But here the division is masked by a great rigour in the perspective construction and composition which play on a calculated ambiguity: the two scenes in the lunette seem to be only one, with the perspective lost in the tumultuous waves in the distance, but each of these scenes has its own distinct vanishing point determined by each of the two opposite sides of the Ark. The strictness of its construction, its chromatic richness, its optico-perspectival finesse, its spaciousness, its great descriptive inspiration all distinguish this fourth bay very precisely from the Gothic of the *Stories from Genesis*. It seems that it was deliberately intended to emphasize the individuality of the inner parts of this great cycle, to which it nevertheless belongs.

This was a deliberate choice on the part of the patrons, probably made after an interlude or a postponement in the enterprise. Indeed, Eugenius IV's prolonged stay at Santa Maria Novella, and particularly the presence of numerous fathers assembled there for the council of 1439, forced work to come to a halt: the convent premises had to be made accessible and the cloister cleared of scaffolding. So it was in the post-reconciliation climate, with its renewed interest in patrology, that this biblical episode was created and given a particular prominence, as a sort of extrapolation from the thematic sequence that had originally been planned. The interpretation of the Ark as a prefiguration of the Church, a building by God on Earth destined to save mankind (and whose dimensions and proportions were directly inspired by divine wisdom) could already be found in Origen and Tertullian, and was supported by Saint Augustine (*Civitas Dei*, XV, I and XXVI: the Ark as a representation of God's City), Philo of Alexandria (in *Genesi Quaestiones*, II, 5: the Ark as a prefiguration of the Cross), and Saint Ambrose (*De Noe et arca*, IV, VI, VII and VIII: the Ark as a prefiguration of the body of Christ from which it took its proportions). Although we

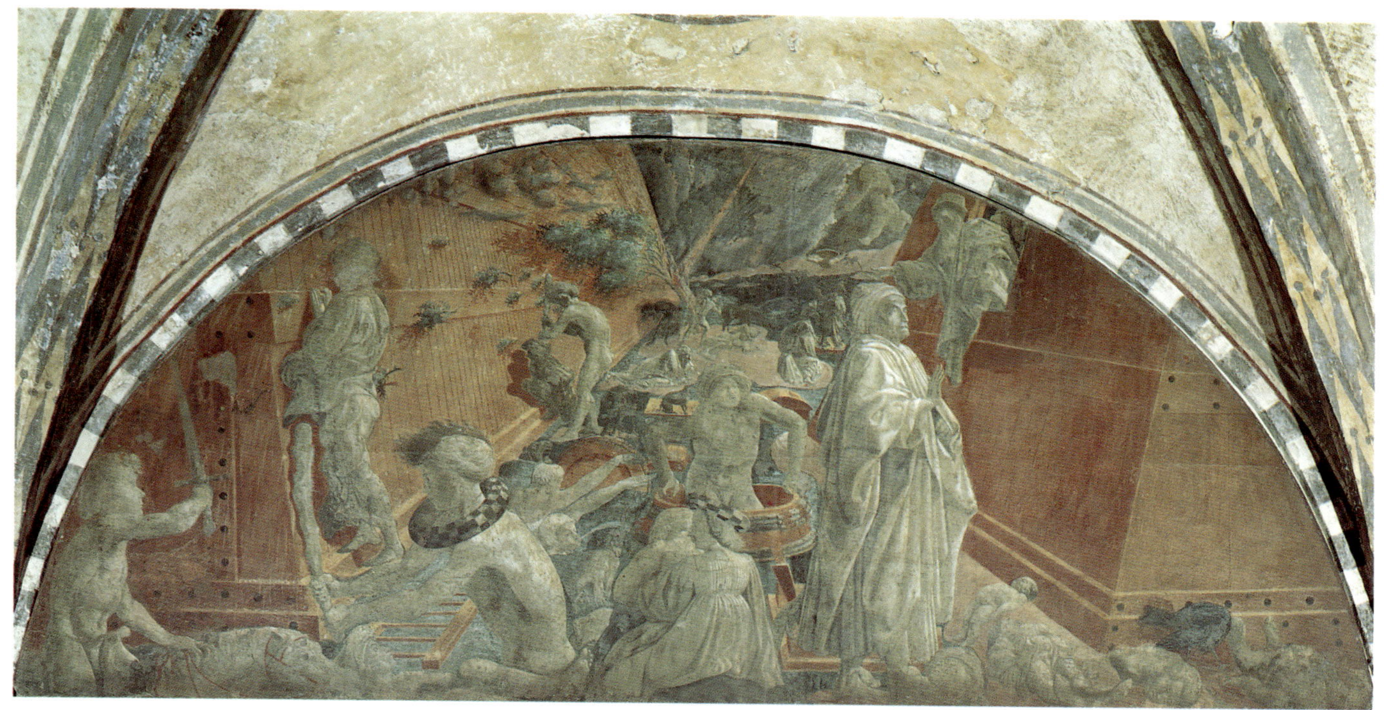

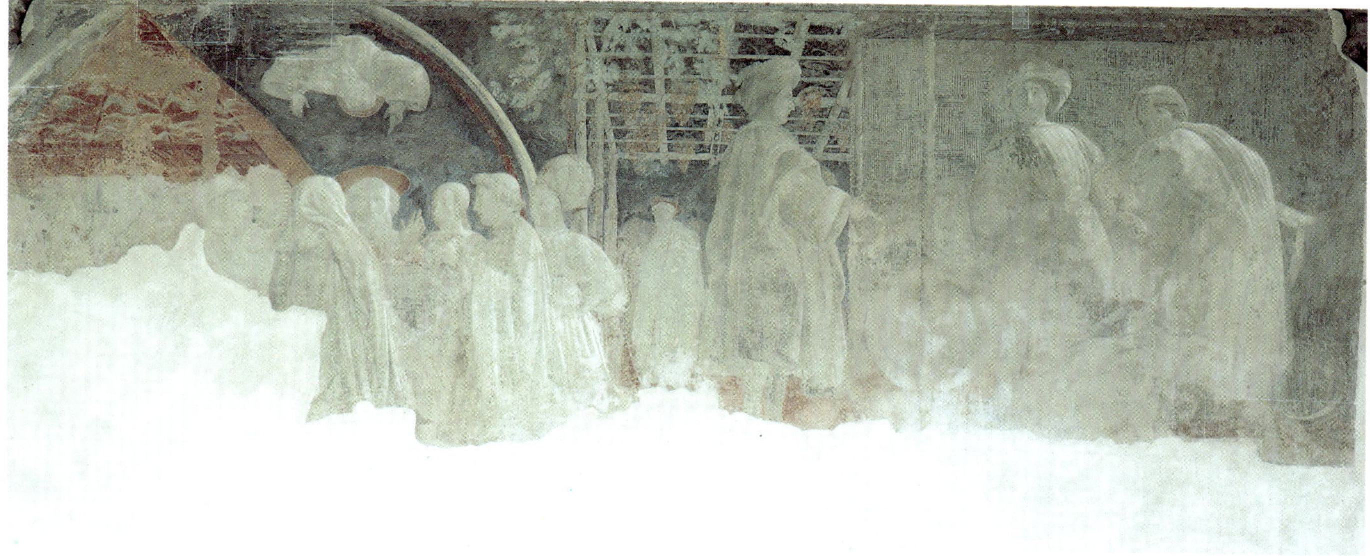

Uccello, *Stories of Noah. Above: The Flood and the Retreat of the Waters; below: Noah's Sacrifice and the Drunkenness of Noah, c.* 1447, mural in tempera transferred to canvas, upper part 215 × 510 cm., lower part 277 × 540 cm. Florence, Santa Maria Novella, Chiostro Verde.

Following pages: Stormy landscape and the Ark, details from *The Flood*.

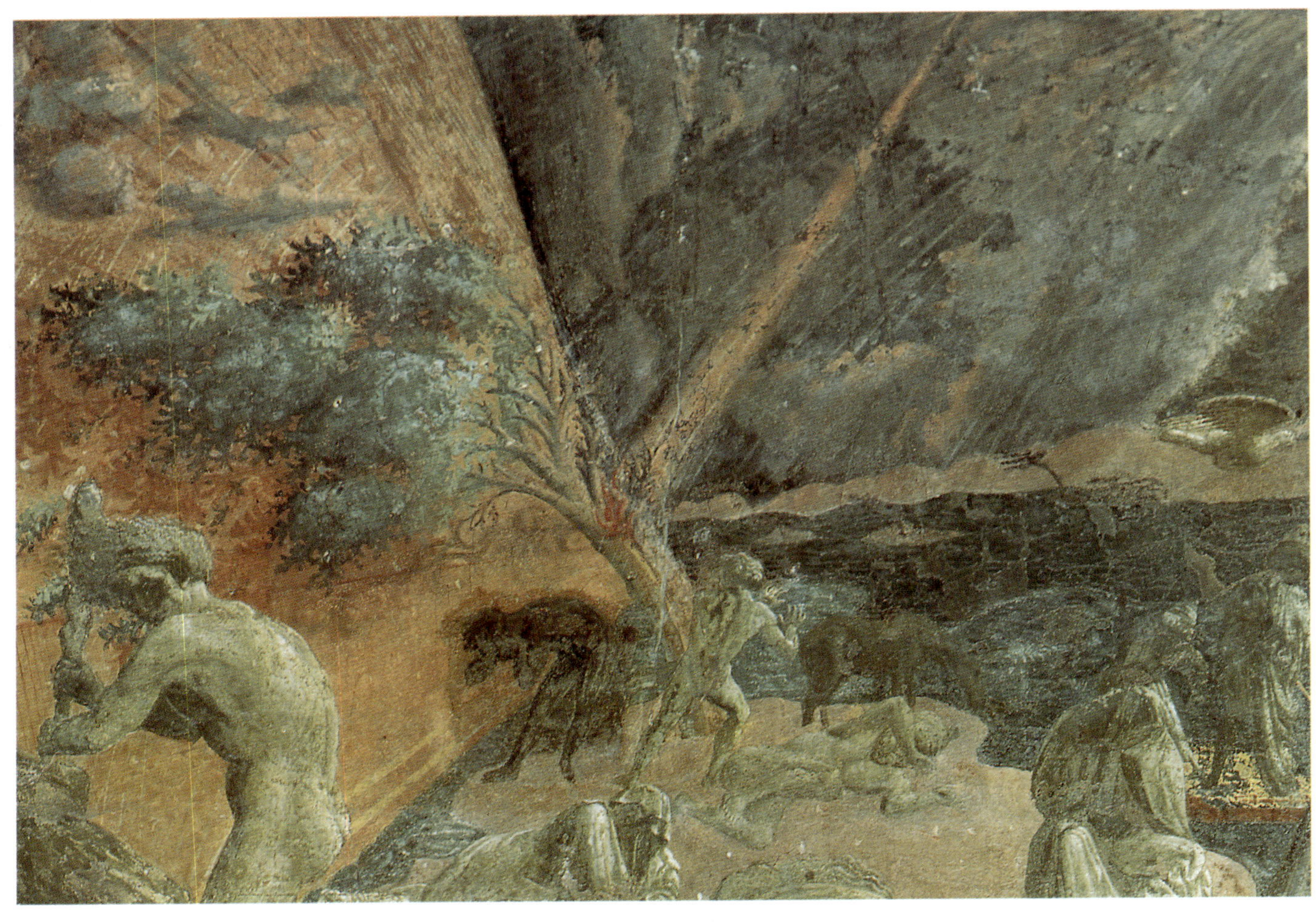

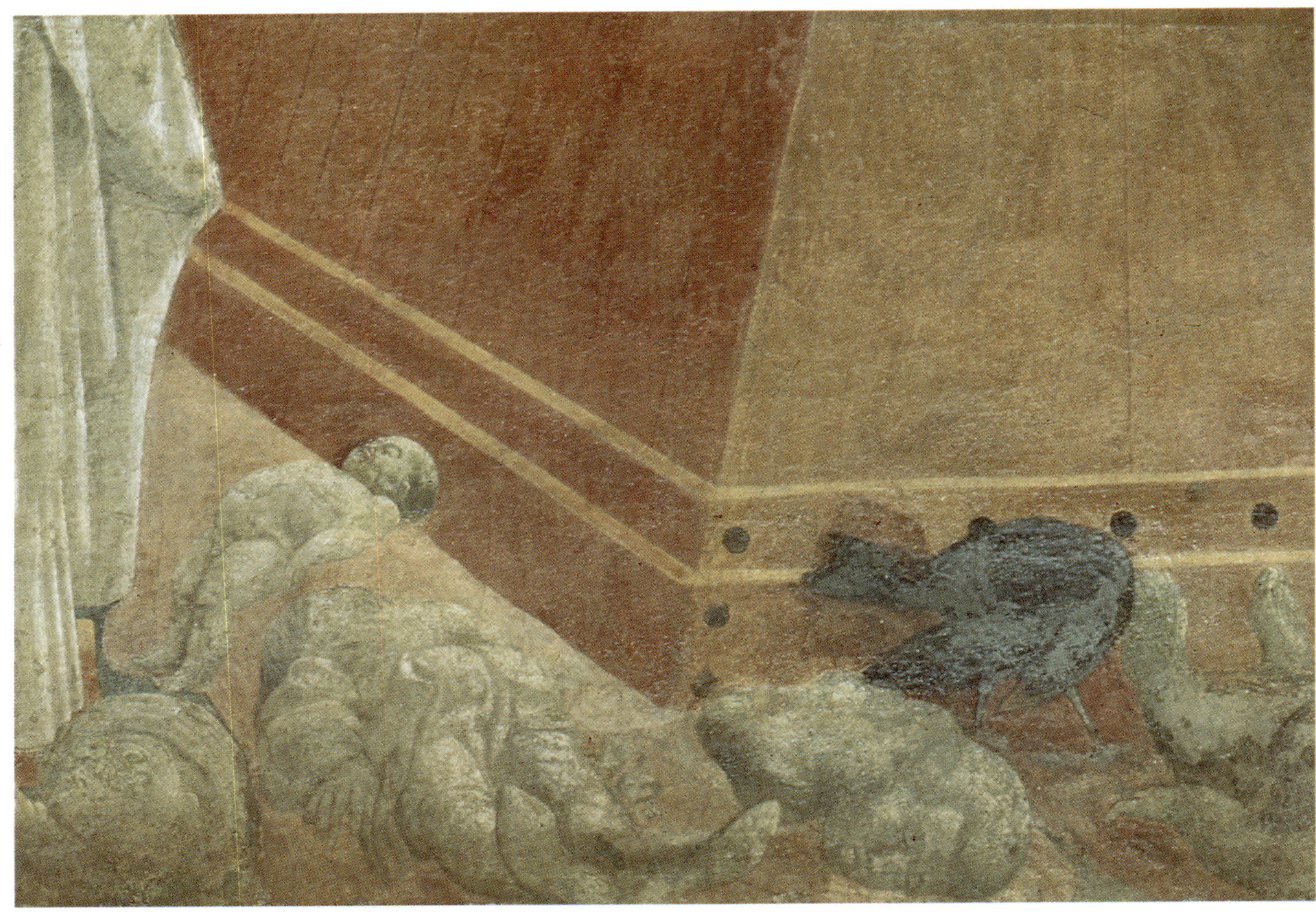

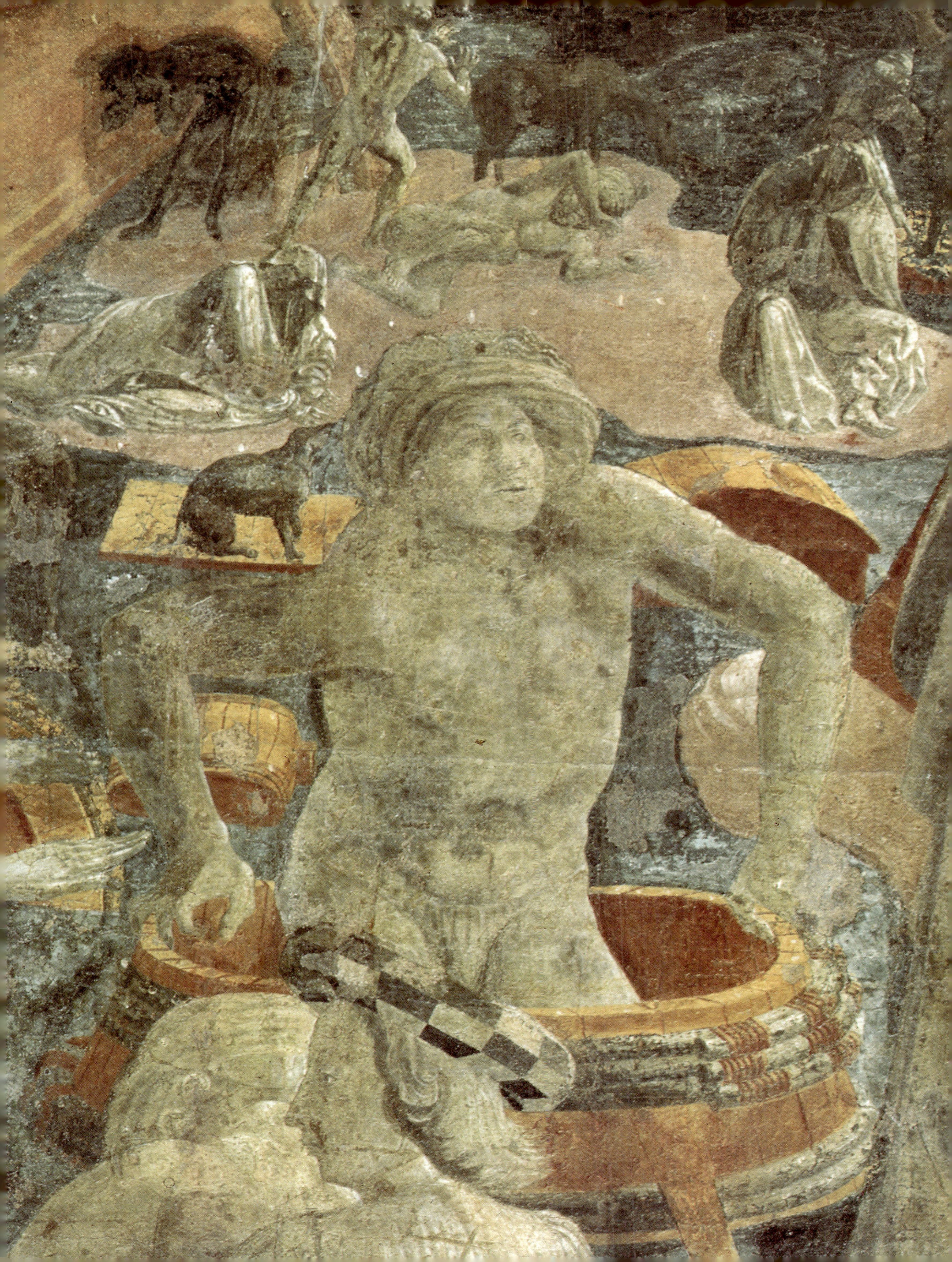

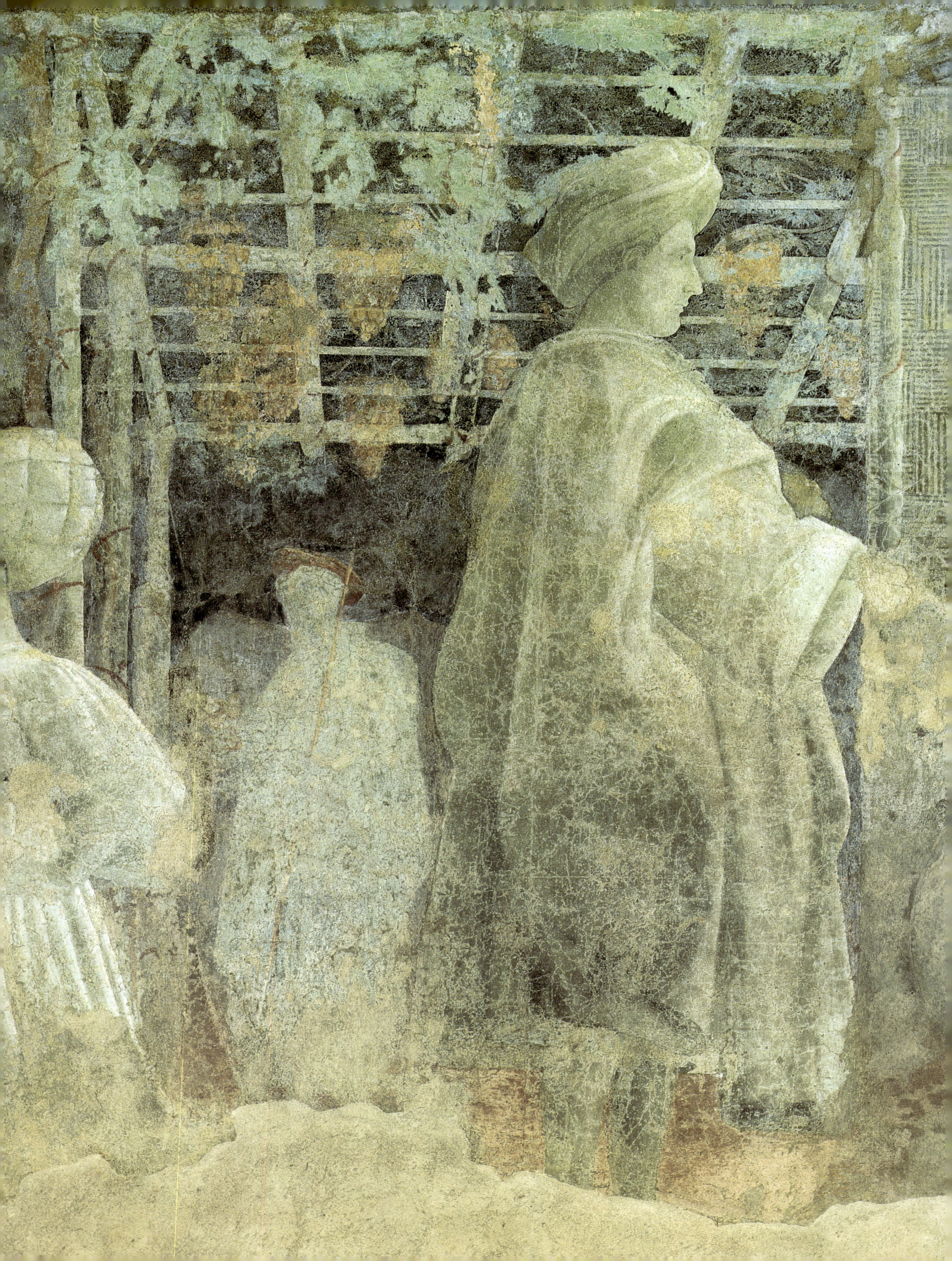

do not know who the patron was, we think the work was inspired by a learned expert in patrology (possibly the Camaldolite Traversari) using this fourth bay to demonstrate his beliefs. On the other side of the wall, inside the church, was *See p. 144* Masaccio's *Trinity*, while in the passage leading from the Chiostro Verde to the Great Cloister could be seen *The Crucifixion with Saint Dominic and Saint Thomas Aquinas*, a fresco Vasari attributed to Stefano Fiorentino. It could be that they had wanted to establish a privileged position in the convent layout for these three 'manifestos' of the complex Dominican theory of salvation, by placing them in a triangle, or *tau* (allusions to the Trinity and Christology). Seen this way, even if the interpretation remains difficult, the charismatic figure of the man standing on the waters, with his gesture of benediction and his gaze fixed on the far distance, out of range (metaphorically out of time), uninvolved in the drama unfolding close at hand, obviously assumes an important function. He is not Noah; he has perhaps a few of Pope Eugenius IV's features, but is not a portrait of him; it could in the ecstasy of his vision be Saint Augustine, like Rembrandt's *Doctor Faustus*.

His presence serves to emphasize the exceptional nature of the scene depicted, as if to invite us to meditate on its profound implications. It is significant that, for a painting of such complexity and importance, Uccello was chosen rather than one of those unknown 'minor masters', those docile interpreters of Gothic's final hours who were at work on the rest of the cycle. His earlier participation had undoubtedly not been forgotten, when his preoccupation with perspective and his curiosity for things optic had seemed uselessly to slow down an enterprise which had already been waiting since 1348. In spite of the uncertainties of attribution and dating, it is nonetheless impossible not to see the exceptional character of the *Stories of Noah* and how different they are from the *Stories from Genesis*.

Facing page: detail from *The Drunkenness of Noah*, with the famous trellis.

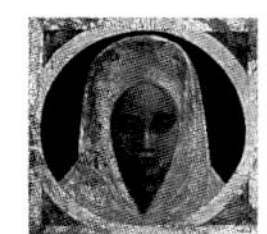

PRATO CATHEDRAL

All the frescoes in Prato cathedral are dominated by a centralized perspective construction, even though the perspective of the *Birth of the Virgin* and the *Presentation of the Virgin* is articulated on a lateral and not centralized vanishing point situated beyond the edge of the picture. In both cases, in order to give the space balance, Uccello has used figures emerging from the wings (the women on the right in the *Birth of the Virgin* are particularly monumental, and have a totally Gothic elegance); these are almost lifesize and are shown in orthogonal projection, in profile, as though they do not belong to the spatiality of the story but rather form a static anchorage for the lateral perspective's diminishing vista. A balanced spatial layout can also be seen in *The Disputation of Saint Stephen*, in the ogival lunette placed very high up for the viewer, with a rigorous symmetry in the architecture and positioning of the figures; while in *The Stoning of Saint Stephen* (only the background architecture and landscape are attributable to Uccello) we can already glimpse the beginnings of a balanced composition, with the great gateway to the city as a central point. There is a corresponding chromatic richness to this richness of construction: the stories are articulated with a liveliness of colour which also extends to the architecture. There are allusions to unexpected or impossible materials, such as green cornices – inspired perhaps by the serpentine that can be found in Florentine medieval architecture in Prato – curiously combined with Gothico-Renaissance ashlar-work on the building on the left in the *Presentation of the Virgin*; or again, the polychrome border of the temple, the intense colour of the *maforion* around the Virgin's head that recurs in the material curtaining off the area behind the colonnade, an iconographical allusion to the relationship of Temple/Church/Virgin – or yet again the intense red of the marble on the cornices of the temple gallery, which might be Tuscan marbles from Amiata and Collemandina used to reface Santa Maria del Fiore and used here in a free interpretation of reality and local tradition.

Cat. no. 10

In this way the architecture harmonizes with the colours of the figures and their clothing. It mingles echoes of the past with contemporary themes: the church in *The Disputation of Saint Stephen*, though on a completely different scale, has similarities to Santa Maria del Fiore's octagonal drum (perhaps in a version that was closer to Ghiberti's interpretation) and combines Quattrocento semi-circular arches with Gothic flying buttresses, while the pinnacles are capped with noble *Vasenkunst* in gilded bronze. We can see borrowings from Florence in the city in *The Stoning of Saint Stephen*: there is the Bargello tower, the bishop's palace of San Miniato al Monte, the Old Sacristy of San Lorenzo with its lantern's twisted cone, the Badia's campanile studded with Gothic ornaments like flowers. There are Classical themes such as the spiral column which finishes in a sort of red *mazzocchio* and cone crowned by a ball,

Ill. p. 167

Ill. p. 166

Facing page: details of the borders of the frescoes in Prato cathedral.

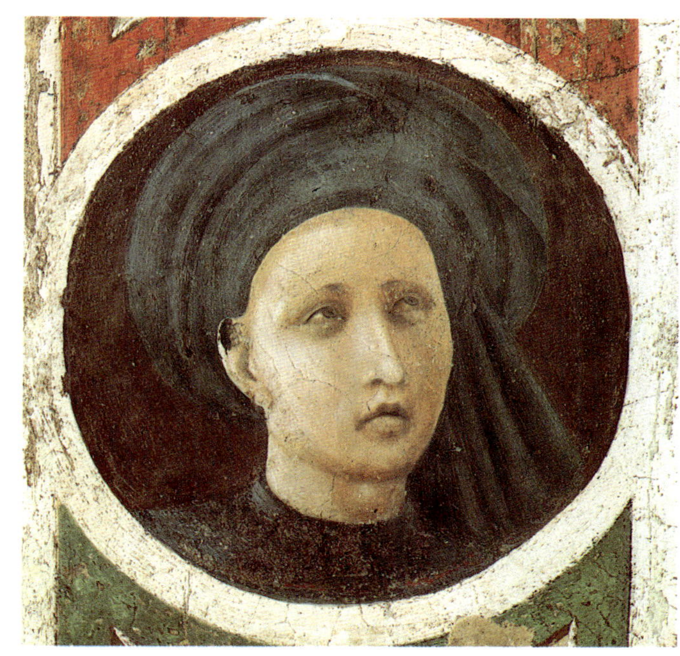

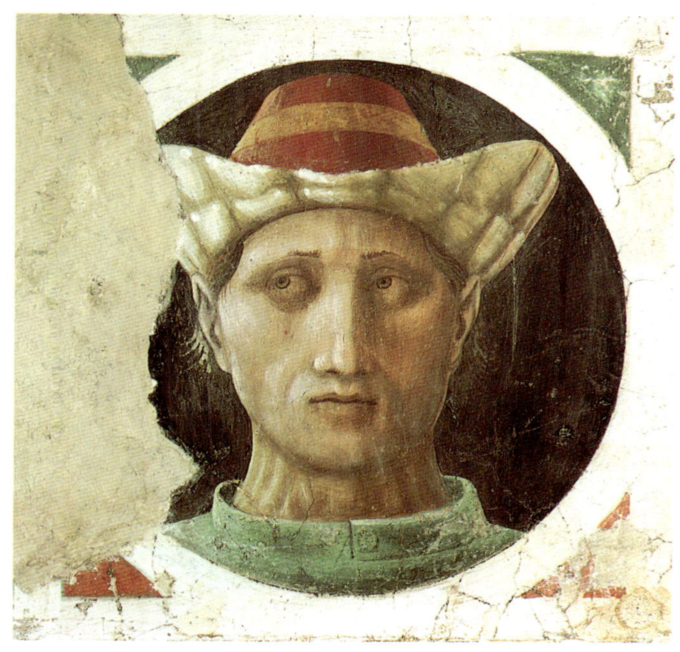

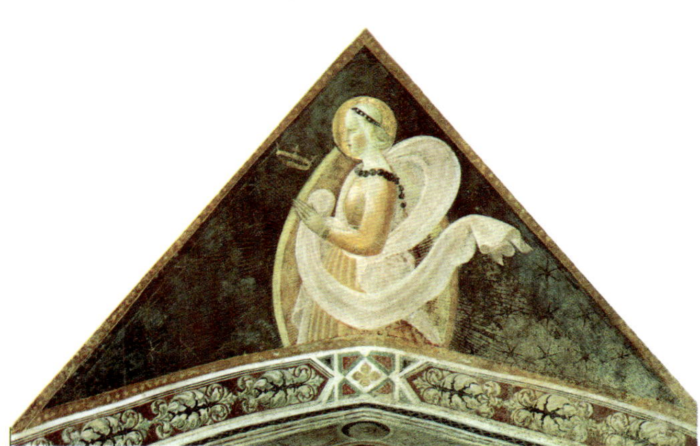

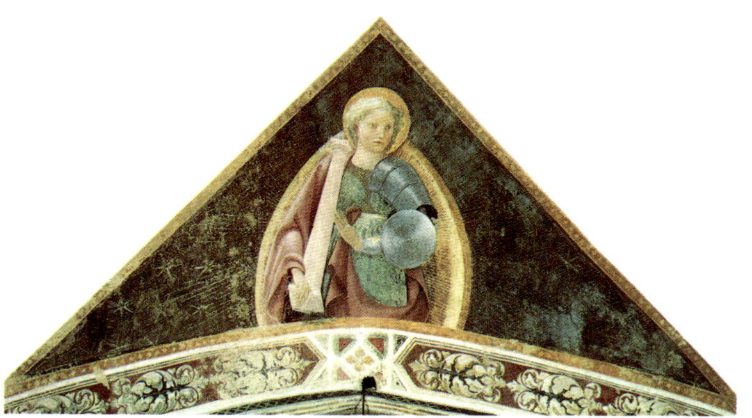

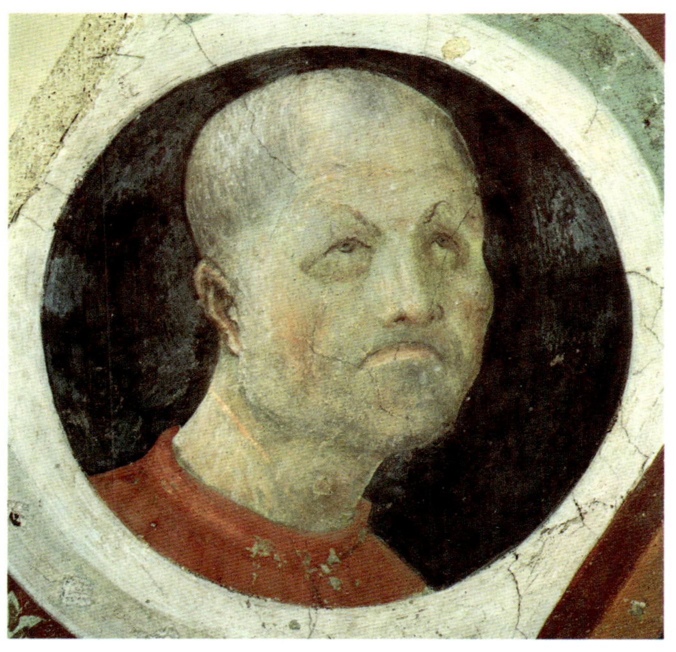

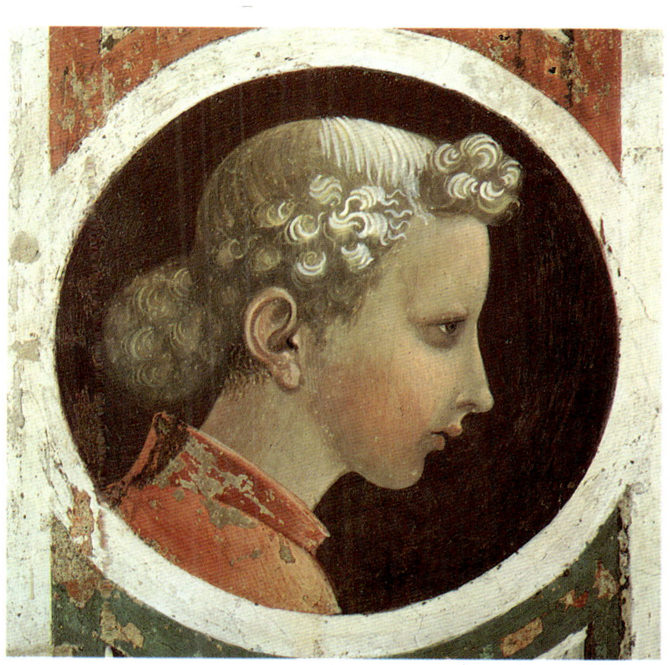

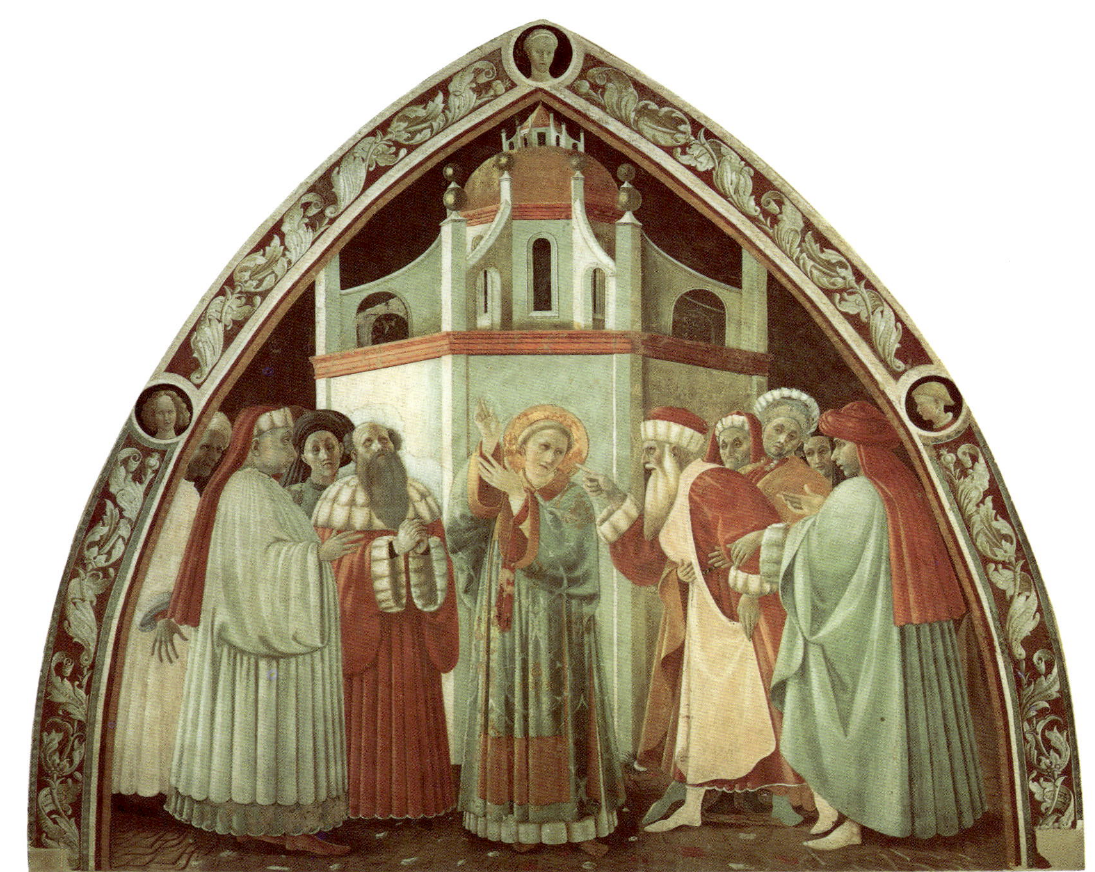

Frescoes in Prato cathedral, Assunta chapel, *c.* 1434–5.

The Disputation of Saint Stephen, 300 × 360 cm. This work is remarkable for the variety of expressions in the figures.

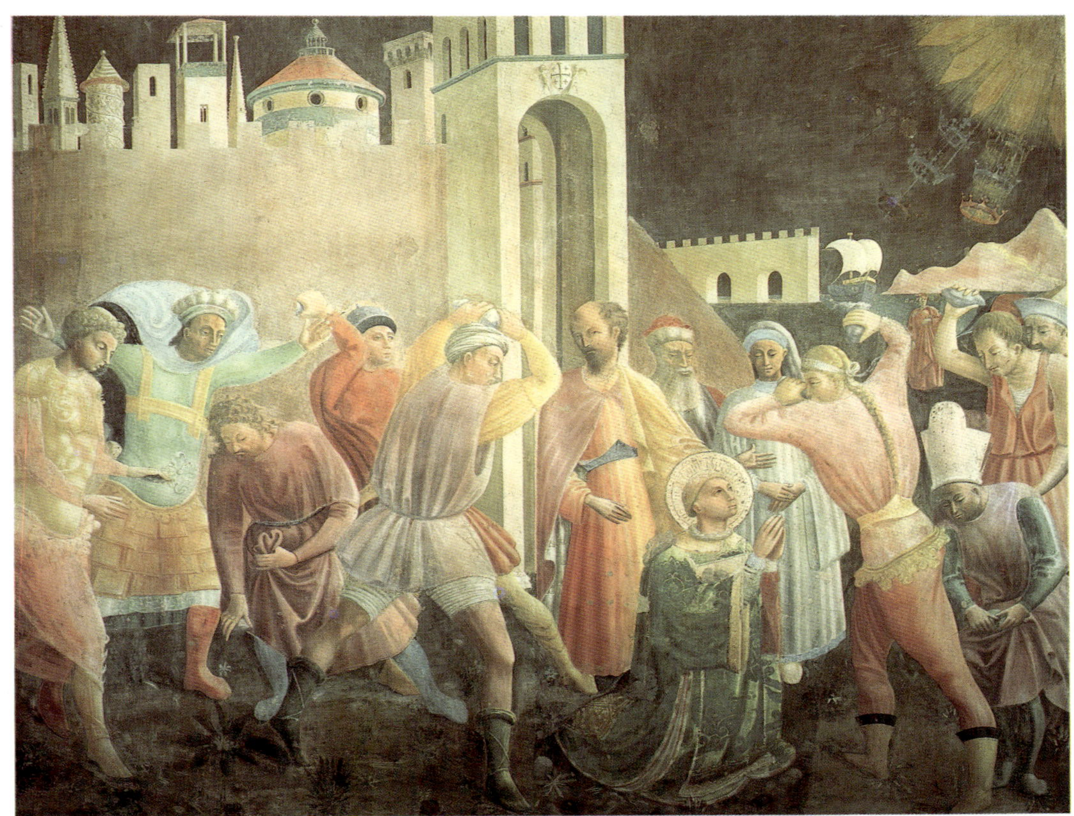

The Stoning of Saint Stephen, 310 × 420 cm. The lower part with the figures is by Andrea di Giusto. For the architecture, see p. 166.

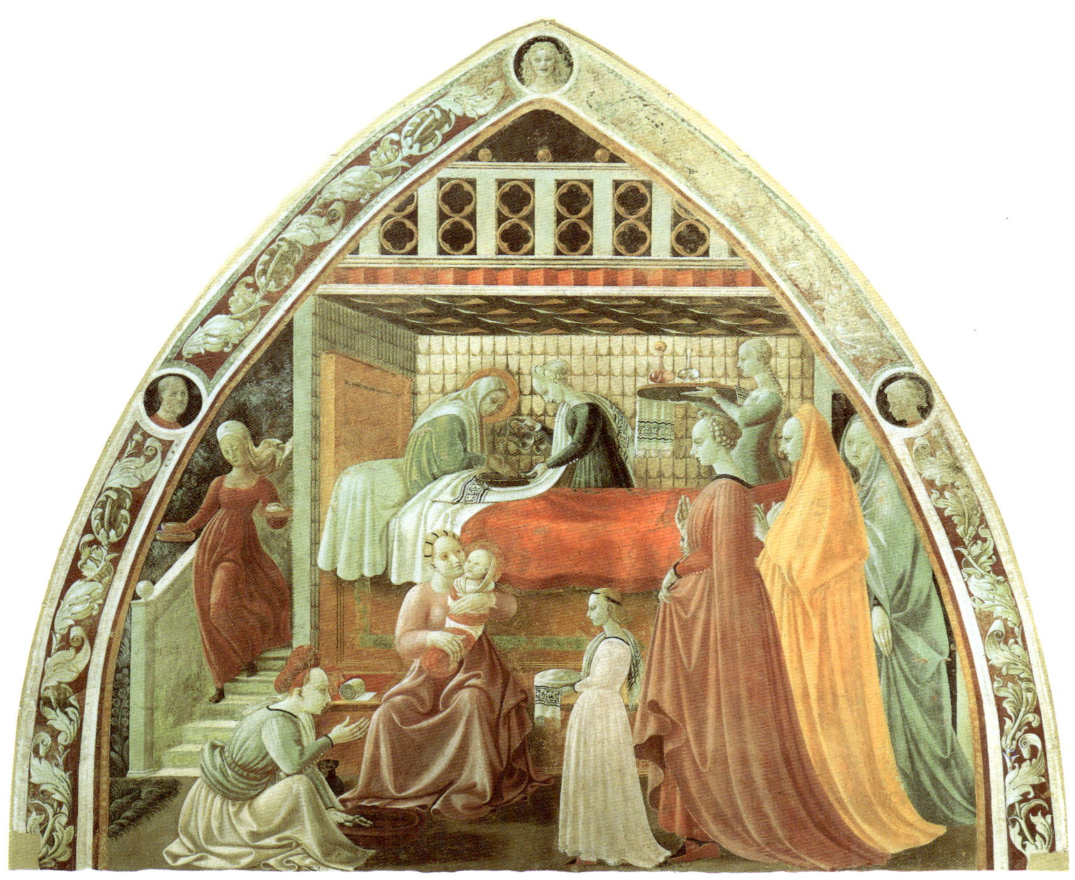

The Birth of the Virgin, 302 × 361 cm.

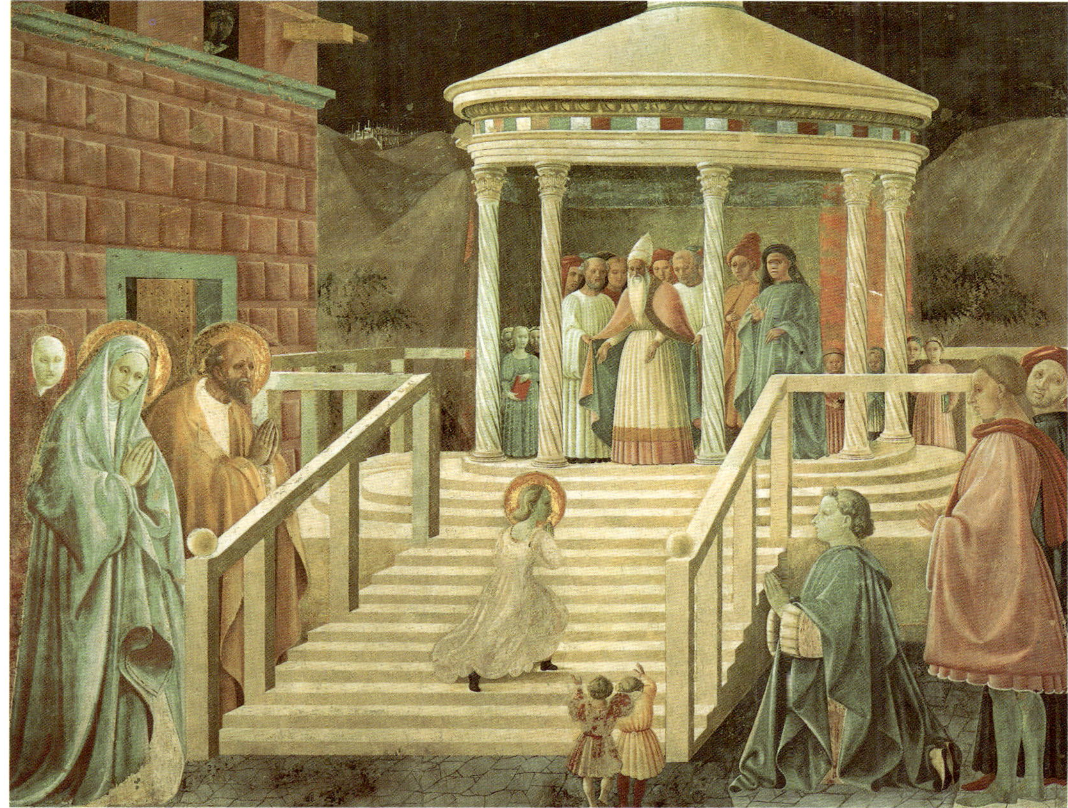

The Presentation of the Virgin, 335 × 420 cm.

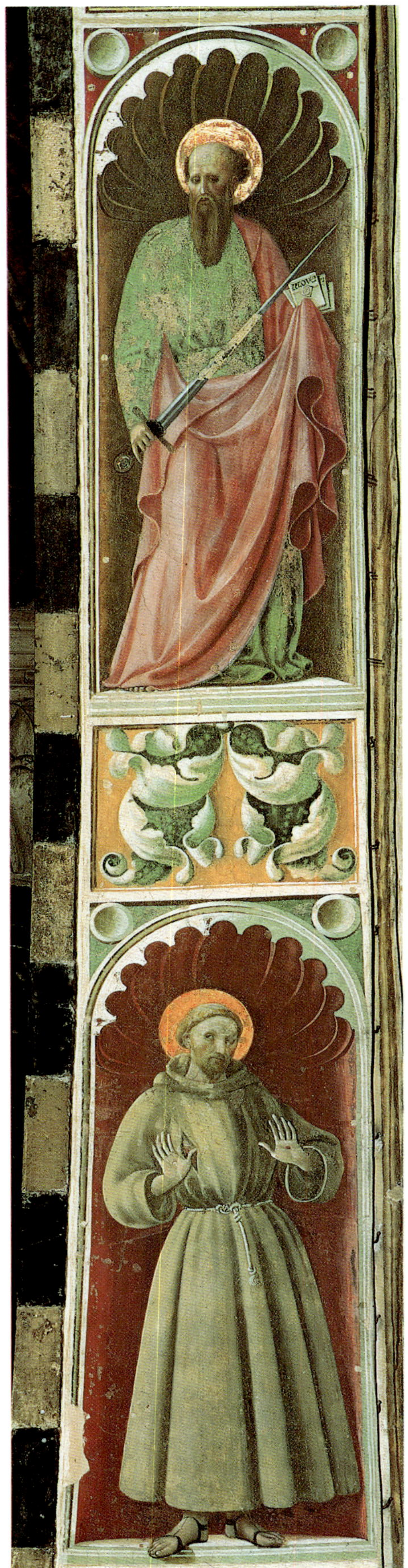

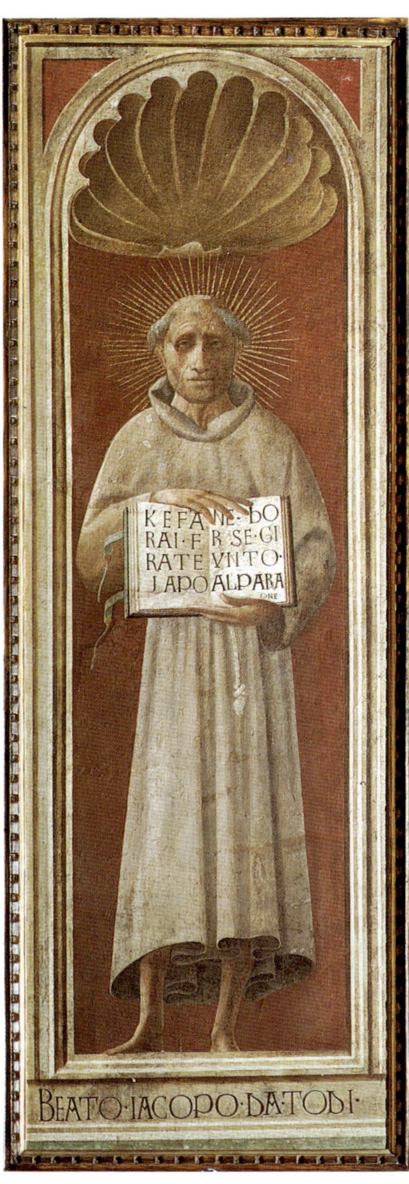

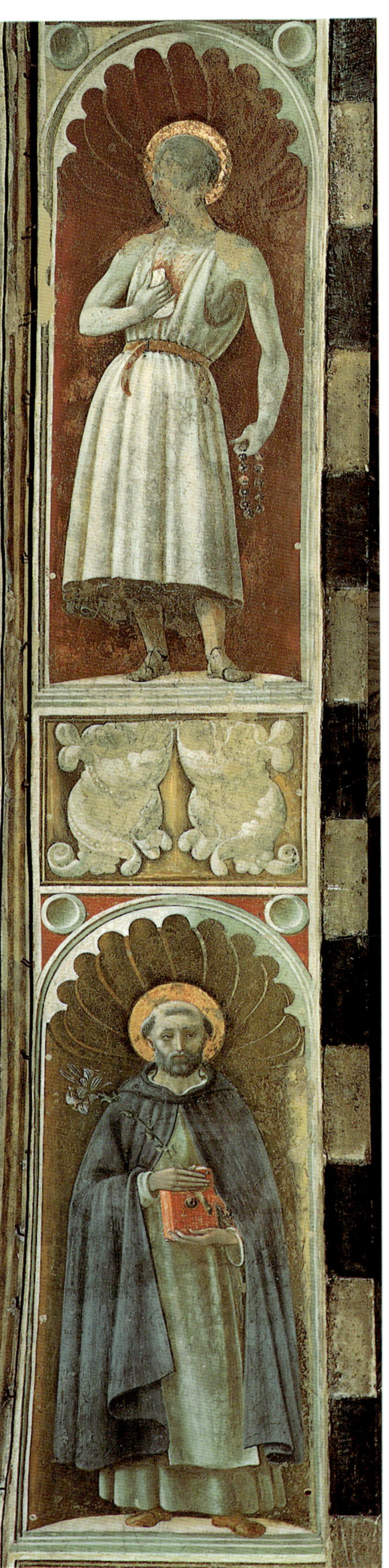

Uccello, frescoes from Prato cathedral, Assunta chapel, *c.* 1434–5. *Left: Saint Paul and Saint Francis; right: Saint Jerome and Saint Dominic* 120 × 46 cm. *Centre: The Blessed Jacopone da Todi,* 181 × 59 cm. Prato, Museo dell'Opera del Duomo.

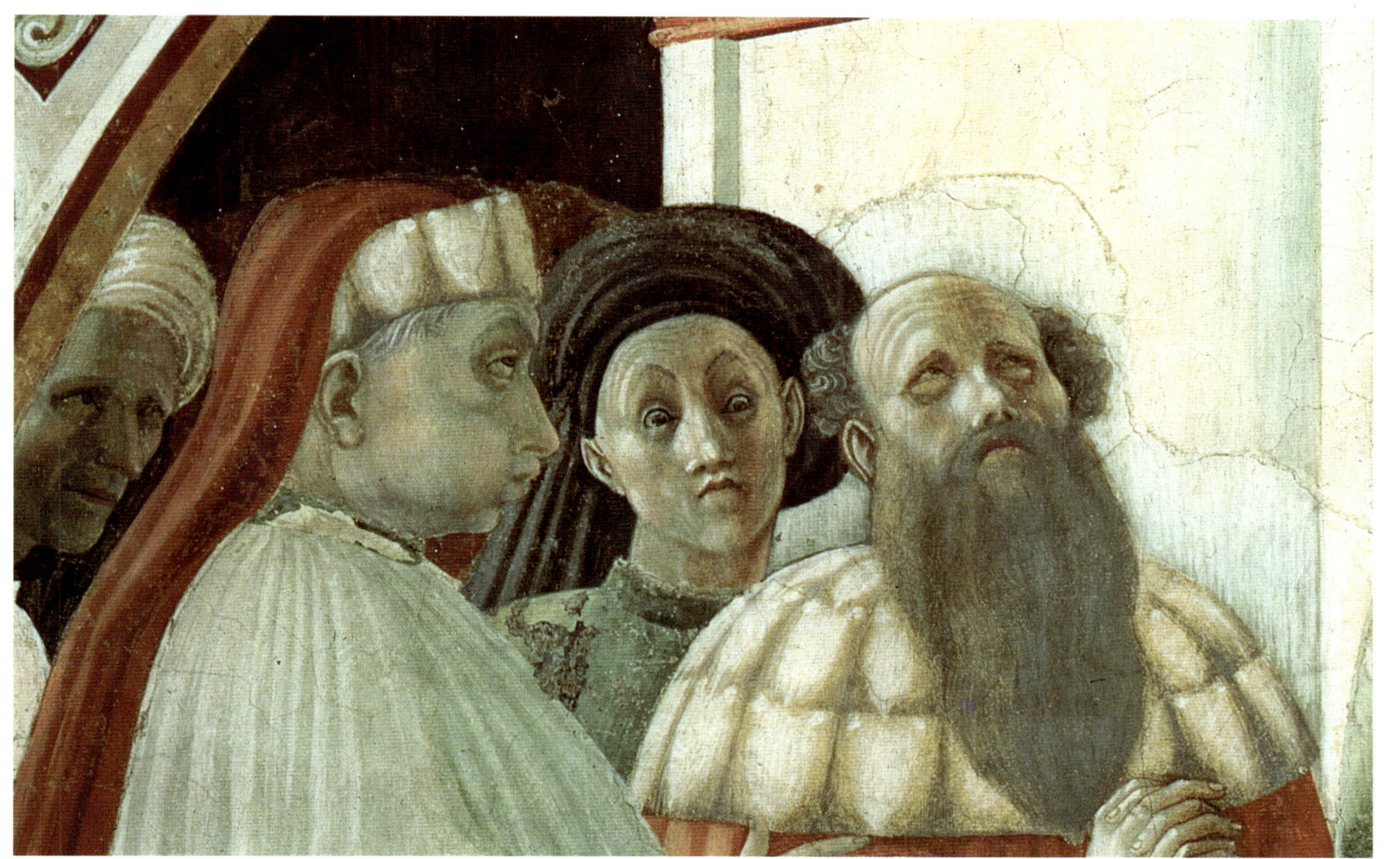

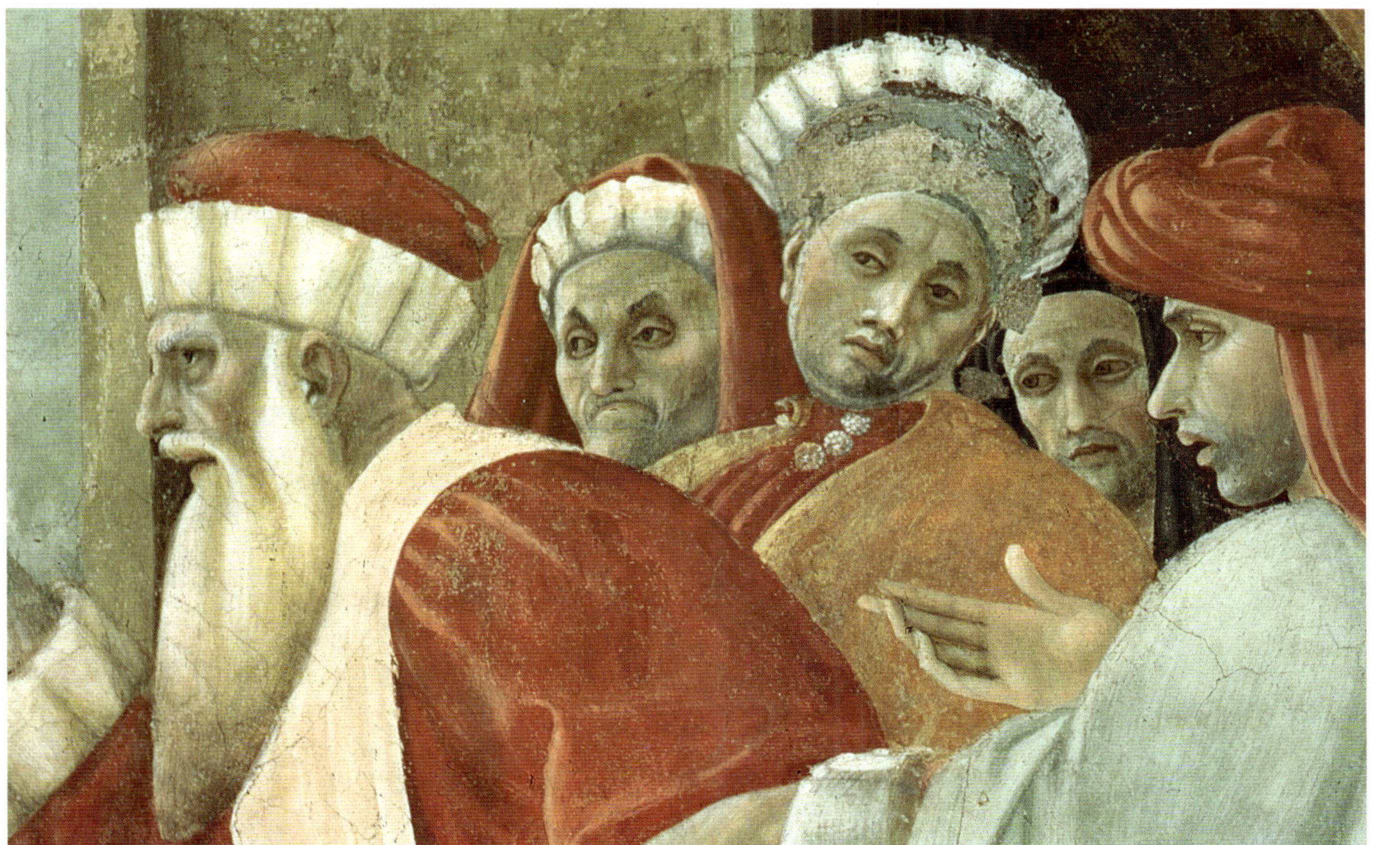

Details from *The Disputation of Saint Stephen* showing the 'attitudes'.

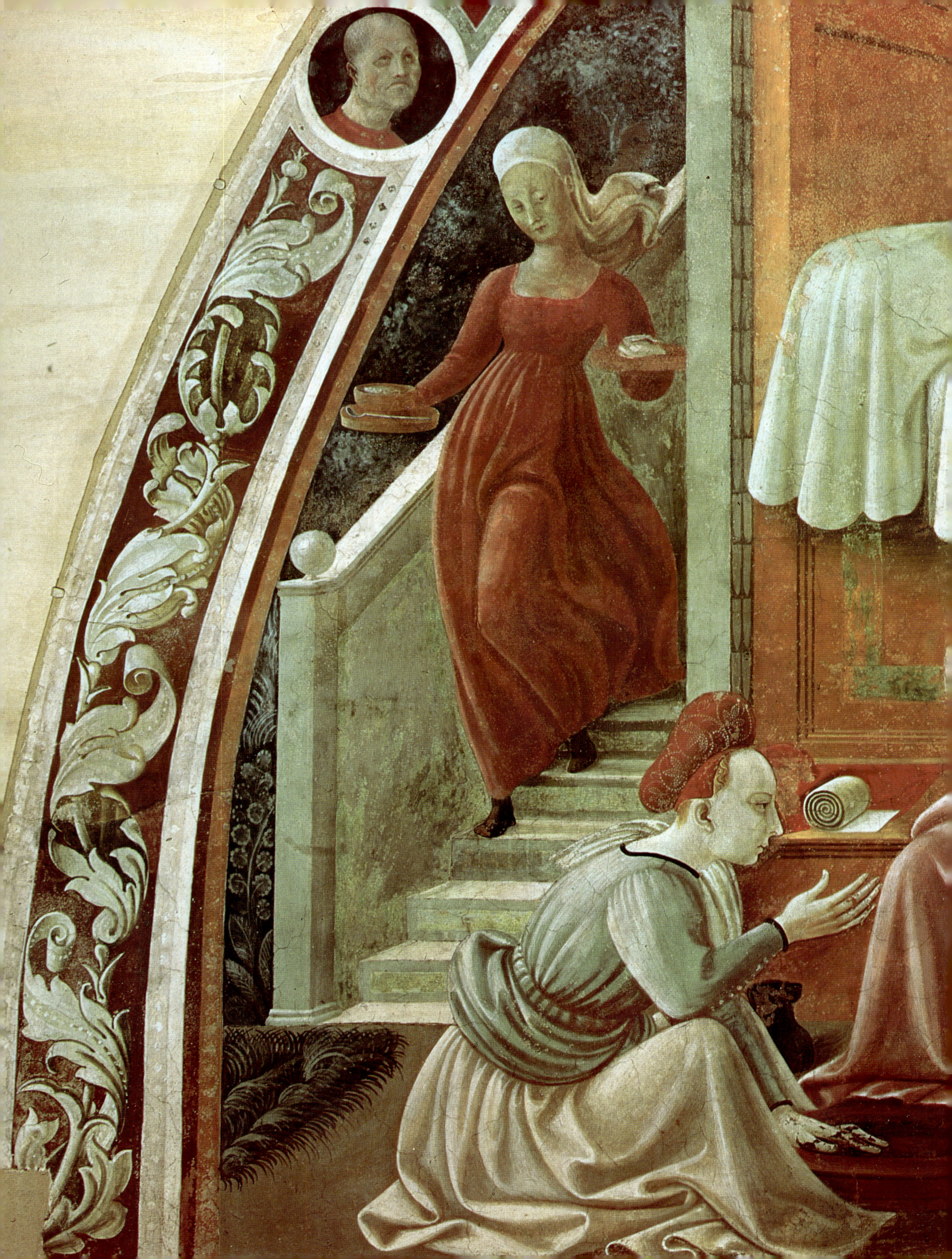

whose twisted decoration is reminiscent of the small lantern on Brunelleschi's sacristy. Then there is an unusual belvedere, that looks almost Pompeian, high up on a tower (which vaguely imitates the Torre delle Ore in Lucca), and other square towers: it is a town poised between imagination and historical fact, but, like Jerusalem, heraldically defined in the Templars' great coat of arms above the gateway in the perimeter wall; a town which, in its eclecticism, is redolent with all the themes and problems of time, from the mythical idea of Classical Antiquity, in its quotations and borrowings, to its organic, fundamental medieval presence and those same Brunelleschian and Ghibertian experiments with which Uccello was familiar on his return from Venice. The interior architecture of the Virgin's room is just as noteworthy (the balustrade imitates the famous bronze grill in the Sacro Cingolo chapel in Prato cathedral, commissioned from Maso di Bartolomeo in 1438): the polychrome ceiling, the leather
See note 45 (*corame*) decoration in Trecento taste, the great *spalliera* of the austere but totally and accurately modern chest-bed, the small marble staircase, the newel post with its ball finial: all have a touch of realism but have been simplified by geometry and a quest for purity of form. Intensely coloured borders, spheres, balustrades that we could easily
See note 112 date to the twentieth century explain the infatuation for Uccello during the *Valori Plastici* period.

When we come to the interpretation of the human figure, we find Uccello disencumbered of the aura of nobility found in *Stories from Genesis* and deploying a naturalism strongly tinged with irony. *The Disputation of Saint Stephen* covers a wide variety of psychological and physiognomical reactions to the saint's inspired teaching. The almost apodeictic intensity of these reactions is not repeated elsewhere, except in encapsulated form in some of the small heads found in the frieze of leaves bordering the Prato frescoes. As the narrative develops we see yet another example of the painter's experimentation that was always changing, as once more he took up the debate on 'attitudes', begun by Starnina at the start of the century, then abandoned in favour of an erudite interpretation of 'Antique' statuary, intiated by Masaccio's celebrated *Sagrà* in the Carmine.

Facing page: detail of *The Birth of the Virgin.*

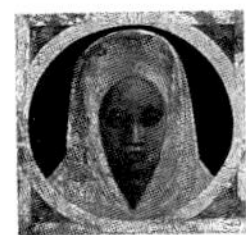

SAN MINIATO

Cat. no. 24

After recent restorations, and recovery of the sinopias and the return of the frescoes to their original site (1976), the San Miniato cycle seems to be one of the most unusual in Quattrocento Florence. However, it is in poor condition and difficult to decipher because of large blank patches and damage done to the walls by installing roof beams, as well as the sixteenth-century addition of a fresco that has nothing to do with it. By the 1950s, any hope of preserving the cycle intact was already in jeopardy, from problems arising in preserving the pigments: the monk's head in profile in the eighth story on the wall appears to be a sixteenth-century addition and not a retouching by Uccello. The frescoes are framed with faint architectural elements in terre-verte, with large niches in bright red, the whole forming a *trompe-l'oeil* which was clearly linked to the cloister's real architecture and which had a complex layout for the refined perspective of the scenes shown.

These, accompanied by long, only partly legible, inscriptions, illustrate episodes in the life of the Holy Fathers and the history of the Benedictine Order, which follows Gregory the Great's biography of Saint Benedict. An exact interpretation of the different episodes is extremely difficult because of the blank patches and it will take patience to reconstruct the inscriptions underneath. However, the importance of these

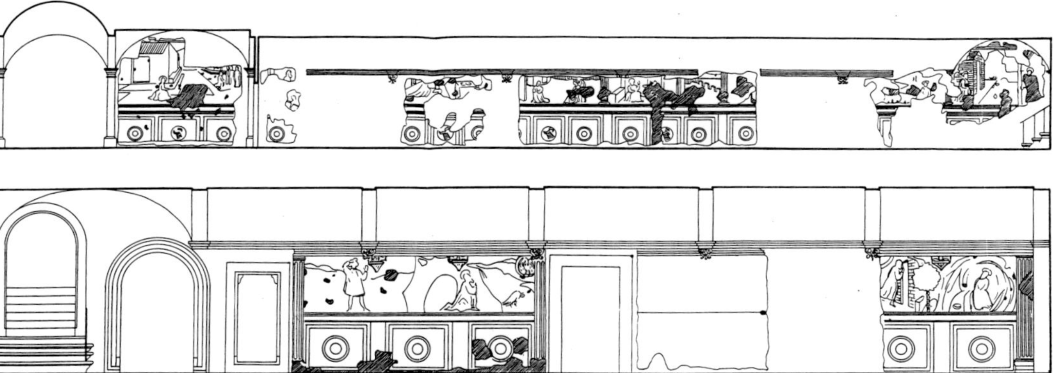

Layout of Uccello's frescoes in the cloister of San Miniato (after R. Balduccini). *Above:* the east wall; *below:* the south wall.

inscriptions clearly shows that this is not a cycle with a hackneyed theme nor one that was readily understood. These rarefied atmospheric scenes, situated in deep space and painted in pale delicate colours, with long explanations underneath, correspond to the 'long period' in monastic meditation.

As with the Chiostro Verde, we do not know who inspired the series. Uccello

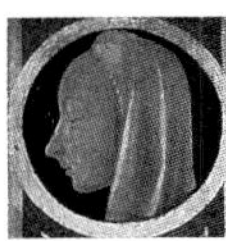

seems increasingly to have used collaborators, the further we move from the east to the south wall, and to the extreme west wall with the monk drinking, who appears to be by a later hand – perhaps in an attempt to add a third wall to the cloister. Two aspects of the cycle struck Uccello's contemporaries more negatively than the rest: these were the extreme, absolute 'metaphysical' character of the perspective construction – the great vistas into the distance forming a counterpoint to the monumental solitude of the figures – and the unreal, intellectual choice of colour. The inflexible perspective plan, the almost maniacal attention to detail (in order to improve the definition of spatial depth, seen for example in the foreshortened cubic well and the striped amphora in the sixth scene of the east wall), and the refinements in the architectural frame all explain Uccello's slowness of execution, the root cause of his arguments with the Abbot.

for Vasari's judgment see p. 325

In its present state the compositions are difficult where not impossible to decipher, but there are still passages that retain their freshness, particularly landscapes. The first scene on the east wall is a good example: here a meditating monk gestures to an angel who pours out water which makes the desert bloom, while in the background there is a vast bay full of fish, which is bordered by a rocky promontory, dominated by a red-

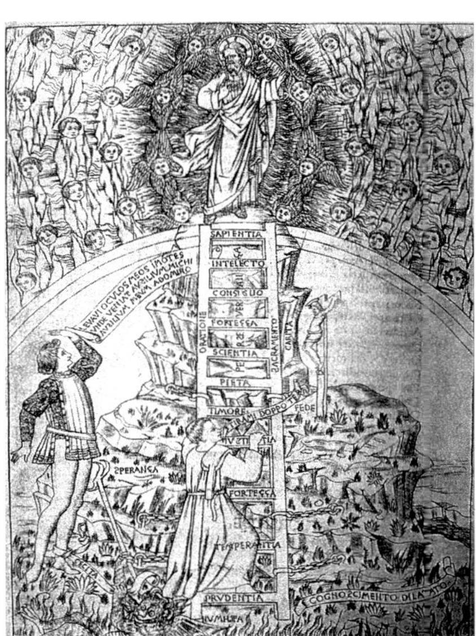

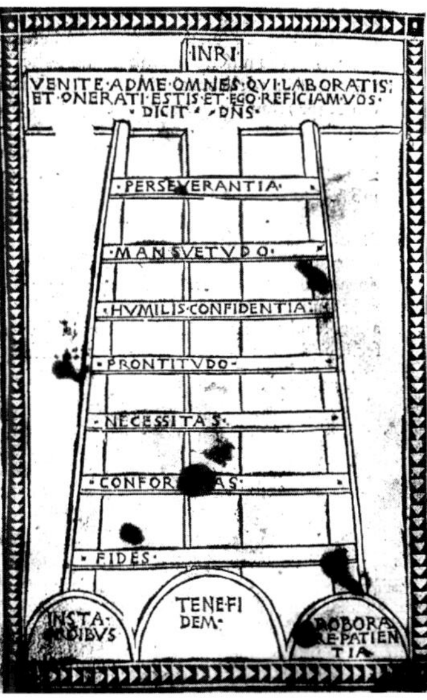

The mystic ladder, painted by Uccello on the lower part of the east wall of the cloister of San Miniato, had an influence on religious illustration in the second half of the century. Traces of it can be found in Savonarola's *Seven Virtues Leading to the Cross* (in *Epistola a tutti gli eletti di Dio*), *c.* 1497, Florence, Biblioteca Nazionale, C 40v), in an engraving by Baccio Baldini on the same theme (in *Il Monte Sancto di Dio*, 1477), and in Botticelli's illustrations for the *Divine Comedy*.

roofed church. On the south wall, the research into perspective is once more linked to the positioning of the figures. In the spatial depth, complex, theatrical rocky structures act as substitutes, through which could once be glimpsed a dense, wooded background – today we can just make out the shape of the tree trunks – like a prefiguration of the Oxford *Hunt*.

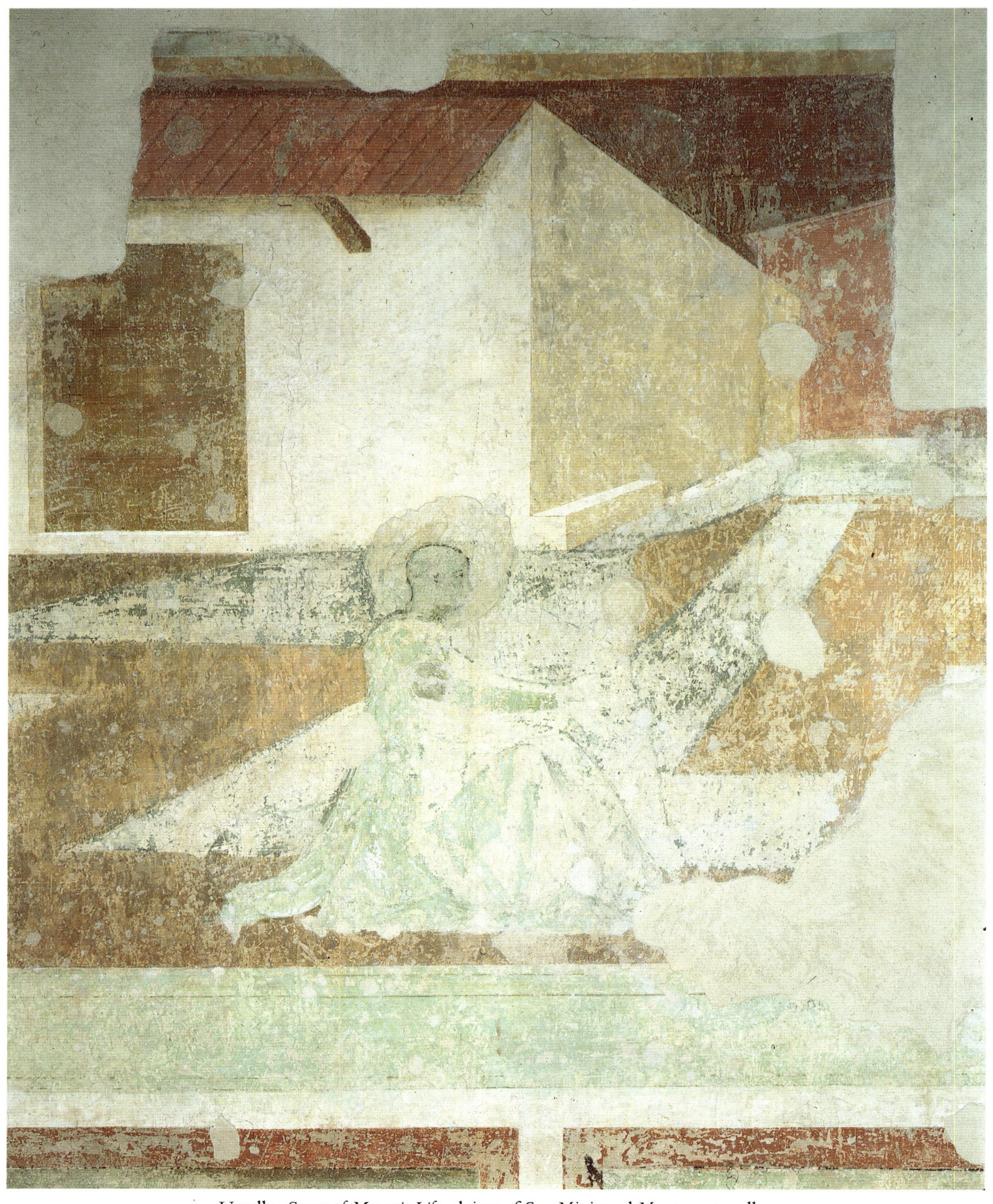

Uccello, *Scenes of Monastic Life*, cloister of San Miniato al Monte, east wall.

Above: Detail of the eighth scene. The monk's head is obviously a later restoration.

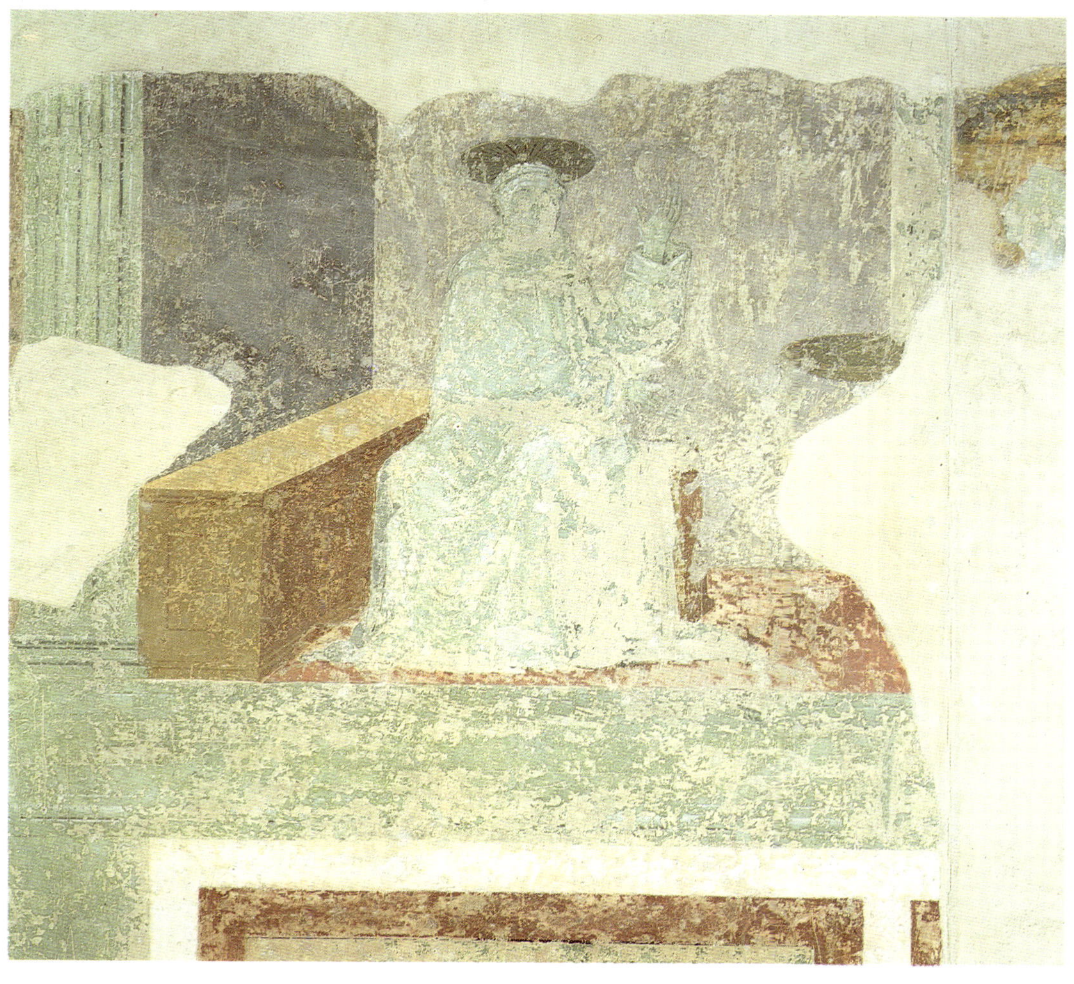

Detail of the fourth scene. The subject is not obvious: the monk-saint (Saint Benedict?) spurns a second figure's gesture of offering.

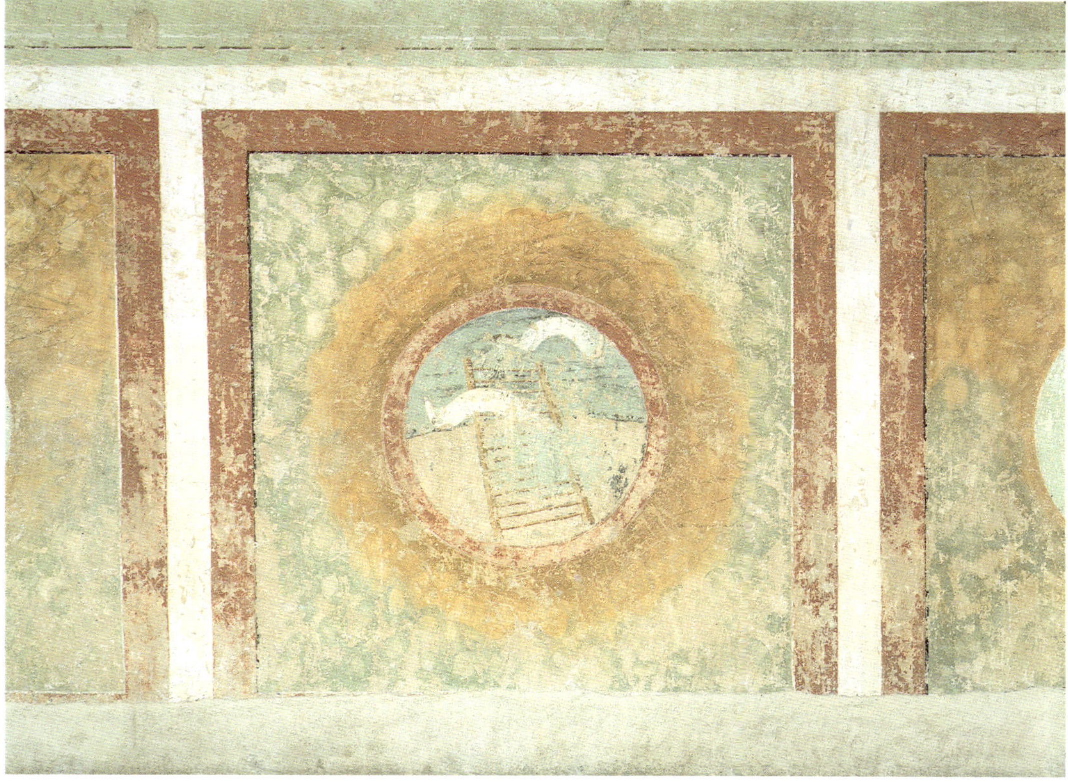

Detail of the lower part of the frescoes on the east wall, with large *trompe-l'oeil* frames imitating marble. The centre is occupied by the emblem of the mystic ladder.

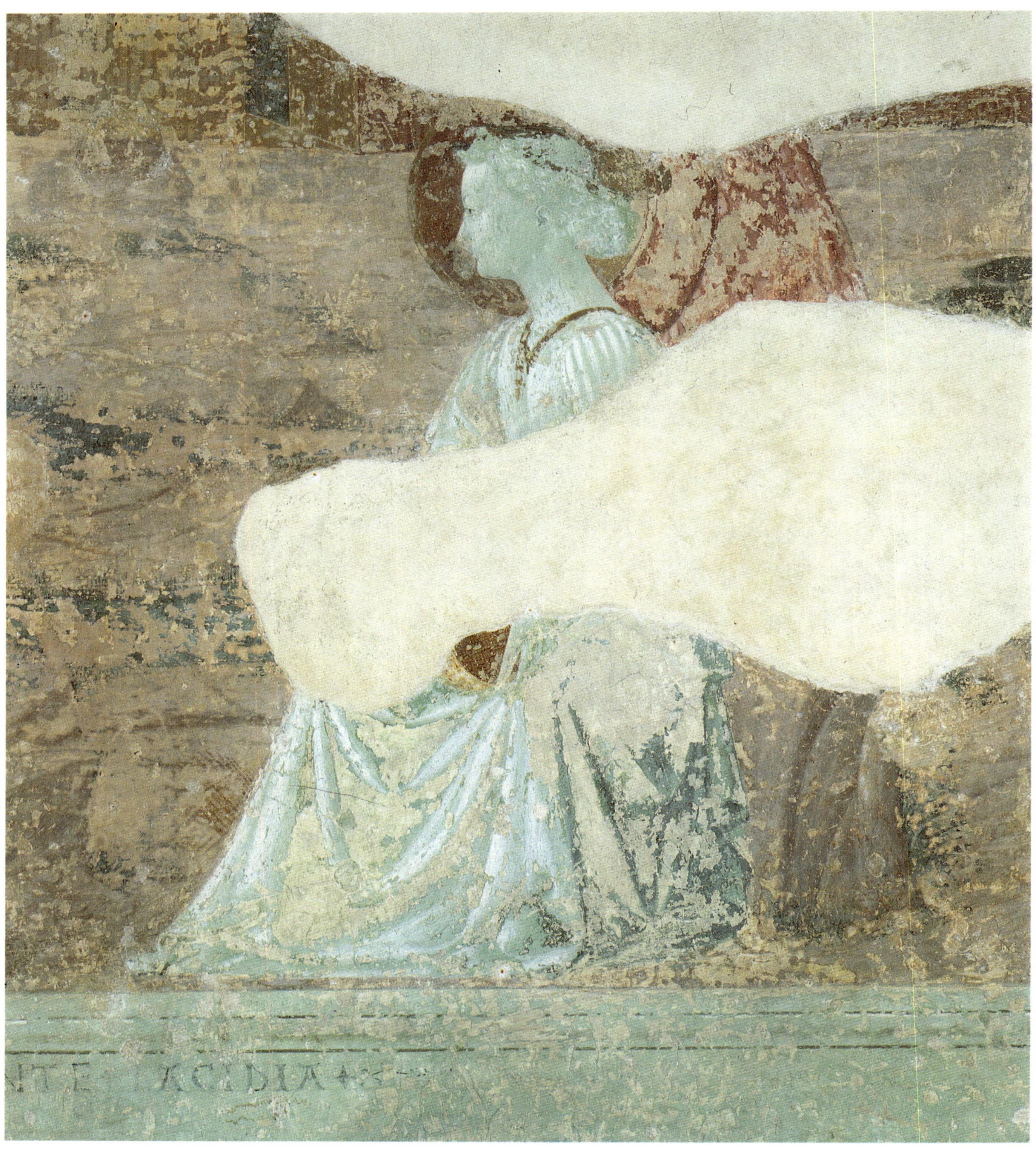

Uccello, *Scenes of Monastic Life*, cloister of San Miniato al Monte, east wall

Above: detail of the fifth scene, in which a praying saint is given encouragement by the silent presence of an angel; the inscription below indicates that with the Benedictine rule of prayer and work ('ORANDO E LAVORANDO') it is possible to overcome sloth ('PE[R]FETAMENTE L'A[C]CIDIA').

Facing page, above: detail of the second scene: a monk meditating in a landscape suggestive of the Nile (Paul the Hermit?) represents 'PERFETTA ABSTINENTIA'. *Below:* two details of the first scene: in the desert, at the behest of the hermit saint, the desert is watered and plants spring miraculously from the sand.

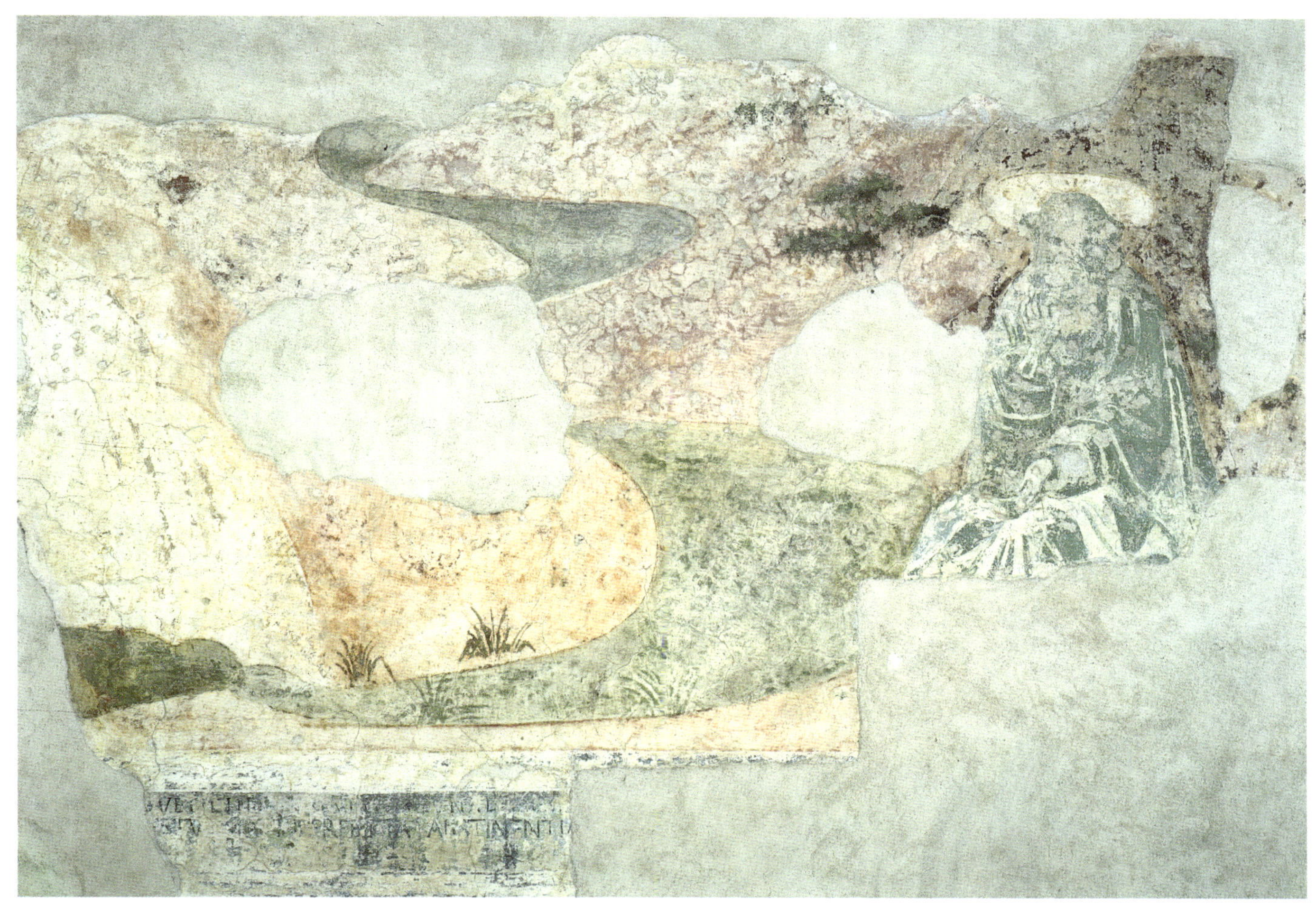

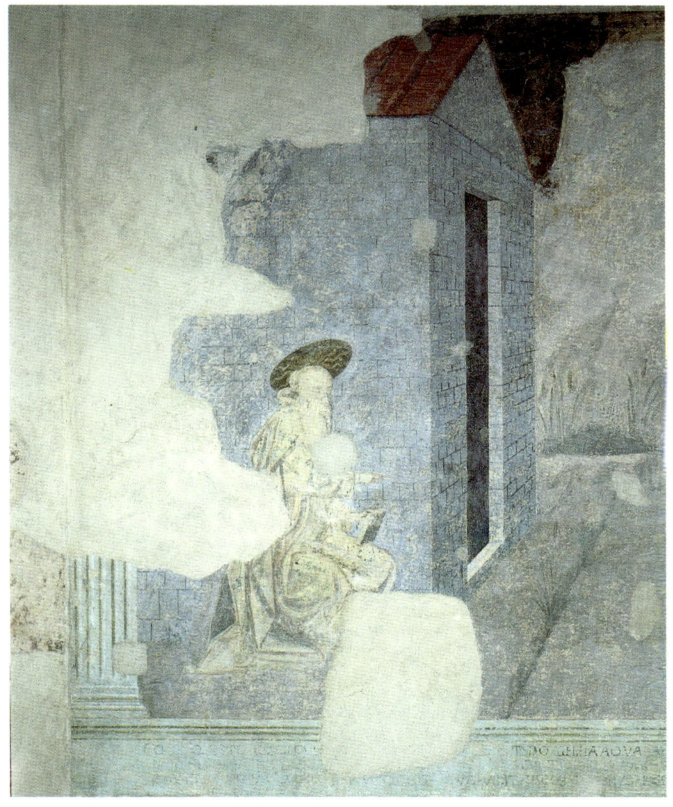

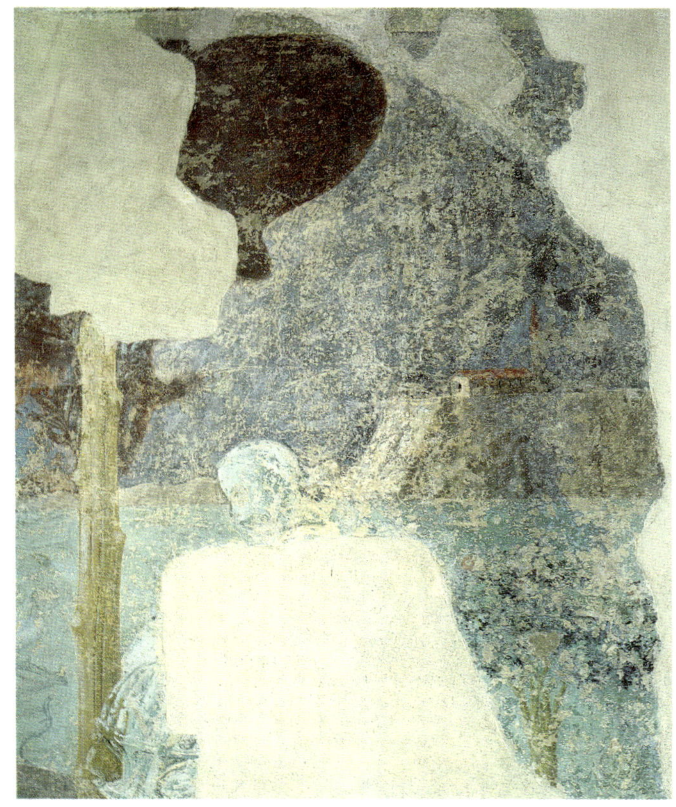

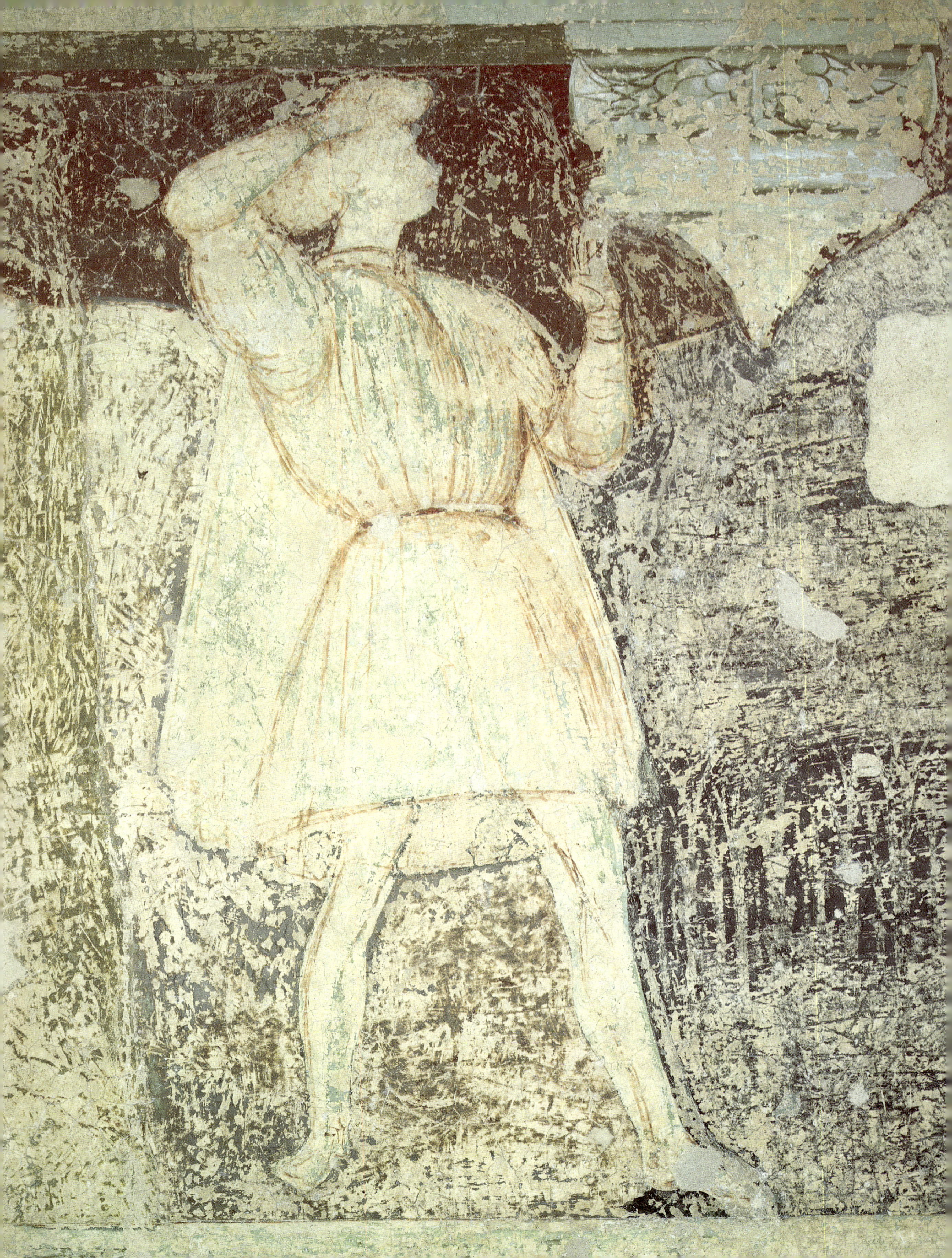

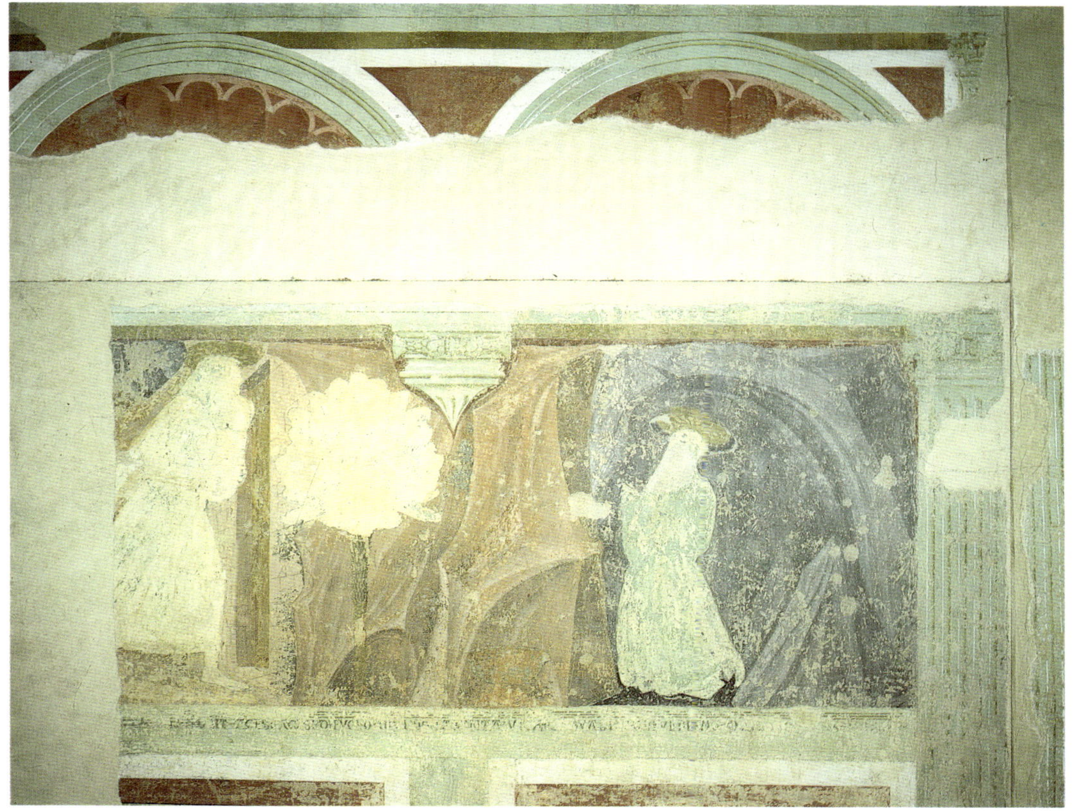

Uccello, *Scenes of Monastic Life*, cloister of San Miniato al Monte, south wall.

Facing page: detail of the first scene.

The second scene: a monk prays in a cave, while another enters his house. The two apparently unrelated episodes are linked by a palm tree (of which only the trunk survives) which marks the perspectival axis.

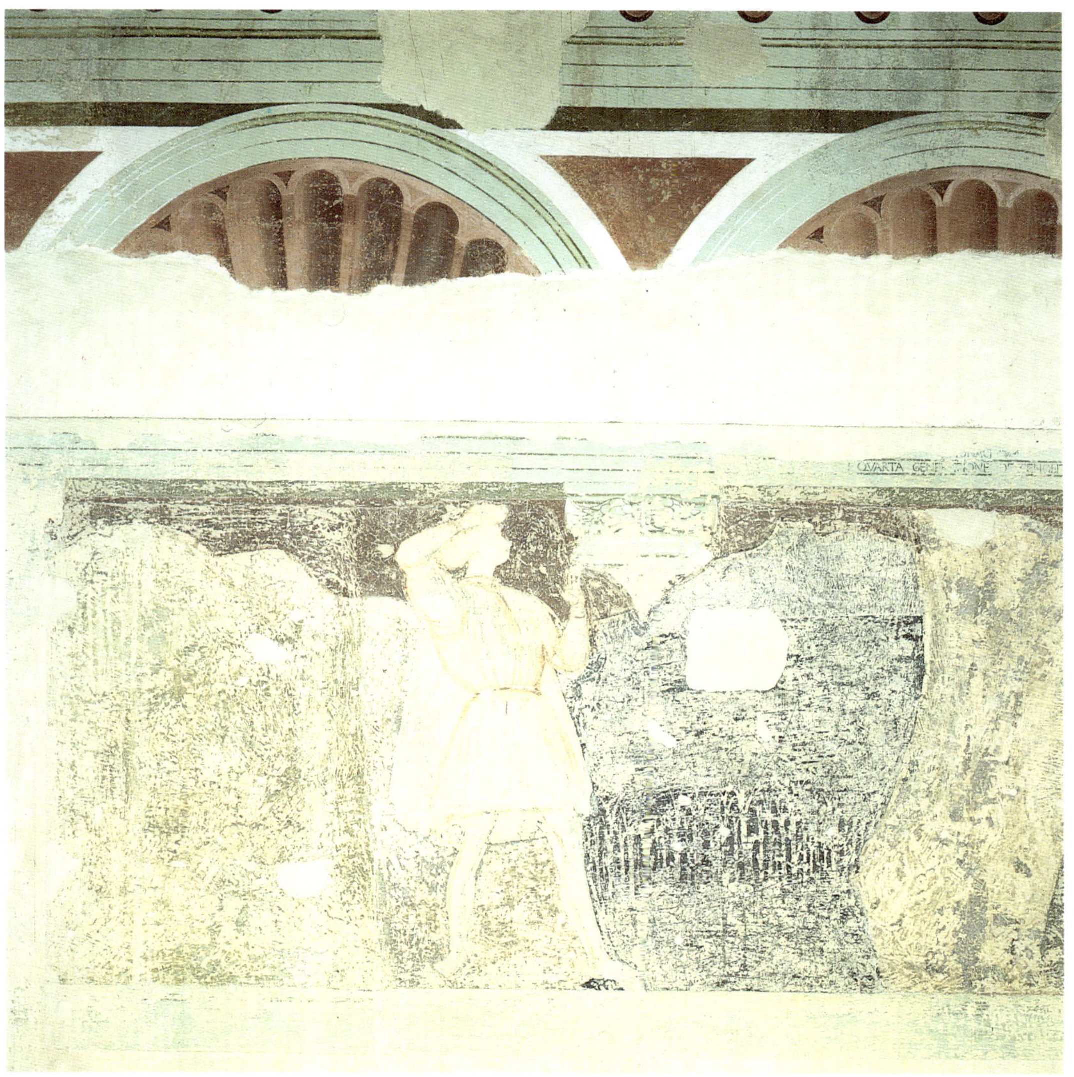

Left part of the first scene: a monk-saint has a vision of God appearing to him in a mandorla on the right. A young man on the left, in layman's clothes, reacts in fear. The monumentality of the figures is accentuated here, perhaps under the influence of Andrea del Castagno (also active at San Miniato).

2 THE REPUBLICAN EPOCH

THE HAWKWOOD

The monument to Sir John Hawkwood marks the height of Uccello's adherence to the ideals and interests of Florentine humanism. The original initiative, which dated back to the end of the Trecento and which had envisaged a sculpted group, had been changed and over the years substantially reduced to just a painting – and a monochrome one at that. But the culture of Classical Antiquity and the literary references used by the humanists supporting the project were to ennoble it through the choice of terre-verte, intended to imitate the bronze of Classical sculpture. There was a chronological coincidence worth noting between this painting and the publication of studies and translations of Plutarch's *Lives*, in particular that of Valerius Maximus to whom a monument in bronze was erected, on the Capitol, in front of the capitoline Temple of the Triad. The monument to the English *condottiere* was to be on the inside of the temple of Santa Maria del Fiore, on the initiative of the cathedral's Office of Works (backed by Cosimo de' Medici). The final product, which is now on the side

Cat. no. 12

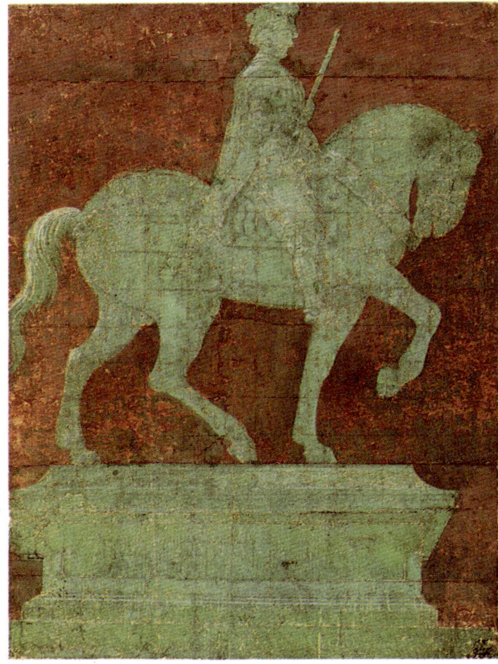

Uccello, *Study for the Equestrian Monument to Sir John Hawkwood*, greenish wash with white highlights on a purple background, 45 × 32 cm. Florence, Uffizi, Gabinetto dei Disegni, cat. fig. no. 31. This is one of the earliest examples of a drawing made on squared paper for transfer.

wall of the cathedral, in a position lower down than the original one, was the result of a series of amendments. A play of curves, often mentioned by critics, characterizes the figure's almost numismatic profile (the *condottiere*'s facial features are heavily restored), while the tomb and plinth are seen from *sotto in su*. As he worked on his plan, Uccello was undeniably inspired by Luca della Robbia's studies for the gallery in the

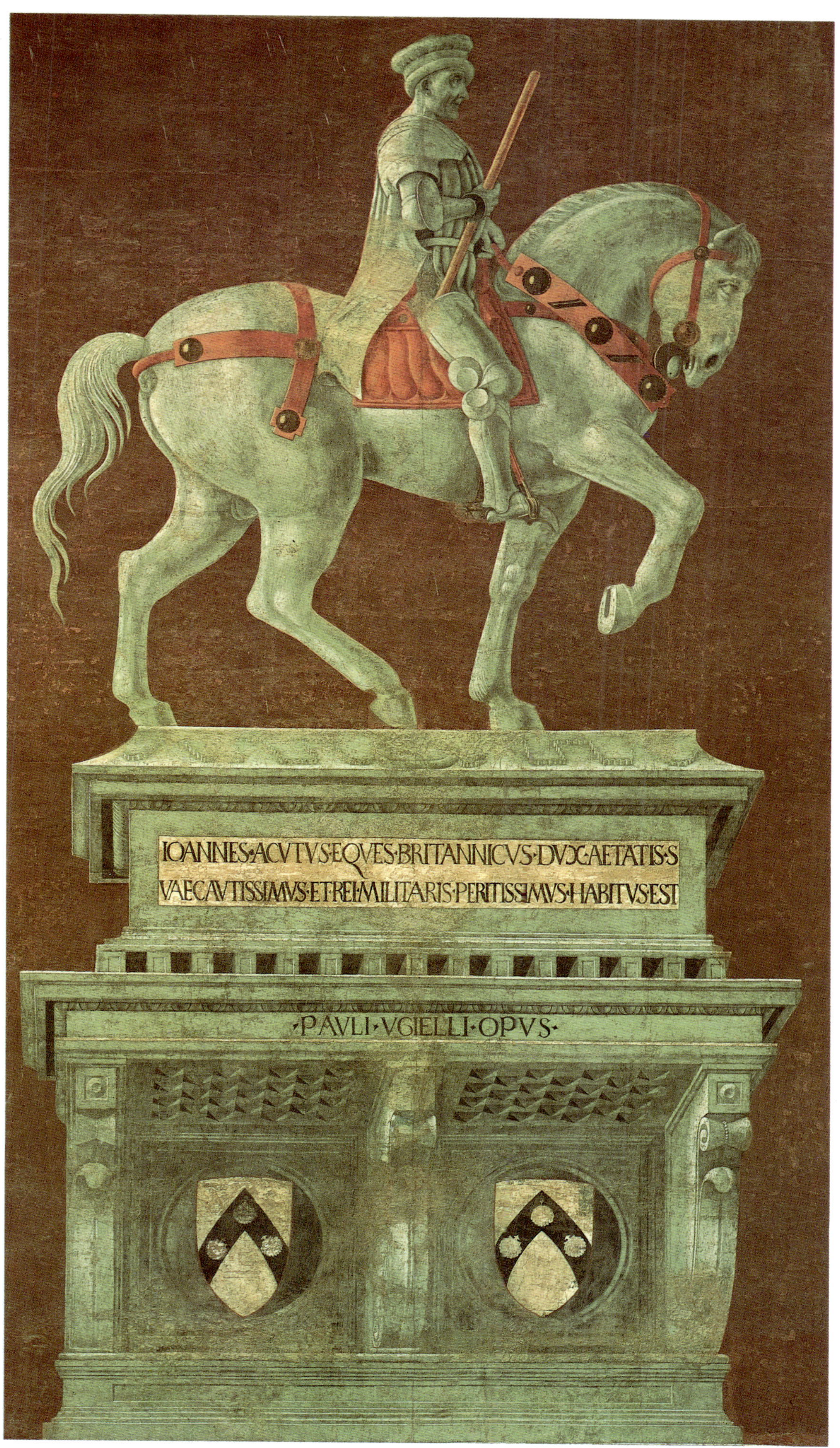

Uccello, *Equestrian Monument to Sir John Hawkwood*, 1436, fresco transferred to canvas, 820 × 575 cm. Florence, Santa Maria del Fiore.

Cantoria of the cathedral, and he seems to have taken the great foliated consoles from them. Uccello's shrewd idea of lighting the work to coincide with the real lighting that came from the double window in the nave had not been used in his lost frescoes in Santa Trinita, in which the accent of low-angled light on the remoulded Corinthian pilasters appeared completely at odds with the real sources of light in the church. In the *Tolentino*, painted much later, Andrea del Castagno adopted the same expedient as Uccello in the *Hawkwood*, accentuating the plastic quality of the monument with even more violent, low-angled lighting, that was vaguely Donatellian in style. The spirited naturalism of Castagno's bad-tempered horse further emphasizes the noble, wide geometry of the *Hawkwood*'s 'Thessalonian warhorse' (mentioned in late Trecento sources).

Ill. pp. 92–3

In all, what is dominant is the epic theme, that involves a series of resplendent enlargements of all the composition's elements: first the architecture, in which the heraldry with its great coats of arms has a rhetorical function, along with the inscriptions in Roman epigraphic capitals and the learned *contaminatio* of Classical and Gothic. Then the horse, whose bends and curves perhaps caused the quarrel involving objections from the cathedral Office of Works. There was a divergence from the preparatory drawing in the final product, in which borrowings from Classical art were mixed with experiments in geometry and stylized abstraction, and the horse was given an unrealistic gait, so criticized in the sources until Baldinucci's time (see catalogue). Finally, there is the harness with its intense colouration and 'purist' shapes and the figure with its geometric armour, like a sort of anatomy of war, all of which reduce the naturalistic element of the face to a detail in relation to the whole. Uccello was experimenting here, in a way which became even more marked in the *Battles*, using a kind of geometric naturalism and realistic geometry which elevated mimesis to an area of abstraction, where openly, if not aggressively proclaimed Classical echoes, Gothic stylistic elements and geometry all converged.

Ill. pp. 168, 171

Facing page: Uccello, detail of *The Battle of San Romano: Bernardino della Ciarda Unhorsed*, *c.* 1435–6, tempera on wood, 181 × 322 cm. Florence, Uffizi.

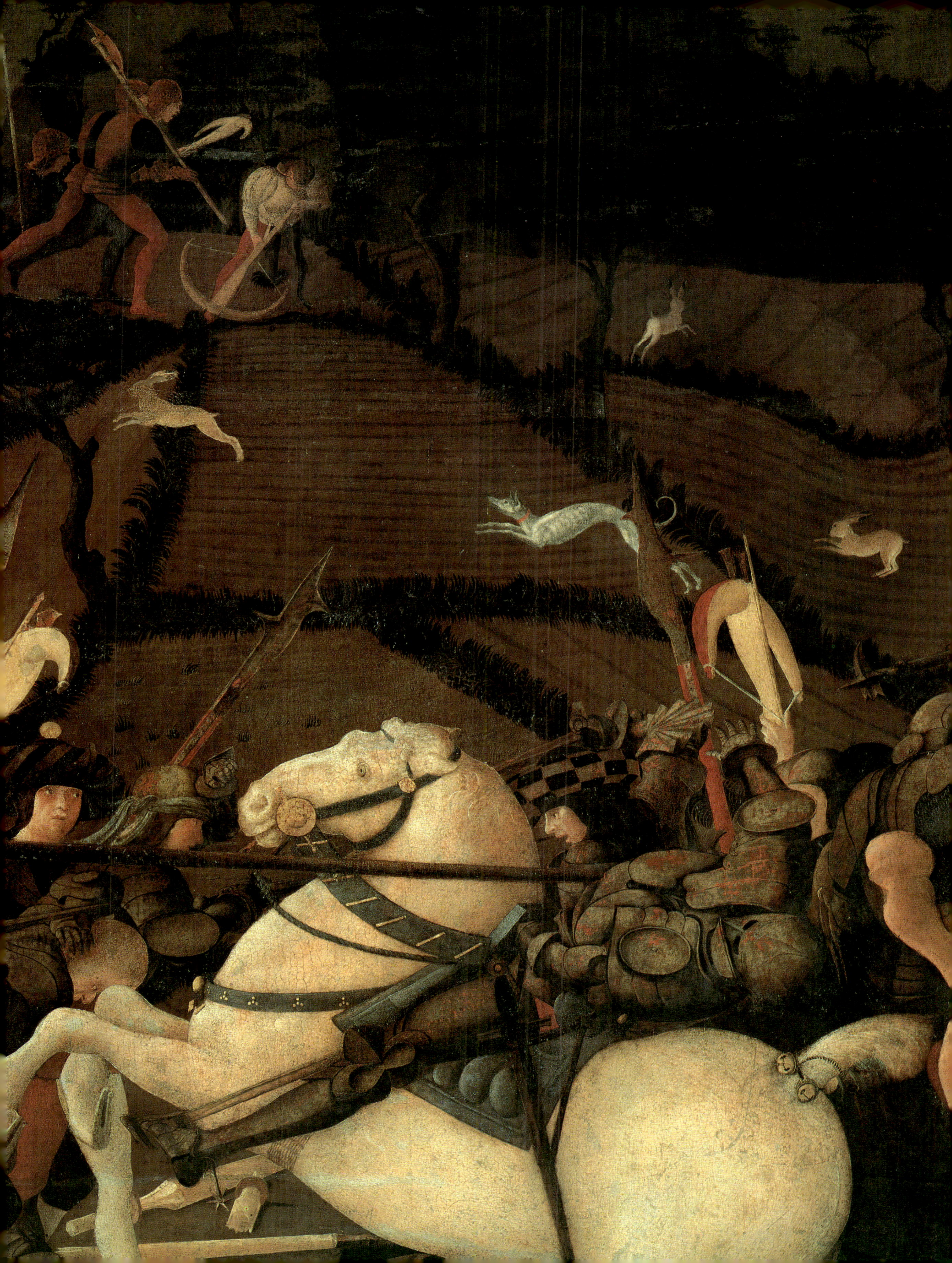

Following pages: Uccello, *The Battle of San Romano: Bernardino della Ciarda Unhorsed*, *c.* 1435–6, tempera on wood, 181 × 322 cm.
Florence, Uffizi. Complete work and detail.

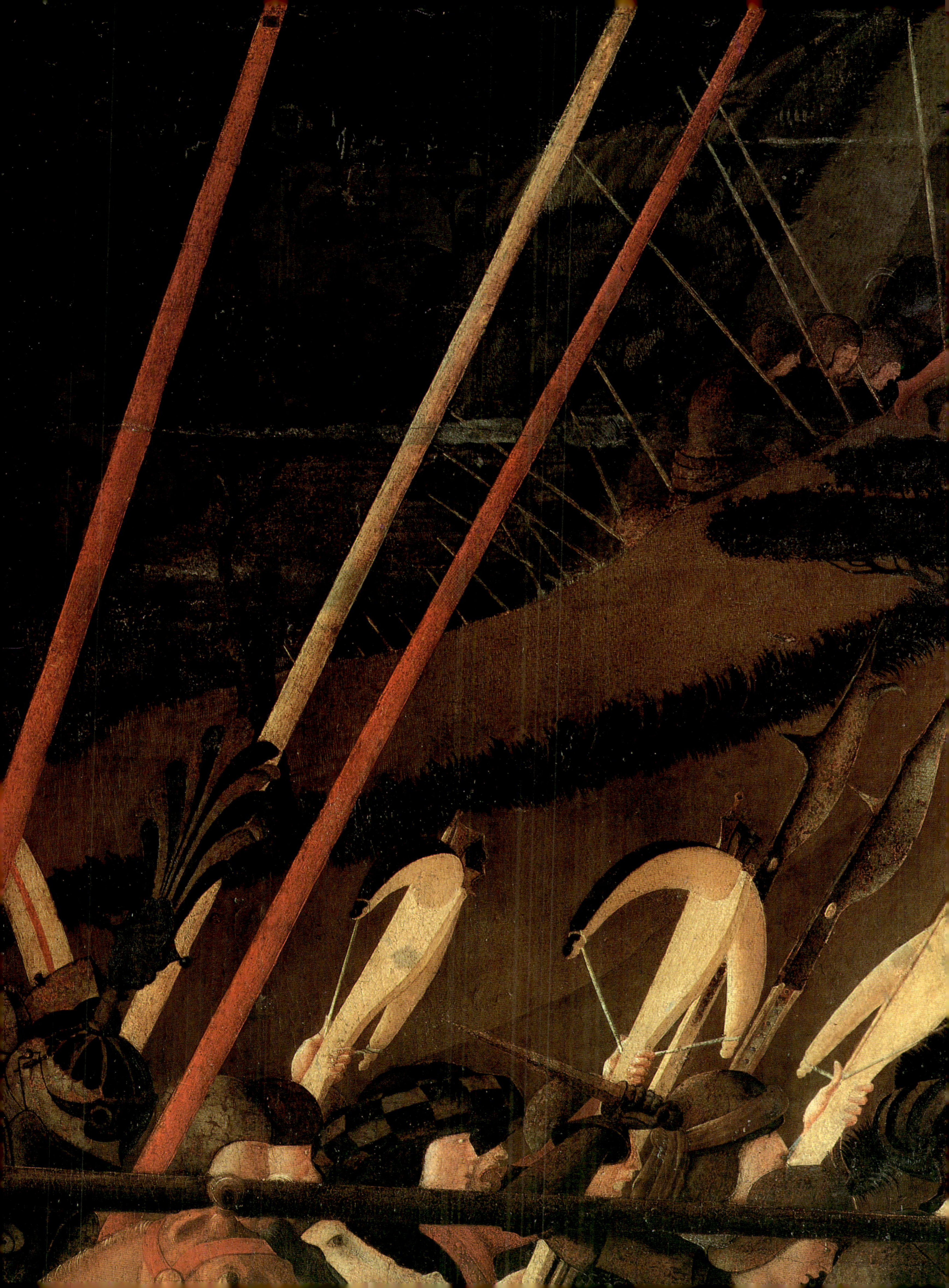

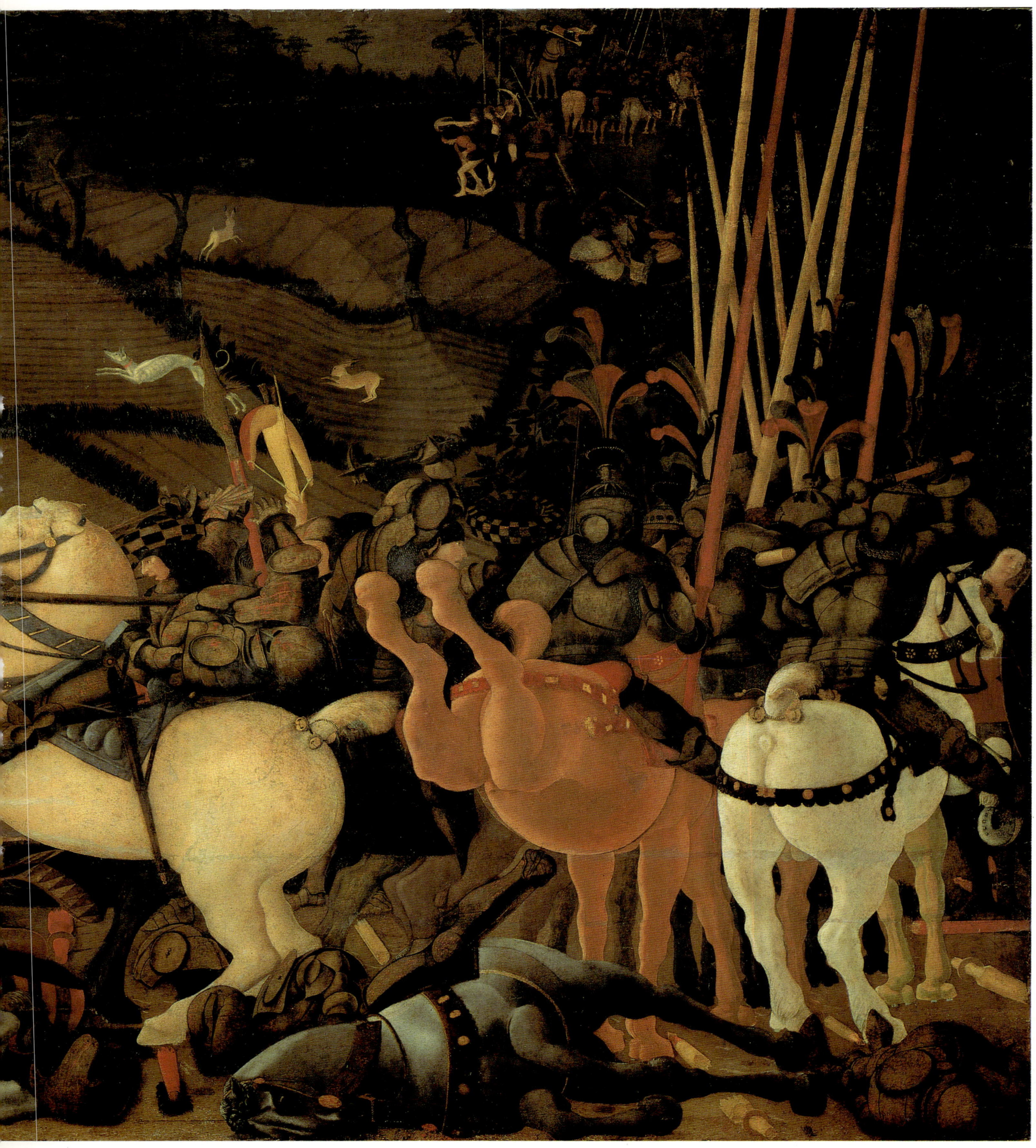

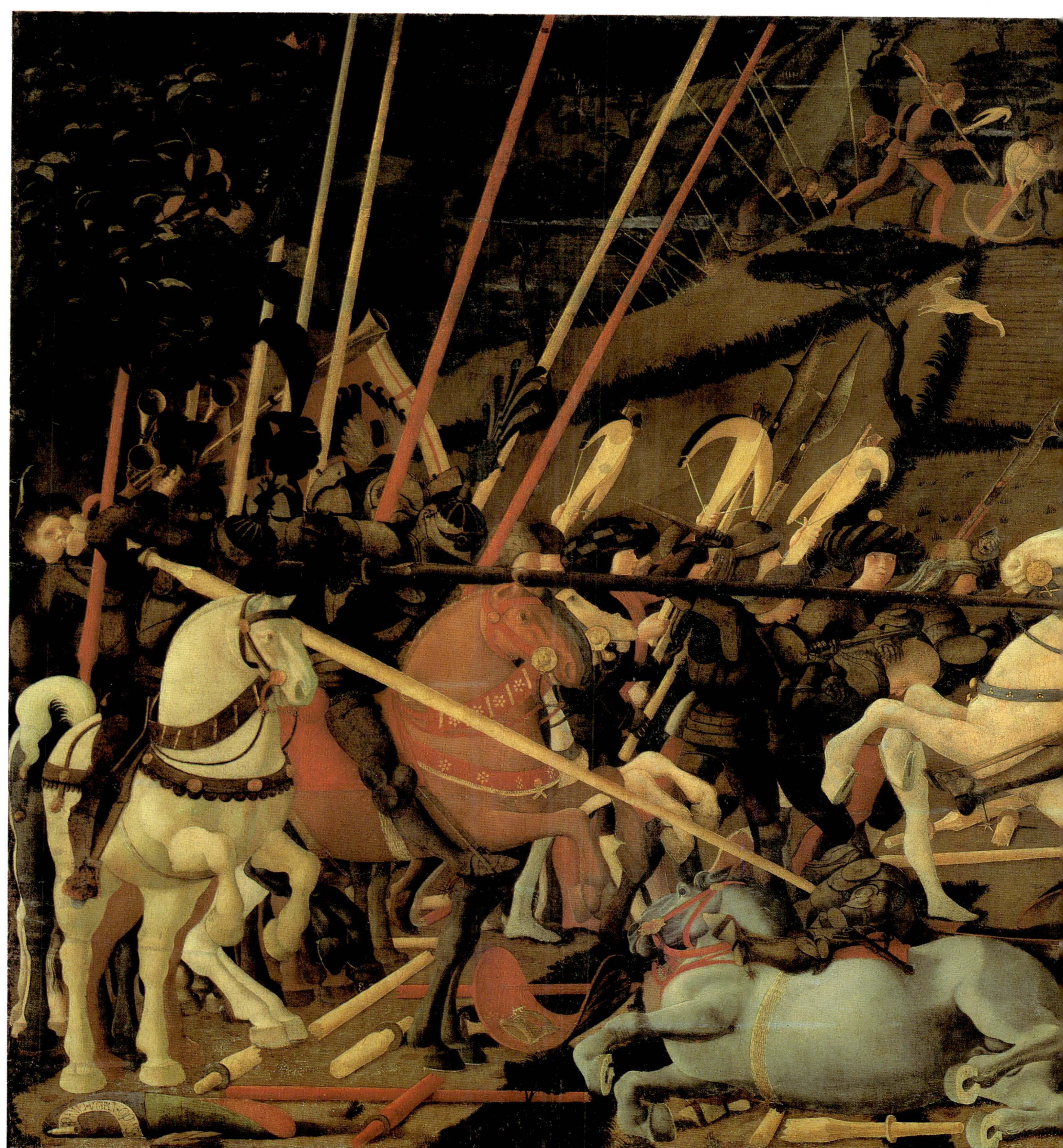

THE BATTLES

The three battle scenes which Cosimo probably ordered for his house in homage to Niccolò da Tolentino mark a new stage in Uccello's experimentation. Here he has used picture-making materials which are particularly rich, full of burnishing and metallic effects – silvering, gilding, lacquers and varnishes – in a sort of material transfer between the depicted object and the depiction itself: almost as though the precious armour, the elegant harness had transferred their preciousness and intrinsic matter rather than a depiction of themselves into the painting. So we have a picture which is like a colossal miniature: it adds objective registers to the usual painterly techniques, quite beyond the range of chiaroscuros, aerial perspective and *sfumati*, which are there to depict an objective aggression in the forms. In the arrangement of the three compositions, the main encounter takes place in the centre of the episode in the Uffizi panel, while in the wings, in the two panels (now in London and Paris) which were originally positioned on either side, the lances move in a progressive dynamic from vertical to horizontal in order to translate the attack. Uccello introduced the story into a limited space, defined by a sort of perspectival 'paving' in which the converging grid pattern of *costruzione legittima* was suggested by bits of broken lance, which localized single episodes, the foreshortened prone bodies, horses and men on foot as though on a draughts board. This ground plane rises in the background to form a landscape – in a part which originally extended into lunettes and has since been cut off – where there are references to Tuscany, terraced hills, harvesting and the season (June) in which the event took place. There the battle mingles with another reality: that of the hunt, and dogs, game and secondary characters go about their business in a series of isolated episodes at the outer edges of the principal action. If the *Hawkwood* evoked statuary and Classical Antiquity, here the ambience is one of chivalrous jousting and Gothic narrative – to which the type of heavily harnessed horse in the paintings referred and which was quite different from the Renaissance horse Alberti described in his *De equo animante*. Here again, as in the *Hawkwood*, the armour, fabrics, Tolentino's enormous, preciously damasked hat, the (now partly incomplete) standards flapping in the wind, the helmets and ornaments all play an important role in the almost cinematographic modernity of the centring, even if over time those triumphantly coloured elements in the painting have deteriorated. This dazzling material and his insistent use of geometry apart, Uccello appears in his refined, rather subdued manner to have given up on chromatic allusions to atmosphere which might have articulated the episodes in the 'day', as morning, or midday or evening. (This is now difficult to prove because of the different degrees of conservation and cleaning on each panel.) Uccello's geometric abstraction that makes him so popular in our own age should not blind us to his

Cat. no. 14

Facing page: Uccello, detail of *The Battle of San Romano*. Florence, Uffizi.

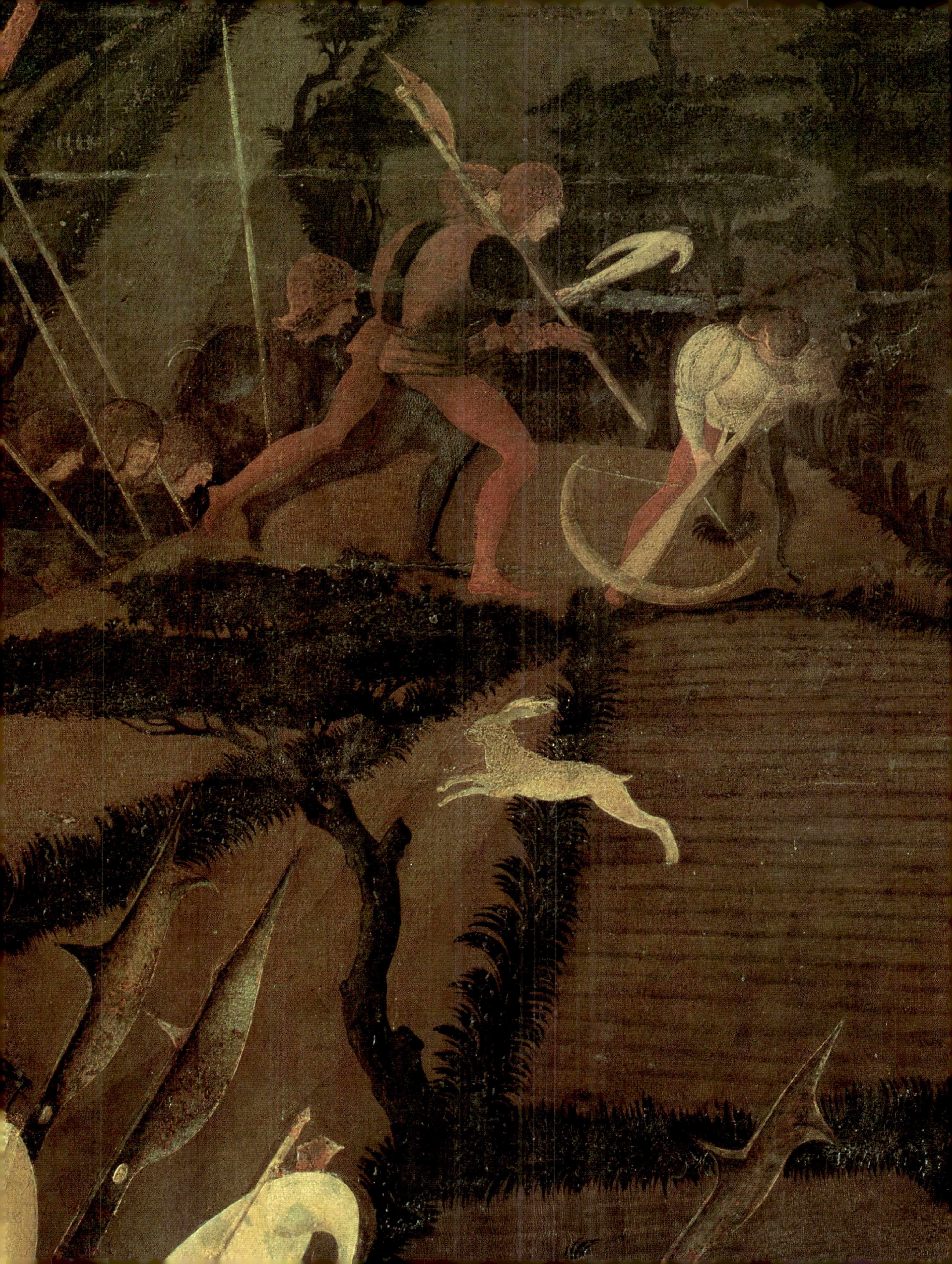

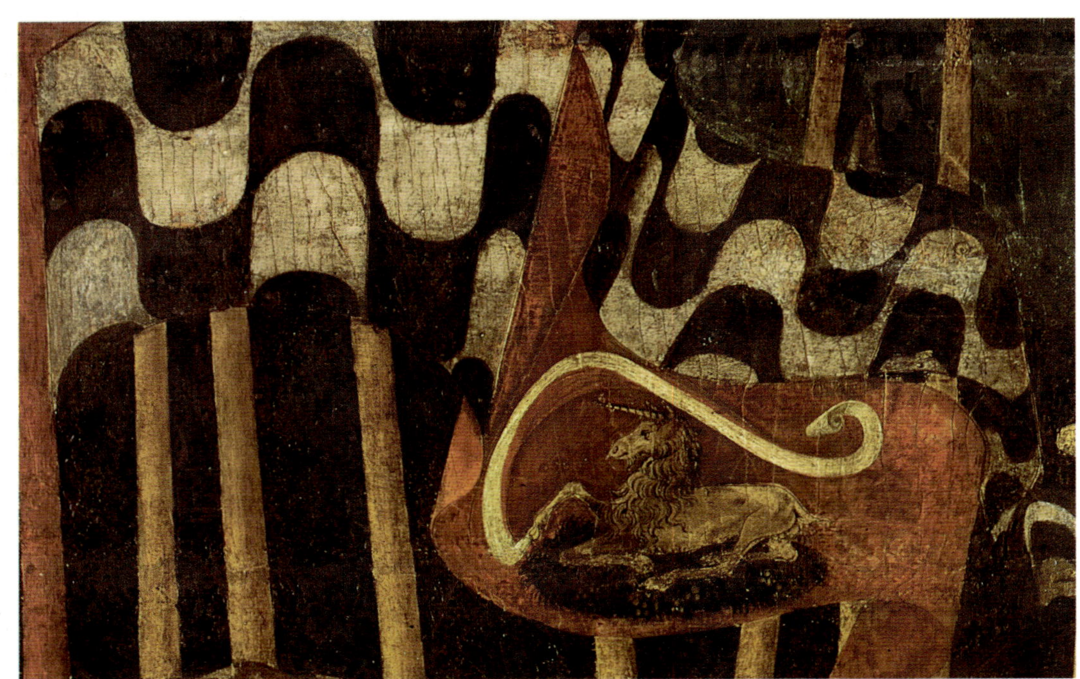

Detail of the Paris *Battle of San Romano* panel showing that the upper part has been cut.

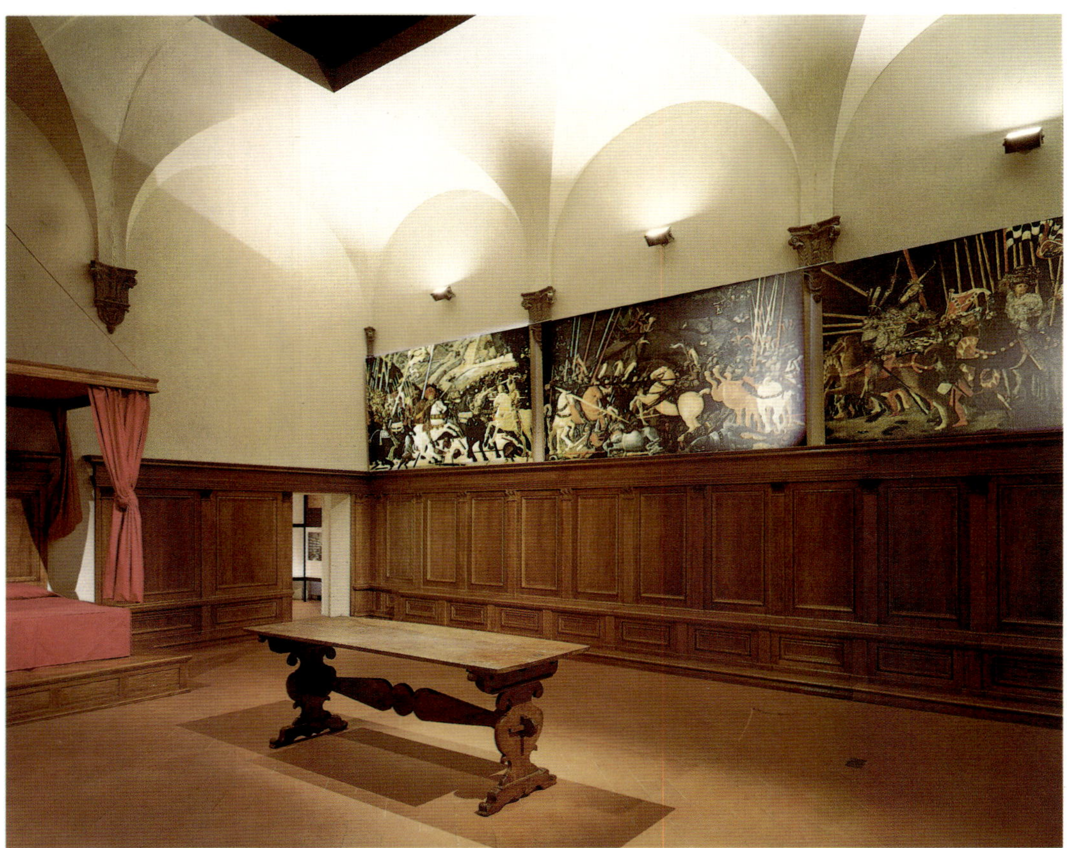

Lorenzo the Magnificent's *camera* with the three *Battles*, reconstructed actual size in the Foundling Hospital for the exhibition, 'The Architecture of Lorenzo the Magnificent', 1992.

Facing page: Uccello, detail of *The Battle of San Romano*: *Niccolò da Tolentino at the Head of the Florentines*. London, National Gallery.

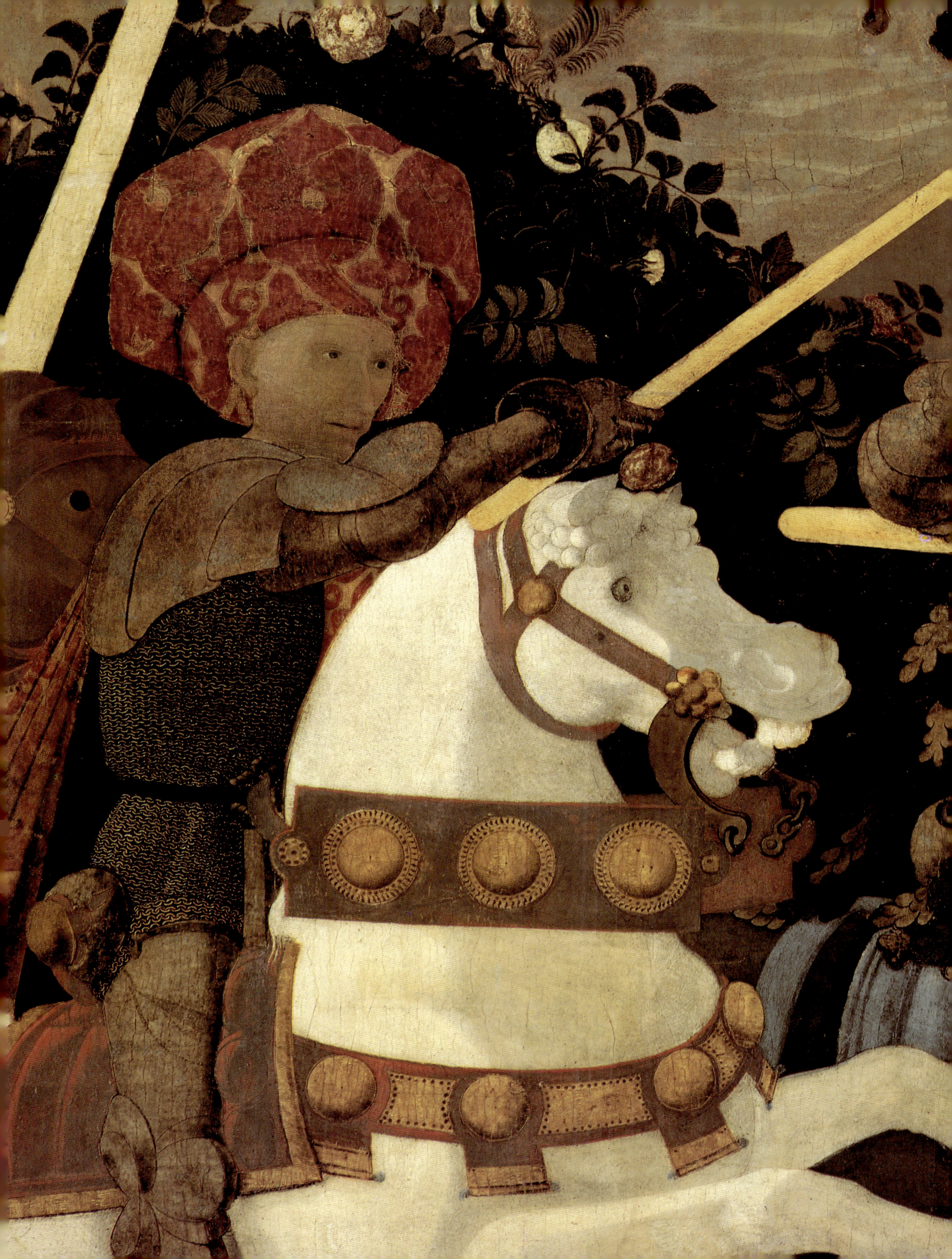

Leonardoesque prefigurations of 'air' and 'humours', reflections and lights, and the relativity of visual phenomena; this prefiguration is still only implicit here, but nevertheless it is significant in the variations it introduces into the very heart of three pictorial moments. The three panels represent a cycle, or the fragments of a cycle, but stylistically each stands on its own and is not just a fragment of a single work, of a single *spalliera*. This atmospheric component contributes strongly to the identity of each panel, although it is a component that is difficult to appreciate today because of Uccello's complex use of patinas, varnishes and other surface treatments, which were quite out of the ordinary in the Florentine tradition of his times, and are now hopelessly damaged.

The entire composition of the three panels is concentrated on the principal episode shown in the frontal impact of the Uffizi panel, which, not by chance, is the only one the artist signed. The signal for attack (daringly, according to many contemporaries) given by Niccolò da Tolentino in the London panel, like the symmetrically placed (later) intervention of the other Florentine troops led by Cotignola, in the Paris panel, depict two movements converging towards the central episode. This latter is commonly interpreted as the unhorsing of Bernardino Ubaldini della Ciarda, commander of the Sienese and Milanese forces. However, none of the sources on the actual sequence of events in any way authenticates this episode. From what is known, the encounter at San Romano began with Tolentino's daring attack against superior forces, and was followed by a mêlée in which he ran the risk of being killed; finally, Cotignola intervened with his forces, after he had been informed of the course the battle was taking. Perhaps the enemy had neglected him, because they thought his contract (*condotta*), which allied his militia to Florence, had expired. Once Cotignola had intervened, the army of the anti-Florentine alliance began a swift withdrawal: a decision made by Ubaldini in spite of contrary advice given by some of his captains. The whole episode is depicted in front of Michelotto da Cotignola's standard, and Uccello would have been quite conscious of the significance of this heraldic element, which, before its amputation, would have dominated both the National Gallery and Louvre panels. Leaving aside the contradictions and lack of precise detail in the sources, obviously Uccello's interpretation of the event should not be read as a narrative or chronicle of that day on 1 June 1432, but rather as a poetic evocation. The Florence panel therefore marks the central focal point of the composition, both in the sense of space and interpretation. The unhorsing of the Sienese knight undoubtedly symbolized Florentine success, which is what the patrons wished to emphasize, even if the sources disagreed in this regard and were very partisan (see catalogue).[140]

Facing page: Uccello, detail of *The Battle of San Romano.* London, National Gallery.

As later in the Oxford *Hunt*, Uccello was more interested in an evocation than in a

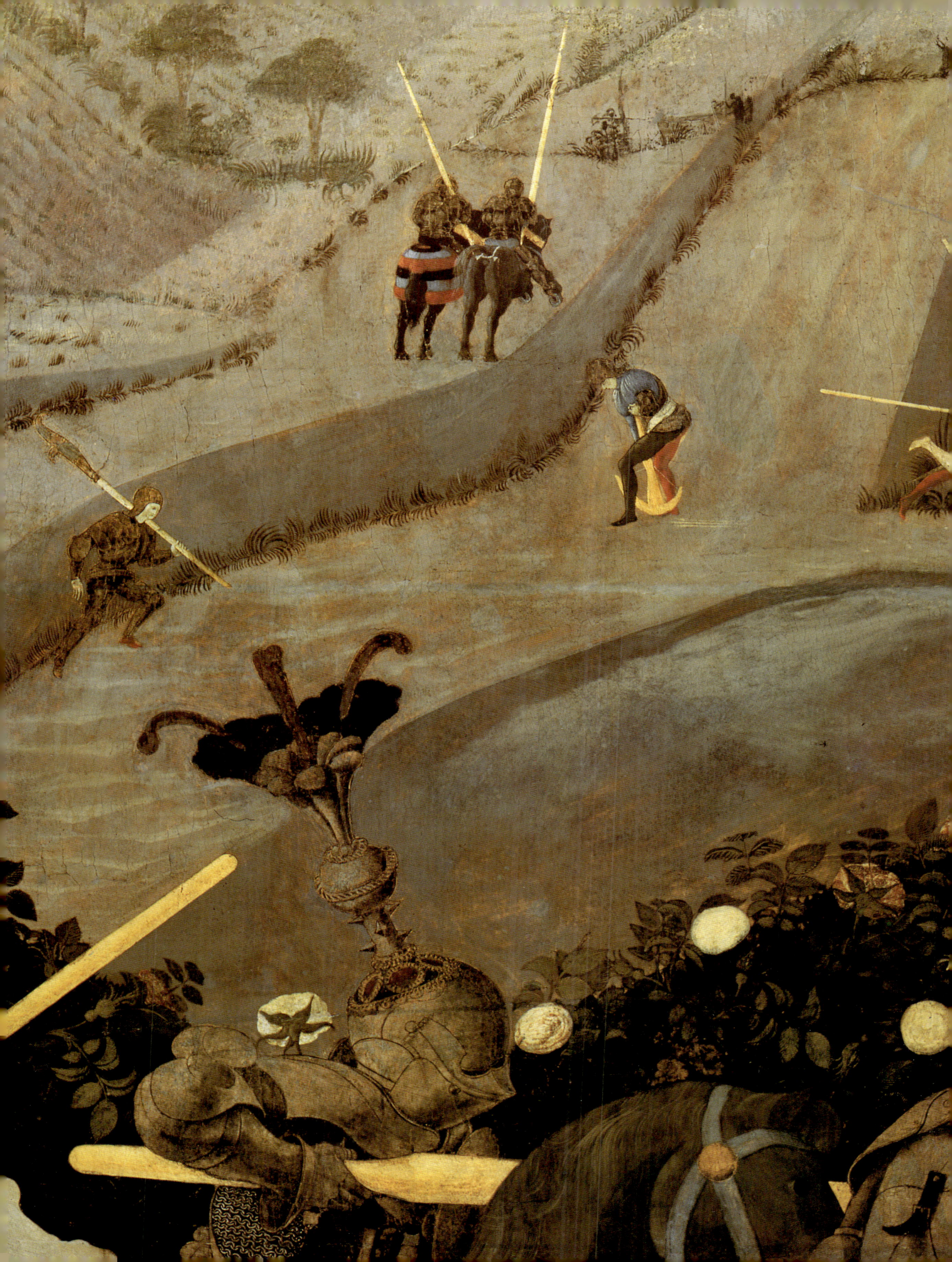

Following pages: Uccello, *The Battle of San Romano: Niccolò da Tolentino at the Head of the Florentines,* *c.* 1435–6, tempera on wood, 181 × 320 cm. London, National Gallery. Complete work and detail.

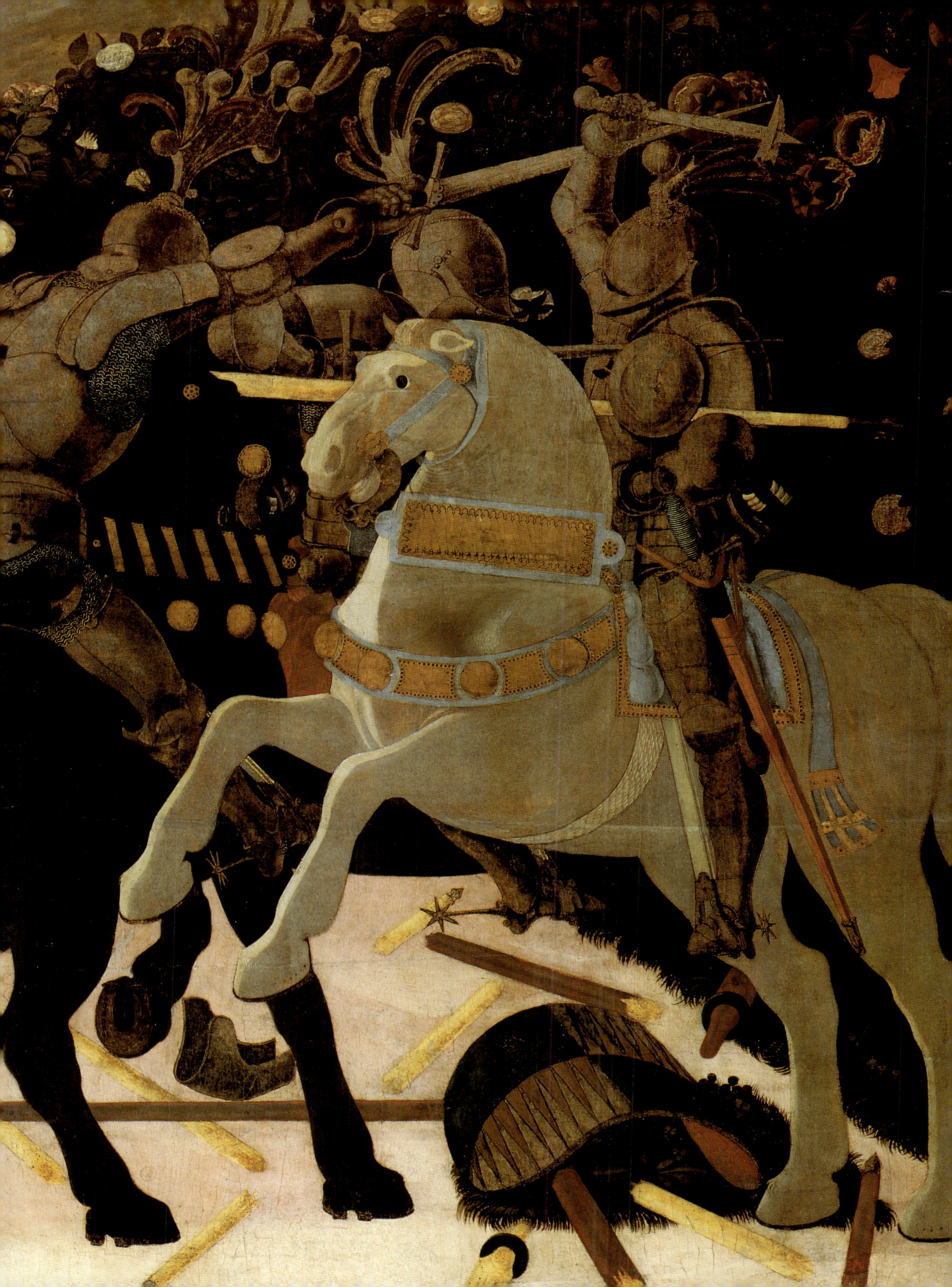

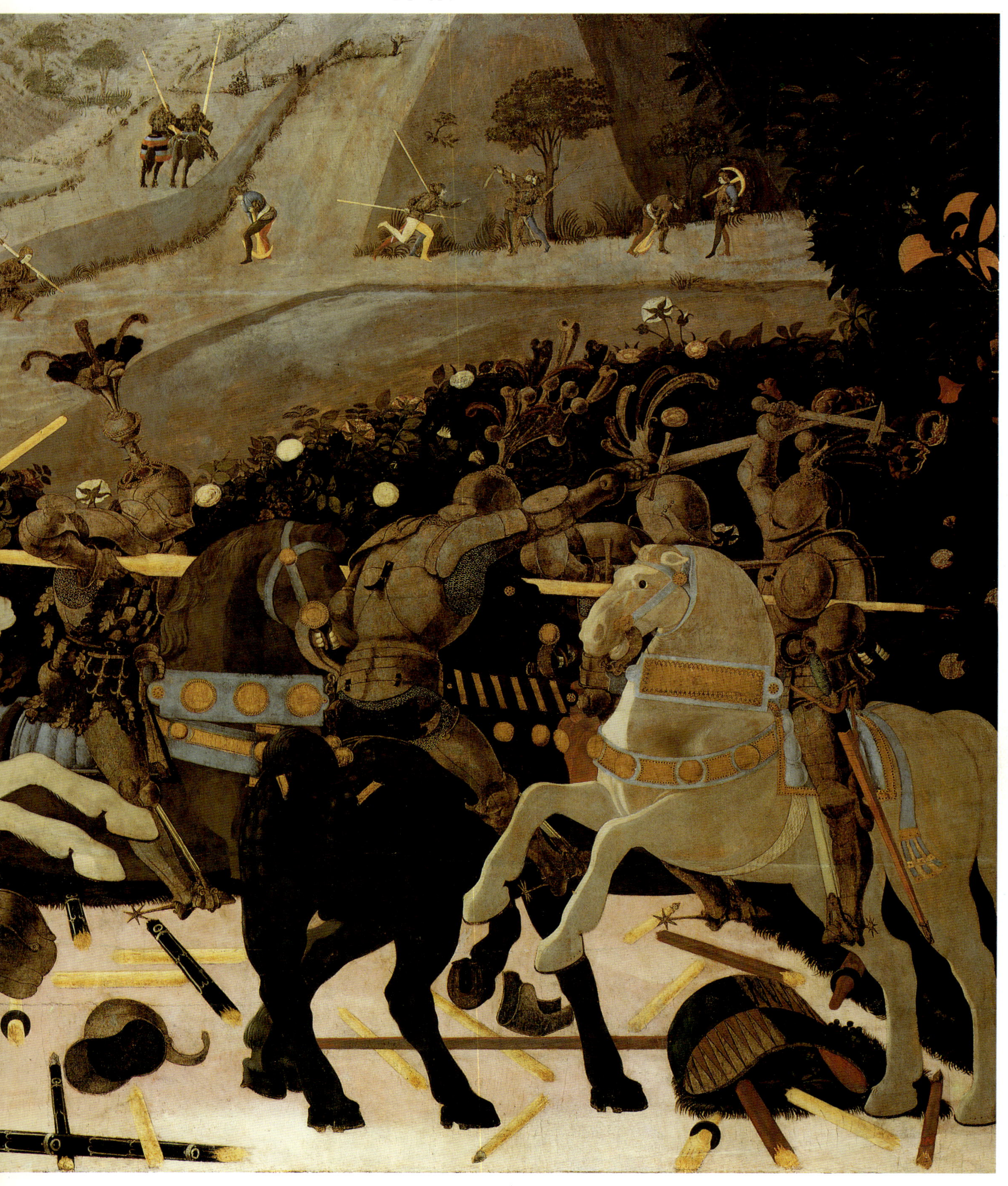

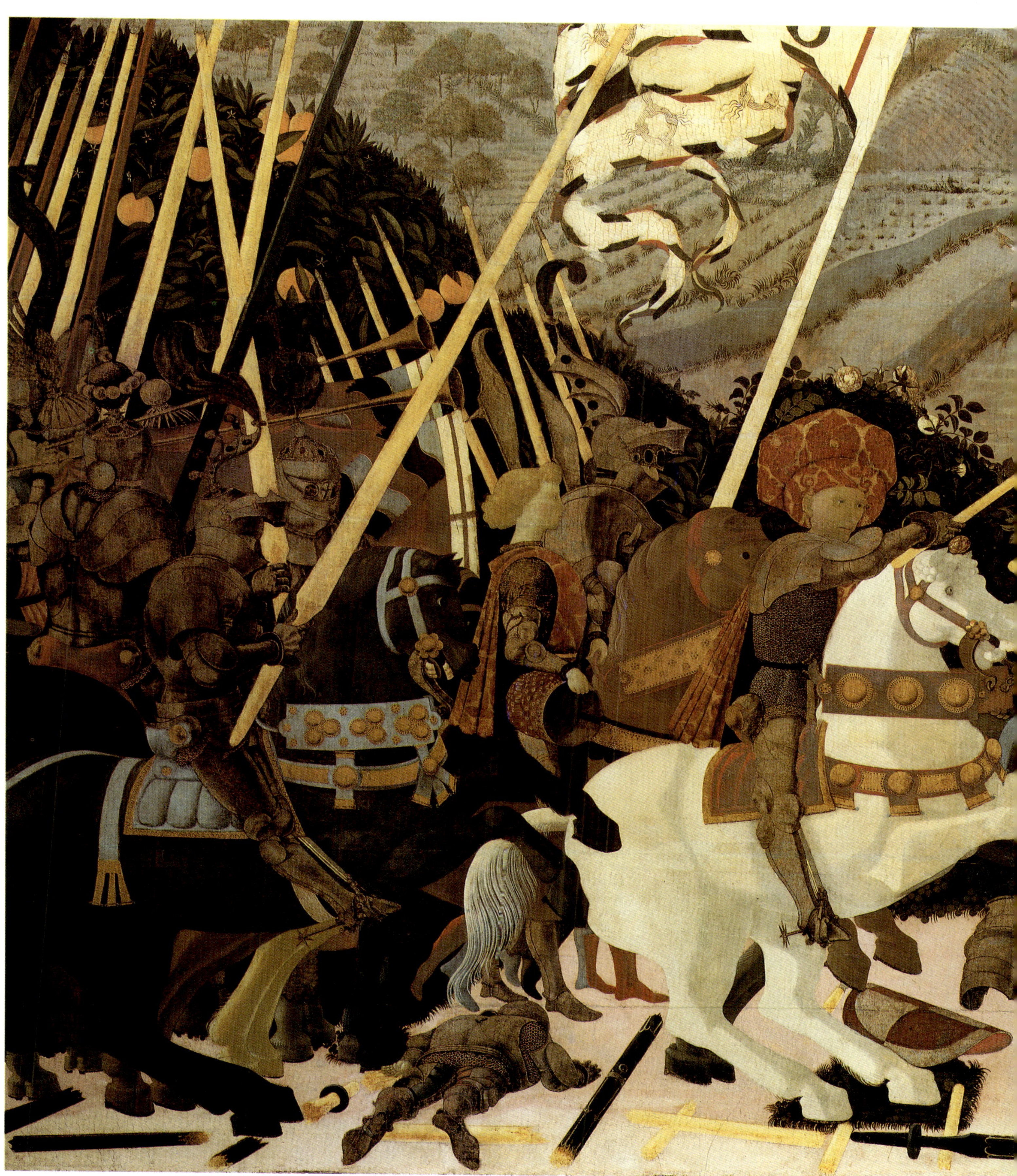

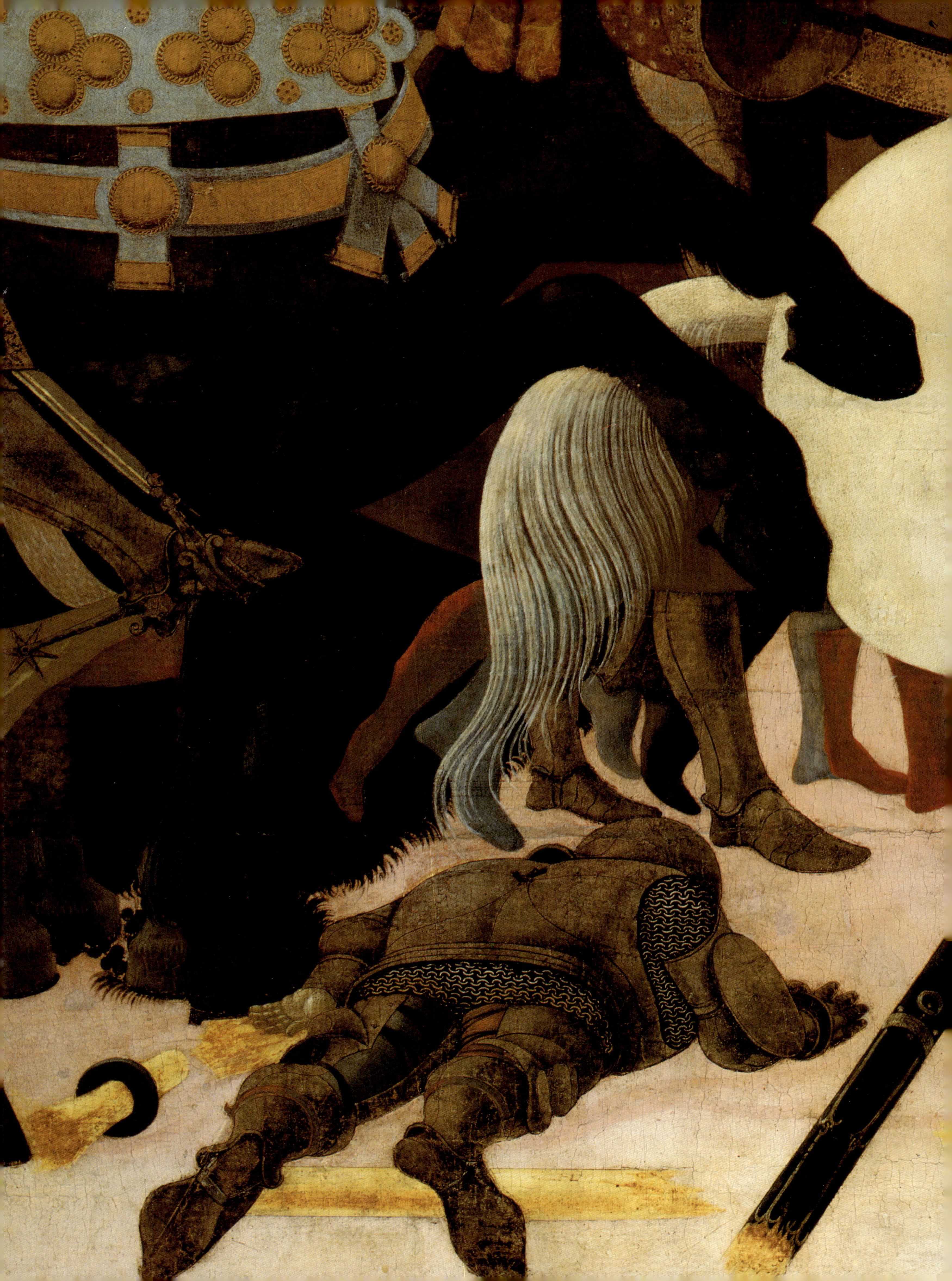

concrete description of hunting practice in Tuscany. So in the distance in the *Battles*, the narrative gives way to poetry and the precision of the chronicle becomes blurred. As though the public were well aware of the facts and the patrons had wanted to emphasize their political wisdom in the painting, the republican era discreetly began to become a self-celebration of the house of Medici, who had given political and economic support to the venture at San Romano. As in the *Hunt*, the agitated human figures contrast with the calm and peace of the natural world. Undoubtedly a more generous description of nature existed before the panels were cut.

We can see in the great standards that immediately identify the two Florentine commanders, and the symmetry of the whole sequence that implied an equal share of merit to both Tolentino who took the initiative, and Cotignola who carried the day, shining through, Cosimo's homage to Averardo, his dead cousin who had been Cotignola's friend and financial backer, a fact that makes us doubt that the panels were linked to the Tolentino celebrations around the 1450s and confirms, even if indirectly, their earlier dating.

Facing page: Uccello, detail of *The Battle of San Romano*. London, National Gallery.

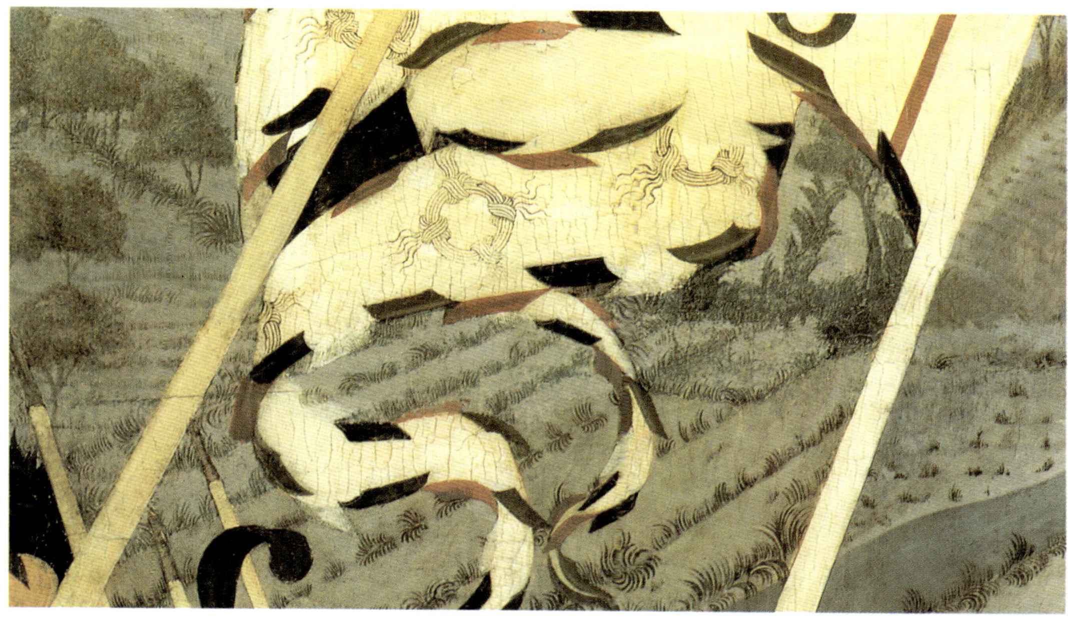

Detail of the London *Battle of San Romano* panel showing the cut-down standards.

Following pages: Uccello, detail of *The Battle of San Romano: the Counter-Attack by Micheletto da Cotignola*. Paris, Louvre.

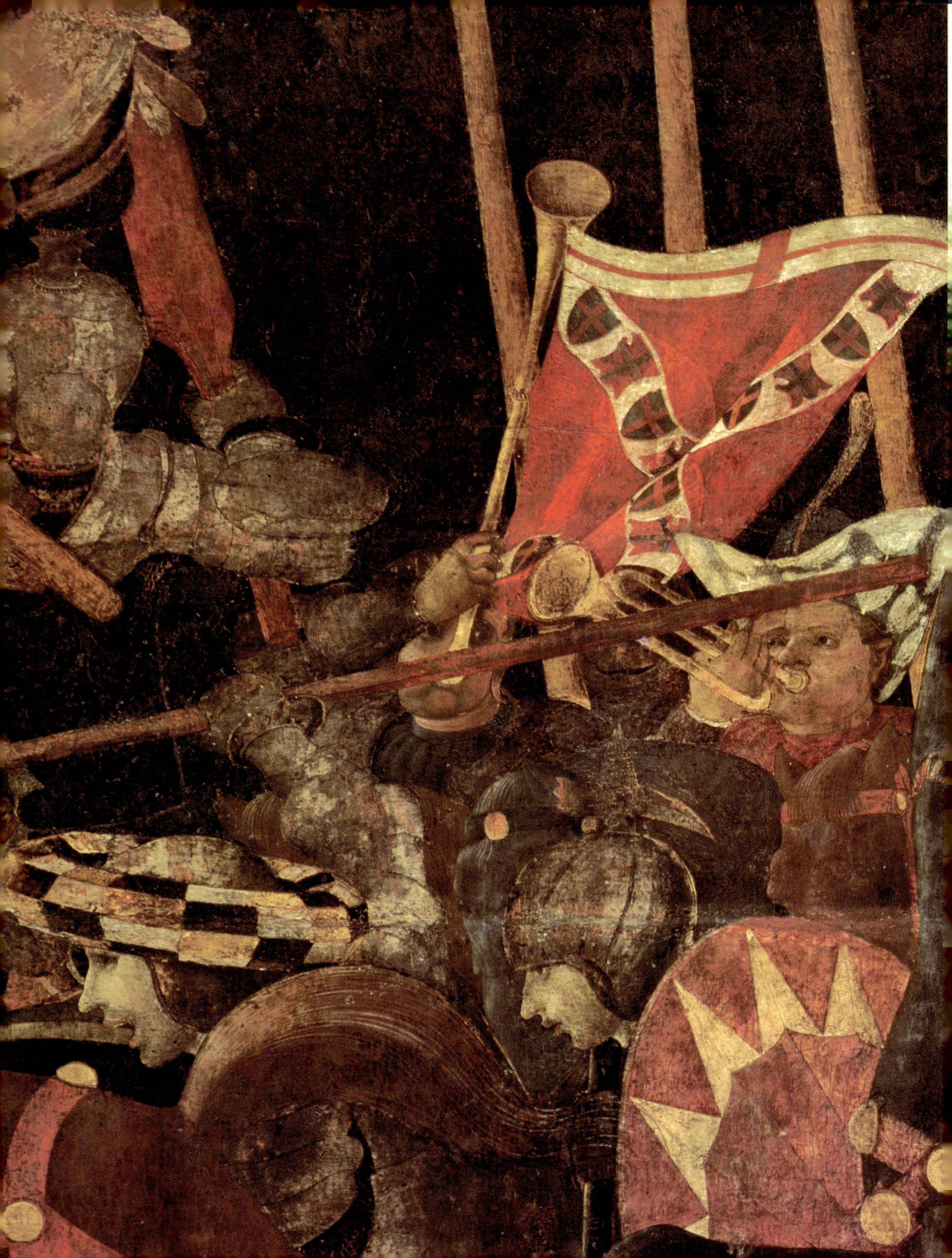

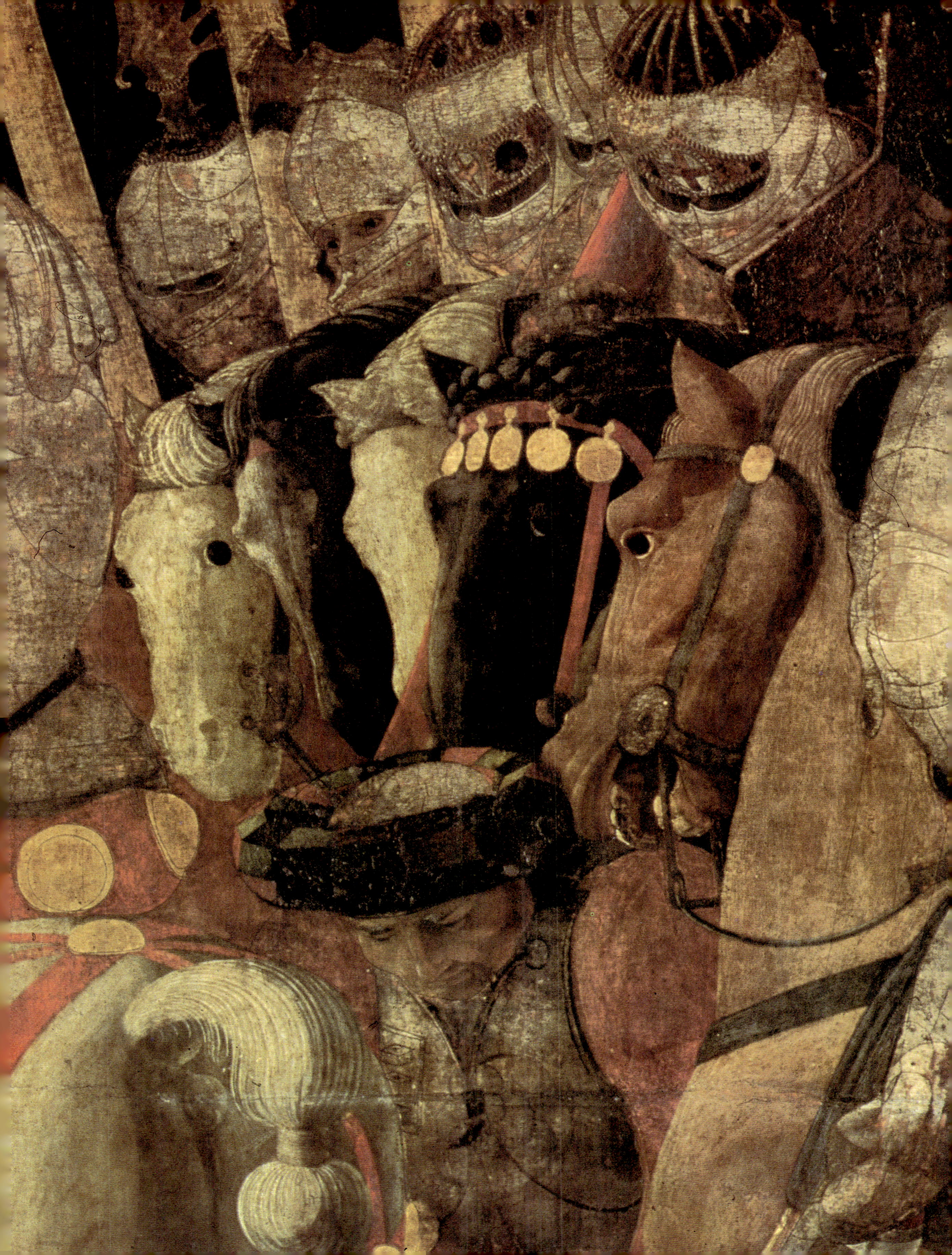

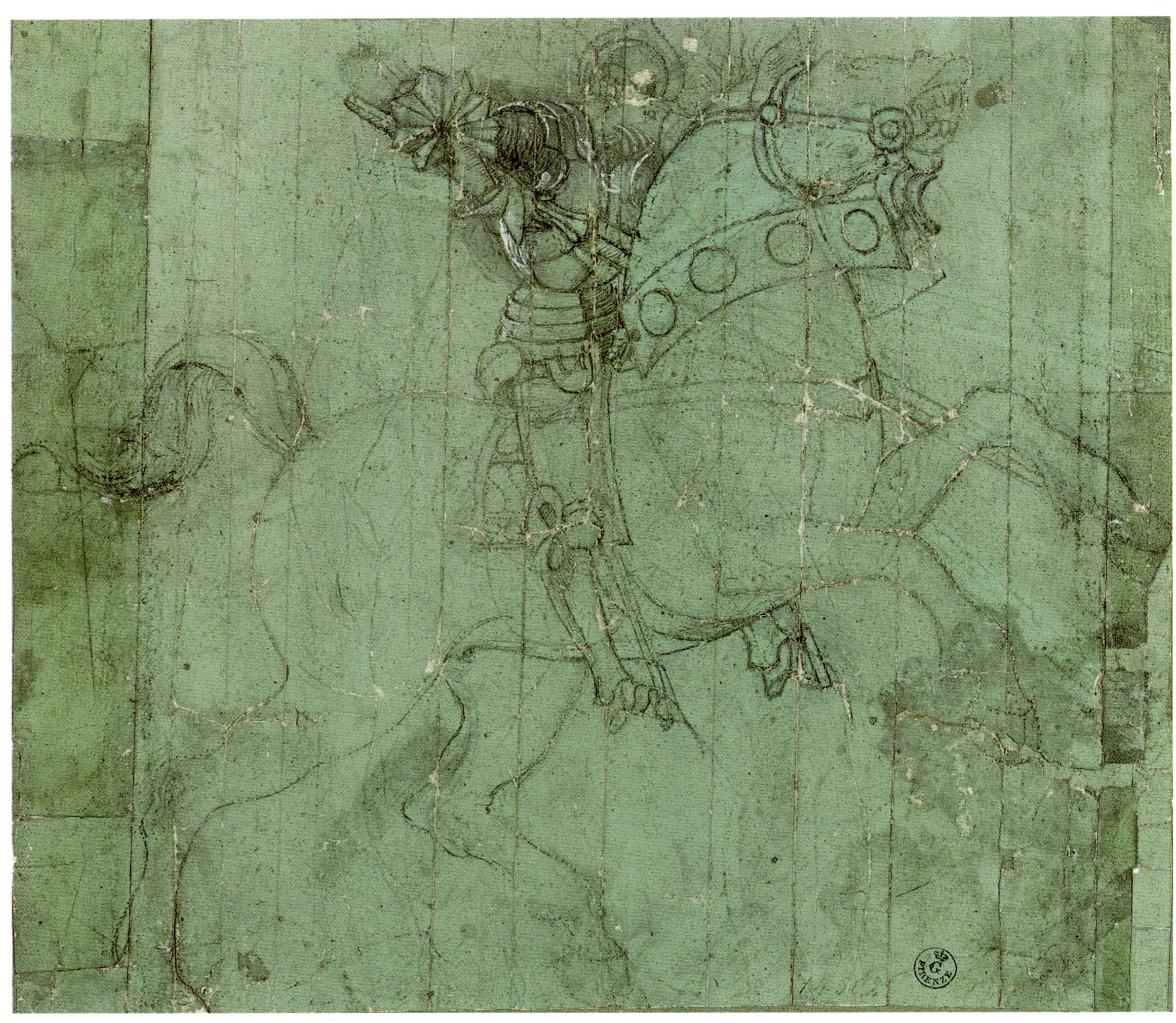

Uccello, *Study of a Knight* (Saint George?), *c.* 1460–65, pen and silverpoint on paper with green wash, heightened in white. Florence, Uffizi, Gabinetto dei Disegni, no. 14502. The paper is perforated for transfer of the design on to canvas, Uccello's usual procedure in his mature period. The pose is a more dynamic version of that of one of the figures in the Florence *Battle*.

Facing page: Uccello, detail of *The Battle of San Romano*. Paris, Louvre.

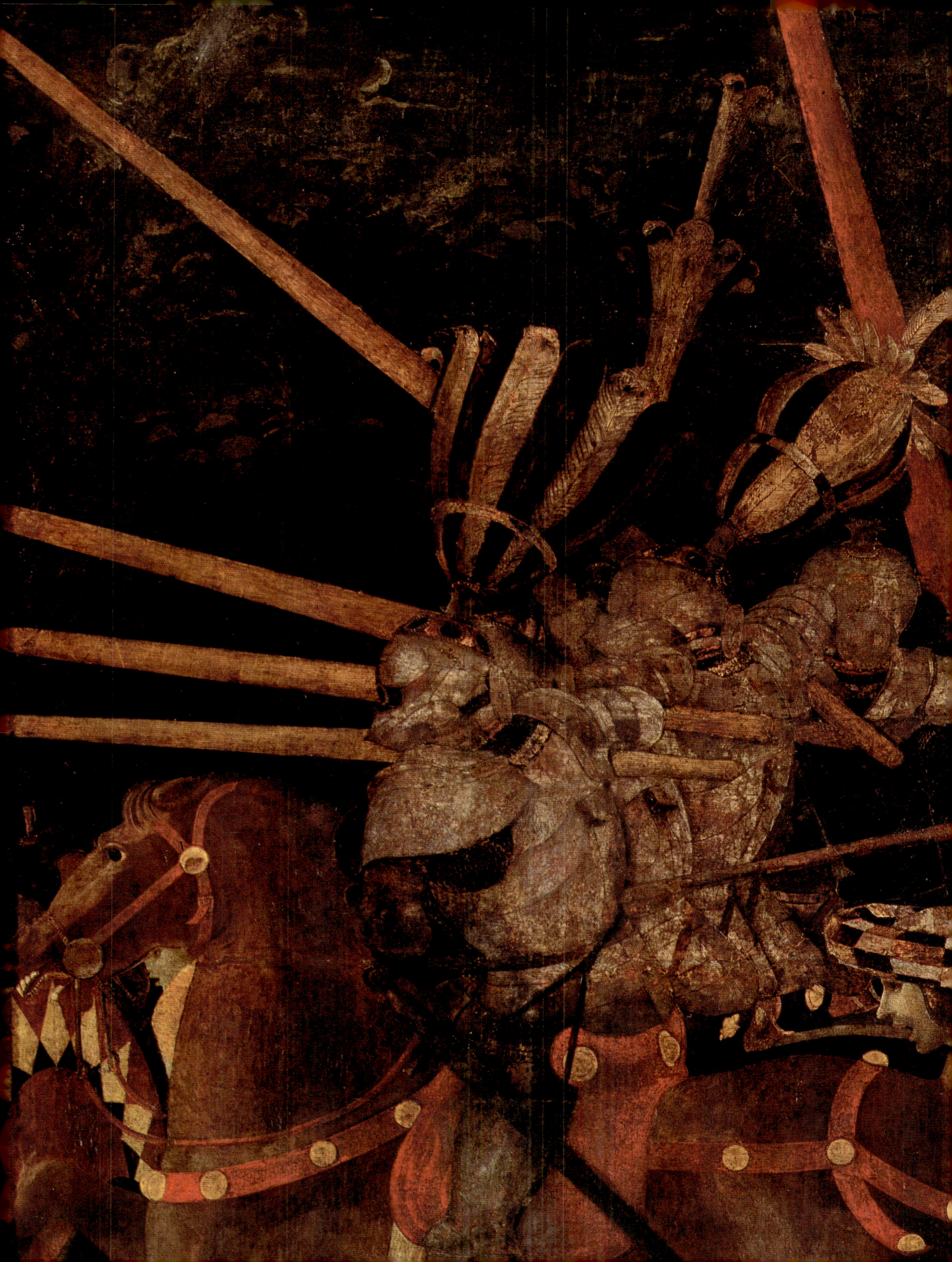

Following pages: Uccello, *The Battle of San Romano: the Counter-Attack by Micheletto da Cotignola*, *c.* 1440, tempera on wood, 180 × 316 cm. Paris, Louvre. Complete work and detail.

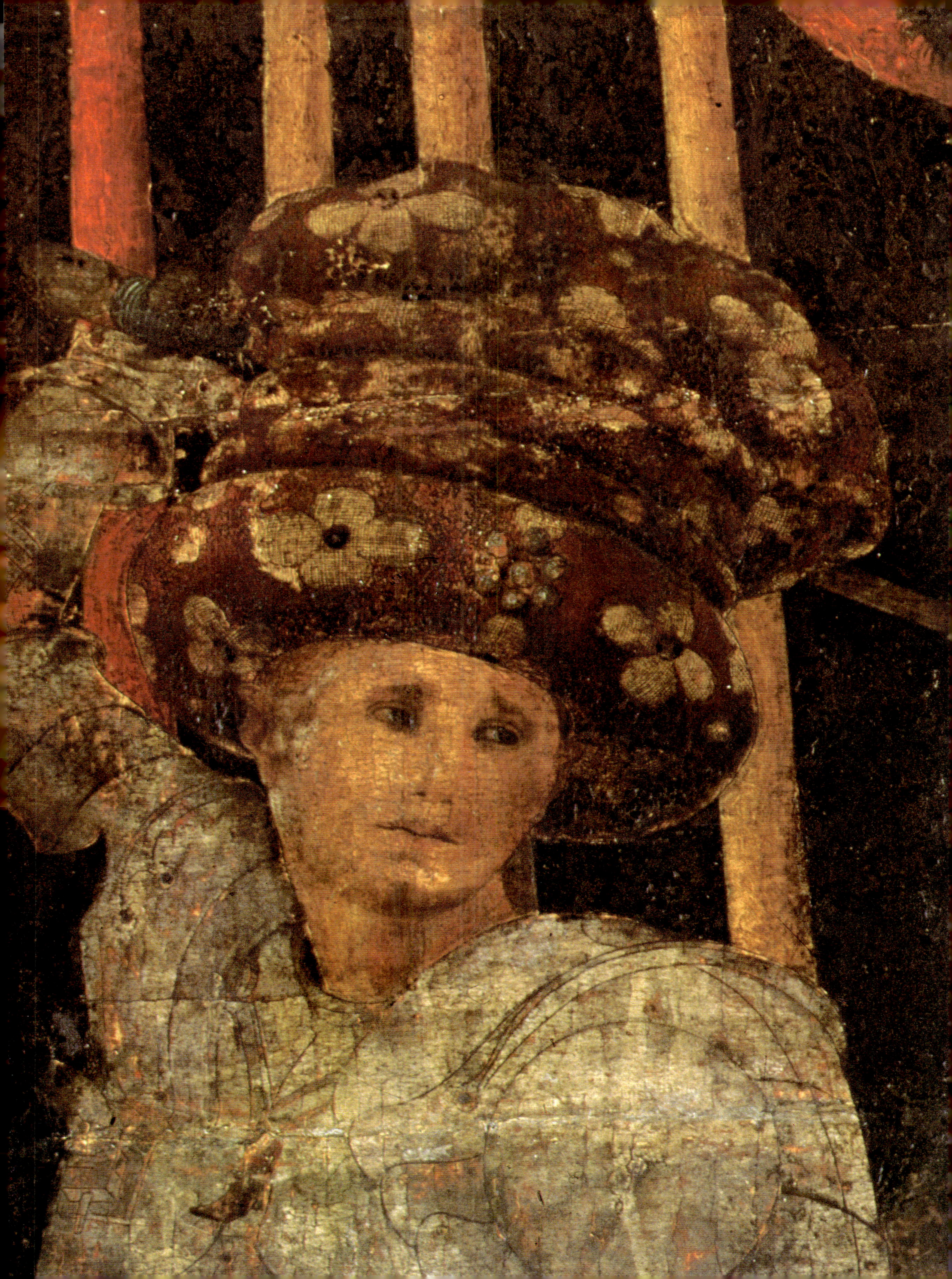

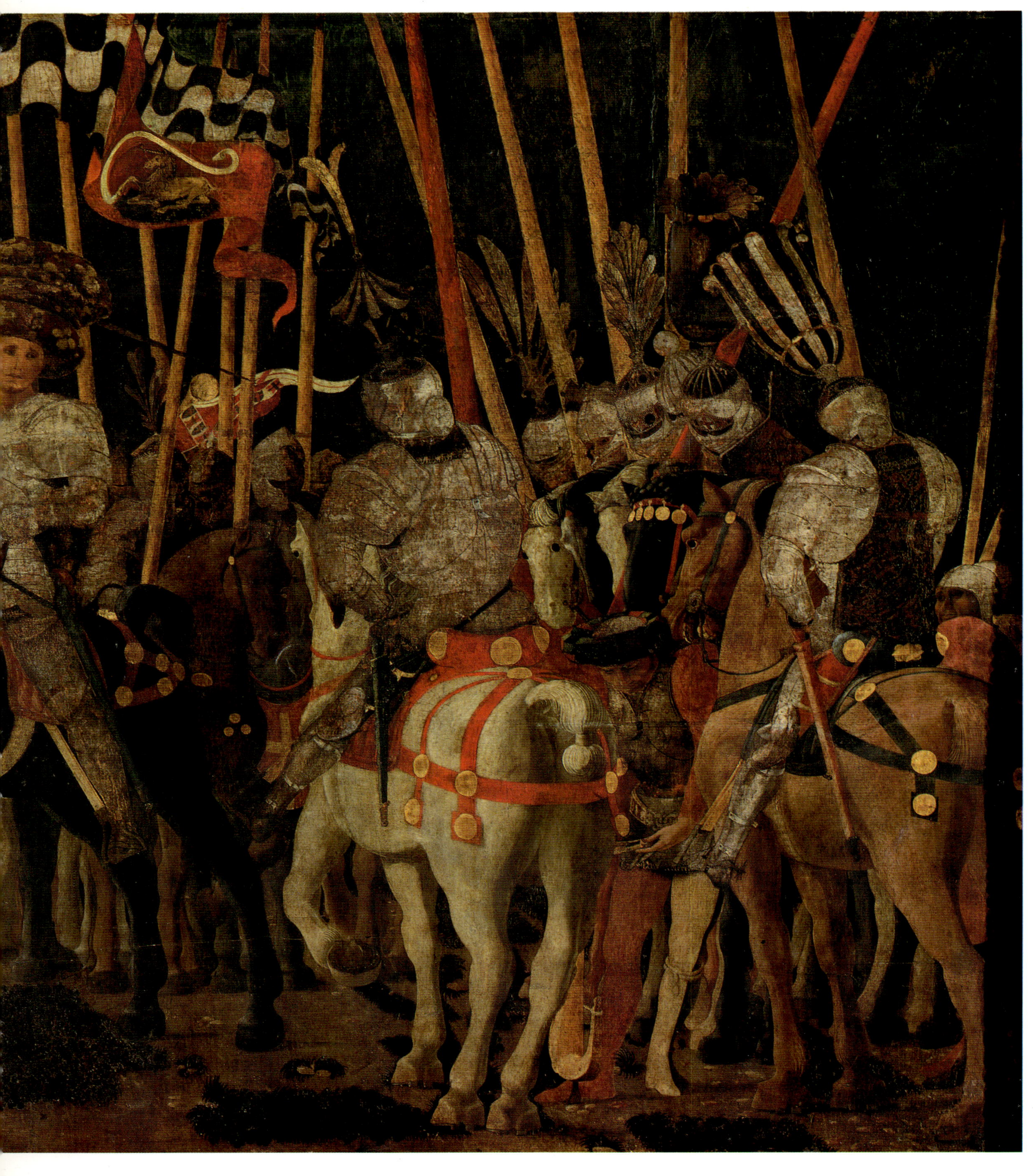

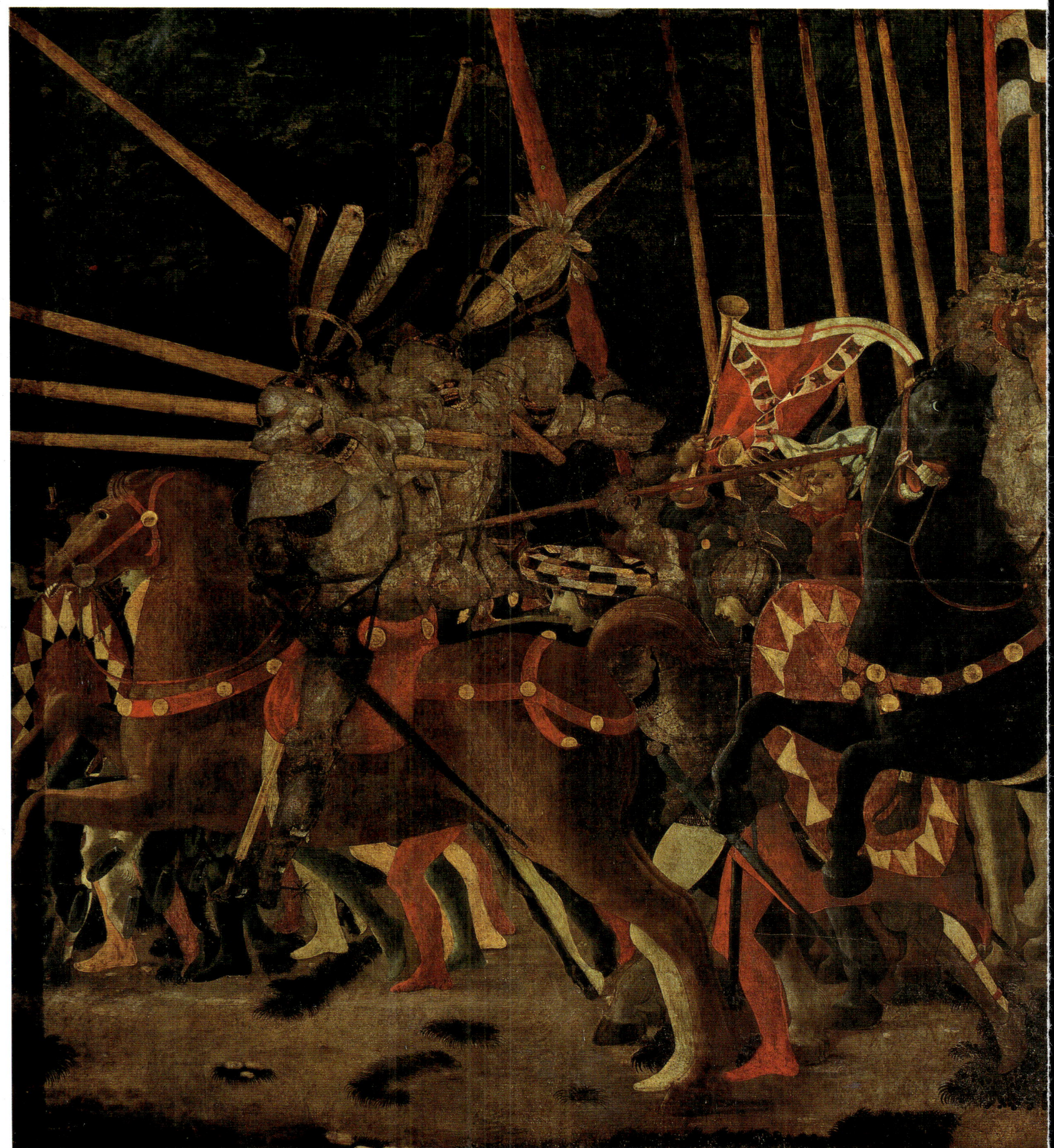

3 RELIGIOUS COMMISSIONS

During his lifetime, Uccello's success relied basically on his being a lay painter: the post-Giottoesque, Gothic tradition of sacred painting was foreign to him, just as was popular, realist secular painting in the manner of Donatello and Castagno. The mystical refinements of the Sienese or Fra Angelico were similarly unknown territory, although he took an interest in them. For Uccello, sacred painting consisted of simply conforming to a type of commission that involved special requests, and thus provided him with an additional opportunity to explore extraordinary phenomena and symbolism. So a miracle took the form of a rainbow, the mysteries, nocturnes, and earthly life, storms. Within what could be described as these limitations – which in reality were elements of modernity and innovation and which gave positive proof of his unusual gifts for fantasizing – there was a sort of internal progression through a variety of experiments. This can be only pieced together rather generally from the few works that survive, but need to be discussed here.

THE KARLSRUHE ADORATION, THE NUN-SAINT

Starting with the Karlsruhe *Adoration* in which Gothic traditions, iconological and symbolic subject matter, conventions relating to the *ductus* (a term used in Italian painting to mean 'making' or 'manufacture') and physiognomical peculiarities were all explored within a framework of refined traditionalism, Uccello moved on to the bare, synthetic and most delicate austerity of the Contini *Nun-Saint*, with its monumentality and aggressive blacks. It has an anaemic pallor and glimpses of a spatiality made up of customary themes, a polychrome border in angular relief and Classical-styled flat cornices, now barely discernible given the fragmentary nature of the panel which, in cinematic terms, has been brutally cut to a 'close medium shot', so that the architectonic space and neighbouring figures are barely visible.

Cat. nos. 5, 11

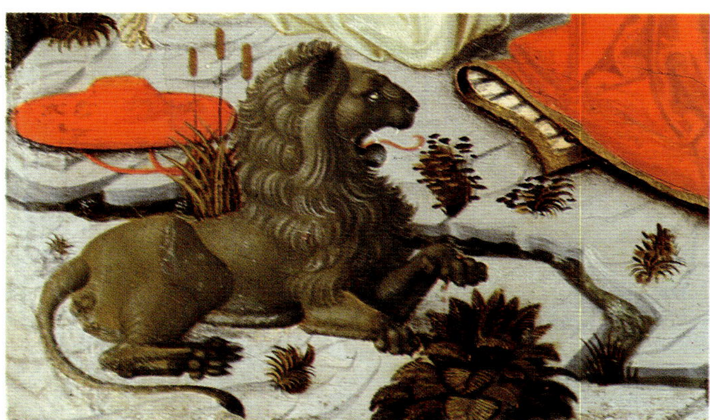

Detail of *The Adoration of the Child* (*see facing page*).

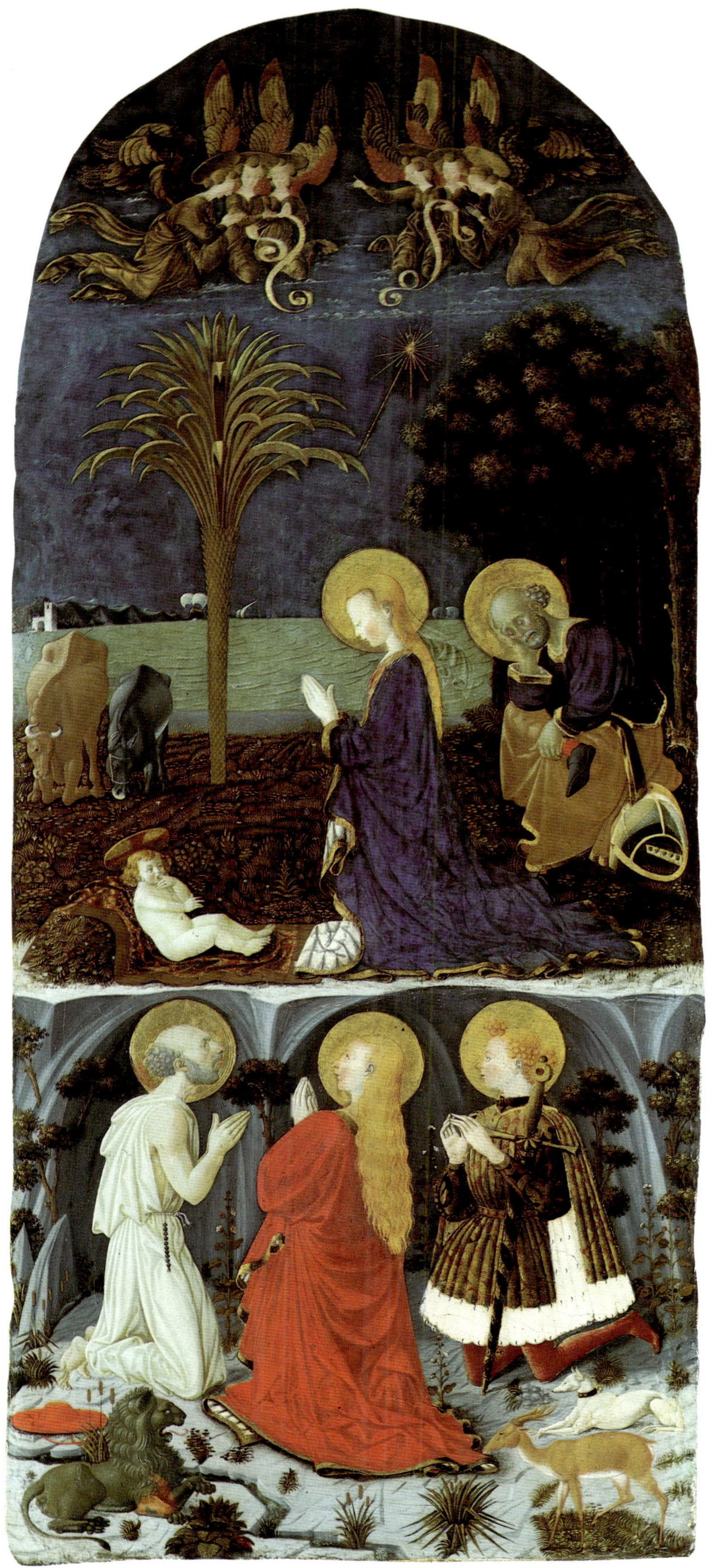

Uccello, *The Adoration of the Child with Saint Jerome, Saint Mary Magdalen and Saint Eustace*, *c.* 1431–2, tempera on wood, 110 × 47 cm. Karlsruhe, Staatliche Kunsthalle.

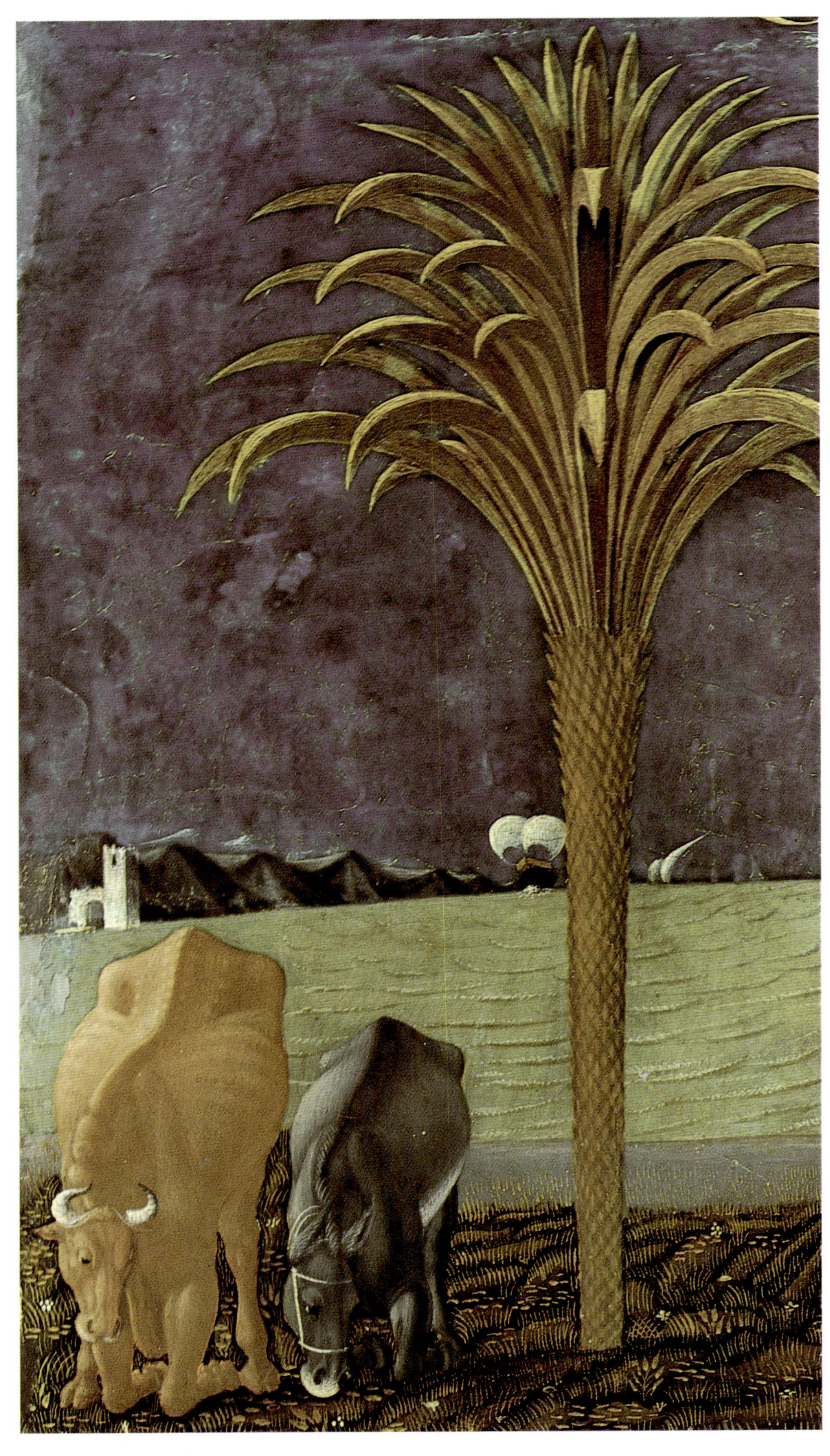

Uccello, detail of *The Adoration of the Child.*

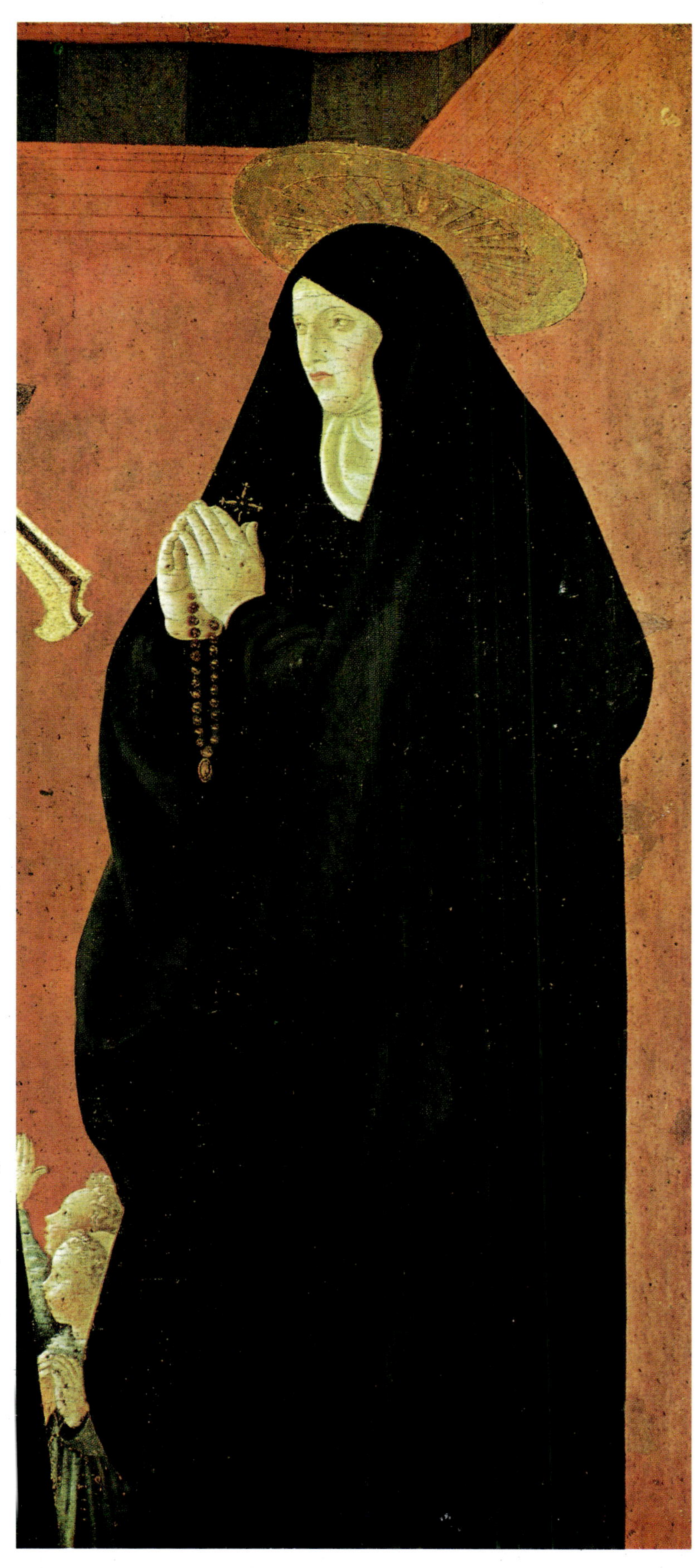

Uccello, *Nun-Saint with Two Children*, fragment of the right-hand section of a retable, *c.* 1434–5, tempera on wood, 79 × 35 cm. Formerly Florence, Contini-Bonacossi Collection.

THE DUBLIN MADONNA AND CHILD, CARTOONS FOR WINDOWS

Next came the most Donatellian of Uccello's experiments, which can be seen in the Dublin *Madonna and Child*, with the Infant Jesus looking almost like a miniature Bacchus: there is a courageous uninhibited naturalism in the faces, and the sacred has been given a feeling of warmth through its assimilation of everyday language. But Uccello the experimenter did not stop here: in the cartoons for the Duomo windows, which show a more direct though not totally demonstrable Ghibertian influence (we know in fact that Ghiberti had the greater part of the enterprise), he was using a technique not unknown to him (through his experience in Venice) and employing elements of a more solemn *goticitas*. He confined figurative synthesis to joining the different coloured pieces of glass, using a tracery of lead; gave his work a structure with different characteristics from those with which he is usually identified. But in another way his sense of colour made him tend to group together areas of intense blue, luminous figures, reds, and the golden yellow of the ox in the *Nativity*. Uccello was working on the window as though it were a painting made up of intense colours; it was like a sort of enlarged mosaic that had an enduring splendour, rather than an austere, ascetic, graphic exercise based on drawing. Next to Ghiberti, Uccello was to be the most 'translatable' of artists and for many years he worked alongside the master

Cat. nos. 16, 20, 21

See p. 121

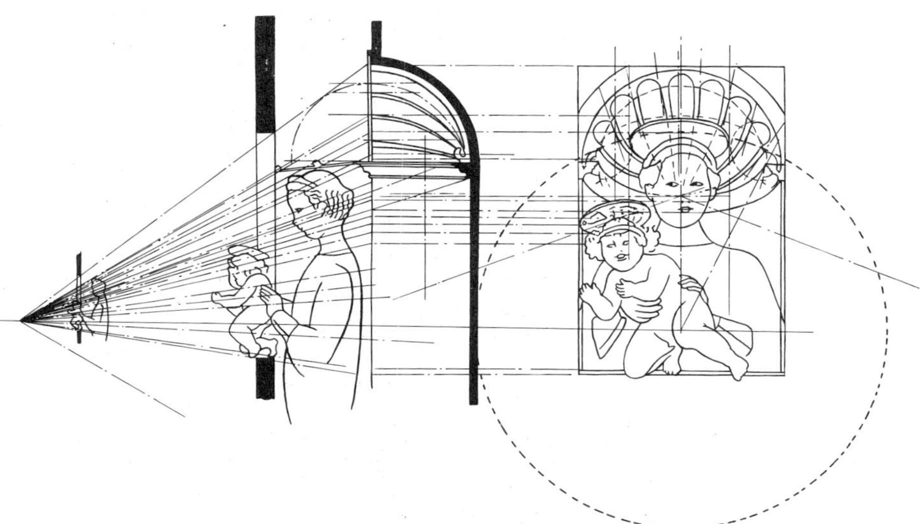

Reconstruction of the perspective used in the Dublin *Madonna and Child* (after Sindona-Rossi).

glass makers for the cathedral's Office of Works. In the *Nativity* the composition is centred on a kind of square inscribed within the circular field of the oculus, and takes on a decorative, superficial form, with the element of the hut, completely lacking any perspective on its thin rustic supports; the only hint of spatial depth is found in the foreshortened ox and ass. By contrast, in the *Resurrection*, the module of compostion is

Facing page: Uccello, *Madonna and Child*, *c.* 1437–40, tempera on wood, 57 × 33 cm. Dublin, National Gallery of Ireland.

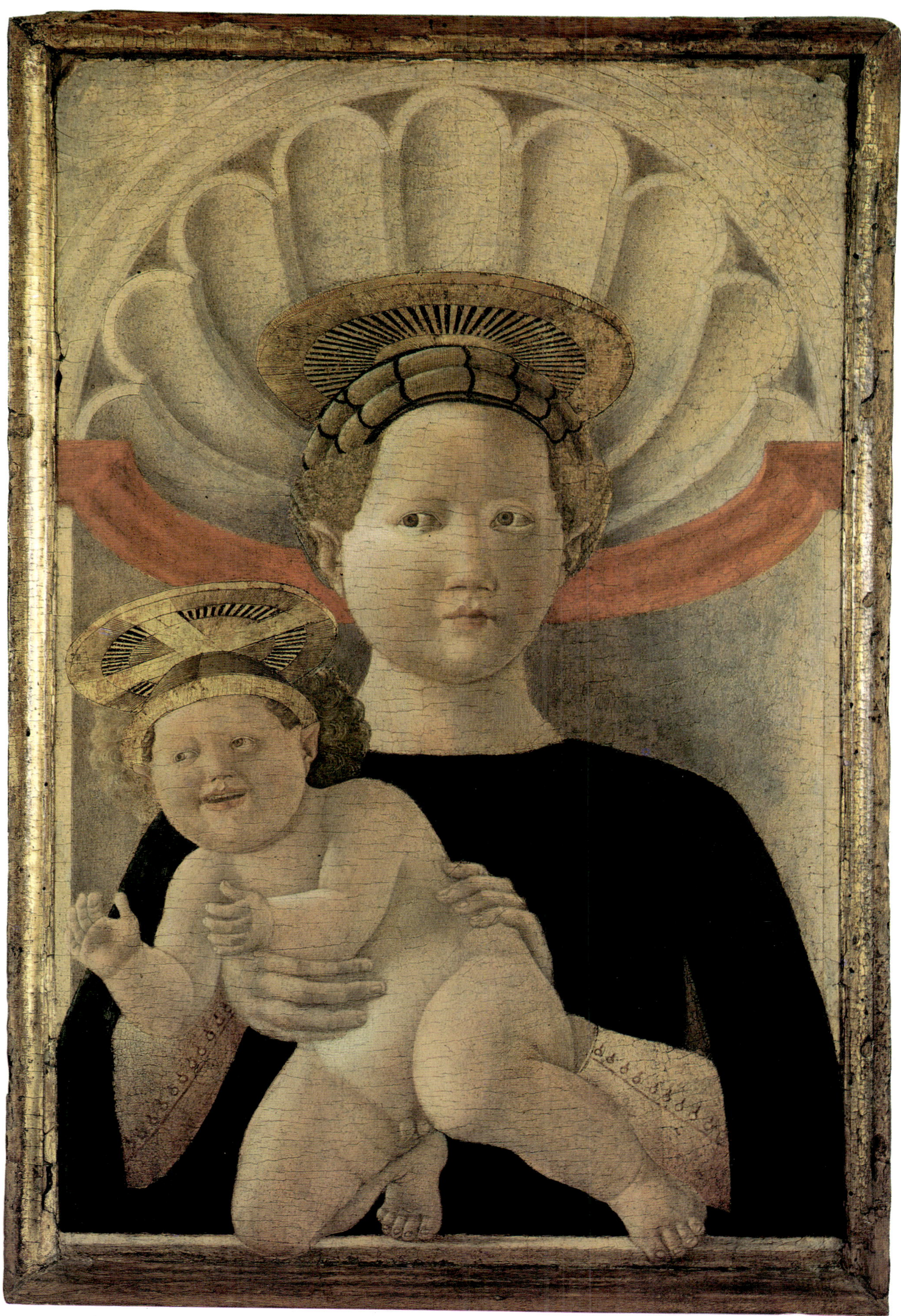

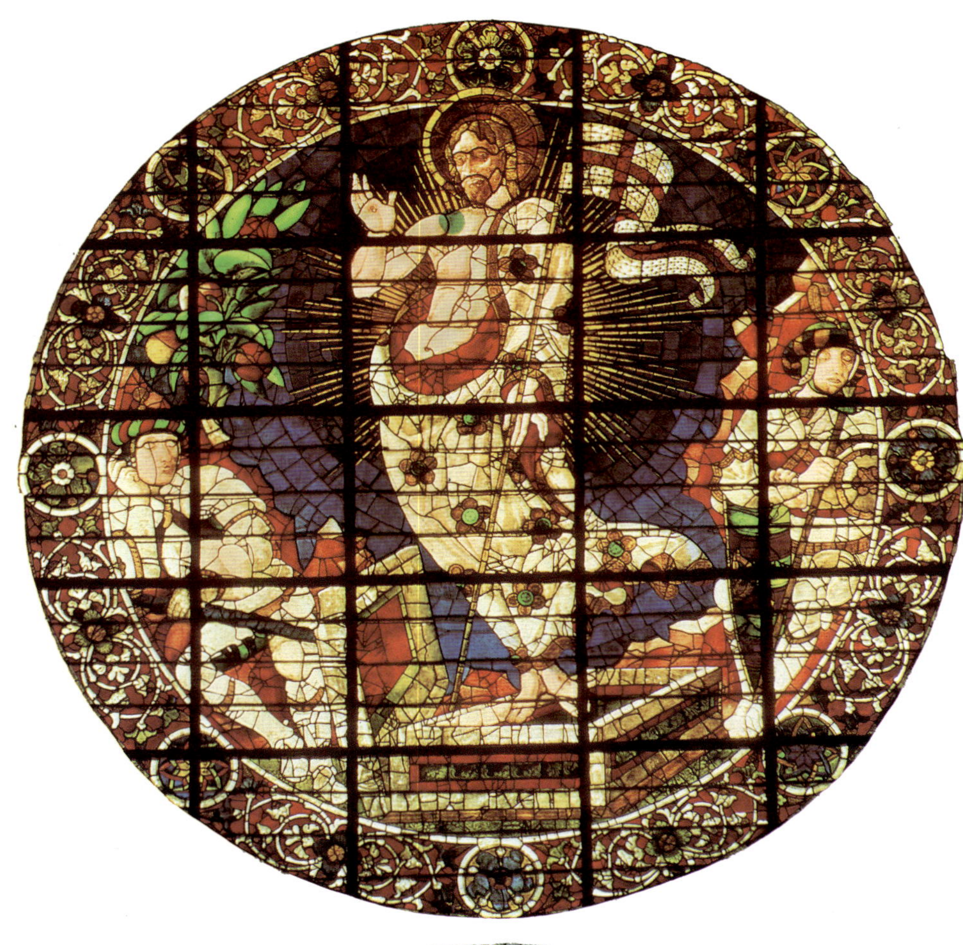

Uccello's two stained-glass windows for the drum of the cupola of Santa Maria del Fiore, 1443–4.

Above: The Resurrection, 468 cm in diameter.

Below: The Nativity, 473 cm in diameter.

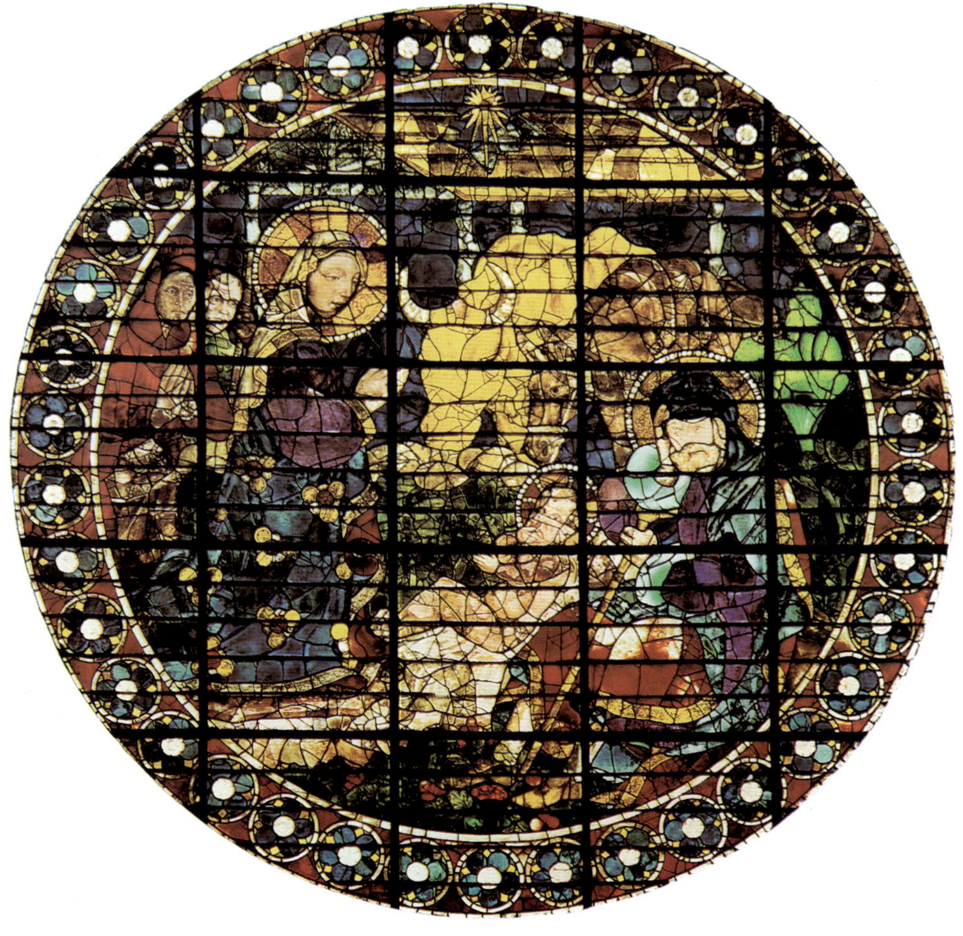

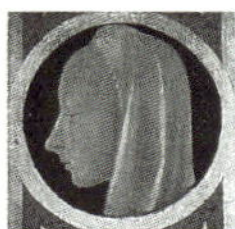

more complex: the figure of Christ is enlarged to the point of almost overlapping the edge, the top of his halo rests on the circular border and the tomb has an accentuated perspective. The radiation of light, in the gold ray-shaped designs (*razzature*), which transpose the art of the illuminator on to a grand scale, is enhanced by the concentric haloes in the sky, graduating from the central image of Christ. The *mazzocchi* and orange trees suggest a date near the *Battles*.

THE ADORATION OF THE CHILD

Cat. no. 13 The imaginary world of the Karlsruhe *Adoration* with its fantastic atmosphere can be seen again, but in a more hieratic style and employing a more rigorous perspective, in the fragments of the *Adoration of the Child*, a fresco discovered recently in San Martino Maggiore in Bologna. Unfortunately it is very fragmentary.

The Bologna *Adoration* is stylistically close to the frescoes in Prato cathedral, but it lacks their nocturnal poetry. Nor does it have the marked facial 'effects' found in the saints in the Karlsruhe retable; it reveals a preoccupation with perspectival layout, almost as though Uccello were looking at Masaccio's *Trinity* afresh, having learnt from his recent experience with the *Hawkwood*, to which this fresco seems close in time.

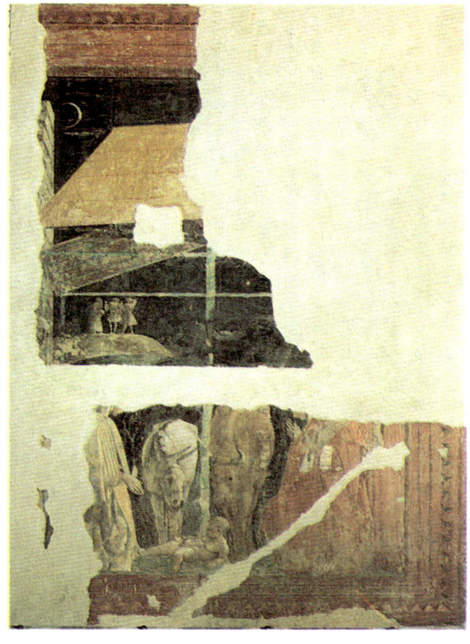

Left and following pages: Uccello, *The Adoration of the Child*, *c.* 1435–7, fresco, 350 × 237 cm. Bologna, San Martino Maggiore. Complete work and details.

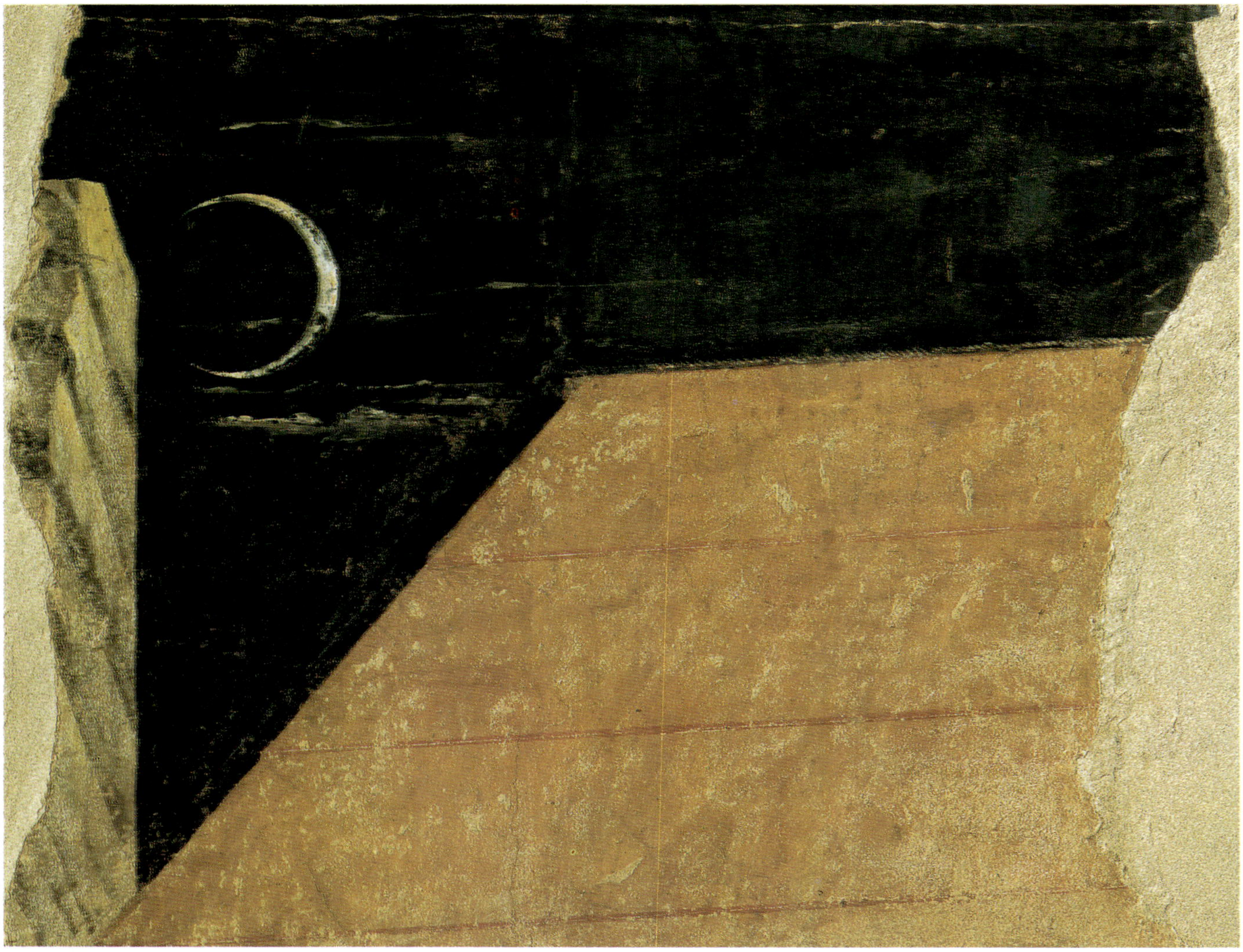

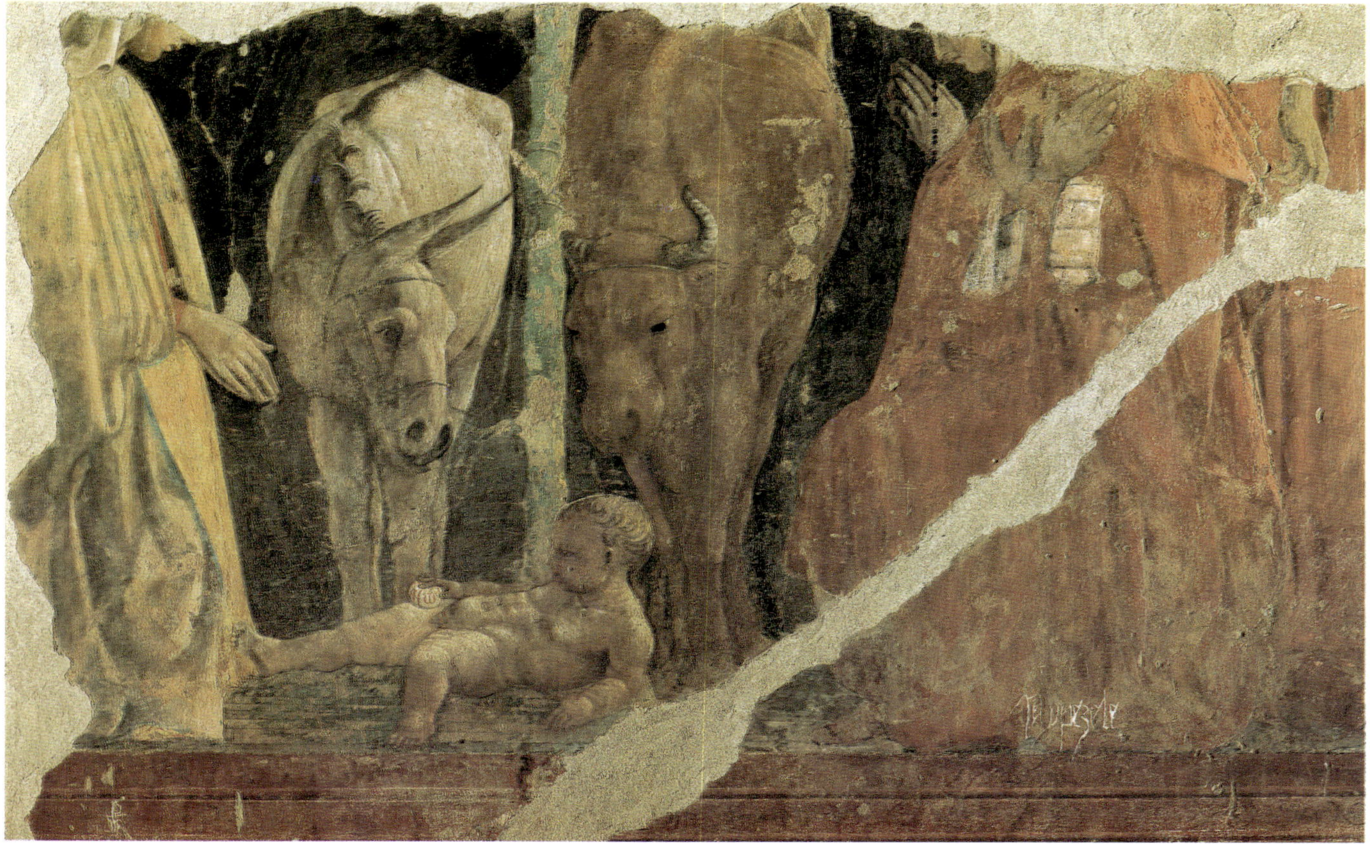

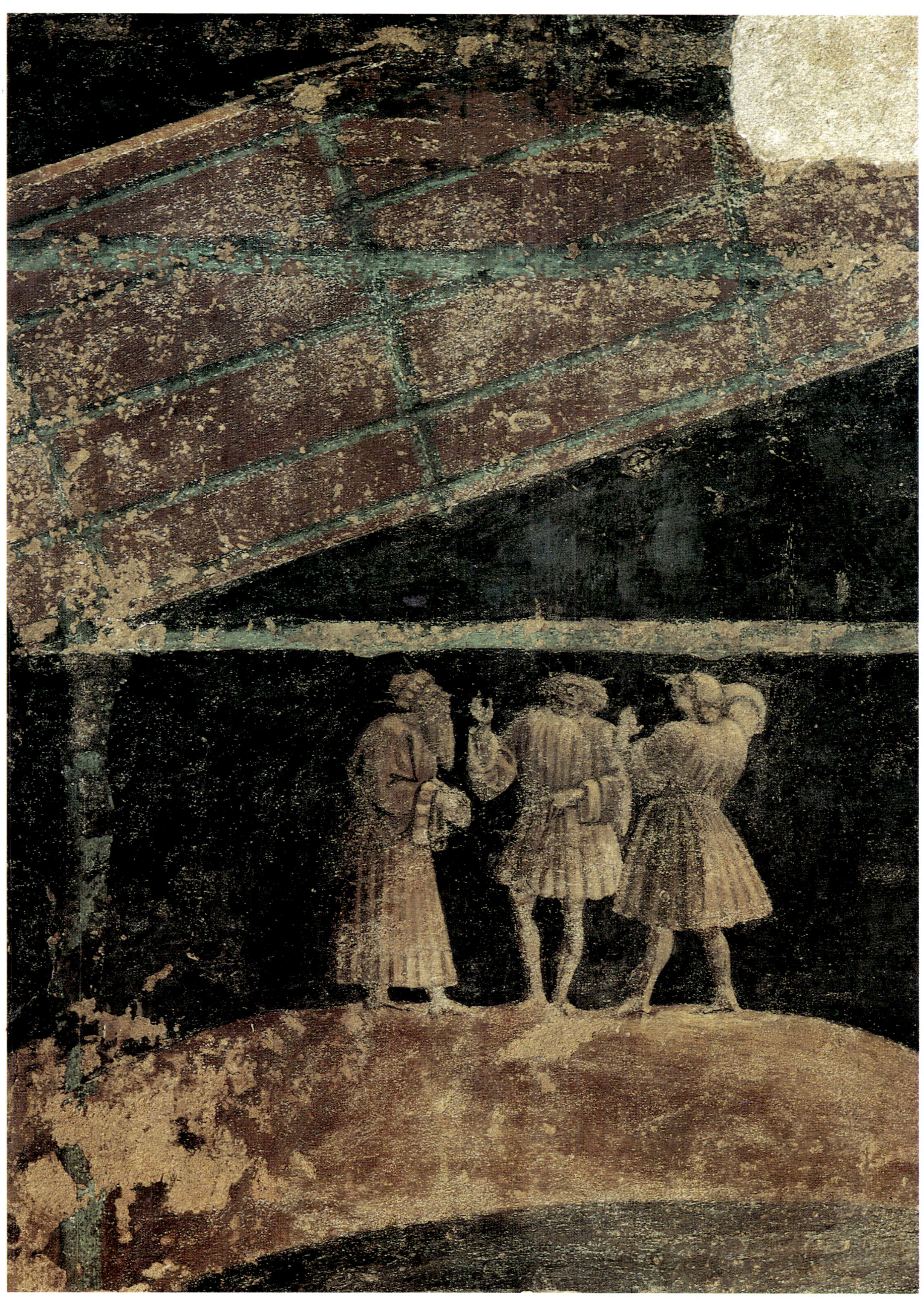

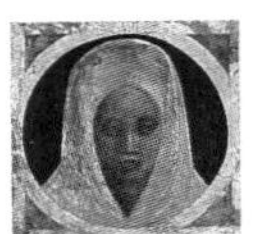

THE THYSSEN CRUCIFIXION

Uccello seems to have given up his usual experimentation in the Thyssen *Crucifixion*, possibly painted after the plague of 1457. It has a kind of austerity that reduces landscape notations to their minimum, like the snowy summits of the Apennines or patches of green grass which become continuous in the foreground and serve to indicate the perspective grid; their horizontality competes with the vertical movement of the figures, dramatizing and breaking up the scene. These isolated figures, each shown walking towards the Cross, are sharply outlined and have pointed profiles (as Vasari was to comment); they are thin and haggard and there is nothing to connect one with the other, either in the composition or in the space that seems to remain completely in the background. This is a deliberate kind of simplification that reflects austere religious preaching. The (much restored) image of Christ conforms to a well-established pattern, with Gothic notes in the loincloth and the rock into which the Cross has been inserted; there is a contrast between luminous calm and death and the slightly frenetic dynamism of the participants. In the plane on which the perspective is constructed and which is suggested by the converging mountain ridges and patches of grass like paving-stones, just as in the assemblage of figures in movement, Uccello seems to be developing the dramatic theme of disarticulation, a way of depicting the grief and tragedy of events, so much so as almost to breach the rigorous *ratio* of his usual system of perspective. All balance is disrupted: the very construction of space is dynamically ambiguous. In his solitude, man confronts his grief and becomes schizoid; the intense colour identifies objects and figures with a synoptic efficiency; a fixed, sinisterly violent light obliterates every nuance of skin tone and all atmospheric allusion. *Cat. no. 30*

THE LIFE OF THE HOLY FATHERS, OR THE THEBAÏD

In the *Thebaïd*, as the small canvas in the Florence Accademia is commonly known, we see a more complex experimentation: this is a story in several episodes, organized with a sort of simultaneous perspective in the scenes. This simultaneity is only valid in an overall view of the picture: the inside reads like an itinerary, punctuated by the dynamics of the different episodes, from right to left and bottom to top, which culminate in the scene where Saint Francis is receiving the stigmata. (The upper edge showing the sky and Christ and his band of angels has obviously been cut off.) This canvas is an edifying, devout enterprise and follows an iconological programme that was much more complex than the traditional Tuscan *Thebäid* of the Trecento and Quattrocento, of distant Byzantine origin. This unity in plurality that *Cat. no. 32*

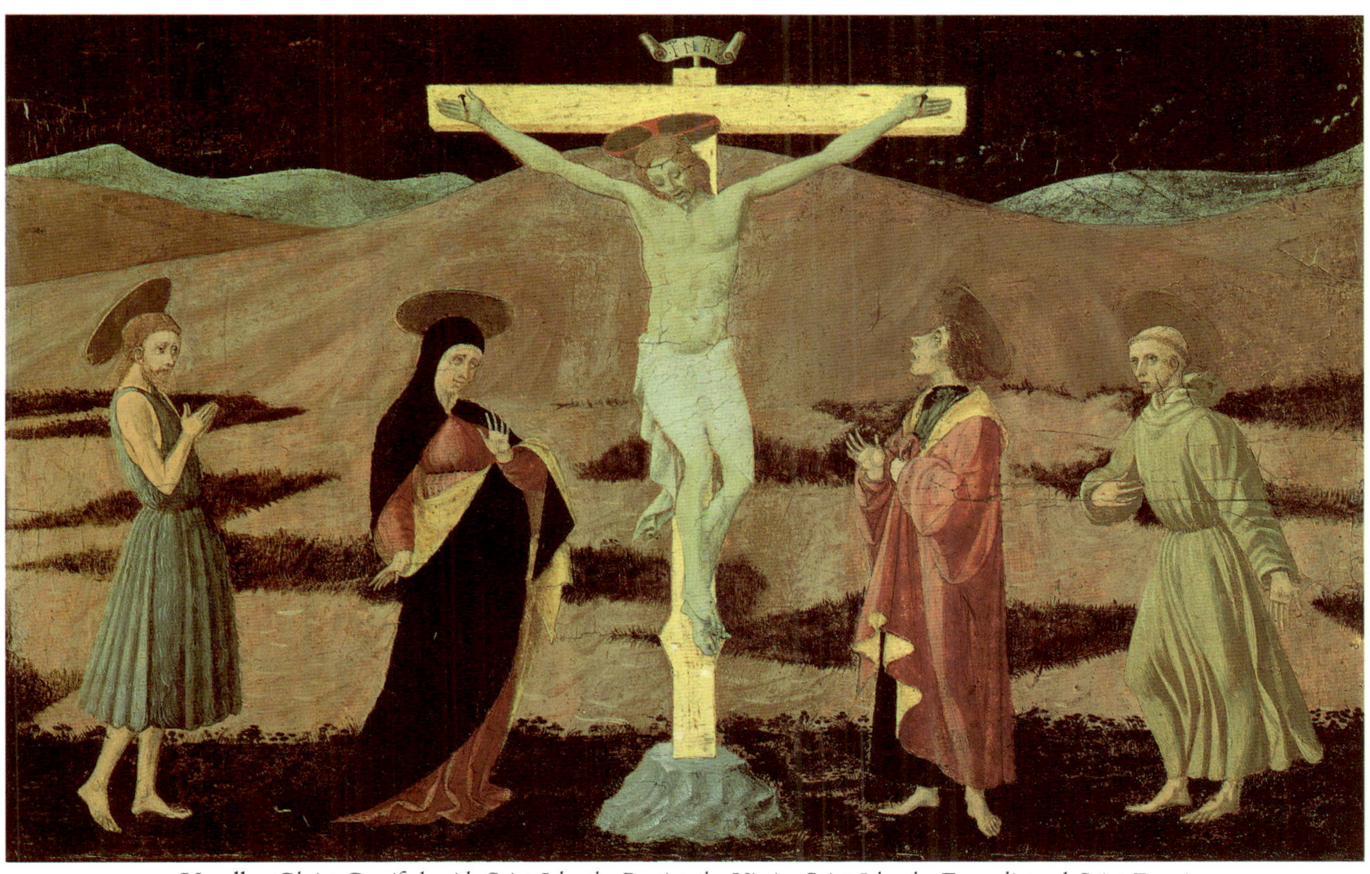

Uccello, *Christ Crucified, with Saint John the Baptist, the Virgin, Saint John the Evangelist and Saint Francis*, *c.* 1457–8, tempera on wood, 46 × 67.5 cm. Madrid, Thyssen-Bornemisza Collection. Complete work and detail.

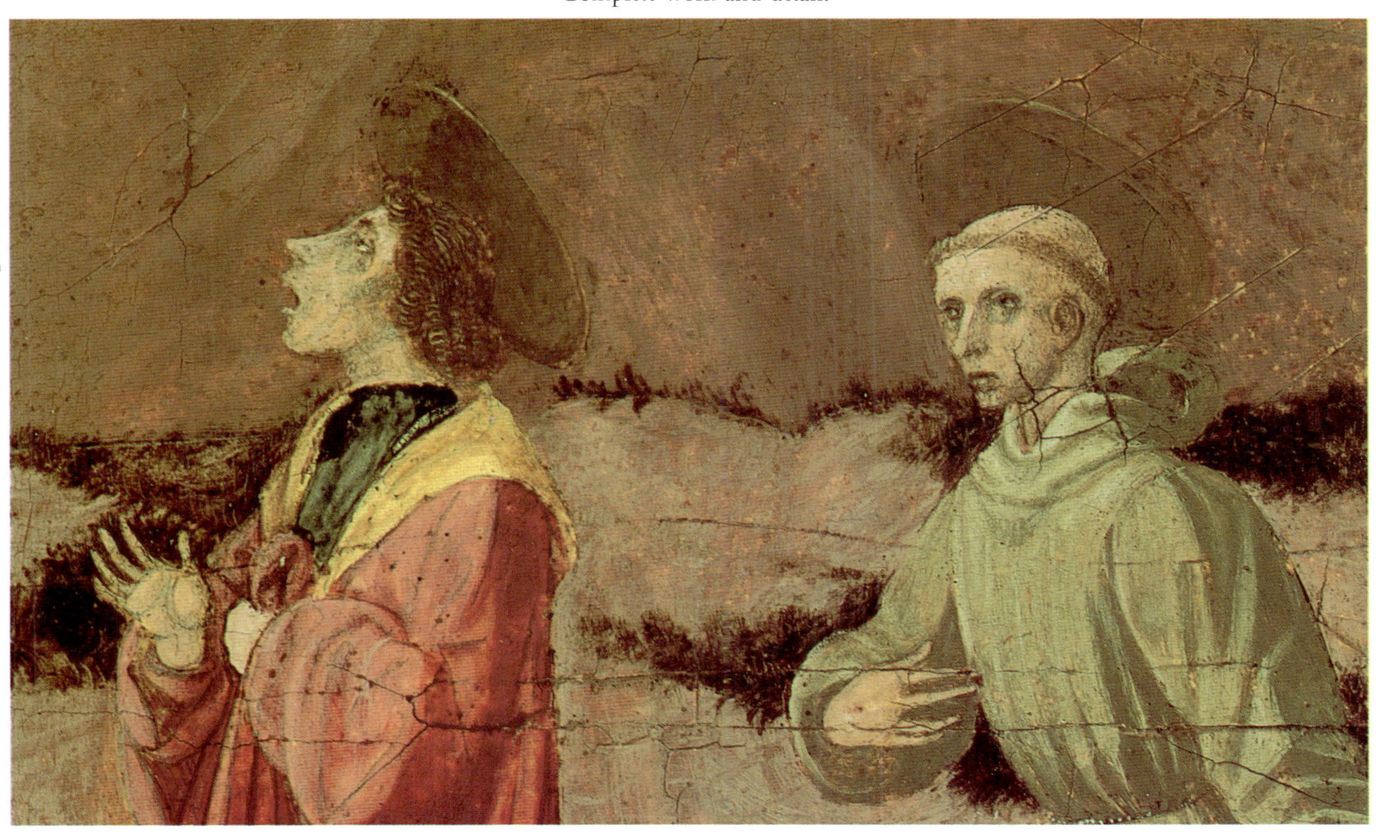

has given rise to so much talk of medieval optics and philosophical painting (see catalogue) was made possible by the rock whose structure and deep cavities were painted to imitate what were originally Gothic architectonic features: the accentuated arches of the two caverns on the left, separated by a sort of polylobed pillar; the recurring theme of small flights of steps which mark the route ascending into the rock (almost like an Alpine *ferrata* with its fine, robust, high railings); and on upwards until the *sotto in su* foreshortening, which is very dynamic in its diagonal axis and in the parallel lines of perspective in the layers of the rocks. On what is almost like the deck of an aircraft-carrier, between heaven and earth, Saint Francis is shown receiving the stigmata, on an unlikely overhanging crag that dominates the luxuriant Tuscan countryside dotted with churches, castles and fortified towns. It is a countryside similar to Valdarno, just as the mountain reminds us of Mount Verna, where, according to a Franciscan tradition, the miracle took place. Between these spaces in the shape of lunettes or altar retables that have been extended to accommodate the most important scenes, or in rectangles at the edges (above left and lower right), Uccello developed his iconographic theme which brought the different elements together. In San Miniato al Monte, the different scenes of the hermits' lives have links with subjects of eastern origin (there are inevitably great difficulties in identifying each of the subjects and the complete iconographic programme). Here, in the Accademia's *Life of the Holy Fathers*, the organization of the themes is based on an easy identification and gives us a sort of synoptic vision of different degrees and types of religious experience. They are graded according to an in-built hierarchy which is similar to the journey along the path to perfection and true beatitude.

The order in which it is read follows the tortuous, rugged, uphill path, whose symbolic significance is clear. It begins with the episode on the lower right, probably Saint Romuald reading to his brothers, an image that emphasizes the importance of a grounding in the Holy Scriptures. In the lower right-hand border, the neo-Early Christian detail of the doe drinking appears to allude to the purity of the spring. The scene unfolds in a sort of open-air chapter-house, with an exedra of spear-headed cypresses echoing the design of a Gothic choir and serving as a backdrop to the holy abbot's solemn, raised pulpit. The foreground of this unusual piece is rhythmically interspersed with slim pine trees which mark the perimeter of the monks' seating arrangements in two semi-circles: these are stylized pine trees that evoke memories of the Vallombrosa forest and form a sort of open pavilion *sub tegmine* through the repetition of their rigorously horizontal clusters of foliage. The scene in the lower left-hand corner refers to another stage in religious experience. There, reading and meditation on the Bible give way to direct solitary mystical experience, illustrated by

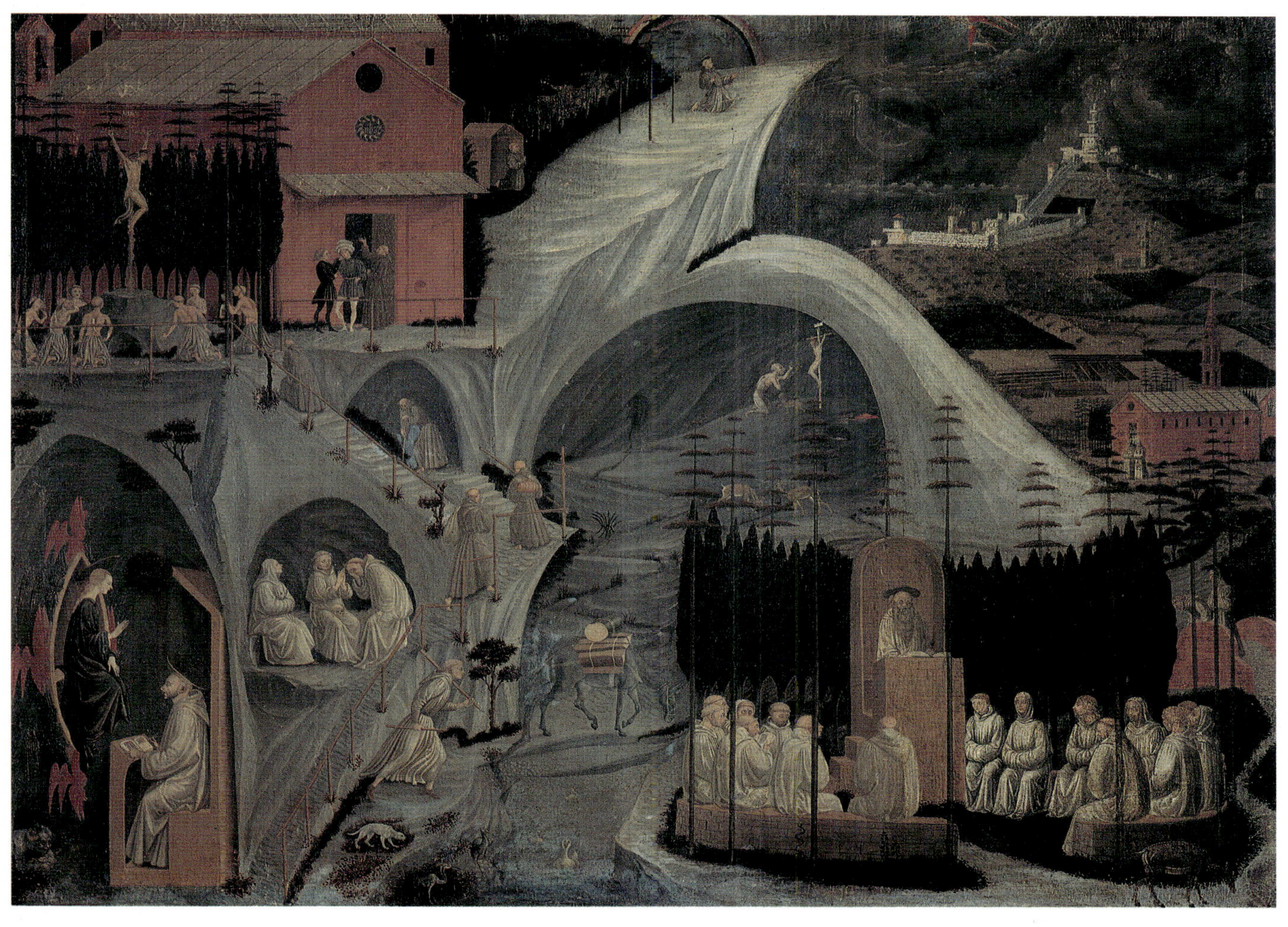

Above and following pages: Uccello, *Life of the Holy Fathers*, or *The Thebaïd*, *c*. 1460–65, tempera on canvas, 80 × 109 cm. Florence, Accademia. Complete work and details.

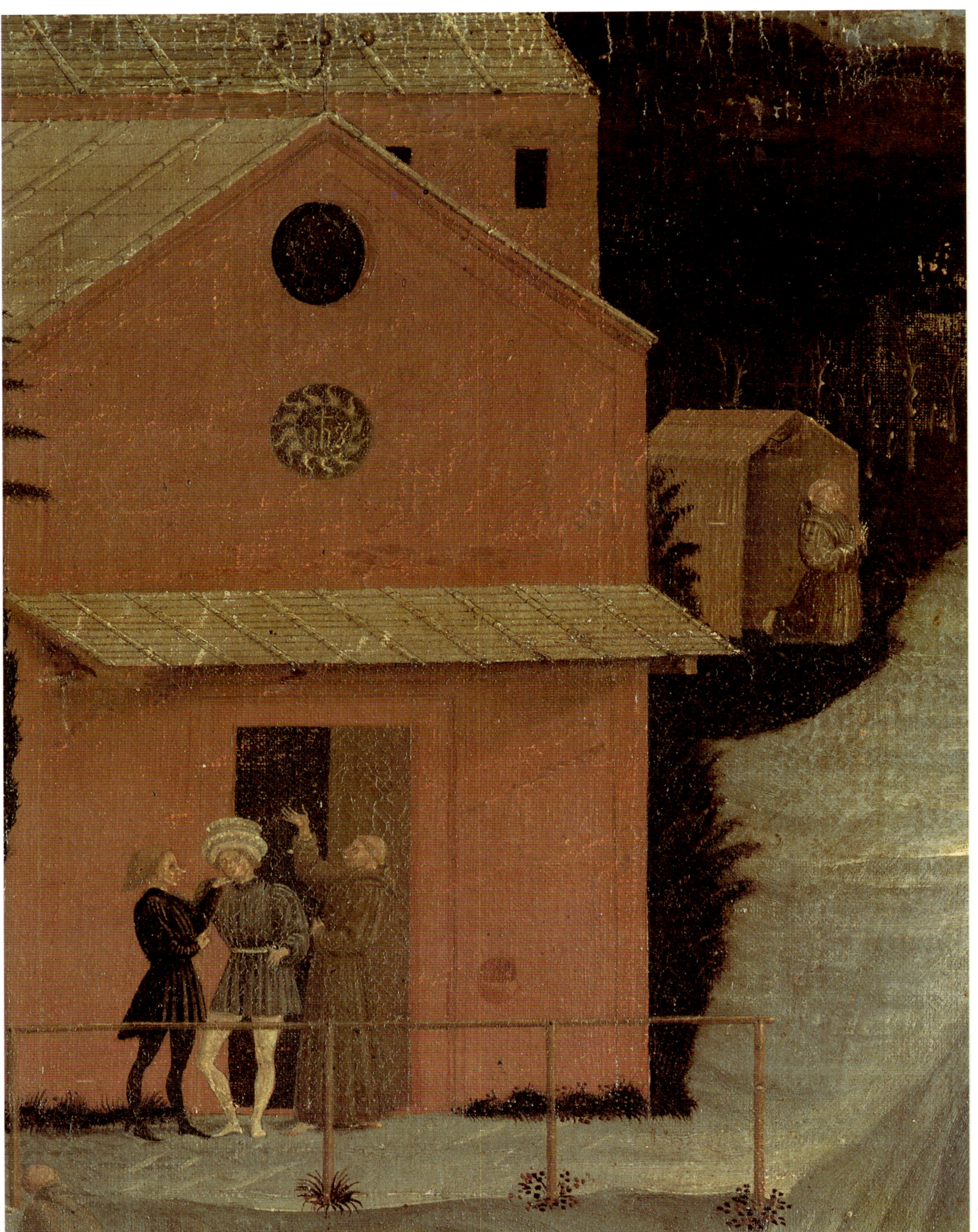

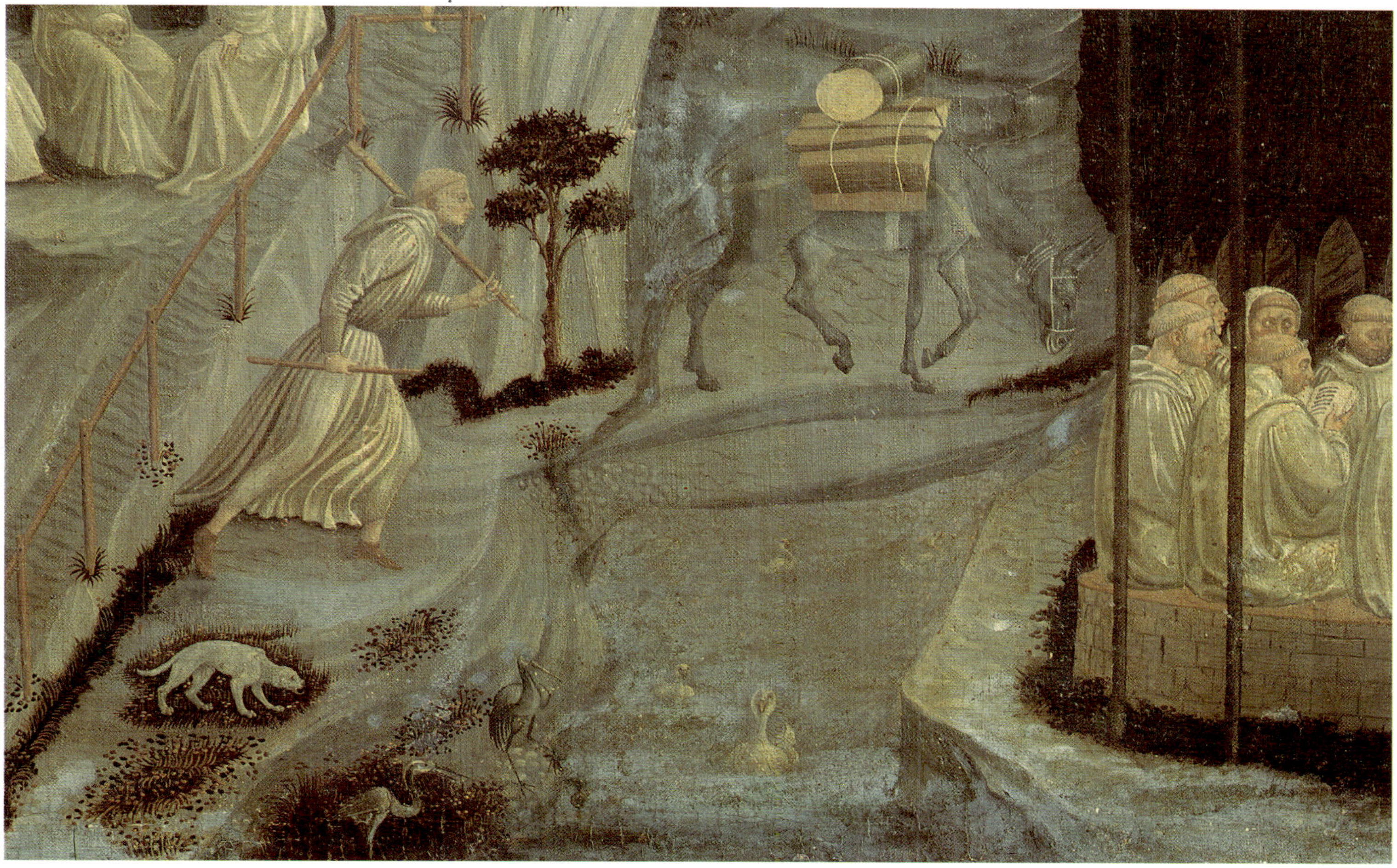

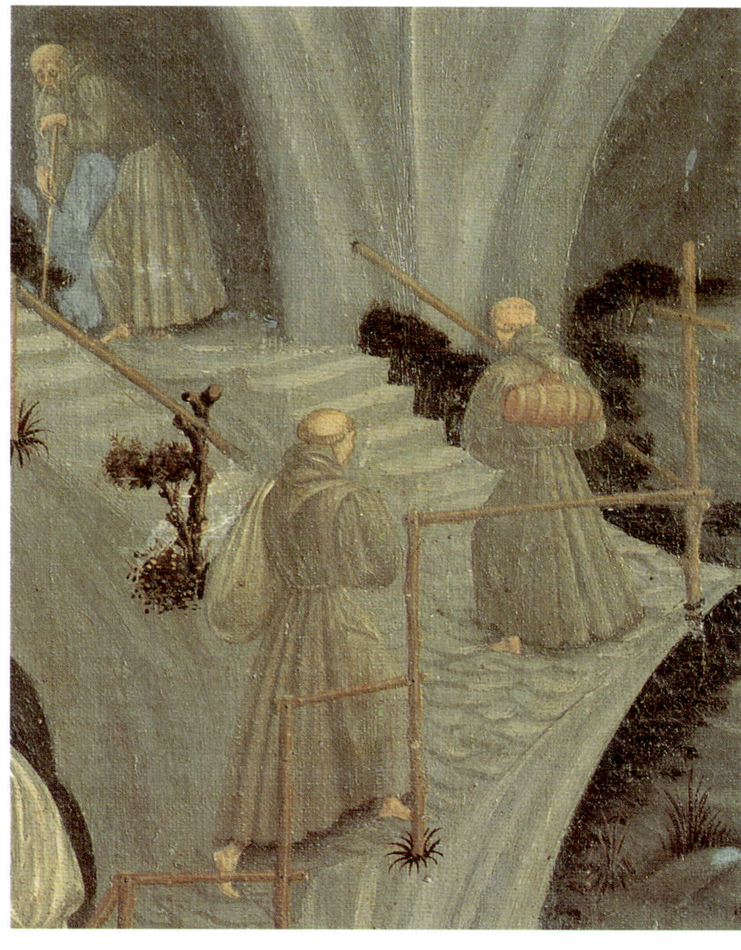
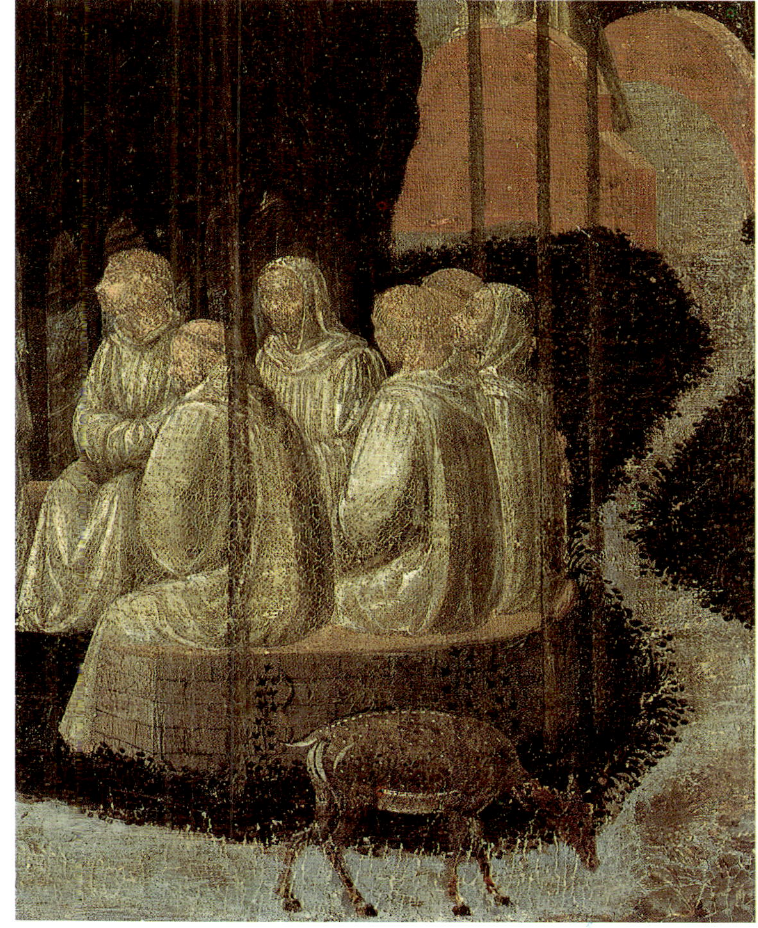

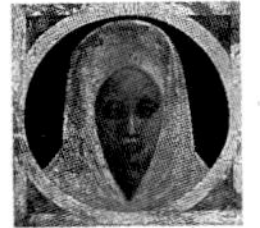

the Florentine iconographic theme of Saint Bernard's vision: the Virgin appears to him in a foreshortened mandorla. The next stage on the ideal road to perfection is depicted in the act of contrition with the group of monks, the youngest of whom is crying, while in the centre, a brother with a skull in his lap is lost in prayer, thus inviting meditation on the transitory nature of earthly things. The episode is probably drawn from the Eastern tradition of the lives of Abbot Anthony and Paul the Hermit, now held to be an autographic work of Saint Jerome. Contrition of the soul is the preamble to punishment of the flesh and the elimination of the last traces of bodily lust, represented by the group of beaten men (*battuti*) whose number, seven, may allude to the founders of the Servite Order of Mary – around whom the Compagnia dei Battuti or Bianchi (White Canons) della Santissima Annunziata gravitated – a probable reference to a typically Tuscan religious experience. The scene of self-flagellation takes place around a slim crucifix, vaguely three-quarter view but lacking any perspective, with an exedra of cypresses and pines as backdrop, echoing the motif in the opposite corner and forming a kind of diagonal relationship across the picture. There is another example of corporal punishment, this time penitence on a strictly personal basis, in the central figure in an obviously important position in spite of his relatively small size: this is the penitent Saint Jerome. (The grotto might also have been an allusion to Saint Philip Beniti, except that the identification is confirmed by the Cardinal's hat at the foot of the cross.)

After the purification of sins, the following stage is the worldwide mission to spread the Christian word and support the faltering; Uccello depicts this in the episode in front of the simple church which bears Saint Bernardino's monogram and which relates specifically to the Franciscan world. A brother, perhaps Bernardino of Siena himself, is comforting a drunken layman dressed like an affluent burgher and somewhat unsteady on his feet, supported on the other side by another layman: a sort of Hercules at the crossroads, a contrast between sacred and profane love, secular and religious life, depicted in this young man who is still vacillating in his choice. The backdrop to the scene is a type of extremely simplified religious building, which Uccello repeated in the background and which had its origins in the tradition of the Ill. p. 165 Franciscan barn-church (the convent in the background bears a certain resemblance to the Bernardine convent of Montecarlo near Arezzo) of which there are echoes in early Raphael.[141] There was a monogram of Saint Bernardino on the façade of the Franciscan convent of Santi Girolamo e Francesco alla Costa[142] and it is depicted as being on the pediment of Santa Croce on a Florentine chest of the period (see catalogue). In keeping with this Franciscan insignia, the final episode at the top of the painting depicts Saint Francis receiving the Stigmata on Mount Verna. This follows

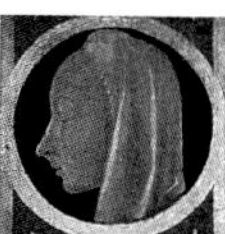

a substantive post-Giottoesque iconography that Uccello had already used in the fresco at Santa Trinita. As an ideal conclusion to this guided tour, there is, in the background, the full reconciliation with God, shown in the juxtaposition of the rainbow, a tangible natural sign – already used in *Noah's Sacrifice* in the Chiostro Verde to signify the end of the Flood – and a realistic landscape of Tuscan farmland with the clouds of a hurricane sweeping over them, a dramatization that alludes specifically to the upheavals and uncertainties of secular life. If this type of interpretation is correct[143] it may be possible to deduce who its patrons were and its original siting from clues in the picture. In fact the painting probably came from the convent of 'Pinzochero Franciscans' (Franciscan Tertiaries who had vowed poverty, but not obedience to the hierarchy) of Santi Girolamo e Francesco alla Costa, an originally Sienese institution. This is suggested in the monogram of Saint Bernardino of Siena, which was a relatively unusual detail in contemporary Florentine painting. It was not the first occasion on which Uccello had introduced Sienese stylistic references into a Florentine setting.

The great coherence in the use of colour and light in all the scenes, with no chiaroscuro or play of shadows, the constant fresco-like austerity, the contrast between green fields and the red brick walls of rustic buildings give way in the top right-hand corner to another register dear to Uccello, with the depiction of the storm. This is a painting that records atmospheric moods, refractions of light and violent shadows caused by the storm, and supernatural lighting, the dialectic contrast between the serenity of monastic life, protected even from uncertainties in the weather, and the uncertainties of the outside world.

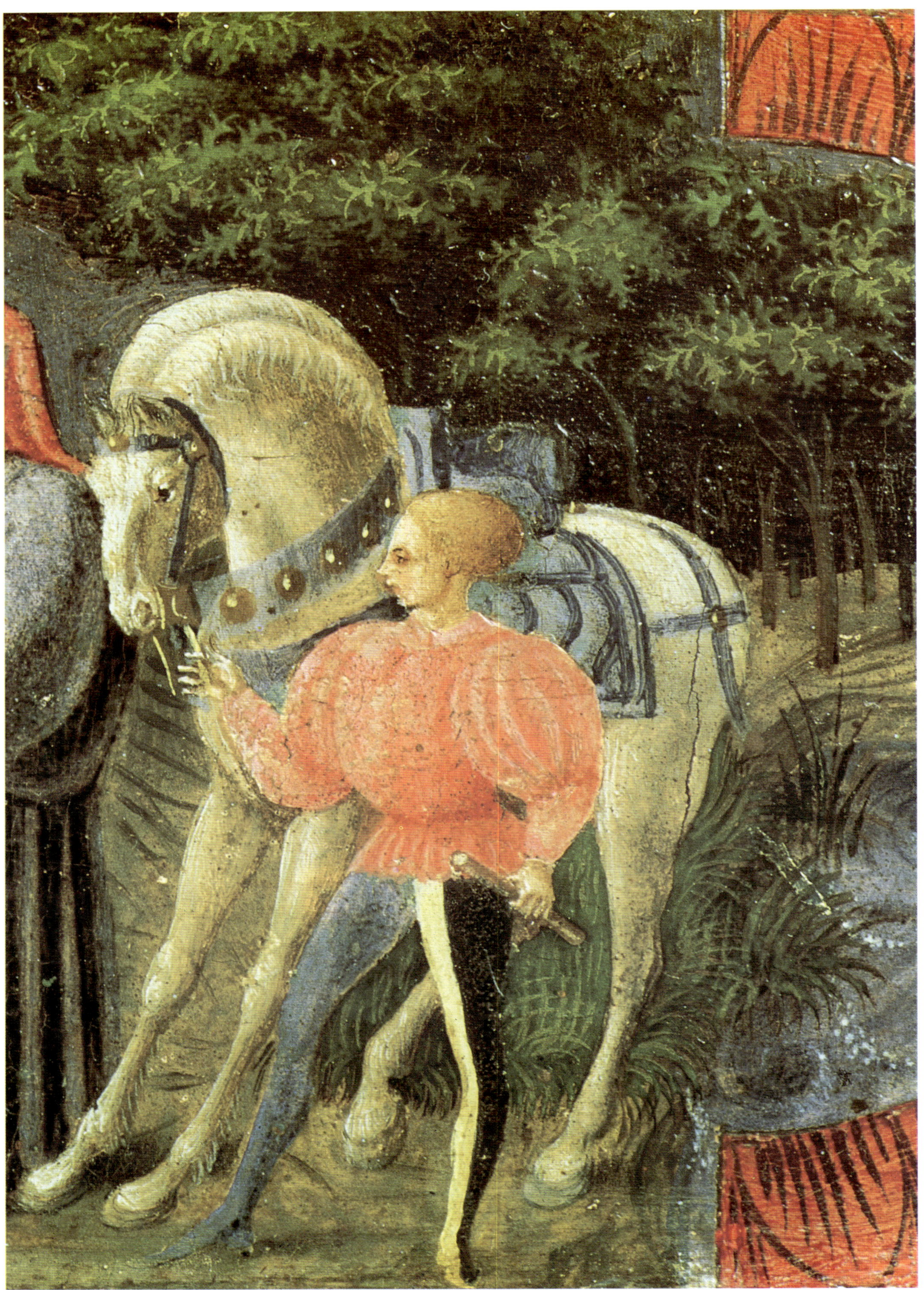

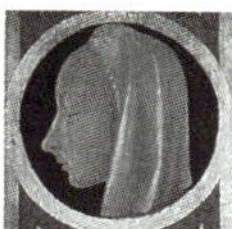

4 THE 'SMALL ITEMS' ('COSE PICCOLE')

When Vasari defined works as 'small items' he was creating a distinction with the craft of picture-making. As a critic and painter himself, he was well aware of the problems of size, and the technical and stylistic relationships between format and representation. What he meant by 'small items' were mostly paintings intended for private patrons: 'In many of the houses in Florence, paintings in perspective on chests, beds and other small items are to be found by the same artist's hand' (1568, I). The 'small items' have nothing in common except that they are nearly all predelle, with a format that extends the area of the perspective space to between fifty and sixty degrees, beyond the normal angle of vision, producing an effect of rhythmic repetition (like the early Japanese stage). This must have delighted Uccello because of the possibilities it held for division, fragmentation, individualization and plurality, that were the driving force in his compositions whether large or small.

In molte case di Firenze sono assai quadri in prospettiva per vani di lettucci, letti et altre cose piccole, di mano del medesimo

Uccello did not adopt fixed positions, nor even very coherent ones as a consequence of these special dimensions: his experimentation was always mercurial, innovatory, even bizarre. However, in the classification we have adopted for the sake of convenience here, we can say that the group of 'small' works comprises the most

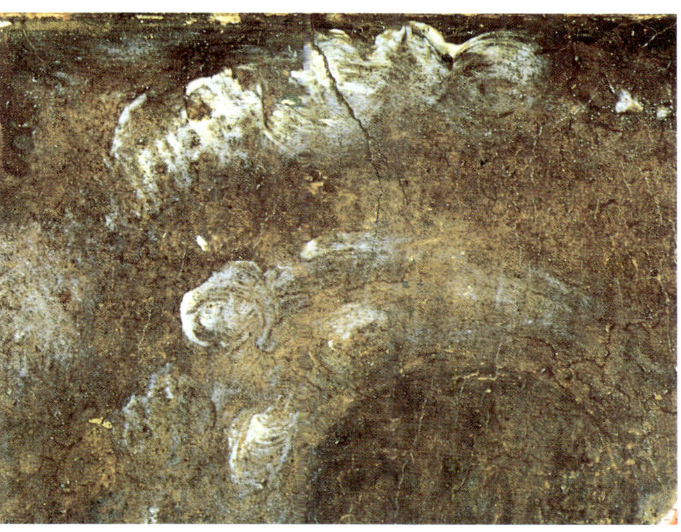

Facing page and left: Uccello, details of *The Adoration of the Magi* (centre panel of the Quarate predella).

strongly dialectic element in the whole of Uccello's research. This was patient research undertaken during the long years of his solitary old age, when he had no significant commissions. They mark his final isolation, the end of his polemic with Donatello (witness Vasari's spicy anecdote that probably had a grain of truth): 'forsaking the certain for the uncertain' was at the heart of Uccello's proud,

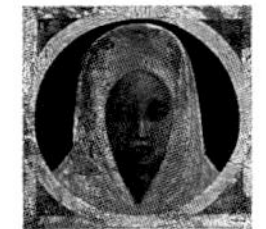

anachronistic position within the Florentine context. Only six of these 'small items' have come down to us – all of excellent quality – and in spite of continuing controversy over attribution, here is a *corpus* in which a common autograph can be discerned. They deserve attention not only as a series of episodes which highlight the delightful quality of Uccello's painting compared with the austerity and avant-garde courage of his frescoes, but as works that play a conclusive role in defining his personal language.

THE QUARATE PREDELLA

In spite of its commonly accepted early dating, which is close to the experimental period in which the Prato frescoes were painted, the Quarate predella already contains many themes that were important in Uccello's later poetics. In the small format, his pictorial technique became precious and extremely refined in the delicate stratification of the detail of the forest in the dark background (as in the Oxford *Hunt*), or in the stormy sky, full of clouds and obscure vapours that accompany *The Vision of Saint John the Evangelist on Patmos*, and in the atmospheric whirlwinds, already encountered on several previous occasions (in the *Flood*, the *Thebaïd* and the London *Saint George*). In the *Adoration of the Magi* there are, once again, the rough countryside and rugged rocks, the experiment in perspective in the peasant hut, with the central axis which serves both as a pivot for the scene and as a rustic support for the simple rafter construction of the roof. There is also a delicate chromatism reminiscent of Fra Angelico on the one hand and on the other of the rich tradition of Florentine Gothic Cat. no. 9

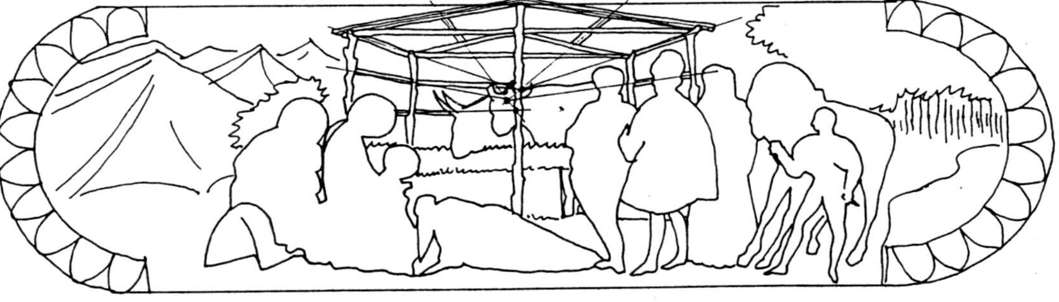

The Quarate predella (*right:* a drawing of the centre panel) probably formed part of a reliquary of the True Cross and not a retable: it bears traces of a ciborium or reliquary. The patrons of the oratory of San Bartolomeo at Quarate were the Quaratesi family, who had also commissioned work from Gentile da Fabriano.

that had been given fresh life by Starnina, not to mention references to Gentile da Fabriano and Masaccio. The predella is a remarkable example of experimentation, where youthful elements – the arched-necked horse held back by the groom, closely related to the horse in the Melbourne *Saint George* – coexist with innovatory elements such as the precious, vibrant colours, the unusual brilliance of the forest greens (one of See Cat. p. 344

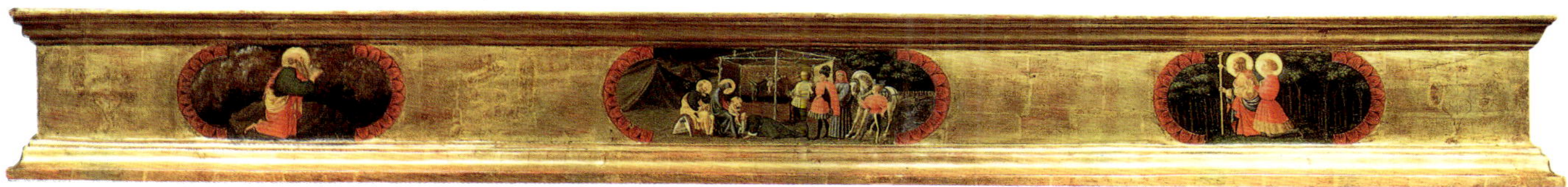

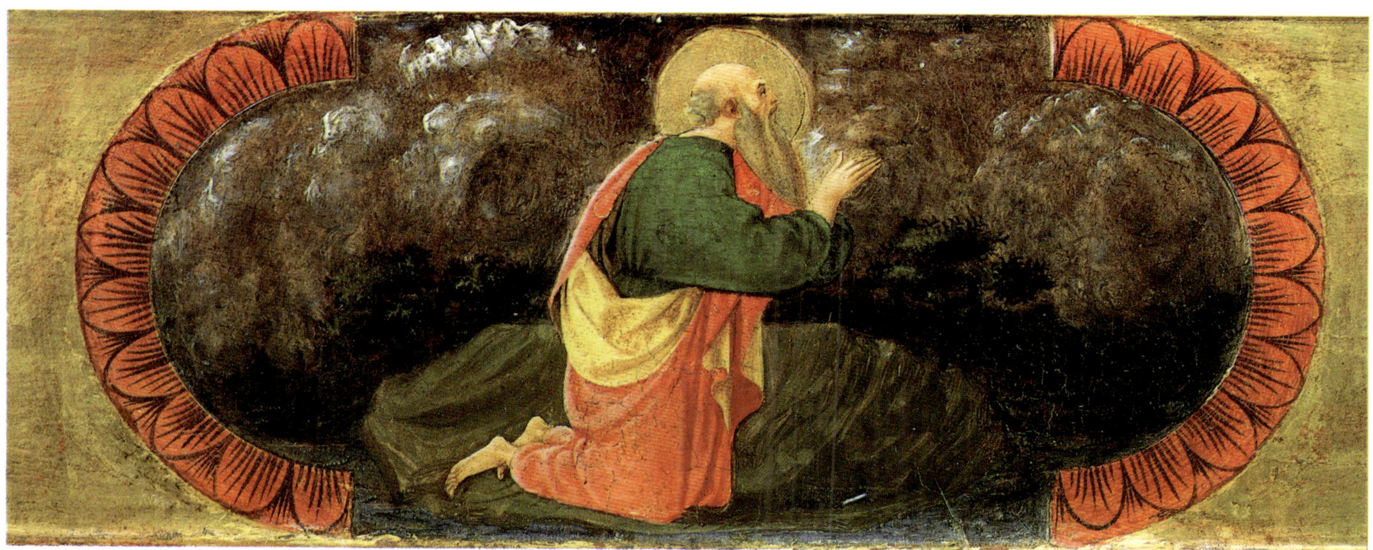

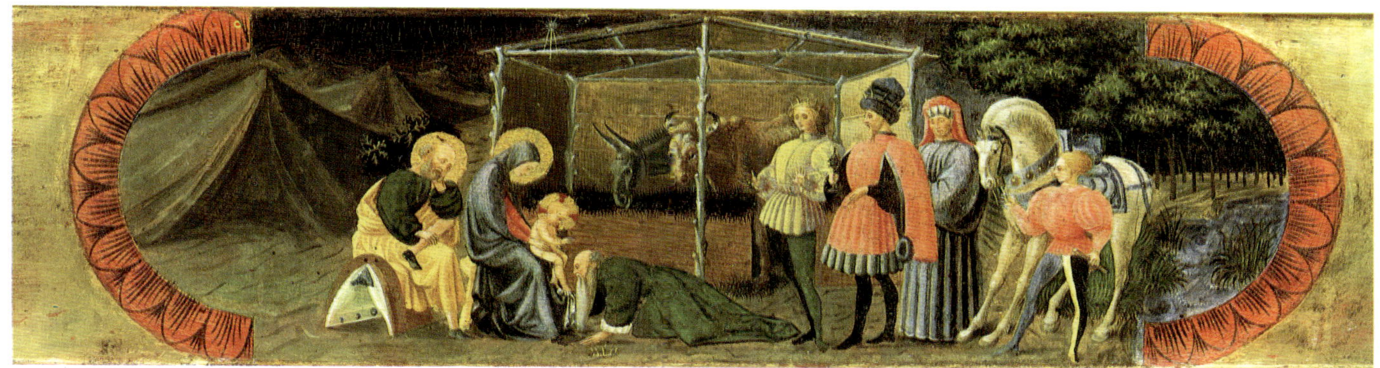

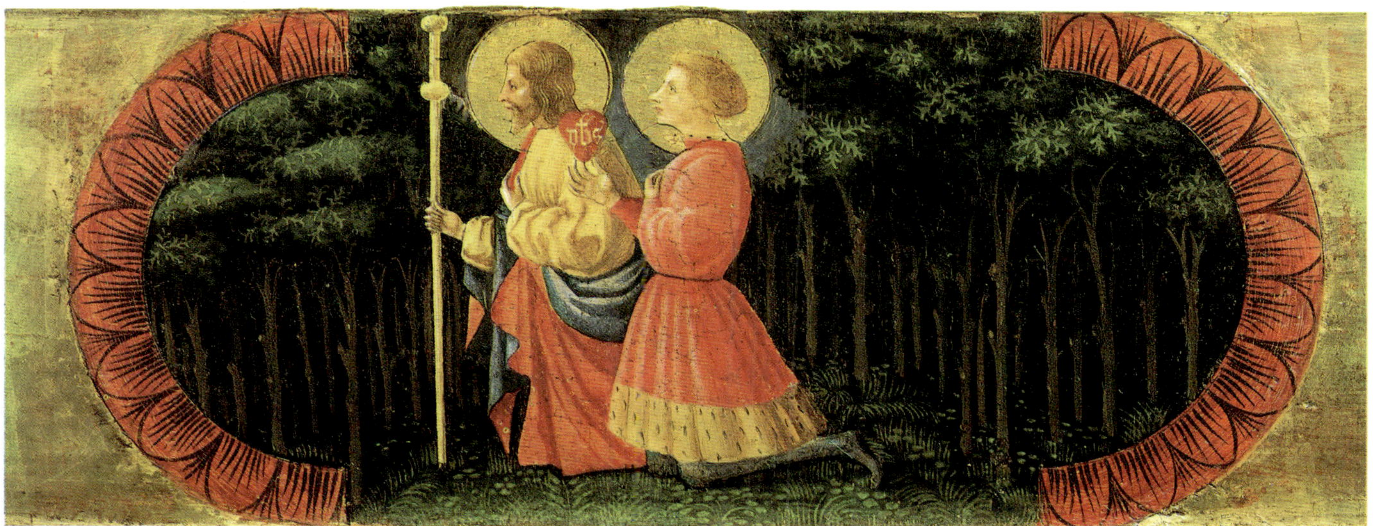

Uccello, Quarate predella, *c.* 1433, tempera on wood, 20.4 × 178 cm. From top to bottom, the complete work and the three panels: *The Vision of Saint John the Evangelist on Patmos*, *The Adoration of the Magi*, and *Saint James and Saint Ansano of Siena*. Florence, Museo Arcivescovile di Cestello.

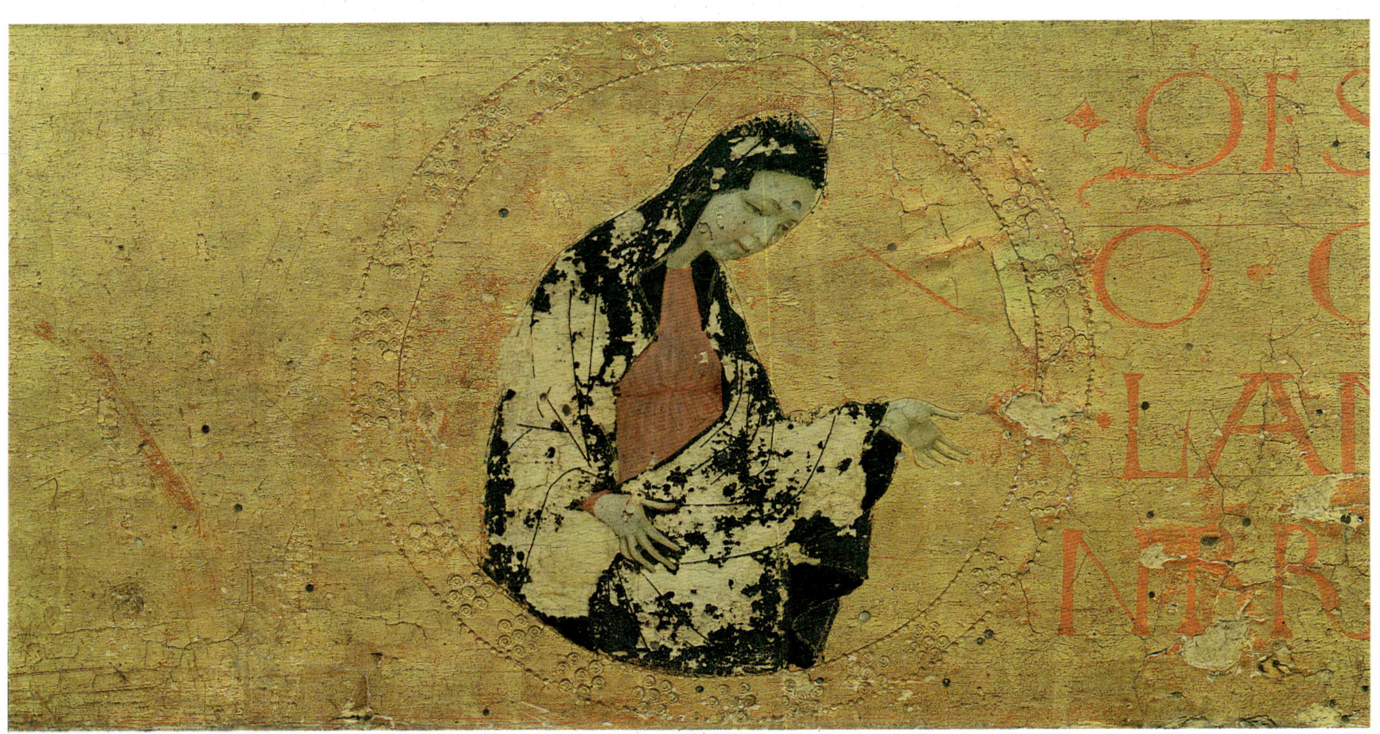

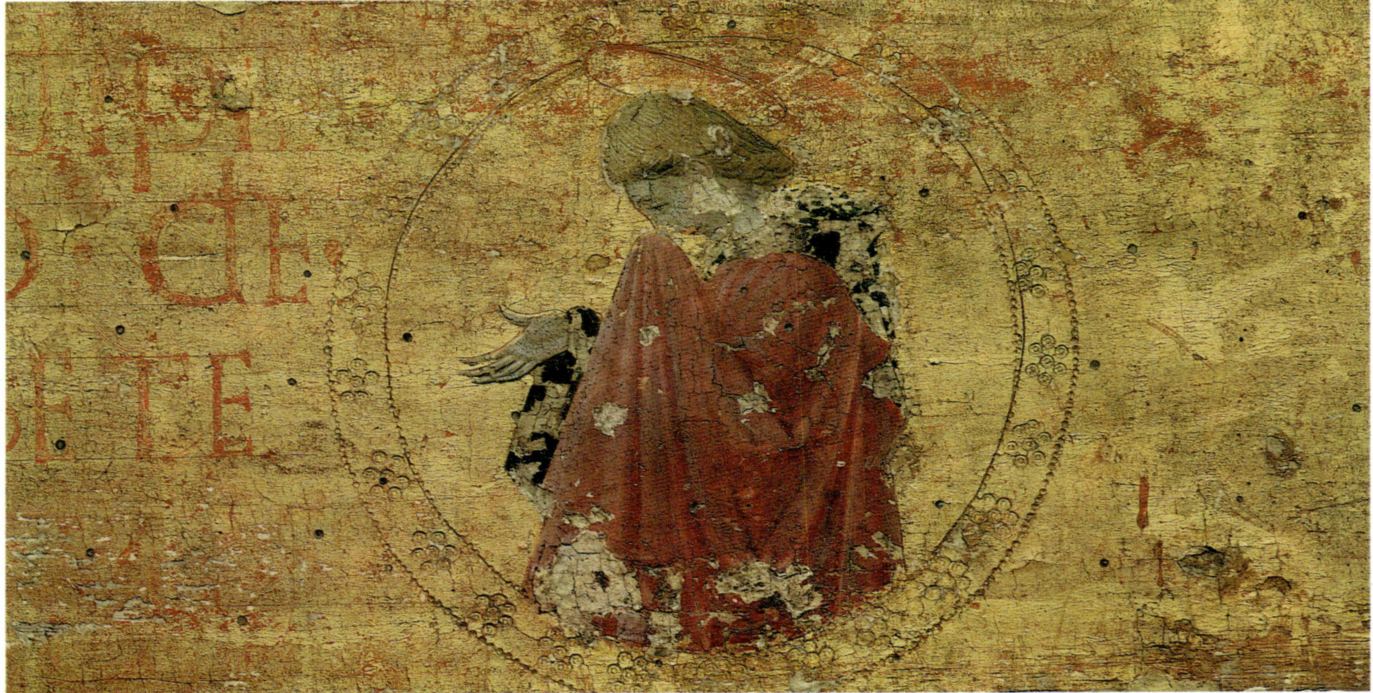

Details of the Avane predella: the *Virgin and Saint John the Evangelist*.

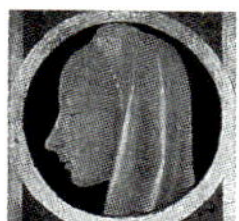

Uccello's specialities) and the eddying clouds in the sky in the episode on the left. Religious experience is once again turned into a lively phenomenological curiosity; there is a calibrated ratio between figures and space and a poetic evocation of nature. This a personal contribution to solving the exigencies of religious painting and sacred story in the years when Fra Angelico's message was beginning to spread.

THE AVANE PREDELLA

Cat. no. 26 The now almost ruined Avane predella is not one of the compositions that have a one-point perspective. It belongs rather to a typology where two medallions frame a central composition of *Man of Sorrows* (now very damaged). However, in spite of its poor state of conservation and loss of the upper retable, and the composition's intentional simplicity, the predella is an example of a rarefied stylistic experiment that uses traditional Sienese 'elegant' profiles, and Gothic, which seems unusual for the beginning of the 1450s (the predella is dated 1452). There is in Uccello's way of articulating profiles (Vasari was to stigmatize it as a 'dry manner, full of profiles' typical of Uccello's late period) an attempt to integrate the figures at the sides into a single perspective that has to take the wide angle of vision into account; there is also an attempt to adapt the style of the miniature to this horizontally extended format. The colour too (although now difficult to assess) marks a development in his experimentation, with its delicate juxtapositions and subtle variations of harmonies of blues, malachite greens and reddish purples; he has deliberately reduced the range of colours used, but treated them with extreme care. In this almost undocumented period in Uccello's career, the disappearance of the upper panel, about which nothing is known, is even more regrettable.

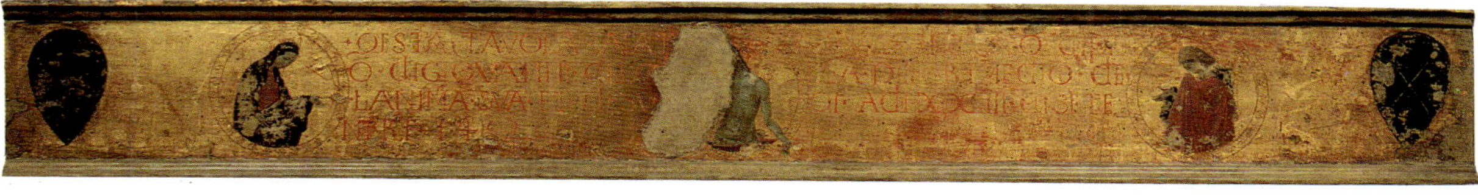

Avane predella, 1452, tempera on wood, 22 × 172 cm. The subject is *The Man of Sorrows between the Virgin and Saint John the Evangelist*.

Compared with the experimentation in the Quarate predella, the Avane predella shows a return to tradition. This may perhaps have been because of its patrons: it seems it was not intended for a sophisticated urban clientèle, but for an oratory in the country. The dedicatory inscription in red lead paint is a formal element which is almost more significant than the figures inside the gold-leaf medallions.

THE TWO SAINT GEORGES

The two Paris and London versions of *Saint-George and the Dragon* theme raise issues about several important aspects of Uccello's work. The Paris *Saint George*, which is earlier, aligns all the figures in profile on a plane immediately adjacent to the bottom edge of the painting, presenting the perspective space in a converging landscape which is seen from a bird's eye view (i.e. from higher up than the observer's normal viewpoint). The London *Saint George*, on the other hand, takes place in a much more complex space: the figures are further back in relation to the bottom edge of the painting, with an area of green grass forming a perspective 'paving' (as in the Thyssen *Crucifixion*) in front of them. The convergence of the landscape in the background is more precise here and more centralized; the scene is articulated on the crossing of two diagonals, which enables the daring foreshortening of the dragon and knight, and carries the dragon's bleeding head, pierced through by the lance, into the foreground. The countryside in the Paris canvas is reminiscent of the *Thebaïd*, with its well-organized, cultivated strips of land (the 'ploughed fields' drawn in perspective which Vasari mentioned), a humanized natural world where hills are encircled by turretted walls and where the dragon's cave is like an extraordinary accident in the agricultural landscape and background woodland, where wild animals and people are barely visible. This cave, which looks like a tent or artificial refuge (as in the *Thebaïd*), seems alien to the natural world, constructed as it is like a stylized Gothic arcade. The London cave with its dark cavity taking up a third of the composition is made up of layered rock, with a geometry of alternating broken dihedrals; it has a more obviously naturalistic structure.

Cat. nos. 17, 28

The Paris panel, like the *Thebaïd*, is bathed in a midday light which covers the scene uniformly and gives it the elegance of a tournament; it is an heraldic-chivalrous interpretation emphasized by the importance given to the horse's harness. In the London painting, the whirlwind, the clouds painted in perspective in the light blue sky, the lighting concentrated on the front of the scene, emphasizing the foreshortening of the figures, all highlight the most significant, most dazzling and most Leonardoesque motif of the tornado behind the knight-saint, evoking the noxious, putrid fumes emitted by the dragon. Unconcernedly, the knight in unison with the movement of his horse has broken through it with a dynamic leap.

Facing page, above: Uccello, *Saint George and the Dragon*, *c.* 1439–40, tempera on wood, 52 × 90 cm. Paris, Musée Jacquemart-André. This panel, which was probably a *spalliera* (see note 45), has been cut down and has suffered from drastic cleaning. It also seems to have been retouched by Uccello some time after it was originally painted.

Below: Uccello, *Saint George and the Dragon*, *c.* 1455–60, tempera on canvas, 56.5 × 74 cm. London, National Gallery.

The Paris panel seems well enough preserved, but an old cleaning and recent restorations have to a large extent jeopardized the original precious treatment of the top layers of varnish. In the top right-hand corner of the sky is the almost invisible moon; the personification of the north wind, which has brought the first snows to the faraway mountain tops, blows down on the almost translucent city behind its curtain of walls. Even the brilliant green of the vegetation, probably obtained through using a semi-

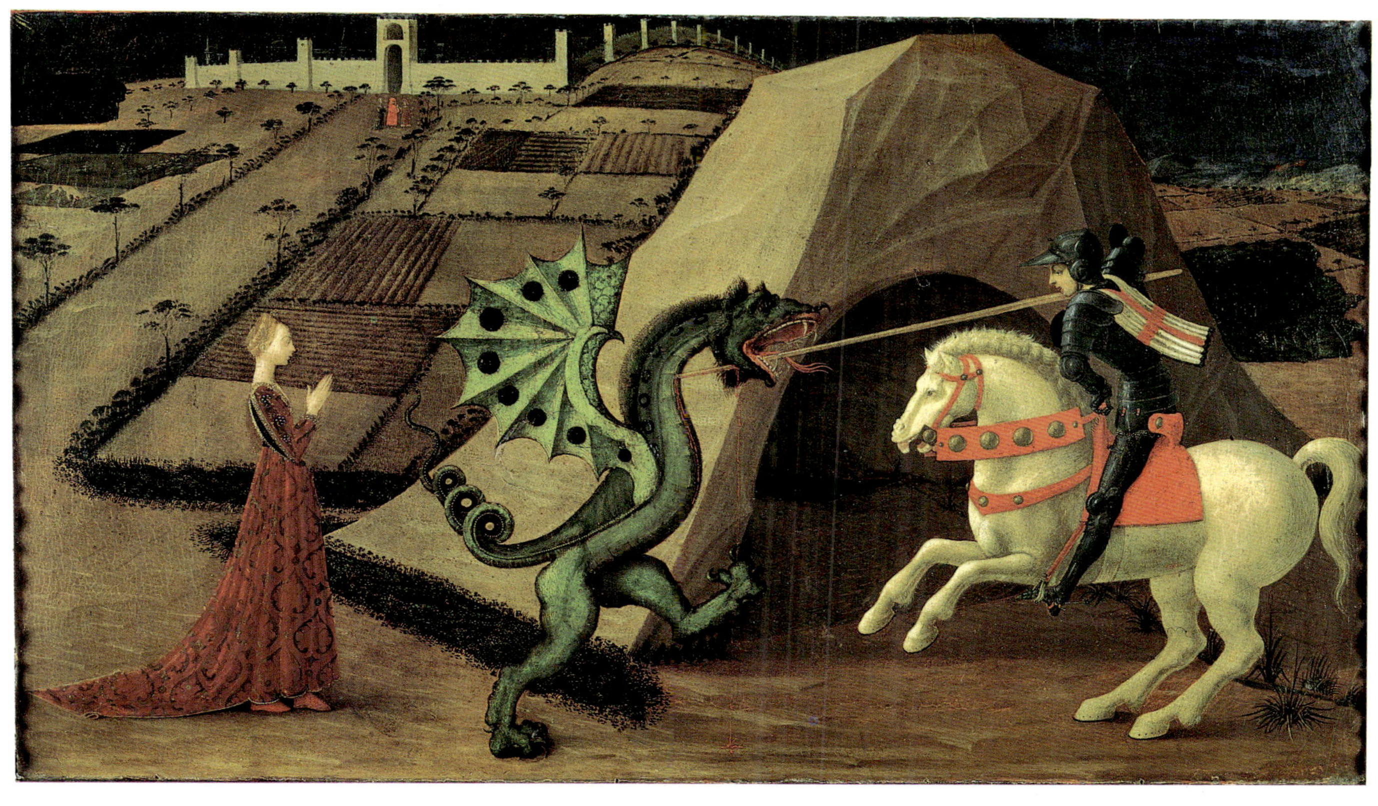

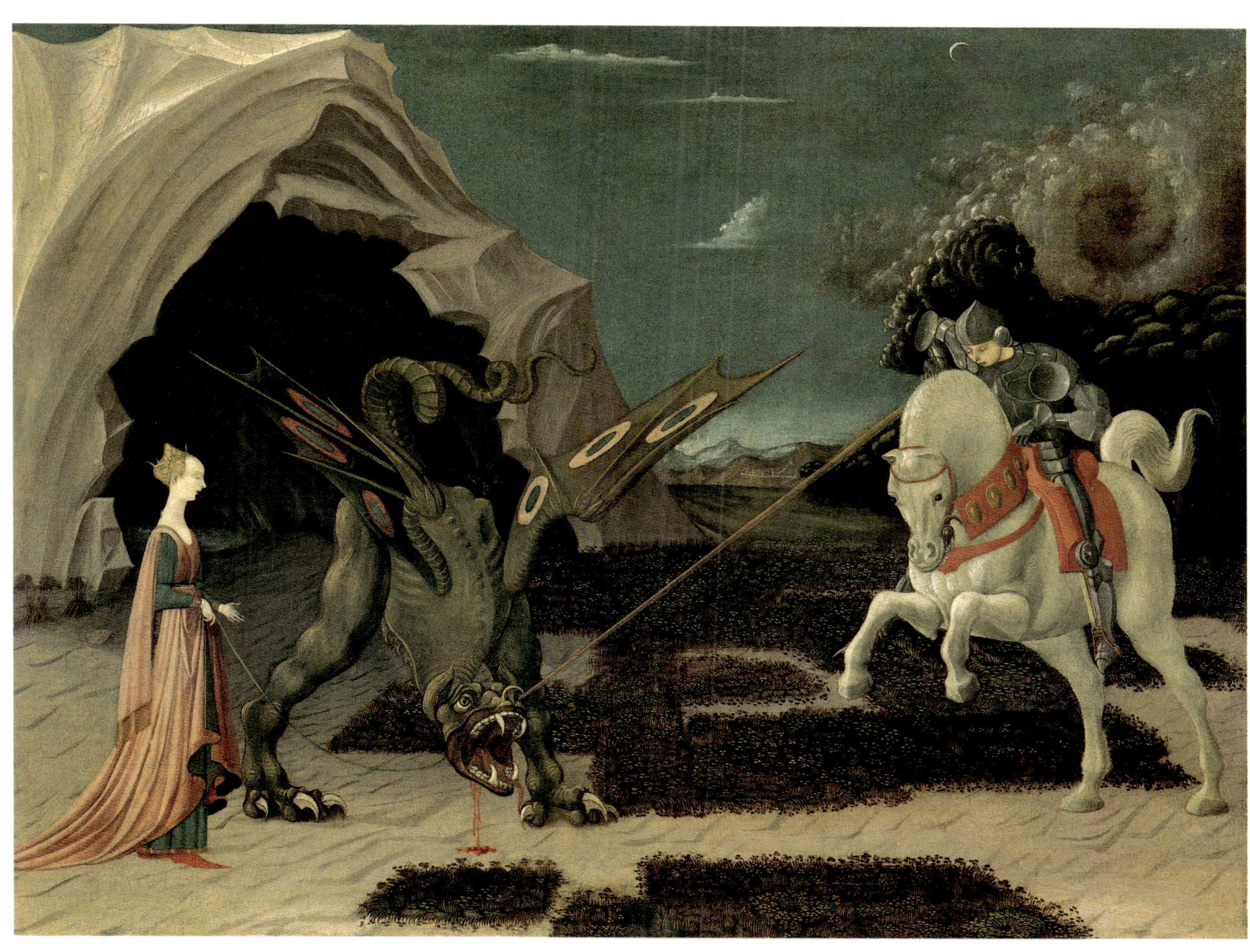

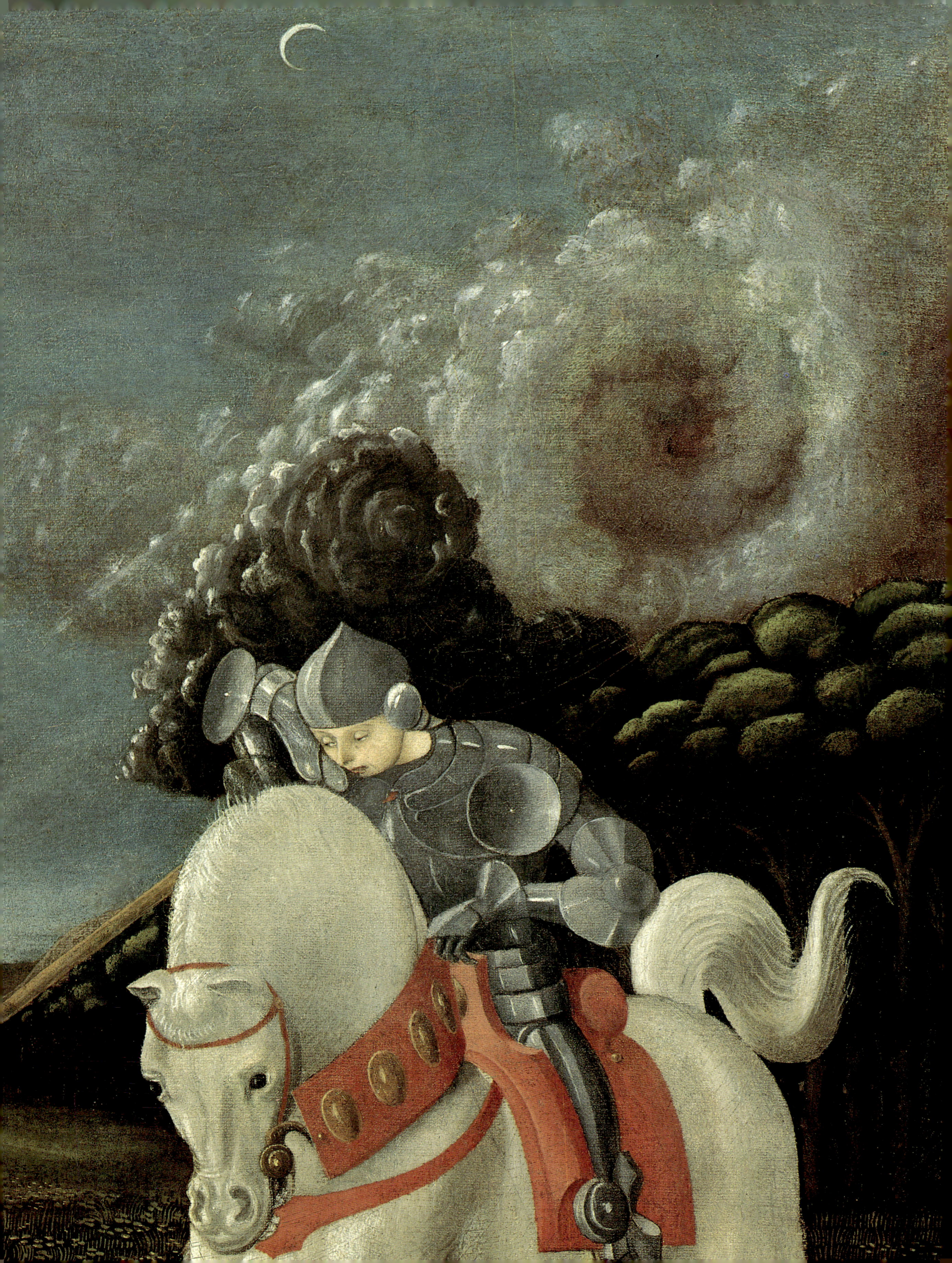

Facing page: Uccello, detail of *Saint George and the Dragon*. London, National Gallery.

transparent varnish which had a resin of copper base, now has a muted appearance in its transformation to an opaque brown. The London painting is colder, more elaborate and better preserved in spite of modern, vigorous restoration; it can be considered as one of the earliest examples of textile support in Quattrocento Florence.

There are different interpretations of the story to correspond with the different dynamics of the two paintings. The Paris panel shows the dragon arrested in his impetuous assault, the knight presenting his lance in a classic move and the anguished princess in prayer, both witness and protagonist in the drama. In the London canvas, the dragon has become an inoffensive giant lizard, held docilely on a lead by the pale princess: a bizarre courtly animal submitting to the unjust violence perpetrated on him by the knight-saint: more victim than aggressor, more pet than ferocious captor. The princess – haughty and self-assured like a Byzantine noblewoman – makes a contained demonstrative gesture: it lacks any emotion but it shows her awareness of the deep reasoning behind the event and its symbolic and emblematic significance.[144] In the Paris picture – which has a much more bourgeois tone – the town takes on great importance, while in the London canvas it appears far in the distance, in the depth of space, in an almost natural dawn light. In the Paris picture where the girl's anxious parents are shown in miniature standing in front of the city walls, the entire countryside is nothing but a necessary suburban and agrarian complement to the city itself. *Ill. p. 164*

THE URBINO PREDELLA

Cat. no. 33 In the Urbino predella the articulation is complex: it has six episodes, each with a format that almost resembles a double square. This proportion suits the centralized perspective to which most of the scenes conform, with the exception of just one, which has the vanishing point on the right edge of the picture (the module for each episode is roughly one Florentine *braccio* in length, i.e. 58.36 cm.). The alternation of outdoor and indoor scenes has a unifying element in the repetition of balusters with cable moulding, in pure Tuscan Quattrocento style, which suggest the architecture of a villa or garden in their orthogonal rhythm and serve as a frame for the action. The dominant colour is an intense cinnabar red, which appears as much in the abstract architectural features with their unlikely cornices as in the clothing, whose repetition, rhythm and balance of colour give a structure to the different episodes. A further unifying element is the dark, dusky sky, far removed from the 'daylight painting' of

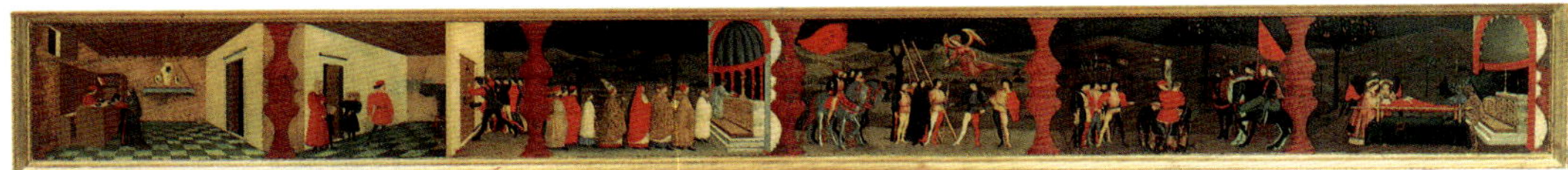

Above and following pages: Uccello, *The Miracle of the Profaned Host*, 1467–8, tempera on wood, 42 × 361 cm. Urbino, Galleria Nazionale delle Marche. Complete work and details.

Fra Angelico, Domenico Veneziano or Piero della Francesca. And there are the natural burnt-earth colours of the Sienese countryside, cultivated fields, farmhouses, churches, sparse trees and luxuriant orchards.

This coherent use of colour, executed in meticulous detail and repeated to give balance, can also be found in the indoor scenes with their bare architecture, whose synthesis depends on the perspectival checker pattern used in *costruzione legittima*, or the wooden furniture, beamed ceilings and whitewashed walls – a typically Tuscan ensemble, in which only a few discreet elements of moulding relieve the surface of the stone. Here the architecture is most realistic, contrasting with the abstract quality of the great niches in the altars in the two open-air liturgical episodes. In the scene with the pontifical procession the pope has a Gothic bearing and a triple crown, in the style of Boniface VII, perhaps in order to place the event chronologically. We have here, as in the last episode – where the demons are quarrelling with the angels over the body of the woman in front of the studded altar – a sense of calm serenity. The whole work has an almost gentle intimacy in the development of the scenes, which neither the violence of the guards as they attack the door to the Jew's house nor the unspeakable sacrilege can dissipate. Even in the scenes showing the hanging and burning at the stake, the composition's balance and the elegance of the knights and their standards create an atmosphere more akin to a tournament. The panel, which was later used for

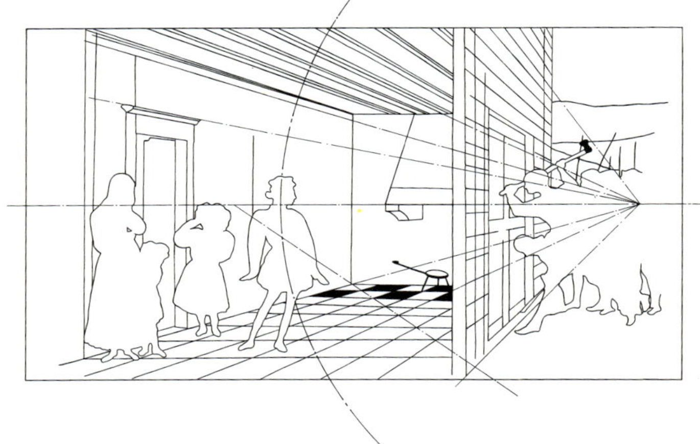

Reconstruction of the perspective in the second scene of *The Miracle of the Profaned Host* (after Sindona-Rossi).

construction work, has undoubtedly suffered over the years: the surface of the paint is damaged and the dazzling Urbino 'scarlets' have lost their depth. More to the point, Uccello's technique, in his late period particularly, was refined and sophisticated, and it is now difficult to appreciate this aspect in the predella. In spite of that, this represents the most magnificent example of Uccello's narrative coordination, both in

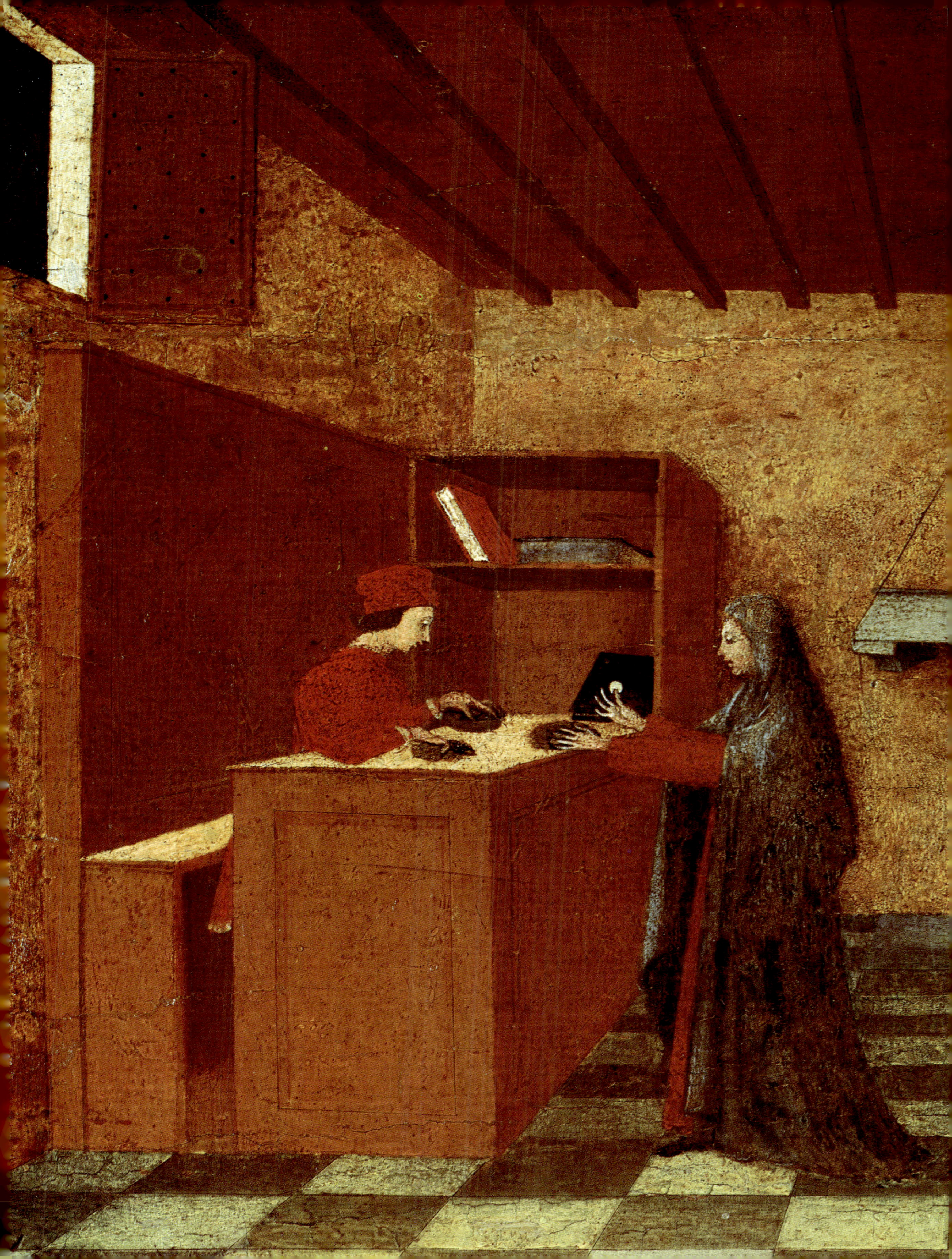

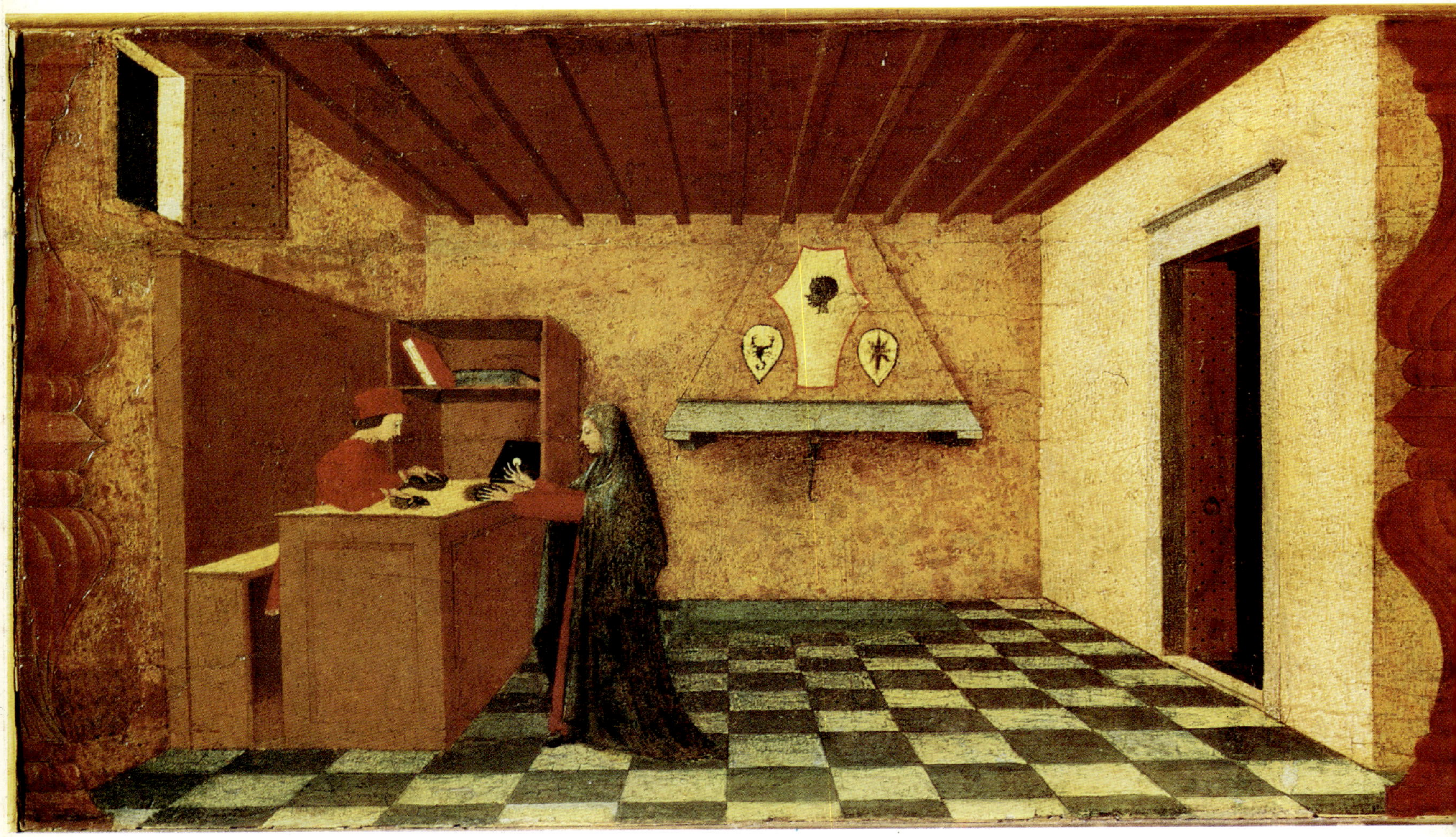

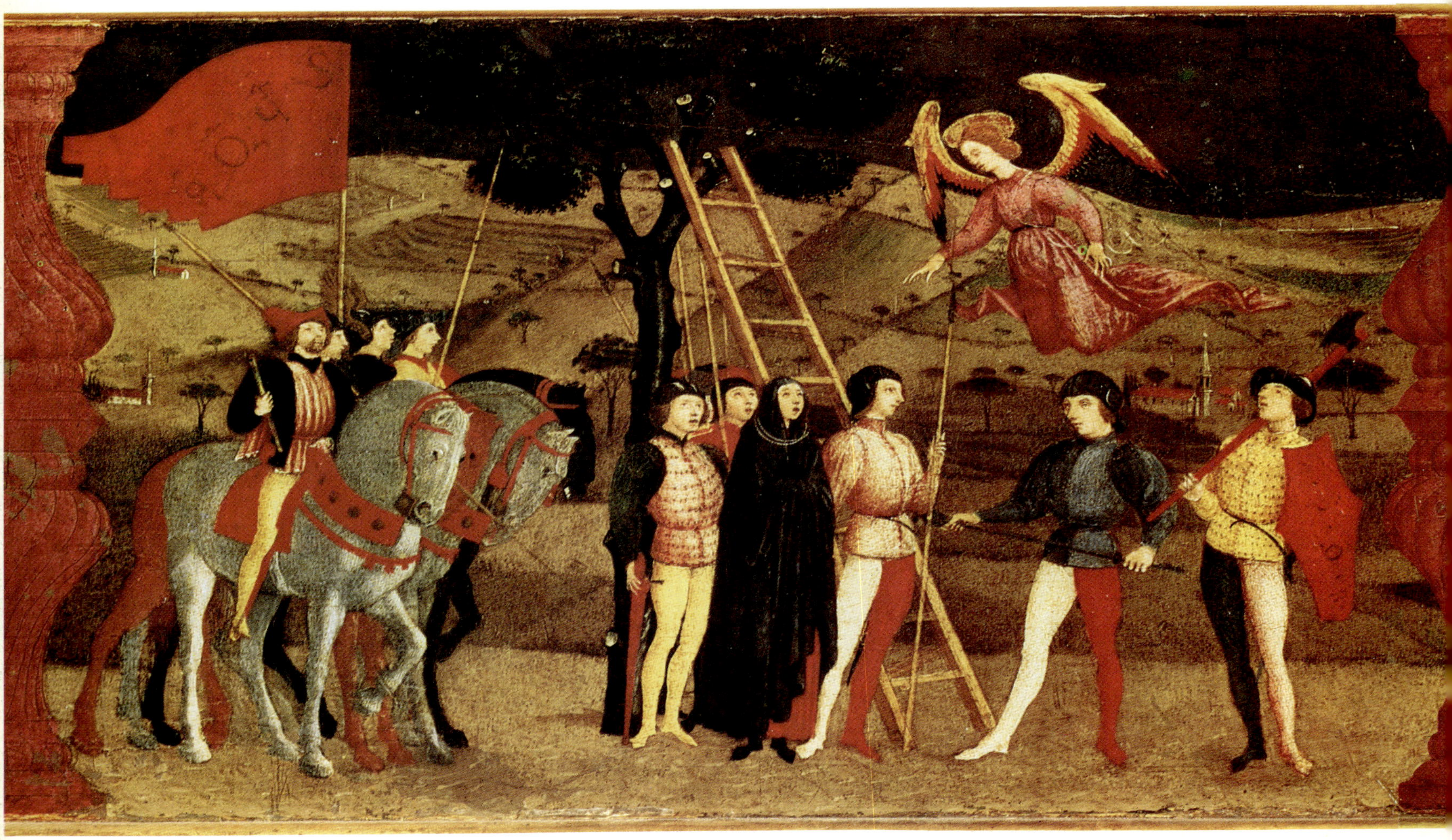

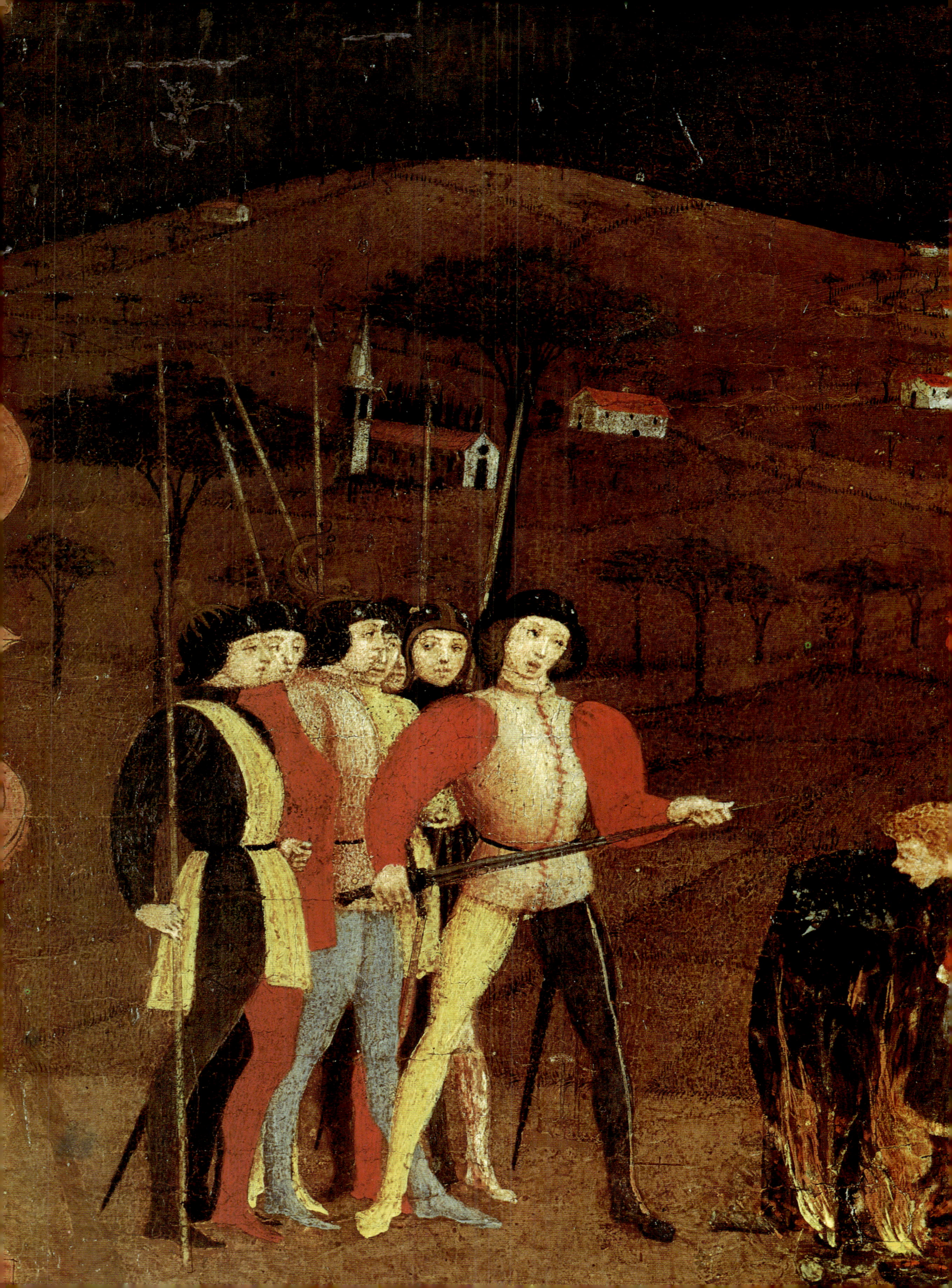

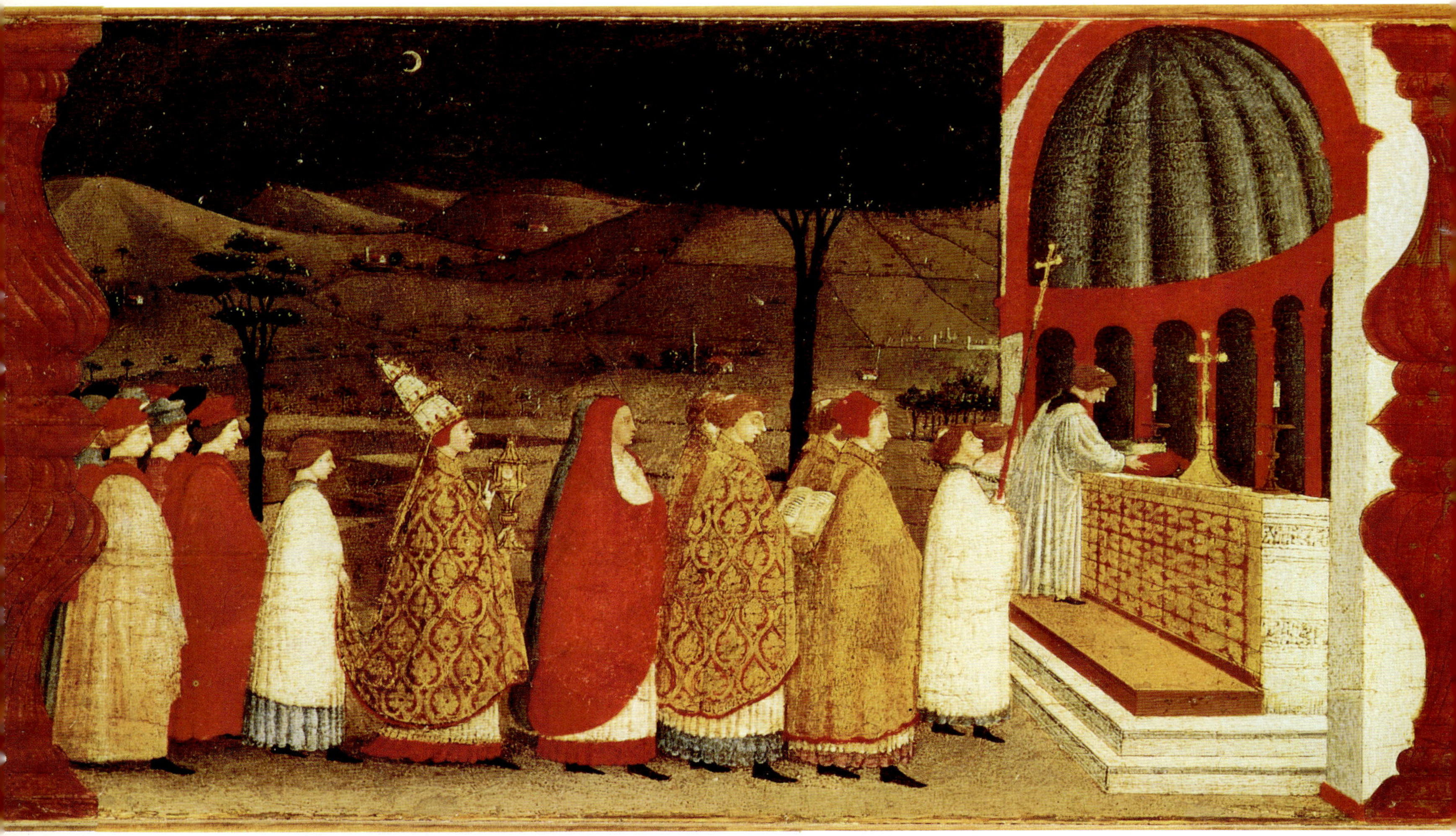

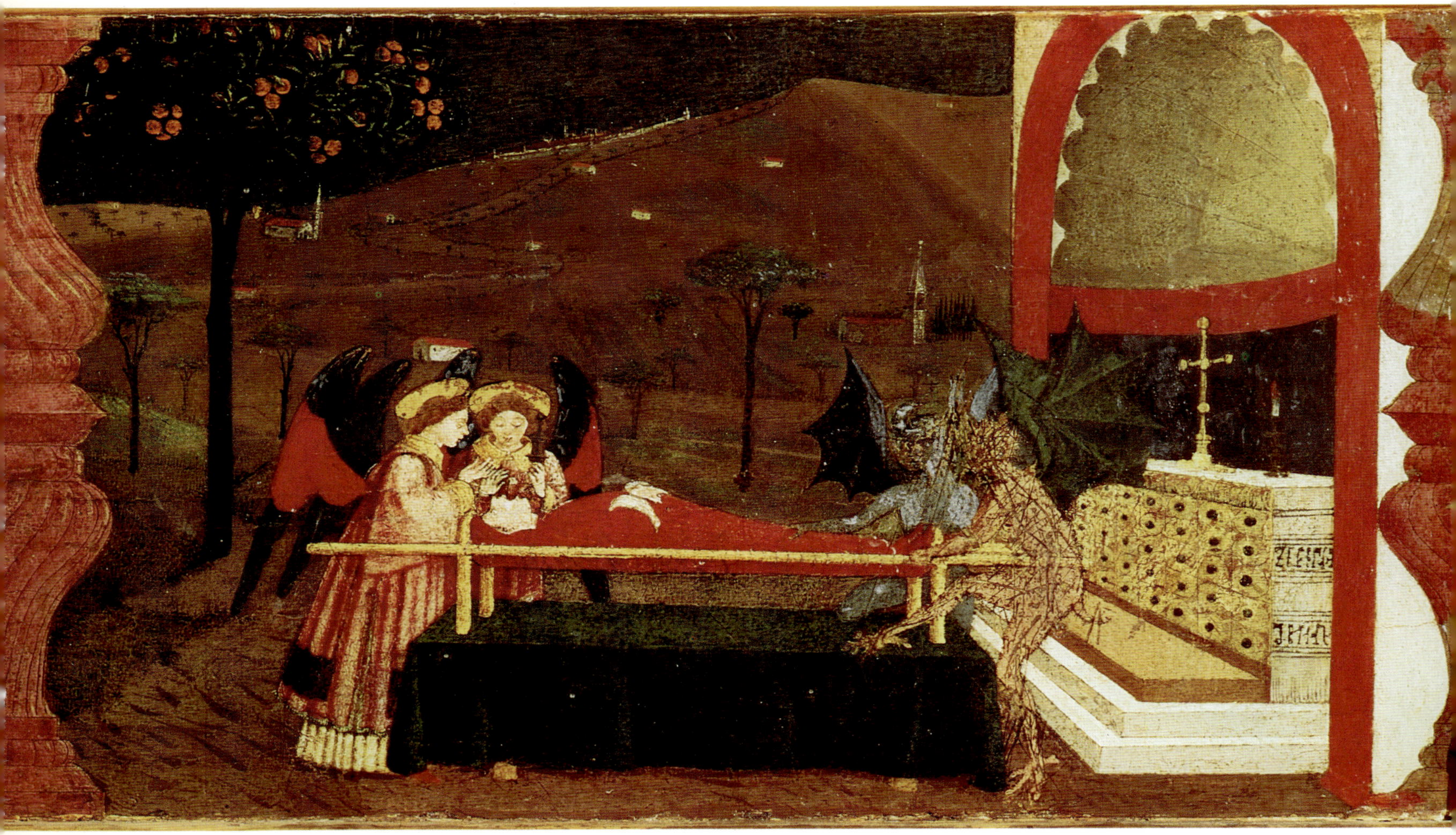

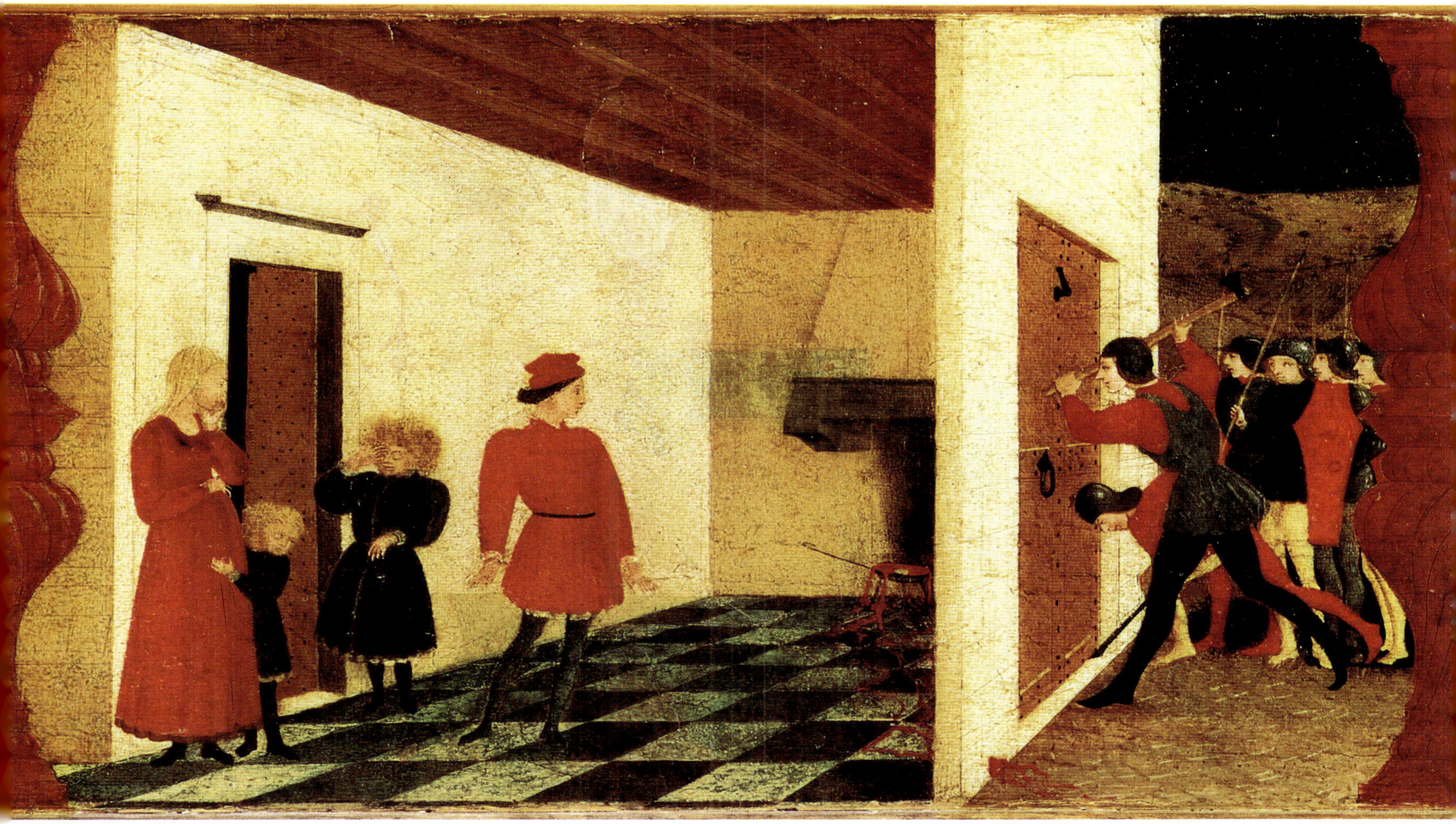

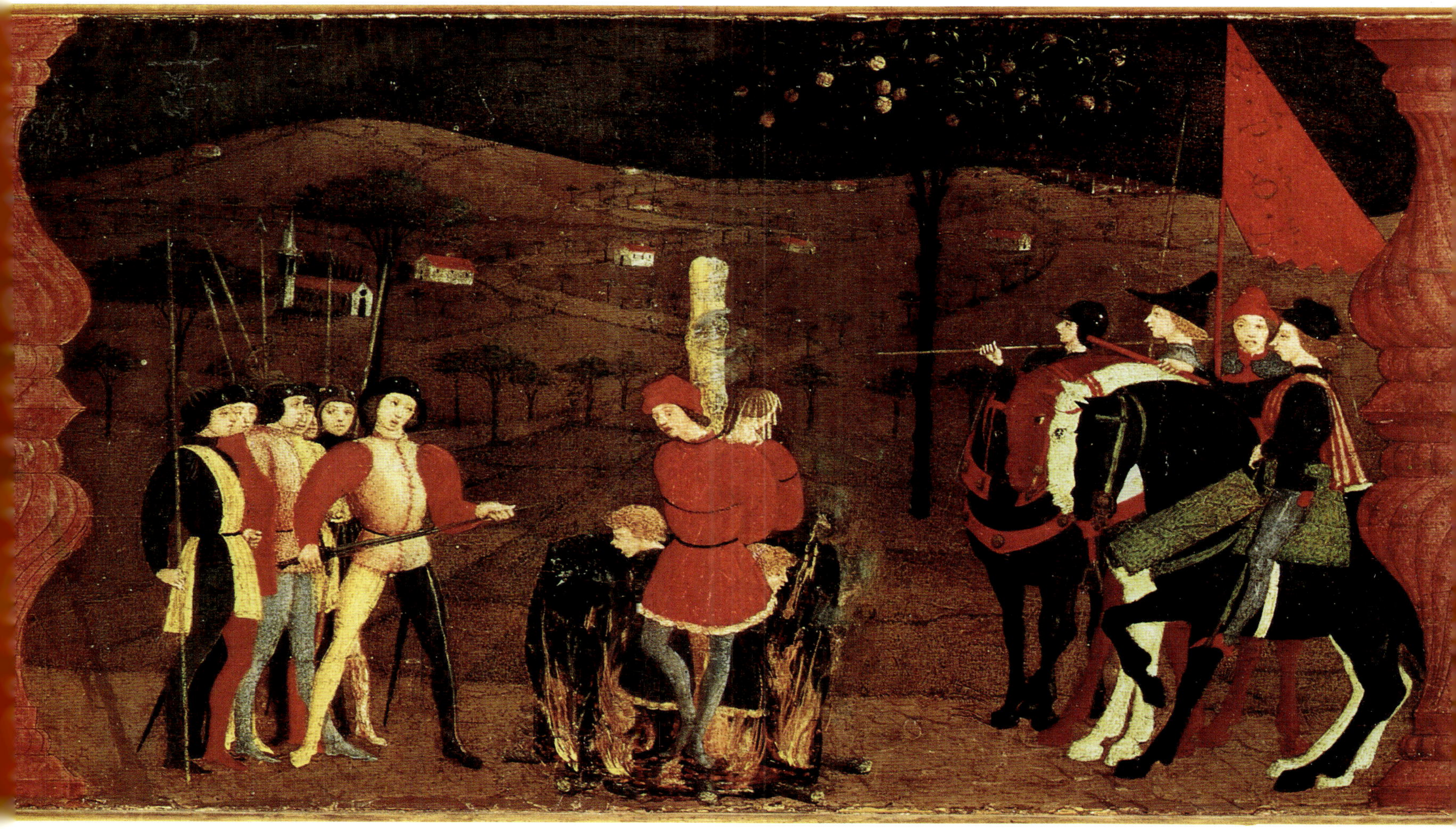

the complexity of the theme – which is rare in an Italian painting of this period – and in the variety of composition. This coordination depends on chromatic balance and on a style that gives every object a dimension of fantastic realism, and relegates curiosities of physiognomy and materials or attempts at naturalism to a secondary role. The result is an elegant choreography which completely omits any emphasis on the miraculous element, in order to document everyday life, where the presence of the sacred is reabsorbed into a ritual in which the real and the miraculous coexist normally. Francastel wrote of this painting in terms of a great celebration of a guild.[145]

THE OXFORD HUNT

Cat. no. 34

The *Hunt* in the Ashmolean Museum in Oxford is probably the last painting of Uccello's to have survived. It is also the best preserved. It is a large wooden panel (classed here among the 'small items' more for its stylistic and thematic affinities than, obviously, for its size) which some sources believe probably formed part of a *spalliera*, or of some sort of painted wooden furnishing. Its origins, initial destination, patron and provenance are unknown (though it has occasionally been linked – groundlessly – with the court at Urbino). Uccello has used a complex series of technical innovations and followed a laborious procedure that has no parallel in the traditional decoration of *cassoni* at that time. The forest's density, volume and colouring are exceptional. In its present state, however, the original pigmentation has undergone changes: the luminous green has turned brownish because of the alteration in the copper resins used in the glazes, and the thinning of the surface layer has allowed the unusual blackish preparation of the ground to show through; the figures, on the other hand, were painted directly on the underlying gesso so that with the passage of time they contrast even more strongly with the darkness of the forest. Successive cleanings in the past have intensified the brilliance of these notes of colour, which now make the figures stand out in such a distinctive way. If the vibrancy of the scarlet clothes is due to Uccello's special technique and the action of time on the panel, the exaggeration of the colour red in the darkness of the green forest had already been noted in medieval and Quattrocento sources on optics (up until Filarete: see catalogue). The trunks of the great parasol-shaped oaks give a rhythm to the space which has been constructed in a carefully researched, erudite manner in pyramid form, and part of its outline is finely incised on the panel itself. The perspective construction is emphasized by the converging dead branches lying in the foreground (a rustic equivalent of the broken lances in the *Battles*). However, the space here is less regular than was normally acceptable.[146] Certainly the trunk standing in the centre of the middle ground identifies the vanishing point, towards which the leaping, syncopated rhythm of dogs and fawns converge in the background. But in his division of the scene, Uccello placed the meeting in the centre, with the dynamic of horsemen and dogs in the wings, but subtly varied the distribution of the movement by placing the action in front of the trees on the left and behind the trees on the right. The movement of the horses in the mêlée of dogs follow lines that are diagonal or parallel to the picture plane in a complexity of perspectival vistas that emphasizes the dynamism, the agitation, the centripetal force of the whole system, in contrast to the immobile rhythm of the tree trunks in the forest. This double register is not translated through mechanical perspective – by using geometrically shaped meadows, as in the *Battles* or elsewhere – but it explores the dialectic between two continuities: the motionless order of things and the chance disorder of the hunt. This reveals the degree of mastery Uccello had achieved in depicting space through imagination rather than through recourse to the contrivances of optics and geometry.

The pictorial execution is an example of the refined formalism found in Uccello's final period. There are few instances where he changed his mind: recent investigations show that these were limited almost exclusively to variations in the position of the legs and tails of the animals in motion. The remarkable effect of the dense forest was

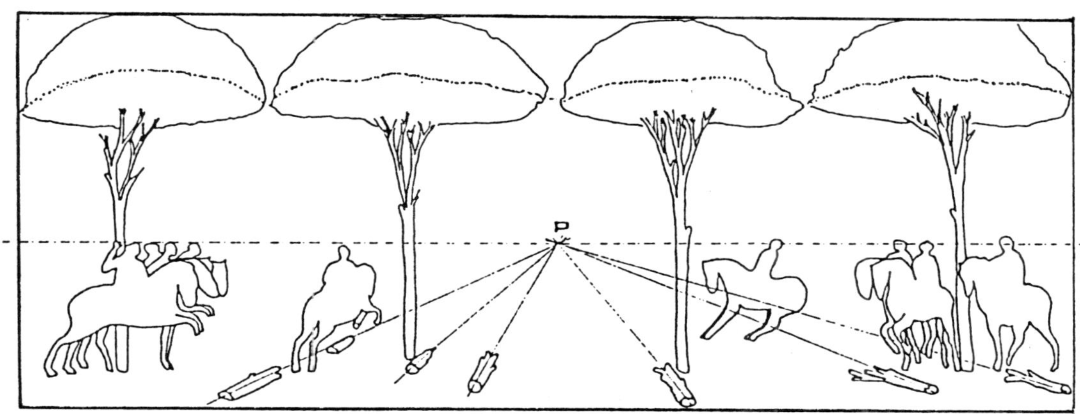

Reconstruction of the perspective in *The Hunt* (after *Paolo Uccello's Hunt in the Forest*, Ashmolean Museum, Oxford).

achieved by a number of successive layers of paint, until the final luminous accent which were obtained by the application of gold leaf; Uccello had borrowed this technique, which enhances the painting's richness, from late Gothic tradition and from miniaturists. This hunt taking place in the thick oak forest was not an accurate depiction of the techniques of deer hunting at that time, in spite of the realism of lances, daggers and horns. Still less was it a description of a Medici hunt in the forests near Pisa: in spite of precise detail, this is a poetic evocation of the world of hunting.

Chromatic distortion and the barely perceptible presence of the crescent moon in the sky in the centre suggest that, contrary to Italian custom at the time, the hunt is taking place at night. In reality, Uccello was attempting to use colour to render the continual changes of light that occur under the canopy of the forest. From a technical viewpoint, subtle variations were produced by limiting the lower part of the umbrella crown of the trees, through a fine circle drawn in perspective, like the foreshortened haloes around saints' heads.

In all this complex perspective, one detail can be isolated: the river crossing the forest on the right leads to a second vanishing point which is distinctly separate from the centralized one. This is because the river, which is deliberately not orthogonal, exacts its own complementary vanishing point as a result. This secondary vanishing point is situated on the same skyline, using a procedure that had already been used in the Karlsruhe *Adoration*. The element, which in itself is marginal, slightly disturbs the balance of the composition because of its linear appearance, which is more like an artificial canal than a natural stream, but it does confirm that Uccello almost never used a single vanishing point; instead, he always retained a certain plurality and ambiguity in his quest for a more complex, more articulated perspective space. It was a quest he never renounced. Of all Florentine Quattrocento paintings, the Oxford panel undoubtedly remains the richest in effects and chromatic passages: it is a painting that must have seemed truly unusual, if not disconcerting, to his contemporaries.

Following pages: Paolo Uccello, *The Hunt*, *c.* 1470, tempera on wood, 65 × 165 cm. Oxford, Ashmolean Museum. Details and complete work.

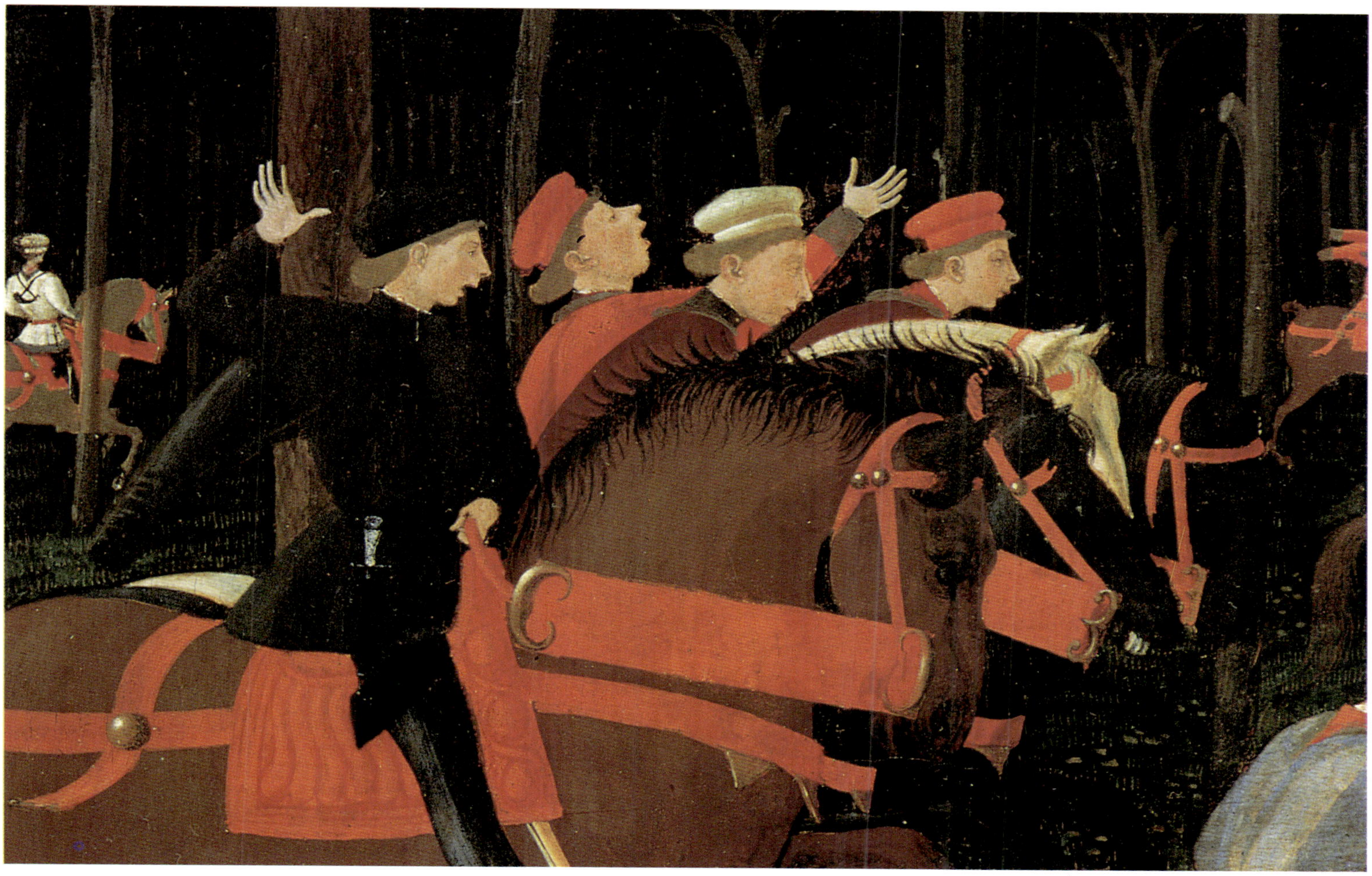

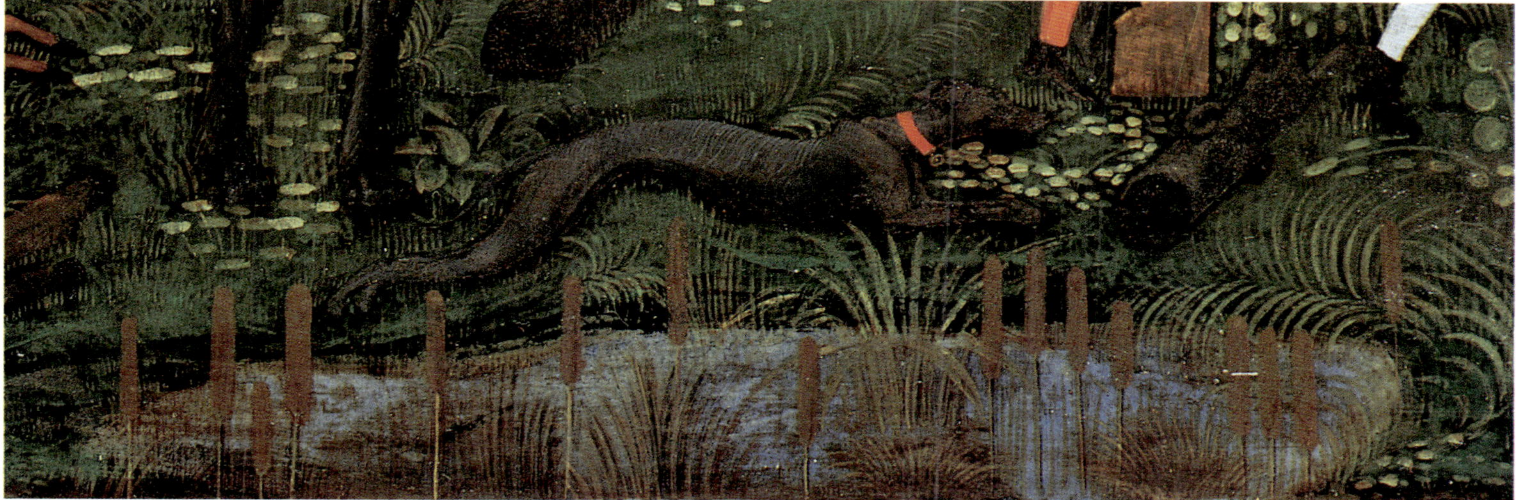

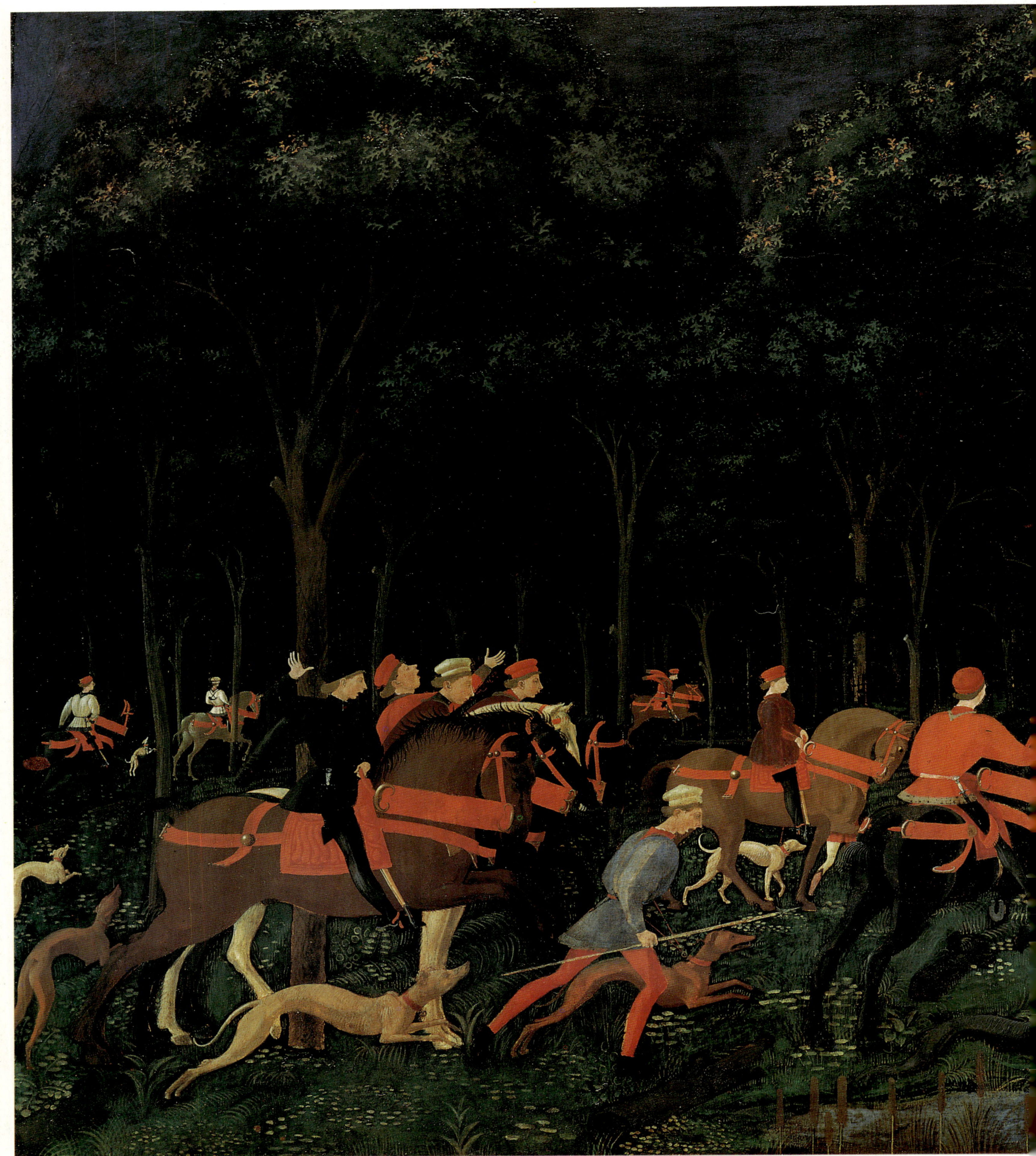

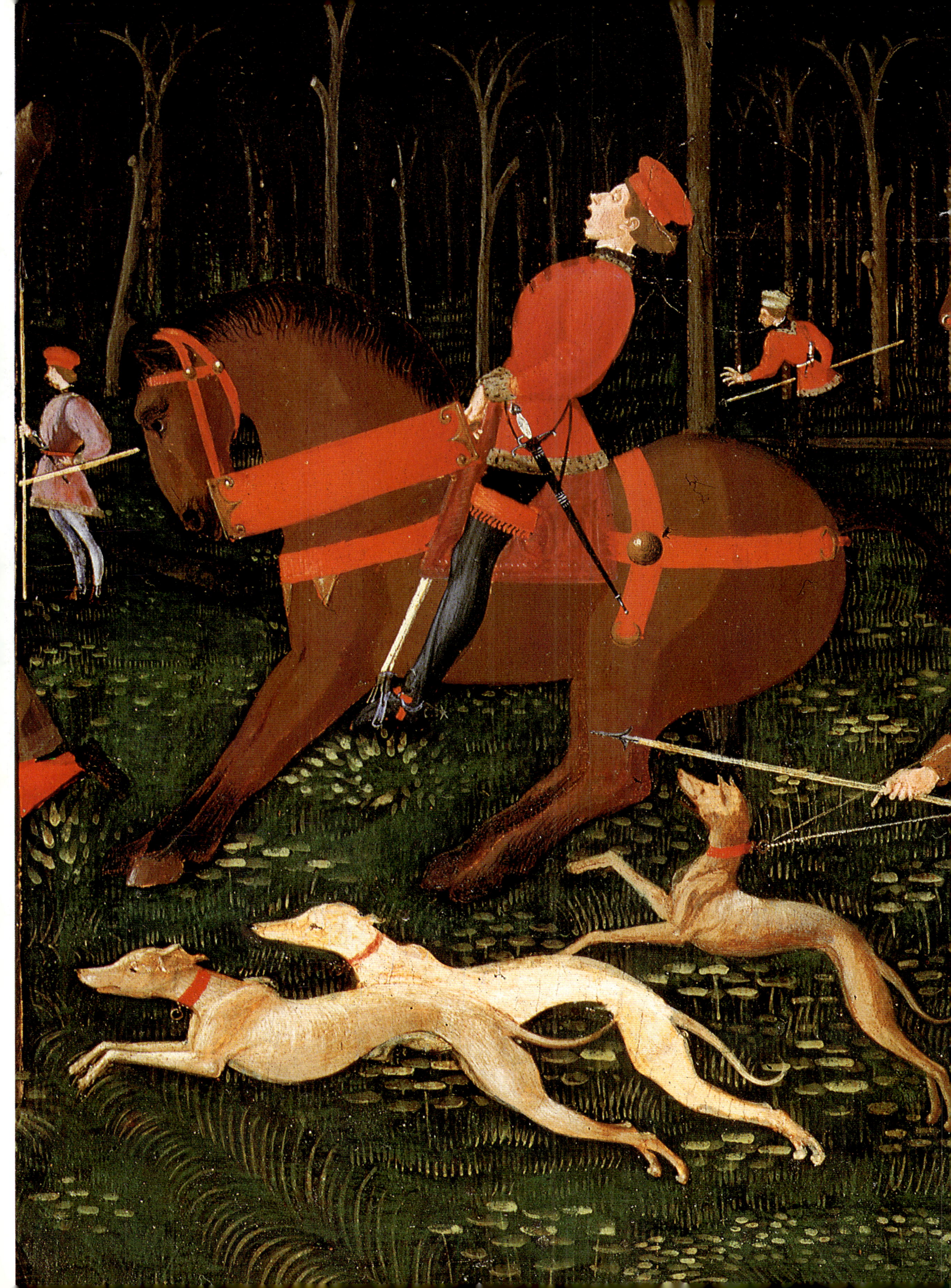

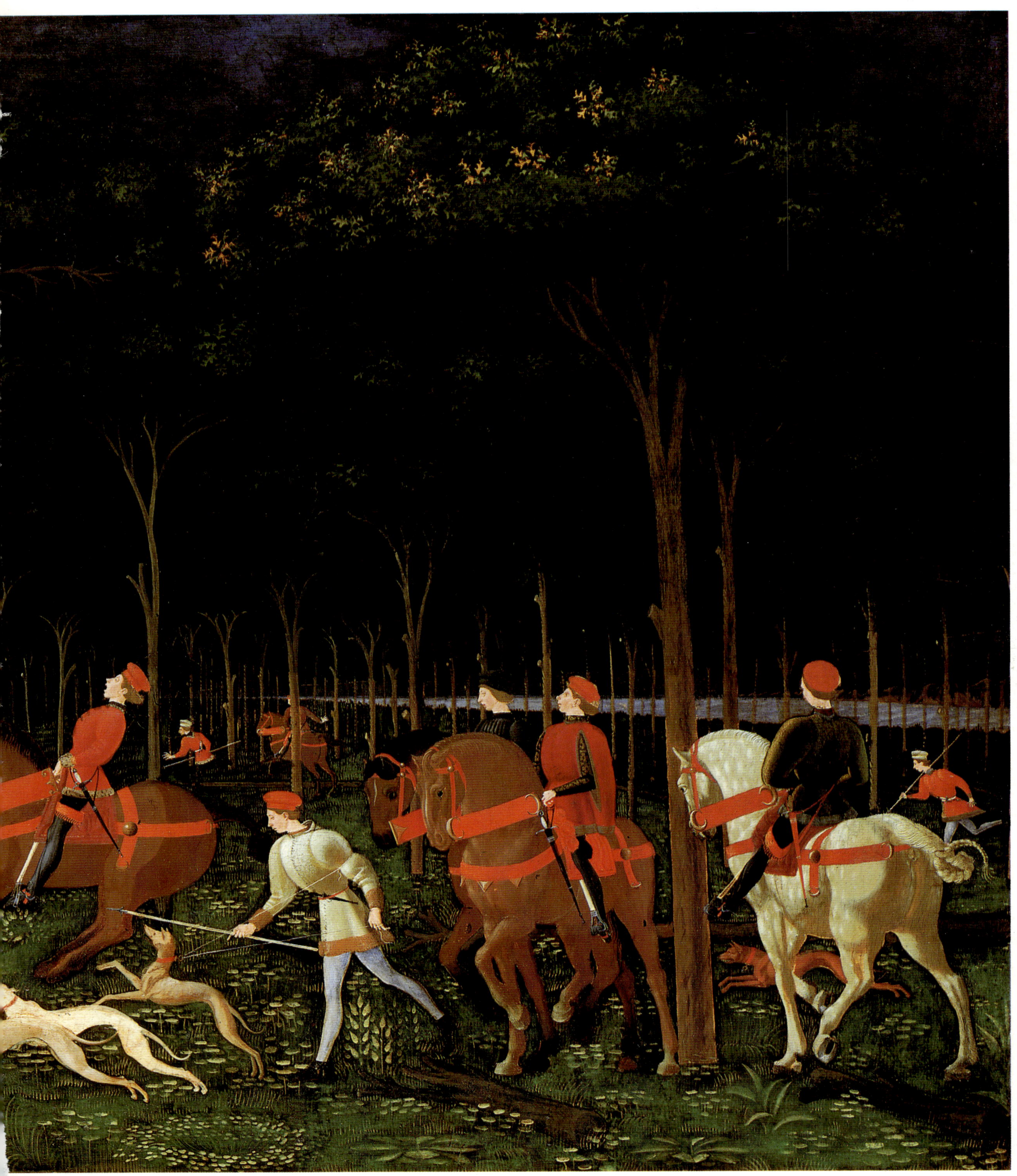

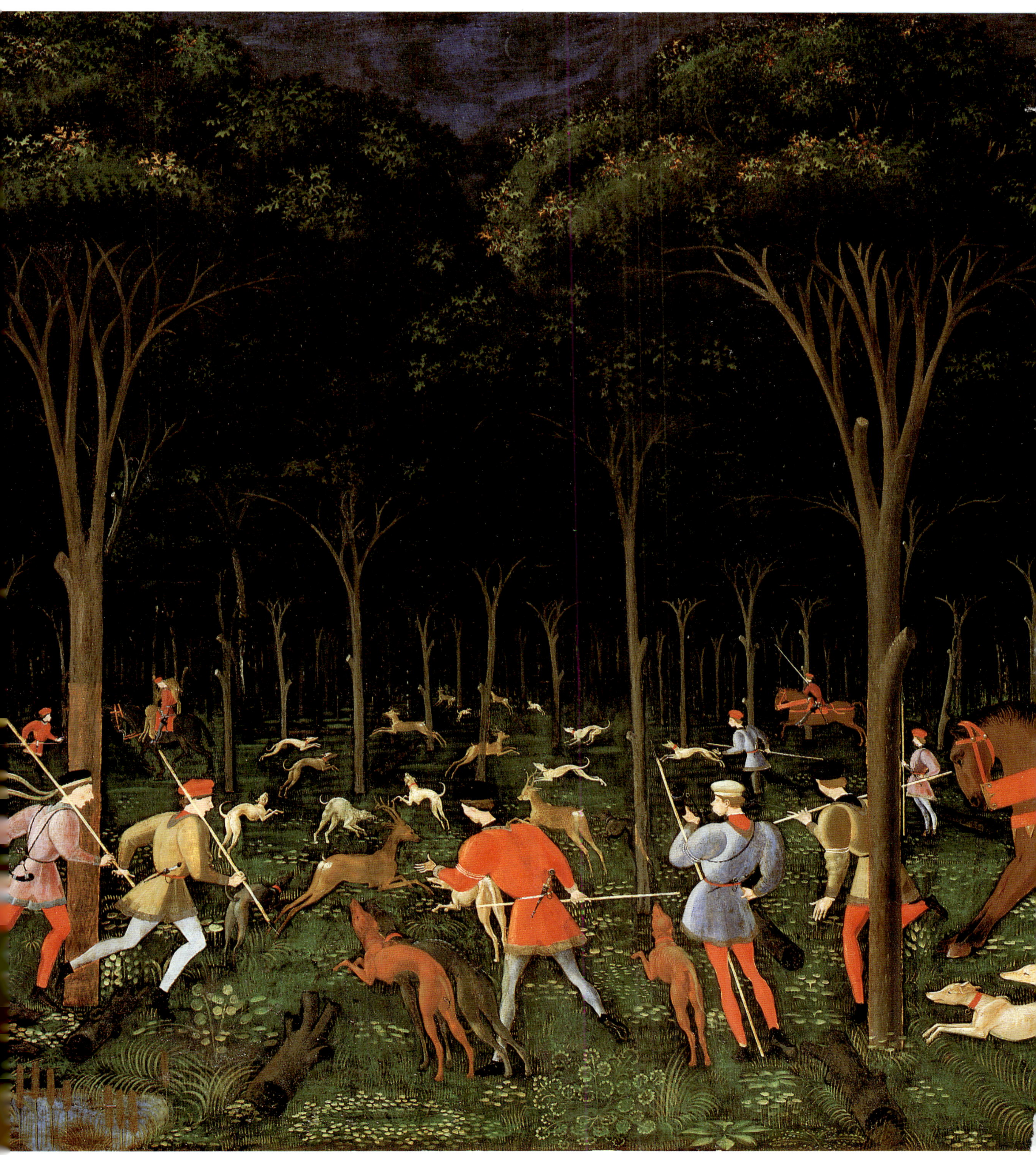

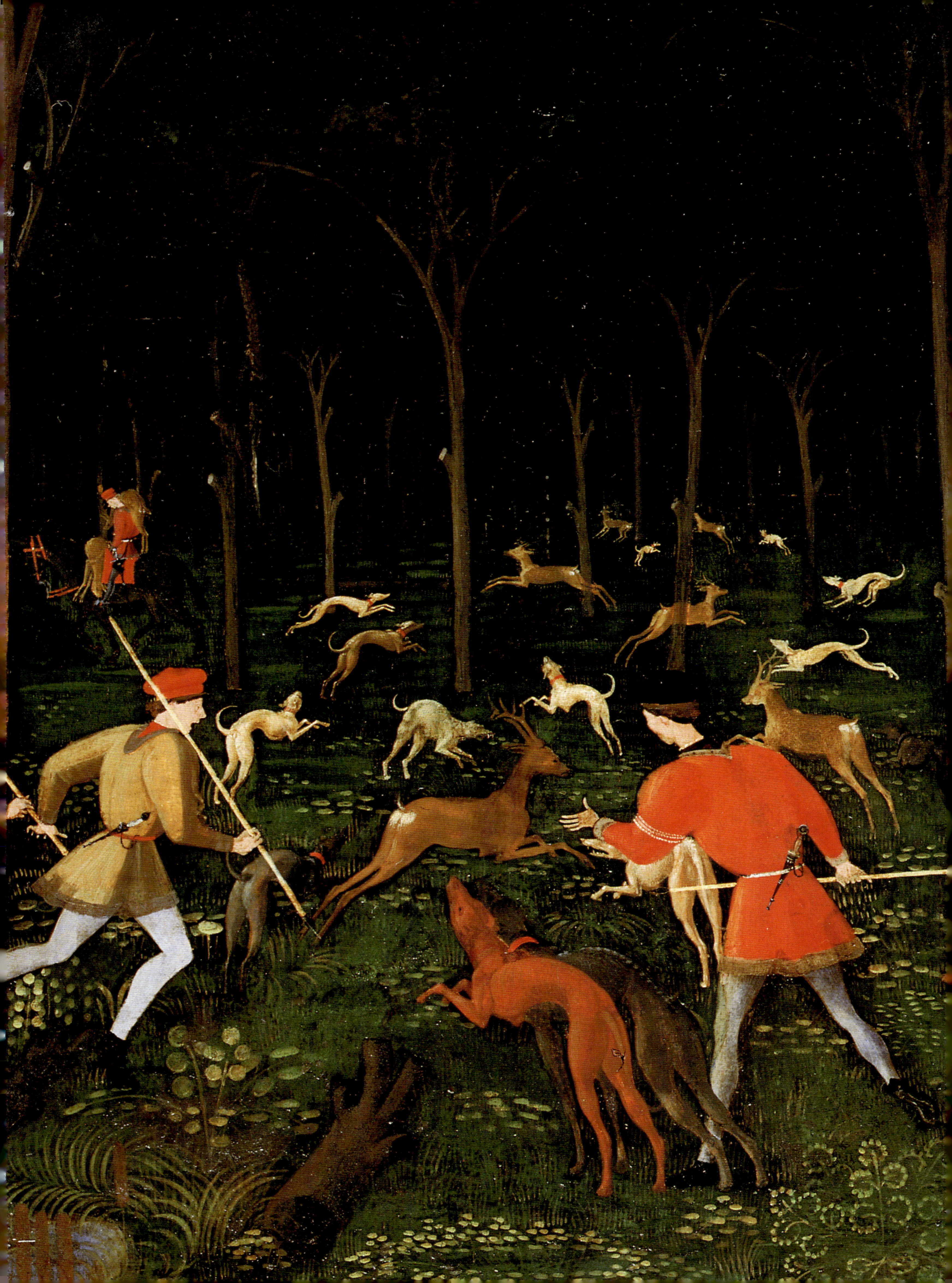

NOTES

Introduction

1 In the prologue of *De Pictura* (*c.* 1426), which takes the form of a dedication to Filippo Brunelleschi, Alberti mentions Donatello '*quel nostro amicissimo Donato Scultore*' ('our great friend the sculptor Donatello'), Ghiberti, Luca della Robbia and Masaccio, the only painter in the list (L. B. Alberti, *De Pictura*, ed. C. Grayson, Bari, 1980, p. 7; *On Painting*, Penguin Classics, 1991, p. 34). Brunelleschi was born in 1377, Ghiberti in 1378, Donatello in 1386, Luca della Robbia *c.* 1400, Masaccio in 1401 and Alberti in 1404. Uccello was born in 1397.

2 '*Truovomi vecchio e senza inviamento e no(n) mi posso asercitare, e la don(n)a inferma*' ('I am old and without resources, I can no longer work, and my wife is ill') Uccello declares to the Cadastre on 8 August 1469 (Archivio di Stato di Firenze [ASF], *Decime* Quartiere S. Giovanni, Gonfalone Drago, Vol. 926, c. 259.

3 L. Bruni, *Panegirico della città di Firenze*, Florence, 1974, pp. 16–17: '*Florentiam vero usque adeo mundam atque abstersam cernimus ut nusquam aliquid reperiatur nitidius.*'

4 L. Bruni, op. cit., pp. 20–21.

5 L. Bruni, op. cit., pp. 22–3.

6 *Novecento*: artistic movement current in the 1920s in Italy which extolled a 'return to order' and the great tradition (Giotto, Masaccio, etc.). Its protagonists were Sironi, Rosai, Soffici, De Pisis, Morandi and Casorati. The group nonetheless tolerated a number of different viewpoints within it.

7 '*Michelozzi architettore, e scultore di tutto*': Benedetto Dei, *Memorie notate* (1470), Florence, Biblioteca Riccardiana, Ms. Ricc. 1853, c. 49; in G. C. Romby, *Descrizioni e rappresentazioni della città di Firenze nel XV secolo*, Florence, 1976, p. 72.

8 L. B. Alberti, *I Libri della famiglia*, ed. R. Romano and A. Tenenti, Turin, 1969.

9 L. Ghiberti, *I Commentari*, ed. O. Morisani, Naples, 1947.

10 G. Roscoe, *Vita di Lorenzo de' Medici detto il Magnifico*, Pisa, 1816, Vol. I, p. XLIII. *Di suggello* florins were coins kept in a small sealed leather purse, *sigillato cuoio* (*suggellato* in Florentine dialect) to prevent the gold coins being scraped, thereby losing weight and value.

Chronology

11 Archivio di Stato di Firenze (ASF), *Medici e Speziali*, ref. 21, c. 69; in W. Boeck: *Paolo Uccello, Der Florentiner Meister und sein Werk*, Berlin, 1939, p. 95.

12 '*Paulus olim doni pictor populi S. Marie nepoticose*', in Boeck, op. cit. p. 95, 15 October 1415; '*Paulus olim doni pictor, populi S. Marie Novelle de Florentia*', in the testament of 5 August 1425 (G. Gaye, *Carteggio inedito d'artisti*, Florence, 1840, I, p. 147; Boeck, op. cit. pp. 95–6). For Santa Maria Nepoticosa, or del Giglio, or degli Adimari, cf. G. Richa, *Notizie istoriche delle chiese fiorente divise ne'suoi quartieri*, VII, Florence 1758, pp. 219–26. Cf. also G. Carocci, *Studi storici sul Centro di Firenze*, Florence 1889, and *Il centro di Firenze restituito*, under the direction of M. Sframeli, Florence, 1989.

13 There is disagreement as to whether the attribution should be made to the Santa Verdiana Master, the albeit elderly P. Nelli or the young Uccello. The dating of 1416 as well as the attribution to Uccello goes back as far as its restoration in 1716 Attention was drawn to the work in U. Procacci, *Sinopie e Affreschi*, Milan, 1960, pp. 234–5 (see catalogue).

14 D. Reggioli, 'La Porta Nord. Paolo Uccello e Masolino', in *Lorenzo Ghiberti, 'Materia e Ragionamenti'*, exhibition catalogue, Florence 1978–9, Florence, 1978, p. 104.

15 F. Ghiberti, *Commentario Secondo*, ed. O. Morisani, Naples, 1947, pp. 37–8: 'Ambrogio Lorenzetti was a very famous and very original master, and created a great many works. His compositions were very noble ...'; 'He was a Master of great perfection, and a man of great talent. He was a great draughtsman, very expert in the theory of that art'; 'Ambrogio Lorenzetti seems to me to be superior to all the others, and very much more knowledgeable.' Cf. G. Sinibaldi, 'As Lorenzo Ghiberti might have considered Giotto and Ambrogio Lorenzetti', in *L'Arte*, 31, 1928, pp. 80–82; G. Ercoli, 'The Trecento Sienese in the Commentaries of Lorenzo Ghiberti' in *Lorenzo Ghiberti nel Suo Tempo*, Proceedings of the International Congress, Florence, 1978, Florence, 1980, II, pp. 317–41.

16 Ashmolean Museum, Oxford, n. inv. A/80. Attributed to Uccello by C. Volpe, *Paragone*, 1980, p. 18. For a review of the dating of the panel, relating to the Master of Bambino Vispo (Starnina?) as much as to the Master of 1419 or to Dello Delli, see the museum catalogue: C. Lloyd, *Earlier Italian Paintings*, Oxford, 1977, p. 61.

17 As an example, we need go no further than consider the works dated *c.* 1420: Mariotto di Nardo, *Trinity and Donors* (Impruneta, Collegiale), 1418; the master of 1419, *Maestà* (Cleveland Museum of Art) 1419; Rossello di Jacopo Franchi, *Coronation of the Virgin* (Florence, Accademia) 1420; *Madonna and Child with Saints* (triptych of San Leolino at Panzano), by Mariotto di Nardo, 1421; Masaccio, triptych of San Giovenale, formerly San Niccolò Oltrarno, 1422; Alvaro Pirez, *Madonna and Child with Saints* (Volterra triptych, Pinacoteca) 1423; Bicci di Lorenzo, triptych in the Collegiale at Empoli, 1423; Fra Angelico, *Crucifix* of Santa Maria Nuova, 1423; (now lost); Gentile da Fabriano, *The Adoration of the Magi* (Florence, Uffizi) 1423.

18 ASF *Notarile antecosimiano* (Pre-Cosimo Notaries' Archives), registration of Ser Matteo di Domenico Sofferoni, in Gaye, I, p. 147; Boeck, 1939, pp. 95–6. Uccello left his worldly goods to the hospital of Santa Maria del Fiore, except for 30 *soldi* for the fabric of Santa Maria del Fiore (for the building sites which remained open). He asked to be buried in the family vault at Santo Spirito.

19 ASF, *Decime*, Quartiere di S. Giovanni, Gonfalone Drago, 1427, Vol. 55, c. 707, v.; Gaye, I, p. 146, Vasari-Milanesi, II, 1878, p. 204, n.; Poggi, 1933, p. 328; Boeck, 1939, p. 96.

20 ASF, *Decime*, Quartiere di S. Giovanni, Gonfalone Drago, 1431, Florentine style 1430, col. 381; c. 779 and A; c. 282 v; Vasari-Milanesi, II, p. 204 n; Poggi, 1933, p. 328; Boeck, 1939, pp. 96–7 'Paolo di Dono painter ... 33 years'.

21 'Paolo Uccello, master of painting, painted the flood in the

cloister of Santa Maria Novella and the story which is below it. The first two stories, the one above and the one beneath, are below the staircase which leads from the church to the cloister. And he painted many other things at Santa Trinita and elsewhere,' in Antonio Manetti, *Uomini Singhularii in Firenze*, Florence, Biblioteca Nazionale (BNF), Ms. 1501, G.2, c. 141 v; ed. P. Murray in *The Burlington Magazine* 99, 1957, p. 330–36 (with bibliography).

22 G. Vasari, *Le vite de' piu eccelenti pittori scultori et architettori*, Florence, 1568, I, p. 272. The description is only in the second edition of the *Vite* (*Vita di Paolo Uccello, Pittore Fiorentino*), as well as the passage mentioning the vault of the Peruzzi with the chameleon/camel. The Benedictine theme of the cloister of Santa Maria degli Angeli is a reminder of the cycle of Spinello Aretino in the sacristy of San Miniato (1386–7) and more particularly of the predella of the *Coronation of the Virgin* by Lorenzo Monaco for the master-altar of Santa Maria degli Angeli of 1414 (Florence, Uffizi). Certain indicators which we can deduce from Vasari's writing are reminiscent of the great Lorenzo Monaco's style, who died *c.* 1425–6: for example, the detail of the ruins, the architectonic simplification of the background, the clothes 'swirling gracefully', the 'attitudes' of the characters, the 'strained' Gothic which becomes 'a drawing of quality'. The attribution to Uccello can be traced back to Antonio Billi's *Libro* of *c.* 1524; before that, Albertini's *Memoriale* reported the cycle as belonging to 'Thomaso Masacci' to whom he also attributed the *Sir John Hawkwood*. Given that the cycle would be a difficult assignment for a young master, and given that the great master of the convent was still alive, the Benedictine cycle of Santa Maria degli Angeli could have been done between 1431 – when Ambrogio Traversari became superior of the Order – and *c.* 1437 (cf. M. Horster, 1980, pp. 173–4, with bibliography).

23 Vasari, 1550, p. 253. 'His first figures were for the Hospital of Lelmo in Florence, in the women's sector, a saint Antony with a Saint Cosmas and Saint Damian in fresco'; 1568, I, p. 269: 'Paolo's first paintings were some frescoes in an oblong niche drawn in perspective, at the Hospital of Lelmo' or Lemmo Balducci (died 1388–9). Originally it was dedicated to his patron saint. Nicolas of Bari, and it was only intended for men. The women's sector was added in 1447, funded by the Money Changers' Guild (*Arte del Cambio*) who dedicated it to its patron saint, Matthew; since 1784 it has housed the Academy of Fine Arts. Vasari's note: 'in the women's sector' (*infra le donne*) in the first edition is explicit: Uccello painted in that part of the building only from 1447 onwards. The relatively late dating is thus confirmed (it is therefore not a question of 'early paintings' as Vasari claims); the difficult perspectives of the pictures 'in an oblong niche' are therefore fully justified. F. L. del Migliore (*Firenze Città Nobilissima Illustrata*, Florence, 1684, pp. 248–57) dwells on the history of the hospital, recalling Uccello's paintings and taking note of Vasari. G. Milanesi (in Vasari-Milanesi, op. cit., II, 1878, p. 206, n. 1): 'The paintings which Paolo did here are no longer visible.'

24 Vasari-Milanesi, op. cit. II, 1878, pp. 7–9. Vasari cites an 'abundance of expressions and emotions in the characters' attitudes', 'like someone who let their mind wander around the things of the natural world', 'a beautiful, rapid style', 'very considerable fame' acquired with the cycle at the Carmine, 'for having expressed in such a lively manner feelings and attitudes never achieved till then by earlier painters'. Cf. A. Paolucci, 'Firenze 1400–1420: la stagione delle "attitudini" e degli "affetti" ' in *L'Età di Masaccio*, Florence, 1990, p. 25. We must point out the episode quoted by Vasari of the child punished by the master in Gozzoli's frescoes at San Gimignano: a game of mirrors enters Vasari's description of Starnina's *Death of Saint Jerome* at the Carmine and that of Uccello's *Death of Saint Benedict* at Santa Maria degli Angeli. The immediate effects of Starnina's teaching are obvious when we compare them with two of Lorenzo Monaco's works of the same year (1404): the *Man of Sorrows* in the Accademia in Florence, in traditional *Trecento* style and – coming after Starnina – the refined triptych of the Collegiale museum at Empoli. The two works, dated and signed, provide a reliable reference for the fellow painter's conversion to 'internationalism', parallel, moreover, with that of Lorenzo Ghiberti.

25 ASF, *Decime*, Quartiere S. Giovanni, Gonfalone Drago, 1433, Vol. 477, c. 392; Gaye, I, p. 146; Vasari-Milanesi, II, p. 204; Boeck, 1939, p. 97; ASF, *Decime*, Quartiere S. Giovanni, Gonfalone Drago, 1442, Vol. 625, c. 224; Gaye, I, p. 146; Boeck, p. 100.

26 In the *Vita di Filippo Brunelleschi* attributed to Antonio Manetti, (ed. D. De Robertis-G. Tanturli, Milan, 1976, p. 60) Uccello is quoted in connection with Brunelleschi's second perspective panel (see p. 143). A. Parronchi (*Le Due Tavole Prospettiche del Brunelleschi*, in *Studi sulla Dolce Prospettiva*, Milan, 1964, pp. 277–81) establishes a connection between the bifocal view of Brunelleschi's second perspective panel and the sinopia drawing for *The Adoration of the Child* at San Martino alla Scala (see p. 155). He emphasizes the deep contrast between the two results.

27 F. Albertini, *Memoriale di molte Statue et Picture sono nella inclyta Cipta di Florentia Per Mano di Sculptori & Pictori excellenti Moderni & Antiqui tracto della propria Copia di Messer Francesco Albertini prete Flore(n)tino Anno d(omi)ni 1510*, Florence, 1510, (reprinted, Farnborough, 1972). The frescoes of Santa Maria degli Angeli are also attributed to Masaccio: 'and in the same cloister of Thomaso Masacci'.

28 M. Bacci, 'Le vetrate del tamburo della cupola' in *Lorenzo Ghiberti 'Materia e Ragionamenti'*; op. cit. 1978, p. 245. Documents in the archives of the Office of Works of Santa Maria del Fiore, *Deliberazioni 1425–1436*, c. 156 v.; in G. Poggi, *Il Duomo di Firenze*, Berlin, 1909, doc. 773; Boeck, 1939, p. 97.

29 *Pittura di luce. Giovanni di Francesco e l'Arte Fiorentina di Metà Quattrocento*, (ed.) L. Bellosi, exhibition catalogue, Florence, 1990, Milan, 1990, p. 19, ill. 6.

30 G. Poggi, 'Paolo Uccello e l'orologio di Santa Maria del Fiore', in *Miscellanea di Storia dell'Arte in Onore di I. B. Supino*, Florence, 1933, pp. 323–36, doc. 757; Boeck, 1939, p. 102.

31 Poggi, 1933, doc. 761; Boeck, 1939, p. 102.

32 Gaye, I, p. 146; Vasari-Milanesi, II, p. 208, n. 3; Boeck, 1939, p. 102.

33 G. Rucellai, 'Il Zibaldone quaresimale', c. 69, in *Giovanni Rucellai ed il suo Zibaldone*, ed. A. Perosa, I, London, 1960, p. 24. The editing of the manuscript covers a wide period, from 1457 to 1481, the year Rucellai died. The note for folio 69 must

be later than 1471 (A. Perosa, *Introduzione*, 1960, op. cit. p. XV). The works belonging to the Rucellai family are not detailed and among the different artists described as 'painters' are only 'Master Domenico da Vinegia' (Veneziano), 'frate Filippo' (Lippi), 'Paolo Uccello' and 'Andreino dal Chas-tagno, detto degl'impichati' (Andrea deal Castagno, 'of the hanged men'), while Verrocchio is defined as 'sculptor and painter' and Antonio Pollaiolo and Maso Finiguerra as 'masters of drawing'.

34 'Paolo Uccello for the painting of the Tabernacle of San Gio(vanni) and of Our Lord/Lady? [*N(ostro/a) S(ignore/a)*], shall be given in total, when he has finished f(lorins) 22.131', Florence, Biblioteca Marucelliana, *Quaderno di Ricordi Se-g(nat)o o cominc(iat)o dal 1450 al 1453* c. 230 v, in Boeck, 1939, pp. 102–3.

35 Vasari-Milanesi, II, p. 211; Boeck, 1939, p. 103. Stefano d'Antonio, born *c.* 1405–7, died in 1483, was associated and collaborated with Bicci di Lorenzo (cf. D. Colnaghi, 1928, pp. 257–8).

36 L. Berti in *L'Età di Masaccio*, op. cit. 1990, pp. 34 and 118: the work, commissioned by the Castellani family, was originally in San Lorenzo. It is cited as having among immediate echoes the Quaratesi polyptych of Gentile da Fabriano. This latter work is emblematic of this period along with Masaccio's *Annunciation* (now lost), the Goldman *Annunciation* by Masolino painted at a time when he was very influenced by Gentile, the Carrand triptych of Giovanni di Francesco and the *San Ansano* attributed to Francesco d'Antonio.

37 Florence, archives of the Office of Works of Santa Maria del Fiore, *Deliberazione 1450–1454*, c. 113; Poggi, 1933, p. 336; Boeck, 1939, p. 103.

38 M. Haines, *La Sacrestia delle Messe del Duomo di Firenze*, Florence, 1983, pp. 287–8, docs 29, 33, 40, 43.

39 Vasari-Milanesi, I, p. 202; A. Chastel, *Fables, Formes, Figures*, Paris, 1978, p. 59, n. 4.

40 Lorenzo di Matteo Morelli, *Giornale-Ricordi 1464–1479*, in J. Beck, *Gazette des Beaux-Arts*, 6, 93, 1979, 1320, p. 3.

41 A. Schumarsow, *Melozzo da Forlì, Ein Beitrag zur Kunst- und Kulturgeschichte Italiens im XV. Jahrhundert*, Berlin-Stuttgart, 1886, pp. 359–60, after the *Libro B del Corpus Domini* (now lost); Boeck, 1939, p. 104.

42 Gaye, I, pp. 214–15; A. Bruschi in *Scritti Rinascimentali di Architettura*, Milan, 1978, pp. 19–22.

43 M. Aronberg Lavin, *The Art Bulletin*, 49, 1967, pp. 10 and 11, n. 60.

44 ASF, *Mercanzia*, Vol. 1483, c. 781, 25 August 1474: 'Paolo di Dono Uccello painter, to whom Domenico de ... del Taxo [?] cabinet maker is debtor for more than three florins by reason of two painted pictures, both sold to him and handed over'; in J. Beck, 1979, op. cit., p. 4.

45 *Lettuccio*: a large chest-seat, with a low backrest behind and armrests, mounted on a dais. It was finished off with a tall *spalliera* (see below) against the partition, divided by pilasters (*lesene*) framing decorative panels, most often in marquetry. The *lettuccio* which had a practical use as a divan was very fashionable in the 1460s. Other than those found in the inventory of the Medici house, the most important to have been documented are those made in Florence by Benedetto da Maiano for Ferdinand of Aragon, King of Naples, and by Giuliano da Maiano for Ferdinand's son Alfonso, Duke of Calabria (cf. M. Trionfi Honorati, 'A proposito del "lettuccio" ', in *Antichità Viva*, 1981, 3, pp. 39–47). *Spalliera*: a painted panel placed behind and above Florentine chests (*cassoni*) which reached shoulder (*spalla*) height of a man standing, hence their name. The oldest documents mention of a pair of *spalliere* painted to go with a pair of *cassoni* is found in the *Ricordi* of the Florentine banker, Bernardo di Stoldo Rinieri, who ordered them in 1459 from Apollonio di Giovanni, a well-known specialist in chest decoration (cf. E. Callmann, 'Apollonio di Giovanni and Painting for the Early Renaissance Room', in *Antichità Viva*, 27, 1988, p. 3 *et seq.*). The *spalliera* can be considered as the ancestor of the easel painting of Florentine High Renaissance palaces.

46 L. C. Ragghianti, *Il Libro de'Disegni del Vasari*, Florence, 1974, pp. 46–8 (with bibliography).

Chapter One Florence 1397–1475: Portrait of a City

47 A. Chastel, *Art et Humanisme à Florence au Temps de Laurent le Magnifique*, 1st edn 1959, Paris, 1982, p. 2.

48 L. de Medici, *Lettere*, ed. R. Fubini and N. Rubinstein, Florence, 1977, Vol. II, p. 201.

49 F. Guicciardini, *Storie Fiorentine*, Bari, 1969, pp. 2–3.

50 E. C. Vasoli, *Leonardo Bruni*, in *Dizionario Biografico degli Italiani*, Rome, 1960, Vol. XIV (1972), pp. 619–33.

51 L. Bruni, *Panegirico della Città di Firenze*, Florence, 1974, p. 95.

52 Bruni, op. cit., ibid.

53 Bruni, op. cit., p. 97.

54 Accursio or Accorso, a famous thirteenth-century Florentine lawyer who held important office in the Republic. He had been buried in Bologna.

55 The house of Apollonio Lapi, a Florentine merchant, in Via del Corso (now incorporated into a large shop, 'il 48', and recently damaged during rebuilding; considered possibly as Brunelleschi's first architectural work. Although still Gothic, its porch and the two symmetric rooms on the sides herald the beginning of Brunelleschian *ratio*.

56 F. Borsi, '*e specialmente nella edificazione ...*', in *Lorenzo Ghiberti nel suo Tempo*, Proceedings of the International Symposium, Florence, 1978, Florence, 1980, II, pp. 541–2; F. Borsi, 'Ghiberti e Brunelleschi', in *Lorenzo Ghiberti, 'Materia e Ragionamenti'*, exhibition catalogue, Florence, 1978, pp. 455–8; F. Quinterio, *Lorenzo Ghiberti 'Capomastro per l'Edificazione della Cupola nel Duomo di Firenze' (1420–1436), loc. cit.*, pp. 458–62.

56a Mariano di Jacopo, known as Il Taccola (1382–*c.*1453) Sienese engineer, author of several treatises (*De Ingeneis, De Machinis*), who had met Brunelleschi in Siena and who had advised him not to divulge his inventions but to mention them only to experts on the subject. This attitude is in keeping with the Gothic corporate spirit as found in the Statutes of Ratisbon, which forbid the spread of secrets connected with one's art.

Chapter Two Art in Florence at the time of Uccello

57 Very few works of art have survived from the last decade of the Trecento, when Uccello was born: these are the eponymous triptych of the Master of San Martino at Mensola (1391), Spinello Aretino's triptych of 1391 (Florence, Accademia),

another by an anonymous follower of Orcagna (Honolulu Academy of Arts), and the *Madonna* of Master Francesco (Florence, Accademia), both of that same year; Giovanni del Biondo's *Madonna and Child* (1392) at Figline Valdarno; Cenni di Francesco's *Madonna del Latte* in the Palazzo Comunale of San Miniato al Tedesco, Spinello Aretino's triptych at Santa Maria in Quinto (1393); 'Maestro Brunelleschi's' *Coronation of the Virgin* (New York, Metropolitan Museum) of 1394; the Master of San Martino's *Madonna and Child with Two Donors* at Mensola (1395, present location unknown); Mariotto di Nardo's triptych for the oratory of Fontelucente (1398) and the anonymous *Madonna Enthroned (Maestà)* at the Serristori hospital of Figline Valdarno.

58 L. Ghiberti, *Commentario Secondo*, ed. O. Morisani, Naples 1947, pp. 42 and 47; D. Reggioli in *Lorenzo Ghiberti, 'Materia e Ragionamenti'*, exhibition catalogue, Florence, 1978, p. 104.

59 Vasari-Milanesi, II, Florence, 1878, pp. 8–9 (*Vita di Gherardo Starnina Pittore Fiorentino*). Vasari's comparisons between Starnina's cycle at the Carmine and Uccello's in the cloister of Santa Maria degli Angeli are enlightening.

60 The second agreement for the doors is dated 1 June 1407, but Uccello is mentioned twice and for different sums of money, in an undated document, but undoubtedly very soon afterwards, among those 'who are working on the said door after the second agreement with the said Lorenzo' (R. Krautheimer-T. Krautheimer-Hess, *Lorenzo Ghiberti*, Princeton, 1956, rep. 1982, doc. 31, pp. 369–70). Uccello's experience of working under Ghiberti would be of cardinal importance. More than a simple practical apprenticeship or a stylistic debt, it would be an important professional preparation, a network of connections, a technical inquisitiveness which went beyond the limits of painting practice, *perspectiva naturalis* and empiricism in the philosophy of nature, explorations into ancient Arab and medieval optic sources, a deep awareness of the Byzantine, Roman and Gothic past and the optico-psychological interpretation of figures. Ghiberti shaped Uccello's early career: a probable journey to Siena to study (Ghiberti was working there on the baptismal fonts in the cathedral); experience as a mosaicist and painter of stained-glass windows (which were closely linked to the options Lorenzo envisaged for Santa Maria del Fiore: mosaics for the sacristies and for the vaulting of the cupola, stained-glass windows for the oculi of the cupola); a journey to Venice, just at the time when Ghiberti was returning there; early experience at pictorial calligraphy, the precious *de re metallica* which would characterize the *Battles*, youthful enthusiasm for Gentile da Fabriano, high esteem for the painter-philosopher Ambrogio Lorenzetti. Also Ghibertian in concept was the composition of the bays in the Chiostro Verde, with the Stories in four sensory perceptions, (*effetti*) following the recommendations given in the *Commentari* (II, p. 45): 'The *effetti* of four stories appear in each panel.'

61 L. Pellosi, 'Il "Maestro della Crocifissione Griggs": Giovanni Toscani' in *Paragone. Arte*, 17, 1966, 193. pp. 44–58, p. 56; F. Zeri, *Diari di Lavoro*, Turin, 1976, pp. 29–31; L. B. in *Arte Lombarda tra Gotico e Rinascimento*, Milan, 1988, p. 197. On Toscani's relations with Ghiberti, cf. M. Sfameli in *L'Età di Masaccio*, exhibition catalogue, Florence, 1990, Milan, 1990, p. 96.

62 L. Berti, *Masaccio*, Florence, 1988, p. 26; A. Paolucci, *Il Museo della Collegiata di Empoli*, Florence, 1985, pp. 62–3, n. 15 (with bibliography); also in *L'Età di Masaccio*, p. 122.

63 G. C. Argan, 'L'Architecture de Brunelleschi et les origines de la théorie perspective au xve siècle', in G. C. Argan–R. Wittkower, *Perspective et Histoire au Quattrocento*, Châtillon-sous-Bagneux, 1990, p. 25 (already published in *Journal of the Warburg and Courtauld Institutes*, 9, 1946). Argan believes (p. 21) that like Masolino, when Uccello wished to represent empty space independently of solid forms and not as a 'comparison', he 'reduce[d] perspective to the Trecentoesque idea of infinite spatiality'.

64 Note among other things: adaptation to Angolo Gaddi's narrative tone (Gaddi painted the frescoes in the chapel of the Sacro Cingolo around 1395); repeated borrowings from Starnina's *affectiones*, apparent in *Saint Stephen's Disputation*; his receptiveness to Fra Angelico, who was already a great authority in the field of sacred Stories; the probable reference to Ambrogio Lorenzetti, to whom Ghiberti attributed a *Birth of the Virgin* and a *Presentation at the Temple* among the lost frescoes (1335) of Santa Maria della Scala in Siena. The Prato cycle is not an homogenous ensemble: certain aspects of it are disconcerting, it was a collaborative effort (with another master from Bicci di Lorenzo's circle, who had been converted at an early stage to Fra Angelico's style and who had probably painted the vaulting); he has given rise to confusion that stretches as far as the invention of a 'Prato Master' *alter ego* who has had a good run with the art critics.

65 The *Hawkwood* is a humanist commorative monument in praise of active life and military discipline that Cosimo encouraged even though it was a legacy of the late Trecento exhumed by the preceding Albizzi regime (see catalogue). The Adroit Medici probably supported the enterprise because he had an analogous celebration of Tolentino in mind: a *condottiere* who died in 1435 and who was closely linked to the public fortunes and rise of Cosimo, who mentioned him as a friend in his *Ricordi*.

66 C. Volpe. 'Paolo Uccello at Bologna' in *Paragone. Arte*, 31, 1980, 365, pp. 3–28, p. 8. Echoes, which in other respects are modest, have been observed in illuminated work of the period by V. Gebhardt, *Paolo Uccellos 'Schlacht von S. Romano'*, Bochum Univ., 1990, Frankfurt-Berne-New York-Paris 1991, pp. 170–71.

67 F. Ames Lewis, 'Domenico Veneziano and the Medici', in *Jahrbuch der Berliner Museen*, 21, 1979, pp. 67–90.

68 Excluding illuminated chronicles like those of Leonardo da Besozzo – for which it is possible to cite other sources and different models – an indirect echo of Uccello's cycles at Padua can be found in the giant *Philosophers* painted in fresco by Bramante in 1477 on the façade of the palace of the Podestà at Bergamo, then under the domination of Venice (S. Borsi, 'Bramante at Bergamo', in F. Bori, *Bramante*, Milan-Paris, 1990, 1st edn Milan, 1989, pp. 152–4, with bibliography). But perhaps the influence of Uccello's lost cycle at Padua has been exaggerated. The *oriolo* (clock) in Florence, of slightly earlier date, in spite of its very visible position in the Duomo, does not seem to have left any significant impression on Florentine painting. In Padua the real driving force was Donatello. Michiel thinks he notices a rapid, simplified pictorial technique which is intentionally poor in the choice of terre-

verte, paid for by the day. But these figures would not have lacked interest for the young painters at the Eremitani, especially Mantegna (Vasari). But the *Cronaca Crespi*, or the '*Libro di Giusto*' derived rather from common sources and referred to a solid iconographical tradition. Perhaps explicit echoes of Uccello can be found in the narrative decorations by the Maestro dei Cassoni Walter as Volpe suggests (1980, op. cit., p. 28, n. 24). They amount to very little: Uccello's presence, between Guariento's and Squarcione's, was scarcely noticeable in the great international centre as had already been the case in Venice and Bologna, and as it would be in Urbino.

69 G. Fossi, *Filippo Lippi*, Florence, 1989, p. 62.

70 The *Codex Magliabechiano*, kept at the Biblioteca Nazionale in Florence (published under the direction of C. Frey, Berlin, 1892) is one of the most important sources for the history of art before Vasari. Written *c.* 1546 by an anonymous Florentine (referred to as the Anonimo Magliabechiano), it contains '*Notizie sopra l'arte degli antichi et quella de' fiorentini da Cimabue a Michelangelo Buonarroti*'.

71 E. Gombrich, in 'The Early Medici as Patrons of Art' (1960), *Norm and Form* (London, 1966) ventures the hypothesis that Cosimo took a personal interest in the architectural commissions and, if they were important, in the commissions for sculpture too, leaving to his sons 'negotiations with painters and decorators'. The reconstruction of the historical background to the *Battles* (see catalogue) gives a glimpse of Cosimo's personal interest in Uccello's panels.

72 The frescoes in the first audience chamber of Count Federico, discovered in 1939, have been attributed to Boccati by P. Rotondi, *Il Palazzo Ducale di Urbino*, Urbino, 1950, I, pp. 163–4 and 168, with a dating of earlier than 1458. The dating has been extended to 1475 by F. Zeri, *Due Dipinti, la Filologia e un Nome. Il Maestro delle Tavole Barberini*, Turin, 1961, p. 85, while keeping the attribution to Boccati. W. Fontana's hypothesis, 'Affreschi di Paolo Uccello nel Palazzo Ducale di Urbino', in *Federico da Montefeltro. Lo Stato, la Cultura, le Arti*, Rome, 1986, pp. 131–49, in favour of Uccello, has not been followed up. Moreover, there is nothing to substantiate the hypothesis of an earlier visit by Uccello to Urbino between 1446 and 1450. The chamber is already *picta* in a document of 28 November 1467. P. Zampetti, in *Urbino e le Marche Prima e Dopo Raffaello*, Florence, 1983, pp. 37–9, opts for Giovanni Boccati and the school of Camerino before 1466. See also M. Bacci, 'Il punto su Giovanni Boccati' in *Paragone. Arte*, 20, 1969, 233, pp. 3–21. For the precedent of Domenico Veneziano in Perugia, cf. F. Santi, 'L'affresco baglionesco della Galleria Nazionale dell'Umbria' in *Commentari*, 21, 1970, pp. 51 *et seq.* and H. Wohl, *The Paintings of Domenico Veneziano. A Study in Florentine Art of the Early Renaissance*, Oxford–New York, 1980, pp. 210–11.

73 A. von Schmarsow, *Melozzo da Forlì*, 1886, pp. 359–60; W. Boeck, *Paolo Uccello*, Berlin, 1939, p. 104. We know that Uccello was preceded in Urbino by Giovanni di Francesco (died 1459) to whom is attributed (M. Laclotte, *Revue de l'Art*, 40–41, 1978, pp. 65–70) the *Hunt* in the Musée des Augustins, Toulouse, which can be identified with the one mentioned in the inventories (1599, 1609 and 1631) of the Palazzo Ducale collections in Urbino (cf. E. Calmann, *Bolletino d'Arte*, 65, 1991, pp. 67–70). The painting was probably executed in Florence at the end of the 1450s, shortly before the artist died. The patrons at Urbino, in asking Uccello, had possibly been looking for a master whose style was similar to Count Federico's *Hunt*.

Chapter Three Places associated with Uccello

74 L. B. Alberti, *Kleinere Kunsttheorischen Schriften*, (ed.) H. Janitscheck, Osnabruck, 1970, p. 47.

75 The Florentine merchant Turino di Baldese (or Baldesi) had left the convent a sum of a thousand florins, which was subsequently increased, to have two cycles of frescoes painted inside the church.

76 L. Ghiberti, *I Commentari*, Naples, 1947, I, p. 24.

77 E. Battisti, *Filippo Brunelleschi*, Milan, 1976, p. 339.

78 M. Bacci, 'Le vetrate del tamburo della cupola', in *Lorenzo Ghiberti*, op. cit., pp. 245–8.

79 Francesco della Luna, a rich burgher from the Santa Maria Novella quarter (second only to the Rucellai), Gonfalonier of Justice from 1418, 'dilettante' architect, died shortly after 1446. He had altercations with Brunelleschi at two worksites: the Spedale degli Innocenti (where as one of the patrons he obliged Brunelleschi to modify his plan) and the Palazzo di Parte Guelfa, when it was Brunelleschi's turn to modify Francesco's initial plans (cf. F. Borsi, G. Morolli, F. Quinterio, *Brunelleschiani*, Rome, 1979, pp. 17 *et seq.* and pp. 235–46). Battista d'Antonio, Brunelleschi's loyal collaborator and deputy on the cupola site, is mentioned repeatedly in the Duomo's Office of Works' documents.

80 C. Guasti, *La cupola di Santa Maria del Fiore*, Florence, 1857, p. 76.

81 Guasti, op. cit., p. 77.

82 Guasti, op. cit., p. 75.

83 Giovanni di Gherardo da Prato, archivist and lawyer, was a consultant to the Office of Works and Ghiberti's deputy at the cupola. He was Brunelleschi's tenacious adversary and argued with him not only about the darkness of the cupola, but about his invention of flat-bottomed boats to bring stone along the Arno for the site (because of the difficulties of crossing the rapids upriver at Empoli. This invention was not one of Brunelleschi's most brilliant successes). He wrote an acerbic sonnet attacking him which began with: '*O fonte fonda et nissa d'ignoranza*' (Oh deep spring and well of ignorance). Because of the bitterness of this argument and Filippo's response, he was forced to retire to Prato.

84 L. B. Alberti, *L'architettura*, ed. R. Bonelli and P. Portoghesi, Milan, 1966, Bk VII, p. 618; see also E. Battisti, op. cit., p. 142.

85 L. Ghiberti, op. cit., p. 47.

86 In Giovanni Pascoli's *Poemi italici e Canzoni di Re Enzio*, Bologna, 1914, p. 14.

87 F. Ferrara, F. Quinterio, *Michelozzo di Bartolomeo*, Florence, 1984, pp. 353–5; F. Gurrieri, 'Il Monastero', in *La Basilica di San Miniato al Monte*, Florence, 1988, pp. 79–82.

88 H. Saalman, 'Paolo Uccello at San Miniato', in *The Burlington Magazine*, 106, 1964, pp. 558–63.

89 *Codex Magliabechiano* (see note 70), p. 100.

90 W. Roscoe, *The Life of Lorenzo de' Medici*, Pisa, 1816, Vol. I, ap., p. IV.

91 Roscoe, op. cit., p. V.
92 The Balía was an extraordinary magistrature. The Eight, and later Ten members (1364) made up a council (which on a number of occasions was modified in composition and duration) and which had judiciary powers, among others. The Balía condemned Cosimo to ten years in exile and a heavy fine.
93 Roscoe, op. cit., p. VII.
94 D. Carl, 'La Casa Vecchia dei Medici e il suo giardino', in *Il Palazzo Medici Riccardi di Firenze*, Florence, 1990, p. 39.
95 G. Vasari, *Le Vite*, ed. G. Milanesi, Florence, 1878, Vol. I, p. 651.
96 Vasari, op. cit., Vol. II, p. 150.
97 Vasari, op. cit., Vol. II, pp. 148–9.
98 Vasari, op. cit., Vol. II, p. 50.
99 A. Filarete, *Trattato di Architettura*, ed. A. M. Finoli and L. Grassi, Milan, 1972, Vol. II, pp. 695–6.
100 Filarete, op. cit., Vol. II, p. 696.
101 *Il Libro di Antonio Billi* (also published by C. Frey, Berlin, 1892), is a sixteenth-century codex which was compiled before the *Codex Magliabechiano*, and which is held at the Biblioteca Nazionale in Florence. Like the *Magliabechiano*, which it resembles in many ways, it contains the lives of Florentine artists from Cimabue to Michelangelo. One of the most developed is Brunelleschi's (*'Di Pippo di ser Brunellesco'*) in which it is reported that Brunelleschi had made a maquette (*modello*) for Cosimo's house on Piazza San Lorenzo in the axis of the church. Cosimo had turned it down because it seemed 'too large and sumptuous an enterprise' (*troppo grande e sontuosa impresa*). Brunelleschi must have destroyed his maquette in irritation.
102 B. Preyer, 'L'architettura del Palazzo Mediceo' in *Il Palazzo Medici*, pp. 58 *et seq.*; see also M. Ferrara–F. Quinterio, op. cit., pp. 210 *et seq.*
103 The palace belonging to the Davanzati (a rich family from the fourteenth to fifteenth century, who also numbered poets among their members) was the prototype for the Trecento palazzo (133), which was pre-Renaissance in its spacing, its ashlar-work and the rationality of its plan (even though there were shops on the ground floor and the courtyard was very small). Inside, the painted decoration had a rich chromatic quality. Today it has become a museum of the Florentine house, with reconstructions of period furnishings.
104 W. A. Bulst, 'Uso e trasformazione del Palazzo Mediceo fino ai Riccardi' in *Il Palazzo Medici*, p. 110.
105 Bulst, op. cit., ibid.
106 Francesco di Stefano known as Pesellino (Florence, 1422–57) because he was the nephew of Giuliano d'Arrigo, known as Pesello. A pupil of Lippi and famous decorator of *cassoni*, he had painted hunting scenes that were similar to the *Battles* in the *camera di Lorenzo*.
107 W. Boeck, *Paolo Uccello. Der Florentiner Meister und Sein Werk*, Berlin, 1939, p. 107.
108 Salvi d'Andrea, master stonemason at the Santo Spirito site from 1476 to 1481. On Brunelleschi's death he became an architect and built the apse – for which he would be reproached for departing from Filippo's plan – and the elegant reverse side of the façade, making a decisive choice when he had three doorways made instead of the four originally planned. This was a virtuoso interpretation of Brunelleschian conventions, often with a tendency to deviate from the master's plans, in the artisan sense (*quattrocentismo artigianesco*), characteristic of Florence at that period (cf. F. Borsi, *Brunelleschiani*, op. cit., p. 64 *et seq.*).
109 F. Borsi *et al.* ibid., p. 324.

Chapter Four La Dolce Prospettiva

110 L. Venturi, 'Paolo Uccello' in *L'Arte*, XXXIII, Vol. I, pp. 52–87.
111 J. von Schlosser, 'Problemi artistici della Rinascenza italiana: il semi-artista Paolo Uccello', in *Xenia*, 1939, 1st edn 1929.
112 *Valori Plastici*: Art review published in Rome from 1918 to 1921, ed. M. Broglio. Contributors included Carrà, de Chirico, Savinio, Aragon, Cocteau, van Doesburg and Soupault. It re-evaluated the great tradition, going beyond the uncertainties of the avant-garde and anticipating the 1930s' 'return to order'. In its metaphorical sense, the term designates a critical attempt to retrace in the artists of the past those permanent values (space, form, composition) which are the source of an enduring modernity.
113 'We have looked for proof of these points of similarity to medieval optics in the work of Paolo Uccello, without claiming that this link came through the bias of Ghiberti's collection of theories in his *Commentario Terzo*. While the *Commentario* is impenetrable without much slow, painstaking effort – it is much more complex that the "*ragione dell'occhio*" (reasoning of the eye) that Ghiberti prides himself on in his work – we can see the admirably successful figurative transpositions of it which Paolo Uccello achieved through his subtle, often sophicated genius: in them can we see proof that he had direct access to it': A. Parronchi, 'Le fonti di Paolo Uccello', in *Studi sulla "dolce prospettiva"*, Milan, 1964, p. 498. This is an interesting hypothesis, but totally undemonstrable in the links he had with Ghiberti that we can be certain of.
114 *The Life of Brunelleschi by Antonio di Tuccio Manetti*, ed. H. Saalman, London, 1970, p. 45.
115 G. Federici Vescovini, 'Il Problema delle fonti ottiche medioevali del Commentario Terzo di Lorenzo Ghiberti', in *Lorenzo Ghiberti nel suo Tempo*, Proceedings of the International Symposium, Florence, 1978, Florence, 1980, Vol. II, pp. 349–87, particularly p. 349.
116 Like Fancelli or Biagio Rossetti, for example.
117 For a graphic reconstruction, see L. Vagnetti, *De Naturali et Artificiali Perspectiva*, Florence, 1979, pp. 200–201 and A. Parronchi, op. cit., Ill. 90–100.
118 *Opere volgari di Leon Battista Alberti* annotated and illustrated by A. Bonucci, Florence, 1843–9.
119 K. Bergdolt, *Der dritte Kommentar Lorenzo Ghibertis. Naturwissenschaften und Medizin in der Kunsttheorie der Früherenaissance*, Wurzburg, 1988, pp. 40–42.
120 Alhazen, the Westernized name of the famous physician, mathematician and astronomer Abu Ali Al-Hasan Ibn al-Haitham (born in Bassorah in 965 and died in Cairo in 1039) whose writings on optics were translated into Latin by Witelus *c.* 1270 and published in 1572 under the title of *De Aspectibus in Opticae Thesaurus Alhazeni Arabis Libri Septem, eiusdem Liber de Crepusculis et Nubium Ascensionibus* by F. Risner in Basel (rep. New York, 1972).

121 C. Maltese, 'Ghiberti teorico', in *Lorenzo Ghiberti*, op. cit., Vol. II, p. 407–49, particularly p. 409.

122 K. Bergdolt, op. cit., p. 42.

123 C. Maltese, op. cit., p. 408.

124 L. Ghiberti, *I Commentari*, 1947 edn p. 42.

125 G. Federici Vescovini, op. cit., pp. 367 *et seq.*

126 Witelus, German–Polish mathematician and philosopher (*c.* 1230–1300), a Dominican, present in Italy *c.* 1270, author of a treatise on perspective in which he referred to the Arab texts and which was an essential work for many centuries. Through him, Neo-Platonic metaphysics of light became a basis of scientific research. See G. Federici Vescovini, *Studi sulla Prospettiva Medievale*, Turin, 1965, pp. 132 *et seq.* and pp. 228 *et seq.* Witelus' text was also published by F. Risner in Basel in 1572 (*Opticae Thesaurus*, op cit.): *Vitellionis Thuringopoloni Libri X.*

127 L. Ghiberti, op. cit., p. 131.

128 A. Parronchi, op. cit., pp. 482–3.

129 In his *Commentario Primo*, Ghiberti wrote: 'Sculpture and painting form a science which involves numerous disciplines and areas of study, and of all the arts is the supreme invention; it is achieved through a certain amount of meditation, which is accomplished *through matter and reasoning*' (L. Ghiberti, *I Commentari*, Naples, 1947, p. 3).

130 Parronchi, op. cit., ibid.; S. Orlandi, *Necrologio di Santa Maria Novella a Firenze*, Florence, 1955, Vol. I, pp. 131 *et seq.*

131 L. Ghiberti, op. cit., p. 112.

132 Ibid., p. 114.

133 Ibid., p. 116.

134 A. Parronchi, op. cit., p. 486.

135 Ibid.

136 In *De prospectiva pingendi*, Piero della Francesca calls a *torculo* a sort of round head-covering made by winding a piece of cloth.

137 Parronchi, op. cit., p. 490–1.

138 J. L. Schefer, *Le déluge, la peste, Paolo Uccello*, Paris, 1976, p. 149.

Chapter Five Uccello's Imprint in his Works

139 Lorenzo Ghiberti, *Commentario Secondo* in *I Commentari*, Naples edn 1947, p. 45.

140 A collection of sources can be found in V. Gebhardt's recent book, 'Paolo Uccello's "Schlacht von San Romano"', *Bochumer Schriften zur Kunstgeschichte*, 17, Frankfurt-Berne-New York-Paris, 1991, pp. 189–207, ap. II.

141 If we think of the churches in the background to *Saint Francis* in the Old Oratory of the brotherhood of Sant'Agostino in Perugia, and the Berlin-Dahlem *Madonna and Child with Saint Jerome and Saint Francis* (Staatliche Museen) or the *Crucifixion* in the same oratory in Perugia. Cf. F. Todini, 'Una "Crocifissione" del giovane Raffaello a Perugia', *Studi di Storia dell'Arte*, I, Todi, 1990, pp. 113–44.

142 G. Richa, *Notizie Istoriche delle Chiese Fiorentine*, X, Florence, 1762, pp. 233–4.

143 The interpretation as *Exemplum vitae perfectionis* can be found in A. Malquori, in *Bernardo di Chiaravalle nell'Arte Italiana dal XIV al XVIII Secolo*, ed. L. Dal Prà, exhibition catalogue, Florence, 1990, Milan, 1990, pp. 128–30. Cf. also D. Arasse, *Les Primitifs Italiens*, Geneva, 1986, pp. 192–208; D. Russo, *Saint Jerome en Italie. Etude d'iconographie et de spiritualité (XIIIe–XVe siècles)*, Paris-Rome, 1987, p. 218; G. Bonsanti, *La Galleria dell'Accademia di Firenze. Guida e Catalogo Completo*, Florence, 1987, pp. 42 and 48, and the catalogue. R. Salvini, 'The Frescoes in the Altana' in *Giovanni Rucellai e il suo Zibaldone, II: A Florentine Patrician and his Palace*, The Warburg Institute, London, 1981, p. 246, attributes the commission for the picture in the Accademia to the Vallombrosans, narrowing down its provenance to the Florentine covent of San Giorgio dello Spirito alla Costa. Recently the lively monograph by A. Padoa Rizzo (Florence, 1991) has appeared, too late for it to be included in the catalogue. In it, the Accademia canvas is attributed to Uccello's two children (after 1480). Also withdrawn from Uccello's *oeuvre* are the Karlsruhe *Adoration* (attributed to his daughter Antonia, following Parronchi's suggestion, with an unconvincing date of after 1470); the Hyland *Madonna* (Malibu) attributed to the painter's children after 1480; the Kress *Madonna* (Raleigh) attributed to Uccello *c.* 1470–75; the Berlin *Madonna* and the one which was formerly in the Hamilton collection (Uccello *c.* 1475–80). The following works are attributed to Uccello: the Lippi tabernacle, ousting Pietro Nelli; the del Beccuto lunette; the *Stories from Genesis* in the Chiostro Verde (after 1431); the Prato frescoes (*c.* 1434–5); the Contini *Nun-Saint* (*c.* 1440); the San Martino alla Scala *Nativity* (after the windows and clock in the cathedral, 1443); the San Miniato al Monte frescoes; the Avane predella; the Allentown *Madonna* (after 1452); the Quarate predella (after 1452); the Lehman portrait (Battista Sforza? *c.* 1465–8); the Paris *Saint George* (1465); the London *Saint George* (after 1470); the Oxford *Hunt* (kept implausibly as a commission from the Duke of Urbino, *c.* 1465–8); the Thyssen *Crucifixion* (after 1470, with his children's collaboration); the five portraits in the Louvre (after 1470); and finally the fragment of the Santa Trinita (with no date indicated). The catalogue is arranged in chronological order, into which is mixed the group traditionally attributed to the 'Karlsruhe Master', the source of which he attributes to the activity of Uccello's children and pupils.

144 For information on the iconography, see M. Davies, 'Uccello's St George in London' in *The Burlington Magazine*, 101, 678–9, Sept.–Oct. 1959, pp. 309–16. For the humanistico-pedagogical, allegorico-political and analytico-naturalistic implications, but without references to Uccello's work or to the Florentine Quattrocento, see the recent B. Blass-Simmen *Sankt Georg Drachenkampf in der Renaissance. Carpaccio, Raffael, Leonardo*, Berlin, 1991.

145 P. Francastel, *Peinture et Société. L'espace figuratif de la Renaissance au Cubisme*, Paris, 1951: 'There is no doubt that the predella . . . was intended to record the great celebration of a guild.'

146 P. A. Rossi, 'Indagine sulla prospettiva nelle opere de Paolo Uccello' in E. Sindona, 'Introduzione alla poetica di Paolo Uccello. Relazioni tra prospettiva e pensiero teoretico', in *L'Arte*, 17, 1972, pp. 7–100, in particular pp. 96–100; the interpretation is taken up in the Ashmolean Museum monograph, *Paolo Uccello's Hunt in the Forest*, Oxford, 1981. More recently it has been corrected by M. Kemp-A. Massing, 'Paolo Uccello's "Hunt in the Forest" in the Ashmolean Museum, Oxford', in *The Burlington Magazine*, March, 1991, pp. 164–78, in particular p. 173, n. 34.

CATALOGUE RAISONNÉ

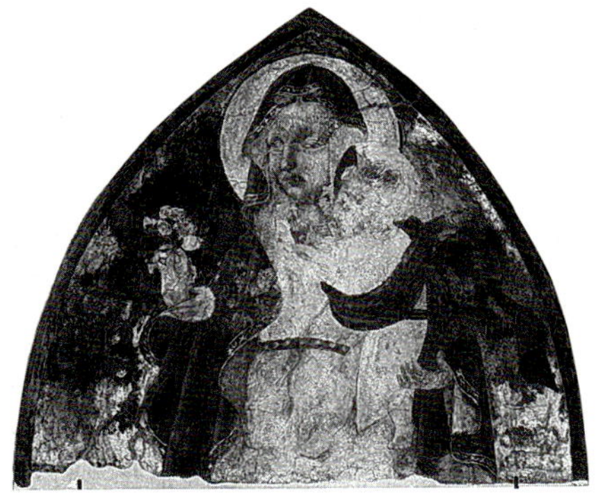

1. VIRGIN AND CHILD

Detached fresco, 57 × 100 cm.
Florence, Museo di San Marco.
About 1415–20

This detached fresco originally came from the del Beccuto family's house in the street of the same name. The house was demolished during the redevelopment of the historic centre of Florence in the nineteenth century (Carocci 1900; Cecchi 1989). Its state leaves much to be desired. Parronchi was the first to draw attention to the fresco ('probabili aggiunte a Dello Delli Scultore' – probably added to Dello Delli Sculptor, *Cronache di archeologia storia dell'arte*, 7, 1968, p. 104; 1974, pp. 22 and 89) and attributes it to Uccello, pointing out that the artist's mother belonged to the del Beccuto family. For Parronchi, the similarities in style to *The Virtues* and St Paul in the lower part of the frescoes of the vault at Prato would indicate a date of *c.* 1435. Volpe (1980, p. 18) using as evidence the 'purest quality lapis-lazuli' and the 'marvellously repeated rhythms in the roomy draperies' of an Iberian and Ghibertian type, finds it similar to the lunette of *The Annunciation* in the Ashmolean Museum, Oxford, which he himself attributes to Uccello and dates to 1420. This attribution has recently been accepted by C. Cecchi (1989, p. 110, n. 44) and Sframeli (in *L'Età di Masaccio*, 1990, p. 94) and the work was shown in the exhibition at the Palazzo Vecchio in 1990 as being by Uccello. The rebuilding of central Florence in the nineteenth century has deprived us of further evidence on the original context of the work, which was probably commissioned by Deo di Deo del Beccuto, the painter's rich maternal uncle, to help him make his professional début: almost like patronage on a strictly private basis.

All the stylistic elements recall the influence of Starnina and of Ghiberti's style as expressed in the second doors of the Baptistery, but in the flower held out in the Virgin's hand we can already perceive a remarkable sense of space, even if this hand is harshly grafted on to the ample coat. It may be that the emphasis placed on the flower, in a gesture of blessing, is linked to the solemn dedication of the Duomo to S. Maria del Fiore (St Mary of the Flower) on 22 April 1412, at the time when Giovanni Aldobrandini was Gonfalonier (Del Migliore 1684, p. 8).

The condition of the fresco allows only a summary evaluation, but the ATTRIBUTION to Uccello seems convincing, with a DATE not far from his registration with the Guild of Doctors and Apothecaries (1415) or with the Guild of St Luke (1414). The lunette in the del Beccutos' house, indicative of the influence on Uccello of late Gothic, probably predates Masolino's early pictorial work (about 1423) and perhaps the arrival in Florence of the young Masaccio (1417). Thus, well before he could have been influenced by Masaccio's humanism, Uccello had begun to absorb the lessons of contemporary monumental sculpture. It was the first step in an exploration he would pursue with passionate dedication throughout his life.

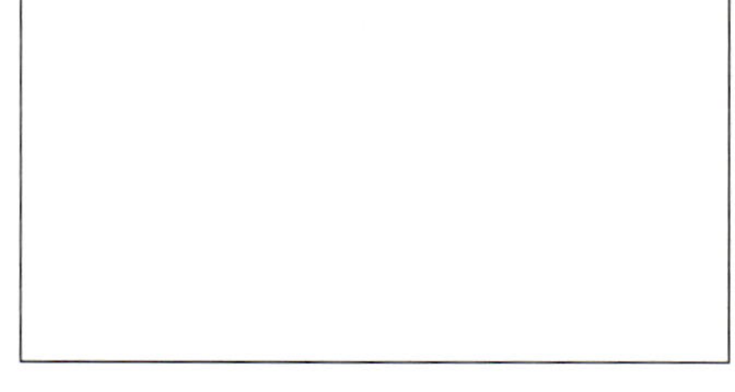

2. THE ANNUNCIATION

Fresco (now lost).
Formerly Florence, Santa Maria Maggiore, Carnesecchi chapel.
About 1424–5 (?)

In his *Memoriale* (1510), Francesco Albertini mentions S. Maria Maggiore and that inside the church 'is a retable by Masaccio: the predella and the arch above it are by Paolo Uccello', but gives no further details. These were provided much later by Vasari (1550, p. 253): 'He also worked in S. Maria Maggiore, for a chapel next to the side door leading to S. Giovanni which contains the retable and predella by Masaccio. There he painted an Annunciation in which he tried to show columns foreshortened through the use of perspective, which break the sharp angle of the vaulting where the Four Evangelists are: this was held to be a fine and difficult achievement.' In the second edition (1568, I, pp. 269–70) other elements have been added: 'a fresco of the Annunciation in which he painted a building which is worthy of attention, being both new and a difficult achievement in those times, for it was the first to show with a fine style of craftsmanship how, with grace and proportion, lines can be made to recede to a vanishing point, and how a small and confined space on a flat surface may be extended so that it appears distant and wide-ranging: and then when colouring is used with judgment and grace to add shadows and lights in the right place the eye is deceived so surely that the painting appears lifelike and in relief. But this did not satisfy him, he wanted to show how to solve even greater problems; and this he did in some columns foreshortened in perspective which curve round and break the sharp angle of the vaulting where the four evangelists are.' This seems to be the same talent Vasari recognized earlier in Uccello, at the beginning of his biography (1568, I, p. 269): 'He also discovered the way to turn the intersections and arches of vaulted roofs, to foreshorten ceilings with their coffers and beams, and to paint round columns in the corner of a wall which, while following the angle, correct it and appear as though painted on a flat surface, through his use of perspective drawing.' There is no doubt that Vasari was struck by the experimentation of the vaulting painted in perspective.

Vasari's text was corrected and abridged by R. Borghini (1584, p. 309); however F. Bocchi's guide (1581) makes no mention of the fresco, perhaps because the church had been closed for building work for a long time. In the next edition (F. Bocchi–G. Cinelli 1677, p. 213) following Gherardo Silvani's work in 1650–15, the Renaissance layout of the church had disappeared. Filippo Baldinucci (1686, 1845 edn, I, p. 447) corrects Vasari, adding a significant passage and updating it: 'He painted an Annunciation, in which he showed some very beautiful houses, a great novelty for this period by reason of the perspective: in this same Annunciation, he showed a very fine invention, that of painting the columns which broke the sharp angle of the wall but curving it, by means of perspective, making it appear round; he was later imitated in our time by Giovanni di San Giovanni in his marvellous work in the ground-floor chamber of the Palazzo Serenissimo.'

Mannozzi's frescoes in the Palazzo Pitti can still furnish us with an example of Vasari's problematical 'breaking of the sharp angle'; an angular *trompe-l'oeil* perhaps already imagined by Giotto in the Bardi Chapel in S. Croce (Parronchi 1962, and 1964, p. 189). We are talking here of an optical effect to correct the right-angle of the walls, which had already been used by Masaccio for the embrasures and irregularities in the walls of the Brancacci chapel. For F. L. del Migliore the retable of the altar in question is attributed to Giotto, and restored by Masaccio according to Father Richa (1755, III, p. 281), who alludes to 'a small Annunciation by Paolo Uccello at the height of the first entrance pillar on the left', thus introducing a fundamental 'innovation': the small format which makes us think, contrary to Vasari, of a painting. L. Biandi (1824, p. 139) returns to the idea of the Annunciation being a fresco and F. Fantozzi (1842, pp. 488–90) mentions only the seventeenth-century altars.

We must add to these summary and problematic indicators the partial data published by W. Stechow (1929–30, pp. 125–6), U. Procacci (1954, p. 37 and 43) and A. Parronchi (1962, pp. 1–38 and 1964, pp. 182–225). From these publications it appears that the Carnesecchi chapel, dedicated to Saint Catherine, was decorated with a retable (by Masolino, not Masaccio) integrated into an archtectonic ensemble made of stone (Parronchi, 1964, p. 183). J. Mesnil (1927, pp. 27 and 136) is the first to mention a document (ASF, *Conventi soppressi, Santa Maria Maggiore*, bundle 43, book 83) according to which the Santa Caterina chapel was granted to Carnesecchi in 1406; a date Stechow corrects (1929–30, pp. 125–6) to January 1427, the time of Masolino's retable, consequently delaying Uccello's intervention to 1428. U. Procacci (1954, p. 37, n. 51, and p. 43, n. 60) corrects Stechnow's erroneous dating: the works in the Carnesecchi chapel would have already been realized by the date of the document (29 January 1428), and would not be able to be used as a precise reference either for Masolino or for Uccello. Consequently the DATING, bearing in mind Uccello's presence in Venice between 1425 and 1430, must fall between 1424 and 1425 (in September 1425 Masolino went to Hungary). Masolino was chosen by the Carnesecchi patrons because of the privileged connections he already had at the time of the Bremen *Madonna of Humility* (*c.* 1423).

There are numerous unresolved problems: the links between the two artists, the possibility of a final intervention by Uccello, the imprecise sources, the obscure trials and tribulations of those commissioning the work and the uncertainty in the attribution of the sources themselves. F. L. Del Migliore (1684, pp. 427–9) mentions three chapels patronized by the Carnesecchi family and two by the del Beccuto family. The two families, according to the declaration to the Cadastre of 1427, lived opposite one another. It is therefore possible that there may have been a certain confusion in the older sources, stemming from the fact that Uccello's mother belonged to the del Beccuto family, who helped Uccello at the beginning of his professional career (see earlier). If we take into account that there may have been good neighbourly relations between the two families, it is quite possible that del Beccuto or other members of his family put in a good word for Uccello with the Carnesecchi. Uccello's fresco – always supposing it was in the Santa Caterina chapel – would have been made to blend harmoniously into a context dominated by Masolino, if we consider the work he had done and his age, born in 1383 and registered with the Guild in 1423. The references they share in common with Ghiberti and Starnina would perhaps have favoured a meeting between the two painters. The hypothesis, already advanced (C. L. Ragghianti, 1977, p. 516), of a link between *The Annunciation* in perspective in the Carnesecchi chapel and Masolino's at San Clemente seems convincing, as opposed to another hypothesis (G. Pudelko, *Early Works*, 1934, p. 244) which sees echoes of Uccello's lost work in the fresco of Paolo Schiavo, on an analogous subject at Castiglione Olona. M. Salmi (1939, p. 15) considers Uccello's fresco not as a youthful work but rather as belonging to the 1430s, and he sees a reflection on Brunelleschi's propositions in it. L. Berti (1964) dates the fresco at 1425. He sees (1961, p. 307, n. 18) an overture from Uccello towards Masaccio in the 1425 mosaic *Saint Peter* in San Marco in Venice, having a connection with Masaccio's *Saint Paul* at Santa Maria del Carmine or with the *Saint Ivo* in the Badia. A. Parronchi accepts the dating of 1424–5 (1962, rep. 1964, pp. 205) and to him we owe a well-argued attempt at reconstructing the chapel. He centres his research on the identification of the *Small Annunciation* (Richa) with the Goldman and Mellon *Annunciation* (Washington, National Gallery) and in consequence on the attribution to Uccello of the latter. His hypothesis is not considered very convincing by C. Volpe (1980, p. 25, n. 1) and justly so. The Goldman and Mellon *Annunciation* is by Masolino under the strong influence of Gentile, and was at San Niccolò Oltrarno (G. Damiani, 1982), with two polyptychs by Gentile, the Quaratesi and the other, heavily damaged, in the reserve collection of the Florentine Soprintendenza (L. Berti, 1990, p. 142). We must therefore put aside Parronchi's ingenious reconstruction: the Santa Maria Maggiore ensemble must be closer to Ghiberti, the Goldman *Annunciation* is not by Uccello (its lateral perspectives would be beyond the normal limits) and, in addition, Uccello's *Annunciation* must have originally been situated in the lunette or on the triumphal arch, as was the solution chosen by Masolino at San Clemente.

The link with Masolino can be illustrated by comparing works relating to the period when their common pictorial references are at their closest: the figures of Adam and Eve in the first story in the Chiostro Verde, and the corresponding ones at the Brancacci chapel. Masolino is pleasanter and more worldly, more natural and descriptive. The young Uccello is disturbing, full of movement, decorative and abstract. And in spite of a certain receptivity in Masolino towards his younger colleagues, especially Masaccio, light remains to be thrown on the shape of an encounter that seems a rather isolated event in the evolution of Uccello's style: the beginning of a dialogue that was abruptly disrupted by Uccello's departure for Venice and barely referred to again on his return. Parronchi's hypothesis (1962; 1964, p. 195) according to which the *Small Annunciation* was a painting transferred on to a wall (as Baldovinetti would subsequently do in the chapel of the Cardinal of Portugal at San Miniato) (H. R. Wedgwood Kennedy, 1938, p. 146) – an hypothesis based on Richa's imprecise indications in the eighteenth century – completely contradicts Vasari who, two centuries before, had had plenty of time to see the initial conversion of the chapel; it is equally rejected by J. Pope-Hennessy (1969, p. 178).

3. SAINT PETER BLESSING

Mosaic (now lost).
Formerly Venice, San Marco, façade.
1425

After making his will on 5 August 1425, Uccello set out for Venice where he remained for almost five years. On his return to Florence he asked the Office of Works of Santa Maria del Fiore if, as a master of mosaic, he could be given work. The essential facts about his Venetian work come to us from the letter the Office of Works sent to Piero Beccanugi, the Florentine ambassador in Venice, in which he is asked for information on the artist: '*qui Venitiis laboravit en faciei s. Marci a parte exteriore unam figuram s. Petri in quodam angulo faciei s. Petri (?) suttus orologium de anno domini 1425, tempore cuius erant operarii dominus Leonardus Mozanighi et dominus Marinus*' (who was working in Venice on the façade of San Marco, on the exterior, on a figure of Saint Peter in a certain corner of the façade Saint Peter next to the clock in the year of our lord 1425, at a time Leonardus Mozanighi and Marinus were masters of the works) (in G. Poggi, 1909, n. 773; W. Boeck, 1939, p. 97). Leonardo Mocenigo of Padua, procurator of San Marco, was in charge of the works and had to ensure that the work of restoration was done to the basilica where damage had occurred during the fire of 1419. A meeting of the Venetian council of 11 March 1424 noted that, following the death of a certain Master Jacobello, the local school of mosaics had died out and cast doubts on the possibility of finding, for San Marco, the associate of the dead master, who was staying in far-off Liguria, at that time enemy territory. Venice and Florence were now united in the struggle against the Visconti of Milan, and the alliance of 1425 between the two republics offered favourable conditions for the employment of a Florentine, although in Venice the Painters' Guild had a closed mind (M. Murano, 1961, pp. 263–74).

Uccello's stay in Venice was perhaps due to the good offices of Ghiberti, who went to Venice in the winter of 1424–5, and possibly returned there in 1430 (G. Fiocco, 'I Lamberti a Venezia', *Dedalo*, 8, 1927–8, p. 346; R. Krautheimer, 1956, p. 5; *Lorenzo Ghiberti, 'materia e ragionamenti'*, 1978, p. 16); these two dates possibly coincide with the beginning and end of Uccello's long Venetian visit. We might think that the motive behind Uccello's training in mosaics was that Ghiberti had set his sights on Santa Maria del Fiore, envisaging a grand decorative scheme of mosaics like that of San Marco in Venice. The most problematic point is Uccello's relatively unimportant contribution in comparison with the length of his stay in Venice. The *Saint Peter*, which probably deteriorated over time, was replaced *c.* 1617–18 with mosaics by Gaetano (after cartoons from Verona). M. Salmi (1950, p. 22) gives an iconographical reference in the detail of the façade of San Marco in the *Procession of the Relic of the Cross* by Gentile Bellini (1496), now in the Accademia in Venice. In it Gentile shows us that Uccello's *Saint Peter* made a matching piece, in the opposite corner of the façade, to a *Saint John the Baptist*. According to certain documents, it seems that Uccello was also called to Venice with the intention of reactivating the school of mosaics at San Marco so that it could be given new commissions, which could explain his limited contribution in the decorative ensemble of the basilica. Current historians differ on the importance of Uccello's period in Venice: G. Fiocco (1925–6, p. 110) presents Uccello as 'fanatical about perspective' and as bringing innovations in this area to the Venice region (1926, 2, pp. 144–7; *L'Arte di Andrea Mantegna*, Bologna, 1927, p. 44) and playing a decisive part in Mantegna's training. R. Longhi (1926, I, p. 129) corrects this innovatory view of Uccello in Venice, where he would only have taken his 'Late fabulous, nocturnal and silvan Gothic', but attributes the architectural drawing of the *Visitation* in the Mascoli chapel at San Marco to him, a mosaic executed by Michele Giambono. This indicator is taken up and developed by G. Pudelko (1934, *Early Works*, p. 254) who imagines a collaboration between Giambono and Uccello, for which no proof exists. M. Murano (1953, pp. 58 and 66; 1955, pp. 197–9) attributes certain geometric motifs in the pavement of the basilica to Uccello (in Tongiorgi Tomasi, 1971, p. 85, n. 5), and in the mosaics of certain minor cupolas. The attribution is accepted by E. Sindona (1957, pp. 57–8) who also grants Uccello the ideation (cartoons) of fragments of mosaics in the decoration of the ante-baptistery of San Marco, which were detached during the rebuilding of 1875 and kept in the San Marco museum. C. L. Ragghianti (1977, p. 348) accepts the attribution of the pavement mosaics and indicates as a source the geometric marquetry in San Miniato in Florence. E. Micheletti (1956, p. 5) reduces Uccello's 'modern' contribution: 'He brought to Venice none of the Florentine innovations, for they had as yet made no impression on him.' L. Berti (1961, p. 307, n. 18) draws attention to *Saint Peter*'s foreshortened forearm, and puts forward the hypothesis that the painter had drawn his inspiration from certain figures by Masaccio, such as *Saint Paul* in the Carmine and *Saint Ivo* in the Badia in Florence (now lost). M. Salmi (1938, pp. 10 and 102) could already see echoes of Uccello's presence in the pavement rosettes of San Marco.

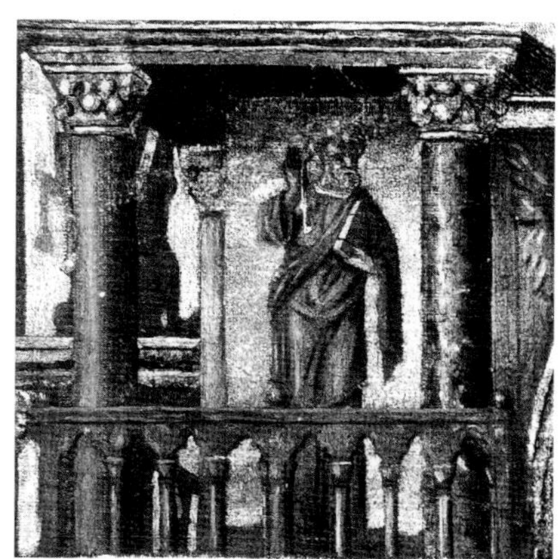

Gentile Bellini, *Procession of the Relic of the Cross* (detail) 1496, Venice, Accademia.

C. Volpe (1956, p. 38) disagrees with Fiocco on the Venetian period (1524–30), attributing to Uccello both the mutilated fresco of *Saint Gothard* at Asolo and the angular compositions of Giambono's *Visitation*, but recently (1980, p. 26, n. 11), he radically reduces Uccello's contribution, whose only trace can be the *Saint Peter* (now lost). Salmi (1938, p. 10) puts forward the hypothesis that Uccello's departure for Venice sprang from his curiosity about the world from which the much admired Gentile da Fabriano came, and he established a friendship with the Lamberti brothers, Florentine sculptors who had worked on the statues of the façade of San Marco after the 1419 fire. But it is not certain that Uccello would have been in a position to entertain any professional aims other than the difficult reorganization of the school of mosaics at San Marco. The early dating of the *Saint Peter* would lead us to think that the mosaic was merely a sample done as a test of his skill. But the fact that in the letter to Beccanugi of 1432 they ask for precise references on the artist and mention only the *Saint Peter* of 1425, shows that perhaps this is indeed the only public work on which we can base our knowledge of whether Uccello '*bene laboravit prefatam figuram*' and justified the salary which he was asking: '*cuius est in civitatis Venetiarum extimationis et pretiis*.'

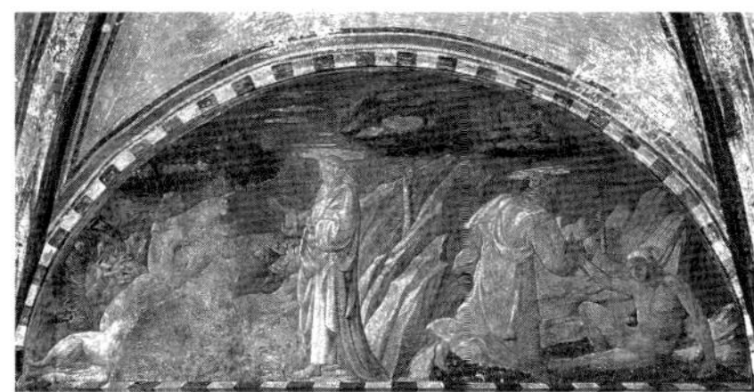

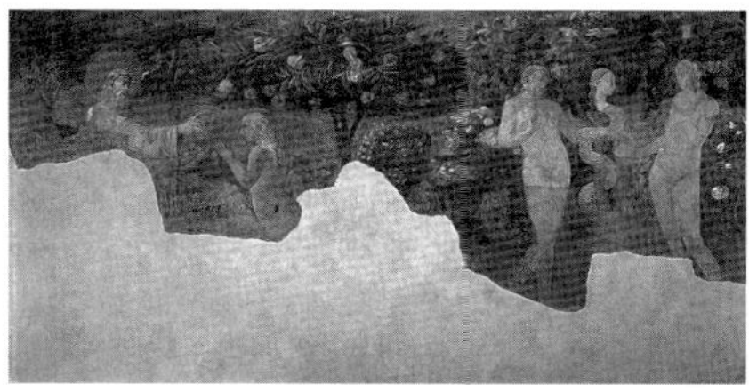

4. STORIES FROM GENESIS: CREATION OF THE ANIMALS AND CREATION OF ADAM, CREATION OF EVE AND THE FALL

Mural in tempera (transferred),
lunette 210 × 452 cm,
lower section 244 × 478 cm.
Florence, Santa Maria Novella, Chiostro Verde, first bay of the east side.
About 1424–5

There is no documentation on this project and a number of aspects relating to it which remain obscure have unleashed the most disparate interpretations and hypotheses. It dates back to the time when Turino di Baldese, who died on 22 July 1348, left a thousand gold florins for his legal executor, Fra Jacopo Passavanti, to have the nave of Santa Maria Novella decorated with stories from the Old Testament (V. Fineschi, O.P., *Memorie istoriche che possono servire alle vite degli uomini illustri del Convento di Santa Maria Novella di Firenze*, I, cc. 66–7; Bibl. Naz., Florence, Conv. Sup. S. M. N., ms. F. V. 491, eighteenth century). Passavanti died in 1357 and the decoration was deferred. Meanwhile the Dominican order embarked on the great New Testament cycles inside the nave, cycles that stretched from the Salvation in the Strozzi chapel to the Triumph of the Church and the Dominican order in the Spanish chapel (*c.* 1365). The Old Testament cycle, which in some ways has become iconographically linked with the other fourteenth-century cycles, came last, in the cloister erected *c.* 1350–60. The names of the patrons for this enterprise – whose size is unrivalled by other cloister cycles of the early Quattrocento in Florence – remain unknown. From 1434 onwards, Pope Eugenius IV, who had been obliged to leave Rome possibly because of the Council, or for reasons of internal security, was living at Santa Maria Novella; his presence gave the work a decisive impetus. We do not know the names of the many artists who were working, without much unity in style, on three sides of the cloister – east, south, west – each comprising five bays. The pillars on the east side (built in the fourteenth century) bear the insignia of the Castiglioni family, who were among the donors when building began, but there are no data to confirm that their successors still exerted a kind of patronage *c.* 1425–35. In any case it is clear that the Old Testament cycle was attentively supervised by the Dominican chapter and that it fits into the vast iconographic programme begun in the fourteenth century. It should be noted that the Chiostro Verde cycle was organized around subjects from the Book of Genesis, in 1424–5, almost at the same time as the second doors of the Baptistery, commissioned in 1425 (although they would not be finished until 1452), whose projected first twelve panels also illustrate scenes from Genesis. The mosaics in the Baptistery were based on this same source.

The Creation scenes do not include the creation of Heaven and Earth, of light and darkness, or of the stars, but begin with the creation of the animal kingdom. It is a simplification of the medieval mosaic model and the one which Leonardo Bruni proposed for Ghiberti's doors. The scheme, on two levels, one above the other (the upper is in the lunette), grouped the 'effects' of four 'stories', as Ghiberti refers to them when speaking of the panels on the Doors of Paradise (*Commentario Secondo*, ed. O. Morisani, 1947, p. 45). Bruni's famous letter to Nicolò da Uzzano on the programme for the doors dates back to June(?) 1424 and stipulates two essentials: variety in design and 'an importance worthy of remembrance'. 'The person to whom the pictorial work is assigned must be well instructed in each story, so that he organize both the characters and events well, and he must have gracefulness, in order to decorate them well' (in G. Richa, V, 1757, p. 21; H. Baron, 1928, p. 134). Bruni's instructions could apply equally well to the Dominican cycle. Ghiberti's strong imprint in the first bay is not surprising and has often been noted by the critics: examples are the figure of Adam, which is derived from antique models in Ghiberti's workshop (R. Krautheimer, 1956, pp. 208–10) the Masolinesque Adam and Eve, and the plastic and monumental Creator. It remains to be seen if Ghiberti participated directly in this first bay, which would have served as a formal model for the rest of the cycle. In this context, it should be noted that the quality and 'modern' aspect progressively diminish in the scenes that follow, except for Uccello's *Stories of Noah* which are generally ascribed to a later campaign. The fact that the first bay is exceptional might eventually be explained by the Dominicans' using the (costly) Ghiberti so that, once the doors for the Baptistery were underway, he could offer useful suggestions on the arrangement of the rest of the cycle which was to be given to less expensive masters. This principle of economy was also adopted in the choice of the monochrome technique.

This probable contact with Ghiberti lends authority to the ATTRIBUTION of the composition of the first bay to his workshop and therefore also to Uccello, even if by this time Uccello was already a painter in his own right. The lack of documentation does not allow any definitive opinion, but the old sources seem clear enough. The identification of the patrons remains equally mysterious. Among them is Fra Giovanni di Zanobi Masi (died 1434), who probably commissioned reliquaries from Fra Angelico: he was sacristan in 1418, then deputy prior, treasurer of the convent in 1419, and once again sacristan at the beginning of 1424 with Fra Andrea Rucellai. (Later, Uccello worked for the palace belonging to the principal branch of this family, where another master painted a *Thebaïd* in terre-verte.) Among the Dominicans in the field of art, we should note Fra Alessio Strozzi di Ubaldino, a mathematician and geometrician whom Brunelleschi consulted on the cupola of the Duomo (S. Orlandi O.P., *Necrologio di Santa Maria Novella*, Florence, 1955, I, pp. 131–2, 152–3, 168) and who was also consulted by Ghiberti (A. Parronchi, 1964 [1957], p. 482, n. 2; M. C. Improta, 1990, p. 70).

The attribution to Uccello dates back to the fifteenth century (from the time of the painter's death). Antonio Manetti (*XIV Uomini singhularii in Firenze*, *c.* 1495, ed. P. Murray, 1957, p. 335) recalled: 'Paolo Uccello master of painting painted the flood in the cloister of Santa Maria Novella and the story which is below, as well as the first two stories, the one above and the one below, at the bottom of the steps from the church to the cloister. And many other things at Santa Trinita and elsewhere.'

The first two stories are the *Creation of the Animals* and the *Creation of Adam* (upper part), and the *Creation of Eve* and *The Fall* (lower part). Francesco Albertini's *Memoriale* (1510, repr. ed. P. Murray, 1972) is more explicit: 'In the first cloister are the old stories; the first of Adam and Eve, and that of Noah, by the hand of Paolo Uccello.' The *Libro di Antonio Billi* (1516–24, ed. C. Frey, 1892, p. 24) said: 'In the first cloister of Santa Maria Novella he painted a story of when God created Adam and Eve, and they were chased from the paradise of delights. And another story of the flood, in which there were very beautiful things.' Parallel to this, the Anonimo Magliabechiano (ed. C. Frey, 1892, p. 99): 'In Florence, in the first Cloister of Santa Maria Novella, he painted God when he created Adam and Eve, and as they were chased from paradise. And in the said Cloister he also painted the story of the flood in which there are some very beautiful things.' Antonio Petrei's *Memoriale* (*c.* 1564–70, ed. C. Frey, 1892, p. 58) reported: 'The Story of Ysac in terre verte in the cloister: Dello Fiorentino. The story of the creation and the flood was made by Paolo Uccello in terre verte.' Vasari lingers over the work, describing it before the *Hawkwood*: 'Then he was asked for some stories: the first of which, at the entrance into the cloister from the church is the creation of the animal kingdom, in an endless variety of aquatic, terrestrial, winged animals. Where he who was so full of imagination and took such a lively pleasure in drawing them very precisely, showed the lions ready to bite, the superb allure of these wild animals and the swift, terrified flight of the stags and fallow-deer; the birds and fishes have strikingly lifelike feathers and scales. He painted the creation of man and woman and their sin, in a beautiful and accomplished style. In this work, he took pleasure in painting the colour of the trees, which it was not customary to do at that time. He was the first among the old painters to make a name for himself for landscapes, which he did very well' (1550, pp. 254–5; with additions in 1568, I, p. 271). Vasari's description leaves us perplexed, as some of these elements are no longer visible, either in what remains of the fresco or in the sinopia, something on which G. Milanesi (Vasari-Milanesi, II, 1878, p. 210, n. 1) remarked even before the sinopias had been uncovered. In his *Vita* of Dello Delli, Vasari attributed to Dello the first story on the west side (Vasari-Milanesi, II, 1878, p. 150, n. 3). Uccello was in Venice between 1425 and 1430, Dello Delli in exile from Florence in the summer of 1424, returning there in 1430 and then away in Spain from 1433 to 1446. He was six years younger than Uccello since he had been born in 1403. Critics are divided on the attributions. If Borghini and Baldinucci repeated Vasari's text, F. Bocchi-G. Cinelli's guide (1677, p. 260) extended Uccello's merits: 'One can see Cain's murder there, the tower of Nembrot and on the same side, the other stories all in chiaroscuro, painted by Paolo Uccello: their meeting is obscure but they are well drawn, which is especially admirable for at that period painting was gross and not as perfect as today. The two other sides have been painted by other artists whose names I am not mentioning because they do not have the same perfection as the first. In the story of Noah's drunkenness, his son Cham is the portrait of the painter Dello, which was done by Paolo.' L. Lanzi (1789, 1834 edn, I, p. 48) limits himself to recalling Uccello's 'stories of Adam and Noah'. F. Fantozzi (1842, p. 519) has a negative opinion of the cycle, but the stories 'which are on the walls of the Church are held in great esteem by connoisseurs, and they were painted by Paolo Uccello, except for the story which represents Jacob blessing Isaac, painted by Dello, Gaddi's pupil'. J. Burckhardt (1855, 1952 edn, p. 881) states that Uccello 'finished the series of frescoes for the Chiostro Verde of Santa Maria Novella begun by himself or by others in the old style of Giotto', noting a distinction in style between the *Stories of Noah* and the rest. G. B. Cavalcaselle (Crowe-Cavalcaselle, 1864, ed. Langton Douglas-De Nicola, 1911, pp. 114–15) points out the superior quality of the *Flood* and attributes the whole cycle to Uccello and Delli. G. Milanesi (Vasari-Milanesi, II, 1878, pp. 158–60, west and south walls, pp. 210–11, east wall) accepts Vasari's details, but makes distinctions between the anonymous painters of the cycle.

H. P. Horne (1905, p. 229) was the first to propose a DATING of 1425, attributing the first bay to Uccello before he left for Venice. E. G. Campani (1910, pp. 203–10) takes the restorations of 1909 into account, and dates all the cycle at 1447. J. Mesnil (1927, p. 129) attributes the *Creation* to Uccello, before 1425. R. Longhi (1928, p. 36) and G. Fiocco (1929, p. 42) propose Dello Delli. R. van Marle (1928, X, p. 226) thinks it might be by a pupil of Uccello's. D. Colnaghi (1928, p. 265) gives a date for Uccello's frescoes of between 1446 and 1448. P. Soupault (1929, pp. 28–9) confirms the attribution to Uccello but draws attention to the extreme deterioration of the paintings. L. Venturi (1930, p. 77) attributes the *Creation* to him, dating it before 1436. For the attribution of the first bay to Uccello, there is B. Berenson (1932, p. 582; 1936, p. 500); J. von Schlosser (1933, p. 37, after 1443); M. Salmi (1934, pp. 168 and 174, with the help of pupils); W. Paatz (1934, p. 118: a work of his youth); G. Pudelko (1934, *Early Works*, p. 238: related to Ghiberti's Doors of Paradise, p. 243: *c.* 1430–36 but nearer 1436; 1935, *The Minor Masters*, p. 71: after Venice, 1430–35, only the first bay; 1936, p. 133, *c.* 1425, before Venice; 1939, T. B., p. 525: about 1431, after Venice, among definite work by Uccello); C. L. Ragghianti (1937, p. 239: emphasizes the 'refinement similar to Masolino'); M. Salmi (1938, pp. 11–14: *c.* 1431, with echoes of Ghiberti, Masolino and Jacopo Bellini); M. Wackernagel (1938; 1981 edn, p. 123: with collaborators, 1433–40 and after; p. 42 *Creation*: Uccello 1430–35) while W. Boeck (1939, p. 118) omits the first bay from Uccello's oeuvre. The following confirm the attribution to Uccello: V. Guzzi (1941, p. 18); M. Pittaluga (1946, p. 9: 'almost as Gothic as Masolino', *c.* 1431); E. Somaré (1946, p. 28: among Uccello's mature works. *c.* 1435, even if stylistically inadequate. in the line from Masolino to Michelangelo); J. Pope-Hennessy (1950, pp. 6–7, and 142; 1969, pp. 5–6 and 139–40: immediately after Venice, a work of great quality, example of his youthful style before the *Hawkwood*). E. Micheletti (1954, exhibition catalogue, p. 26: towards 1431, after Venice; reaffirmed in 1956, p. 6: with echoes of Ghiberti and throwbacks to Masolino and Gentile); E. Carli (1954, 1959, p. 53: between 1430 and 1436); M. Muraro (1955, p. 197: immediately after Venice); E. Sindona (1957, p. 58: around 1431); D. Gioseffi (1958, pp. 137 and 145, n. 98: references to the *Saint Peter* of San Marco in Venice, after 1430 'or perhaps just before', in the style of Ghiberti); P. D'Ancona (1959, p. 6: among the 'first of Paolo's pictorial expressions we can be sure about', *c.* 1431–2, after Venice); U. Procacci (1960, pp. 64–5 and 230: superiority of [Uccello's] sinopia, fourth bay done by an atelier, at the same time as the *Stories of Noah* around the fifth decade); E. Borsook (1960, p. 148: before Venice, therefore before 1425; 1980, pp. 71–4: echoes of Ghiberti, foreshortened haloes, period of transition between Ghiberti's and Donatello's influence). R. Krautheimer (1956, p. 344) maintains that Uccello knew Ghiberti's studies for the Doors of Paradise, before they were executed: if we retain the date of 1425, this possibility cannot be excluded. Krautheimer (p. 209) relates the opinion of M. Meiss who attributed the first bay to Uccello and did not envisage (p. 209, n. 7) the possibility of Uccello briefly returning to Florence during the years of his Venetian sojourn. L. Berti (in L. Berti-U. Baldini, 1957, pp. 63–4; 1958, II, pp. 34–7) confirms the attribution to Uccello *c.* 1431. He sees in it an example of Uccello's leanings towards animal painting (1961, p. 301; 1964, n.p.) and dates it to 1425 or more probably to *c.* 1431. A. Parronchi emphasizes the composition based on the circle (1964 [1957], p. 476) and offers the hypothesis of a date before 1425 (p. 471) at the 'beginning of the third decade' (p. 513). He compares the animal subjects of the lunette with the medieval *summae* of the Aristotelian school. For Parronchi (1963, col. 464) the sinopias are a remarkable experiment by Uccello, who drew in a Ghibertian style before 1425, while the pictorial execution is rather closer to Masolino. A. Chastel (1965, p. 375) accepts the attribution to Uccello with a later date, around 1445, G. C. Argan (1968, 2, p. 183; 1988, 2, p. 185) emphasizes Uccello's return to Ghiberti's artistic authority immediately after his journey to Venice, thus confirming the dating of the bay to around 1430–31. Tongiorgi Tomasi (1971, p. 86) accepts the attribution to Uccello with a slightly later dating of 1430; P. A. Rossi (in E. Sindona, 1972, p. 42) takes into consideration 'the border which, with its segments drawn in perspective, suggests the base of a semi-circular surface on which the scene is developed' (fig. 19). L. H. Heydenreich (1972, p. 291) dates the *Creation* just after 1430, close to Ghiberti but with Masaccio's and Donatello's pathos. Parronchi confirms the dating of before 1425 proposed by Horne in 1905, and more recently (in *Santa Maria Novella*, 1981, pp. 135–41) he admits as 'more than likely' that Uccello conceived the whole of the east side of the cloister; he considers the reference to Dello as pure hypothesis and confirms a date of before 1425. C. L. Volpe (1980, p. 12) agrees on the dating and considers the cycle 'as the most impassioned and innovatory Florentine venture of those generated by the Brancacci chapel'. He attributes (p. 27, n. 12) the third bay of the same side of the cloister to Francesco d'Antonio or to one of his followers. C. Brandi (1980, p. 124) accepts the early dating of the first bay, before 1425, and thinks that the lower part was taken up again in 1431 (p. 125). D. Gioseffi (1980, II, p. 398) sees in it a confirmation of Ghiberti and Brunelleschi's use of perspective, as in the Quarate predella, and considers the *Stories of Adam and Eve* as the 'point of greatest convergence' with Ghiberti. E. Wakayama (1982, p. 94) thinks it possible that Uccello was asked to execute the fresco in 1424–5 and that he did not finish it because of his move to Venice. R. Lunardi (1983, p. 39) also attributes the first bay to Uccello, in *c.* 1425, while the second and third would be due to his school. A. Chastel (1984 [1983], p. 66) resumes the attribution to Uccello, correcting the chronology: 1435–44. De Marchi (in Vasari, 1986, p. 239, n. 12) dates the cycle from 1445 to 1450 and again thinks (p. 227, n. 3) the first bay should be attributed to Dello Delli. W. Fontana (1986, p. 139) attributes the four bays on the east side of the Chiostro Verde to Uccello. A. Angelini (1990, pp. 75–7) dates the stories of the first bay after 1425, excluding the attribution to Uccello, after Venice, on stylistic grounds, and again offering Longhi-Fiocco's hypothesis in favour of Dello.

The technique is correctly described as fresco: in fact it also involved painting *a secco*, although on *arriccio* with a sinopia (Campani, 1910, p. 204). This allowed for changes of mind and retouching. The basic colours were terre-verte, malachite green and red earths (Borsook, 1989, p. 73). Baldinucci (1845, p. 449) noted that already in the seventeenth century the *intonaco* or top layer of plaster was bulging considerably and had fallen away in some places, as had the *arriccio*. We know nothing of early restoration work other than that it took place. The *a secco* technique contributed to the paintings' deterioration. The *Genesis* scenes were restored between 1938 and 1940 under the direction of the Istituto Centrale in Rome (Baldini-Berti, 1957, pp. 56–61), detached and transferred to canvas. In 1954–7, Leonetto Tintori carried out cleaning and transferred the paintings to masonite. After the flood of 1966 new work had to be done, mainly to remove the filth deposited by the floodwater. Procacci (1960, p. 65) and Parronchi (1981, p. 139) noted traces of *spolvero** on God the Father in the *Creation of Adam*, whereas Wakayama (1982, p. 94, n. 12) saw traces of small ornamental dots on the hem of God's robe in the same scene. Before Tintori's restoration, the work was shown in Florence in the *Quattro Maestri* exhibition in 1954, and later in the *Affreschi staccati* exhibition in the Belvedere in 1957. The fresco is still difficult to decipher, with major gaps in the lower part.

**Spolvero*: In order to transfer the design from the preparatory drawing to the final support, the outlines of the drawing were pierced with a series of small holes. The drawing was then applied to the support and the outlines patted with a small, loosely woven bag containing dry pigment (*spolvero*). The pigment filtered through the holes in dots on to the support.

The cycle raises many questions that remain unanswered particularly as regards the first bay (the first to be painted is in fact the second on the side of the cloister (next to the church). Its sinopia is distinguished by its elaboration from the others which have been recovered (those of the *Stories of Noah* are unfortunately lost); clearly, considerable changes were made in the translation into paint. The characters show a strong Ghibertian influence (Paatz, 1934, p. 142, saw the *Creation* as 'an obvious counterpart of the same scene by Ghiberti') and Krautheimer (1956) pointed out Ghibertian sources and models for it. But there is also an obvious reference to Masolino, which extends from the naturalistic clouds to the graceful figure of Eve, similar to that in the Brancacci chapel. The use of light which is reminiscent of Masaccio confirms the modernity of the composition, and the partial use of *spolvero* (pointed out by R. Oertel, 1937–40, p. 303, n. 146) shows the link between the practices of Ghiberti's workshop and Masaccio's *Trinity*, on the inner wall of the church, just the other side.

The rest of the cycle, entrusted to different masters, represents more of a pocket of resistance for traditional painting: critics have found in it influences of Rossello di Jacopo Franchi, Lorenzo Monaco, the Pseudo Ambrogio di Baldese, the Master of the *Judgment of Paris* in the Bargello, but with diverging opinions (Salmi, 1934; Pudelko, 1935; Parronchi, 1981; Lunardi, 1983). The drapery is reminiscent of Ghiberti's designs for the doors of the Baptistery and for statues such as the *Saint Matthew* of 1419–21 for Orsanmichele (Pope-Hennessy, 1969, 5; Borsook, 1980, p. 73, n. 9). If Ghiberti's and Uccello's 'modern' imprint is evident in the *Creation* (first bay) and if it becomes increasingly less so in the second, it almost entirely disappears from the third onwards (excluding the *Stories of Noah* in the fourth), while the fifth and last bay on the east side is indecipherable. The possibility (Procacci, 1960, *loc. cit.*) that the first and fourth bays were contemporary appears unconvincing (Pope-Hennessy, 1969, pp. 139–40). Critics who accept the attribution to Uccello are divided on the chronology: either around 1425, before Venice, or immediately after his return to Florence in 1430–31. The attributions to Dello Delli, which are even more problematic, range from the year of his return from exile (1430) to that of his departure for Spain (1433). Krautheimer's hypothesis, according to which Uccello was familiar with Ghiberti's preliminary studies for the doors, ordered in 1425 and not executed until 1427–52, is attractive and allows for a dating of 1424–5. This would be the date of the first project for the cycle, of which the execution would appear to be spread ove time, with rather disparate contributions, which are generally difficult to evaluate because of the poor state of preservation and also because of probable restoration and later retouching. The paintings were already 'invisible in many places' in 1836 (V. Fineschi-G. Giuliani, *Il forestiere istruito di Santa Maria Novella*, 1836, p. 42). It is still not known why the Dominican fathers gave their support or favoured the return to a more traditional style than the model furnished by the sinopia of the first bay (apart from the 'peak' the *Stories of Noah* represent). The Dominicans of Santa Maria Novella, who depended on Santa Maria sopra Minerva in Rome, chose a sort of Trecentism, while those of San Marco, who depended on the Congregation of Lombardy, would choose Fra Angelico's modernity. We cannot evaluate how that could have influenced the choice of Uccello, whom we could imagine reluctantly agreeing to participate in a collective enterprise which was strictly supervised by the Dominican chapter. The homage that he renders to Masolino – a remarkable fact in view of young Uccello's preferences – is given original and critical concrete expression, and in connection with this, the comparison of the *Ancestors* with a more sculptural, less pictorial result is enlightening. Pope-Hennessy (1969, p. 140), in order to support a later dating (at least in the mid-1430s), points to the close similarity between the image of Eve and that of Christ in the window of the *Resurrection* (1443). The monochrome, as in Masaccio's work in the cloister of Santa Maria del Carmine, is enriched by different localized colours, almost anticipating the ambiguities between naturalism and the abstract vision of false relief in perspective, which would become evident in the monastic stories of San Miniato. The Ghibertian distribution of the 'effects' in four 'stories' was not taken up by the other painters with Gothic leanings who were working in the cloister, and the quality of the sinopias goes down suddenly: there is no lack of fairly vigorous characters, but the drawings are extremely simple, in the Trecento tradition. The sinopia of the first bay is thus a one-off, as if its main purpose had been to furnish a model for a venture intended from the outset to be collective. The representation of the Creator's halo, in space an Albertian 'reference' incorporated in the sinopia, in the painting appears only in the lunette; in the *Creation of Eve* it is replaced by a more conventional depiction. Finally, all the research into effects of depth seen in the lunette disappears in the Ghibertian Late Gothic of the Garden of Earthly Delights – the first probable sign of Uccello's disengagement.

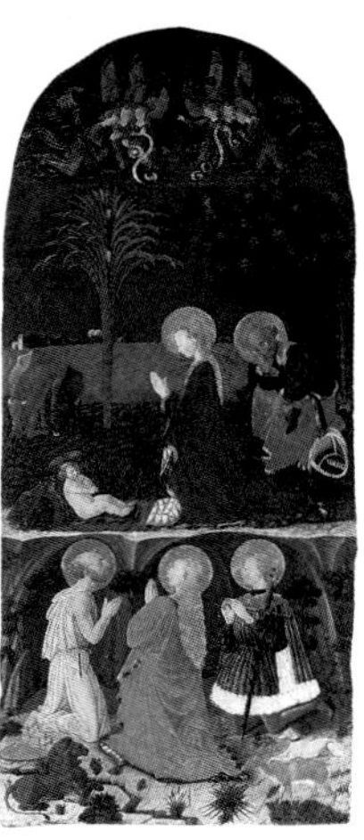

5. THE ADORATION OF THE CHILD WITH SAINT JEROME, SAINT MARY MAGDALEN AND SAINT EUSTACE

Tempera on wood, 110 × 47 cm.
Karlsruhe, Staatliche Kunsthalle.
About 1431–2

This is one of the works in Uccello's *oeuvre* which poses the most problems. We can easily understand the long quarrel over its ATTRIBUTION: we know practically nothing of the retable's origin, its patrons, its original placing nor of its chronology. It was initially attributed to Pisanello; it was associated with Uccello (or his school) for the first time by Loeser (1898, pp. 89–90) and considered as a work characteristic of his Late Gothic style. Before that H. Thode (1890, pp. 249–50) had placed it in the Florentine school linked to Baldovinetti. Other suggestions followed: W. Weisback (1901, pp. 44–5) favoured an anonymous artist much influenced by Gentile; J. Guthman (1902, p. 295, n. 89) an anonymous artist trained in Umbria; P. Schubring (1907, pp. 111–12), Matteo de'

Pasti, until G. Gamba (1909, pp. 28–9) attributed it once again to Uccello (or his school) but with influences from Domenico Veneziano and Baldovinetti. A. Venturi (VII, 1, 1991, p. 269, n. 3) proposed Giovan Francesco da Rimini (refuted by R. Buscaroli, 1931, p. 59). A. Schmarsow (1900, ill. 25–6) was the first to suggest the Master of the Carrand Triptych, later identified with Giovanni di Francesco del Cervelliera. This direction was first taken up by R. Longhi (1928, p. 39), followed by B. Berenson (1932, pp. 341–2), M. Marangoni (1932, p. 345, with a dating of 1426–32) and R. Offner (1933, p. 177, n. 34). R. Van Marle attributed the retable to the school of Baldovinetti (1928, X, p. 250), while G. Gamba (1933, p. 156), V. Giovannozzi (1934, p. 356: 'Uccello's inspiration is obvious'), G. Poggi (1933, p. 324, n. 2), W. Boeck (1939, p. 119) and M. Davies (1959, pp. 312–13: 'eclectic master') came out in favour of an unknown disciple of Uccello. G. Pudelko (1935, pp. 123–30) introduced the work into the catalogue of the Karlsruhe Master, an unknown Florentine active between 1440 and 1445. Agreeing with this were J. Lauts (1947, p. 31; 1957, p. 44; 1966, pp. 187–8, cat. n. 404); E. Carli (1954 and 1959, p. 70: 'the closest disciple to the Master'); D. Gioseffi (1958, p. 138: 'a disciple influenced by Paolo's late work'); P. D'Ancona (1959, p. 10: 'Paolo Uccello's climate is obvious', the Karlsruhe Master was not the same person who painted the Quarate predella). Partisans of the Karlsruhe Master were challenged by M. Salmi (1934–5, p. 27, n. 18), who attributed the retable to the Quarate Master, M. Salmi (1938, p. 113, in dubious fashion), followed by B. Degenhart (1941, p. 83). M. Salmi (1950, p. 26) chose the Prato Master, an unknown late disciple of Uccello whose catalogue was described by J. Pope-Hennessy. The latter (1950; 1969, p. 168) attributed the *Adoration* to the Prato Master. A. Parronchi (1965, p. 178) retracts it in order to give weight to the 'sentimental hypothesis' that it was Uccello's daughter, Sister Antonia di Paolo, nun and painter (A. Parronchi, 1974, pp. 66–7), as a 'proof of the freedom her father gave her'. Prior to this ([EUA,X] 1963, col. 467) he had placed it, along with the 'Prato Group', in the second half of Uccello's *oeuvre*.

Loeser's attribution to Uccello was supported by C. L. Ragghianti (1938, p. 24; 1940, p. 11; 1977, p. 13) and taken up again by R. Longhi (1952, p. 32, who removed it from Giovanni di Francesco) and, with some hesitation, by E. Micheletti (cat. 1954, n. 19), E. Sindona (1957, p. 57), L. Berti (1961, p. 304; 1964, n.p.), L. Tongiorgi Tomasi (1971, p. 96), F. Zeri (1983, p. 555) and A. Angelini (1990, p. 73).

The painting's DATING is equally controversial: a work of his youth, before 1425, according to Sindona (1957, p. 57, second work in the catalogue), between 1426 and 1432 for Marangoni (1932, p. 345), around 1432 for A. De Marchi (1990, p. 199), at the beginning of the 1430s for Angelini (1990, p. 73), *c.* 1440 for Pope-Hennessy (1969, p. 168), between 1443 and 1456 for Tongiorgi Tomasi (1971, p. 96), towards 1445 or after for Salmi (1950, p. 26), between 1445 and 1450 for G. Pudelko (1935, pp. 124 and 129) and J. Lauts (1957, p. 44), a work of the 1460s for D. Gioseffi (1958, p. 138) and L. Berti (1961, p. 304, with references to the Oxford *Hunt*).

There are no references in the sources to the retable and it abounds in apparently contradictory elements. It is unusual in a number of ways: its elongated form (perhaps it was completed with lateral panels?); the bipartite levels (with the saints of the lower part separated from the main scene by a rough, rocky platform); the almost heraldic, graphic quality of certain elements; the geometric simplification of shapes and its characterization by a refined stylization. The very decentralized focal point of the composition is the 'legitimate construction' of the palm tree, which is in perspective, abstract, 'metallic', less 'natural' than in Ghiberti's reliefs or Gentile da Fabriano's predellas. This is a painting steeped in nostalgia, with something of the visionary, nocturnal character of Lorenzo Monaco and far removed from Filippo Lippi's naturalistic interpretation for the Medici retable of 1459. The dating is almost always limited to the painter's late period, but it is difficult to interpret the varied intonations we find in the 'small items' at the end of Uccello's career. In fact, this work has affinities with the fresco at Bologna which has an analogous subject, and has the landscape scenery of the *Stoning of Saint Stephen*, the last scene in the Prato cycle (completed by Andrea di Giusto). A dating of between 1430 and 1435 would therefore seem more plausible, unless we consider the hypothesis of a disciple (but of extraordinary calibre) or, less probably, a deliberate, nostalgic return to the past on Uccello's part. The figures of Saints Jerome, Mary Magdalene and Eustace seem closer to the Prato cycle, while Saint Joseph seems to replicate the Quarate predella's. The angels in the upper part suggest Baldovinetti and remind us of Fra Angelico's in the San Domenico retable at Fiesole (1428–30) and of Francesco d'Antonio's at Orsanmichele (1429). To the experiences Uccello had acquired during his stay in Venice he was adding memories of the period prior to that, of Gentile da Fabriano and Lorenzo Monaco. We could say that Uccello was attempting here to 'loop the loop' as regards his time in Venice (1425–30), passing from experience to experience with a disconcerting speed and plumbing the rich figurative culture that existed before Masaccio. This would explain the 'international' character of the retable. This mysterious retable represents a moment of heightened Ghibertian calligraphism, with scrolls that unwind 'like woodshavings' (Vasari). Certain elements are very interesting, such as his explorations in perspective – with the foreshortened shoreline in contrast to the Albertian skyline and especially the palm tree, which seems to capture the painter's attention – the dynamism of the composition with the 'Lorenzettian' shooting star and, finally, perhaps the similarities between the three saints and their animal counterparts (Parronchi, 1974, pp. 66–7). There are already many elements here that would be developed later in Prato, in the Quarate predella, in Bologna, and the references that Uccello drew on after his long stay in Venice are clearly visible.

The composition remained on view for a long time: in the 1470s it inspired Verrocchio – who, like Ghiberti, was also a master in metalwork – in his palm tree in perspective in *The Baptism of Christ* (Florence, Uffizi; see Ragghianti, 1977, p. 10). That one of the formal characteristics of the work should be 'the atonic and rigid lifelessness of automatons' (F. Zeri, 1983, p. 555) could be explained by a sort of stiffening, a total Ghibertism on the painter's part. The atmosphere of the nocturnal religious fable is far from the natural moonlight of Fra Angelico's theological certainties, a painter with whom Uccello started a close, complex liaison at the beginning of the 1430s which would last until towards the middle of the decade. But at this stage the two artists were still very far apart.

Because of the lack of explicit documentation, the Karlsruhe retable will probably continue to be the subject of discussion, even if the attribution to Uccello gains acceptance from now on. The dating, which also merits discussion, should not stray too far from 1431–2, thus preceding the frescoes at Prato and Bologna.

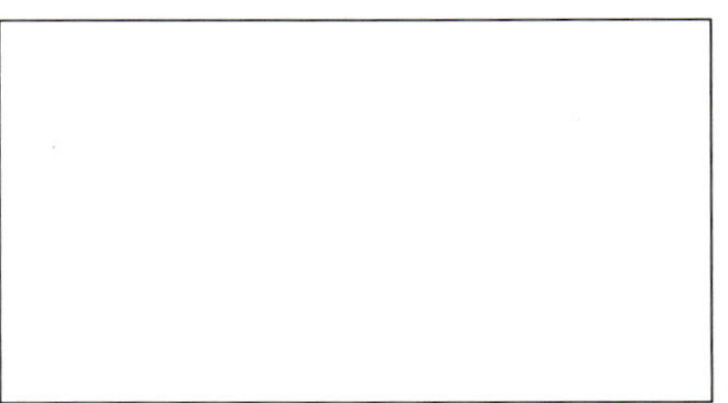

6. STORIES OF SAINT FRANCIS

Three frescoes (now lost).
Formerly Florence, Santa Trinita.
About 1431–4

Uccello's frescoes at Santa Trinita are now reduced to remnants worthy only of archaeological interest (J. Pope-Hennessy, 1969, p. 160). There is a fragment of cartouche with a seraph below, the last trace of *Saint Francis Receiving the Stigmata*. The seraph, in foreshortened form, is the most important image, other than the remains of the architectonic frame with Corinthian pillars, of a style reminiscent of Michelozzi in the 1430s and 1440s. From the fragments of inscription we can decipher: '[F]RAN[CESCO] [R]EGIE LA [C]HIESA' (Francis Upholds the Church); the upper scene was therefore *The Dream of Pope Innocent III*, with the emblematic image of the Lateran basilica supported by Saint Francis. Vasari provided other details: 'and in Santa Trinita, above the left door inside the church, some stories of Saint Francis' (1500, p. 253) 'in which he receives the stigmata, he protects the church by bearing it on his shoulders and he meets Saint Dominic' (1568, I, p. 269). The iconography in the three scenes one above the other is thus defined: *The Dream of Innocent III*, *Saint Francis Receiving the Stigmata*, *The Meeting between Saint Francis and Saint Dominic*. We can gather as much from its position as from its location in a Benedictine church, that the cycle must have been very important. This is borne out by the fact that it is the only work mentioned, along with the Chiostro Verde of Santa Maria Novella, in Antonio Manetti's *XIV Uomini singhularii in Firenze (c.* 1495) even if he gave no details. Nor did Francesco Albertini mention it in his *Memoriale* of 1510: 'Not to mention Paolo Uccello's paintings between the doors on the side of S[an]c[t]a Maria Magd[alena], begun by Desiderio' (and finished by Benedetto da Maiano and intended for the Cerbini tomb).

The cycle was probably jeopardized by repairs to the façade of the church which began in 1592 (by Bernardo Buontalenti and Alfonso Parigi): the frescoes were mentioned by F. Bocchi-G. Cinelli (1677, p. 192) as well as by F. Baldinucci (1681; Florence edn 1845, I, p. 447) among works that had disappeared or faded away ('they can no longer be seen today').

These frescoes are not documented, and neither the PATRONS nor the DATING is known. However, we should remember that the presence of a Franciscan cycle in a Benedictine church was unusual: the stories of Saint Benedict or Saint Giovanni Gualberto would have been more likely. Obviously this was due to precise requests from the patrons (it would be the same for Ghirlandaio's Sassetti chapel). Uccello's frescoes were part of the old tradition, of Giotto and Gaddi, in the context of the Albizzis' regime, which was stylistically disinclined to 'modernism', where they represented an important concession for the period. They revolved around compositions that were strongly entrenched in Late Gothic, among the most important of which were the frescoes of Francesco di Ser Cenni (Gianfigliazzi chapel, *c.* 1400–1410), Lorenzo Monaco's work in the Bartolini-Salimbeni chapel (*c.* 1420–21, followed by the unfinished Strozzi retable), Gentile da Fabriano's sumptuous retable for Palla Strozzi (1422–3), the decoration of the Ardinghelli chapel by Giovanni Toscani (1423–4), the Compagni chapel (1431) by Bonaiuto di Giovanni and his pupils, the Doni chapel (*c.* 1431–4) by Bicci di Lorenzo and his pupils, and the bold 'return to Gothic' by Giovanni del Ponte in the Scali chapel (1434). Uccello may have been summoned to work at Santa Trinita from as early as 1418–23, at a time when Lorenzo Ghiberti was coordinating work ordered by Palla Strozzi (sacellum, family tomb, sacristy, library; R. Jones, 1984, p. 9–106) and when Gentile da Fabriano's *Adoration of the Magi* was already a basic reference for young painters, from Toscani to Giovanni di Paolo, who came from Siena to study it. However, certain stylistic indicators – the foreshortened seraph, the architectonic, historical and epigraphic frame – incline us towards a dating later than 1430. It was the year of Uccello's return from Venice and the death of Giovanni Toscani, painter to the Ardinghelli family, who had close ties with the Strozzi family and who financed the work on the façade of the church. It is perhaps no accident that *Saint Francis Receiving the Stigmata* can be found on the predella of the Ardinghelli retable painted by Toscani. What narrows the uncertain dating of Uccello's intervention still further is Cosimo de' Medici's accession to power in 1434, which was accompanied by a serious crisis between the government and the Benedictines, with repercussions on artistic commissions and enforced exile for Palla Strozzi and the Ardinghelli family. It seems that Cosimo had trouble in controlling the Church politically, although in 1435 he had succeeded in getting Pope Eugenius IV to agree that the convent should observe Saint Giustina of Padua's reform, in spite of strong opposition from the Benedictines: even in 1444, the Strozzi Sacristy of Santa Trinita was harbouring a citizens' conspiracy (G. Cavalcanti, *Istorie fiorentine*, X; 5, ed. G. Pino, Milan, 1944, p. 300). We can advance the hypothesis that the Ardinghelli family, in part supported by Palla Strozzi, had replaced the defunct Toscani with Uccello, due yet again perhaps to Ghiberti's good offices. These were the years when Fra Angelico was finishing Lorenzo Monaco's retable for the Strozzi (A. Padoa Rizzo in *La Chiesa di Santa Trinita a Firenze*, 1987, p. 130) and it is possible that Uccello wished to vie with him in the field of religious painting. The Santa Trinita frescoes could therefore be placed at a time not too distant from those of Prato.

The fragment of Uccello's work was identified for the first time, using information from Vasari, by G. Pudelko (1932–4, p. 157; 1934, *Art Bulletin*, p. 231) and considered a youthful work. More recently L. Bellosi (1990, p. 21 and fig. 10) moved the chronology to between 1430 and 1437, a convincing dating, but we must still limit it to 1431–4, if we consider the serious crisis that hit Santa Trinita with Cosimo's arrival and the exile of a number of *boni homines* variously linked to the Benedictine convent. During this crisis Ghiberti, Michelozzo, Fra Angelico and Uccello managed to survive: it seems that even the clever Cosimo de' Medici hastened to exploit the artistic choices of his great adversary, Palla Strozzi to his advantage. Giovanni Rucellai, in his *Zibaldone* (1960 edn, I, p. 49) mentioned the following as among the exiles – with the Strozzi – : Piero di Neri Ardinghelli and Ridolfo and Bartolomeo Peruzzi. The two latter were probably patrons of *The Four Elements* that Uccello painted on the vault of the loggia of their palace in the Santa Croce quarter.

7. THE FOUR ELEMENTS

Fresco (now lost).
Formerly Florence, Palazzo Peruzzi loggia.
About 1432

Vasari is the source for this lost fresco, and he mentions it only in the second edition of his *Vite* (1568, I, p. 273), immediately after recalling Uccello's trip to Padua in 1445. This work is not mentioned in older sources, but Vasari provides us with an exhaustive description: 'Paolo worked on the Peruzzi's vault in fresco with triangular elements in perspective; in its corners he painted the four elements in quadratures, each symbolized by an appropriate animal; a mole for earth, a fish for water, a salamander for fire, a chameleon for air, since it feeds on this element and takes on every colour; but as he had never seen one, he painted a camel which opens its mouth and swallows air to fill its stomach, revealing a very great simplemindedness in confusing the names and turning a simple little lizard into an enormous, unbecoming beast.' This text was repeated, and synthesized, in Raffaello Borghini's *Riposo* (Reggio Emilia, 1826 edn, II, p. 59): 'Deceived by the similarity in name, he mistook a camel [*camello*] for a chameleon [*camaleonte*]': the episode occurred between the cycle of Santa Maria degli Angeli and the fresco of Saint Thomas in the Mercato Vecchio. Filippo Baldinucci, in 1686, was still mentioning the work (Florence, 1845 edn, I, pp. 450–51) and added a precious detail: 'I have been fortunate, thus I shall not be accused of inventing, for this figure has remained until now entire and intact, as if it had just been painted; while those of the mole, the fish and the salamander, even though I can still recollect them, have, one after the other, gradually become soaked with water leaking across the vault which has no covering over it, and they have all fallen to the ground.' We can then consider that the work disappeared in the second half of the seventeenth century, and the image which benefited from the longest life would seem to be the camel-chameleon which had aroused Vasari's curiosity. The loggia was converted by descendants of the Peruzzi in 1777, as an inscription bears witness, and in the Fantozzi's guide (1842, p. 233) it is described as 'reduced, through petty interests, to a wheelwright's shed and workshop'.

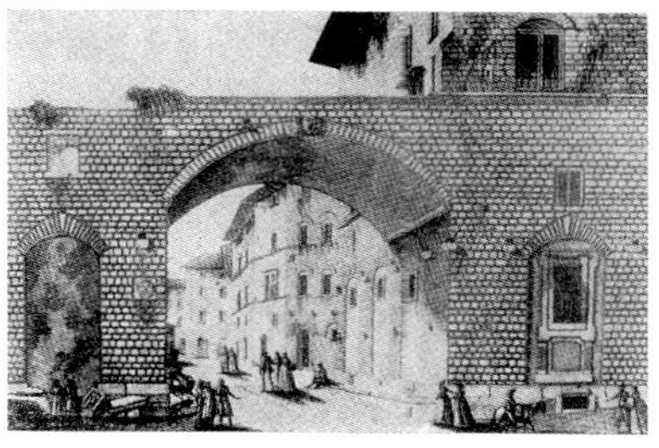

The loggia of the Palazzo Peruzzi, site of the lost fresco. Engraving from *Guida di Firenze e d'altre città principali della Toscana*, Florence 1820.

The iconographical theme of the fresco seems to have been suggested by frescoes on the vault of the theatre of the Orsini palace in Montegiordano near Rome, which closely resembled Leonardo di Besozzo's miniature on a similar subject (R. L. Mode, 1972, p. 374 and ill. 25) inspired by one of Masolino's cycles. Parronchi (1962, p. 65; 1974, p. 76, n. 91) suggested that a drawing in the codex of Bartolomeo Rustici (Florence, Seminario Arcivescovile library (f. 4 verso, *c.* 1447) might be a drawing of the Peruzzi vault. This is a seductive hypothesis but it raises some questions: the drawing, which divides the area into four sectors of a circle, only vaguely corresponds to Vasari's precise

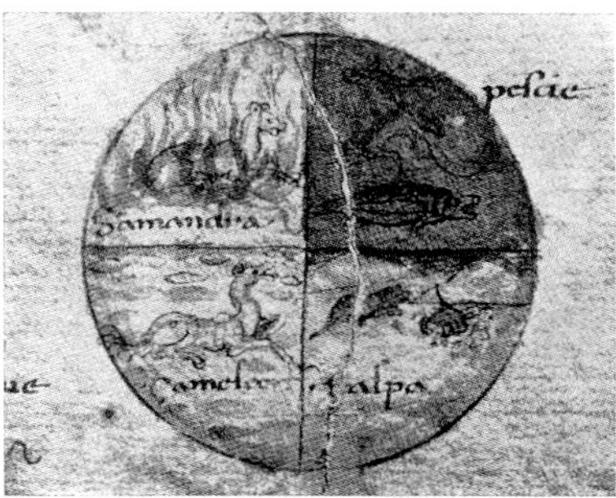

The Four Elements, drawing in the *Codex Rustici*, *c.* 1447. Florence, Biblioteca del Seminario Arcivescovile di Cestello.

description, in which he mentions 'triangular elements in perspective ... in its corners', – in the four corners of the vault. We might conclude from this (Parronchi, 1962, p. 65) that Vasari had not seen the frescoes in their original positions, but it is barely conceivable, given the *a fresco* technique, that it could have been successfully detached before 1568. The drawing in the Rustici manuscript must then be considered as a diagrammatic transposition of the subject, rather than a faithful though summary reproduction of the vault of the Peruzzi loggia.

The work's DATING can be defined more easily. Parronchi (1962, p. 66, n. 2) supposed that the decoration of the vault was connected with the Council of Florence, for in 1438 the Eastern Emperor and his retinue were entertained in neighbouring houses. Parronchi also considered (1957; 1964, p. 513) that Uccello's animal painting was more traditional here than in the *Creation* in the first bay of the Chiostro Verde. He suggested a more conventional source of the type seen on the Canons' door in Santa Maria del Fiore and concluded with an earlier dating, 'an earlier period of shallower culture' compared to the *Creation*. The hypothesis of a close link with Masolino's Roman fresco at the Palazzo Orsini (*c.* 1430–32) is also plausible, even if it appears difficult to accept Mode's hypothesis (1972, p. 577) suggesting that Uccello may have travelled to Rome with Masolino and Donatello.

We can be more precise about the PATRONS, an undocumented aspect and one on which the critics have not pronounced until now. The most probable patron is Bartolomeo Peruzzi, who had a significant fortune at his disposal and who in 1430–31 was a member of the Dieci di Balìa at the same time as Cosimo de' Medici. Their involvement in politics dated from the eve of the battle of San

Romano against Siena in June 1432. The commission would therefore have been contemporary with the richest and most influential member of the Peruzzi family's entry into the political arena, and it is no coincidence that the work was destined for a site which was open to the public, the family's merchant loggia. Unfortunately, Peruzzi was fighting on the wrong side: with the Albizzi and the Strozzi against Cosimo and Averardo de' Medici. If we accept this hypothesis, the dating that follows – of *c.* 1431–2 – could only with difficulty stretch beyond 1434, the date when Bartolomeo and other members of the family, who had been compromised with the oligarchic regime of the Albizzi, were struck down by Cosimo's vengeance when he returned from exile in 1433 and they in turn went into exile. It was not the only occasion (if we think of the three frescoes at Santa Trinita) in which Uccello found himself linked with an anti-Medici faction.

It is possible too that a fresh impression of the fresco and of Uccello's 'admired' choice of colour came together in a passage of Alberti's *De Pictura* (1435–6): 'There is fire-colour which they call red, and the colour of air which is said to be blue-grey, and the green of water, and earth is grey and ash-coloured' (Book I, ed. C. Grayson, Bari, 1980, pp. 22–4). The chameleon (mentioned in Tolomeo's *Optica*) had special details that aroused great interest among specialists in optics and perspective, as is confirmed in a singular passage in *De Pictura* (Book I, par. 7, 1980 edn, p. 20): the 'median rays' of the optic pyramid 'do what they say the chameleon and other like beasts are wont to do, who assume the colours of nearby objects: from the point where the rays touch the surface to the eye itself, they show the same light and the same colour as that surface'. And there it is, within Alberti's text: an acknowledgment of the little animal's bizarre virtues, which certainly would have intrigued a man like Uccello.

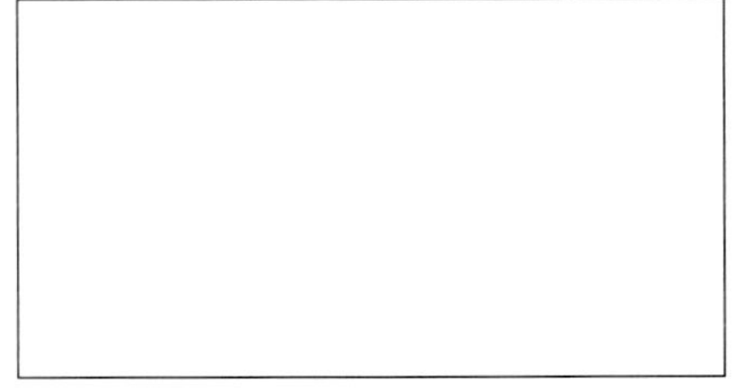

8. STORIES OF SAINT BENEDICT

Murals in monochrome tempera (now lost). Formerly Florence, Santa Maria degli Angeli, cloister.
About 1431–7

Albertini's *Memoriale* (1510) is the first source to mention this cycle, positioning it 'in the cloister' and attributing it to 'Thomaso Masacci', to whom he also attributed the *Hawkwood*. The *Libro di Antonio Billi* (1516) cites it as a work by Uccello: 'In Santa Maria degli Angeli, in the great garden of the cloister, he painted many pictures in terre-verte with great bravura which were much admired' (ed. C. Frey, Berlin, 1892, p. 24). The Anonimo Magliabechiano (*c.* 1546) adds little: 'And he also painted in the monastery of the brothers of the Angels, in the cloister of the garden, many pictures in terre-verte, with great deftness and esteemed by connoisseurs to be quite rarte' (ed. C. Frey, Berlin, 1892, p. 100). In the first edition of Vasari's *Vite* there is a brief reference: 'He worked in the cloister of the garden of the Angeli' (1550, p. 256), while the second edition provides us with the essentials of what we know of the lost cycle: 'He worked again in the colour of terre-verte in the loggia of the garden of the Monastery of the Angeli, facing west: under each arch he showed the stories of the acts of Saint Benedict the Abbot' and he also added certain ecphractic scenes. These are precious details, not only in their thematic information but also because they allow us to form a picture of the stylistic references. The 'clothes, unwinding around a naked body, floating gracefully' make us think immediately of Lorenzo Monaco, the great painter at the convent of Santa Maria degli Angeli. The effects of 'fear', 'solemnity', 'devotion' and 'amazement' demonstrate the interest in *affetti* and *attitudini* already shown by Starnina, and extended to physiognomy in *The Disputation of Saint Stephen* at Prato. Vasari's description of the death of Saint Benedict has many characteristics in common with the death of Saint Jerome in the Carmine cycle, which is described for us in his biography of Starnina. The developments in perspective that we witness in later works are very limited here and Vasari clearly says: 'In this work, there are neither coloured landscapes nor a great number of buildings and learned perspectives, but fine *disegno* and many felicities.'

Iconographic sources are found in Spinello Aretino's frescoes in the sacristy of San Miniato (1386–7) and above all in Lorenzo Monaco's predella of the *Coronation of the Virgin* for the high altar of the convent church painted in 1414 (Florence, Uffizi). The economy of media (a mural in terre-verte tempera, as in the Chiostro Verde, wrongly called fresco), the simplicity of the composition and the choice of monochrome all suggest an atmosphere imbued with austerity, and recourse to a monastic tradition whose tone had been set by Niccolò di Pietro Gerini (who was painting there around 1380) and by Lorenzo Monaco. Since it is unlikely that a commission of this importance would have been given to a beginner while Lorenzo Monaco was alive (he died in 1425 or 1426), and since Uccello was in Venice between 1425 and 1430, we can deduce a DATING certainly later than 1431. At that moment the covent embraced the culture of humanism and welcomed modernity, to become one of the most progressive religious centres in the city for at least a decade. The election of the humanist Ambrogio Traversari as the new Abbot General of the Order (21 October 1431), and the commissioning of Fra Angelico's retable of the *Last Judgment* (financed by the Arte di Calimala) for the oratory of the convent, were all part of this movement (San Orlandi, 1964, pp. 29 and 184; M. C. Improta, 1990, p. 72). Traversari, who was already in contact with Ghiberti (P. Castelli, 1978, p. 532), gave a new impetus to the decoration of the monastery. His correspondence mentions the purchase in Venice of glass for the windows (*Epistolae*, lib. VII, ep. XVI) and of costly paintings destined for the convent's *scriptorium* (*Epistolae*, lib. XXIV, ep. XX). M. Bacci (in *Lorenzo Ghiberti 'materia e ragionamenti'*, 1978, p. 246) suggests that the presence of Pope Eugenius IV in Florence from 1434 onwards had prompted the many decorative works recorded during those years in the convents of the town. The enterprise could only with difficulty be dated after

1439 (Traversari's death) but already in 1437 work on Brunelleschi's Rotunda – one of the most 'modern' works of the convent, made possible by large bequests from the Scolari family – had been abandoned. In 1426 Matteo Scolari, Pippo Spano's brother, had left money for the foundation of a convent for ten Camaldolites, dedicated to Saint Anthony Abbot and Saint Julian. Later (E. Battisti, 1976, p. 379) the most important festivals of the convent, other than those in honour of the Virgin Mary, manifested a special devotion to those two saints. The choice of a Benedictine cycle, as with the Olivetans of San Miniato or the Vallombrosans of Santa Trinita, might have been suggested to Traversari for 'political' opportunistic reasons on which it is now difficult to pronounce. On the great humanist abbot's death, the convent swiftly changed the direction of its stylistic preferences, as is shown in the first *Crucifixion* by Andrea del Castagno, generally dated between 1440 and 1444 (M. Horster, 1980, pp. 20–21 and 173–4).

An echo of the Angeli cycle can be found in the remarkable Benedictine cycle in the Chiostro degli Aranci in the Badia in Florence, which can be dated 1436–9. C. L. Ragghianti finds it 'directly influenced by Uccello' (1937, p. 239) while for M. Salmi (1938, p. 19) the frescoes 'show influences from Fra Angelico, but are closer to Paolo in their tendency to geometric forms'. Certain authors have attributed the *Nun-Saint* formerly in the Contini-Bonacossi Collection to an anonymous painter associated with the Badia. For the debate on the attribution of the cycle, cf. *La Badia fiorentina*, Florence, 1982, pp. 139–40, notes 219–24.

The cloister in which Uccello worked is shown in a drawing in the *Rustici Codex* (*c.* 1447). The work on Brunelleschi's Rotunda took place between 1434 and 1437, the probable date of Uccello's cycle. Several authors have suggested that echoes of the Santa Maria degli Angeli murals may be seen in the painting in the Accademia wrongly called a *Thebaïd* (G. Pudelko, 1934, p. 246, n. 23; M. Salmi, 1950, p. 27); but this does not seem convincing, because of Vasari's precise description. Uccello's cycle was completed by an episode painted by Ridolfo del Ghirlandaio (Vasari-Milanesi, V, 1880, p. 196) which F. Bocchi-G. Cinelli

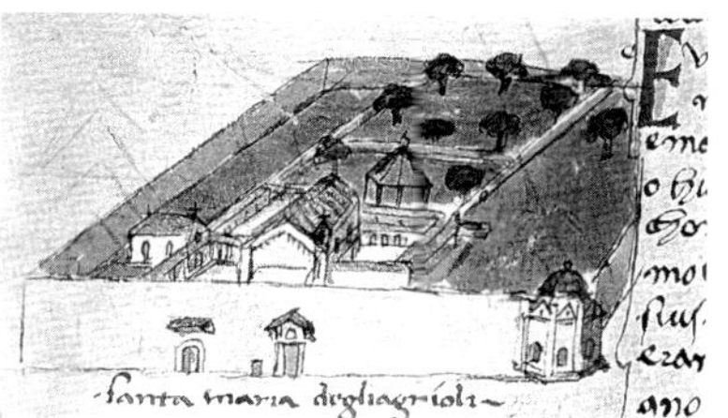

The cloister of Santa Maria degli Angeli, drawing in the *Codex Rustici*, *c.* 1447. Florence, Biblioteca del Seminario Archivescovile di Cestello.

(1677, p. 493) also placed 'in the garden loggia'. F. Baldinucci (1686) restricted himself to emphasizing the important innovation of the draped monk (1845, p. 450), as had Vasari. The Uffizi drawing 97/E, with four seated monks, which Salmi (1950, p. 28) likened to Uccello's cycle (B. Berenson, *Drawings*, 1938; II, n. 168: school of Fra Angelico) can be linked to him only with difficulty. Father Richa (IX, 1761, p. 216) attributed the lunettes, painted green, in the cloister of the Cistercian abbey at Settimo near Florence to Uccello. The Quattrocento lunettes disappeared with the rebuilding of the convent in the sixteenth and seventeenth centuries, when new cloisters were built by Bartolomeo Ammannati, Gherardo Silvani and Matteo Nigetti. Bernardino Poccetti's frescoes were dedicated to the founder of the order, Saint Romuald, while Lorenzo Monaco's and Uccello's iconographical choices privileged the order's affiliation to the great Benedictine family.

9. THE VISION OF SAINT JOHN THE EVANGELIST ON PATMOS, THE ADORATION OF THE MAGI, SAINT JAMES AND SAINT ANSANO OF SIENA

Tempera on wood, 20.4 × 178 cm.
Florence, Museo Arcivescovile di Cestello.
About 1433

Illustrated on p. 296

The predella probably formed part of a triptych, of which nothing is known, formerly situated in the church of San Bartolomeo at Quarate near Bagno a Ripoli, on the southern outskirts of Florence (not to be confused with Quarrata, on the Pistoia road). It consists of three panels, each contained within a red semi-circular border. The centre panel is the largest (in the ratio of 8:5). On the left is the *Vision of Saint John the Evangelist on Patmos* with its modern, extraordinary, nocturnal, stormy sky, which seems to anticipate Leonardo (A. Parronchi, 1963, col. 467). Uccello already seems to be veering towards those Aristotelian 'natural causes' dear to Ghiberti (*Commentario Terzo*: 'when the air is filled with large clouds, which resist the light' (ed. Morisani, 1947, p. 51; ed. Bergdolt, 1988, p. 12) which he developed in the *Flood* in the Chiostro Verde and in the extraordinary *Saint George*, now in London. The monumental image of Saint John is characterized by nervous, vibrant drawing, with references that range from Ghibertian statuary to Masaccio, but it is the brilliant, lively landscape that captures the painter's interest. The sharply profiled saints, kneeling on the right of the composition, in the dark, dense wood, are two pilgrim knights, Saint James Major and Saint Ansano. In accordance with a rare iconography of Sienese origin, Ansano is holding up a heart marked with Christ's monogram, whose cult was promoted by Saint Bernardino (G. Kaftal, 1952, p. 59; V. Kiererk, 1961, I, pp. 134–6). This representation of him could already be seen in Florence by about 1425, in the controversial fresco in San Niccolò Oltrarno, attributed to Francesco d'Antonio and strongly influenced by Gentile: the monogram is in the medallion on the frame. In the Quarate predella, the references to Gentile are less marked than in the Karlsruhe *Adoration* that preceded it. This scene heralds Uccello's later compositions (in particular the late *Hunt* now in Oxford, where the shadowy forest has been exposed to complex research into perspective). In the central scene, the remarkable, reined horse (M. Salmi called it 'displaced', 1934–5, pp. 20–21 and thought it derived from the horse in the earlier Saint George) also heralds the Oxford *Hunt*, but it also shows affinities with the Melbourne *Saint* George.

The central scene, *The Adoration of the Magi*, has a delicate coloration with significant explorations into the way space is rendered. The dignitary in the Magi's retinue is reminiscent of the sovereigns of Trebizond in the background of the Paris *Saint George*; apart from a few details, the tired, dreamy Saint Joseph closely resembles his namesake in the Karlsruhe retable. The work fully reveals Uccello's

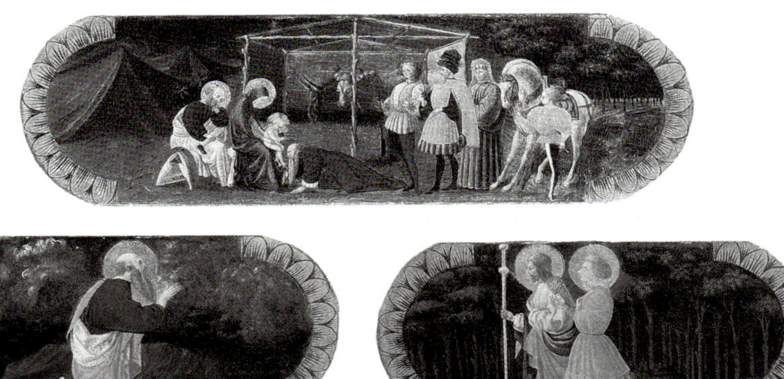

feverish progress at the beginning of the 1430s on his return from Venice: from International Gothic in the Melbourne *Saint George* (*c.* 1430–31) to the Gentilian atmosphere of the Karlsruhe *Adoration* (here much attenuated by a conscious response to modernity) and at the same time to monumental work in Prato cathedral, which was perhaps slightly later. This responsiveness to modernity stems from his interest in Fra Angelico rather than Masaccio's innovations in his Pisa polyptych. He was attracted to Fra Angelico not only for his delicate chromatic nuances (the Tabernacle predellas of Linaiuoli, 1433, and Cortona, 1433–4) but above all for his preoccupation with space in the years immediately following Masaccio's disappearance.

The Quarate predella demonstrates the closeness between Uccello and Fra Angelico, but their incompatibility is already evident: Uccello systematically refused the Dominican painter's light morning atmosphere. Domenico Veneziano's controversial *tondo*, *The Adoration of the Magi* (*c.* 1438–9) would later enrich the panorama of Florentine painting, which, at the beginning of the decade, still remained indebted to Gentile da Fabriano: a particular example was the anonymous *Adoration of the Magi* of Santa Felicita (*c.* 1430–5, Mariotto di Cristofano? Cf. *L'Età di Masaccio*, 1990, pp. 222–3) whose cabin, painted in perspective, is similar to Uccello's in the Quarate predella. These different *Adorations* all owed much perhaps to Fra Angelico's views on the rendering of space (Prado retable predella, Madrid, *c.* 1428–30). The most plausible DATING for Uccello's predella is 1433 or 1434, after the Karlsruhe *Adoration* and close to the Prato cycle.

Following G. Carocci's clues (1907, II, p. 164) which established a connection betwen this predella and Fra Angelico's school, R. Longhi (1928, p. 40) ATTRIBUTES it to Giovanni di Francesco (W. Weisbach's Master of the Carrand Triptych, 1901, identified by P. Toesca in 1917). After W. Boeck (1931), pp. 276–7) suggested it could be one of Uccello's youthful works, the predella was examined in detail by M. Marangoni (1931–2, pp. 329–47) who attributed it to Uccello, dating it between Masaccio's polyptych of 1426 and the *Battles* which he dated at 1432. B. Berenson (1932, p. 342; 1936, p. 278) favoured Giovanni di Francesco, but indications of Uccellian workmanship prevailed: it was attributed to Uccello's school by G. Poggi 1933; R. Offner, 1933, p. 177; V. Giovannozzi, 1934, p. 359; M. Salmi, 1934–5, pp. 20–21 who considered it the product of a workshop; D. Gioseffi, 1958, p. 148, n. 107, as having possible autographic interventions by Uccello in the centre panel, as an eponymous work by the anonymous Quarate Master (M. Salmi, p. 154; p. 44: 'it accentuates the legendary aspect, with colours similar to a miniature' and is also reminiscent of Domenico Veneziano); P. D'Ancona, 1959, p. 10: 'faithful disciple', with 'exceptional qualities as a colorist'; as a work of the Karlsruhe Master (G. Pudelko, 1935, pp. 123 and 126; 1939, T. B., p. 526); of the Prato Master (J. Pope-Hennessy, 1950, p. 162, 1969, p. 167, rep. 1980) and as a work by an unknown painter close to Uccello (G. Kaftal, 1952, p. 59; J. Lauts, 1966, p. 187).

The attribution to Uccello argued by Marangoni was widely echoed: W. Paatz (1934, p. 124, who was reminded of the fresco at San Martino alla Scala), L. Malkiel-Jirmounsky (1932, p. 64), C. L. Ragghianti (1938, p. 24), W. Boeck (1939, pp. 74–5), R. Longhi (1940, p. 179, who thereby corrected his 1928 attribution to Giovanni di Francesco), L. Serra (1933, p. 45), E. Carli (1954; 1959, pp. 33–4 and 58), E. Sindona (1957, p. 57), L. Berti (1961, p. 306; 1964, n.p.), A. Parronchi (1963, col. 467; 1974, pp. 24–5 and 89), L. Tongiorgi Tomasi (1971, p. 90), C. Volpe (1980, p. 17), D. Gioseffi (1980, II, p. 398), F. Zeri (1983, p. 554), L. Bellosi (1987, pp. 33–4) and A. Angelini (1990, p. 78). The work's DATING has also been a source of contention: Boeck (1931, pp. 276–7) considered it a youthful work; Sindona dated it as 1425 (1957, p. 57); between 1426 and 1432, said Marangoni (1932, pp. 340–46), Malkiel-Jirmounsky (1932, p. 64), Serra (1933, p. 45), Paatz (1934, p. 124) and Ragghianti (1938, p. 24); at the beginning of the 1430s, said Volpe (1980, p. 17) and Angelini (1990, p. 78); perhaps towards 1434, said Parronchi (1974, p. 89); the 1430–40s, said Bellosi (1987, pp. 33–4); but it was 'shortly after 1440' for Carli (1954, p. 58); around the same time for C. Gamba, who, however, considered it to be by a disciple of Fra Angelico (1933, pp. 155–6); perhaps earlier, about 1445, Salmi thought (1934–5, p. 21; 1938, p. 44, echoes of Domenico Veneziano and therefore post 1439–45); it was 1435–40 for Tongiorgi Tomasi (1971, p. 90); between 1436 and 1443 for Berti (1961, p. 303; date changed to 1450 in 1964, n.p.); 1440–47 for Gioseffi (1980, II, p. 398); 1440–50 for Pope-Hennessy (1969, p. 167), 1445–50 for Longhi (1940, p. 179); a late work, close to the Oxford *Hunt* for Boeck (1939, pp. 74–5); a studio work after 1468 for Gioseffi (1958, p. 148, n. 107).

There are no documented sources nor written references on this predella and it is not signed: we do not know where it was intended for – perhaps an urban setting before Quarate? – and we know nothing of its patrons. Critics seem to have struggled to put the painting back in the painter's catalogue, where the predella (we do not know if the upper part of the retable was ever done, or if it has been lost) represents an extraordinary moment, reconciling the religious *ratio* of Fra Angelico – whom Uccello considered, with reason, to be the most modern master at the turn of the 1430s – and an irresistible empirical curiosity. Even if Ghiberti's stylistic *imprinting* diminished from then on, Uccello continued to translate a number of his theories pictorially. It was at this point that he set out with determination on his own creative journey.

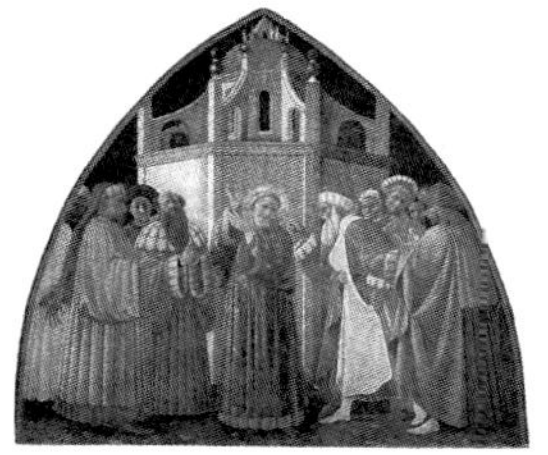
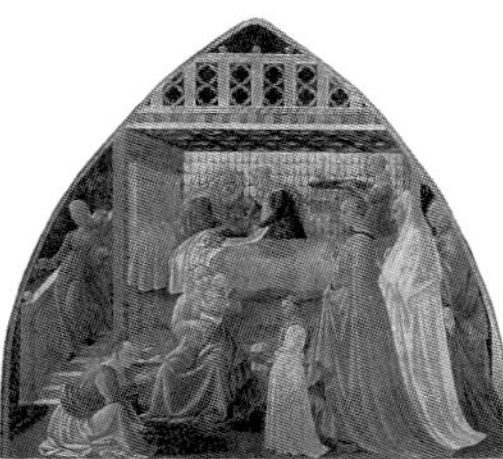
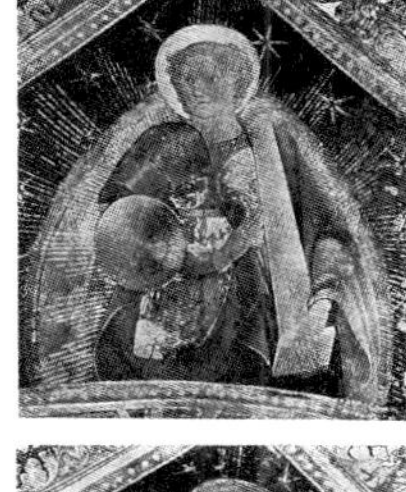
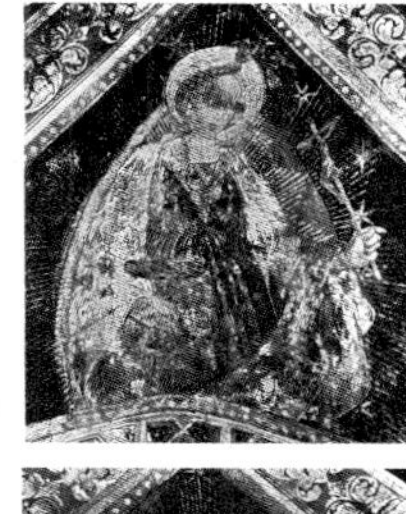
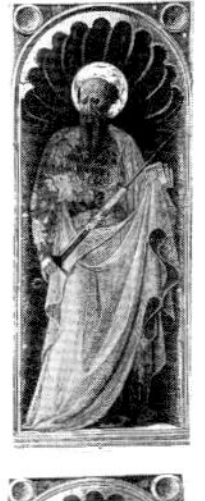
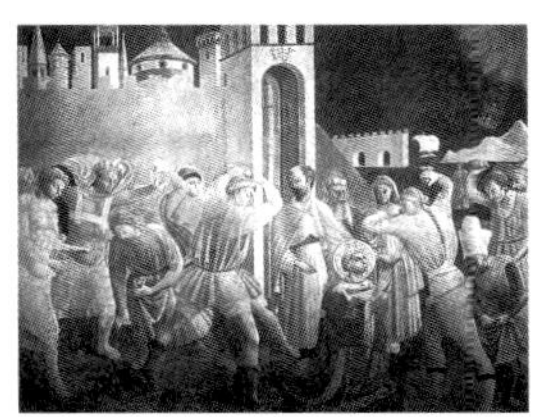
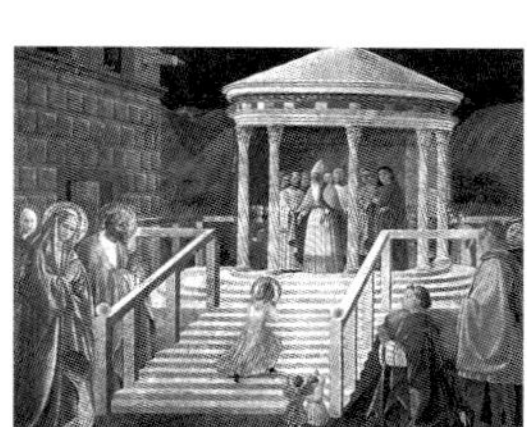
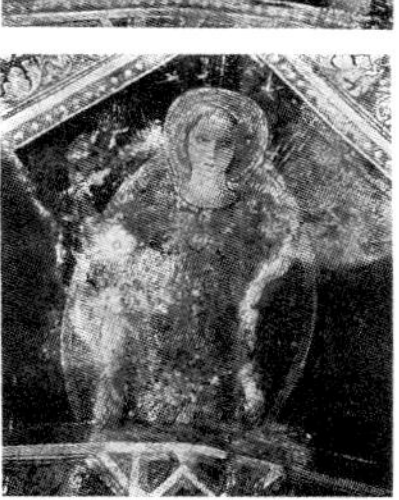
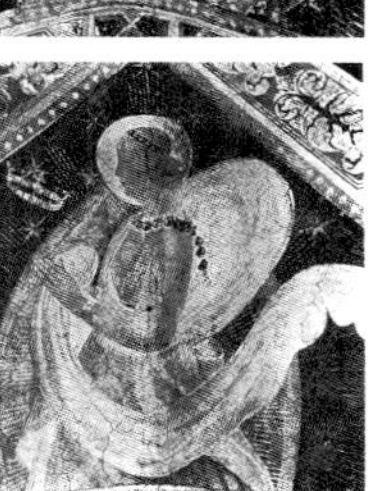
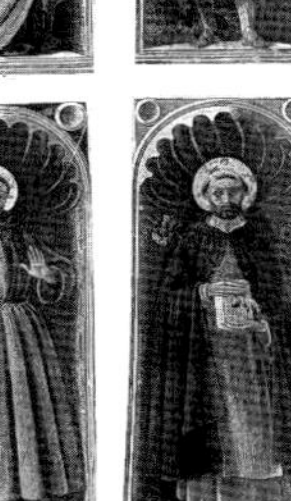
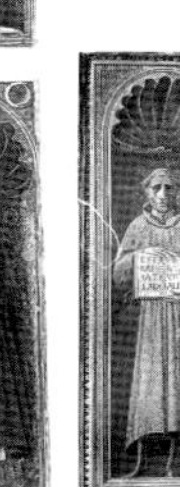
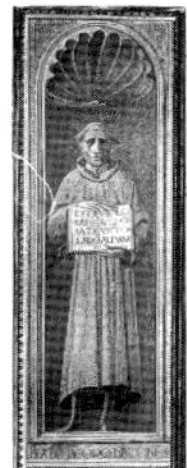

10. DECORATION OF THE CAPPELLA DELL'ASSUNTA, PRATO CATHEDRAL

Frescoes.
About 1434–5

This group of frescoes has been detached and replaced in its original site, with the exception of the *Blessed Jacopone da Todi*. The series consists of the *Virtues*, on the vaulting of the transept, two lunettes (*The Disputation of Saint Stephen* and *The Birth of the Virgin*), two scenes in the central section (*The Stoning of Saint Stephen* and *The Presentation of the Virgin*), two scenes in the lower part (*The Discovery of the Bodies of Saint Stephen and Saint Laurence* and *The Marriage of the Virgin*) and *Saints Paul, Francis, Jerome* and *Dominic* in *trompe-l'oeil* niches on the intrados. These frescoes clearly reveal the presence of several artists and the debate on their ATTRIBUTION remains closely fought. The enterprise is not documented and the cycle is not mentioned by Florentine sources: even Vasari, who knew the cathedral at Prato well, did not mention it. In 1665, the back wall was altered and a great Baroque altar was erected there (Carlo Dolci's retable). This was removed during the restoration of 1870–71, which led to the recovery of the *Jacopone*. The first people to mention the Prato cycle considered it a Trecento composition: the work of an anonymous disciple of Giotto according to F. Baldanzi (1846); of Lorenzo di Niccolò Gerini and Niccolò di Pietro for L. Mazzei (1880, II, p. 410); of Tommaso del Mazza for G. Milanesi (I, 1878, p. 609, n. 3; G. Milanesi-C. Pini, 1876, I, p. 9); and of Antonio Vite and Gherardo Starnina for G. B. Cavalcaselle (1883, II, p. 234; 1903, pp. 293–4). In A. Schmarsow's view (1893, p. 159), the frescoes should be credited to a late disciple of Giotto, but had been entirely restored by Domenico Veneziano: this opened the way to a more correct historico-critical interpretation. F. Witting (1910, p. 495) was alone in opting for an attribution to Domenico Veneziano; but the frescoes were considered to be by a follower of Domenico Veneziano by W. Bode (1897, p. 187 f.), K. Escher (1922, I, pp. 78–9) and W. Wackernagel (1938, p. 121). O. Siren (1904, p. 343) retained the attribution to a disciple of Domenico Veneziano (assisted by Pesellino), but he made a fundamental distinction between these and the lower stories, which he attributed for the first time to Andrea di Giusto, an identification which later critics continued to accept. R. van Marle (1928, IX, p. 331, X, pp. 244–50) associated the whole cycle just with Andrea di Giusto. R. Longhi (1928, p. 40) modified the range by proposing Francesco del Cervelliera (for the parts that were not by Andrea di Giusto), followed by B. Berenson (1932, p. 342; 1936, p. 279) and J. Pope-Hennessy (1939, p. 118). Longhi takes the credit for first suggesting the link with Uccello. The frescoes, which L. Testi (1916, p. 432) considered weak and crude and by an anonymous Florentine, were withdrawn from Giovanni di Francesco (1934, pp. 353–4) by V. Giovannozzi in favour of an anonymous disciple of Uccello influenced by Domenico Veneziano's frescoes at Sant' Egidio, while J. Lipman (1936, p. 118) was in favour of a minor, eclectic master deriving from Uccello, Domenico Veneziano and Castagno. M. Salmi (1934–5, pp. 1–27) favoured a Quarate Master, a disciple of Uccello, with eclectic tendencies. This suggestion was retained by D. Gioseffi (1958, p. 138: composed by Uccello but perhaps carried out by 'the disciple who was working at Quarate') and, in small measure by H. Wohl (1980, p. 171) who veered towards a work by the unknown disciples of Uccello, the Quarate Master and the Karlsruhe Master. The attempt to include the Prato cycle in the *corpus* of the Karlsruhe Master fell to G. Pudelko (1932–4, pp. 174–5; 1935, p. 123; 1936, p. 133; 1939, T. B., p. 526), but it was not subsequently upheld.

The frescoes were attributed to Uccello's circle (except for those by Andrea di Giusto) by M. Salmi (1938, p. 28), R. Kennedy (1938, pp. 204–5), W. Paatz (1940, II, p. 104), P. D'Ancona (1959, p. 12: an unknown artist who was inspired by Uccello but who reveals only 'generic similarities' with his art), L. H. Heydenreich (1974, p. 297: 'very close in style to Paolo'), G. Brandi (1980, p. 190: the comparison between the sinopias made him resolute in rejecting the attribution to Uccello), and – already quoted – H. Wohl (1980, pp. 170–71: a collaboration between two disciples of Uccello). V. Giovannozzi's suggestion (1934, pp. 353–4) which, while refuting Longhi's hypothesis in favour of Giovanni di Francesco, gave substance to the existence of an unknown disciple of Uccello, was developed by M. Salmi (1850, p. 26) who made him the 'Prato Master'. J. Pope-Hennessy (1950, 1969, pp. 163–4) finally developed the profile of the Prato Master, thus creating the most enduringly famous of Uccello's *alter egos*. G. Marchini agreed (1957, p. 77; 1969, pp. 51–130) and (1987, p. 12) recognized the same hand that had already created the cartoon for the stained-glass window of the *Nativity* at Santa Maria del Fiore, a documented work of Uccello's); M. Meiss (1970, pp. 126), R. Fremantle (1975, p. 597, suggested the young Uccello, which is incompatible with the dating he proposed: 1443–55), and A. Chastel (1984 [1983], p. 78: derived from the Sant' Egidio cycle begun in 1439 by Domenico Veneziano).

The first direct reference to Uccello was formulated by C. L. Ragghianti (1938, p. XXIV) followed by R. Longhi (1940, p. 179; 1952, p. 10) who renounced his earlier attribution to Giovanni di Francesco. Later Ragghianti (1976, p. 74) elaborated his views, removing the *post quem* deadline of 1445 (linked to the rebuilding of the window in the back wall of the chapel, according to a document published by Canon Baldanzi (1846, p. 47; G. Marchini, 1963, p. 109, doc. 75)), thus making the attribution to Uccello more convincing. This was accepted by C. Volpe (1956, p. 45), E. Carli (1954 and 1959, p. 22: revising – to Uccello's advantage – the link with Domenico Veneziano at Sant'Egidio), E. Sindona (1957, p. 59 excluding the *Virtues* on the vaulting; 1970, pp. 68 and 73; he suggested, pp. 82–3, a considerable intervention by assistants, Domenico Veneziano among them, p. 73, and the young Piero della Francesca), L. Berti (1961, p. 302: after the San Miniato cycle, but with more conventional results; 1964, n.p.), A. Parronchi (1963, col. 467; 1964 [1957], p. 518: incongruous and archaic, without any connection with Sant'Egidio; 1966, pp. 53–4: perhaps Uccello's first work after Venice; 1974, pp. 17–18: Uccello, after Venice and before the *Hawkwood*), P. Dal Poggetto (1968, p. 144: in attributing it to the Prato Master, all the minor production mentioned by the sources must be withdrawn from the catalogue), L. Tongiorgi Tomasi (1971, pp. 87–90), while C. Volpe (1980, p. 12) considered the insistence on a Prato Master an 'artificial problem', reaffirming Uccello's paternity, and dating it before the *Hawkwood*. F. Zeri (1983, p. 554) accredited Uccello with different anonymous compositions at Quarate, Prato and Karlsruhe. The attribution to Uccello (as a relatively early work) was taken up by A. Padoa Rizzo (1987, pp. 130–2), followed by M. C. Improta (1990, p. 72), L. Bellosi (1990, p. 21), A. Angelini (1990, p. 73) and E. Andreatta (in *L'Età di Masaccio*, 1990, p. 263), while E. Borsook (1980 [1960], pp. 79–84) attributed it once more to the Prato Master. C. Shell (1961, p. 206) tried to give substance to an unknown artist to whom he attributed the Prato cycle and Lippi's youthful work, including the fresco at the Carmine and the *Trivulzio Madonna*, but his attempts were not followed up.

The Prato cycle's DATING has also given rise to close debate. The nineteenth-century documents quoted earlier considered the frescoes as a Trecento work; Schmarsow (1893) was the first to change the dating to the Quattrocento when he proposed Domenico Veneziano. The different proposals can be summarized as follows: the 1430s for Ragghianti (1938); 1430–35 for Shell (1961) and Parronchi (1966); after 1432 and before 1435 for Padoa Rizzo (1987) and Improta (1990); *c.* 1433 for Bellosi (1990, p. 21: in any case before Andrea di Giusto's triptych dated 1437); 1433–4 approximately for Angelini (1990); *c.* 1435 for Parronchi (1974, p. 22) and Volpe (1980; p. 14); *c.* 1436 for Carli (1954, 1959); before 1438–9 (first phase) for Sindona (1957, p. 33; 1970, p. 73: he advances the hypothesis of a collaboration with Domenico Veneziano before Sant' Egidio); a little after 1436 for Andreatta (1990); 1435–40 for Berti (1961, p. 303), M. Boskovits (1970, pp. 38 ff.) and Tongiorgi Tomasi (1971); between 1436 and 1440 for Sindona (1970); about 1440 for Berti (1964) and Heydenreich (1972; 1974); about 1440–45 for Gioseffi (1958); 1442–4 for Sindona (1957); 1442–3 and the following years for Chastel (1983; 1984); before 1445 for Ragghianti (1946); *c.* 1445 for Pudelko (1932–4; 1935; 1936; 1939) and Longhi (1940; 1952); after 1445 for Salmi (1950) and for Bode (1897), Esher (1922) and Wackernagel (1938) who thought it might be a disciple of Domenico Veneziano; *c.* 1445–6 for Salmi (1934–5); towards 1446 for Giovannozzi (1934); between 1445 and 1447 for Wohl (1980); between 1443 and 1445 and 1450 for Borsook (1960; 1980); between 1443 and 1455 for Brandi (1980); and about and after 1450 for all those who think it is by a disciple of Uccello.

The debate remains open. However, we must initially emphasize the receptivity to the new Florentine language in the work at Prato cathedral, with the commissions given (in 1428) to Donatello and Michelozzo for the outside pulpit (work began in 1433), and where from 1434 work was directed by Maso di Bartolomeo. Cosimo de' Medici himself intervened to ensure that Donatello and Michelozzo respect the engagements they had undertaken with the Masters of Works of the Sacro Cingolo. Uccello could have been on the scaffolding of the Assunta chapel around 1434, afterwards preferring more stimulating opportunities in Florence, patronized by Cosimo (the first *Battles* project and the *Hawkwood*) in 1435 and 1436.

Andrea di Giusto's involvement seems to date from 1435, the year of his polyptych for the convent of San Bartolomeo della Sacca near Prato, which would perhaps have given him the opportunity to gain the confidence of the Prato patrons. The *Saint Francis* on the intrados clearly inspired the *Saint Francis* in Andrea di Giusto's polyptych at the Accademia, dated 1437, a convincing *ante quem* date. In the predella, *The Laying on of Hands in the Name of Saint John the Baptist* is a replica of Fra Angelico's famous little panel, while traditionalist borrowings prevailed at Prato, notably from Bicci di Lorenzo. The *Saint Paul* on the intrados (Padoa Rizzo, 1987, p. 130–32) seems to be derived from Fra Angelico's polyptych for the Strozzi in Santa Trinita, dating from *c.* 1432. The shape of Uccello's niches at Prato is similar to those on the pillar of the pulpit inside the cathedral, of uncertain attribution (Pasquino di Montepulciano?), recently given a dating of the 1430s (A. Natali in *L'Età di Masaccio*, 1990, p. 59). The allusion in the documents to work on the back wall (*c.* 1445–7), with the consequent displacement of the window, cannot be considered a firm chronological reference. It must be considered as a 'restoration' of a vaguely Albertian type, like the transformation of San Francesco de Rimini into the Tempio Malatestiano which affected the cathedral choir and made the window unharmonious. In any case, work in the seventeenth century altered the layout of the choir. E. Borsook (1980, pp. 80–83) suggested that the removal of the window (stained glass in 1407) in 1445 could have had something to do with work by a disciple of Uccello (the Prato Master), itself linked to the confirmation of the Roman relics of Saint Stephen in 1447. However, the cults of the relics of the Virgin of the Assumption – the Sacro Cingolo, or Holy Girdle – and of Saint Stephen preserved in the cathedral were already strongly rooted in the Prato region, and the initiative could well have been quite independent. In 1438, the Masters of Works ordered a bronze grill for the Sacro Cingolo chapel from Maso di Bartolomeo.

It is possible that underlying the strictly Florentine spirit of Prato cathedral's artistic renovation there was political calculation on the part of the Medici, perhaps connected to Donato de' Medici's episcopate in the diocese of Pistoia, to which the curacy of Prato was attached. There are several signs in favour of a dating of 1434–5 that destroy the theory of dependent connections with the cycle of the Virgin at Sant' Egidio, envisaged by Pudelko (1935, p. 126) and contested by Carli (1954; 1959, p. 22). The aspirations and certainly more limited inspiration of the *Birth of the Virgin* and the *Presentation* are quite different from Domenico Veneziano's significant efforts, while in the stories of Saint Stephen the painter's orientation towards experiment is accentuated. The *Birth* was painted in the lunette of the right wall (302 × 361 cm). There is no doubt that it was painted first, because the areas of painting achieved in one day (*giornata*) are very irregular, while in the following scenes the painter, unlike Andrea di Giusto, manages a remarkable simplification of his daily plan that in the lower part – the *Presentation* – has the greatest regularity.

The *Birth* is the most complex scene as regards perspective: the lines do not converge into a single vanishing point but space is solidly constructed, with refined details such as the foreshortening of the dishes carried by the servant girl with swaying hips (a Hispanic/Ghibertian touch) on the staircase (taken from the 'great drawing' and the '*foriture*' of the cloister at Santa Maria degli Angeli), or the servant on the right's round tray and carafes. Here we can see an attention to ambience which heralds Lippi in his *Corneto Madonna* (1437), a balance between a mastery of geometric forms and an 'intellectual' colour which preludes the 'bluish fields and red-coloured towns' of San Miniato, and diaphanous flesh tones obtained through a preparation described as *a verdaccio*. The recent restoration of the frescoes (G. Rosi, 1965–8), their detachment and transfer on to masonite, have meant that the sinopias could be recovered with the exception of those on the vaulting. Comparing the *Birth* with the sinopia shows variants: the woman with the tray and the disappearance of the child on the extreme right (Marchini, 1969, p. 100). The sinopia, which was first done in charcoal, then in sinoper – a red earth pigment – is less elaborate than the others, a further sign of its earlier date. (Marchini, 1969, p. 100, suggested that the *Disputation* was painted first.) The story below is the *Presentation of the Virgin* in rectangular form (335 × 420 cm.). Here the painter has introduced a notable softening and technical refinements: the sinopia is reduced to the minimum and in its stead is a large grid pattern which is partially painted. The perspective is done on top of the first coat; the principal lines were marked with string attached to nails which had been hammered in at the vanishing points. Certain elements reveal that the artist's system here

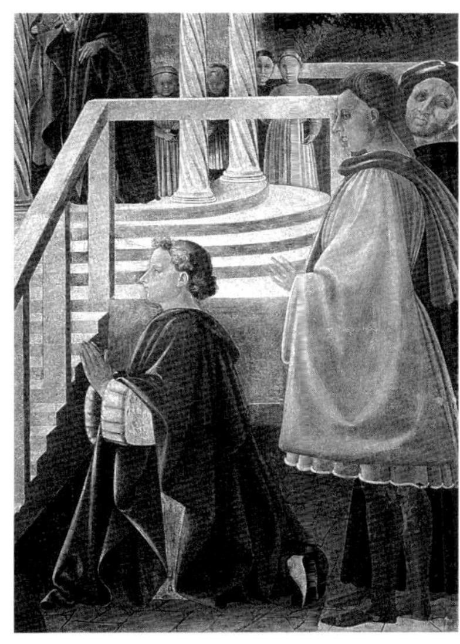

Detail of *The Presentation of the Virgin*. The figure on the right could be a self-portrait of Uccello.

is similar to that used on the *Hawkwood*: the drawing on paper is transferred to a larger scale (a device used in Ghiberti's workshop) and there has been an attempt at borrowing Masaccio's technique for the *Trinity*. For certain elements, such as the small twisted columns of the round temple, Uccello used a cartoon and *spolvero* (see footnote, p. 289).

The avant-garde character of the Prato frescoes is remarkable. Of particular note are the background landscape and the architecture of the temple-tabernacle, whose entablature of white-red-green is reminiscent of the colours of the towers of Jerusalem in the *Entry of Heraclius*, Agnolo Gaddi's fresco (*c.* 1395) at Prato cathedral. Perhaps this choice of colour was an attempt to harmonize the Quattrocento cycle with its illustrious predecessor in the Sacro Cingolo chapel. Sindona (1970, p. 83) supposed that the girl who is holding the red book between the columns of the Temple was by Uccello, who also reveals a preference for an accentuated green preparation for flesh tones. The steps of the building and the Virgin-child who is mounting them are the least happy moments in the spatial research of the entire scene. On the right is the kneeling donor and at the edge of the painting is probably the artist's self-portrait in the role of master of ceremonies (*festaiuolo*, drawing attention to the sacred picture (M. Baxandall, 1972, p. 75). This was a custom Alberti himself followed: 'In a story I like there to be someone who points things out and instructs us as to what is going on there' (*De Pictura*, Florence edn, 1950, p. 94).

The lower story, *The Marriage of the Virgin*, can be attributed entirely to Andrea di Giusto. On the opposite wall, the lunette bears *The Disputation of Saint Stephen*, in a balanced and simplified composition, dominated by the image of the saint. Behind him, high up in the middle ground, is a temple of 'Gothico-Brunelleschian' construction, perhaps there to form a link with the Ghibertian model of the lantern of Santa Maria del Fiore's cupola. The composition is entirely devoted to research into Albertian attitudes (*affectiones*) (*De Pictura*, 1435–6, Book II, ch. 43) and gives many examples. The fresco illustrates the differing reactions to the saint's sermon and '*Aliud enim est superbum pingere, aliud avarum, aliud ambitiosum, aliud prodigum*' (Bartolomeo Fazio, *De viris illustribus*, Rome, Biblioteca Nazionale Centrale, ms. Vitt. Eman. 854, c. 22; in M. Baxandall, *Giotto and the Orators*, Oxford, 1971, p. 163). A. Parronchi (1964 [1957], p. 518) names the *Secretum Secretorum* or the pseudo-Aristotelian *Physiognomica* as Uccello's probable sources of research into physiognomy. Starnina had already indulged in this tendency and it was probably elaborated by Uccello during his time spent with Ghiberti. The sinopia reveals several variants: the image of the saint was originally less isolated. The sequence of *giornate* appears more regular, and we must emphasize the striving towards a monumental quality in the figures.

The scene below this is *The Stoning of Saint Stephen*. The first three large *giornate* (the town in the background) are surely attributable to Uccello, for Andrea di Giusto worked in a more fragmented, irregular manner and his *giornate* are more numerous. The gateway in the form of a tower bears the emblem of Jerusalem, thus individualizing a city whose 'modern' architecture was inspired by the Old Sacristy of San Lorenzo and perhaps too by the plan for the Pazzi chapel. It is a rare example of an open-mindedness towards Brunelleschi. Marchini (1969, p. 118) pointed out similarities with the marine landscape in the Karlsruhe *Adoration* (with echoes of Lorenzo Monaco), while the series of crowns in the sky, symbols of martyrdom, had already been used as emblems by Palla Strozzi. The sinopia is entirely by Uccello. It shows a part of the basic grid (only the vertical lines) allowing us to glimpse his technique as he worked first on the background, reserving the addition of parts lower down for himself, with other drawings transferred as he went along, using the grid. The confident spatial composition of the characters' lower limbs (Marchini, 1969, p. 130) totally disappears in Andrea di Giusto's uncertain execution, as can be seen in the lower scenes on the two opposite walls, *The Marriage of the Virgin*, and *The Discovery of the Bodies of Saint Stephen and Saint Laurence*. Andrea di Giusto's death (1450) is obviously a *terminus ante quem*, but he could have worked after Uccello from as early as 1435–6.

Equal attention should be given to the decorative motifs on the borders, whose Ghibertian influence has been emphasized (Borsook, 1980, p. 83, n. 10). The heads in the medallions are vivacious and characteristic and some can be found again in the large compositions. *Spolvero* was also used for the borders, and, in one case, the pattern has been made over the entire surface of the vaulting. However, the attribution of the *Virtues* to Uccello (one of which, *Charity*, has no sinopia) appears less clear and convincing. It seems more likely that it was an artist linked to Fra Angelico in anticipation of the direction the Prato patrons would take in 1452, when they thought of the Dominican painter for the major chapel, which ultimately Lippi would paint (Fra Angelico was in Rome). We know that even before Andrea di Giusto arrived, Uccello was not working alone. The Prato Master was invented because of the difficulty in reconciling the frescoes – for various reasons dated *c.* 1445 – with Uccello's style of 1443 seen on the clock at Santa Maria del Fiore. Other factors come into play: the firmly rooted axiom of Uccello's 'integral perspective' and the consequent difficulty in attributing work of a more liberal invention to him, which different disciples and his *alter ego* would inherit. The rebuilding of the window in 1445 is not a *terminus post quem*. On the contrary, it could even be taken to mark the end of the work: once the walls were uncovered and scaffolding dismantled, people could have noticed problems of lighting, leaks or other things.

This is a cycle whose uneven but remarkable quality has – with rare exceptions – been underestimated, in particular because of the controversies over attribution. Only recently have critics recognized Uccello's paternity and the importance of the cycle. The problem of the chronology have been set out more correctly, with a relatively early dating, probably towards 1434–45 and perhaps even a little earlier. The *Birth of the Virgin* after its resotration in 1965–8 was part of the travelling exhibition *The Great Age of Fresco* (1968–9). An earlier restoration was done by Pietro Pezzati in 1880–81. An exhibition on the resotrations, detached frescoes and corresponding sinopias took place in Prato in 1969 (Palazzo Pretorio). The sinopias were then put in a museum in the convent of San Domenico at Prato. The frescoes, which had been transferred on to masonite, were put back *in situ*. The current nomenclature of 'Bocchineri' for the chapel is inappropriate, since it refers to a later patronage. Marchini's hypothesis (1969, p. 52) in favour of a commission from the Zuccherli family has not been followed up, and the appelation 'cappella dell' Assunta' (the 1435 dedication) is preferable.

The Blessed Jacopone da Todi (181 × 59 cm.) is a significant and unique fragment of the decoration of the Assunta chapel which has not been returned to the walls of Prato cathedral: it is now in the museum of the Opera del Duomo at Prato. Discovered in 1870 on the back wall to the right of the window behind a Baroque altar, it was detached – on that occasion the sinopia was lost – restored by Pezzati in 1871 and transferred on to canvas. It is difficult to evaluate because of numerous repaintings. The lifesize image on a base a Florentine *braccio* wide clearly possesses the twice baked (*biscottate*) character of many heads in Uccello's cycle, and, more than anything else, reveals a remarkable awareness of perspective. The monumental ascetic character is seen from below and we can (Marchini 1969, p. 116; Berti, *L'Età di Masaccio*, 1990, p. 218) detect an echo of a lost fresco by Masaccio, the *Saint Ivo* of the Badia in Florence.

The history of the ATTRIBUTION has seen the same development as the rest of the cycle, inclining towards the possible intervention of an assistant. Nevertheless, here is a painting of great importance, which seems to herald the perspectival construction of the *Hawkwood*: the Blessed Jacopone is seen from below, with a marked foreshortening, to the extent that one foot is hidden: a daring solution perhaps initiated by Masaccio, but pushed here to the extreme, but his bust is almost frontal. The knight and his stone tomb will be treated in the same way but using a different system of perspective. In the book the Blessed Jacopone holds, we can decipher the first two lines of one of his poems: 'KE FARAI FRATE JA[CO]PONE HOR SE GIUNTO AL PARA[G]ONE' ('What will you do Jacopone? Now you are put to the test'). The inscription beneath identifies the character: 'BEATO JACOPO DA TODI'. The niche in perspective appears slightly off-centre from a lateral viewpoint. The rear wall must therefore have had several rows of niches in *trompe-l'oeil* with saints and the blessed, probably Franciscan and Dominican, in view of the founding saints on the intrados.

The fresco, which was detached and transferred to canvas, was shown in the exhibition *L'Età di Masaccio* (Florence, Palazzo Vecchio, 1990). The *Guido di Prato* of 1880 records that the fresco was found on the right side of the window. It could therefore have been part of the main wall, along with the *Assumption of the Virgin* (now lost) which gave its name to the chapel. Other than the iconographical rarity of Jacopone, it should be noted that he was not an official saint beatified by the Church: rather, the motivation for his cult seems to have come from Franciscan circles, probably those associated with the Osservanza (Saint Bernardino of Siena). Recently (A. Angelini, *Prospettiva*, 1991, pp. 49–53) the Prato cycle has been linked to Saint Bernardino's second visit to Prato and to the discovery at Todi of the remains of Jacopone. Both events occurred in 1433, an early date which argues in favour of an attribution to Uccello.

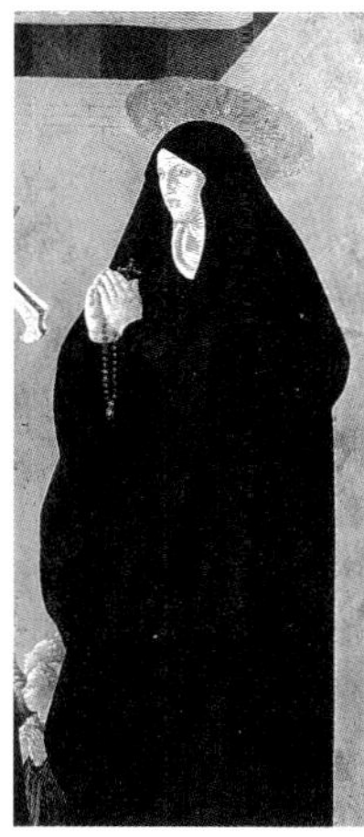

11. NUN-SAINT WITH TWO CHILDREN

Tempera on wood, fragment, 79 × 35 cm.
Formerly Florence, Contini-Bonacossi Collection.
About 1434–5

This is an unsigned, undocumented work: date, patrons, place of origin and historical background are all unknown. Only the truncated image of a nun-saint in prayer remains: this was a peripheral part of a central composition, with the praying figures of two small children in modern dress. This leads us to think that the patrons were either a private family or an institution providing care for children, such as the Spedale degli Innocenti (the Foundling Hospital). In its present state, we can only speculate – even the reconstruction of the composition is pure conjecture. M. Salmi (1938, p. 24) imagined that it was a fragment from a triptych of three saints, a proven Trecento formula. R. Longhi first drew attention to the work (1928, p. 44); he attributed it to Giovanni di Francesco but gave it back to Uccello in 1940. He identified the saint with Saint Scolastica (therefore from a Benedictine background); if this is accurate, there may be a connection with Scolastica Rondinelli, abbess of the Murate (Immured), who in 1449 was godmother to Lorenzo the Magnificent.

However, there are several elements that make a Dominican background more likely. This is reinforced by the depiction of the rosary (the Dominican Pius V would make the cult official) with perhaps Saint Peter Martyr in the centre of the composition, with his coat hem just visible and the handle (?) of what perhaps was the great knife, symbol of his martyrdom, above his head. A possibility would be the female Dominican convent of Santa Scolastica, which Julius II suppressed in 1553, the nuns being transferred to San Felice in Piazza (L. Meoni, 1989, 2, p. 27), a convent for which Fra Angelico painted his early triptych of *Saint Peter Martyr* (*c.* 1428–9 or perhaps earlier). Vasari had seen the triptych, which showed strong influences of Masaccio and Gentile, at San Felice (it is now in the Museo di San Marco). A number of indicators, such as Rosello di Jacopo Franchi's and Ventura di Moro's Bigallo cycle of 1446, confirm that the cult of the Dominican saint was particularly active in Florence. As to the PATRON, Sebastiano Benitendi – a Dominican of Santa Maria Novella at the time when Uccello was painting the *Stories of Noah* – might be a possibility: he commissioned Fra Angelico's *Lamentation* *c.* 1440 (Museo di San Marco), with an iconographical source drawn from Lorenzetti, a 'Ghibertian' choice. Benitendi, who was said to have among his ancestors the blessed Villana delle Botti, a Dominican nun who died *c.* 1360, could have had the prestigious Villana depicted as a saint, or could even (since he had been a Benedictine before entering the Dominican order) have set Saint Scolastica (if we accept Longhi) next to Saint Peter Martyr.

This is a painting of extreme formal refinement and intellectual mastery of an advanced kind: the panel marks the moment when Uccello's painting was at its closest to Fra Angelico's. This is not just a question of having distant sources such as Starnina or Lorenzo Monaco in common, for from then on the painter-monk had also been won over by Masaccio's modernity and in a more direct way than Uccello. Here, Uccello goes beyond the homage to Fra Angelico that we have already seen in the Quarate predella: he is clearly going back to his sources. He has grasped Masaccio's sense of monumentality in the grave, noble, unornamented profile of the nun, and also the vibrations of Masolino's blending of colour (after Starnina?): Uccello knew how to analyse and assess the merits of the Brancacci chapel masters. He could see that Masaccio's *Trinity* developed the problem of the relationship between figure and space his *Nun-Saint* is successor to Masaccio's monumental *Madonna*. C. L. Ragghianti (1977, p. 12) noted the use of the foreshortened halo as a spatial 'reference' in accordance with Alberti's definition. Uccello also perceived that in Florence, in the middle of the 1430s, neither Masaccio nor Masolino represented the limits, for it was the time of Fra Angelico's and Filippo Lippi's irresistible official débuts. He preferred the more atmospheric Masaccio, as could be seen at San Niccolò in the *Annunciation* (now lost, but described by Vasari). But even while he openly flaunted his adherence to figurative humanism, for which Brunelleschi was the standard-bearer, we can discern a formal distancing as he became more and more engrossed in his own reveries and involved in resisting the spread of 'Lippism', which, during the 1450s, would finally stifle some of the best artists, among them Giovanni di Francesco. This refined, intimist panel with its pinks and browns has no equal in the Florentine Quattrocento; it is Uccello's powerful hallmark and we can already see elements that Domenico Veneziano would borrow: those pale pinks come from immersion in natural light. The idea for this pink was possibly prompted by Uccello's memory of the pink woollen cloth used on pontifical feast days and supplied to the Curia by Florentine merchants, and perhaps by Pope Eugenius IV's presence at Santa Maria Novella. Just as remarkable is the *trompe-l'oeil* frieze which stands out from the upper frame and is picked out in two different browns: a clever inventiveness that has not been compromised by the painting's theoretical commitment.

Since Longhi's ATTRIBUTION to Giovanni di Francesco the Master of the Carrand Triptych, critics have generally favoured Uccello, who had already been proposed by V. Giovannozzi (1934, p. 358), followed by G. Pudelko (1936, pp. 128, 133 and 136, with doubts), M. Salmi (1938, p. 24), R. Longhi (1952, p. 10), E. Carli (1954; 1959, pp. 21, 22 and 57), E. Sindona (1957, pp. 59–60; 1970, p. 67), D. Gioseffi (1958, p. 137), P. D'Ancona (1959, pp. 12–13), C. Berti (1961, p. 300; 1964, n.p., who considered it a 'minor production'), A. Parronchi (1963, col. 467; 1974, p. 89), L. Tongiorgi Tomasi (1971, pp. 91–2), C. L. Ragghianti (1977, p. 12) and A. Angelini (1990, p. 73). B. Berenson (1963, 5, p. 88; previously 1932, p. 582; 1936, p. 500, when he had removed it from Uccello's catalogue) came out in favour of Giovanni di Francesco, while W. Boeck (1939, pp. 119–20) and R. Oertel (1937–40) chose the Chiostro degli Aranci Master (Florence, Badia) and J. Pope-Hennessy inserted it into his Prato Master's catalogue (1950; 1969, pp. 165–6).

The DATING is equally contentious and so is the scope for comparisons: Angelini favoured 1434–5; D'Ancona *c.* 1435; Carli, Parronchi (1963) and Ragghianti (1977) 1440; Salmi (1938) 1443; before 1443 for Berti (1961); between 1440 and *c.* 1445 for Tongiorgi Tomasi (1971); *c.* 1443–5 for Gioseffi; about 1445 for Longhi (1928) and Sindona (1957) while Pope-Hennessy favoured the decade from 1445 to 1455. The work is thus narrowed down to within more or less a decade, like the Dublin *Madonna and Child* which is not chronologically close to this painting (Sindona, 1970, p. 67). The *Madonna* presents a coherent solution in a 'modern' perspective but is already veering towards Donatello. The Contini *Nun-Saint* looks towards Masaccio but its true reference is Fra Angelico, with whom Uccello vied in a subtle, courteous polemic. The beginning of the 1430s was a moment of delicate balance for Uccello, which would not be repeated; he was revising his bearings and drawing on the same sources as Fra Angelico in order to achieve a modern religious paintings. After his work on the Quarate retable (?), which we can judge only by the predella, Uccello produced an admirable work, full of movement and the fruit of the feverish researches he undertook directly after his return to Florence.

Until now the *Nun-Saint* has been undervalued by critics, not so much because of its fragmentary state or its uncertain historical background or because of doubts as to its authenticity, but rather because of its isolated position within the catalogue. Its fate among the critics is to be linked with the Dublin *Madonna* – in this case the comparison is pertinent – for although it is generally associated with it, it is in fact representative of a different period. Uccello's stylistic journey was never as uncertain or contradictory as we might think and the time has come to stop feeding his contentious *alter ego*. Rather we should be considering this work as proof of a process of elaboration in his mature period, a process triggered by his attempt to recover bearings he probably felt he had lost during his time in Venice. Thus his style now became free of earlier Hispano-Ghibertian influences and in this phase which is marked by the *Hawkwood*'s humanism, Uccello can certainly be seen as having links with Brunelleschi's group. It was perhaps a question of professional opportunity which, towards the middle of the 1430s, decisively changed the direction of Uccello's research. On the one hand, there were the opportunities offered by a different generation of Florentine painters and the chain reactions triggered by the explosion of Masaccio's comet; on the other the uncertainties and interminable meetings of the Duomo's Office of Works council who were prevaricating on the mosaics and the stained-glass windows for the cupola's drum, abandoning the first and delaying the second for about a decade.

The stylistic evidence and the interpretation of Uccello's progress which we propose here suggests the *Nun-Saint* in the Contini Collection could be dated at 1434–5. This was a time marked by Uccello's intense activity and professional maturity, which would enable him to survive the great changes in the political system of 1433–4 when the disbandment of the Albizzi's oligarchic regime and Cosimo de' Medici's accession to power affected many earlier patrons.

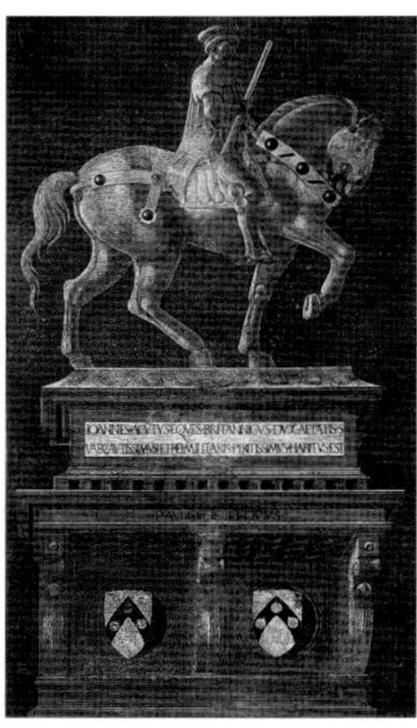

12. EQUESTRIAN MONUMENT TO SIR JOHN HAWKWOOD (GIOVANNI ACUTO)

Fresco, 820 × 515 cm.
Florence, Santa Maria del Fiore.
1436

Giovanni Acuto was the italianized name of the English *condottiere* John Hawkwood, in regular service as a war captain with the Signoria in Florence from 1377. After fighting in the Hundred Years' War, he settled in Italy with his famous company of mercenaries. The humanist Coluccio Salutati had persuaded Florence to secure his services, which John Hawkwood provided professionally and consistently for almost eighteen years until his death on 17 March 1394. For Florence, he became a kind of guarantor of institutions, probably the oldest example of a political *condottiere*. He was still alive when the Signoria, at Salutati's suggestion, decided to honour him with an equestrian monument in the cathedral, an act without precedent for a living person. This was on 22 August 1393 (ASF, Commissions, 82, c. 211; Gaye, 1839, I, p. 536; Poggi, 1933, p. 330). In December 1395 the painters Agnolo Gaddi and Giuliano d'Arrigo (the mysterious Pesello) were awarded the commission for the monument. It was to be part painted, part in relief, in honour of Hawkwood and his predecessor Pietro Farnese who had died in 1363 (Poggi, 1933, p. 332–3; B. Cole, 1977, p. 66, doc. 30). A document dated 16 June 1396 testifies that Gaddi's fresco, which replaced an earlier project for a statue, was in place at that time, for it mentioned a window in the nave of the Duomo which was situated '*iuxta figuras domini Johannis Aghuti*' (Cole, 1977, p. 70). Thirty years later, Gaddi's fresco must have been damaged, possibly from water leaking through the window, for the project was taken up again by the Office of Works and the Arte della Lana, under Albizzi's declining regime (Poggi, 1933, p. 333; Boeck, 1939, p. 98). A competition was organized so that 'anyone who wished to provide either a model or a drawing should submit it to the Purveyor, and the Masters of Works will assess who will best execute the work' (Archives of the Operai of Santa Maria del Fiore, Vol. P.Q., c. 25; Poggi, 1933, p. 333; Boeck, 1939, p. 98). This was on 13 July 1433, but we do not know if Uccello was one of the artists who presented plans or models. According to certain indirect information, it appears that he was hoping instead for the commission for the cartoons for the stained-glass windows. But here history becomes obscure. A number of changes occurred. First, the political scene had radically changed, with the downfall of the Albizzi government and the consolidation of Cosimo de' Medici's, who had returned from exile in 1434. Cosimo unexpectedly relaunched the project, perhaps secretly intending to celebrate his friend Tolentino, who had died in 1435, in like manner. On 18 March 1436, the Office of Works decided that '*rificiatur figura domini Johannis Hauto eo modo et forma prut alias fuit picta*' (Archives of the Operai of Santa Maria del Fiore, *Deliberazioni 1425–1436*, c. 253v; Vasari-Milanesi, II, 1878, p. 212 n.; Poggi, 1933, p. 333; Boeck, 1939, p. 98). The document leaves us to understand – unfortunately not in the clearest of terms – that it had simply been decided to renovate the already existing fresco: the limitations and methods of implementation were not precise. Events now progressed rapidly, undoubtedly under pressure from the Medici: on 26 May, the Masters of the Office of Works: '*deliberaverunt quod fiat sepultura domini Johannis Hauto prout fuit ordinatum per consilia oportuna populi et communis Florentie*' (ibid., c. 254; Vasari-Milanesi, II, 1878, p. 212; Poggi, 1933, p. 333; Boeck, 1939, p. 98). If these additional deliberations were necessary, it was probably because they were veering towards a more complex painted monument – not a *figura* but a *sepultura* – and that the plan for a simple restoration of Gaddi's fresco had been discarded.

Uccello now entered the scene in a procedure which does not seem to have copied the previous regime's competition in 1433. Cosimo probably intervented before the direct order was given to Uccello (see the entry for the *Battles*). On 30 May 1436, the Masters of the Office of Works '*conduxerunt Paulo Uccello ad pingendum dominum Johannem Hauto in facie ecclesie maioris ubi erat pittus prius dictus dominus Johannes de terra virdi et pro salario alias per eorum offitium ordinando*' ibid., c. 254; Vasari-Milanesi, II, 1878, p. 212 n.; Poggi, 1933, p. 333; Boeck, 1939, p. 99). The choice of terre-verte monochrome shows that the fresco was to imitate a bronze equestrian monument and not a marble one (rendered superfluous by the elimination of sculptured parts). Not a month passed without some disconcerting and unexpected event: the Office of Works deliberated on 28 June 1436: '*quod caput magister destrui faciat quemdam equum et personam domini Johannis Hauto factum per Paulum Uccello, quia non est pictus ut decet*' (ibid., c. 255 v; Vasari-Milanesi, II, 1878, p. 212 n.; Poggi, 1933, p. 333; Boeck, 1939, p. 99). For reasons that remain obscure, there was an order for the monument to be completely redone. Historians have pulled out all the stops to try to find reasons for such a draconian measure, but it must be pointed out that it was redone at the patrons' cost, not the painter's, who had not defaulted, since his commission was reconfirmed. It was therefore not a question of a deficiency on the painter's part but a fault in the organization and planning that the Office of Works acknowledged. On 6 July 1436, they decided that '*Paulus Uccello de novo pingat et figurat in viridi terra figuram domini Johannis et equi dicti domini Johannis pro salario et pretio alias stauendo*' (ibid., c. 255v; Vasari-Milanesi, II, 1878, p. 212 n.; Poggi, 1933, p. 333; Boeck, 1939, p. 99; also documents in G. Temple-Leader-G. Marcotti, *Giovanni Acuto*, Florence, 1889, p. 232; previously in F. Baldinucci, 1845 edn, I, p. 441). On 10 July, the Office of Works reviewed the situation with the painter and on 31 August, Francesco di Benedetto di Caroccio Strozzi and Simone di Nofri Bonaccorsi were asked to estimate Uccello's already completed work (*Deliberazioni 1436–1452*, c. 3; Vasari-Milanesi, II, 1878, p. 212 n.; Temple-Leader-Marcotti, 1889, p. 232; Poggi, 1933, p. 334; Boeck, 1939, p. 99). After so many delays, the whole matter was finished with remarkable speed in three or four months while the business of the stained glass for the drum of the cupola dragged on for a decade.

One question which remains is the link between Uccello and his fresco on the one hand and the two great masters of Santa Maria del Fiore, Brunelleschi and Ghiberti, on the other. Ghiberti, who was fighting for the invitation to tender for the sculptural decoration and for the cartoons for the stained glass, would have been delighted that one of his ex-apprentices had landed an important commission; but he probably did not take kindly to the commission for the stained-glass windows being postponed in favour of other decorative enterprises. Brunelleschi did not seem to be interested in the problem and was not opposed to Uccello, but he did not establish the close theoretical and practical relationship with him that marked Masaccio's *Trinity*. Nevertheless, in spite of a very different approach to perspective, if not to say an antithetic one, Uccello's monumental cenotaph had a 'modern' connotation which put him into the militant figurative humanist camp for some time, arousing both Donatello's and L. B. Alberti's admiration. Donatello would be remembered for his *Gattamelata* and it was perhaps for that reason that he asked Uccello to visit Padua; Alberti would praise such lay commemorative monuments inside sacred buildings (*De re aedificatoria*, Lib. VII, ch. XVII, 1966 edn, II, p. 658). On 30 August 1436, Pope Eugenius IV solemnly consecrated the Florentine cathedral: the following day, '*Pagholo di Dino degli uccegli*' was paid 54 lire in a final settlement of accounts, the 'price of his exertions for having twice painted Mr Giovanni Aghuto and his horse' (*Stanziamenti* CC, c. 135; Poggi, 1933, p. 334; Boeck, 1939, p. 100). Finally, on 17 December 1436, a decision was made to redo the inscriptions on the fresco '*eo modo et forma prout declarabitur per Bartolomeum ser Benedicti ser Landi Fortini*' (*Deliberazione 1436–1452*, c., 9 v.; Poggi, 1933, p. 334; Boeck, 1939, p. 100; for B. Fortini see Vespasiano da Bisticci, *Le Vite*, Florence edn, 1976, II, p. 409–13; N. Rubinstein, *The Government of Florence under the Medici*, Oxford, 1966, p. 18, n. 5; E. Borsook, 1982, p. 47).

Over the centuries the *Hawkwood* has undergone many restorations: in 1524 Lorenzo di Credi gave it the Renaissance framework with candelabras; in 1688 it was restored for the marriage of Ferdinand de' Medici and Violante of Bavaria (with 'a light coat, or in popular parlance, a reflourishment', F. Baldinucci, 1697; 1845 edn, I, p. 441); in 1842 it was restored by Giovanni Rizzoli, at which time it was detached, transferred to canvas, and installed on the inside of the façade of the Duomo (F. Fantozzi, 1842, p. 777: 'an operation which, several centuries before, would have been considered diabolical'). In 1947 it was moved to its present site – lower than its original position – and in 1953–4 it was taken down to be shown in the 1954 *Quattro Maestri* exhibition in Florence.

A very interesting drawing for the *Hawkwood* also exists (Uffizi, UF 31). This is on squared paper, an innovatory technique, probably learnt from Ghiberti's

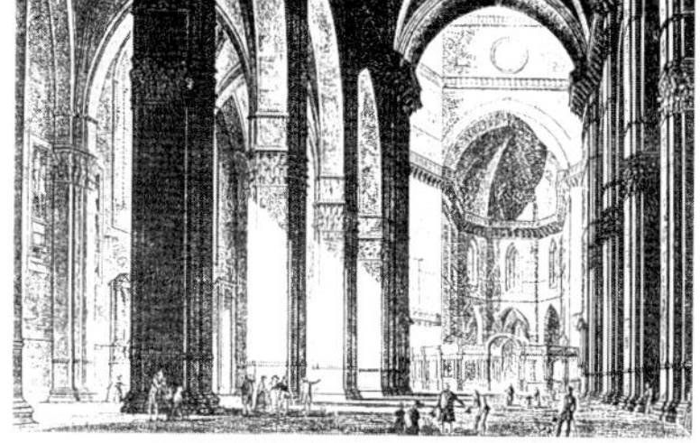

View of the interior of Santa Maria del Fiore, showing the original position of the *Hawkwood (far left)* before its move in 1842. Engraving by L. Rupp after a drawing by C. Giglio.

workshop (R. Krautheimer, 1956, pp. 248 and 250–51; E. Borsook, 1980, p. 49) and already used for Masaccio's *Trinity* (R. Oertel, 1937–40, p. 307). M. Salmi (1938, pp. 16–17) thought that this drawing related to the first version of the fresco, which was too clumsy, and that Uccello was asked to redo it to correct the 'erroneous' perspective of the whole; Salmi pointed out a link with the bronze horses of San Marco in Venice. M. Pittaluga (1946, pp. 10–11) also noted that 'the extolment of sculptural modelling' was more marked in the drawing which is confined to the upper part, while in the fresco it was less strong. K. Clark (1944, p. 55) observed the geometric perfection of the drawing, ignored by the succession of restorers down through the years and saw in it a remark-able example of the popularization of Brunelleschian perspective of *c.* 1435. R. Longhi (1947, p. 157, followed by E. Carli, 1954; 1959, pp. 54 and 57) thought the horse belonged to Uccello's mature years (*c.* 1455) and that he might have repainted it himself when Andrea del Castagno was painting his fresco for the Tolentino celebrations in 1456. On that occasion, Uccello's fresco was probably retouched, but Longhi's suggestion is unacceptable for it relies on too late a dating and on a limiting interpretation of Uccello.

The fresco (which without its sixteenth-century frame measures 732 × 404 cm.) bears two Latin inscriptions in epigraphic characters: 'IOANNES ACVTVS EQVES BRITANNICVS DUX AETATIS SUAE CAUTISSIMUS ET REI MILITARIS PERITISSIMVS HABITVS EST' and 'PAVLI VGIELLI OPVS'. There are significant differences in the A, the P and the breadth of the letters in the latter inscription: one explanation might be that it belongs to the second version; another, that the epitaph came from an external source, being dictated by the humanist Fortini, one of Rinaldo degli Albizzi's protégés. Uccello's signature was apparently illegible before 1524, for Francesco Albertini, in his *Memoriale* of 1510, talks of the 'terre-verte horse from Masaccio's hand' a significant error in attribution. The importance of the DOCUMENTS relating to Uccello's fresco is remarkable, particularly because of its positioning. It is mentioned in the *Libro di Antonio Billi* (1516, ed. C. Frey, 1892, pp. 24–5) and by the Anonimo Magliabechiano (*c.* 1546): 'At Santa Maria del Fiore he painted the figure of messer Giovanni Aguto, English captain of the Florentines, on horseback, in terre-verte' (ed. C. Frey, 1892, p. 99). Vasari (1550, pp. 255–6) mentions the work as 'a horse in terre-verte, which is considered very beautiful and is of an extraordinary size, on which he put his name in huge letters: "PAULI UCCELLI OPUS"'. In the second edition (1568, I, p. 272) the passage is repeated with significant additions: 'A horse in terre-verte, considered very beautiful, and of extraordinary size, and above it, the portrait of that captain in terre-verte chiaroscuro, placed in the middle of a wall of the church, in a frame ten *braccia* high. Paolo drew a great tomb in perspective, that appears to contain the body: and above it, he painted the portrait of the captain, in armour and on horseback. This painting was, and still is, considered as a masterpiece of the kind; and if Paolo had not shown the horse lifting both legs on the same side, a thing no horse could do without falling over (which occurred perhaps because he was not accustomed to ride and therefore was not as familiar with horses as he was with other animals), the work would be perfect.' Thus began the myth of the error in the horse's gait, an academic observation which gave rise to Baldinucci's even more academic defence (1697; 1845 edn, I, pp. 442–6). Vasari's objection was taken up in F. Bocchi-G. Cinelli's *Guida* (1677, pp. 50–51), while F. L. Del Migliore (1684, pp. 34–5) championed the artist's freedom and his 'great pictorial licence'. L. Lanzi (Florence edn, 1839, I, p. 48) recalled 'the portrait of Gio. Aguto on horseback, done in terre-verte by Paolo, of colossal proportions. This was perhaps the first time that painting was so daring, without being too daring.' F. Fantozzi's *Guida* (1842, pp. 349–50) repeated Vasari's passage but also mentioned Baldinucci's defence. Rizzoli's account of the restoration (p. 777) is very full; this was one of the earliest occasions when a fresco was detached successfully (by the *strappo* method). Before that, R. Borghini had been content to summarize the passage in the second edition of Vasari (1826 edn, II, pp. 58–9).

Modern criticism dwells much on the *Hawkwood*, since it is one of Uccello's rare documented, dated and signed works. C. Loeser (1898, p. 83) considered it a youthful work and cited Paolo Savelli's equestrian monument at the Frari in Venice as a late Trecento model. Even though P. Soupault (1929, p. 10) had remarked that Uccello was about forty years old at the time of the fresco and that it could not therefore really be considered a youthful work, Loeser's conjectures were upheld by G. Pudelko (1934, p. 232, n. 2) who offered as evidence the lack of unity between the powerful horse and the timid knight, a unity that he found more assured in Donatello's *Gattamelata*. He also insisted on the reference to the horses of San Marco in Venice, and did not think the perspectival construction of the horse very rigorous, since it is depicted as if seen at eye level, unlike the sarcophagus (p. 333). B. Berenson (*Drawings*, 1903, I, pp. 14–15), in his analysis of the Uffizi drawing, found it lacking any artistic interest, badly preserved and adding nothing to our knowledge of the fresco. His critical approach was contested by M. Marangoni (1919, pp. 37–42) for whom the drawing was more telling than the much amended fresco, and who stressed the geometricization of forms, especially in the horse 'drawn more by compass than freehand' (p. 40). J. Pope-Hennessy (1950, pp. 142–3; 1969, pp. 140–41) considered that the fresco had undergone less damage than Marangoni thought, apart from the knight's obliterated face. Meanwhile, the cleaning undertaken on the occasion of the *Quattro Maestri* exhibition in 1954 (cat. no. 26, pp. 63–4) gave rise to a more detailed examination of the fresco's state. A. Parronchi (1957; 1964, pp. 514–15) conjectured that the artist had used a popular version of Giordano Ruffo's thirteenth-century *Mascalcia Equorum* or similar treatises. He wondered if the decision to repaint the fresco were not connected 'to too literal and abstract an interpretation of those rules'. In his seminal essay of 1957 (p. 14), Parronchi stressed the spatial complexity of the fresco, with two different vanishing points corresponding to different viewpoints. W. and E. Paatz (1952, III, pp. 369, 419 and 491–3) collected the whole history surrounding the fresco. D. Gioseffi (1958, pp. 111–12) wondered why Vasari raised the problem of the horse's gait only for Uccello and not for Andrea del Castagno. He suggested that the repainting, limited to horse and knight, was intended to correct the effect, deemed unsuitable, of the excessive foreshortening of the horse, which appeared to be falling inward. This proposition was partly accepted by E.

Sindona (1972, pp. 28–9), who saw the fresco in its definitive version as a sort of compromise, referring to its 'execution which shows signs of technical fudging'. P. D'Ancona (1959, p. 9) was the first to suggest that the terre-verte was meant to imitate bronze. L. Berti (1961, p. 308) put forward the theory that the lost frieze, repainted by Lorenzo di Credi in the sixteenth century, was made up of foliage in the Gothic style, and thought that Uccello himself had instigated the repainting of the *Hawkwood*. According to Berti (1964, n.p.), the fresco was the 'second example of the new system of perspective in painting' following Masaccio's *Trinity*, but with 'more geometric abstraction'. R. Oertel (1937–40, pp. 303–6) was the first to point out that the Uffizi drawing 31 F represents the pasting together of five sections (fig. 34, p. 305) and closely analysed the sheet with the modifications made by Vasari who later owned the drawing. He emphasized the importance of the grid pattern, perhaps a modular layout of proportions mentioned by Ghiberti in his *Commentari*, I, p. 233, II, p. 38). A. Schmitt (1957–9, pp. 125–30) established the relation between the drawing and the execution of the fresco in its second and definitive version, emphasizing that the changes and repositioning in the recomposition of the cut and pasted sheet were perhaps the outcome of a later intervention, which had altered and corrected the Quattrocento design. He confirmed the innovative nature of the grid system (p. 130) and thought that the second version had been shown for to correct the original, over-accentuated foreshortening of the equestrian group (p. 129). H. E. Mittig (1969, pp. 235–9) considered that the lowered viewpoint, as in Masaccio's *Trinity*, originally involved the monument being positioned about two metres higher than its present location (since 1947) and that the lack of concordance in the perspective was intentional, like an allusion to two different spheres of existence, with no connection to the historical fact documented by the fresco. M. Meiss (*The Great Age of Fresco*, 1970, p. 124 and *Art Bulletin*, p. 231) developed Mittig's thesis and suggested an even higher original position, publishing a nineteenth-century engraving of the Duomo (by L. Rupp, before 1838–42) which provides a valuable picture of it. From this we see that the height would appear to have been about 820 cm. above the stone border of the wall, with the tops of the *Hawkwood* and the *Tolentino* aligned with the abaci of the Gothic capitals of the left-hand aisle. A. Parronchi (1974, pp. 31–2) and C. Volpe (1980, p. 14) returned to the problem of Uccello's repainting of the fresco and suggested that he was concerned only with colour, while the design remained the same, given the brevity of his intervention. C. Brandi (1980, pp. 189–91) once more promoted Longhi's hypothesis of Uccello repainting it after Andrea del Castagno had finished his *Tolentino*. He insisted on the 'light from behind, like Masaccio' (p. 190) increasing the volumes without resorting to illusionism, an example of 'anti-naturalist synthesis' which would influence Piero della Francesca. E. Borsook (1960; 1980, pp. 74–9) found a Florentine precedent in the Corsini cenotaph (*c.* 1422); she connected the inscription with Plutarch (*Life of Fabius Maximus*), stressed the connection between the humanist Fortini and the Albizzi family, took up the suggestion again that the terre-verte (malachite) was intended to be an imitation of bronze, as in Plutarch's text, and linked the fresco to the solemn consecration of the Duomo on 25 March 1436. Borsook went on to develop the argument in a well-documented essay (1982, pp. 44–51), establishing connections with Alberti's *De Pictura*, with Lapo di Castiglionchio's translation finished on 30 May 1436, the date of Uccello's commission), with the *De Militia*, and with Leonardo Bruni's eulogy of Hawkwood (1421, cf. H. Baron, *Leonardo Bruni Aretino*, Leipzig-Berlin, 1928, pp. 166–7), dedicated to Rinaldo degli Albizzi.

Hawkwood, a dead Englishman, became the symbol of impartiality: the loyalty of the mercenary militia was a recurring and pressing theme. The change from mock marble to mock bronze would, for Borsook (1982, p. 46) tie in with the literary model of Plutarch and not with models from imperial Rome. That the loyalty of the *condottiere* assured him his fame was the message that the Florentine republican regime wished to broadcast in the principal temple of the city. Already Giovanni di Pagolo Morelli's *Ricordi* (ed. V. Branca, Florence, 1956, p. 316) reported praise for the English *condottiere* and called for him to be included among the *Uomini Illustri* whom Salutati wished to represent at the Palazzo Vecchio: 'He was a very loyal and faithful man to our city, and as he was dead, he was painted in the Camera del Comune because of his fame.' The first monument was dedicated to Pietro Farnese, the conqueror of Pisa, who died in 1363, in a privileged position nearer the altar. The *Hawkwood* was supported by Cosimo when he was Gonfalonier of Justice, but his initiative was shelved during his exile until after Leonardo Bruni's public eulogy of Niccolò da Tolentino, delivered from the balcony of the Palazzo Vecchio (1433: *De Laudibus exercitii armorum*) after the victory at San Romano. Cosimo's interest in the enterprise must have been more active than is generally admitted: the very choice of painter can be explained by Uccello's previous links with the patrons in connection with the design (if not the execution) of the Tolentino *Battles* cycle. L. Boccia (1970, pp. 56–8) analysed the knight's armour and judged it archaic, dating it from 1430–35, close to the *Battles*, and pointing out that the hands had been restored. The fresco, transferred to masonite at a height of 324 cm. above the ground, had originally been 'in an eminent, high, honourable place' as the archives of the Duomo's Office of Works attest.

As a valuable chronological point of reference, *Hawkwood* is indisputable proof of the artist's maturity in 1436. The fact that he returned from Venice in 1430 loaded with international, ultra-Gothic inspiration, with influences from the north, Bohemia and Byzantium, practised in the ancient sciences of stained glass and mosaic, and that, in 1436, he produced a masterpiece of such resonance, should alert us to a high-level, precocious career. In close chronological succession, it encompassed the Bologna *Nativity* and the London *Battle*. Shortly before, Uccello may have done the fresco in the Spedale della Scala where two buildings in perspective are juxtaposed on a horizontal plane. Here, at Santa Maria del Fiore, they are arranged vertically, with different principles of construction. The sequence was rich in symbolic significance: the terrestrial dimension of the tomb, built 'physically' from the base upwards, to be seen off-centre from the floor of the nave, and the universal dimension, the eternity of fame, in the abstract knight in profile, without perspective, and cleverly composed, using the method of generative circles which are valid from all viewpoints.

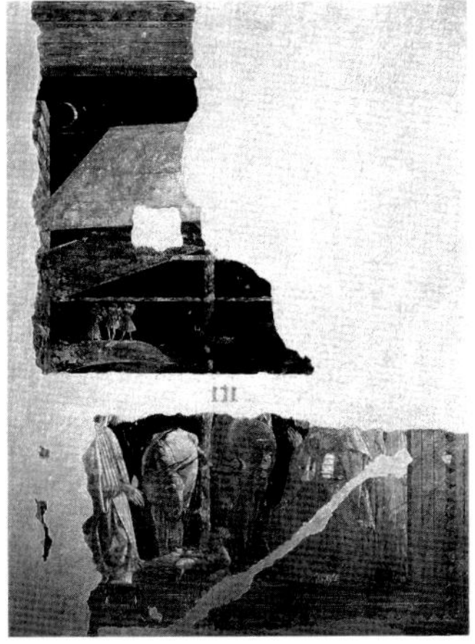

13. THE ADORATION OF THE CHILD (NATIVITY)

Fresco, present state 350 × 237 cm.
Bologna, San Martino Maggiore.
About 1435–7

The Bologna fresco is a recent addition to Uccello's catalogue. It is in the Carmelite church of San Martino Maggiore, but we do not know its original destination. It is neither dated, signed, nor documented, and the original circumstances surrounding its commissioning are unknown. We owe the ATTRIBUTION to Uccello, based on stylistic criteria, to C. Volpe (1980, pp. 3–28) in an exemplary essay that pieces together Uccello's youthful activity. Volpe dates it at 1437 (p. 24) for that year is incised in the top layer and is still visible today. The fresco, which had been recovered, was irreparably damaged when heating was recently installed in the sacristy; Volpe inclines towards an original size of around 270–288 cm., larger than its present dimensions. It is possible that, like the frescoes at Santa Trinita in Florence, it was framed with architechtonic elements which are now lost. The frescoes of Santa Maria Maggiore in Florence (see no. 2) are perhaps a direct precedent (the commissions may have had a common origin) but the date of Uccello's work (now lost) in the Carnesecchi chapel is also uncertain. The Bologna fresco reveals a high-level theoretical commitment in its construction of space, probably just after the *Hawkwood*. It was then that Uccello, in full intellectual maturity, arrived in Bologna, an important centre of Late Gothic, where Jacopo della Quercia had been working in 1425. These two would become the spearhead of modernism in the town, with their progression inhibited by the persistence of International Gothic, in a network of exchanges which gave greater importance to Venice and Milan. In Bologna, where Gothic masters such as Giovanni da Modena, Michele di Matteo and Pietro di Giovanni Lianori were successfully working, Uccello's great lesson went unheeded. M. Lucco's observations (in *La pittura in Italia*, ed. F. Zeri, 1987, I, p. 240) are pertinent: 'No one was in a position to understand his work for a long time, and it is for that reason that it has no immediate echoes: when the time finally arrived for its figurative layouts and the mental conventions it proposed, to enter into the public domain, it was in the curious position of no longer being fashionable without ever having truly been anyway.' The polyptych ordered by the Vivarini brothers through the humanist Pope Nicolas V (1450) – a crucial work – shows to what extent Uccello's work came too soon: they would have to await Marco Zoppo's return in 1461 and Piero della Francesca's mysterious but fundamental journey to Bologna (which Luca Pacioli witnessed) for the 'modern', humanist conception of figure representation to be accepted. The Uccellian parenthesis, during his years of feverish experimentation, had no significant consequences locally. People have tried to catch echoes of it in the unusual monumentality of figures in the anonymous frescoes in the choir of the Crucifix at Santo Stefano (R. Grandi, in *La pittura in Italia*, ed. F. Zeri, 1987, I, p. 225); unaware of the fresco at San Martino, R. Longhi (*Officina ferrarese*, 1934; 1956, p. 13) conjectured a brief stay by Uccello in Bologna, where he would have been influenced by the fresco of the *Inferno* by Giovanni da Modena in San Petronio. In reality, Uccello was an ill-understood, avant-garde artist in Bologna. That he was summoned to do this work can perhaps be explained by the connections within the Carmelite order who commissioned it, and who were probably in touch with the Florentine church of Santa Maria Maggiore where Uccello had already worked. C. Volpe pieces together the Bolognese artistic situation well ('Tre vetrate ferraresi e il Rinascimento a Bologna', in *Arte antica e moderna*, I, 1958, pp. 23–37; and in S. Bottari, *La pittura in Emilia nella prima metà del 400*, Bologna, 1958). The situation in Bologna seemed as closed as in Padua slightly less than a decade later, but in Padua, Uccello could lean on Donatello's support, a much stronger presence than Jacopo della Quercia in Bologna in 1425.

In Uccello's fresco (for its conservation and restoration, see R. D'Amico, *Conoscenza e Conservazione*, Bologna, 1981, pp. 51–61), framed by two very foreshortened buildings – only the one on the left is now visible, but was probably counterbalanced on the opposite side – we can see the simple wooden cabin of the Nativity, slightly from below, as the pergola in *The Drunkenness of Noah* would be later in the Chiostro Verde. It is the same cabin as in the Quarate predella, with the rustic wooden crossbeam holding up the roof. In spite of their mutilation, the kneeling figures have that grave monumentality rendered possible only through a direct knowledge of Masaccio's *Trinity*. The virtuoso perspective has resulted in the daring foreshortening of the donkey and ox, which is even more accentuated than in the Karlsruhe *Adoration*, in which Uccello took up the theme of light from a new perspectival axis. In the background, the three wise men search the night sky for the Star (which should be in the upper part on the right, a perhaps more decentralized position than in the Karlsruhe retable); this way of showing them echoes Gentile da Fabriano's splendid *Adoration of the Magi*, formerly in Santa Trinita (now in the Uffizi). It was also Gentile who, in his *Nativity* on the predella of the Strozzi retable, had introduced the motif of the donkey viewed frontally with accentuated foreshortening. The Bolognese fresco, detached and restored, 1978–9 (cf. Volpe, 1980, p. 7) was on the east wall of the present sacristy; it was transferred into the first chapel on the left, formerly patronized by the Marescotti family. Its striking modernity was originally attenuated by its being placed where it was not directly visible from the nave. In *c.* 1436, it constituted an important stage in Uccello's progress and indicated Masaccio's influence. The representation of the Child (Volpe, 1980, p. 21) seems to be paying homage to Masaccio and anticipates later works such as the Dublin *Madonna and Child*. Certain decorative details are reminiscent of the *Hawkwood*, such as the diamond-pointed frame that we find again in the lower part of the tomb in Santa Maria del Fiore (we might also query whether the original frame of the Florentine fresco was not similar to this Bolognese one). Volpe (1980, p. 22) notes 'a certain similarity to the Prato frescoes', above all in the figure of the Virgin 'lit with an intensity halfway between Masaccio and Piero'. In spite of its fragmented state, the Bolognese fresco appears to be the most important proof of Uccello's 'modernism' in his most experimental period, with a monumentalism in harmony with the dreamy depth and 'nocturnal' feeling of the countryside. This was the Uccello who undoubtedly left the deepest impression on Mantegna in Padua and whom in Bologna only Marco Zoppo could perhaps understand: Zoppo who, in the 1460s, was won over for good to the modernist cause through Piero della Francesca, while in Bologna Uccello was already forgotten. One thing is certain: the Bolognese fragment only confirms that Fra Angelico's sole, true representative, in post-Masaccio Florence, was the 'subtle and sophisticated' Uccello. All this highlights – along with the diamond-pointed frame in perspective in the mock splayed jambs – that the probable theme of this fresco was the Adoration of the Child, since the different characters are adoring the Child facing the Virgin, behind whom we can glimpse the remains of the face of a standing Saint Joseph.

We know absolutely nothing of the patron of such a modern work: it might have been a Florentine in exile after the Medici purge of 1434, or a rich Bolognese in the Carmelite convent. The reference to the magi's caravan, quite visible in the background, does not automatically signify that this was an *Adoration of the Magi*: the three monumental figures in front of the Holy Family are too mutilated to be identified, but two between them seem like female figures and one, kneeling, is holding a rosary in her hand. It is unlikely that this was the patron's family: these are figures who have too much 'importance' (thinking of Masaccio's *Trinity*), they are too revolutionary for the period and surroundings, unless we were compleltely to reconsider the question of Uccello's links with the Flemish world. They are probably saints (Jerome, Catherine of Siena, Mary Magdalen?) as in the lower part of the Karlsruhe *Adoration*.

The date 1437 was read as 1431 by A. Parronchi, (*Michelangelo*, 1981–2, pp. 25–6) and A. Angelini (*Prospettiva*, 1991, p. 53, n. 26), a reading which links the work to his years in Venice rather than to the *Hawkwood*, which in any case it precedes.

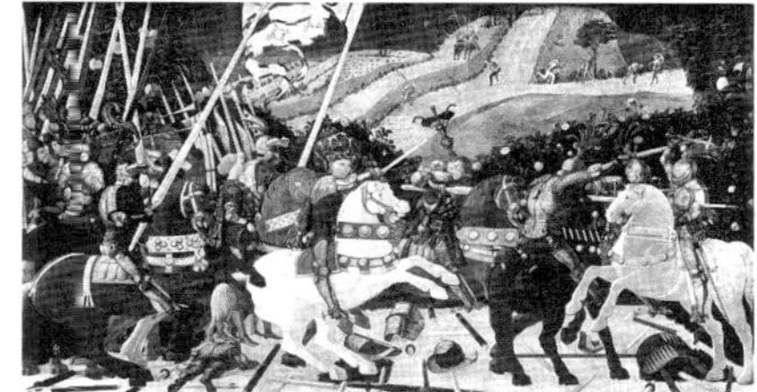

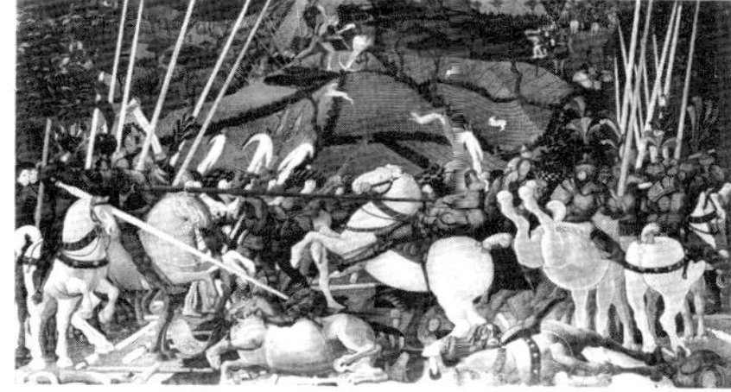

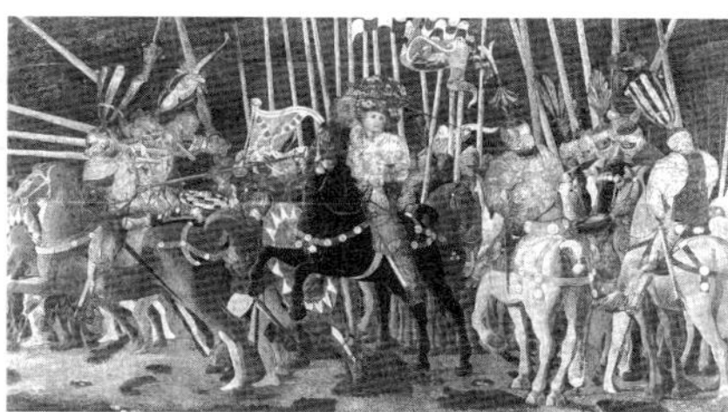

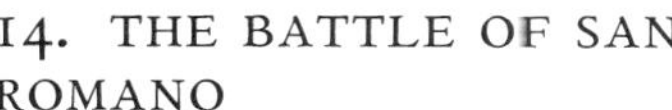

14. THE BATTLE OF SAN ROMANO

Tempera on wood.
(1) Niccolò da Tolentino at the Head of the Florentines, *181 × 320 cm. London, National Gallery, inv. no. 583.*
(2) Bernardino della Ciarda Unhorsed, *181 × 322 cm. Florence, Uffizi, inv. no. 52 (479).*
(3) The Counter-Attack on Micheletto da Cotignola, *180 × 316 cm. Paris, Louvre, inv. M.I. 469 (Ricci 1273; Hautecoeur 1273).*
About 1435–6 (1 and 2)
About 1440 (3)

This series of panels is perhaps Uccello's best-known work. He signed the central panel which is now in the Uffizi. The history of the enterprise is not documented and it can only be reconstructed in broad outline. The identification of the subject goes back to the Palazzo Medici inventory of 1492: 'In the great room on the ground floor, known as the *camera di Lorenzo* . . . six paintings framed in gold above the "*lettuccio*" [see note 45], 42 *braccia* long and three and a half *braccia* high, of which three are of the rout of San Romano, and one of battles and [of] dragons and lions and one of the story of Paris, by the hand of pagholo ucello, and one by the hand of franco di pesello depicting a hunt' (H. P. Horne, 1901, p. 137). In the *camera di Lorenzo* in the palace built by Michelozzo, the panels were framed and hung above the furniture in a room next to the garden (as the inventory of 1531 confirms, in W. A. Bulst, 1990, p. 109, n. 164); their total extent was 42 *braccia* (24.36 m.). The building of the palace, begun in 1444–6, was in greater part completed in 1452, a reason why the three panels are commonly dated in the 1460s, more or less contemporary with Andrea del Castagno's *Tolentino* in Santa Maria del Fiore (*c.* 1456). However, there are serious indicators in favour of a much earlier DATING. By resituating the *Battles* in the years between 1435 and 1440, we can put an end to Longhi's 'very late career' (*curricolo ritardatissimo*) and restore an avant-garde role to the work, even if it owes much to Gentile da Fabriano.

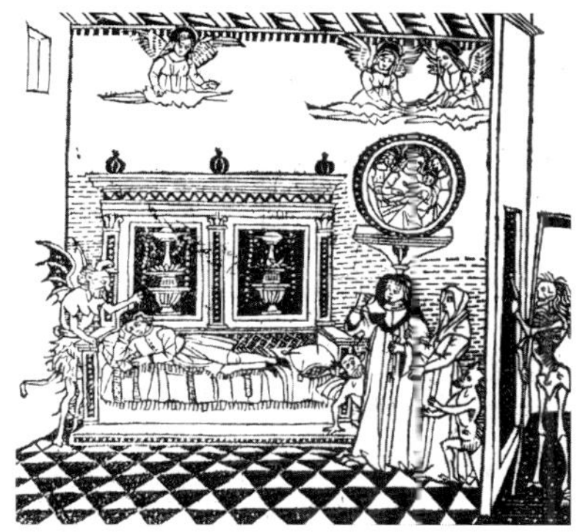

A *lettuccio*, woodcut from Savonarola's *Predica dell'arte del bene morire*, *c.* 1498.

We must therefore list the elements that will provide a better understanding of the 1430s in Florence (post-Masaccio).

(1) The stylistic elements, such as the rhythmic grouping of horses which recalls Ghiberti's *Stories of David* on his second doors (*c.* 1434–7), the vegetal decoration (as in the frames of the same doors), the landscape evoking Gentile da Fabriano (G. Pudelko, 1934, p. 242), the numerous echoes of Gentile and Pisanello (C. Loeser, 1898, pp. 83–94; G. Pudelko, 1934, p. 258; M. Salmi, 1938, p. 37): all these give weight to a chronology rather close to Gentile leaving Florence in 1425.

(2) The political significance of the battle depicted. The clash occurred one Sunday, on 1 June 1432, in the course of

the war between Florence and the Visconti of Milan and Siena, their ally. It developed from a strategy that can be pieced together as follows: (a) the majority of Sienese troops were surprised by Tolentino's advance troops (Tolentino was a captain in the pay of the Florentines); (b) having no cover, he launched recklessly into an attack (his courage and self-sacrifice were stressed later), in contrast to the doubtful reliability of the mercenaries; (c) the enemy, superior in strength, almost had the upper hand; (d) in the afternoon, other militia in Florence's pay arrived from the rear, led by Cotignola; (e) the clash was brief, the Sienese preferred to disengage themselves. The battle's outcome remained uncertain, but in what was a rather unfortunate war for Florence, it was already seen as a success. Giovanni Cavalcanti (1944 edn, pp. 246–7) spoke of a 'remote danger' and reproached Tolentino for his 'habitual' recklessness; Giovanni Rucellai (1960 edn, I, p. 47) admitted that, if the enemy had won, 'we would have been lost'. Florentine sources made it a great victory: Benedetto Dei (ASF, *Man. 119*, cc. 11–12) mentioned 10,000 '*signori e chondottieri*' captured from the enemy; Leonardo Bruni talked of a victory over Milan (1730 edn, RIS, XIX, 3, p. 451); Flavio Biondo da Forlì (1531 edn, p. 468) of the most important battle that had taken place in Tuscany; Poggio Bracciolini (1731 edn, RIS, XX, col. 378) of a violent clash, unheard of for that period; Matteo Palmieri (1906–15 edn, RIS, XXIV, I, pp. 135–6) exalted the great republican victory against tyranny; Neri di Gino Capponi (1729 edn, RIS, XVIII, col. 1177) celebrated Tolentino the victor. Sienese sources proclaimed victory for themselves too, or applauded the fact of having escaped the danger of encirclement: Orlando Malavolti (1599, III, c. 23v), Tommaso Fecini (1939 edn, RIS, XV, 2,2, p. 843), Guerriero da Gubbio (1732 edn, RIS, XXI, col. 768), Pietro Russio (1731 edn, RIS, XX, coll. 37–9) and the exiled Florentine Domenico di Lionardo Buoninsegni (1647 edn, p. 44). Leonardo Bruni disdainfully replied to the Sienese and with slightly suspect animosity the day after the event (L. Bruni's letter to Montepulciano, 2 June 1432, ASF, *Signori, Missive, Prima Cancelleria*, 33, cc. 72v–73v): as if the wound were still open. The humanists exalted the civic republican ideal but, in reality, the economic backing for the enterprise was entirely supplied by the Medici's bank. Later sources are silent or minimize the event, sometimes presented as an episode of chivalry with no loss of blood and of no great consequence (G. M. Mecatti, 1755, I, pp. 390–91: a victory that was not exploited by Florence, 1,500 cavalrymen captured, 160 important prisoners'; San Ammirato, II, 1641–7, a 'tournament', eight hours of battle without losses, as Machiavelli wrote on the Battle of Anghiari). Machiavelli did not mention the episode. Whatever happened, certain facts are irrefutable: the clash was fortuitous but the conditions were carefully prepared. It was one of those rare battles between mercenary troops that Tolentino had truly longed for. It was bloody; the Florentines had an absolute need of victory; the Medici were gambling as much on the economic plan as on the level of personal connections (Cosimo's and Tolentino's friendship, and his cousin Averardo for Cotignola). Victory was especially useful to Cosimo (Averardo died in 1434) to bolster his power in Florence on his return from exile, in the political vacuum created by Niccolò da Uzzano's death (1432) and after freeing himself of his principal opponents (1434). Cosimo had doubtlessly decided to celebrate the unique victory, or what was claimed as such, which was more decisive for him than for Florence in a war that was short on gratification for the town. Meanwhile in 1435, Tolentino was beaten in Lombardy by Piccinino and died in prison in Milan, perhaps from poison (P. Bracciolini, *His. Flor.*, 1476 edn, Bk. VI, ch. III). The solemn funeral was organized in Florence, in the presence of Pope Eugenius IV, and a monument was planned for the Duomo. At the same time, Cosimo ordered Uccello to paint a cycle celebrating the victory for a room in his palace (the Medici's 'Casa Vecchia', not Michelozzo's palace). It was used for everyday business matters relating to family and state and was consequently more open to the public than the future '*camera di Lorenzo*' in the new palace. Citizens and *clientes* could read an episode in the cycle that revealed Cosimo's concern for the fortunes of the state. The celebration of San Romano and Tolentino in particular had a further significance: Tolentino had been bound to Cosimo in friendship and had been prepared to intervene militarily when Cosimo was imprisoned in the Palazzo Vecchio (September 1433); it was Tolentino who had paid the fine so that imprisonment could be commuted to exile in Venice. It is hard to believe that Uccello's cycle could have been painted *c.* 1456 when the political message would have been stale, since other campaigns had taken place which made the memory of that June Sunday in 1432 pale into insignificance. In particular, the victory at Anghiari (1440), which was more clearcut, indeed dazzling, would have been more appropriate for a celebration. As a reward for the two captains, and better to gain their loyalty, the city organized solemn ceremonies awarding them honorary citizenship, ceremonies at which perhaps (like Tolentino's funeral) Uccello was present, drawing precise iconographic and heraldic elements from it. All this points to a commission of *c.* 1434–5, with a few years for the panels to be done, during which we could perhaps insert the *Hawkwood*, another enterprise encouraged by Cosimo (see no. 12). Cosimo did not hide his connections with the captain (*Ricordi*, in W. Roscoe, I, app. II). But who would have recommended Uccello to him? It is now difficult to say, but the two men must have already been in touch. Some further information has a bearing on the political climate on the eve of the campaign of 1432, at the moment when the Medici were making their undisguised entry into Florentine politics. One of the Balia Ten, with Cosimo, and probably his ally until the crisis of 1433–4, was Bartolomeo Peruzzi, who was one of the patrons of the *Four Elements* Uccello painted in the loggia of the Palazzo Peruzzi (see no. 7).

(3) If we examine the heraldic details and the appearance of the armour (L. Boccia, 1970, pp. 55–91), the date of the paintings is *c.* 1435 or shortly afterwards (ibid., pp. 61 and 68).

(4) The changes to the format of the original panels (see p. 214) are a definite indication of their adaptation to a new position. Uccello may not have known the precise measurements of Michelozzo's new palace. But why such radical and visible alterations to the panels? (cf. U. Baldini, 1954, pp. 221–40; M. Davies, 1961, pp. 525–31; P. Joannides, 1989, pp. 214–16). The panels were probably cut to fit the '*camera di Lorenzo*' only after 1452, when Cosimo moved to his new palace.

(5) Restoration work on the London panel (*Report 1962–4*, p. 85; A. Conti, in *Sul restauro*, 1988, p. 78) has revealed

damage to the sizing caused through being upside down over a long period. Even if it is difficult to establish from this the precise time it took place, the *Battles* would probably have been interfered with during the work on Michelozzo's palace, while waiting to be transferred there.

(6) From the little that is known of the Medici's 'Casa Vecchia' in Via Larga, it had a façade 32 m. long facing the street, a 'great hall', a 'beautiful room', among others, and interior decoration of great interest. Vasari records his memory of the 'jousts, tournaments, hunts and festivals' by Dello Delli for Lorenzo the Elder's chamber (who died in 1440): if the information is correct, the dating of that work can only be 1424 at the latest – Dello's exile – or between 1430 and 1433 – his return from exile and departure for Spain.

(7) The *Libro di Antonio Billi* mentions a '*spalliera* with animals' by Pesello, and Vasari recalls Bicci di Lorenzo's cycle of *Famous Men*: a natural context into which the *Battles* would seem to fit well, in a continuity of taste, that must be taken into consideration (on the 'Casa Vecchia', cf. H. Saalman-P. Mattox, 1965, pp. 329–45; D. Carl, in *Il Palazzo*, 1990, pp. 38–43). The discrepancy between the dimensions of the panels and those of the '*camera di Lorenzo*' in the new palace was raised by Joannides and detailed by W. A. Bulst (*Il Palazzo*, 1990, op. cit., pp. 98–124, particularly p. 110), while Baldini (1954, p. 230) mistook the room. It is unimaginable that a commission would fail to take its purpose into account.

(8) The Medici patrons' change in taste in the 1450s while Benozzo Gozzoli was working in the (new) Medici palace (chapel, 1459) and also the Pollaiuolo brothers (Great Hall, 1460) and Filippo Lippi was painting the retable of the chapel altar.

(9) Cosimo de' Medici's promotional activity on Uccello's behalf on the occasion of the *Hawkwood*, a pre-Medici enterprise, resumed when Cosimo was Gonfalonier of Justice and executed after his return from exile, the moment when the painter's name appears for the first time in the registers of the Office of Works at Santa Maria del Fiore.

(10) The fact, established many times, that the Louvre panel is later than the other two and reveals Uccello's closest affinity with Donatello, which would lead to the *Oriolo* (Clock) in 1443 and the journey to Padua in 1445. The humanity of the characters in the third of the *Battles* already presages, which should put it *c.* 1437–40.

(11) The fact that Uccello did not indulge in an archaeological reconstruction. The *Battles* are close in time to the event, they do not follow a literary text and the data are fairly precise because they bring together living protagonists and witnesses to the event.

(12) If the panels formed part of the context of the Tolentino celebrations of 1456, their profound divergence from the stylistic orientation made official in Castagno's fresco would become glaring. Why would Cosimo have had recourse to the painter of the *Hawkwood* – a work of twenty years earlier – and not to Castagno, now public interpreter of the *condottiere*'s fame?

(13) Even if we wanted to create a link between the *Battles* and the Tolentino celebrations at Santa Maria del Fiore, we must take into account that as early as 1435 – directly following the funeral celebrated by Pope Eugenius IV in the Duomo – the Office of Works had decided to erect an equestrian monument in his honour in the cathedral (M. Horster, 1955, p. 112), sculpted and not painted like the *Hawkwood*.

(14) The radical change in Florentine and Medician politics, from fighting the Visconti to a stable alliance with Milan, would make celebrating San Romano somewhat inappropriate, even if it were a matter of portraying Cosimo's rise to power.

(15) On the basis of all this, it was hardly an accident that, in his painstaking descriptions of the Palazzo Medici, on the occasion of Galeazzo Maria Sforza's visit in 1459, we find no mention of the *Battles* cycle, as if the Medici had intentionally not shown the room to their illustrious Milanese guest (R. Hatfield, 1970, pp. 232–49) because in this instance the cycle on the war against the Visconti would have proved a diplomatic gaffe.

(16) This is only a hypothesis but it is noteworthy that the centre of the lunettes, later cut, to give the new rectangular format, is asymmetric in relation to the lower rectangular part. This detail, confirmed by the upper corners being painted later, is repeated twice on the left (London and Paris) and once on the right (Florence). The Florentine panel is therefore the matching piece to the London one and the layout should be repeated for the Louvre panel. We can explain these anomalies of format by the original positioning between the structures of a house like the 'Casa Vecchia' which dated from the Trecento, with dimensions that were probably more irregular than those of the Michelozzo palace.

(17) The balls of the Medici coat-of-arms, which can be found in Gozzoli's frescoes and were already present at the beginning of the 1430s in Domenico Veneziano's famous tondo (F. Ames Lewis, 1979, p. 85), occur in the London and Florence panels, the oldest of the series.

(18) It would certainly seem strange, in this connection, that if the *Battles* were painted between 1435 and 1440, Domenico Veneziano did not mention Uccello in his famous letter to Piero de' Medici in 1438, a letter that was so well-informed on the artistic scene in Florence at the time. His silence could have been intentional, because when the shrewd Domenico mentioned Fra Angelico and Lippi, he was quick to add that they had a great deal of work, and therefore, *a contrario*, recognized in Uccello a dangerous rival. In any case, Domenico clearly showed that he aspired to a commission for a retable, while the *Battles* and the *Hawkwood* revealed a painter who was very specialized in 'profane' subjects.

(19) Echoes of a work by Sassetta, now in Melbourne, reveal a certain closeness between Uccello and the Sienese. F. Zeri's observation (1974, pp. 22–34) in which he saw an echo of Uccello's panels in Sassetta's *Heretic's Death at the Stake* (Melbourne, National Gallery of Victoria) is

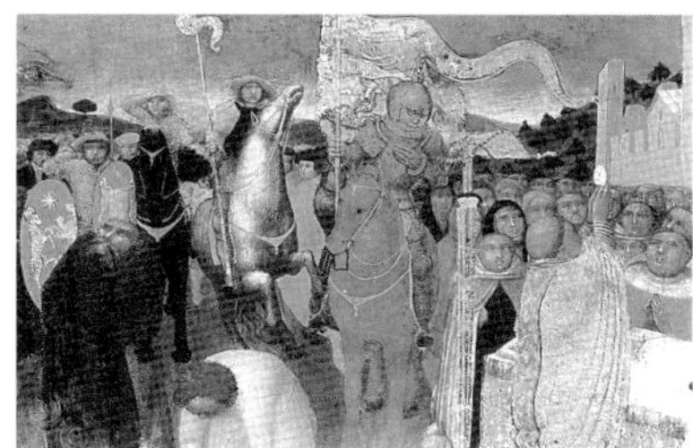

Sassetta, *A Heretic's Death at the Stake* (detail) *c.* 1425. Melbourne, National Gallery of Victoria.

more acceptable in an earlier chronology than the 1450s (which he admits). It is difficult to draw precise information from this suggestion, because of numerous uncertainties that stem from the recomposition and dating of Sassetta's polyptych, commissioned by the Arte della Lana. In the same way, the reference to the *Battles* put forward by B. B. Walsh (1979; 1981, p. 97) with regard to Bonaiuto di Giovanni's Knight at Santa Trinita (Compagni chapel, *c.* 1430–31) is fairly doubtful: a suggestion rejected by C. Frosinini, (*Rivista d'Arte*, 1986, p. 116, n. 40) which supports a dating that is too late for Uccello. R. Varese (1981, pp. 13–14) sees echoes of Salimbeni's frescoes at the oratory of San Giovanni in Urbino in the *Battles*: echoes we can admit as far as stylistic sources (Gentile?) go, but not for a post-1469 dating, when Uccello returned from Urbino.

(20) It might seem surprising (R. Starn-L. Partridge, 1984, p. 53) that Tolentino's emblems should be given greater weight than Florence's: but this confirms the emphasis voluntarily placed on the friendship between Niccolò and Cosimo. By insisting on Tolentino's importance in relation to Cotignola's decisive intervention, the cycle takes on precise connotations of propaganda, as far as Cosimo is concerned.

(21) This might go some way towards explaining Cosimo's intervention in the *Hawkwood*, which was the project of an earlier regime: but perhaps it was a sort of introductory test for the monument he envisaged for his friend Tolentino. He was probably already thinking about it in 1435, but he delayed the project, prudently waiting for the political tensions of 1433–4 to die down, as well as for the divergence of opinion on the *condottiere* who was not unanimously appreciated.

(22) In the Louvre panel, the motif of trumpets seems a direct echo of one of the panels on the gallery of Luca della Robbia's *cantoria* at Santa Maria del Fiore, commissioned *c.* 1431 and documented from 1434–5. This panel is dated 1434–7 (M. Lisner, 1960, pp. 8–11; J. Pope-Hennessy, 1980, pp. 226–8). The year 1437, roughly, could separate the painting of the two first *Battles* from the one in the Louvre which followed immediately afterwards.

(23) If all these considerations are founded, the *Battles* should have a date barely later than the Prato cycle. That Cosimo had an active role in its whole history still remains to be demonstrated, but a link can be established between him and the Master of Works of the Sacro Cingolo in Prato concerning the external pulpit at the cathedral: Cosimo interceded with his brother Giovanni de' Medici to make Donatello return from Rome (M. Lisner, *Münchner Jahrb. der bild. Kunst*, 1958–9, pp. 119–20). They were also probably in touch about Uccello. Donato de' Medici was bishop of Pistoia and Prato at the time and the most plausible chronology of Uccello's frescoes at Prato broadly coincides with Cosimo's Venetian exile. At the moment we lack a number of elements to complete the picture, but Cosimo's intervention in the cathedral's history at Prato is an acquired fact and could be a clue to a subsequent contract with Uccello; this began when he was replaced at Prato by Andrea di Giusto (*c.* 1435, see no. 10) and was almost immediately granted the commission for the *Battles* for the old Medici palace.

(24) The battle of San Romano was not a simple, bloodless spectacle, lasting eight hours. On the contrary, it was singularly violent and lasted only three hours. This does not make M. L. Cristiani-Testi's hypothesis (1981, pp. 3–47) very convincing. His argument is that the painting first show a morning light, then an afternoon one and then dusk to signify the length of the battle. This would explain why Uccello used symbols of death, among them grenades, especially in the London panel. When the paintings were later altered in the fifteenth century – the top corners were extended where the corbels of the room in the 'Casa Vecchia' had formerly been – the orange colours predominate; the symbolic motif is not repeated. It is just as if the battles that had occurred since and the spread of artillery had dimmed the violence of the clash of 1432. These additions to the corners have been attributed to Uccello himself (A. Conti, op. cit., 1988, p. 78) but their mediocre rendering and the non-continuity of the symbols leads us to think more of his studio, if not Pesellino's.

(25) The unique, refined pictorial technique of the panels, with the *sangue di drago* glaze over layers of gold, the use of precious lacquers and varnishes made from resin and copper with a type of Venetian turpentine as binding medium (Conti, 1988, op. cit., p. 75, n. 103) are totally unusual in Florentine painting of this period. They reveal a remarkable sense of experimentation and are proof of a technical knowledge probably acquired during Uccello's time in Venice. On the other hand, the wide use of silver leaf, brushed over with varnish to give an effect of translucent enamel, corresponds to a different technique in the Trecento tradition and would be linked to his experience in Ghiberti's workshop. In one case as much as in the other, the dating is more probably in the 1430s than in the 1450s.

The panels' journey through history is only partially known. After their adaptation to the new site *c.* 1452, and not after 1457, the year of Pesellino's death, who had completed the ensemble with a *Hunt*, the panels were still in place at the time of the Medici's inventory in 1568 (ASF, *Guardaroba* 198, c. 26). In the sixteenth century they were restored – at least the Louvre panel was – and the silver leaf was replaced by tin leaf. When the Palazzo Medici was sold to the Riccardi in 1659, the panels left the place and were inventoried – still together – among goods belonging to Cardinal Carlo de' Medici's inheritance in 1666 (S. Meloni Trkulja, 1975, pp. 108–11). Between 1784 and 1787 two of the *Battles* were restored by Carlo Magni and one of them, numbered 642, entered into the Uffizi collection; the one that was signed by the painter was probably kept as an historic document. The two others were given up at an unspecified date, probably between 1787 and 1844. From the Giraldi collection they were sold to the antiquarians Baldi and Lombardi and then passed into the Campana collection in Rome. The Paris panel was bought in 1861 by the Musée Napoléon III (S. Cornu, 1862, n. 166) and went to the Louvre in 1863 (F. Reiset, 1863, n. 99). The London panel was bought by the National Gallery in 1867 from the Baldi-Lombardi Collection (M. Davies, 1961, p. 529).

The *Battles* were considered as youthful work by G. B. Cavalcaselle-J. A. Crowe (1911, ed. Langton-Douglas-De Nicola [1864], IV, pp. 109–11) who claimed that the paintings' subject was Malatesta's victory at Sant'Egidio in 1416. G. Milanesi (in *Vasari*, 1878, II, p. 214 n.) identified them with the four battles described by Vasari, which were formerly at the Casa Bartolini at Valfonda. H. P. Horne (1901, loc. cit.) was the first to describe their theme as the 'rout of San Romano', which figured in the Medici inventory of 1492. He put forward the hypothesis of a London-Paris-Florence sequence which was taken up by Cristiani-Testi (1981, loc. cit.) and proposed a dating (pp. 120–1) of between 1451 and 1457 (Pesellino's death). F. Antal (1925, pp. 8–14) also thought it a work of youth; R. van Marle (1928, X, p. 218) favoured a dating of 1456–60 and reversed the order of the panels. P. Soupault (1929, p. 14) returned to the identification of the *Battles* with those described by Vasari at the Casa Bartolini, although according to Vasari they were in terre-verte and heavily restored by Giuliano Bugiardini. G. Gronau (1932, p. 176) supported a dating close to Gozzoli's frescoes (1459), while M. Marangoni (1931–2, p. 346) thought the panels a mature work, but with a date near the event (1432), followed by M. Malkiel-Jirmounsky (1932, p. 64). B. Berenson (1932, p. 582; 1936, p. 500), J. von Schlosser (1933, p. 37: after the Green Cloister) and W. Paatz (1934, pp. 143–4: a humanist exhumation of paintings of Antiquity such as *Alexander's Victory on the Issos* in the Museo Nazionale in Naples) were inclined towards a late dating, as was G. Pudelko (1934, p. 249) who, however, (1936, p. 133) dated the Louvre panel at about 1445 (but in T. B., 1939, p. 525, the *Battles* were dated 1456–7). R. Longhi (1940, p. 179; 1952, p. 32, n. 8), believing Uccello to be a late developer as a painter, gave it a date of 1456 and rebuilt the composition from a basis of circles and their derivatives, evoking cubism. E. Somaré (1946, p. 37) put the panels a little earlier than Urbino and pointed out the grouped rhythms and the greatest unity in the Louvre panel. M. Pittaluga (1946, p. 9) gave 1456–9 as the date; E. Micheletti (1957, p. 7) 1457; E. Carli (1954, 1959, p. 40) 1456–60, at the same time as Castagno's *Tolentino*. For E. Sindona (1957, p. 61) it was a late work, just before the Oxford *Hunt*. P. Francastel (1957, p. 97, n. 44) connected the panels with jousting and tournaments rather than military tactics and emphasized the symbolic and spatial values of the works (p. 77) and the novelty of a single battlefield, while (p. 51) the shadows did not always coincide with the shapes nor with the lighting which was not provided by a unified source of light. If E. Micheletti (1956, p. 18) saw it as an affectionately ironical evocation of the world of chivalry, U. Baldini (1954, loc. cit.) tried to reconstruct the original context in Lorenzo's room, imagining a position where the Uffizi panel and the Louvre panel were at right angles, gives information on the cleaning of the Florentine panel for the *Quattro Maestri* exhibition. D. Gioseffi (1958, pp. 135–6) saw a link between the red and green horses and the *Flood* and the technique of the anaglyph; he spoke of 'totally indifferent colour' and 'plastically inert chiaroscuro' and dated the works at 1456 (p. 137), still identifying them as the Bartolini panels. He maintained there would not have been lunettes and the three panels would have been aligned on a single wall, cut down by about 30 cm. to fit Lorenzo's room. P. D'Ancona (1959, p. 18) dated the works after Padua, near the time of the *Flood*. Baldini's reconstitution was welcomed with reserve by M. Davies, with metric measurements (1961, pp. 525–31). A. Parronchi's hypothesis was that the panels were surmounted by lunettes on canvas, on which skies and standards were painted. He considered the London and Florence panels as 'obsessed' by the principle of composition by circles, pointing out that the foreshortened corpses could be seen as an anticipation of axonometry (p. 474). He noticed that the composition by circles was absent in the Louvre panel. He gave prominence to the 'anguishing light' obtained through the reflection of mirrors and armour painted in silver leaf, seeing a connection in it with theorem 3 of Book IV of Witelus's *Perspectiva* (every reflection weakens light and colours) and with theorem 60 of Book VIII (reflection in the air from mirrors which are not visible), an interesting but perhaps exaggerated attempt. The foreshortened horse which is kicking out would be *scalmaticus* according to Giordano Ruffo's (p. 516) source of the *Mascalcia Equorum*. Parronchi (1963, col. 468), like Horne, dated the *Battles* at 1455–60, a dating subsequently corrected to 1450 or later. L. Berti (1961, p. 303; 1964, unnumbered) linked the panels to the Tolentino celebrations of 1456. A. Chastel (1965–6, p. 375; 1983–4, p. 67) placed them between 1456 and 1460 or perhaps even later. G. C. Argan (1968, 2, pp. 186–7; 1988, 2, p. 189) agreed on the dating and wrote of an 'almost Socratic irony' in the intention of demonstrating how 'strange and incoherent appearances are when collected through empirical experience'; everything is revolved on the surface: light, colour, form, perspective, lines. J. Pope-Hennessy (1950; 1969, pp. 152–3) took account of the alterations made to the Paris panel (the first to be restored in modern times) and the Uffizi panel (1954); he considered that the three panels were not contemporaneous with other canvases in the '*camera di Lorenzo*' but he held to a late dating for the *Battles*, followed by Sindona (1970, p. 83) and F. Ames Lewis (1979, p. 72: the middle of the 1450s for the new Medici palace).

The question was reopened by L. Boccia (1970, loc. cit.) who, in analysing the knights' armour and the horses' harness, datable from before 1440–5, veered towards *c.* 1435 and gave the Medici's 'Casa Vecchia' as its destination. The silvering (p. 69) would imitate an effect that the armour of the period produced and among immediate precedents Boccia cited the armour of *Saint George* on the Gentile da Fabriano's polyptych in the Uffizi (p. 87, n. 13). A. Conti (1988, loc. cit., p. 77) agrees, while F. Hartt (1971, pp. 257–8) dated the panels at *c.* 1445 and Tongiorgi Tomasi (1971, p. 97) returned to a dating solidly anchored at 1456. For L. H. Heydenreich (1972–4, pp. 291–2) the date was 1456–60; among the reasons that would have inspired Uccello's technique he quoted Cosimo's desiderata, the marquetry and tapestry. For F. Zeri (1976; 1989, p. 7) the vision of the countryside was crushed in the 'capricious network of perspective'; he considered the panels as late works, near to the Urbino predella. L. Bellosi (*Storia dell'Arte italiana*, 4, 1980, p. 29) quoted the memory of Gentile da Fabriano's 'Gothic nocturnes'; C. Volpe (1980, p. 19) saw them as 'bloodless battles in a garden' with a date close to *c.* 1440 and the *Hawkwood*, and in any case not beyond 1443. C. Brandi (1980, pp. 203–5) wrote of the pictorial process that was the opposite of Donatello's plane (*stiacciato*) and a formal, not natural light, without shadow, without chiaroscuro, which could however be linked to the deterioration over the years and successive alterations. For Brandi the panels were a mature work and showed the 'abnormal, almost incomprehensible position' Uccello held in relation to his period, but also 'the most original interpretation of Masaccio's plasticity', this latter observation having taken on a special value, in its link with the 1430s. M. Wackernagel (1938; 1981, p. 165) dwells on Lorenzo's room in the Medici palace (height: 6.5 m.; dimensions: 9 × 10.5 m.), emphasizing the substantial size of the mural (including Pesellino's work) which measured about 25 m. M. Trionfi Honorati ('A proposito del "letuccio"', *Antichità viva*, 1981, 3, pp. 39–47) gave details on the Florentine Quattrocento chest with backboard (see note 45 for *lettuccio*) which in the layout of Lorenzo's room formed a unit with the *Battles* 'with a surrounding frame' (*chorniciatj atorno*). R. Starn and L. Partridge (1984, pp. 33–65) drew attention to the semi-public function of the panels, the importance of Cosimo's commission and Cotignola's role as Averardo de' Medici's confidant; they veered towards a probable dating of *c.* 1435, in hypothetical *rapport* with the public ceremonies of October–November 1432 when Florence made the two victorious (or reported as such) *condottieri* honorary citizens. The political significance of the three panels was emphasized by G. Griffiths (1978, pp. 313–16) who still dated them in the 1450s but correctly highlighted the personal connections between Cosimo and Tolentino. F. Zeri (1983, p. 554) dated the work 'not before 1450', while M. Baxandall (1972; 1985, p. 138) noted the calculated geometric ambiguity of Tolentino's cylindrical-annular-polygonal turban in the London panel painted in *sangue di drago* over gold leaf. W. Fontana (1986, p. 142) placed the paintings towards 1460, P. Adorno (1986, 2, p. 160) towards *c.* 1456. A De Marchi (in *Vasari*, ed. L. Bellosi, 1986, p. 238, n. 10) followed L. Boccia as regards the chronology, *c.* 1435–40. F. Petrucci (1987, I, p. 285) upheld the late dating and put the *Battles* on a parallel with Castagno's researches, while H. W. Janson (1962; 1986, p. 418) considered them contemporary with Piero della Francesca's at Arezzo. L. Berti (1988, p. 275) conjectured that the paintings' patron was Piero de' Medici, Cosimo's son, who, almost simultaneously, was encouraging the creation of the tabernacle in San Miniato (1447–8). P. Joannides (1989, pp. 214–16) reconsidered the transformations and combinations of the three panels and highlighted the differences in scale, measurements and composition of the Louvre panel; he rejected the *terminus post quem* of 1450–51, the date when the new palace was finished, stressing that the integration of the bottom left-hand corner (of about 90 cm.) into the Paris panel could not be linked to the presence of the door in the '*camera di Lorenzo*', for which (p. 215) the panels were not made. Following Davies (1961, p. 529), their original height from the ground was established at about 2 m. A. Conti (1988, pp. 74–111) accepted Boccia's conclusions on the early dating. A. Angelini (1990, p. 75) thinks the paintings were done slightly before 1440 and were destined for 'Cosimo's room' and, therefore, not for the Medici palace, on which work was not begun before 1444 after Cosimo Salviati's *Zibaldone* (BNF, *Magliabechiano*, XI, 42; cf. A. Warburg, 'Der Bau Beginn der Palazzo Medici', in *Gesammelte Schriften*, Berlin, 1932, pp. 166–8; M. Gerrara-P. Quinterio, *Michelozzo di Bartolomeo*, Florence, 1984, pp. 207–12).

The painter deliberately chose to present foreshortened elements which are not in harmony with the perspective of the whole, and lines which do not converge towards a vanishing point, in order to accentuate the dramatic character of the event. Leonardo put it well when he wrote in his *Trattato della pittura* (II, c. 59 v; quoted in Parronchi, 1957, rep. 1964, p. 352): 'The many foreshortenings and numerous bent forms ('*infiniti scorciati et piegamenti*') among the participants in such a mêlée, signify a very bestial madness.' In depicting this 'madness' with such sombre, rhythmic, chromatic and geometric beauty, Uccello created one of the most sublime, morally committed masterpieces of fifteenth-century European painting.

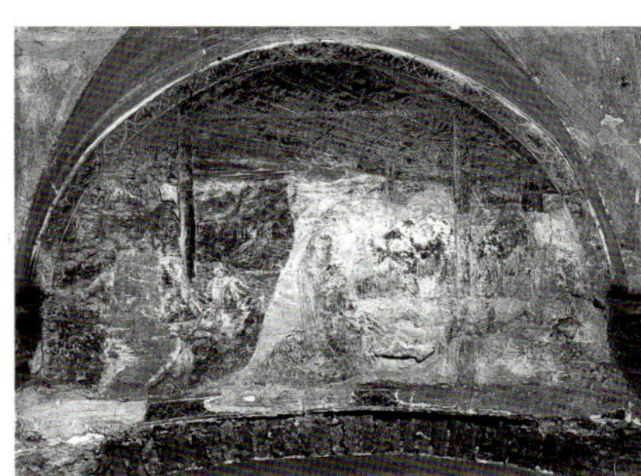

15. THE ADORATION OF THE CHILD (NATIVITY)

Fresco, upper lunette 140 cm, base 215 cm. Formerly Florence, San Martino alla Scala (originally Santa Maria della Scala). Florence, Uffizi, Reserve Collection. 1435–43

The hospital of Santa Maria della Scala, built in 1313 as a hospice and shelter for pilgrims (G. Richa, III, 1755, p. 328; R. Bencini-A. Busignani, 1979, p. 217) is a direct offshoot of the hospital of the same name at Siena. In 1530–31, it became home to the Camaldolite nuns of San Martino a Mugnone and took the name of San Martino alla Scala. In Uccello's day (at least from 1313 to 1532), the successors to the founder, Cione di Lapo Pollini, were patrons of the church and adjoining hospital. The circumstances surrounding the COMMISSIONING of the work from Uccello are not known: the commission formed the conclusion to an obscure series of works in the cloister *c.* 1435. We can in fact find affinities with the Chiostro degli Aranci of the Badia in Florence (*c.* 1436) (M. Tyskiewicz, 'Il chiostro degli Aranci della Badia Fiorentina', *Rivista d'Arte*, 27, 1951–2, pp. 203–9; W. Paatz, 1934, p. 146) and with the women's courtyard of the Foundling Hospital (*c.* 1437–8) (G. Morozzi, 'Ricerche sull' assetto originario dello Spedale degli Innocenti di Firenze', *Palladio*, 15, 1964, pp. 186–201).

Uccello's lunette was originally in the north-west corner of the cloister, above the door to the narthex of the Trecento church. It was restored in 1934 and in 1952, the date at which the sinopia was discovered; it was detached in 1958. On 21 April 1434, Uccello bought a house in Via della Scala (W. Boeck, 1939, p. 100) and he probably gained the commission through local connections, so this local work could not have been done before 1434. Research on the hospitallers (*spedalinghi*) from 1435–45 might contribute towards narrowing down the origin of the commission; relations between the institution and the Dominicans of Santa Maria Novella also need to be clarified, especially if we accept that Uccello's painting of the lunette was close in date to his second campaign in the Chiostro Verde (the *Stories of Noah*). The fresco is almost indecipherable; we can best evaluate its composition from Rosini's nineteenth-century engraving (1840, ill. XXX) or from the drawing of the same work attributed to Rossi (Uffizi, UF 4622; Paatz, 1934, fig. 2). The sinopia reveals an elaborate perspectival construction that Uccello only partially used in the final work. In contrast, the fresco shows a great freedom in the adaptation of the extreme perspectival options in Uccello's *modus operandi*; it would not be repeated in later works and is here at its most experimental stage.

Even if the poor state of conservation prevents us appreciating its quality, the work is important proof of everything that separates Uccello from the Brunelleschi-Alberti theory of perspective, which was developed as a system *c.* 1435. In this intense and subtle debate, Uccello's original stance can already be plainly seen. He developed a deliberate antithesis to the teaching found in Masaccio's *Trinity*. We can see a symbolic intention in his choice of construction: with Masaccio, the rigorous unifying layout visually expresses the dogma of the Unity/Trinity; with Uccello, the accentuated double focus alludes to the mystery of the Incarnation, of the God Made Flesh. The Virgin, in the foreground, in the space common to two lateral vanishing points, is almost projected towards the onlooker as she humbly kneels in accordance with the iconography cherished by the Florentines (but of distant descent from the Trecento Sienese) and is interpreted as the great mediator between humanity and God. In 1335 the Lorenzetti brothers had painted *Scenes of the Life of the Virgin* in the Sienese hospital of San Scala, and Ghiberti alludes to an *Annunciation* by Ambrogio Lorenzetti (*Comm. Secondo*, 1947 edn, p. 38): the patrons would probably have encouraged Uccello to imitate the 'singular' Lorenzetti, so dear to his master Ghiberti. The iconographic motif of the hanged men had already been used in Lorenzetti's *Good Government* and Giotto's *Last Judgment* in Padua.

As far as technique is concerned, Uccello continued his experimentation on the monochrome fresco 'enriched' with different pigments, as in the Chiostro Verde. The freedom of execution, when compared to the sinopia, is linked with a technique which is perhaps incorrect to define as a fresco (*affresco*): it undoubtedly included an element of *mezzo fresco* and *a secco* which has not helped preserve the work. Uccello's preference for a limited range of colours, which are used for an intellectual representation of the different planes of space rather than for a naturalistic rendering, explains his popularity as a provider of cartoons for glass and marquetry artists. This tendency would later be radicalized in the frescoes at San Miniato, criticized by Vasari.

The SOURCES are silent on the fresco at San Martino alla Scala. The first to publish it was W. Paatz (1934, pp. 111–48). He emphasized the importance of the auxiliary construction and the elaborated character of the perspective (contrary to Loeser's 'Gothicizing' interpretation of Uccello, 1898; Longhi, 1914; and L. Venturi, 1930), the links with Ghiberti, to which he added Lorenzo Monaco (polyptych predella at Santa Trinita), the dramatic components and the Nordic character of certain details, such as the hanged men in the background landscape, a motif he considers Pisanellian. Among the Ghibertian elements he emphasized the stable, the arbour and the donkey, which recall the *Sacrifice of Isaac* on the 'Doors of Paradise' of the Baptistery. He dated the work *c.* 1446, near in time to the *Flood* in the Chiostro Verde. Elsewhere, substantially in agreement were M. Salmi (1938, pp. 34 and 147) who thought there might have been a 'rather poor collaborator' working from a drawing by the master around 1440, and W. Boeck (1939, p. 114) who considered the fresco a studio work, based on one of Uccello's drawings, only done in part, of the same date. G. Pudelko (1939, T. B., p. 525) had doubts about the attribution and did not date the work. J. Pope-Hennessy (1950, pp. 18 and 152–3; 1969, pp. 154–5) reaffirmed the attribution to Uccello, emphasizing the composition with its double *costruzione legittima*, indicated the regularity of the principles of the composition and proposed a later date, during the 1450s (after the *Flood*). W. and E. Paatz (IV, 1952, p. 142) suggested a date of *c.* 1450, while E. Carli (1954; 1959, p. 61) attributed the fresco to a pupil based on a composition imagined by Uccello, and resumed the chronology of *c.* 1446. E. Micheletti (1956, p. 6) limited herself to mentioning the lunette 'which says nothing to us about Paolo other than his passionate, almost loving investigation of space and perspective'. U. Procacci (1957, p. 56) and E. Sindona (1957, p. 60) considered the fresco to be by Uccello's own hand and dated it at 1446. J. White (1957, p. 205) found the perspectival construction of the sinopia irrational and thought it consisted of a construction that used 'circular vision', was bifocal and not centred, obtained by fusing two Albertian constructions into one 'synthetic vision' of space as opposed to Brunelleschi's 'analytic vision'. D. Gioseffi (1958, pp. 106–7) proposed a dating of towards 1430, immediately after Venice, and in open opposition to White's and Parronchi's hypotheses (see below) which he judged 'fantasies'. He considered that the sinopia followed Albertian orthodoxy: for him, it was a question of an Albertian construction being applied to spaced-out vanishing points for the first time in painting, and the geometricized foreground would not be a pavement – after all, this is the country – but a grid to measure the diminutions that occur in perspective.

A. Parronchi (1957; 1964, pp. 484–5), the first to publish the sinopia, emphasized that the unity of structure in Quattrocento painting, with vanishing points spaced at intervals, 'remains curiously unused because of the two lateral vanishing points, instead of serving the unitary construction, were used to develop the composition in two diverging diretions'. He linked the sinopia with theorems 2–15 of Book III of Alhazen's *De Aspectibus* and with theorems 27–47 of Witelus's *Perspectiva* on binocular vision: 'One can only suppose that in the fresco in question, the artist wanted to concentrate the pictorial effect of this phenomenon.' Uccello would have defined the visual rays, which reached both eyes from opposite directions, by taking good care that the two vanishing points lay outside the edges of the picture. Parronchi (ibid., p. 485, n. 2) linked Uccello's design with Brunelleschi's second panel, in which the bifocal construction creates an effect of unity, an effect that is provocatively disjoined in Uccello's fresco. Parronchi (1962, p. 60) considered Klein's hypothesis on binocular perspective 'extravagant', and noted that, at that period, it could not have been known among artists' studios. For him, it was more a question of a response to the problem of binocular vision. He considered as 'an anomaly pure and simple' that 'the construction with spaced-out vanishing points would make the pictorial development diverge curiously into two directions' (EUA, X, 1963, col. 466). U. Procacci (1960, p. 233) insisted on the value of the sinopia, which was shown in the Florentine exhibition of detached frescoes in 1966. R. Klein (1961, pp. 211–30) noted (p. 222) that in this unique scene Uccello used Masolino's method of connecting two adjacent scenes, at San Clemente: Uccello 'has found a way to stretch the bifocal system to a representation of unified space, all on his own'. He returned to the largely accepted dating of 1446 'or before' and noted (p. 222, n. 32) that: 'the disconcerting effect due to the orientation of objects through using vanishing points at spaced-out intervals suggested this intentional anti-

Albertian polemic'. L. Berti (1961, p. 304) reconfirmed the attribution to Uccello and dated the work at 1450; L. Tongiorgi Tomasi (1971, p. 94) returned to *c.* 1446, after Padua and before the *Flood*. Parronchi (1974, pp. 30–1) emphasized the 'absurd' experimental perspective which he had probably intended to 'demonstrate that human vision can find a dichotomy in painting that translates binocular vision'; he noted that the two lateral vanishing points are to be found in the decoration around the lunette. C. L. Ragghianti (1977, pp. 371–2) chose an early dating, towards 1430; he interpreted the fresco as a disagreement with Alberti (p. 128), a perfect antithesis of the Masaccio *Trinity*'s unified construction. H. Wohl (1980, p. 20) pointed out that in the sinopia of Domenico Veneziano's *Marriage of the Virgin* in Sant'Egidio, there was a bifocal construction similar to Uccello's lunette, but he did not wish to broach the problem of chronological priority. Gioseffi (EUA, XI, 1963, col. 143–4) interpreted the fresco in Albertian fashion: Uccello 'strongly accentuates the central vertical line . . . the axis of symmetry corresponding to Alberti's auxiliary perpendicular', even if the diminution of the pavement polygons is obtained through 'the intersection of a single diagonal on the fan of orthogonals receding towards the principal point'. More recently Gioseffi (1980, 2, pp. 403–4) affirmed that the sinopia provided the standard for all the interpretations (*Battles, Hunt*) and emphasized the importance of the construction with spaced-out vanishing points; the dating proposed is *c.* 1445.

In spite of the divergences in interpretation, the theoretical importance of the fresco emerges clearly. It was painted in a period when Uccello's position *vis-à-vis* perspective and visual problems was close to that of the *Flood* in the Chiostro Verde. Perhaps such a position would have been provoked by Brunelleschi's second perspective panel, the one seen from a 'corner', *c.* 1435. The deciphering of the lunette is made difficult by the poor condition in which the work has reached us; it was restored for the first time in 1932 by Italio Zetti, which has encouraged researchers to concentrate their attention on Uccello's interesting essay into perspective as seen in the sinopia. The finished work was without doubt less revolutionary and more conventional, and not inevitably through interference from the patrons. It was conceived to close off the view of an aisle of the cloister; Uccello had perhaps wanted to put some diversity into the perspective by playing on several viewpoints, both near and far. Datable between 1437 and 1447, and probably towards 1443, the *Nativity* of the hospital of Santa Maria della Scala is a problematic complication in Uccello's complex work.

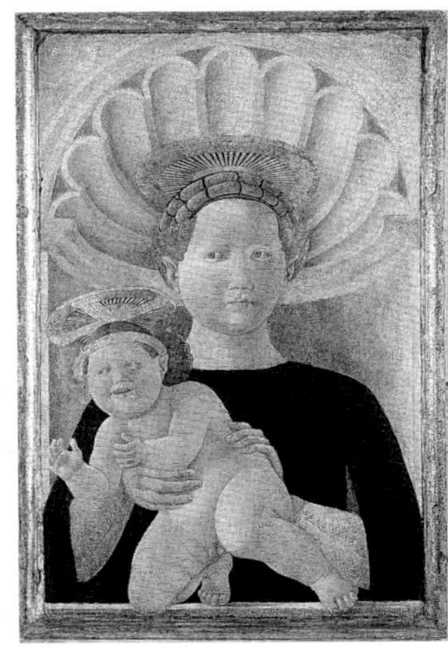

16. MADONNA AND CHILD

Tempera on wood, 57 × 33 cm.
Dublin, National Gallery of Ireland (inv. no. 603).
About 1437–40

Here again is a debatable work which is neither dated, signed nor documented. It was attributed first to Lorentino d'Andrea, Piero della Francesca's successor from Arezzo, and sold as such in London on 5 June 1899, auctioned by the Bardini Collection of Florence. It then passed into the Butler and Langton Douglas Collections, before being acquired by its present owners in 1910. The attribution to Lorentino of Arezzo was rejected by R. Fry (1909, p. 274) who suggested an unknown follower of Domenico Veneziano working in Florence from 1439, who achieved a great deal of success in the fifth decade. The ATTRIBUTION to Uccello was advanced by G. Pudelko (*Art Bull.*, 1934, pp. 231–59) and debated in *Art in America* (1936, pp. 127–34), followed by C. L. Ragghianti (1939, p. 25), R. Longhi (1940; 1975 edn, p. 45), E. Carli (1954; 1959, p. 58), E. Sindona (1957, p. 59; 1970, pp. 67–107), D. Gioseffi (1958, p. 137), P. D'Ancona (1959, p. 13) and L. Berti (1961, p. 303; 1964, unnumbered). The attribution was confirmed in the catalogue of the *Centenary Exhibition of the National Gallery of Ireland* (Dublin, 1964, n. 4) and by L. Tongiorgi Tomasi (1971, p. 93), P. A. Rossi (in Sindona, 1972, p. 41 and pp. 105–6; 1986, pp. 40–5), A. Parronchi (1963, col. 467; 1974, p. 88), F. Zeri (1974, pp. 88–9), C. Volpe (1980, p. 17) and A. Angelini (1990, p. 73: 'adventurous experimentation in perspective'). It was attributed to Uccello with a certain amount of doubt by M. Salmi (1938, p. 30), W. Boeck (1939, p. 120: attributed but with some reserves) and by E. Micheletti (*Quattro Maestri* exhibition, 1954, n. 15); G. Pudelko considered it the work of Uccello's studio (T. B., 1939, p. 525), L. Colletti (1953) of a pupil of Lippi's. It was attributed to the Prato Master by J. Pope-Hennessy (1950 and 1969, p. 25; in opposition to G. Marchini 1957, p. 82), C. H. Shell (1961, p. 208) and more recently H. Wohl (1980, p. 187).

The work's DATING is also controversial, wavering between about 1430 and 1450 (the nineteenth-century repaintings were removed in 1969). Pudelko considered it a relatively early work (1934, op. cit.: 1430–36; 1936, p. 134: second half of the 1430s, before 1445); Volpe thought it dated back to 1432–4 (1980, p. 17: in keeping with the Prato frescoes, with Lippi's early career, and Domenico di Bartolo's 'best' period, that of the Siena *Madonna* of 1433); between 1434 and 1435 was Angelini's opinion (1990, p. 73); *c.* 1435, Ragghianti (1938, p. 25: in keeping with the Prato cycle which he considered early) and Parronchi (1974, p. 88: his thesis was strengthened by the Prato frescoes' restoration); Sindona's dating was between 1435 and 1445 (1970, pp. 67–107); Berti's between 1436 and 1443 (1961, p. 33), Wohl's, *c.* 1440 (1980, p. 187: he saw a strong influence of Lippi, the child being similar to the one in the Corneto *Madonna* of 1437); Pope-Hennessy dated it after 1440 (1969, p. 25: 'wrongly attributed' to Uccello); Longhi, before 1443 (1940/1975, p. 45); Pudelko, still before 1445 (T. B., 1939, p. 525, as a studio work); *c.* 1443–5 for Gioseffi (1958, p. 137); *c.* 1445 for Tongiorgi Tomasi (1971, p. 93), not much before 1450 for Carli (1954, p. 58).

The attribution to Uccello is generally accepted and the uncertainties over its chronology are less marked than for his other paintings: critics are more or less agreed on Donatello's influence and references to the Prato cycle, which in any case preceded this previous panel. In spite of its extreme iconographical simplicity (Longhi saw it as a successful portrayal of a 'peasant Madonna', like Donatello's peasant Christ of the Cross), the panel is a remarkable example of perspectival research (see Sindona and Rossi's observations, 1972, pp. 41 and 105–6) and rare evidence of the period when he was close to Donatello (the putti on the pulpit at Prato cathedral, and the Santa Croce *Annunciation*). Perhaps it was conceived for Prato, but not at the same time as the cathedral's frescoes. This period of Uccello's influence on Filippo Lippi, on his return from Padua, is in any case obvious. Tangential points in style, due partly to the common reference to Donatello, all work in Uccello's favour. The panel, about one Florentine *braccio* high (58 cm.), is skilfully calibrated with guidelines but in subtly decentralized perspective, and enlivened by the child's oddly angled face, similar to those found in Donatello and Lippi. It veers away from Brunelleschi's and Alberti's *costruzione legittima*. The rapport with Donatello can be partly explained by the two artists' common antipathy to Brunelleschi and by the similarity of their researches into space; this was to last from the mid-1430s until *c.* 1445 when they were in Padua, where their paths diverged for good. The Dublin *Madonna*, whose 'secular tonality' was commented on (Sindona, 1970), as well as its archaic idol-like appearance (Pudelko, 1936), is also a moment of refined chromaticism. Its most likely dating is *c.* 1440, after the *Hawkwood* and Bologna fresco, well after the Prato frescoes and before the clock at Santa Maria del Fiore of 1443, the nadir of Uccello's 'Donatellism'.

This is a work of very high quality, which points the way for Filippo Lippi (the link with the *Madonna* of 1437 is reversed in Uccello's favour); but it is also a very characteristic moment, of limited duration, in the Tuscan painter's complex career. It has some traditional references, such as the Virgin's typical headdress (recovered in the 1969 restoration) which, under the guise of a modern *mazzocchio*, takes on a Lorenzetti motif (see the female figure on the right in Ambrogio Lorenzetti's *Lamentation*, Siena, Pinacoteca Comunale). A subtle tension has created a perspectival balance: if we stand back about two *braccia* (1.17 m.), that is to say double the height of the panel, you will see an original, complex relationship developing between image and background, but without the rigorously theoretical aspect of Masaccio's *Trinity*. The Dublin panel marks a moment of great formal research, and although there is little among Uccello's other works that can be truly likened to it – it is unique among the surviving paintings – it fits into a more coherent development than is generally recognized. The approximative dating proposed is due to this panel's unique quality, sole proof of the period before 1443 when Uccello was so close to Donatello.

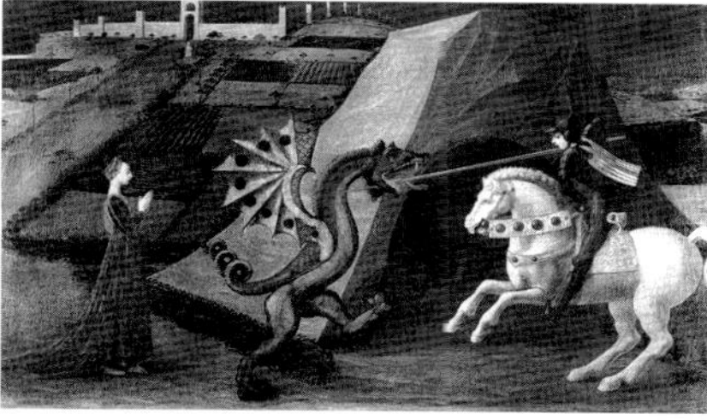

17. SAINT GEORGE AND THE DRAGON (SAINT GEORGE FREEING THE PRINCESS)

Tempera on wood, 52 × 90 cm.
Paris, Musée Jacquemart-André.
About 1439–40

This is a convex panel, perhaps a *spalliera* (see note 45) or a piece of decorative panelling (less probably, the front of a *cassone*) painted in tempera and retouched a number of times; some of the retouching is attributed to the original painter. As a result there are significant difficulties in dating and a necessarily controversial classification within the catalogue. It is an unsigned work and it is not mentioned in the sources, although documentary evidence attests that Uccello painted the subject on several occasions, without ever providing elements that would definitely identify the paintings. In our present state of knowledge, it can be considered as one of Uccello's works, as can the early Melbourne *Saint George* (National Gallery of Victoria) and the later one in London, as well as the Uffizi drawing 14502/F, probably intended to be copied on to a panel (*c.* 1465?). The Paris panel, which predates the London one, came from the Florentine antiquarian market: it reached its present location through the Stevens sale (London, 5–7 June 1899, lot 488) of the Bardini Collection in Florence. The year before, C. Loeser (1898, p. 89) had been the first to suppose that this could be a work by Uccello, an hypothesis generally welcomed by later studies. In favour of the ATTRIBUTION to Uccello were R. Fry (1914, pp. 79–80: he was the first to linger on the quality of the panel, the stylization of the faces and space, the 'scientific and abstract realism'), L. Venturi (1914, p. 64: similarities with the Urbino predella), D. Colnaghi (1928, p. 265: among Uccello's foremost works), P. Soupault (1929, p. 18: of all Uccello's work, the closest to Quattrocento popular taste; p. 25, one of Uccello's least personal works), M. Marangoni (1931–2, p. 415: similarities with the Chiostro Verde and San Miniato), B. Berenson (1932, p. 582; 1936, p. 500; 1963, p. 209: Uccello's late period), W. Wackernagel (1938/1981, p. 157: with doubts), M. Salmi (1938, pp. 22–3: similar to the San Miniato cycle in its construction of space), W. Boeck (1939, p. 112: a little later than the San Miniato frescoes, which he considered youthful work), K. Clark (1944, p. 73: authentic Uccello, but late), M. Pittaluga (1946, p. 13: before the London one; 'coexistence of congenital naïveté and acquired intellectual tendencies'), E. Somaré (1946, p. 37: between the *Hawkwood* and the Clock in the Duomo), J. Pope-Hennessy (1950; 1969, pp. 153–4: the state of the work prevents a definite attribution, quality less high that Fry claimed, similarities to the landscape of the *Battles*), E. Carli (1954; 1959, pp. 20 and 55: mediocre state of conservation, similar to San Miniato frescoes), E. Micheletti (1956, p. 10); E. Sindona (1957, p. 58: youthful work), M. Davies (1959, p. 314: doubts about its autograph status, inferior quality compared to London version, a number of incoherencies in the construction), P. D'Ancona (1959, p. 13: an example of the 'small items' painted by Uccello and mentioned by Vasari), L. Berti (1961, p. 304: after the London *Saint George*, influence of Giovanni di Paolo in the landscape, similarities to the *Battles* which he dated 1456; 1964, n.p.: before the London painting and similar to the San Miniato cycle). A. Parronchi (1963, col. 466: similar to the experimental research in the San Miniato frescoes; 1964/1967, p. 481, n. 4: the town in the background is similar to the reliefs on Ghiberti's shrine of St Zenobius; p. 486: links with theorem 35 in Witelus's Book IV: same vision on different axes, shifted in relation to the perpendicular of the eye looking at it; landscapes which do not converge into a single vanishing point; 1974, pp. 25 and 90: has similarities with the San Miniato cycle, with references to Fra Angelico and Ghiberti); G. C. Argan (1968, 2, p. 184; 1988, 2, pp. 186–7: theoretical space is unreal, for Uccello 'things exist in relation to space'; no chronological information). L. Boccia (1970, p. 70: the saint's armour resembles that in the *Battles* – which he dated *c.* 1435 – and to the drawing in the Uffizi), L. Tongiorgi Tomasi (1971, p. 98: after the London *Saint George*), P. A. Rossi (in E. Sindona, 1972, p. 42: 'errors in perspective through lack of theoretical bases', therefore an early dating), C. L. Ragghianti (1977, p. 375: composition of concentric, tangential and overlapping circles; two regrouped perspectives, raised viewpoint as in Ghiberti; p. 433: Uccello's dragon was perhaps inspired by a theatre automaton, like the illuminated *Romuleon* by Vespasiano da Bisticci's workshop, *Life of Cato of Utica*, Paris, Bibliothèque de l'Arsenal; more archaic landscape than in Giovanni di Paolo; *c.* 1445), J. Beck (1979, p. 2: suggests that this was the *Saint George* documented in 1465 for the Florentine merchant Lorenzo di Matteo Morelli – an unacceptably late date), A. Angelini (1990, p. 75): along with the London one, the painting, which is similar to the *Battles*, should be viewed as avant-garde; Gothic echoes and research into perspective).

Considered the work of a studio by G. Gamba (1909, p. 22), by R. Van Marle (1928, X, p. 208) and D. Dioseffi (1958, pp. 137 and 148; n. 106), it was mentioned as a painting by Uccello's school by A. Venturi (1911, VII, p. 340: included in a group along with Veneziano's Berlin tondo and the Accademia's *Life of the Holy Fathers*) and by P. Schubring (1915, p. 241). Pudelko's proposal (1934, p. 250, n. 41) that it was by the Karlsruhe Master was not followed up, and the same researcher in the Thieme-Becker's article limited himself to including the painting among Uccello's attributed but not definite works (T. B. 1939, p. 525).

Much more controversial than the attribution, and not without reason, is the DATING of the work: *c.* 1425–30 for Boeck (1939), *c.* 1430 for Sindona (1957; 1959 a work of youth), *c.* 1435 for Boccia (1970) and Ragghianti (1977), *c.* 1439 for Angelini (1990), *c.* 1437–40 for Carli (1954; 1959), between 1436 and 1443 for Somaré (1946), *c.* 1440 for Salmi (1938) and Micheletti (1956), the 1440s for Parronchi (1963), *c.* 1440–5 for Pittaluga (1946), *c.* 1445–7 for Marangoni (1931–2), between 1450 and 1455 for Pudelko (1934), near 1456 for Berti (1961, too early in 1964), *c.* 1456–7 for S. L. Faison (1940, *à propos* of W. Boeck, 1939, pp. 242–4, has links with the *Battles*) and for Pope-Hennessy (1969, p. 154); later than 1456 for Gioseffi (1958, p. 137), towards 1456–60 for Clark (1944) and Tongiorgi Tomasi (1971 and reprints and later coeditions), dated 1465 for Beck (1979, as a suggestion), *c.* 1467–9 for L. Venturi (1914), a late work with similarities to the Urbino predella for Loeser (1898) and Berenson (1932; 1936; 1963); uncertain or indeterminate for the others.

The uncertainies can be explained by the numerous interventions that the work has undergone: the most likely hypothesis is that of a first version in tempera at the turn of the 1403s/1440s (the princess's costume is reminiscent of the Eastern dress at the time when the Council was in Florence, and Uccello's interest in Domenico Veneziano) and later additions of oily tempera, lacquers and resins, which have mostly deteriorated and are barely visible but which remain in the remarkable traces of animal painting in the background, in the green, regular fields and in the nocturnal wood on the right. There are many stylistic elements in favour of Uccello: the treatment of the fine scales in the immediate foreground, the extreme stylization of the rocks, the impressive spread of the town in the background (already shown in the Melbourne *Saint George*, but somewhat deadened with its references to Ghiberti and Fra Angelico), the vivacious sketch of the rulers of Trebizond standing before the town – in accordance with the *Golden Legend*, the snowy mountains (as in the Thyssen *Crucifixion*), the dreamy 'nocturne' (with the now almost vanished personification of the wind and the crescent moon), the landscape on the right, not to mention the principal characters. These latter have not escaped retouching, especially the knight-saint and the princess whose enormous hands are undoubtedly the result of ill-advised restoration. The dragon, which is energetically drawn, is faithfully taken from the *Thebaïd* in the Camposanto at Pisa, a probable indication of first-hand knowledge of the cycle. In the upper corners, the moon and golden rays designate instant dusk, while the wind, crouched over the already snowy mountains, indicates that the cold season has arrived: for it is in the freshness of the landscape details rather than in the activity itself that the painter's gifts for fantasizing are confirmed. The construction of space once more deviates from Albertian-Brunelleschian perspective. If the fantastic tone of the tale, within the confines of a private room, in part justifies a little theorizing, it is significant that the construction of space is not reduced to a principle of unity: the two parts of the landscape are structured according to different angles of vision. The great avenue leading to the town does not converge in accordance with the rules of perspective; the town itself has an open, symbolic shape in the buildings' propitious surrender to night. Once again it is a question of a 'Lorenzettian' attitude (which would be pushed to extremes by Giovanni di Paolo from the mid-1440s onwards) but in Uccello's work demonstrates a mature sympathy for Ghiberti.

The Paris panel therefore implicates Uccello's links with the Sienese world, a knowledge of Lorenzetti's work and a certain familiarity with Giovanni di Paolo (who made a veritable cult of Ambrogio). Ghiberti's work on the baptismal fonts in Siena (*c.* 1424), and the preferences he expressed in his *Commentari*, his friend Dello's exile in Siena in the autumn of 1424 and Gentile da Fabriano's time there (June 1425) could have greatly encouraged Uccello's interest in Sienese art. In his youth, Uccello could possibly have encountered Giovanni di Paolo in Florence, when he went there to study the famous Strozzi retable at Santa Trinita, in real workshop sessions. In Uccello's work there are several specific references to Sienese iconography (San Ansano, Bernardino of Siena, the monogram of Christ in the Quarate predella or in the Accademia *Life of the Holy Fathers*) and he probably knew the reliefs of the Fonte Gaia by Jacopo della Quercia. Ghiberti executed the shrine of St Zenobius (Florence, Santa Maria del Fiore) between 1432 and 1440, and the landscape of the town which is reproduced there derives from the final phase of his work (1439–40): Ghiberti's work is a useful reference in dating

Uccello's monochrome town, lit faintly by the light of dawn, as in the bronze relief. Theorem 35 of Book IV of Witelus's *Perspectiva* (quoted by Parronchi, 'Le fonti di Paolo Uccello', in *Studi sulla 'dolce prospettiva'*, pp. 485–6) tries to demonstrate that vision can operate on different axes; these can be moved back and forth in relation to the orthogonal position of the eye, which automatically corrects itself as a result. The Paris panel has two distinct vanishing points converging at its centre, on axes which are vertically out of place. Uccello's interest in these phenomena and in the problems of optics would therefore have gone beyond Ghiberti's teaching, since his *Commentario Terzo* only picks up a few of Witelus's themes, theorems and problems from Book II and none from Book IV. In any case it remains difficult to imagine how, apart from Ghiberti, the painter could have had access to basic texts on optics.

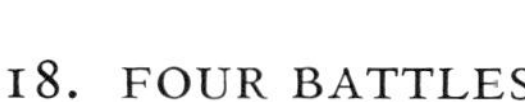

18. FOUR BATTLES

Medium unknown (now lost).
Formerly Florence, Casa Bartolini in Valfonda.
After 1440?

In Vasari's biography of Uccello in the first edition of the *Vite*, he recollects that: 'In a number of Florentine houses, [we can see] many pictures in perspective by him ... four of them very large scenes in chiaroscuro with a great number of people, horses, animals and landscapes which today are in the garden of the Bartolini family: in the attempt to revive the colours which were half faded, they have been spoilt rather than improved.' The passage comes after the *Hawkwood* and before the final one on Saint Thomas in the Mercato Vecchio, with Donatello's criticisms. The pictures were four *Battles* almost in monochrome (as in San Miniato or the Chiostro Verde) – probably mural paintings in tempera. In the second edition

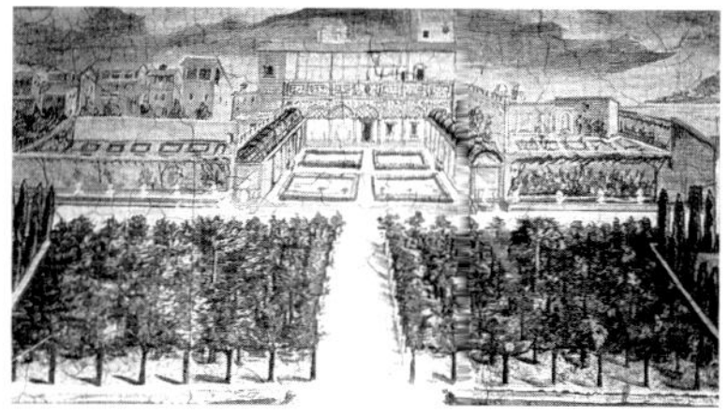

Renaissance garden at Valfonda (fresco in the Palazzo Giuntini, Florence). This garden is typical of the 'palazzo-villas' of Via di Valfonda in the sixteenth century. In one of them Vasari saw Uccello's *Four Battles*, already heavily restored by Giuliano Bugiardini.

(1568, I, pp. 272–3), Vasari furnished greater details, although they should be subject to caution: 'and, at Gualfonda, particularly, on a terrace in a garden which once belonged to the Bartolini, there are four stories in his hand, on wood, representing battles: horses and men at arms are painted wearing the beautiful costumes of those times. Among the men are portraits of Paolo Orsini, Ottobuono da Parma, Luca da Canale and Carlo Malatesti, Lord of Rimini, all captain generals of that time. And the said paintings – because they were in a very poor state and were damaged – have been restored in our time by Giuliano Bugiardini who has ruined them rather than improved them.' What is perplexing is on the one hand the notion of painting on wood – unless sections of panelling had been moved from another residence (belonging to the Bartolini?) – and on the other hand the names of the characters portrayed. Vasari's notes leave us to suppose a cycle devoted to several Florentine victories (Carlo Malatesti and the battle of Sant'Egidio in 1416, and Pietrogiampaolo Orsini, victor at Anghiari in 1440). If indeed Orsini was portrayed, the victory at Anghiari over Piccinino who was in Milan's pay could provide a good *post quem* date, indicating a later period than the Medici *Battles*. The interest shown in the armour, standards and breastplates, if we believe Vasari, should be of prime interest in the paintings. Giuliano Bugiardini's restoration undoubtedly occurred between 1530 and 1540. The place-name 'Gualfonda' indicates a place in the environs of the Porta Faenza which corresponds to today's Via Valfonda, now shorter than in Renaissance times. In his biography of Tribolo (Vasari-Milanesi, VI, 1881, pp. 57–8) Vasari recalls the 'garden and house' belonging to Giovanni Bartolini at Valfonda and Jacopo Sansovino's *Bacchus* sculpted for it, probably at the same time as the restoration of Uccello's panels which had undoubtedly lost the lustrous effect of the metallic leaf. Bugiardini was a painter of *cassoni* and the fact that Vasari metnions his intervention suggests a wooden support, which makes an outdoor site for the panels – in the loggia of a 'terrace' – seem improbable. The Bartolini house was destroyed in 1638 and with it all trace of the paintings. Carlo Malatesta, who, according to Vasari, was portrayed in them, was the Signore of Rimini and not the *condottiere* of the same name, defeated at Maclodio by Carmagnola, as we had supposed (D. Gioseffi, 1958, p. 147, no. 105). In the margin of Vasari's biography of Uccello, G. Milanesi (1878, II, p. 214, n. 1) takes up the Crowe-Cavalcaselle suggestion which identified one of the four Bartolini *Battles* as the Medici *Battle* in the National Gallery, London. This identification was corrected (H. P. Horne, 1901) after publication of the Medici inventories which itemized the subjects of the three Medici panels: '*la rotta di San Romano*'. Gioseffi is alone (1958, pp. 147–8) in having recently tried to resuscitate the old identification of the Bartolini panels with Uccello's three famous masterpieces. The attempt is unconvincing; moreover the Medici panels show no trace of sixteenth-century restoration visible enough to justify Vasari's criticisms; nor do they show any superimposition of colours on top of an originally almost monochrome composition, nor damage that would have justified Bugiardini's draconian intervention. If the chronology of the *Battles* lies between 1435 and 1440, that of the Bartolini *Battles* is doubtless later and comprises what is perhaps a strictly decorative work.

19. CLOCK FACE

Fresco, 583 × 583 cm; heads 68 cm. in diameter.
Florence, Santa Maria del Fiore, inner face of the façade wall.
1443

Illustrated on p. 318

Vasari mentions the episode only in the second edition of the *Vite*, immediately after the *Hawkwood*: 'At the same time and in the same church he painted the round

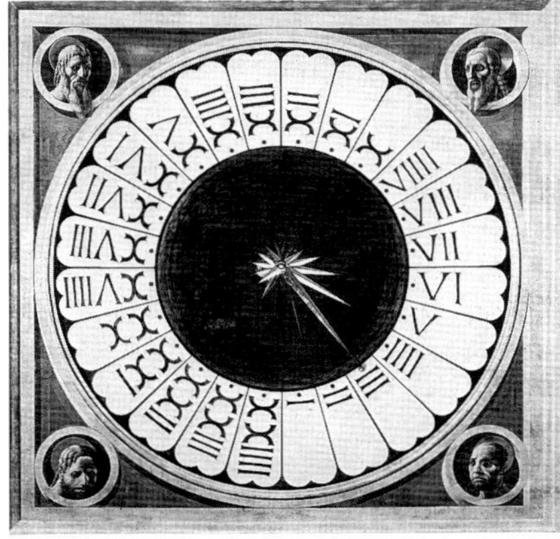

clock face in colour above the main doorway inside the church, with four heads coloured in fresco in the corners' (1568, I, p. 272). However, the documents published by Poggi (1933, pp. 323–36) date Uccello's work at 1443, at the same time as the cartoons for the three stained-glass windows in the drum of the cupola. Vasari completely misses this and attributes all the stained-glass windows (except for the one by Donatello) to Ghiberti's drawings. Uccello was paid on 22 February 1443 and on 2 April of the same year he received a new amount 'for gilding the star of the clock and likewise an orb at the tip [i.e. of the hand], and in remuneration for his work in putting an azure field around the star'. So there were two different work sessions: the first for the fresco (the clock face), the second for the precious blue and gilding of the hand, paid for separately, and perhaps requested by the patrons on a second occasion.

The composition was within a square framework, each side being ten Florentine *braccia* (583 cm.) in length. The face was divided into twenty-four hours and laid out in an anti-clockwise direction. Each section was edged with a double scallop. The restoration in 1968 (under Dino Dini's direction) revealed Uccello's modification at the time of his second and final intervention (the one to which the known documents refer), which was probably done to make the Roman numerals for the hours more legible. The modern restoration has revealed successive stratifications on the clock – it was repainted in the Baroque period and again in the nineteenth century (U. Baldini, 1970, pp. 44–50) – and the process the painter used to draw his composition on the plaster (G. Botticelli-S. Giovanni, 1979, pp. 177–81). Uccello used diagonals of the square as his basic structure and direct engraving to transfer the drawing on to the plaster. In the original version, the clock face was green (Baldini, 1970, p. 45). Proof can be found of earlier interventions or repaintings in the sources, before the restoration of 1963–70: between 1838 and 1842, there was one by the painter Antonio Marini (F. Fantozzi, 1852, p. 775; p. 332: 'Above the main door is the clock, which of Paolo Uccello's painting retains only four proudly expressed Prophets' heads in the tondi near the corners, and little else'); and one in the seventeenth century (F. Bocchi-G. Cinelli, 1677, p. 46: 'the round clock face is by Paolo Uccello, even if its centre has recently been restored'). F. Baldinucci limited himself to recalling that Uccello 'painted four heads in fresco in the corners of the square' (1686; 1845 edn, I, p. 447). These appeared so damaged to Cavalcaselle (1864, in 1911 Langton-Douglas-De Nicola edn, IV, p. 114, n.) that it was impossible to judge Uccello's original authorship. G. Pudelko (1934, pp. 233, 237 and 243) pointed out how the heads jutted out towards the nave, and interpreted them as the Prophets, watching the faithful from on high. The heads reminded him of Ghiberti's in the frames of the Baptistery doors, but were particularly influenced by Masaccio's frescoes in the Brancacci chapel and Donatello's statues for the campanile of the Duomo, thus revealing a 'rapport with the humanity of Masaccio's figures'.

W. Boeck (1939, p. 39) thought the two upper heads well enough preserved, and the lower left in a poor condition; he saw in them similarities to the Saint John in the Thyssen *Crucifixion* and with the Masaccian expressivity and assertive shading that are found in the Louvre group portrait (see p. 350). Pittaluga (1946, p. 14) considered the clock Face to be one of Uccello's mature works, an example of his 'rebellion against the century's artistic ideal', with a liking for Andrea del Castagno and 'under Masaccio's influence and even more under Donatello's'. E. Carli (1954; 1959, p. 57) agreed with Boeck on the state of preservation, while P. D'Ancona (1959, p. 14) confirmed the reference to Andrea del Castagno and Donatello's *Prophets*. A. Parronchi (1957; 1964, p. 477) was the first to suggest that the heads might depict the Evangelists, pointing out Uccello's marked interest in physiognomy, an art in which the lines of a face relate to a corresponding symbolic animal (p. 518). Parronchi again (1974, p. 41) thought that the old clock of San Marco in Venice could have been a precedent for Uccello's. L. Berti (1961, p. 303) linked the four heads with those at Prato and the sculptural 'corkscrew curls' of the hair. J. Pope-Hennessy (1950; 1969, pp. 144–5) expressed doubts on the iconography of the heads and was not sure that they portrayed the prophets. It was, however, as these that they were repeated by Giovanni di Francesco in a polychrome stucco frame in the Kaiser Friedrich Museum in Berlin (L. Bellosi, 1990, p. 21, and ill. 6); Francesco was directly inspired by Uccello's fresco. C. Volpe (1980, p. 190) was somewhat scathing about the clock face, emphasizing its 'less felicitous accents', while for C. Brandi (1980, p. 190) it was 'a composition in bursts of darkness and light'; he compared the fresco to the *Battles*, which he thought came later. F. Zeri (1983, p. 555) also noted adherence to the Donatellian model, the unilateral interpretation of perspective without overmuch knowledge of anatomy and the construction in fragmented planes. He was also inclined to interpret the heads as those of the Evangelists and not the Prophets.

In fact, the accentuated disarticulation, the brutality of the lighting which referred to bronze, the popular taste, all remind us of the *Schermidori* or fencers (as Filarete nicknamed Donatello's Apostles on the doors of the Old Sacristy at San Lorenzo) and the statues on the Campanile. This is one of Uccello's less happy and inventive moments – when he was slavishly following his sculptor friend – which would be followed shortly afterwards in 1445 by the journey to Padua. It is not surprising that Uccello accepted such a commission: it was not only prestigious, but it put him in contact with the scientific milieu of modern humanism and in the wake of the painter-philosopher Ambrogio Lorenzetti's *Mappamondo* in the Palazzo Pubblico in Siena. A comparison might be suggested between the cathedral clock and Brunelleschi's *oriolo* (clock) or *destatoio* (alarm) (cf. E. Battisti, 1976, p. 339, with bibliography), Filippo's passion when he was a young man. The choice of Uccello seems to be in keeping with the complexity of his researches and in particular with his orientation towards scientific problems: he was certainly more suitable than the other official providers of cartoons for the stained-glass windows. Baldini (1970, pp.

45–6) pointed out that there is an example of a Quattrocento Florentine clock in Botticelli's fresco of *Saint Augustine* in the church of Ognissanti in Florence, which is similar to the great clock in the Duomo. The star of the *Nativity* (identical to that in the Karlsruhe altarpiece) served as a model for the reconstruction of the hands in the restoration of 1968 (begun in 1963).

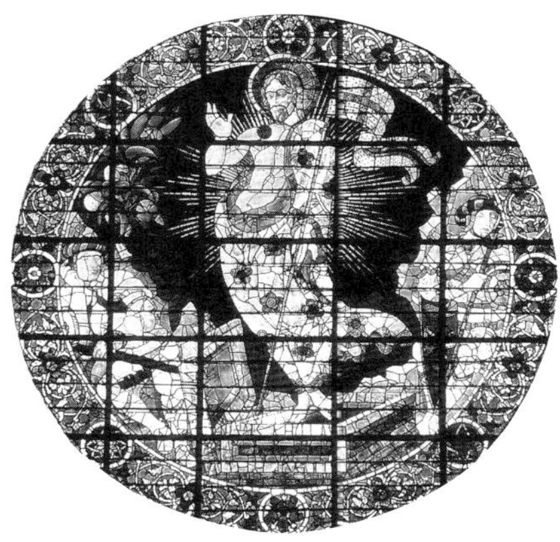

20. THE RESURRECTION

Stained-glass window, 468 cm in diameter. Florence, Santa Maria del Fiore, cupola drum.
Also The Annunciation *(lost).*

The eight large circular windows (oculi) of the cupola drum were put in place in 1431 (G. Pozzi, 1909, p. LXXXVII) and on 24 April 1433 three were boarded up '*propter ventos et frigora et alia pericula*' (C. Guasti, *La Cupola di Santa Maria del Fiore*, Florence, 1857, p. 75). In the meantime, the Duomo's Office of Works wrote to Piero Beccanugi, the Florentine ambassador in Venice, asking for information on Uccello as '*magistro musayci*': they wanted to know if he '*bene laborevit*' on the Saint Peter on the façade of San Marco and '*cuius est in civitate Venetiarum extimationis et pretiis*', '*et an de vitreis potest haberi et reperiri et cuius pretii sunt*' (G. Poggi, 1909, doc. 773; W. Boeck, 1939, p. 97). Not only did they want to know whether Uccello was a good master (an indication that he was barely known in Florence), but also whether he was available. The inquiry was linked directly with that for stained glass, so a connection with the enterprise was probably being planned, even if there are some uncertainties. Continuation of work on the cathedral and the advance of the cupola saw the opposition between Brunelleschi and Ghiberti coming to a head. In 1429 Ghiberti had been asked to do the cartoons for the stained-glass windows in the chapels and apse, and in December 1433 he was commissioned to make the cartoon for the first window, the *Coronation of the Virgin*, intended for the oculus above the chapel of Saint Zenobius. This window, which is the first we see on entering the church, was to be the model to which all the others had to conform. But in April 1434, an analogous cartoon on the same subject was ordered from Donatello. In spite of Ghiberti's long-standing privileged links with the Office of Works, they surprisingly chose Donatello's cartoon. Ghiberti could probably thank Brunelleschi for this professional blow, at a time when his presence on the cupola worksite was becoming less frequent. It is possible that because Ghiberti lost this contest, Uccello's involvement was hindered or slowed down, since information had already been asked about him in March 1432.

Donatello's window gave the general tone and the monumental inspiration to the whole series. The glazing was done by Domenico di Pietro da Pisa and Angelo Lippi, and finished in December 1437. In 1439 the Office of Works decided to call in the master glassmaker Bernardo di Francesco, but the order for the cartoons was postponed. There were doubts and dissensions which transpired in the meeting of 20 January 1443, which Brunelleschi and Ghiberti attended. In spite of the objections about the lack of clarity distance would impart to the coloured pictures of the windows, the prevailing opinion, led by Francesco della Luna, was to follow the model of the first window (Guasti, 1857, pp. 76–7). In the meantime, Ghiberti must have strengthened his position by providing the windows for the apse (1434–7) and now, with the new commissions, he carved the lion's share for himself. He provided cartoons for the *Ascension*, the *Agony in the Garden* and the *Presentation in the Temple* (1443–4), the last window to be put in place on 25 February 1445. Uccello was commissioned to do three other cartoons, if not at Ghiberti's behest, then at least with his agreement: the *Nativity*, the *Resurrection* and the *Annunciation* (lost in 1828) for which Uccello was paid in February 1444. The last cartoon, provided by Andrea del Castagno, was of the *Pietà*; the name of the glazier for this is not known. All these masters increased the diameter of the window compared with Donatello's (evidently profiting from that first experiment), because of the distance from which people would see it, following the objection by the Franciscan Jacopo di Giorgio del Biada during the 1443 deliberations. Work on the window was carried out by Bernardo di Francesco with whom Uccello formed a friendship that lasted beyond this professional occasion. In January 1444, Francesco was in debt to Uccello '*pro suo labore in pingendo unum oculum factum per dictum Bernardum*': the expression *pingendo* leads us to believe that the cartoon was already broken down into different coloured compartments; or (M. Bacci in *Lorenzo Ghiberti, 'Materia e ragionamenti'*, 1978, p. 255) that the painter himself intervened at the time the windows wre made. For that he could have profited from the experience he had gained during his long stay in Venice. However, after the restorations and the damage the window has undergone, it is extremely difficult to pronounce on this with any certainty. At the time Ghiberti's window of the *Presentation in the Temple* was put into position on 25 February 1445, Uccello's *Resurrection* was already in place. The history of this is therefore relatively well documented (G. Poggi, 1909, doc. 749, 750, 757, 770). In January 1445, Uccello was paid by the Office of Works '*pro ristoro et additione quod fit pro suo labore picture duorum ocularum*': this related to interventions on two unspecified cartoons, probably already being worked on. We can therefore only think that the Office of Works kept the cartoons in view of future possible interventions. It was probably a question here of the *Nativity* and the *Resurrection*, for the drawing of the now lost *Annunciation* was ordered in February 1444 and was the first of Uccello's series.

In his *Commentari* Ghiberti records that 'in the cupola there are three oculi designed by me' (II, ed. Morisani, 1947, p. 47) and Vasari extends the attribution to the whole series, except for Donatello's window (Vasari-Milanesi, II, 1878, p. 246), followed by Milanesi's comment (ibid., n. 2). A. Marquand ('Two Windows', *American Journal of Archaeology*, 1900, 2, pp. 192–203) put forward the ATTRIBUTION to Uccello. P. Toesca (1920, p. 4) emphasized the window's powerful chromatic effects, while G. Poggi (1933, pp. 335–6) addressed the problem of the sources and confirmed that the *Ascension* mentioned in the document of 2 May 1443 was really the *Resurrection*. Ghiberti's influence was emphasized by W. Boeck (1933, p. 266; 1939, pp. 36–9, 113) who also pointed out (1939, pp. 38–9) the perspectival refinement of the tomb and the *mazzocchio* of one of the soldiers. G. Pudelko (1934, p. 237) underlined the 'enormous dramatic power' and 'new realism', noting the *mazzocchio*'s first entry on to the scene, an indication of Uccello's preoccupation with perspective. M. Salmi (1938, p. 26) reaffirmed the importance of the research into space, considered the head of the risen Christ 'Donatellian' and thought the result superior to the *Nativity*. H. van Straelen (1938, pp. 87–8) put forward the hypothesis that Uccello had perhaps been paid for restoring the cartoons of the two surviving windows in 1445, work in which he could have improved on the work of the master glassmakers. This suggestion is taken up again by J. Pope-Hennessy (1950; 1969, p. 145). After brief commentaries by R. Oertel (1937–40, p. 269) and W. and E. Paatz (III, 1941, p. 374 and 515), M. Pittaluga (1946, p. 15) issued a negative judgment: Uccello 'loses ... all coherence', and in the *Resurrection*: 'the accentuated research into solid forms and foreshortenings is not effective, perhaps because of a lack of spatial depth.' E. Carli (1954; 1959, p. 58) examined indication (from H. van Straelen) of reworkings or restorations in the window, particular in Christ's body. In fact the window, which is better conserved than the *Nativity*, underwent interventions in the nineteenth century and in 1954, when it was reinforced with bitumen and restored at the time of the *Quattro Maestri* exhibition. On that occasion the surfaces were abrased, thus attenuating or eliminating the effects of relief and chiaroscuro. L. Berti (1964, n.p.) admired the 'gigantic sagging Christ, as archaic as a Cimabue, and the two admirable, contorted soldiers'. A. Parronchi (1957/1964, p. 477) noticed that the lines of the tomb in the *Resurrection* did not converge on a vanishing point, demonstrating (ibid., p. 484) connections between the layout of the stained-glass window's composition and the illustration of theorem 84 in Book I of Witelus's *Perspectiva* (Parronchi, 1964, ill. 167a). 'Paolo moves in circles, with a felicitous effect, an ascending rhythm of composition, taking absolutely no account of the depth, and in that he demonstrates the greatest knowledge of the material at his disposal: coloured glass, a simple diaphragm interposed against the light, as the most ancient of masters understood' (Parronchi, 1974, pp. 40–1). G. Marchini (1987, p. 12) also stressed the knowledgeable use of the lead framework which became a medium of expression. The painter's curiosity about optics emerges in his analyses of the diffusion of light into a halo and perhaps the effects of projecting a hemispherical concave surface on to a flat one, since, thanks to Witelus, via Ghiberti, he had knowledge of the specific problems of depicting the circle. Perhaps he also developed Euclid's concept of the squared image which, seen from far away, appears circular, which might indicate a slight adaptation to the demands of a viewpoint from the nave.

The *Annunciation* was made by Bernardo di Francesco based on Uccello's cartoon and paid for in February 1444 (documents in Poggi, 1909, doc. 761, 768, 769, 770), and taken down in 1828. It had occupied a position opposite Donatello's window. Since it marked both the beginning of Christ's and the Virgin Mary's stories, it had an introductory role in the complete programme. As the last of the three windows based on Uccello's cartoons, it probably revealed a deepening of his researches into space and vision, in the oculi of the drum. M. Bacci (1978, p. 256) reported G. Marchini as saying that the remains of the original window, never reassembled (and not restored in 1954), survived in pieces in the cathedral's stores.

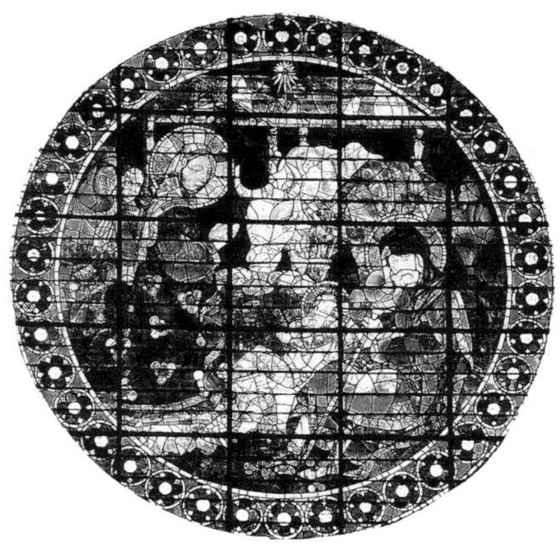

21. THE NATIVITY

Stained-glass window, 473 cm. in diameter. Florence, Santa Maria del Fiore, cupola drum.
1443–4

Uccello's cartoon, executed by Angelo Lippi, was the second one he provided, even though the results undoubtedly seem more conventional and the whole less solidly structured than the *Resurrection*. G. Pudelko (1934, p. 250) examined the spatial deficiencies of the *Nativity* and thought it showed an influence of Lorenzo Monaco (O. Siren, *Lorenzo Monaco*, 1905, pp. 136–7). He raised the question of how much Uccello was influenced by the Sienese, with regard to this window, even suggesting that in his youth the painter could have been an apprentice of Lorenzo Monaco. M. Salmi (1938, p. 26) thought that the lack of innovation in the window was due to his having to bring his window into alignment with Donatello's and Ghiberti's. The *Nativity*, with its links with Lorenzo Monaco, was successful. Salmi (p. 79) was the first to suggest that the important commission for providing the cartoons fell to Uccello because of Ghiberti's good offices, and this likely hypothesis was taken up again by A. Parronchi (1957/1964, p. 481). M. Pittaluga (1946, p. 15) was also somewhat scathing about Uccello's cartoon; however, the windows showed a remarkable attempt at simplification so that it could be seen from a distance. More significant reserves (G. Pudelko, 1934, p. 237; W. Boeck, 1939, pp. 36–9, 113) were expressed about its executant, the glazier Angelo Lippi, to whom H. van Straelen (1938, pp. 86–7) attributed important responsibilities in the conception of the whole work. Certainly the large flowers on the Virgin's cloak, which spoil the composition's structure, are foreign to Uccello's style. On the other hand, there are characteristics in the regular geometry of certain details – the shape of the donkey, the ox and the shed – which are reminiscent of the Karlsruhe retable and the Prato and Bologna frescoes. The glazier translated Uccello's scene by using some of his chromatic intellectualisms, like the artificial colour of the two animals (G. Marchini, 1956, pp. 42 and 230). Uccello was undoubtedly one of the most 'translatable' painters for glaziers, which would explain his long association with Bernardo di Francesco, beyond the important period of the two stained-glass windows for the drum of the cathedral. Unfortunately the 1954 restoration (for the *Quattro Maestri* exhibition in Florence) provided no precise documentation on the former state of the window, which appears to have been repaired in different places and damaged on a number of occasions. The Virgin's face, which is completely out of keeping, is undoubtedly the most visible, strident addition. Uccello's cartoon seems to have followed a different tack from Ghiberti's, with a denser composition and structure, a style which was at its height in the *Resurrection*. It was 'a staging point in his experimentation in space' (M. Bacci, in *Lorenzo Ghiberti*, 1978, p. 254) where his non-adhesion to Brunelleschi's theory of space made it easier to follow a traditional style (like the echoes, already mentioned, of Lorenzo Monaco). W. Paatz (1934, p. 138) used the *Nativity* to uphold his thesis that 'Paolo Uccello's first ventures must have taken place in the circle of Lorenzo Monaco.' The master Angelo Lippi's colours were judged 'powerful' by P. Toesca (*Vitraux*, 1920, p. 4) and criticized by H. van Straelen (1938, op. cit.). Recently, G. Marchini (*Antichità viva*, 1987, p. 12) considered the *Nativity* to be 'by the same hand as the frescoes at Prato' (frescoes whose attribution he had formerly denied to Uccello, see no. 10).

The historical evidence, which can, to a great extent, be reconstituted, directly implicates Uccello. In February 1443, the Office of Works at the cathedral decided to commission two cartoons from Uccello (on the identical subject) for two different glaziers: Angelo Lippi and Carlo Zati. On the following 5 November, Uccello was paid by the Office of Works for the drawing of the *Nativity* which had been given to Angelo Lippi. He received payment for the window in the months of April and June 1444, even though the documents are not precise on the reason for the payment. On 25 February 1445, the window of the *Nativity* was brought to the site (G. Poggi, 1909, doc. 654, 747, 754, 766, 772). The *Nativity* is less well preserved than the *Resurrection*. L. Berti (1964, unnumbered) thought it had 'great beauty' and saw in it 'the mood of the Quarate predella and the small Karlsruhe panel'.

22. GIANTS

Frescoes? (now lost).
Formerly Padua, Casa Vitaliani.
1445

These were mentioned by Marcantonio Michiel (Anonimo Morelliano, between 1524 and 1543) in *Notizie d'opere del disegno* (ed. G. Frizzoni, Bologna, 1884, p. 66): 'In the Eremitani, in the Vitaliani's house, the giants in chiaroscuro are by the hand of Paolo Uccello, a Florentine; he painted one a day for a ducat each.' The monumental construction of the figures, the speed of execution and the relative economy of means used suggest that this was not a question of *buon fresco*, but rather of murals in tempera, in terre-verte (*terretta verde*) as in the Chiostro Verde, and consequently running a greater risk of deterioration, even more so if painting on the outside of a building was involved. The *Giants* were probably painted on the inside front wall of a loggia looking on to a courtyard, in an arrangement using *trompe-l'oeil* niches in perspective, with real architectonic elements and archaeological fragments, following an idea for which we can see a precedent in the decoration of the Carnesecchi chapel at Santa Maria Maggiore. Other details can be deduced through analogy, from the description by Michiel of the Carraresi palace cycle (*c.* 1368–79) in Padua: 'The Lords of Padua painted in green and life-size' (quoted in M. M. Donato, 1985, p. 121); in the same palace, at the back of the loggia, there was another monumental decorative cycle in terre-verte. This was the most undisputed precedent in the region, from which the unidentified patrons could have taken their idea. Uccello, for his part, could have drawn some inspiration from his direct knowledge of Niccolò Gerini's *Famous Men* in terre-verte in the Palazzo Datini in Prato, and of those by Bicci di Lorenzo (*c.* 1420) at the Medici's 'Casa Vecchia' in Via Larga in Florence. As for the Carraresi cycle, Petrarch's stay in Padua has been pointed out as a significant factor (Donato, 1985, II, p. 106); in Florence, *c.* 1435, Leonardo Bruni wrote a biography of him. The patron of the 'Casa Vecchia' cycle was Giovanni di Bicci, Cosimo the Elder's father, while an assessment of Uccello's influence in regard to the lost cycle in the Palazzo Baglioni in Perugia (*c.* 1437–8), attributed to Domenico Veneziano (I. Toesca, 1952, p. 19; H. Wohl, p. 210–11, with bibliography) has been made (F. Santi, 'L'affresco baglionesco della Galleria Nazionale dell' Umbria' in *Commentari*, 21, 1970, p. 51 f.). C. L. Ragghianti (1937, p. 237) suggested that Filarete, on his travels to Padua in 1449, had perhaps been inspired by Uccello's cycle for the decoration of the portico shown in his Book IX, although Uccello is not mentioned among the masters referred to by the Utopian essayist: these were Mantegna, Tura, Foppa and Piero della Francesca. Foppa, a master of Paduan culture, painted eight emperors (?), now lost, for the Medici bank in Milan, in which echoes of the Vitaliani cycle could be found.

The other source concerning the *Giants* is, as usual, Vasari, who mentioned them in the second edition of the *Vite*: 'When Donatello was working in Padua, he asked Paolo to go there, and, at the entrance to the Vitali's house he painted some figures of Giants in terre-verte, which were so fine – according to what I have read in a letter written in Latin by Girolamo Campagnola to the philosopher Leonico Tomeo – that Andrea Mantegna set the greatest store by them' (1568, I, p. 273). According to Vasari's source (now lost), Donatello would have called Uccello to Padua, probably because he considered him an expert in the *quadratura* of the horse: Uccello's trip can be linked to the elaboration of Donatello's designs for the *Gattamelata*. Not only had Uccello given convincing proof of his talent in the *Hawkwood* and in the *Battles*, but he could easily have studied the bronze horse of San Marco in Venice, and could have seen them close up, from the scaffolding for his mosaic decoration of the façade. His sculptor friend was undoubtedly aware of these studies. A reciprocal interest is perceptible in the Louvre *Battle*, the latest of the series: great attention to the humane element and a more accentuated monumentality of the figures distinguish this panel from the two others, in a phase when Uccello was in close contact with Donatello. When we think of the evolution of painting in Padua, we can detect details in the splendid Louvre panel which seems to anticipate Mantegna. It was in this period, which is barely documented elsewhere, that the Vitaliani cycle was done, at the moment perhaps when Donatello's existential, heroic humanism and Uccello's intellectual, imaginative refinement were at their closest. Mantegna, Niccolò Pizzolo and Ansuino da Forlì held this fresco in high regard and were perhaps inspired by it for the neighbouring frescoes at the Eremitani.

Uccello and Donatello were not the first Florentine artists active in the city of Padua. Besides earlier ones (Giotto, Giusto de' Menabuoi), there were Ghiberti (he mentions it himself in the *Commentari*), the sculptors Marco and Andrea da Firenze in 1424, Nanni di Bartolomeo (from 1429, then, with Donatello, from 1443 to 1449), Pietro Lamberti, the Donatellian sculptor Francesco d'Antonio, Dello Delli and Filippo Lippi. Palla Strozzi was exiled there from 1434; the city would give two bishops to Florence, Ludovico Scarampo Mezzarota and Bartolomeo Zabarella. Leonardo Mocenigo, procurator of San Marco from 1418 (M. Muraro, 1961, p. 271) and Uccello's patron in the years 1425–30 also came from Padua. Remember that Uccello had been to the city once before, during his period in Venice, when he may have had a strong interest in Altichiero's frescoes. That a presence as qualified as Uccello's – with Donatello's backing, who for a decade was the incontestable leader of the local artistic world – should have ended with such a relatively modest outcome, and had no great imitators, leaves us somewhat perplexed. The political context was not the most favourable: the danger represented by the Visconti had become less distinct, relaxing the ties between Florence and Venice, and the arrival of the Sforza, in 1450, imposed a radical reversal of alliances, sanctioned by a final break. But, already, it was extremely difficult for a foreign painter to penetrate the rigid corporative structure of the city (Muraro, 1961, p. 272), in 1450 they discouraged Florentine painters and painters from other places in general: Bono da Ferrara, Cecco da Roma and Baldassare da Francia are examples (Muraro, 1961, p. 273).

One of the most controversial themes that has a bearing on Uccello's activity in Padua – once the Vitaliani cycle had disappeared – was the identification of echoes he left and their effects on the local artistic milieu. P. Toesca (1912, p. 482) noticed a connection between the drawings in Leonardo da Besozzo's *Cronaca* in the Crespi Morbio Collection, Milan, and Florentine naturalism, and also suggested a Tuscan model for the *Libro di Giusto* (of Andrea di Giusto) in the Gabinetto delle Stampe in Rome (A. Venturi, *Le Gallerie nazionali italiane*, IV, 1899, pp. 345–76) and for a collection in the Biblioteca Reale in Turin (n. 102). C. L. Ragghianti (1937, p. 241) thought, for chronological and stylistic reasons, that the three collections did not derive directly from the Vitaliani cycle, but from another of Uccello's models, an earlier notebook. M. Salmi (1938, pp. 28–30) considered the Crespi *Cronaca* earlier than 1442, and excluded any connection with the Vitaliani frescoes of 1445; he suggested that the layout of the niches could be found in the *Men of Arms* in Casa Panigarola in Milan (S. Borsi in F. Borsi, *Bramante*, French edn, 1990, pp. 163–6, with bibliographical notes) and in the architecture of Giambono's *Visitation*, a mosaic in the Mascoli chapel at San Marco in Venice, perhaps through the intermediary of Jacopo Bellini. G. Pudelko (*Early Works*, 1934, pp. 246–9) established a relationship between the *Giants* and the painting of a young man, seen foreshortened from below, in the frescoes at San Miniato (south wall, an attribution not universally accepted). I. Toesca (1952, pp. 16–20) attributed the Cockerell *Cronaca* at Kew to an unknown French follower of Piero della Francesca, after 1445; he considered the links between Uccello's Paduan work and the *cronache* drawings to be groundless and was in agreement with C. Volpe (1980, . 28, n. 4) who found, not without some contention, echoes of Uccello's Paduan work in the Master of the Walter *Cassoni*. For R. L. Mode (1972, p. 373) the drawings in question derived from the Masolino cycles; the three hundred or more figures in these drawings would in any case be too numerous for a façade. In Leonardo da Basozzo's miniatures where the drawings include doors and windows, the figures seem to be men of normal height and not giants, and their style is alien to Uccello's mature period. These are pertinent observations, while Mode's hypothesis of a journey to Rome by Uccello with Donatello around 1430 is unconvincing, and even less that of his collaboration in the Masolinian cycle at San Clemente (op. cit., 1972, p. 377). W. Fontana (1986, p. 140) rejects the drawings and proposes an immediate echo of the Vitaliani cycle in the *Famous Men* of the Palazzo Ducale in Urbino, which he unconvincingly attributes to Uccello at too early a date, *c.* 1446–50.

The monumental monochrome decorations of the Casa Vitaliani were probably a stimulus for the young Mantegna, even if his true source remained Donatello. The exaggeration of Uccello's merits in this way is taken up again by G. Fiocco ('Riposta a Roberto Longhi' in *Vita artistica*, 2, 1926, pp. 144–7) for whom Uccello is the decisive Florentine presence in Venice for Mantegna. A contrary opinion had been expressed by R. Longhi ('Lettera pittorica a Giuseppe Giocco' in *Vita artistica*, I, 1926, pp. 129–32) which relativized Uccello's role in favour of Squarcione's. Fiocco (*L'Arte di Andrea Mantegna*, Bologna, 1927, pp. 44–5) later reaffirmed the importance of Uccello's role in Venice. Ragghianti (1937, p. 242) pointed out Uccello's influence in fresco work at the beginning of the Cinquecento, formerly in the castle of Ghedi, near Brescia (Brescia, Pinacoteca Tosio-Martinengo). Bramante may have been influenced by Uccello to a certain extent in his Bergamo cycle (1477; S. Borsi, op. cit., 1990, pp. 152–4); after his training in the Marches between Urbino and Pesaro, Bramante must have passed through Venice and Padua (Bergamo was also part of the Serenissima's domain). Ragghianti (1977, p. 128) established a link between Uccello's time in Venice and the Paduan studio where studies on optics and perspective flourished, and where Paolo del Pozzo Toscanelli had worked. Uccello's 'differentiated experimental compositions' (p. 484) and Uccello's and Donatello's earlier experiences did not prevent Vasari voicing criticisms of Uccello, in the Brunelleschian milieu, for which Donatello was spokesman. What is certain is that the artistic alliance with Donatello did not last: and by the time they were both back in Florence, they had grown very far apart.

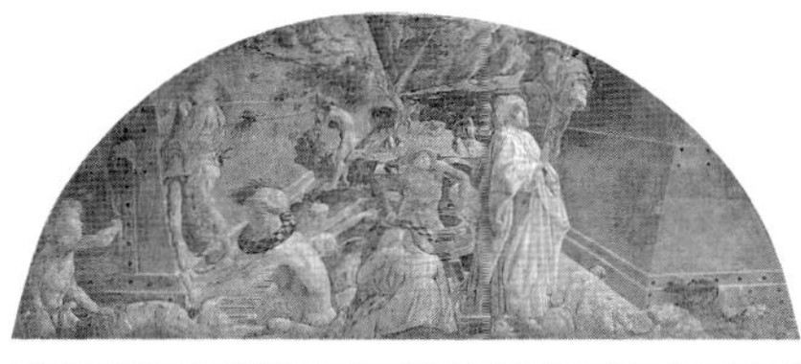

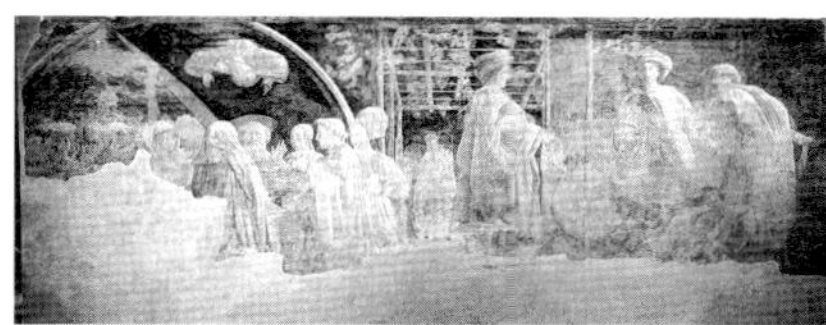

23. STORIES OF NOAH: THE FLOOD AND THE RETREAT OF THE WATERS, NOAH'S SACRIFICE AND THE DRUNKENNESS OF NOAH

Mural in tempera (transferred);
lunette 215 × 510 cm.,
lower part 277 × 540 cm
Santa Maria Novella, Chiostro Verde, fourth bay of the east wall.
About 1447

We have no documents for this great Florentine Quattrocento masterpiece: the ATTRIBUTION to Uccello comes from the sources, which are reliable, since they cite it as the master's most significant work. This was the opinion of Manetti, Albertini, Billi and the Anonimo Magliabechiano (see cat. no. 4), who considered the *Flood* his best work and felt it was closest to Renaissance sensibility. Vasari described a naturalistic work: 'in the same Cloister . . . he painted the Flood and Noah's Ark, with such effort and skill and diligence. He painted corpses, a tempest, the fury of the winds, bolts of lightning, trees torn down, and human fear better than one can say; and he painted the body of a dead man, in perspective and foreshortened, with a crow pecking out its eyes, and a drowned child whose corpse was filled with water and all bloated. He showed the whole range of emotions (*effetti*): there were two men fighting on horseback totally unafraid of the water, and a woman and a man in extreme fear of death, riding a buffalo which was sinking under the waves: they had lost all hope of being saved. It is a work of such good quality and excellence that he acquired the greatest fame. He made figures smaller still through lines of perspective, and painted *mazzocchi* and other things so beautifully. Below this story, he painted a picture of Noah's drunkenness with Cham his son looking at him in contempt, and he gave Cham the features of his friend Dello the Florentine painter, and showed Sem and Japhet, his other sons, covering Noah's nakedness and revealing his shame. Paolo painted a barrel in perspective, being tossed about, which was thought to be very fine, and a trellis laden with grapes, of which the wooden latticework squares can be seen diminishing to a vanishing point, but he made a mistake, because the perspective of the ground on which he placed his figure's feet harmonized with the line of the pergola, but the vanishing point for the barrel was different: I was therefore amazed that such an accurate, diligent painter should have made such a notable error. He also depicted the Sacrifice, with the open Ark, drawn in perspective, with rows of perches one above the other, where the birds were kept, and one could see them flying out, foreshortened more correctly; and in the air could be seen God the Father who appeared above the sacrifice that Noah was making with his sons; and of all the figures that Paulo painted in this work, it was the most difficult, for he was flying head first, in foreshortened form towards the wall, and it had such force that it seemed that this prominent figure would make a hole and bury itself in it. Noah is surrounded by a very great number of animals as beautiful as varied. In sum, Uccello gave the whole work such delicacy and grace that it is without comparison, superior to and better than all other painting; so that no just then, but even now it is greatly praised' (1568, I, pp. 271–12; with variants from 1550, p. 255). In this text there are many references to Ghiberti's description of the hailstorm and tempest painted by Ambrogio Lorenzetti in Siena (*Commentarie Secondo*, 1847 edn, pp. 37–8).

In 1909, the works were detached by *strappo* under the direction of Domenico Fiscali and the sinopie were then lost. Since that time the frescoes have undergone the same treatment as those in the first bay (see cat. no. 4). As far as technique is concerned, this is a mural in tempera, with large elements painted *a secco*. E. Gaspari Campani (1910, p. 210) mentioned three different versions of the head of one of Noah's sons in the sinopia. Today, the chromatic range still appears different from the rest of the cycle, due to the use of ochre and warm earth colours, with a predominance of reds and greens. Besides the work done directly on the wall, the use of partial cartoons has been pointed out (R. Oertel, 1937–40, pp. 300–1), even if U. Procacci (1958, pp. 23–4) expressed doubts on this issue. Campani (1910, p. 204) was the first to notice the alterations and say that it was not a true fresco, but that only the later restorations were done in fresco; he also emphasized certain differences in relation to Calendi's known engraving of the *Drunkenness of Noah (Etruria Pittrice*, 1791, I, n. XIV). The large gaps in the lower, very damaged scenes can be reconstructed in part from the illustrations by Calendi, by Rosini (*Storia della pittura italiana*, Pisa, 1839, I, fig. XXX) and by de Seroux d'Agincourt (*Histoire de l'Art par les Monuments*, Paris, 1823, VI; fig. 146), the latter illustrating *Noah's Sacrifice*. But many of the elements that Vasari describes so meticulously have not been decipherable for a long time.

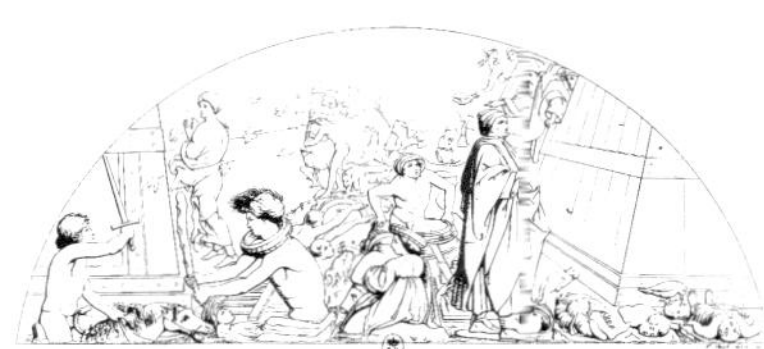

The Flood and the Retreat of the Waters, engraving from Giovanni Rosini, *Storia della pittura italiana*, Pisa 1841, pl. XXX.

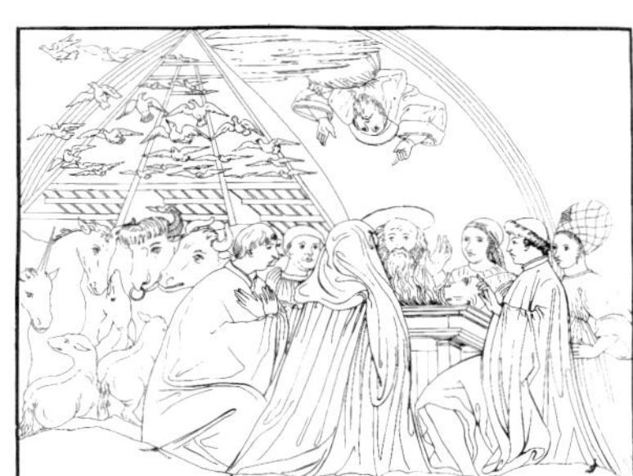

Noah's Sacrifice, engraving by Seroux d'Agincourt from *Histoire de l'art par les monuments*, 1823, VI, pl. 146.

The work's critical fortune is important, with discussions mostly focusing on the DATING, and with little doubt over the attribution. Crowe-Cavalcaselle (1864/1911, Langton-Douglas-De Nicola (eds), IV, p. 115) suggest a date after the *Hawkwood* and Dello's assistance for the whole cycle. D. Colnaghi (1928, p. 265) dated the work from 1446–8, using Vasari's note on Dello's portrait, who returned to Florence in 1446; L. Venturi (1930, p. 72) noted 'Paolo's indifference to the reality of shapes and colours' and although he acknowledged the 'greatest realization of perspective' he saw in it 'a perspectival void filled with great confusion', true to his tendency to give greater importance to Uccello's portraits, even if the *Flood* was 'the culmination' of his talent and one of the 'most heroic moments'. B. Berenson (1932, p. 582; 1936, p. 500) opted for a date later than 1443–4, after the windows; J. von Schlosser (1933, p. 37) agreed with him. M. Salmi (1934, p. 180: around 1445–6; 1934–5: near the Prato frescoes) reduced the chronological limits and W. Paatz (1934, p. 147) proposed *c.* 1446, in agreement with G. Pudelko (1934, p. 231 *et seq.*; 1935, *The Minor Masters*, p. 71; 1936, p. 133; 1939, T. B., p. 525). Salmi (1938, p. 31) identified the large figure giving a blessing in the lunette with Noah (which J. Pope-Hennessy thought doubtful, 1969, p. 147) and suggested (p. 147) that Donatello's relief for the altar of the Santo in Padua, *The Miracle of the Repentant Son*, perhaps derived from Uccello: the date proposed was 1445, the year when Uccello 'began or took up the work again' (p. 31). M. Wackernagel came out in favour of 1445 (1938/1981, p. 142: ten or so years after the first bay), while W. Boeck (1939, p. 113), like Berenson, thought the *Flood* later than 1443–4. R. Oertel (1937–40, pp. 300–302) noted certain contradictions in the composition, suggested the use of different partial drawings and stressed the divergencies between the skyline and vanishing point in *Noah's Sacrifice*. R. Longhi (1940, p. 179), using his interpretation of a 'very late career' for Uccello, proposed a date of 1455–60; he was followed by V. Guzzi (1941, p. 18). K. Clark (*L. B. Alberti on Painting*, 1944, p. 18) established a link between the zephyr in the *Flood* and a recommendation by Alberti (cf. H. Janitscheck, 1877, p. 131) and (1944, *P. Uccello and Abstract Painting*, p. 55) cited links with *De Pictura*; he proposed a date around 1440, observing that the *mazzocchi* around the neck could have depicted what remained of a contemporary head-covering when the wind had blown the fabric about. M. Pittaluga (1946, p. 15) thought the work to be the most representative of Uccello, with a late dating before the *Battles* which he placed in 1456–9. E. Somaré (1946, p. 37) considered the work to be a little later than 1444, while J. Pope-Hennessy (1950; 1969, pp. 145–8) reversed Salmi's suggestion, seeing an echo of Donatello's already mentioned relief (1447) in it with, as a consequence, a date of *c.* 1450–55, a hypothesis taken up by E. Carli (1954; 1959, p. 59: more towards 1450, 'frescoes with finishing touches in tempera'). E. Wind (1954, pp. 412–24) established a link between the *Stories of Noah* and Origen's *In Genesim Homiliae*; E. Micheletti (1956, p. 6) dated the work at *c.* 1446; E. Sindona (1957, p. 60) at 1446–8. J. White (1957, pp. 204–5) saw in it an example of the application of Euclidian rather than Albertian perspective, linked to Ambrogio Lorenzetti; he stressed 'his deep knowledge of phenomena which accompanied the artist's rotation of the head and eyes, like an observer (p. 205), an example of 'synthetic' perspective or *naturalis*. P. Francastel (1957, ill. 6) noted: 'We have two Noahs and two Arks, but the first Noah is looking at himself, enclosed in the second Ark: the plastic unity preceded the symbolic unification.' With the last cleaning for the exhibition of detached frescoes in the Belvedere in Florence, new details emerged, especially in the background (U. Baldini-L. Berti-U. Procacci, *Mostra di affreschi staccati*, 1957, notes 65–6). D. Gioseffi (1958, pp. 123, 129, 134–5) proposed a date of between 1443 and 1456, preferably towards 1445, and a complex analysis of space, and was critical of White and Parronchi's suggestions (1957). He noted a similar construction in the Santa Maria della Scala *Adoration of the Child* (cat. no. 15) and looked forward to seeing (p. 123): 'Paolo's perspectival activity fully restored to being under the influence of Brunelleschian and Albertian orthodoxy'; he saw the work as an example of Uccello's style just before Padua (p. 137), with links with 'the Ptolomeic theory of the double pyramid' reported by Witelus and Ghiberti, and suggested an 'attempt at three-dimensional stereoscopic painting following the technique of the anaglyphs', a hypothesis which was considered as 'fantasist' by Pope-Hennessy (1969, p. 147). P. D'Ancona (1959, p. 14: after Padua) considered Uccello's remarkable work in perspective as the 'expression of a pure fantasy which does not intentionally repudiate scientific accuracy'. U. Procacci (1960, pp. 64–5) dated the entire cycle to the years 1440–50 (more towards 1450), but the rather unconvincing hypothesis of a similar date for the first and fourth bays was rejected by Pope-Hennessy (1969, p. 146). E. Borsook (1960; 1980, pp. 72–4) pointed to the absence of any proper *arriccio* and considered the works to be in tempera *a secco*; for her the 'Dantesque' figure giving a blessing cannot be identified as either Noah or Alberti; she emphasized the variants in the sinopias of the *Drunkenness of Noah* and (mentioned by Gasperi Campani, 1910) proposed a date of *c.* 1450.

A. Parronchi (1957; 1964, pp. 486–92) interpreted the *Flood* as a 'synoptic painting' on the errors of vision, according to the plan proposed in theorem 28 of Book IV of Witelus' *Perspectiva* with regard to perception of size. In the *Flood* 'Euclid's cone, as the principal agent, creates the marvellous view in which objects, near or distant, are in apposition to each other and intersect in the very sophisticated lines of perspective between the two Arks' (1964, p. 487). The gigantic Noah (his interpretation of the large figure in the act of blessing), the shadows which are denser than the figures, the excessive distances, the inconsistent proportions, the 'too solid' *mazzocchi*, the dark, cloudy sky and the lightning can only be the application of errors in *Perspectiva*. Vasari's God the Father would be the image (p. 491) of Noah making the sacrifice, reflected in the concave space of the sky (a seductive, ultimately acceptable hypothesis, as a calculated ambiguity between reflection and representation of the divine), under the influence of Biagio Pelicani. For Parronchi (1963, col. 4667) the 'stylistic rupture' with the first bay is obvious, and the fourth bay is to be dated from 1447–8 (recalling P. Meller's opinion, 1960, in favour of a later dating). Later Parronchi suggested a date of about 1448–50 (after Padua), and then (1981, p. 139) the end of the 1450s, suggesting that the entire conception of the east side could be attributed to Uccello (p. 136). L. Berti (1961, p. 303; 1964, n.p.) stood by this dating of 1446–8, while G. C. Argan (1968, 2, p. 184) opted for 1450–60 and saw in the painting an example of Uccello's argument with Lippi. Berti's dating was accepted by L. Tongiorgi Tomasi (1971, pp. 94–5) while E. Sindona (1972, pp. 26–7) emphasized the 'forced perspectives' of the *Flood* and considered the 'masterpiece of the artist's mature years'. P. A. Rossi (ibid., p. 71–83) made a careful analysis of the composition in perspective of the paintings of the fourth bay of the cloister. L. H. Heydenreich (1972, p. 291) dated the work to the 1450s. C. H. Joost-Gaugier (1974, p. 351) thought the years after Padua were probable and saw a Venetian echo in the image of the crow on the drowned corpse (as in the mosaics of San Marco). C. Volpe (1980, p. 12) put the works after 1443–4 (the cathedral windows). E. M. L. Wakayama (1982, pp. 93–106) dated them at *c.* 1450, recognizing in them a posthumous portrait of Pope Eugenius IV (who died in 1447) and linking the work to the commemoration of the Ecumenical Council of 1439.

In *Noah's Sacrifice* people thought they recognized portraits of Cusano and Traversari, protagonists in the Council, with Noah having the features of Joseph, Patriarch of Constantinople (cf. J. Gill, *The Council of Florence*, Cambridge, 1959). There is a rich bibliography on the identification of the mysterious person issuing the blessing: it is Noah for Cavalcaselle, Salmi and Pittaluga (op. cit.); Pope Eugenius IV for Meller and Wakayama; L. B. Alberti for F. Ames Lewis (1974, pp. 103–5; with doubts: C. Eisler, 1974, p. 259). The Ark, the proportions of which agree with the information given in the Bible (Genesis, 6–13), is partially shown in the same triangular shape as in the panel on Ghiberti's Doors of Paradise. Wakayama's hypothesis, according to which the two arks represent the two Churches, is interesting, but does not take the complexity of the lunette's composition into consideration. This has to be read as a single scene, an effect that Uccello sought by playing on the true/false perspectival representation. F. Zeri (1983, p. 554) and R. Lunardi (1983, p. 42) dated the work at *c.* 1450, while A. Chastel (1983/1984, p. 66) proposed an early dating of 1435–44. D. Covi (1986, ap. 426) examined the inscriptions which are still visible in the cycle; A. De Marchi (notes on Vasari, 1986, p. 239, n. 12) maintained a dating of *c.* 1445–50 and later (*Pittura di luce*, 1990, p. 202) of 1447, while F. Petrucci (1987, I, p. 282) dated it *c.* 1447–8; A. Angelini (1990, p. 76) reaffirmed that the work belonged to Uccello's mature period.

The fresco's importance on a theoretical level is incontestable: Uccello's return to the Chiostro Verde (for reasons still not clarified) is stylistically far removed from the first (already remarkable) bay. A long time afterwards Uccello re-established the 'Ghibertian' design of the subdivision of the wall into 'four stories, that is to say effects'. The work has an ambiguous composition, as if it were a question of a construction involving a single perspective in each of the superimposed levels, but contradicted by the unusual details by differences of composition, by the phenomena of vision, due to the different positions of the observer, with a single viewpoint for the *Flood* and a different one for the lower scenes. The first impression, which was knowingly calculated, is almost that of an urban, axial and infinite perspective between the sides of the Ark (in reality these are two different views of the same enormous Ark). Here Uccello once again achieved the synthesis between symbolic intention, allusive game, narration, rational problem and poetic creation which characterizes his best works. He demonstrates the extraordinary possibilities of expression of his optico-psychological interpretation of 'subjective' space, as opposed to the direction taken by Florentine painting towards the middle of the century. In the absence of any definite data, we can judge the work contemporary with the change of style accompanying his return from Padua. So we can envisage the current chronology of around 1447 as a date, though opinions are not unanimous. It could be that the Dominicans had wanted to link their initiative with a commemoration of Eugenius IV, elected pope in their mother house at Santa Maria sopra Minerva in Rome.

Recently (L. Marin, 1990, pp. 129–32), attempts have been made to give the cycle an Augustinian interpretation, with the Ark as the City of God, the scenes illustrating the building of the Church in the world. According to Saint Augustine, the proportions of the Ark given in the Bible were analogous to those of the human body (metaphor of Christ; the wood of the ark referring to the wood of the Cross). Marin dates the entire cycle (p. 116) between 1445 and 1450 While this interpretation is seductive, it seems strange to attribute Augustinian leanings to the patrons when they are manifestly Dominicans, as is demonstrated in the Spanish chapel.

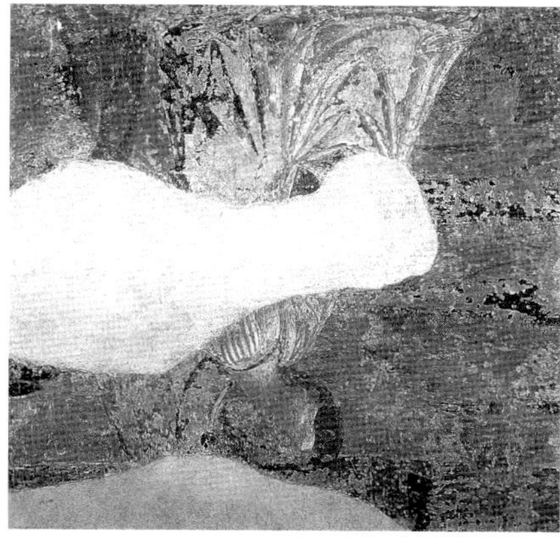

24. SCENES OF MONASTIC LIFE

Frescoes.
Florence, San Miniato al Monte, upper gallery of the cloister.
About 1447–54

The earliest attribution to Uccello dates back to Francesco Albertini (*Memoriale*, 1510): 'In the first upper cloister are XII paintings by Paolo Uccello.' The information given in Antonio Billi's *Libro* (1516; ed. C. Frey, 1892, pp. 24–5) is less precise: 'He did more painting in terre-verte in the Cloister of San Miniato al Monte, but it was not highly thought of.' In the first half of the Cinquecento the frescoes were considered as monochromes of mediocre quality, and this scathing judgment was taken up by the Anonimo Magliabechiano: 'He also did paintings in the upper cloister of San Miniato a Monte, inside, and below by the entrance, but these are not much valued' (ed. C. Frey, 1892, p. 100). Vasari furnished a few supplementary details: 'Outside Florence, in the cloister of San Miniato, he worked in partly coloured terre-verte on the life of the Holy Fathers; but he hardly observed any unity in these stories as he should have done by painting them in one colour – for he made the fields blue, the city red and the buildings whatever colour took his fancy; for articles which imitate stone cannot and must not be tinted with another colour' (1550, p. 254; 1568, I, p. 270). These reserves were an expression of Vasari's naturalistic viewpoint, but Uccello would certainly not have accepted Alberti's suggestions (*De Pictura*, Book I, 9; ed. C. Grayson, 1980, pp. 22–4): 'The colour of fire is painted red, air light blue, water green, and the earth grey and ash-coloured.' However, while 'enriched' monochrome did not correspond to Alberti's tastes, it did have illustrious precedents quoted by the very same Alberti: 'They say that the Ancient painters Polignotus and Timanthes used only four colours, and Aglaophon astonished everybody by painting in a single simple colour' (ibid., Book II, 86). By the middle of the sixteenth century, the frescoes must have already been in a poor state and barely valued, since in 1547 Bernardo Buontalenti was allowed to paint his *Christ on the Road to Emmaus* over one of Uccello's scenes, and sign and date it. Vasari recounts a comic episode, *à propos* this cycle, of Uccello running away because the abbot was so mean that he gave him only cheese to eat, but there was a final reconciliation: the abbot 'brought him back to work and ordered a diet other than cheese for him'. There is no other information to confirm this episode, which was taken up in F. Bocchi-G. Cinelli's guidebook (1677, p. 16) but it contained an authentic element which allows us to glimpse a difficult relationship with his patrons: he abandoned the work, reflected on his decision and returned. This could explain the substantial differences between the frescoes of the two walls, which is often raised by critics and which supposes a chronological gap between the two. In fact the Quattrocento frescoes are situated on the east side (which has eight scenes) and on the south side (of which only two frescoes remain along with the fresco of 1547). There are interesting contrasts between the two: on the south side, the compositions are sparser and more spaced out and the perspectival construction is more simplified. There are other differences, too, in the painted architectonic elements, in the composition of the lower band (on the east side there is the emblem of the mystic ladder, which is missing on the other side), not to mention obvious variations in the pictorial treatment as well as in the sinopie. The hypothesis that its execution was staggered over a number of years seems a likely one, and on the more recent wall (the south side) Uccello appears to have had quite a lot of help. The divergences in perspectival construction and composition result from the different viewpoints which Uccello was taking into account: the spaced-out perspectives on the east side were conceived both for close and distant viewing (from the opposite side, on to which the monastic cells led in the old bishop's palace); the frescoes on the south side were made for a series of close viewpoints and consequently each scene was expanded horizontally. There are also differences in conception of the *trompe-l'oeil* architecture, which on the south side harmonizes with the real, rather like Fra Angelico at San Marco. *Trompe-l'oeil* corbels separate the scenes, with pilaster strips down to the ground; a pediment with red and green niches (three large red niches correspond to the scene below) marks a radical change in the decorative design.

The frescoes were plastered over in the seventeenth century: they were not visible when Baldinucci's book was published in 1845 (I, p. 447, n. I), nor at the time of Milanesi's publication of Vasari (1878, II, p. 207, n. 1). Their discovery dates from 1925 (M. Marangoni, 1930, pp. 403–20), with new fragments found in 1942 (M. Salmi, 1950, pp. 22–3). The discovery of the upper decoration of the south wall dates from 1969, as does the recovery of the sinopias, which were detached and restored under Giuseppe Rosi's direction. The detached frescoes were replaced *in situ* in 1976 (L. Berti, 1988, p. 252).

Marangoni (op. cit.) thought the paintings 'a revelation as far as colour was concerned'; he noted the unusual carmine pinks, an alteration in a halo painted in perspective, compared the frescoes with the London *Battle*, interpreted the colour as 'one of the rarest and most seductive aspects of Paolo's Gothic colouration' in the same way as Loeser (1898) and Longhi (1914), and dated the cycle before the *Stories of Noah*. L. Venturi (1930, p. 77) felt that the contradictions in perspective revealed a 'fragmented way of seeing perspective', while B. Berenson rejected the attribution to Uccello (at least as far as the conception was concerned) and proposed Giovanni di Francesco (1932, p. 582; 1936, p. 278). W. Paatz (1934, p. 118) restored the attribution to Uccello even if he remained a little ambiguous on the autography of the work: he proposed a slightly later date than the Chiostro Verde *Creation* scenes, which he considered a youthful work. G. Pudelko (1934, pp. 243–6) opted for the attribution to Uccello, but with a collaborator (the Karlsruhe Master); he pointed out the division of space into compartments, as can be seen in Masolino's work, and the 'dialectic style' of the perspective, with a dating of *c.* 1440. Later (1935, *Der Meister*, p. 125), he made a distinction between Uccello and the Karlsruhe Master, to whom he confidently attributed the most decipherable scene of the south wall, with about 1440 as a date – a date extended to the two walls – and noted an echo in them of Masaccio's *Trinity*. Pudelko (1936, p. 33) also risked a date of 'probably' before 1440, and catalogued the cycle among the most likely works by Uccello (using an assistant) towards *c.* 1439 (1939, T. B., p. 525). M. Wackernagel (1938/1981, p. 124) took up Albertini's attribution of the twelve scenes to Uccello and dated them towards 1450, while M. Salmi (1938, pp. 19–22) chose an early dating, *c.* 1436–9. He suggested contacts between Uccello and the young Domenico Veneziano, whom he thought might have been Uccello's assistant before his (documented) arrival in Florence: 'the enlarged episodes of a Thebaïd' would have found an early echo in the cycle in the Chiostro degli Aranci at the Badia. W. Boeck (1939, pp. 23–8) attributed the south wall to Uccello, praising the 'rocks painted in the ancient manner' and proposing the impossible date of *c.* 1425 (among other things before the cloister was built). R. Frey (1947, p. 242) talked of 'almost abstract painting, like architecture'. M. Pittaluga (1946, pp. 11–13) thought space was like a 'vital protagonist' in the frescoes; she spoke of 'space that had been meditated upon' and pointed out the unreality of the colours: 'everything is secondary to the perspectival function'. She dated the cycle at *c.* 1440, considering it to be earlier than the *Flood* and *Battles*. E. Somaré (1946, p. 37) dated the Benedictine cycle immediately after the *Hawkwood*. J. Pope-Hennessy (1950, pp. 143–4) made a distinction between the two walls (only the east was attributed to Uccello), with a dating of *c.* 1440. M. Salmi (1950, pp. 22–3) took account of the new fragments discovered in 1942, in a survey of the parts of the cycle which had just been found. He noted the 'homogenous style' of the east wall, a weakened 'power of fantasy' and illustrative styles on the other wall, in which he discerned the intervention of a collaborator, whom he identified with the Quarate Master, a disciple of Uccello's *c.* 1440–5. The date he proposed was *c.* 1440 for the first wall and shortly afterwards for the other (p. 26). He was followed by E. Carli (1954; 1959, pp. 54–5) who made a distinction between the two walls (he attributed only the east to Uccello), with a slightly earlier date of 1439. D. Gioseffi (1958, p. 137) also attributed only the east side to Uccello, after Venice and before the *Hawkwood*; P. D'Ancona (1959, pp. 9–10) 'at least' the east wall in 'the middle of the forties', praising the 'measured, abstract' world of the frescoes. U. Procacci (1960, p. 39) attributed the two walls to Uccello and followed E. Sindona (1957, p. 58), regarding the chronology: slightly later than 1430, after Venice. L. Berti (1964, n.p.) thought the cycle was slightly later than the *Hawkwood*, but not beyond 1443.

A. Parronchi (1957/1964, pp. 476–7) placed the cycle before 1443 and stressed two aspects which were in open contradiction with Alberti: the empty space in the middle of the composition and the restrained number of figures. For Parronchi, the frescoes were an example of 'subtle experimentation' in space and perspective where 'the purpose of spacial depth is allied to a sense of relationships on the flat surface' in a 'purely intuitive, discontinuous and irregular recourse' to the Brunelleschian concept of space (1963, col. 465: after 1443–4, before the *Flood*). Parronchi (1974, pp. 25–6) also thought the frescoes were like an experimental phase after the Prato ones, and favoured a date at the beginning of the 1440s, before the *Hawkwood*. In the meantime H. Saalman (1964, pp. 558–63) and A. M. Fortuna (1957, pp. 40–1) published documents on the cloister of San Miniato and on Uccello's intervention, with Antonio di Papi, in the refectory during 1445 (1964, doc. VII). The outcome was that the building works for the upper floor of the cloister lasted until 1447, a *terminus post quem* for Uccello's frescoes, accepted by J. Pope-Hennessy (1969, pp. 142–4). For him, only the east wall was attributable to Uccello, but he expressed doubts on an early date for the cycle in relation to the *Stories of Noah*: he saw the painter's adherence to *costruzione legittima* in them. Saalman (1964, p. 559) identified Giovanni Schiavo as being the painter who in 1448 was paid for a *Saint Benedict* in the dormitory and other paintings in the refectory (however, only decorative fragments have been found) that formerly L. Dami (1915, p. 244) interpreted as a work by Giovanni da Fogliano. The presence of Antonio di Papi was also mentioned by Berti (1961, p. 306, n. 11; in this essay, p. 302, the cycle is placed after the *Hawkwood* and before Prato). Successive studies of the cloister and its restoration (F. Gurrieri, 1969, p. 49 *et seq.*; C. R. Mack, 1974, pp. 447–8; F. Gurrieri, 1976; M. Ferrara-F. Quinterio, 1984, pp. 353–5; F. Gurrieri in Collected Works, 1988, pp. 79–96) keep the *post quem* limit of 1447, while according to the *Libro di ricordanze di San Bartolomeo a Firenze* (c. 77v) in the central archives of the Olivetan order, the frescoes would have been ordered from Uccello in 1461 (*La Graticola*, Florence, 1976, p. 130, quoted in Gurrieri, 1988, p. 82, n. 44), too late a dating for the east wall, but perhaps valid for the south side (with collaborators). E. Sindona (1970, p. 83) preferred to keep the attribution to Uccello for the two walls, between 1430 and 1436 before the *Hawkwood*. L. Tongiorgi Tomasi (1971, pp. 90–91) found that the attribution of the south wall to Uccello was generally rejected and attributed only the east wall to Uccello, with a date of 1439: the apparently archaic style made him doubt the documents which stated that the cloister was finished between 1443 and 1447, with the construction in 1448 of the staircase leading to the upper floor of the cloister (with the frescoes). P. A. Rossi (in Sindona, 1972, p. 54) analysed the perspectival construction of the two scenes of the cycle, which reveal the application of Albertian *costruzione legittima*, using a single vanishing point. L. Berti (1988, pp. 249–57) took up the whole problem again, analysing in detail the remains of the painting and the sinopias, which are not so well-finished as those in the Chiostro Verde because of the use of the fresco technique. Making a distinction in attribution between the two walls (only the east could certainly be said to be by Uccello), Berti (who nonetheless counts among the 'unifiers' of Uccello's register of work) admitted that the south wall reopened the question of a collaborator (Prato, Quarate) and wondered why this important intervention was not documented. His probably well-founded suggestion is that the painter was not paid directly by the Olivetans, even if we cannot be sure about this. In the period from 1447 to 1448, Piero de' Medici, Cosimo's son, had commissioned the marble tabernacle for the basilica of San Miniato, while works in the cloister were financed by the powerful burgers' guild of the Calimala. A. Angelini (1990, p. 77) admitted that the classification of the frescoes was 'arduous' and in any case he judged them to be later than 1447.

As far as the east wall goes, there is no doubt about the unity of conception; this wall corresponds to rooms added, in the Quattrocento, to the Trecento sacristy opposite the 'Bishop's palace'; the artist probably took this fact into account, considering the place as a residential building giving directly on to the cloister wall. The work probably dates back to *c.* 1448 and the extreme simplification of the organization and scenes, probably requested by the religious order for clearly symbolic purposes, explains the unified character of Uccello's work (as Salmi remarked in 1950). It is not certain that the perpendicular wall, on the south side, was earlier than the intervention in the refectory, nor that Antonio di Papi was implicated in it, but there was probably quite a long time lapse between the two walls, as might be indicated by the episode of the quarrel with the miserly abbot quoted by Vasari. This interruption has prompted a fresh look at the more sparsely spaced design, the closer adherence to the structure, the renunciation of the rigorous perspectival construction of the preceding scenes (also explained by the fact that it was unnecessary to be seen from a distance here, the opposite side not being practicable), and the work being less supervised and largely confided to collaborators. These may have been Giovanni Foliano or Antonio di Papi, already active in convent decoration. Uccello's privileged position can be explained by the recognition of his qualities and advancing years: for this in fact is a mature work. Marking a moment of hardening on theoretical positions, it is deliberately archaic and perhaps polemical (whence the contradictions between the stylistic exegesis and the documented references). The painter is engaged in a rigorous demonstration of the 'eye's reasoning' within a design using central perspective: to show the validity of his theory, he changed colours 'to whatever . . . took his fancy' (Vasari); he used colours to define the quality of perspective planes and not objects, to define space, not nature. Elaborating a simple sermon on monastic life, eliminating the superfluous, composing solid spatial structures that interpret ascetic solitude in a pleasing manner, Uccello distanced himself, towards the middle of the century, from the naturalism and sentimentality that were developing in religious painting through Lippi and his followers. Many problems remain to be cleared up about the execution, the identity of the collaborators, the chronology, the commission (completely obscure), the iconography and the sources of the cycle, the restorations (to which we perhaps owe the refined figure of the monk at table, on the edge of the south wall, recovered in 1969, and shown at the Florentine exhibition, *L'Età di Masaccio* (cat. notice, 1990, p. 216, M. C. Fabbri), attributed by Berti (1988) to Uccello's collaborator and the modern restorations (the remarkable angel in the fifth scene of the east wall seems to have been considerably retouched).

In its present state the cycle on the east wall comprises eight fragmentary scenes, with partially decipherable inscriptions below and plinths composed of three squares for each scene, in mock marble with *trompe-l'oeil* paterae. In them we can see the mysterious emblem of the ladder (possibly Jacob's dream or Saint Bernard's vision). In the first scene, which is more decipherable than the others, a monk-saint is meditating in front of a white building painted in perspective, surrounded by marshy vegetation, while in the background on the right there is a wide bay, an echo of the Karlsruhe *Adoration*. The inscription is hardly legible. There is no element to suggest that the episode has any links with the life of Saint Benedict, painted at San Miniato in the sacristy by Spinello Aretino (1387). In the second scene, a seated monk, with a foreshortened halo, is the only decipherable human presence, while in the centre a river weaves its way through a landscape of clay – almost a desert landscape. The inscription reads '*Perfetta abstinentia*'. In the third scene only a piece of landscape remains: in the sinopia there is a monk and a seated angel. In the fourth a seated monk raises his arm in a gesture of amazement before the arrival of a young man (the scene takes place indoors). Of the fifth a monk-saint remains kneeling in prayer with a seated angel, which is more famous and more frequently reproduced than the rest of the cycle. The fragmentary inscription refers to the very essence of the Benedictine rule: '*[Apparen?] dogli l'angelo, orando e lavorando vinse pe[r]fetamente l'ac[c]idia.*' Behind the monk there are traces of the hermitage, in angular perspective. The ground is treated as overlapping scales, as in Uccello's other works. The heavily restored angel is reminiscent of Tolentino's page in the London *Battle*. The scene refers to Saint Benedict, or in any case figures the exaltation of his rule. Very little remains of the sixth scene: the fragments of a red building, a figure overturning an amphora as he runs, traces of a monk's ear on the opposite side: there is nothing to provide a satisfactory interpretation of the subject-matter. The seventh scene is even more damaged: fragments of a head, the remains of a building and, in the sinopia, traces of another monk. The eighth scene, recovered in 1942, concludes the sequence on the east wall. Published for the first time by Salmi in 1950–51, it is of remarkable quality, showing a seated monk, some buildings, and, on the right, five brothers standing. Berti (1988, p. 272) sees 'an angular, almost mechanical rigidity, but an intentional one' in the principal protagonist, and praises the 'stereometric' and powerful pictorial qualities of the scene.

The south wall was probably divided into four scenes instead of eight, developed horizontally and divided by *trompe-l'oeil* corbels painted in terre-verte. Besides the spacing of the decorative motifs the changes are substantial: among others, the elimination of any attempt at perspective. Today, only the remains of three scenes are visible, of which two are incomplete, while in 1547 Buontalenti introduced one of his frescoes, a sign of the original's poor state of conservation even at that period. In the first scene a monk-saint has a vision of God the Father surrounded by cherubim in the presence of a young man who is raising his arms to acclaim the miracle. The black crow on the ground is reminiscent of an episode in the life of Saint Benedict (Salmi, 1950; Berti, 1988; but in Domenico Cavalca the crow is feeding Saint Paul the Hermit and Saint Anthony Abbot). In the lower inscription, we can read: '*Quarta generatione dei cenobiti oratori.*' This indicates the general theme of the cycle: stories of different generations of monks, with the episodes drawn from the lives of Paul of Thebes, Pacomius and Anthony the Hermit. In the second scene, of which only a third is visible (after Buontalenti's fresco), there is a monk, a palm tree and a kneeling hermit. On the wall, between the south side of the cloister and the first room on the south side, there are the remains of two monks painted in terre-verte – a refined piece of work, perhaps restored in the sixteenth century. On the lower plinth of this side, we can see the remains of two small unidentified figures standing in profile: a king, and a draped nude in the act of haranguing what might perhaps be a leper (Berti) or a penitent Saint Jerome.

The origins of the cycle remain obscure as well as their inspiration, perhaps guided by sources such as Palladio's *Vita Patrum*, Saint Jerome's *Vita Pauli*, Saint Athanasius's *Vita Pachomii* and, finally, the opening up to the eastern world as a result of the Council of 1439.

Payment for the lost fresco in the 'refectory with a crucifix surrounded by a decoration' was made to Uccello and to Antonio di Papi in 1455 (ASF, *Conventi soppressi* 168, ms. 147, c. LV; Saalman, 1964, doc. VII). A supplement of two florins was paid them for the 'said paintings executed in oil when they were not obliged to do it': the relatively modest sum leads us to think it was a painting of limited use, but it is difficult to pronounce on it when the painting itself has disappeared. A Parronchi imagined a panel painted in oils and hung on the wall, a solution adopted by Alesso Baldovinetti in the Cardinal of Portugal's chapel in San Miniato al Monte (R. Wedgwood Kennedy, 1938, pp. 107–8) in combination with the fresco, but this suggestion is doubtful. Uccello and Antonio di Papi worked in the refectory from August 1454 at least (Fortuna, 1957, pp. 40 *et seq.*), while Antonio di Papi and a certain Corsino (his brother?) were paid in 1446 to whitewash the interior of the same church (O. Giglioli, 'La Cappella del Cardinale di Portogallo', *Rivista d'Arte*, 3, 1906, p. 96; Saalman, 1964, p. 559, n. 18). Echoes of the lost *Crucifixion* may have been found in the one in Santa Maria Maggiore attributed to Giovanni di Francesco, with the arms of the cross foreshortened, projecting from the vegetal decoration (*Pitture di luce*, 1990, ill. p. 55), a work which is neither dated nor documented, but which we can probably place between 1452–4 and 1457, the year of Giovanni di Francesco's death. In this case the *terminus post quem* could become 1455, near the painter's death, whose links with Uccello have been established through documents and are often evident stylistically. An as yet unsolved problem is the artistic significance of Antonio di Papi, who was sometimes been promoted to the rank of Uccello's assistant and perhaps even higher, in attempts to identify a presumed *alter ego*. According to some rare information in our possession, he was probably a house-painter who had a long association with the Olivetans, even though the remuneration for the refectory painting was shared equally between him and Uccello.

25. SAINT ANTHONY ABBOT, SAINT COSMAS AND SAINT DAMIAN

Fresco (now lost).
Formerly Florence, hospital of Lelmo (or San Matteo).
About 1448–50?

Vasari was the first to mention this work (1550, p. 253): 'His first pictures were for the hospital of Lelmo in Florence, in the women's section: a Saint Anthony with Saint Cosmas and Damian, in fresco.' In the second edition (1568, I, p. 269), Vasari added several details: 'Paolo's first paintings were in fresco, in an oblong niche, and drawn in perspective, in the hospital of Lelmo: that is a Saint Anthony Abbot, and Saint Cosmas and Saint Damian on either side of him.' It is no accident that in this edition the reference to the women's section has been dropped: the biographer had taken note of his own contradiction when he had referred to this as one of Uccello's earliest works. In fact, the female section of the hospital was not built until 1445–7, with money from the Arte del Cambio, the Bankers' Guild, who dedicated it to their own patron Saint Matthew (F. L. Del Migliore, 1684, pp. 248–57; Vasari also mentioned some paintings by Uccello that have since disappeared). Mariotto di Cristofano's retable, *The Mystic Marriage of Saint Catherine with Saints Mary Magdalen, Agnes, Dorothy and Elizabeth*, formerly in the hospital of San Matteo and now in the Accademia (inv. no. 3162, 1890) dates from these years. If Vasari's first details are accurate, the fresco must have a DATE of after 1447, so it cannot be a question of Uccello's 'first paintings'. The hospital took its name from its founder, Lelmo, or Lemmo Balducci, who died in 1388–9. Since 1784, it has been home to the Accademia di Belle Arti. Uccello would have worked in the wing added in 1447, fully justifying his preoccupation with perspective with his figures 'in an oblong niche', for which a precedent can be found in the *Blessed Jacopone* in the Prato cycle (*c.* 1434–5). The Trecento hospital, which was solely for men, was dedicated to Saint Nicholas, and the absence of this saint in the fresco would confirm that it was indeed situated in the women's wing which had been added. Following Vasari, F. Baldinucci (1686; 1845 edn, I, p. 447), in his piece on the San Matteo frescoes, tells us that they were no longer visible and had probably disappeared at the time of building work in 1560.

Eugenius IV's and Luca degli Albizzi's solicitude for the hospital in the years round 1443 is a factor worthy of attention, especially if we recall that Luca degli Albizzi was a member of Santa Maria del Fiore's Office of Works at the time when Uccello was working on the oculi of the cupola and on the clock. Although there is no definite information on this, Uccello could possibly have continued with the same patrons, hence his comission there. Giovanni di Francesco's *Saint Anthony, Abbot* (formerly in the Brivio Collection, Milan, Pinacoteca Ambrosiana) might have echoes of Uccello's, even though as a mature artist Francesco gradually distanced himself from Uccello's influence. J. Pope-Hennessy's hypothesis (1950; 1969, p. 179) that Uccello's fresco belonged to the youthful period (according to him) of the *Hawkwood* seems unconvincing. M. Salmi (1938, p. 15) had already rejected Vasari's suggestion of a youthful work, preferring to date the frescoes in the 1440s. The hospital of Lelmo's tastes appear to be stamped with an austere religious traditionalism: Lorenzo Monaco painted in fresco in the men's wing (perhaps a fragment of it remains in the detached fresco of the *Man of Sorrows* in the Museo degli Innocenti in Florence, cf. F. Brasioli, in *Santa Maria Nuova, Il tesoro dell'arte nell'antico ospedale fiorentino*, Florence, 1989, p. 50, n. 25). In 1472, the pictorial decoration of the monument to the founder was commissioned from the elderly Stefano d'Antonio (D. Colnaghi, 1928, p. 257: he died in 1483), a pupil of Bicci di Lorenzo who, in 1468, had already painted the story of the *Passion* in fresco in the San Matteo dormitory, a *Saint Christopher* under the outside loggia and a *Mary Magdalen* in the garden. A further probable reason for the patrons' choice of Uccello was his adherence to the tradition of Lorenzo Monaco and Ghiberti in the Santa Maria degli Angeli frescoes (?), or his *Nativity* in stained glass in the Duomo, rather than his inveterate experimental side.

26. THE AVANE PREDELLA: THE MAN OF SORROWS, WITH THE VIRGIN AND SAINT JOHN THE EVANGELIST

Panel, 22 × 177 cm.
Florence, Museo di San Marco.
Sala del Lavabo.
1452

Illustrated on p. 330

This is a 'minor' predella, of simplified traditional design, with coats-of-arms on either side, a gold-leaf background and inscriptions. In the lateral medallions are half-length figures of the Virgin and Saint John, both weeping, and in the centre Christ, the Man of Sorrows. It is extremely difficult to form an opinion on the latter – a pathetic, nervous drawing, since a recent restoration (in the 1960s) removed large sections of repainting. The not entirely legible inscription which took the place of a dedication dates the panel: 'ADI XXIII DI SETEMBRE 1452', while the name of the patron remains fragmentary. This is a non-documented work which has aroused little discussion, despite the great quality of the lateral figures. Their splayed haloes extend up into the area of the stamped circles, while their bent bodies, narrowly contained within these circular compartments, are seen slightly from the side because of the close-up angular viewpoint; they reveal a subtly refined perspective within a composition that is deliberately controlled and austere. This is a work of accentuated formality, with a refined linear elegance, in which a late nostalgia for the Sienese world and Lorenzo Monaco shines through. This interpretation of religious painting is decidedly different from Lippi, at a time when Fra Angelico was living in Rome and working for Nicholas V. The Virgin's head still shows features similar to

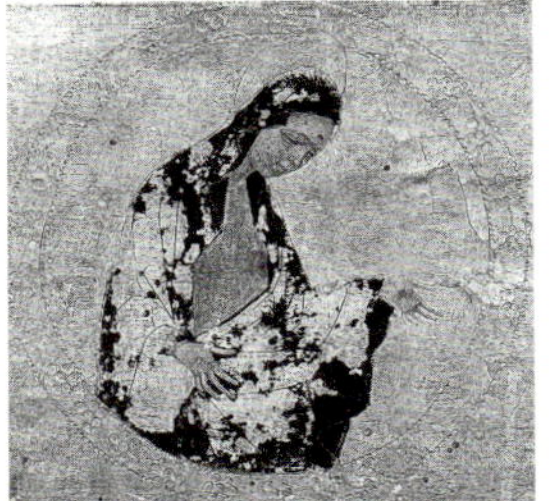

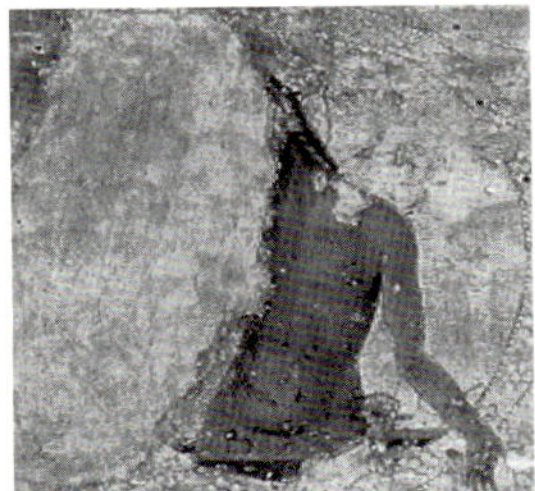

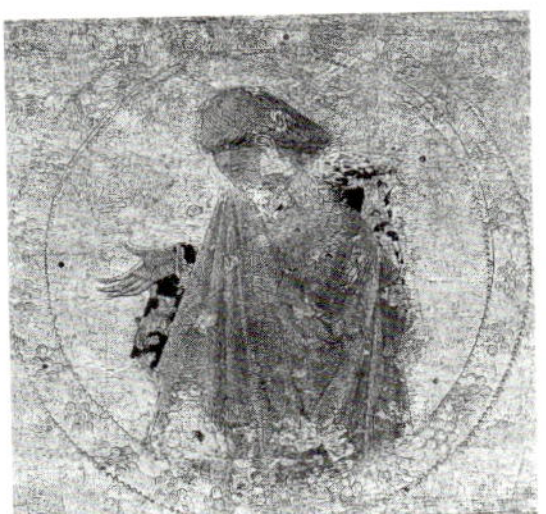

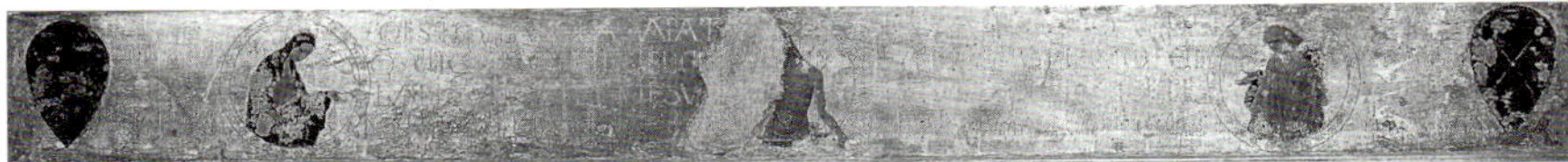

those in the stained-glass *Nativity* in Santa Maria del Fiore, which Saint John – with his skilfully rendered hair, his extended linear elegance and pointed profile, as in Uccello's late works, but with a drapery reminiscent of one of the figures in Ambrogio Lorenzetti's *Presentation in the Temple* – seems to anticipate later figures, some of whom Pudelko attributed to the Karlsruhe Master. 'Proof of a moment one might describe as equidistant between the art of the supposed Prato Master and the equally supposed Karlsruhe Master; with an incontestable quality which leads one to attribute the predella directly to Paolo Uccello' (L. Berti, 1990, p. 221).

The predella was part of a lost retable figuring the *Annunciation*, painted for the oratory of the Santissima Annunziata at Avane in Valdarno: all trace of the principal panel has been lost, for it was stolen during the nineteenth century. The predella was in the Uffizi's reserve collection when Longhi drew attention to it (1940, p. 179) as one of Uccello's works. He found its style uncertain but maintained an 'incredible date' of 1452. He used it to foster his scathing opinion of the painter as an 'ingenious artisan' and 'paradoxical decorator of chests' who appeared to him, even after the middle of the Quattrocento, as late in his conquest of Florentine painting in that century. Longhi dated the masterpieces, from the *Battles* to the *Stories of Noah* in the Chiostro Verde, later than this uncertain attempt in the predella.

The ATTRIBUTION to Uccello was rejected by J. Pope-Hennessy (1950; 1969, p. 173) in favour of the 'Prato Master' for whom this work represented the only definite chronological reference point. Critics have not taken up this proposition and at the Florentine exhibition of 1954 (E. Micheletti, in cat. 1954, n. 21), the predella was exhibited as a work by Uccello, with doubts; it was considered as autograph by E. Carli (1954; 1959, p. 60), L. Berti (1961, p. 300 and 303, with affinities with the Kress *Madonna* at Allentown), confirmed in 1964 'in no way monumental but narrative, with caricatural and humorous sides, but in any case always in a very elegant style' and in 1990 (*L'Età di Masaccio*, pp. 220–1), by A. Parronchi (1963, col. 467: example of the 'small items' which Vasari mentioned, belonging to works attributed to the Prato Master, Uccello's late activity), L. Tongiorgi Tomasi (1971, pp. 96–7, 'generally attributed' to Uccello), A. Angelini (1990, p. 77: similar to the Thyssen *Crucifixion*), and M. C. Improta (in *La chiesa e il convento di San Marco a Firenze*, II, Florence 1990, p. 114). D. Gioseffi thought it a work by the school of Uccello (1958, p. 137) while A. Parronchi has dubiously attributed it to Baldovinetti's early period (1974, p. 23) in an attempt to resolve the question of the Prato Master.

There is little doubt about the DATING, even if the third figure in the date is not easily readable. Before it was cleaned at the end of the 1960s, E. Sindona dated it, on stylistic grounds, at *c.* 1446–56 (1957, p. 60). In 1990 it was exhibited in Florence (*L'Età di Masaccio*, Florence, Palazzo Vecchio, 7 June – 16 September 1990).

In spite of its state of conservation the great quality of this work can still be appreciated. The attribution to Uccello is obvious, given the Virgin's features – which can be compared with the Prato group – and those of Saint John, similar to the Karlsruhe group, given also the incoherence of the different subgroups and *alter ego* that have been proposed and that in no way help towards understanding Uccello's poetic and stylistic progress. The predella of 1452 marks – and this explains the multiple attributions – a little-known moment in the Master's activity: with the disappearance of the portrait of the Blessed Andrea Corsini and the panel for the Lanfredini brothers, there remains only this predella as proof of a trend which would continue to be dominant in the 1460s, until a time when Uccello's activity slackened off (?), but his prestige remained intact, with the election of Giovanni di Francesco as one of the directors of the Company of Saint Luke. No details exist on the patron (Antonio di Piero di Giovanni del Golia) who had the panel made 'for the salvation of his soul and that of his family' as the inscription indicates.

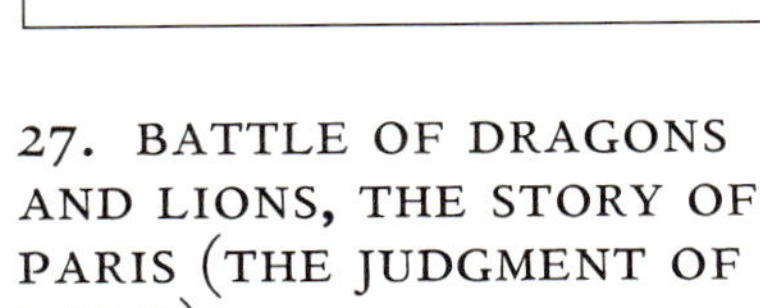

27. BATTLE OF DRAGONS AND LIONS, THE STORY OF PARIS (THE JUDGMENT OF PARIS)

Tempera on canvas (now lost).
Formerly Florence, Palazzo Medici-Riccardi, 'camera di Lorenzo'.
About 1452–9 (?)

The Medici inventory of 1492, compiled at the time of Lorenzo the Magnificent's death, mentioned three other paintings as the same time as the *Battles*: they were 'one of a battle of dragons & lions, one of the story of paris by the hand of pagholo uccello & one by the hand of franc(esc)o di pesello of a hunt'. The Anonimo Magliabechiano mentions only 'paintings of jousting in the Palazzo Medici', that is to say the *Battles* (cat. no. 14). Vasari referred to them in the second edition of Uccello's *Vita* (1568, I, p. 270): 'In the house of the Medici, he painted in tempera on canvas some scenes with animals, a subject always dear to his heart. He studied unrelentingly in order to be a success at it . . . in the same palace, among other animal stories, he painted lions fighting with such terrifying movement and violence that they seemed to be alive. But among other things, the most original was a story in which a ferocious dragon was fighting a lion; and he showed its fierceness with such vigorous movement and the venom spurting from his mouth and eyes; near by a little peasant woman tending an ox is painted most beautifully in foreshortened form ... and similarly, the country girl, who is full of fear and running away from these animals. There were also some very natural-looking shepherds, and a country landscape which was considered very beautiful in its time.' The details in the inventory and Vasari's description bear only a broad resemblance. In the first edition, Vasari had already mentioned the paintings (1550, p. 420; Vasari-Milanesi, III, 1879, p. 37) in his *Vita di Pesello e Francesco Peselli*: 'In the (Medici) Palace today, one can still see several canvases by his hand with lions behind a grill, which seem almost alive; and others roaming free, one of which is fighting a serpent; on another canvas he painted an ox and a fox with other animals, all in a vivacious, vivid manner.' The contradictions and uncertainties in the attribution are obvious (and in Pesellino's *Vita* the canvases are mentioned after the Cavalcanti predella painted by Giovanni di Francesco). At the time of the Medici inventory of 1598, the battle 'of the dragon and lion' is mentioned without any attribution, at the same time as 'several animal hunts with a grumbling little peasant woman': the canvases were mentioned as being in poor condition. It was probably shortly after this date that the *Battles* and the *Hunts* parted company, since the *Hunts* are not mentioned in the inventory of Cardinal Carlo de' Medici's inheritance in 1666.

The information provided by the sources therefore remains problematical, but certain stylistic elements suggest a similarity to the London *Saint George*, which was also painted on canvas. The same could be said of paintings by the Pollaiuolo brothers for the great hall in the Palazzo Medici in 1460. The paintings probably completed a series begun by Pesellino and interrupted by his early death in 1457. If they were put with the *Battles* panels, whose shape had been modified for the occasion, the patrons' change of intention and plan were obviously to move from an explicit celebration of Tolentino to more hermetic political allegories. The dragon fighting the lion (the *Marzocco*, symbol of Florence) could in fact allude to fights with the Visconti (whose heraldic symbol was a grass snake) and the fights between lions could have the underlying meaning of winning political power despite opposition from Florentine aristocratic factions. The *Judgment of Paris* could contain a conciliatory and didactic message for the benefit of his son Piero, or from Piero to his sons, since the whole programme of paintings would perhaps have suited his refined taste.

Praise for Uccello as a landscape painter can be traced back to the Neo-Platonist Cristoforo Landino in his famous 1481

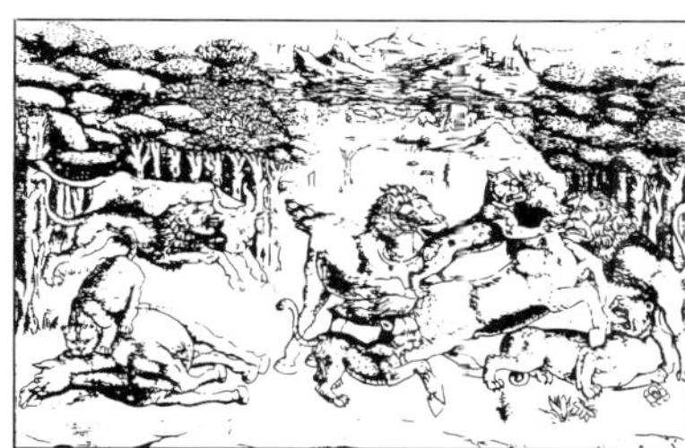

Anonymous Florentine woodcut, *c.* 1460, probably related to Uccello's lost works.

commentary on Dante: 'great master of animal and landscape painting'. K. Clark (1944, p. 72) spoke of these pictures as being in the Burgundian or Flemish taste prevalent in Florence in the 1450s and 1460s. M. Salmi (1950, . 31) dated them 'around 1456' and found echoes of them in certain Florentine engravings of 1470–90 (in A. M. Hind, 1938, I; A.II.2, A.II.3, A.II.17, A.IV.24, D.III.4, E.III.12) but J. Pope-Hennessy (1950; 1969, p. 179) was sceptical and thought the engravings simple proof of the spread of this genre of illustration. It was a genre which later would be even more appreciated in Medici circles, as is borne out by the cartoons for tapestries by Alessandro Allori in 1578. L. Boccia (1970, p. 80) dated the *Battles* at 1435 but the other canvases twenty years later. It is tempting to interpret the lost paintings as political allegories, as did P. Meller (in an oral communication with A. Parronchi, 1974, p. 37) and C. Del Bravo (1983, I, pp. 202 *et seq.*). The anonymous *Terze Rime in Lode di Cosimo de Medici et de Fig[1]i e dell'Honoranza fatta l'anno 1458* [= 1459, see note p. 71] *al fig[1]io del Duca di Milano et al Papa nella loro venuta a Firenze* (BNF, *Codex Magliabechiano*, VII, ms. 1121) contains numerous literary and allegorical motifs that are found in the decorative cycles (including the Pollaiuolo brothers' *Labours of Hercules* of the following year) of the great hall – among which were 'lions behind grilles painted by Francesco di Pesello' (cf. W. A. Bulst, 1990, p. 113, n. 226) – and of the future '*camera di Lorenzo*', which had belonged to his father, Piero. We may think that the reintroduction of the *Battles* into a different figurative context and the subtly allegorical character of the new canvases would be an encumbrance, not to Cosimo the Ancient but to his son Piero (for his orientations, see E. Gombrich, 'The Early Medici as Patrons of Art' [1960] in *Norm and Form. Studies in the Art of the Renaissance*, London, 1966, pp. 35–7). In 1459, hunts and animal fights were held in the Piazza della Signoria, in honour of Pius II's passage through Florence on his way to Mantua, where Galeazzo Mario Sforza and other Italian aristocrats awaited him. These canvases would probably have recorded this event in some way. Commissioned as much by Piero as by Cosimo de' Medici, they would have conformed to a radically modified political framework, centred on the alliance with Milan.

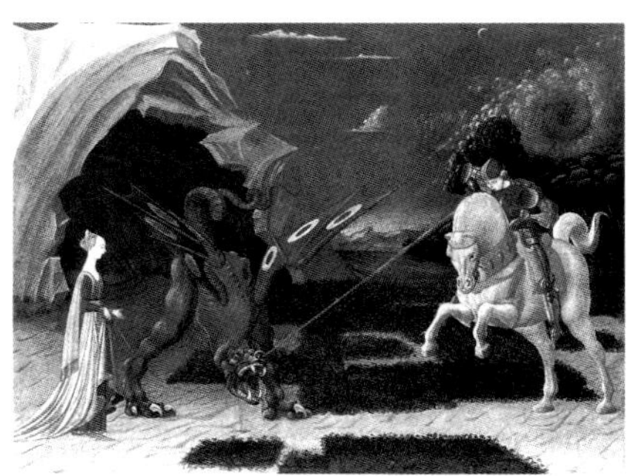

28. SAINT GEORGE AND THE DRAGON (SAINT GEORGE FREEING THE PRINCESS)

Tempera on canvas, 56.5 × 74 cm.
London, National Gallery (inv. no. 6294).
About 1455–60

This painting, using the medium of tempera on canvas, is one of several mentioned by Antonio Billi in his *Libro* (1516) as being made by Uccello on Flanders' 'cloth' and by the Anonimo Magliabechiano (*c.* 1546) as paintings that were 'much discussed' and admired in Renaissance Florence. They were part of the Lanckoronsky Collection in Vienna, where the canvas was mentioned for the first time by Loeser (1898). It was then moved to the castle of Hohenems, and, after the building burnt down, was thought lost in the Second World War until the National Gallery bought it in

1959. At that time, the painting was restored (there is a detailed account in N. E. Brommelle, *Museums Journal*, 1959, pp. 87–95). It has been cut down on the left and at the bottom and has numerous areas of repainting.

The first ATTRIBUTION to Uccello was made by C. Loeser (1898, pp. 88–9), followed by P. Schubring (1915, p. 240), R. van Marle (1928, X, p. 207: before the *Creation* scenes in the Chiostro Verde), D. Colnaghi (1928, p. 265: one of the Master's main works, mentioned erroneously as a wood panel), L. Venturi (1930, p. 63) and M. Marangoni (1931–2, p. 339). Berenson (1932, p. 342; 1936, p. 279), on the other hand, suggested Giovanni di Francesco (Master of the Carrand triptych). V. Giovannozzi (1934, p. 359) rejected this suggestion and reinstated Uccello as its author, an indication J. Lipman (1936, p. 119) thought 'very probable' and M. Wackernagel (1938/1981, p. 157) welcomed, though doubtfully. While rejecting the attribution to Uccello, A. Venturi's proposal (1911, VII, p. 340) attempted to identify the personality of an 'excellent chest-painter' to whom he also accredited the famous Berlin tondo by Domenico Veneziano, but this was not followed up. G. Pudelko withdrew the former Lanckoronsky canvas from Uccello's catalogue in favour of his *alter ego*: the Karlsruhe *Adoration* Master (1932–4, p. 176; 1934, p. 259, n. 41; 1935, p. 127; 1939, T. B., p. 525), a suggestion which was not followed up either. M. Salmi (1938, pp. 23 and 141) announced himself resolutely in favour of Uccello, and suggested (ibid., p. 24) that Uccello had had help from his studio, because the execution of it showed contemporary repaintings. He was followed by W. Boeck (1939, p. 116) who was the first to propose a late dating and saw in the horse echoes of the one in Andrea del Castagno's fresco of Niccolò da Tolentino in Santa Maria del Fiore, 1456. S. L. Faison (1940, pp. 242–4), M. Pittaluga (1946, pp. 13–14: later than the Paris *Saint George*, with a more 'northern' princess), E. Somaré (1946, p. 37), E. Carli (1954; 1959, pp. 31–2), C. Volpe (1956, p. 45; 1980, p. 20), E. Micheletti (1956, p. 6: the world of the Gothic fairytale, with a 'Pisanellian' princess), D. Gioseffi (1958, p. 137), E. Sindona (given as destroyed in the monograph of 1957, rectified in 1959, pp. 293–302, stressed the fantastic elements and noted a 'mysterious pantheist harmony between nature and characters that heralds Leonardo'). M. Davies (1959, p. 309–16, with a wide-ranging discussion on the literary sources; 1961, pp. 532–3: emphasized the variants between Uccello's painting and the text of Jacobus de Voragine's *Golden Legend* and noted how its miraculous character was shown only through a disturbance of nature), L. Berti (1961, p. 303: the work might anticipate the Paris *Saint George* and be linked to the Avane predella; 1964, n.p.: he reversed the order of the two paintings and stressed the way in which the perspectival construction corresponded to the dramatic elements of the story: 'the forms have an identity which is simultaneously dynamic and frozen'), B. Berenson (1963, p. 209, correcting his first attribution to Giovanni di Francesco), A. Parronchi (1957/1964, pp. 495–6: the work lacks precise geometric syntax; studies can be found in it of the deforming effects of dusk, turbulent wind, emanations from bogs, and perhaps the pestilential exhalations of the dragon; the saint is driven forward by the whirlwind; 1963, col. 467: a canvas similar to the Prato group, by Uccello; he pointed out the atmospheric effects; 1974, pp. 24 and 89), J. Pope-Hennessy (1950, p. 152; 1969, p. 154: late date principally because of the fabric backing, of a better quality than the Karlsruhe group), L. Boccia (1970: the saint's armour is typical of the period from 1435 to 1440, with an infantryman's small helmet and 'a northern quality'), L. Tongiorgi Tomasi (1971, p. 98), and A. Angelini (1990, p. 75: stressed the Gothic illusions).

There is far more disagreement over the DATING. It was considered a youthful work by van Marle (before the *Creation* and the *Hawkwood*); around 1435 by Parronchi (1974, pp. 24 and 89, close to the Prato frescoes which he dated at about 1435); after 1436 by Volpe (1980, p. 20); between 1436 and 1443 by Somaré (1946); between 1435 and 1440 and not later than the windows of 1443 by Boccia (1970); *c.* 1439 by Angelini (1990); before 1443 by Salmi (1938); between 1445 and 1450 by E. Borsook (1980, p. 80 [I, 1960 edn]: but attributed to the 'Prato Master', an unknown follower of Uccello); close to 1452 according to Berti (1961); *c.* 1456 for Carli (1954; 1959), Gioseffi (1958) and Tongiorgi Tomasi (1971); a late work after 1456 for Boeck (1939), Faison (1940) and Pope-Hennessy (1950; 1969; 1980); from about 1455–60 for Sindona (1959) and around 1460 for Davies (1961).

It is a painting of extreme delicacy which reveals Uccello's intellectual position in advanced maturity. The fable's tone of fresh invention goes hand in hand with a modern theoretical engagement, whose singularity went unnoticed by his contemporaries, who were however fascinated by the eccentric Master decorator's artisan-like inventiveness. The theme is dear to Uccello who seems somewhat betrayed, here, by his intellectual zeal: the pictorial transcription is disjointed, with some successful bits, sudden afterthoughts and failures – all signs of an unhappy compilation. The research into special effects natural 'accidents' of optic vision, is tormented, from the nocturne of the stormy whirlwind to the atmospheric depth and lacustrine reflections inside the cavern. The miraculous event has no connection with the dramatic action, from which any heroic element is absent: it is translated only through the disturbance of nature. The action is crystallized in a construction of intersecting perspectives; the atmosphere is free on one side and stormy on the other, as in the *Thebaïd* in the Accademia in Florence. Natural disturbances expressing supernatural intervention had already been used in the *Flood* in the Chiostro Verde and here we find again those 'great clouds' which 'resist the light' (Ghiberti, III, Morisani (ed.) 1947, p. 51). A comparison with the Paris panel on the same subject is revealing: what constitutes a structural element in the London one is almost entirely absent from the Paris one. The London picture has an extraordinary spatial depth, brought about by virtuoso foreshortenings and a new sense of atmosphere which came from Flemish painting and Domenico Veneziano. Following on from this are the regular perspectival blocks of grass on the layered ground, the delicacy and depth of the atmosphere, the great airy space, the calm, light clouds in the serene part of the sky. The liveliest traits are the 'dramatic' foreshortenings of dragon and horse, but the monster's wound is more of an unusual fortuitous event than an heroic moment: the long lance becomes the formal linking element between two 'impossible' spatial boxes, colliding prisms, perspectival virtuosities which are absent from the Paris panel. This intellectualism and taste for fantasy (Argan, 1969,

2, p. 186 speaks of an 'almost Socratic ingenuity') characterize the work, in which action is clearly 'useless': the terrible snorting dragon has become an inoffensive puppy, led docilely on a leash by a pale Gothic princess. This is not the maiden's terrible guardian, violence is useless, liberation totally unnecessary: for Uccello, only the validity of his spatial theory had any importance. In the Paris panel, the oposite is the case: the Trebizondian princess anxiously awaits the outcome of the fight, there is violent action, the lance can barely hold back the monster's attack, the hero-knight himself appears to be on the defensive. The grotto, an allusion to the infernal cave which engendered the monster, has been simplified, the ground in the foreground does not have the crystalline regularity of the *Battle* made from rocky layers viewed in perspective. The skyline is lower and the spatial construction more homogeneous than in the Paris panel. The horse's harness and the dragon's form are identical. The strange aspect of the armour can be explained: after the extreme attention paid to it in the *Battles*, Uccello painted armour from memory, with an increasing lack of accuracy and with archaisms. Pudelko (1932–4, p. 176) noticed how much the princess owed to Domenico Veneziano, an acceptable suggestion even if we cannot see an immediate echo of Domenico Florentine activity after 1439, but rather a nostalgic return to the past, a stylistic tendency already noted in the Avane predella of 1452. The textile support favours a late dating (Pope-Hennessy, 1969, p. 154); and in this context, we should mention Pollaiuolo's canvases of 1460 for the Medici palace, and Uccello's lost ones for the same place, while the stylistic solutions, the extreme theoretical engagement, the tormented execution and the technique are all elements which suggest a dating of towards 1455 or a little later, which would extend to the 1460s only with difficulty.

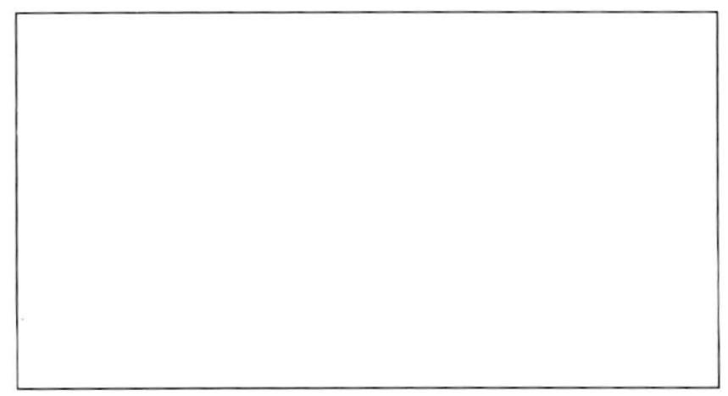

29. TWO UNIDENTIFIED FIGURES

Fresco (now lost).
Formerly Florence, San Vincenzo di Annalena.
About 1455–60(?)

Antonio Billi's *Libro* (1516, ed. C. Frey, 1892, pp. 24–5) tells us that Uccello 'painted two figures on the façade of the Monastery of Baldaccio/Annalena'. The Anonimo Magliabechiano repeated the information: 'On the façade of the Baldaccio nuns' monastery, he painted two figures.' Vasari also repeated it – 'In the Monastery of the nuns of Annalena, he painted two figures' (1550, p. 253; 1568, I, p. 269) – and included them in Uccello's youthful activity: 'Paolo's first paintings were in fresco.' The comment was probably erroneous, for it seem that these were murals painted in tempera. The inclusion of 'two figures' in Uccello's youthful work leaves us even more perplexed. Vasari's chronology was probably already wrong about Uccello's 'early work' being at the hospital of Lelmo (see cat. no. 25), and it was incorrect for the convent of San Vincenzo di Annalena, founded by Annalena Malatesti in 1453–4 and dedicated to Saint Vincent Ferrer, canonized in 1445. Thus we have a *terminus post quem* which dictates a late date, after the *Stories of Noah* and the San Miniato frescoes. F. Bocchi-G. Cinelli's *Guida* (1677) no longer mentions any paintings by Uccello, which were perhaps on the façade of the church. G. Milanesi (1878, II, p. 206, n. 2) imagined that Vasari might have been referring to an earlier building 'on the site where the monastery of Annalena was built twenty-three years later. When the monastery was destroyed, the figures he had painted there were lost.' We have no information on the subject-matter of the paintings: they might have represented Saint Vincent and the pious founder in Dominican habit.

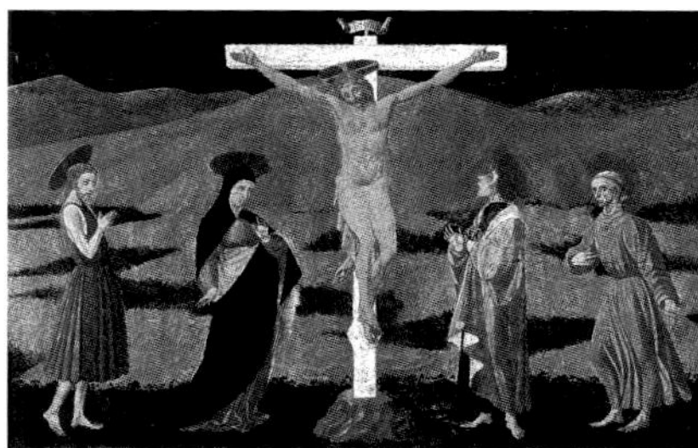

30. CHRIST CRUCIFIED, WITH SAINT JOHN THE BAPTIST, THE VIRGIN, SAINT JOHN THE EVANGELIST AND SAINT FRANCIS

Tempera on wood, present state
46 × 67.5 cm.
Madrid, Thyssen-Bornemisza Collection.
About 1457–8

This is the only painting left to represent a special and little-known period during Uccello's late activity, between his return to the taut style (Vasari's 'dry manner') of the Avane predella and his final works at the end of the 1460s. The work is neither documented nor mentioned by the sources, and was published for the first time by R. van Marle (1928, Pantheon, p. 242; 1928, X, pp. 210–14, with an attribution to Uccello). It belonged to the Goudstikker Collection in Amsterdam, then passed into the Schloss Rohoncz Collection and finally to its present location. It comprises the centre panel of a predella: we do not know what became of the retable, nor do we know its chronology, its destination or its patrons. It is an austere religious sermon in a rough, lunar landscape which has been simplified to the utmost: a moment of *contractio animi* that would not be found in Uccello's final works. It can be placed chronologically at *c.* 1460, in that little-known period that Vasari labelled as 'his dry manner, full of profiles'. It is difficult to voice an opinion on the Christ figure, which is much restored – the central part of the panel has suffered especially – but it seems very distant from the Donatellian interpretation, taken up by Andrea del Castagno at Santa Maria degli Angeli and at Sant'Apollonia, and by Giovanni Francesco at Sant'Andrea a Brozzi and Santa Maria Maggiore in Florence. Uccello returned to a rigidity that reminds us of Brunelleschi's wooden *Crucifix* (C. L. Ragghianti, 1977, p. 362). The figures at the side of the cross have an dislocated, nervous humanity, in a layout which is deliberately simplified and which, in the marked archaism of the composition, denotes only a small preoccupation with space. In this sacred drama, no echo can be found of the noble, luminous sobriety of Fra Angelico, nor of Lippi's naturalistic sentimentality. Returning to sacred painting, Uccello seems to have abandoned himself to a moment of rare emotion, allowing his theoretical researches to go by the board. The Thyssen *Crucifixion* is a work which undoubtedly has a special place in Uccello's catalogue, but we can already glimpse in it the falsely naïve tone of the Urbino predella. At Urbino, Uccello's sacred painting developed into an ample horizontal rhythmic sequence in six episodes; here the very structure of the composition, the iconographical exigencies and the strange fixedness of the light impose an axial rigour and a hierarchy in the distribution of figures. The distribution of the figures through the differentiated perspectival planes is remarkable, forming as it does a rhythm that dislocates the rigid composition. These lateral figures are bathed in a successful chiaroscuro which radicalizes a motif perhaps taken from Baldovinetti in the Santissima Annunziata plate Cupboard (*c.* 1450–1, in collaboration with Fra Angelico; in particular in the *Baptism of Christ*; Florence, Museo di San Marco). The chromatic choice is one of refined elegance: the pink background of the sombre landscape and snow-capped mountains in the distance follow an almost Sienese landscape tradition which we have recently learnt could have been suggested by Masaccio's backgrounds brought to light in the recent restoration of the Brancacci chapel.

The composition of the *Crucifixion* is based on a perspective that has its vanishing point at the height of Christ's knee, a point of the greatest luminous intensity, with the cross seen foreshortened from below and the foreground seen from above: a construction which supposes a singularly high position for an altar predella. Did the lost superior retable hold corrections to this perspective, using the model of Masaccio's *Trinity*? With the total absence of data we can only extrapolate, but we could suppose the influence of a convent setting in Uccello's desire to simplify and in his sparseness, and perhaps too in the reuse of Lorenzo Monaco's motifs, in the obvious renunciation of seductive elements concerned with optics, naturalism and landscape.

The Thyssen panel was ATTRIBUTED to Uccello by Van Marle (1928, op. cit.), an attribution taken up by L. Venturi (1930, p. 63), W. Boeck (1931, p. 276; 1939, p. 14–15 and 110), M. Marangoni (1931–2, pp. 334–5), V. Giovannozzi (1934, p. 358), M. Salmi (1938, p. 41), M. Pittaluga (1946, p. 18), E. Somaré (1946, p. 36), E. Carli (1954; 1959, pp. 64–5), E. Sindona (1957, p. 57), E. Micheletti (1956, p. 26), R. J. Heinemann (1958, p. 110, cat. no. 431, with doubts), P. D'Ancona (1959, p. 20), L. Berti (1961, pp. 300 and 304; 1964, unnumbered), L. Tongiorgi Tomasi (1971, p. 98), A. Parronchi (1963, col. 467; 1974, p. 23) and C. L. Ragghianti (1977, p. 362). The work was exhibited in Munich (Alte Pinakothek, 1930) and in Florence (*Quattro Maestri*, 1954), attributed to Uccello. Against this attribution are: B. Berenson (1932, pp. 341–2; 1936, pp. 278–9, in favour of Giovanni di Francesco, an affirmation rejected by V. Giovannozzi and by later critics), G. Pudelko (1934, p. 259, n. 1: the Karlsruhe Master; 1935, p. 127, a highly restored work of little quality by the Karlsruhe Master), followed by J. Lauts (1966, pp. 187–8), D. Gioseffi (1958, p. 138: an unknown artist in the tradition of Uccello after a Sienese initiation in the work of Giovanni di Paolo), while Pudelko still (1939, T. B., p. 525) and J. Pope-Hennessy (1950 and 1969, pp. 171–2) exclude Uccello's paternity, generally accepted elsewhere today (A. Angelini, 1990, p. 77).

The painting's DATING is highly debatable, even if the stylistic inflections denote a late phase, and perhaps, in all likelihood, the painter's isolation. Van Marle proposed a date of 1425–30 when he published the work (but it coincided with his time in Venice). Boeck (the 1420s) and Sindona considered it a youthful work. With the exception of Parronchi, who proposed a wide variation between the Prato frescoes – that he dated at about 1435 – and 1452 (Avane predella), the other suggestions favour a later date: for Angelini it was just before the Avane predella (definitely close to it because of the taut style and dated at 1452, but still of uncertain attribution); Pope-Hennessy between 1450 and 1460; towards 1460 for Somaré and Berti (1961, p. 304); a late work – close to the Oxford *Hunt* – for Marangoni, Salmi and Pittaluga; close to the Urbino predella, between 1465 and 1469 for Giovannozzi and Carli; and towards 1470 for Micheletti. We suggest a date here of *c.* 1457–8, somewhat closer to the Avane predella than the Urbino one. This detail remains uncertain because of the sparsity of other pictures which could serve as a reference, and through our ignorance of the rest of the retable and Uccello's late activity in general, apart from the two works in Urbino and Oxford. Beyond these considerations of a stylistic nature, a 'sentimental hypothesis' could place this sincere, austere religious commission close in time to the plague of 1457. It might perhaps have been destined for a Florentine convent under Franciscan rule (A. Padoa Rizzo, 1991, p. 128).

31. THE INCREDULITY OF SAINT THOMAS

Fresco (now lost).
Formerly Florence, San Tommaso in Mercato Vecchio.
About 1453–66

Antonio Billi's *Libro* was the first source to mention work in its brief biographical notes on Uccello: 'Above the door of San Tommaso in Florence, a Christ and Saint Thomas' (1516–*c.* 1530, ed. C. Frey, 1892, pp. 24–5). The Anonimo Magliabechiano (ed. C. Frey, 1892, p. 100) repeated: 'He painted Christ and Saint Thomas above the door of the church of San Tommaso in the old Market.' Antonio Petrei's *Memoriale*, written between 1564 and *c.* 1570, reinforced these meagre facts: 'A Christ and Saint Thomas above

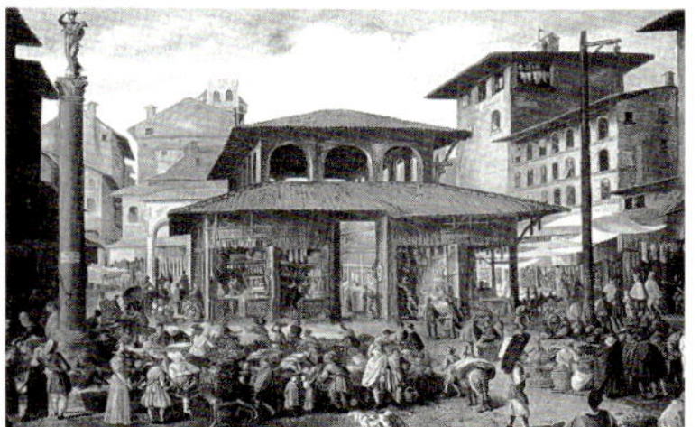

Piazza del Mercato Vecchio, seen in an anonymous eighteenth-century painting. Florence, Private Collection.

the door of San Tommaso in the Mercato Vecchio: Paolo Uccello' (ed. C. Frey, 1892, p. 63). Vasari dwelt longer on the work, which he had already mentioned in the first edition, and which in both editions he saw as the end of Uccello's pictorial activity. 'They say that he received the commission for a Saint Thomas touching Christ's wound, which was to be placed above the door of the Mercato Vecchio which bore the name of this saint; he put all his energy into realizing this work which would be his last, for he was elderly; and he said he wanted to show everything he valued and knew in this work. He put up a wooden barricade all around to prevent anyone from seeing it before it was finished. Donato, who ran into him by chance one day, when he was on his own, asked him: "But what is this work then that you are hiding so well?" To which Paolo retorted: "You'll see: and that's all I'm saying." Donato did not force him into saying more, thinking that he was going to see something marvellous, as on other occasions. Following this it happened that Donato was in the market one morning buying some fruit for dinner, when he saw Paolo in the act of uncovering his work: he went up to him and greeted him courteously. Paolo, anxious to know his opinion, asked him what he thought of this painting. Donato examined it very closely then said: "Eh, Paolo, now's the time you should be covering it up, and you're uncovering it." Uccello was deeply upset, he fully understood that his last work merited more criticism than compliments; discouraged, he shut himself up in his house, and felt no further desire to go out; he became entirely preoccupied with perspective, which kept him poor and obscure until he died' (1550, p. 256–7; with few variations in 1568, I, p. 273). From this emerges an expressive, literary portrait of an irritable, solitary experimenter, like Pontormo.

The anecdote must surely be treated with reserve and read almost as embroidery. The painting was done during the painter's late period of activity, after Donatello's return from Padua in 1452–3, and certainly before 1466, the year of the sculptor's death. This is a relatively obscure period of Uccello's activity, but the ancient bonds of friendship with Donato seem confirmed by the name Uccello gave his own son, born in 1453. After his experience in Padua, Donatello's researches developed in an ever more distant direction from the preoccupations with perspective so dear to his painter friend. We only have to recall the London *Pietà* (Victoria and Albert Museum) of *c.* 1455–60, the famous *Mary Magdalen* in wood of *c.* 1455 (Florence, Museo dell'Opera del Duomo) or the bronze *Saint John the Baptist* in Siena cathedral of 1457 to understand the chasm that separated the two artists' positions. It would seem therefore that Vasari's anecdote did contain some grains of truth.

A precedent for Uccello's fresco can be seen in Bicci di Lorenzo's on the façade of Santa Croce in 1418 (Vasari-Milanesi, II, 1878, p. 51), with *Saint Thomas, Christ and the Apostles*. Uccello's work was remembered by Borghini (1826 edn, p. 59), but not by Baldinucci (1686). In the seventeenth century the fresco (or mural in tempera) had already deteriorated, as F. L. Del Migliore recalled: 'This painting, which was by the hand of Paolo Uccello, had deteriorated, because of the impossibility of preserving the colours for long, because they were exposed to the rigours of the weather.' No trace of the painting appears on the nineteenth-century photograph of the church of the Baccani (Parronchi, 1974, Ill. 18d); the church was demolished at the end of the nineteenth century. It was described as, 'A small church, with no ornamentation, founded before the year 1000' in F. Fantozzi's guidebook (1852, p. 485) which recalled the Medici's patronage of the church, a possible clue to the patrons. A picture of the façade of the church in the Quattrocento is shown in a drawing in the *Codex Rustici* (Florence, Biblioteca del Seminario Arcivescovile di Cestello); the simple façade with a doorway and lunette is flanked on the right by a perpendicular wall. Here was a constraint of some significance, which would have forced Uccello into a lateral displacement of the vanishing point – as in the second scene of the Urbino predella – in order to obtain a decentralized viewpoint. D. Gioseffi (1958, pp. 130–2) supposed the use of the technique of anamorphosis: Uccello would have painted at an angle from close up, inside the barricade, which prevented the work from being seen and the scene appreciated other than from the point of observation foreseen by the artist. A. Parronchi (1974, pp. 76–7) suggested that the scene of *The Incredulity of Saint Thomas*

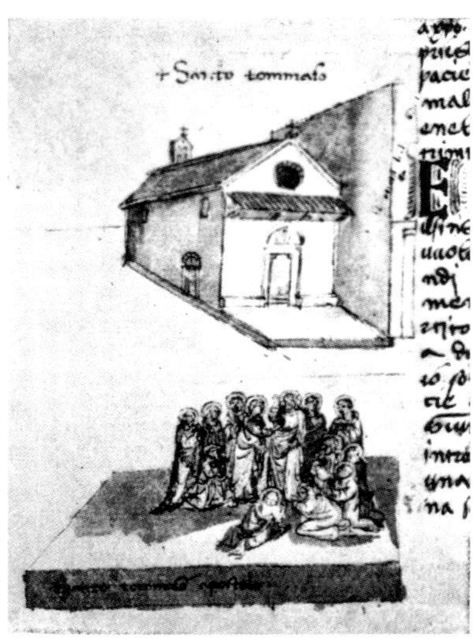

San Tommaso in Mercato Vecchio, drawing in the *Codex Rustici*, *c.* 1447. Florence, Biblioteca del Seminario Arcivescovile di Cestello.

reproduced in the drawing of the church in the *Codex Rustici* was perhaps a sketch of Uccello's fresco, highlighting the oblique position but not hiding his perplexity when faced with the fact that a scene as extended and articulated could be included in the lunette of a doorway (the position of which, moreover, was uncertain). The scene seems to recall Masaccio's compositions at the Carmine, from which Andrea di Giusto's *Exorcism of a Man Possessed*, in Philadelphia (the Johnson Collection) could have equally been inspired. In any case, Parronchi pointed out the uncertainties regarding an exact date for the *Codex Rustici*, generally fixed at 1447–8 but probably elaborated on later (Barlolomeo Rustici died in 1457, but the *terminus ante quem* is not very restricting; the picture could be connected with a work on an underlayer of plaster, before Uccello's intervention). Parronchi (op. cit., p. 77) noted a certain resemblance to the composition of the apostles in Justus van Ghent's retable of the Corpus Domini at Urbino and took up the suggestion again of its dependence on Uccello's drawing. The table covered with a cloth in the Urbino retable would be the repetition (Parronchi, 1974, p. 78, n. 97) of the oblique platform in Uccello's *Incredulity of Saint Thomas*. This work was considered a 'late fresco' by M. Salmi in 1938 (p. 43). We would have to wait for Verrocchio's statuary group at Orsanmichele, *c.* 1472, to have a composition layout of this theme, which was freer and articulated in space. A valuable motive for choosing this theme of the

Incredulity in the Florence diocese could have been in the condemnation by Saint Antoninus, bishop of Florence, of painters who paint hidden things (*apocrypha pingunt*), making an example of those who depicted the Sacro Cingolo, the girdle given by the Virgin to Saint Thomas, and venerated at Prato (M. Baxandall, 1972/1978, p. 55).

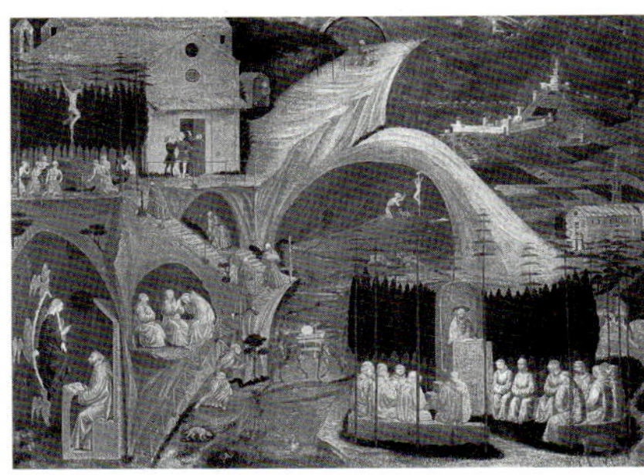

32. LIFE OF THE HOLY FATHERS (THE THEBAÏD, OR PERSPECTIVA RELIGIOSORUM)

Tempera on canvas, 81 × 110 cm.
Florence, Accademia, inv. no. 5381.
About 1460–65

This work originally came from the convent of Vallombrosan nuns of San Giorgio alla Costa in Florence. It was transferred to the Accademia di Belle Arti in 1808. F. Bocchi-G. Cinelli's *Guida* (1677, p. 119) mentioned a painting in the church of the convent dedicated to the Holy Spirit, which may have been this one. Neither dated nor signed, the canvas is not mentioned specifically in the sources nor in F. Fantozzi's *Guida* (1842, pp. 425–8). The first to note it was G. Gamba (1909, p. 22) who ATTRIBUTED it to Uccello's circle, in connection with the Karlsruhe *Adoration*. The suggestion was accepted by Longhi (1928, p. 46), reconfirmed by Gamba (1933, p. 156: a follower of Uccello, author of the Karlsruhe panel), by G. Poggi (1933) and developed in a structured way by G. Pudelko (1934, *Early Works*, p. 259, n. 41; 1935, pp. 124–5; 1939, T. B., p. 526: 'erroneously attributed to Paolo Uccello') who instead attributed it to the Karlsruhe Master. E. Carli (1954; 1959, p. 69) and J. Lauts agreed (1966, pp. 187–8), while M. Salmi attributed the work to the Quarate Master (1938, p. 37) and J. Pope-Hennessy (1950, pp. 172–3) accredited it to the Prato Master's circle. Both the following excluded the work from Uccello's catalogue: A. Schmarsow (1900–2, II), who proposed attributing it to Alesso Baldovinetti (a proposal which was never followed up), and A. Parronchi (1965, pp. 169–80; 1966, p. 55; 1974, p. 54) who thought it a late work derived from Uccello, thus subscribing to the sentimental hypothesis' of Uccello's daughter Antonia as a painter-nun: an hypothesis which is difficult to verify and was not followed up. The Accademia canvas was thought to be a studio work by A. Venturi (1911, VII), R. van Marle (1928, X, pp. 249–50: 'a close pupil' familiar with Uccello's work at Urbino), G. Poggi (1933), V. Giovannozzi (1934, p. 356: not the Prato Master, but a follower of Uccello's during his final period), M. Salmi (1934–5, p. 27, n. 15: late disciple; 1950, p. 27), E. Callmann (1957, pp. 149–55: the work 'would have derived from the Uffizi *Thebaïd* and should therefore be credited to a close follower of Paolo Uccello', P. D'Ancona (1959, p. 10: an unknown follower of Uccello, without his mastery or his 'inventive mind') and A. Parronchi (1974, p. 54). The attribution to Uccello has been supported by W. Boeck (1931, p. 276: a youthful work; 1939, pp. 10–14 and 110); M. Marangoni (1931–2, p. 338: a late work); M. Wackernagel (1938/1981, p. 138, n. 66: Uccello's youthful period); C. L. Ragghianti (1946); R. Longhi (1952); E. Sindona (1957, pp. 20 and 57: 'stylistic reasons suggest a youthful work'; the catalogue starts with this work); A. Parronchi (1957; in 1964, pp. 522–6: he proposed Pierre Lacepierre of Limoges's *De Oculo Morali* as a source; 1963, col. 467: in the Prato group, second half of Uccello's career). L. Tongiorgi Tomasi (1971, pp. 98–9: stressed its great quality) and A. Angelini (1990, p. 77: 'Paolo seems to return with new verve to subjects already experimented with'). B. Berenson (1932, a very early dating, which for different reasons is, objectively speaking, untenable. This synopsis of the pleasures of monastic life is a montage of different iconographical ideas, *topoi* of the blessed life, some of which had already been used in other works by Uccello, such as *Saint Francis Receiving the Stigmata*, painted in fresco in Santa Trinita. On the other hand, any connection with the lost cycle at Santa Maria degli Angeli, as has occasionally been proposed (Pudelko, 1934, p. 246, n. 23; Salmi, 1950, p. 27) must be excluded and links with the San Miniato cycle are also very weak: iconographical echoes of the Benedictine cycles are almost non-existent. The connection with the iconography of the *Thebaïd* (an essentially Thuscan concept, used particularly in a Trecento–Quattrocento Carmelite setting, from the retable predella by Pietro Lorenzetti at the Carmine in Siena in 1329, to the much discussed Uffizi *Thebaïd*, perhaps formerly at the Carmine in Florence) is equally tenuous. In Uccello's painting each episode is relatively identifiable and relates to different communities: Franciscans, Servites, Camaldolites, Cistercians. The absence of explicit references to the Vallombrosan iconographic tradition is fairly remarkable, and might perhaps be linked to specific requests from the patrons (as at Santa Trinita) or to a different original destination for the painting.

The current name of *Thebaïd* given to the Accademia canvas is incorrect and should be replaced by *Vita Patruum* or *Life of the Holy Fathers* following a solid literary and devout tradition, reaffirmed by Domenico Cavalca. The following main scenes can be identified: *Saint Bernard's Vision of the Virgin Mary*, *Seven Flagellants*, *Sermon of the Blessed* p. 341; 1936, p. 278) attributed the work to the Carrand Triptych Master or to Giovanni di Francesco del Cervelliera, but, after V. Giovannozzi published details in 1934, he dropped this hypothesis.

The DATING of the work is equally controversial. It was thought to date from the painter's youth by Boeck (1931; 1939: '*ante* 1420'), Wackernagel (1938/1981; 1941) and Sindona (1957); towards 1445 by W. Paatz (1941, II, p. 167); 'towards the end of the 1450s' by Anghelini (1990); towards 1460 by Pope-Hennessy (1950; 1969; 1980) and Tongiorgi Tomasi (1971; 1972); after 1460 by Schmarsow (1900–2); from 1460 to 1470 by Salmi (1938, in any case after the *Flood*) and E. Callmann (1957); from the Urbino period, *c.* 1465–9 by van Marle (1928) and V. Giovannozzi (1934); a late work by Marangoni (1931–2), late, perhaps by Sister Antonia di Paolo (1456–90) for Parronchi (1965; 1966), with a consequent date of 1480–90 at the latest.

There are certain special aspects of this work that make the chronology uncertain: the fabric backing, the mixed technique, essentially in oil (penetrating research has shown that there is no certainty on this point: in the Oxford *Hunt* both oily and resinous temperas were used), the deliberately archaic character of the painting, the return to a Trecento spatial layout, which is very different from Uccello's usual researches. The model was provided by Trecento *Thebaïds* (Salmi, 1938, p. 44), deliberately simplified, with a limited number of scenes and the smallest of horizontal developments; greater importance was given to each interlinking episode, which necessarily implies an articulated, non-synthetic design, a fragmented space, all of which suggests *Bernardino of Siena* (or less probably, *Miracle of the Lame Man*), *Saint Francis Receiving the Stigmata*, *Saint Jerome in Penitence*, and *Saint Romuald's Sermon to his Brothers*. The old hermit who is turning his back on his disciples is taken from *Thebaïds* of the Trecento, from a Byzantine source, probably the *Death of Saint Ephraim*; as are, on the right of the canvas, the monks leaning over the bridge (which, in Benedictine iconography, becomes the *Miracle of the Bridge*, as in Spinello Aretino's frescoes at San Miniato and those in the Chiostro degli Aranci in the Badia). The landscape is given a moral tone: the sky is stormy; the rainbow signifies rest and reconciliation with God, as in the *Noah* scenes in the Chiostro Verde. The whole painting is given a simplified structure, but one which is a collage of motifs typical of Uccello: the bird's-eye view of the countryside, the rainbow, the dark sky and whirlwinds as in the London *Saint George*, the care given to the botanical elements, the elegance of the animal painting, the dense woodland, the architectonic and scenic simplification of the rocks, the layered treatment of the ground. Among the secondary episodes, there are some that are difficult to relate to one order rather than another, but their significance is obvious, for they are a very free rendering of the iconographic tradition of the *Thebaïds*: the monk-woodcutter returning to Saint Anthony the Hermit, the traveller, the doe in the foreground which has a connection with the stories of Saint Procolus, who fed his brothers with the milk from this animal. The different species of trees are noteworthy, from the wood in the distance to the cypresses that form the Gothic apse-like spaces (and whose lanceolated outlines can be seen in the two diametrically opposed sections of the painting) and the slim conifers, as in the sombre landscape of *Christ Bearing the Cross* of Parma. The idea of an encirclement of trees was rapidly adopted by Baldovinetti in the Museo di San Marco panel (*Saint Antoninus in Adoration before the Crucifix*). Uccello attempted to simplify the composition to the maximum, but it appears rather forced, with a spatial construction that is out of place in his mature work.

Departing from proven iconographic formulae, especially in the main episodes, the painting depicts scenes of different milieux and with a varied chronology. *Saint Bernard's Vision* is typically Florentine; Giovanni da Milano and the Master of the Rinuccini chapel at Santa Croce (S. Janke, 1974, pp. 45–50) were among the first to treat the subject, after the *De laudibus Sanctae Dei Genitricis* of the Cistercian Ogerio da Lucedio (L. Dal Pra, 1989/1990, pp. 345–76); this scene has a link with the Cisterian patrons. The *Flagellants*, on the other hand, are a subject more frequently found in the Sienese Franciscan milieu (as for example in the anonymous tablets in the Musée Condé at Chantilly or in the Musée Bonnat at Bayonne). In any case, there would be groups in Florence such as the Compagnia dei Bianchi, an association of flagellants who ran through the streets of the town during the winter of 1399–1400, leaving a strong impression. The Bianchi gravitated around the Santissima Annunziata, which is perhaps the reason why in the canvas there are seven beaten men, like the founders of the Florentine order of Servites of Mary, patrons of the Santissima Annunziata. The miracle of the spring in the grotto, connected here with Saint Jerome's penitence, also belongs to the Servite community and is linked with Saint Philip Benizzi. The episode on the top left, on the other hand, is of Sienese origin and treats of the sermon of the Franciscan Bernardino of Siena (who died in 1444 and was canonized in 1450), shown here without a halo (perhaps a useful clue to dating the painting?). The identification is authenticated by the monogram IHS on the façade of the church behind him. The same monogram appeared on a Florentine *cassone* of 1439 depicting the façade of Santa Croce (Schubring, 1915, ill. 25). The cult of the Holy Name of Christ was promoted by Bernardino in 1427 and reconfirmed in 1432. The monk and a layman seem to represent a choice of different lifestyles to the hesitant young man. Behind the church, in the simple form of a barn, typical of mendicant orders and also repeated in the landscape in the background, a premeditated choice of confident architectonic rigour is *Saint Francis Receiving the Stigmata*, probably a replica of the fresco on the inside wall of the façade of Santa Trinita, according to the traditional iconography. Salmi (1938, p. 37) suggested that the model for the landscape could have been the Verna mountain. While *Saint Jerome in Penitence* was a theme dear to different religious communities in Florence, from the Carmelites (Starnina's cycle) to the Camaldolites and Servites (Andrea del Castagno's frescoes), the iconography of Saint Romuald was specifically Camaldolite. The saint is reading his sacred texts to his brothers who, with their subtly varied expressions, recall the *affetti* of *The Disputation of Saint Stephen* in the Prato cycle. We should not be surprised if this assemblage of monastic glories of the different orders, which forms a eulogy of monastic life in general, is treated somewhat freely. The early dating proposed in Boeck (1931; 1939) is not acceptable, and Salmi (1950, p. 28, n. 1) had, in regard to this, already noticed the presence of Bernardino's monogram. Uccello nonetheless appeared attentive to Sienese events and the Holy Name is already visible on the figure of Sant'Ansano in the Quarate predella. Fra Angelico shows Bernardino with the monogram, immediately after his canonization, in his predella at Bosco ai Frati. The practice of self-flagellation also played a part in the imagry of the preachers' order: the theme is present in Angelico's frescoes at San Marco, in cells 20 and 26. The destination of the painting remains obscure; as a sort of invitation to taste the 'pleasures' of religious life, it was probably commissioned when vows were taken by some scion of a Florentine family.

An original and interesting interpretation of the work came from Parronchi (1957; 1964, pp. 522–6: 'very subtle in detail and very weak as a whole'. Using *De Oculo Morali*, quoted above, as a guide, the Accademia canvas (provisionally transferred in 1853 to the Uffizi reserve collection) might propose a series of optical problems (similar to Alhazen's *De Aspectibus*) in the form of a moral allegory, even if similarities between text and painting are slight, which posed some problems for Parronchi himself. A happier interpretation is the symbolic one of different views of the landscape, whose moral significance is in any case clear: the shadows of sin, stormy life on earth, the solid firmness of the ecclesiastical citadel. The work might be better called *Perspectiva religiosorum* (or *De Oculo Morali*) like the small Duecento treatise on morals. The weakness of the whole, which has been emphasized on many occasions (since Longhi's incisive definition, 1928, p. 46: as 'a Luna Park [fun fair] for hermits') seems linked to the subject depicted and is not sufficient proof to refute Uccello's authorship, in whose favour are the subtle details and the unusual atmospheric effects. It would be stretching a point to say the construction was weak: here is a composition that can be likened to polyphonic singing, which unifies different scenes through a common theme. The whole, however, is weakened by the episodes' different iconographies. It could be that they were reflecting other lost works by Uccello, but not, as we have seen, the Benedictine cycles in Santa Maria degli Angeli and San Miniato. But it is true of the *Stigmatization* in the Verna wood which has assimilated the Calvary: in three slim trees reminiscent of the crosses on Golgotha in an echo of the Santa Trinita fresco. The perspectival interest comes to the surface in details such as that of the Virgin seated as though on a swing, in a foreshortened mandorla, in the *Saint Bernard's Vision of The Virgin Mary*. The remarkable details of sky and landscape also give weight to an attribution to Uccello, and to a period close in time to the London *Saint George* (also on canvas). If it is an exaggeration to mention the influence of Lorenzo Monaco here (Boeck, 1931, p. 37, who proposed the impossible dating of the 1420s), it is nevertheless true that this work once more highlights the attention Uccello gave to events in Siena. Lippi's retable in the monastery of the Murate, mentioned in Antonio Billi's *Libro* (after 1516; ed. C. Frey, p. 27), also depicts 'the devil bound hand and foot by Saint Bernard', as in the detail in the bottom leftof the Accademia canvas. The fact that *Thebaïds* (or similar pictures) existed in private homes is borne out by the terre-verte decoration in the belvedere of the Palazzo Rucellai in Florence (*c.* 1457–9; cf. R. Salvini in *Giovanni Rucellai*, London, 1981).

33. THE MIRACLE OF THE PROFANED HOST

Tempera on wood, 42 × 361 cm.
Urbino, Galleria Nazionale delle Marche (Palazzo Ducale).
1467–8

Here we have a valuable reference point in Uccello's late period of activity. The predella, commissioned for the oratory altar of the powerful Company of the Corpus Domini in Urbino, was later transferred to the church of Sant'Agata, then to the neighbouring Scolopi college, where around 1859 it was discovered 'chipped in numerous places, with nail holes and with its colours damaged by a combination of lime and water which had soaked through the painting over a long period. It is sufficient to say that blacksmiths and masons for many years have used it to rest scaffolding' (note of 1858 in F. Canuti, 1954, p. 27; E. Sindona, 1957, p. 62). It was restored in 1861 by A. Mazzotti on the occasion of its transfer to the museum. After being exhibited in the Royal Academy, London, in 1930, it was again restored (by L. Tintori) for the *Quattro Maestri* exhibition in Florence in 1954 (U. Baldini, 1954, pp. 34–7). According to documents belonging to the lay company who commissioned it (L. Pungileoni, 1822, pp. 17–18; A. Schmarsow, 1886, p. 359–60), Uccello was in Urbino from 1465, and left again at the beginning of 1469, although it was probably not a continuous stay: he returned to Florence at least once.

Numerous aspects of its history remain obscure: the known documents refer to several payments, mostly in kind, to Uccello and his son Donato (born in 1453), but they do not explicitly refer to the commission for the panel. Nor do we know the reasons for the choice of artist. Privileged links between Urbino and Florence are well known, as were the links between the Medici and Federico da Montefeltro, who spoke of Tuscany as 'a fountain of architects', and the opportunities he had offered to Maso di Bartolomeo, Pasquino di Montepulciano, Luca della Robbia and Francesco di Giorgio Martini (from Siena). Another aspect which remains unclear is that the patrons first approached a painter from Foligno (a completely different choice), after which they summoned Uccello from Florence – but even while he was working, they were still following up contacts with other painters. Uccello probably reneged on his contract and agreed to do only the less time-consuming predella, either refusing or prevaricating over the main altarpiece. Relations with the Company of the Corpus Domini seem to have extended beyond this unfinished work, and Uccello's studies of a chalice in perspective may have been connected with a processional banner or emblem of the confraternity (a commission later given to Justus van Ghent). However, if the elderly Uccello had found the strength to face the journey to Urbino, it seems strange that he painted only a predella. The hypothesis of a setback with the patrons (J. Pope-Hennessy, 1969, p. 156) is probably unjustified, even if it is possible that they expected a different painter in Urbino, perhaps someone close to Filippo Lippi. The best painters of the region were already becoming more closely influenced by Lippi: Giovanni Boccati, Giovanni Angelo da Camerino and Fra Carnevale who declared himself indispensable in the execution of the Corpus Domini retable. Here the first symptoms show a more or less open incompatibility between Uccello's predella and Urbino's cultural horizons, an incompatibility unequivocally confirmed by Piero della Francesca's refusal to paint the retable, when, accompanied by Giovanni Santi, he went to see the site which had been chosen and the almost finished predella. His refusal is not surprising, since Piero would have been unlikely to want to taint his luminous vision with the Florentine's disturbing little stories. The retable was executed in 1473 and 1474 by Justus van Ghent: after Piero della Francesca, Uccello's vision no longer seemed compatible with 'Italian space' in Urbino. W. Bombe (1931, p. 70) suggested that under the Flemish painting there could be traces of the composition that Uccello had envisaged, but this appears most unlikely because Justus van Ghent was working *ex novo*, including the wooden panels. Whatever was the case, for the first time, he had to measure his talents against Italian monumentality, a concept alien to Flemish culture, though not the case for the creator of the Paduan *Giants*. Having to provide true portraits of people in the *Communion of the Apostles* may have been the factor that discouraged Uccello.

Uccello's predella was divided into six scenes, separated by small balusters (a

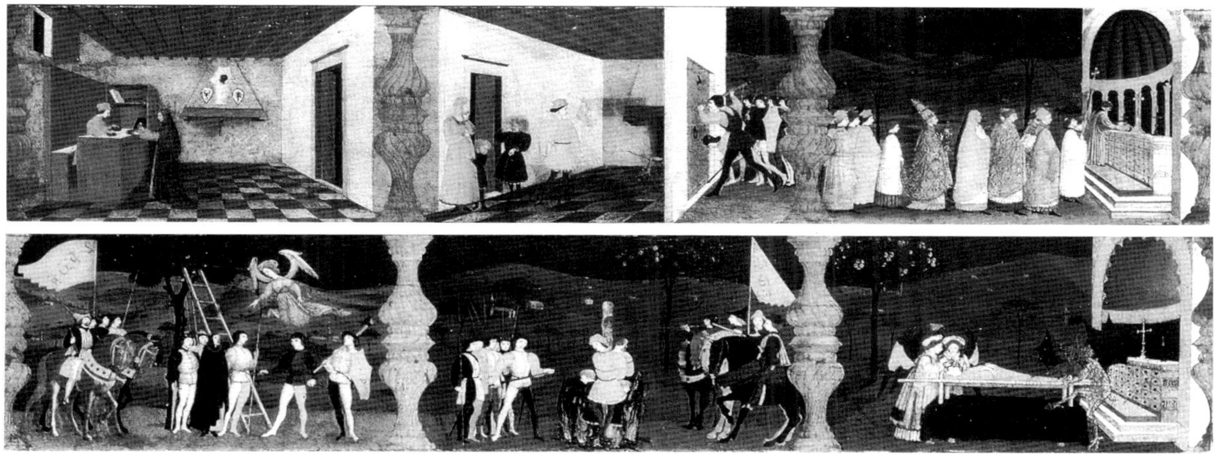

Donatellian motif) on which the auxiliary perspectival constructions converged. The iconography was unusual for Italy: the event had taken place in Paris in 1290 (P. Francastel, 1950; 1952, pp. 180–91) and it was known in Italy through Villani and through *sacre rappresentazioni* (religious plays). M. Aronberg Lavin (1967, pp. 1–24) identified the different Italian and Uccellian variants and established connections between the predella's anti-Semitism and the institution of the Monte di Pietà, patronized by Count Federico to combat usury. Uccello may have remembered Saint Antoninus's inflamed invective when, as bishop of Florence, he preached against Jewish usurers, expressly mentioning the distant events in Paris. Uccello tells the story in six episodes: (1) A Christian woman sells a consecrated host to a Jewish merchant, in order to redeem the coat her husband had lost through gambling. (2) The merchant tries to destroy the host by frying it, but miraculously blood begins to spurt from it, which brings armed men running to his door. (3) The host is solemnly reconsecrated. (4) The woman is condemned to be hanged, while an angel descends from the heavens. (5) The Jewish merchant and his family are burnt at the stake. (6) Two angels and two demons quarrel over the woman's corpse, exhibited in front of the altar. Uccello introduced several variants on the legend. In the first scene, the coat is not shown (Aronberg Lavin, 1967, pp. 6–7); in the third, he introduced the pope (Boniface VIII?) with an iconography derived from the Trecento mode of Arnolfo di Cambio; in the fourth, contrary to the tradition of the Italian *sacre rappresentazioni*, he omits the King of France and Saint Thomas Aquinas (who appears singing the hymn of the Corpus Domini, *Pange lingua gloriosa*). In the fifth, when the Jew has failed to repent, Uccello's depiction has the whole family burnt at the stake. The sixth scene, which is completely independent of the legend, comes from other sources – such as *Ars Moriendi* – as a final admonition, probably at the suggestion of the patrons. M. A. Goukowski (1969, pp. 170–73) published a tablet in the Hermitage Museum in St Petersburg which originally came from Tuscany (perhaps from the studio of Uccello), dated *c.* 1470–80, where we can see the event that preceded these episodes (the husband losing at gambling); Uccello's first scene would then follow. The tablet may be the source of a woodcut, dated *c.* 1490, in the printed text of the *sacra rappresentazione*. Depictions of the legend of the profaned host are relatively rare. The contemporary anti-Semitism of the Monte di Pietà – managed by the rich and powerful Company of the Corpus Domini – does not seem very marked in the main retable, where the *Communion of the Apostles* broaches the problem of the conversion of Jews (by Saint Paul). According to documents, Justus was paid for the first time on 12 February 1473, while the outstanding balance is dated 25 October 1474. G. Neerman (1983, pp. 84–5) supposed that the patrons were not satisfied with the work of the Flemish painter, who had also been engaged to provide the painted emblem of the company – perhaps previously ordered from Uccello? So we have, then, a disturbing collection of events, in which Uccello's predella finally became something of a millstone. Both Fra Carnevale (believed to have taught painting to Bramante) and Piero della Francesca may well both have been alienated by the experiments with perspective, the off-centre visual pyramids and the anamorphic distortions. Piero went on several years later to make a clear demonstration of his own idea of a monumental retable with his altarpiece for the church of San Bernardino (Milan, Brera).

In Uccello's researches in his final years, he wanted to test the possibilities of 'composed' perspective by studying the lateral aberrations that occur with close-up vision. The concept was clarified by Leonardo (ms. G., fol. 13b; J. White, 1949, p. 74): 'composed perspective is that which is painted from the position where there is no part at an equal distance from the eye.' The perspectival construction of Uccello's lively scenes was analysed by J. White (1957, p. 203) who found in the second traces of certain original lines showing three schemes for alternative compositions, modified at the time of the final execution, in a process similar to that used in the fresco of San Martino alla Scala. D. Gioseffi (1958, pp. 105, 108 and 124–5) highlighted the 'fantastic leaps' and the taste for progressive anamorphic distortions due to the angular vision, and as a result of which 'the pointed caricatural profiles instantly become Uccello's normal graceful profiles that can be seen in the *Battles*.' J. Pope-Hennessy (1950, p. 25) saw in it the style of the background landscapes of the *Battles* (which he took to be later), and noted, as had Gioseffi (1958, p. 107) how the painter made the spectator take up a position on the right. The second scene is the one that arouses the greatest interest: R. Klein (1961, p. 222) saw in it Uccello's attempt to show the possibilities of bifocal perspective by taking the vanishing point as the distance point. P. A. Rossi (in E. Sindona, 1972, pp. 56–8) briefly pointed out the composition of the two first interior scenes. The best conserved of the six scenes is the last with a successful piece of landscape. The work shows serveral changes of mind (U. Baldini, 1954, pp. 234–7) which by contrast are rare in the Oxford *Hunt*, even though it is fairly close chronologically. The predella has often been considered Uccello's last work (E. Micheletti, 1956, p. 22; P. D'Ancona, 1959, p. 20; L. Berti, 1964, n.p.).

The documented payments (from 10 August 1467 to 31 October 1468) leave little doubt as to the DATING, but critics are divided in their evaluation of the work. Philippe Soupault (1929, pp. 42–3) emphasized its elevated quality: 'the lyricism of conception', the 'desire for the essential', the absence of grandiloquence in the story's protagonists. L. Venturi (1930, p. 58) relativized the importance of the spatial experimentation: 'By contrast, the predella shows us Paolo Uccello liberated from his excesses of perspective: it is one of his perfections.' R. Longhi (1940; rep. 1973, p. 326) saw in it a fall in tone, an example of his 'artisanal fastidiousness' diminishing. K. Clark (1944, p. 72) thought it had been entirely repainted and that here was a predella of a lost work. M. Pittaluga (1946, pp. 18–19) felt that the 'pure fantastic effervescence' took away any dramatic power the events had, so that the final result was rather uncertain. M. Salmi (1938, pp. 40–43) saw in it 'the chromatic zones of a marquetry-designer' and 'calm and monumental structures that were due to Piero's influence'; E. Carli confirmed the 'very high quality' of the predella 'without descriptive indulgences'. For A. Parronchi (1974, p. 48) there was 'a prevailing look of astonishment in the facial expressions', while C. Brandi (1980, p. 125) noted 'the pure colour, almost without plastic inflexions', 'almost on the verge of popular painting', 'an intentional impoverishment, which not only suggests marquetry but extends to atrophying perspectival representation', 'not senility, but a rigorous style carried almost to the point of self-destruction', 'an extreme effort in Florentine painting to refer to colour rather than drawing', 'a unique and almost blinding source of light' following Masaccio's tradition. The predella, inventoried in 1500 as a work of 'Giusto Todesco' – Justus the German (E. Scatassa, 1902, pp. 438–46) – would have been ill-received by the patrons according to Pope-Hennessy (1969, p. 156; after W. Bombe, 1931, p. 70); A. Padoa Rizzo (1983, p. 79) believed, on the other hand, that right from the time of Uccello's departure he was engaged part time and refused to do the retable. If this was the case, and if the patrons were immediately happy with just the predella, giving up *a priori* the idea of a unified work, we would then have tangible proof of the high esteem in which Uccello was held in the Montefeltro capital. W. Fontana's hypothesis (1986, pp. 140, 142) that Uccello had stayed in Urbino before, between 1446 and 1450 (in order to justify his attribution to Uccello of Boccati's frescoes at the Palazzo Ducale, untenable at such an early date) is unconvincing. G. Gronau's hypothesis (mentioned in Salmi, 1938, p. 152 who rejected it) of identifying the Oxford *Hunt* with the one (only 'a span high') inventoried in the Palazzo Ducale is inconsistent (but for Parronchi, 1974, p. 47, 'the *Hunt* probably came from Urbino').

The COMMISSION doubtless came about through the countess, Battista Sforza, who had a special connection with the Company of the Corpus Domini and was involved in the Monte di Pietà; the predella's eucharistic emphasis was due in part to connections between Federico da Montefeltro, Captain General of the Church, and Pope Sixtus IV, author of *De Sanguine Christi*. The drawing of the angel and the geometric chalice (Uffizi F 1302) were perhaps studies for the predella. 'The two groups of knights near the distance points were surely designed to serve as an angled viewpoint, obtained by placing the panel in an oblique position, with the artist viewing it obliquely as he painted' (L. Tongiorgi Tomasi, 1971, p. 99). Bombe's suggestion (1931, p. 77) that Justus of Ghent used a cartoon left by Uccello for the retable is unconvincing, but Parronchi (1974, p. 49) thought that 'the Flemish painter seemed to have followed Uccello's drawing' in the portrait of the Count of Urbino in the *Communion of the Apostles*. Uccello was present in Urbino from 1465 (A. Schmarsow, 1886, pp. 359–60) until the beginning of 1469; on 8 April 1469, Giovanni Santi was paid to give lodgings and accompany Piero della Francesca to make an estimate for the commission that had been offered him, obviously after Uccello's refusal and departure. Piero would certainly have had difficulty in harmonizing his vision with the subtle Master's taste for narrative in the predella, and his perspectival accidents, his nocturnal landscapes, his knowingly archaic atmosphere that was more appropriate in a sacred painting of medieval origin. Perhaps Uccello had lost his motivation, or was too trapped in positions that were difficult to share, and thus left only a slim trace of his presence in Urbino compared with the length of his stay. Piero della Francesca's distancing of himself is an indication of the gulf that separated their two diverging paths in Italian figurative humanism, throwing Uccello into the shade. His predella, though not a truly *arrière-garde* work because of its powerful experimental character, nevertheless represents a passionate and stubborn defence by a great elderly artist who refused to compromise, and once more affirmed the uniqueness of his own personal course. A different vision defended to the last, even at the price of surrendering an important professional opportunity, in a complex story whose exact details continue to escape us.

34. THE HUNT

Tempera on wood, 65 × 165 cm.
Oxford, Ashmolean Museum.
About 1470

This work, which is painted in tempera on panel with extensive use of resinous pigments, is neither signed nor documented and bears no inscriptions. No documentary or literary reference can be associated with it. It reached its present location in 1850, as a gift from the collector W. T. H. Fox-Strangeways. We know nothing of the painting's previous history, although it must have been put on the Florentine market at an early date. A label on the back bears a note in Italian (in eighteenth-century handwriting): 'A Hunt in the Woods near Pisa by Benozzo Gozzoli'. The first ATTRIBUTION to Uccello dates back to C. Loeser's pioneering attempt (1898, pp. 87–8). This was rejected by A. Venturi (1911, VII-I, p. 340) in favour of an unknown painter to whom he also attributed Domenico Veneziano's Berlin tondo, which R. Longhi would definitively restore to Domenico (1925, pp. 31, 55). P. Schubring (1915, p. 242, n. 101) thought the panel might have been the

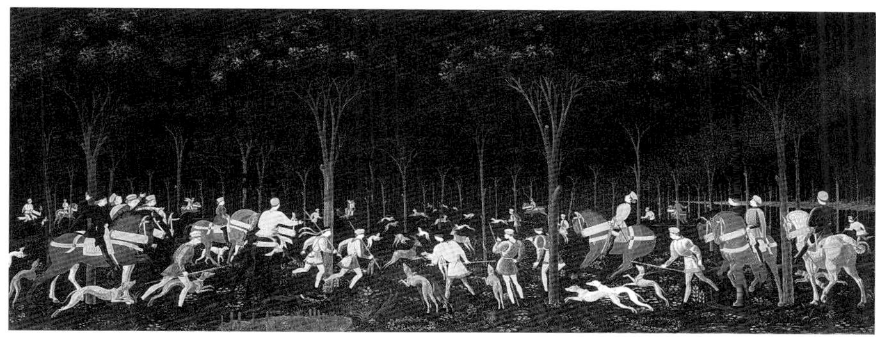

front of a chest and noticed that the hunt was in daylight rather than at night. The attribution to Uccello was proposed again by C. Philips (1919, p. 215) who excluded the idea of it being a studio work. The suggestion was taken up, with some doubts, by R. van Marle (1928, X, pp. 209–10) who was somewhat scathing, stressing the 'almost caricatural' nature of the fitures and suggesting that little care had been taken in the painting's execution because of its utilitarian purpose, probably as the front of a *cassone*. With his artistic sensitivity, P. Soupault (1929, p. 11) proclaimed the work's high quality, considering it Uccello's most important work; D. Colnaghi (1928, p. 365) on the other hand did not include it in his entry for Uccello in his *Dictionary*. L. Venturi (1930, p. 69) saw it as a fantastic example of Uccello's creative freedom, which 'played with perspective' (the *Hunt* was still not nocturnal), while M. Marangoni (1931–2, pp. 334–5) thought the *Hunt* was one of Uccello's youthful works but already close in time to his mature period, and delighted in 'the colourist, fantastic, romantic perspective'. Not only did J. von Schlosser (1933, pp. 37–8) withdraw the work from Uccello's catalogue, but he did not even consider the work Tuscan; however, the attribution to Uccello was confirmed by B. Berenson (1932, p. 582; 1936, p. 500) and by G. Pudelko (1934, p. 242: a late work, with important northern elements, deriving from Pisanello's *Hunt* painted in fresco at Pavia; 1935, *Minotaure*: he invented the apt description of 'lunary painter' for Uccello with regard to this Oxford panel; 1939, T. B., p. 525: a late work). M. Salmi (1938, pp. 151–2) accepted the attribution to Uccello and established a link between the painting and the short poems on hunting by Lorenzo de' Medici in San Rossore wood. He admitted a late dating (pp. 40–41: not intended to be naturalistic, 'magical colour'; rejected an oral communication of Gronau who without any grounds proposed identifying the panel with the one on an analogous subject inventoried in the sixteenth century in the Palazzo Ducale in Urbino). Equally in favour of Uccello, were W. Boeck (1939, p. 116); K. Clark (1944, p. 72: a rare work, after the *Flood*, using perspective in the modern sense of the term: nocturnal, a neo-courtly, Franco-Flemish moment in Florence of 'Burgundian taste'); E. Somaré (1946, p. 31); M. Pittaluga (1946, pp. 16–18: 'fragmented vision', 'ghostly reality', 'a light which is neither day nor night', 'attenuated geometric construction'); E. Carli (1954; 1959, p. 63); E. Micheletti (1956, p. 27: not a nocturnal light but an unreal one); E. Sindona (1957, p. 61); D. Gioseffi (1958, p. 136: stressed the regularity of the irregular, lateral vanishing points but 'the game of anamorphosis had ceased to amuse him' and 'the consequent deformities interested him only in as much as they were a means of expression and style'); P. D'Ancona (1959, p. 18: close in time to the *Battles*); L. Berti (1961, p. 304: eye-level vertical projections, as in the *Battles*; 1964, n.p.); A. Parronchi (1963, col. 468; 1974, p. 47: 'a little play frozen in time by a spell', 'A nocturnal wood', 'reality seen as though it were a cheerful story that had been dreamed'; p. 93: rejected the proposal regarding the Urbino inventory of 1599; the great quality of the work would exclude it from being a *cassone* front); J. Pope-Hennessy (1950; 1969, pp. 23–4) who reconfirmed the link with the Urbino predella and the nocturnal setting of the scene, while the division of the wood into regular geometric spaces suggested a connection with the design of the *Nativity* in San Martino alla Scala. Today the attribution to Uccello is accepted by the following: L. Tongiorgi Tomasi (1971, p. 99: definitely by Uccello); L. H. Heydenreich (1972, p. 293); C. L. Ragghianti–P. A. Rosse (1984, pp. 86–9: an attentive reading of the composition and an example of the reinstatement of perspective; unique central perspective, and 'perspectival construction coinciding with optical reality'); F. Petrucci (in Collected Works, ed. F. Zeri, 1987, p. 289: the perspective would have been 'studied in sections and then unified'); F. Zeri (1976; 1989, p. 7: real landscape of the Tuscan coast and natural nightime effect, 'example of naturalistic perception', but 'the residue of Gothic plays an active role in the painting'); and A. Angelini (1990, p. 77: a 'late masterpiece' of Uccello). The work was shown as by Uccello, in the *Florentine Painting before 1500* exhibition at the Burlington Fine Arts Club, London, in 1920 (as no. 22).

Positions taken regarding the DATING vary rather more. The panel was seen as a youthful work by van Marle (1928) and Marangoni (1931–2: before the *Hawkwood* of 1936), he has generally been considered to belong to a later period. D'Ancona (1959) dated the work between 1450 and 1455, a hypothesis that was not taken up; Clark (1944), Tongiorgi Tomasi (1971–2) and Heydenreich (1972; 1974) dated it *c.* 1460; Pittaluga (1946) suggested *c.* 1459: Salmi (1938) thought it later than 1460 and so did Carli (1954; 1959), Zeri (1976; 1989) and Petrucci (1987). Pudelko (1934) thought the beginning of the 1460s; Berenson (1932; 1936) between 1460 and 1470 (before the Urbino predella), as did Somaré (1946), Sindona (1957) and Berti (1961). Parronchi (1974) placed it in the Urbino period of 1468–9, while Gioseffi (1958) considered it only just a little later, around 1470, as did Pope-Hennessy (1950; 1969; 1980), Parronchi (EUA, 1963) and Angelini (1990). E. Micheletti (1956) and Pudelko (T. B. 1939) thought it undoubtedly late, but were not specific.

Analyses of the perspectival construction of the work were proposed by P. A. Rossi (in E. Sindona 1972, pp. 97–100) and in the Ashmolean Museum's later publication devoted to the painting (anon. no date, ill. 5-6-7-9 with corrections), and by P. A. Rossi-C. L. Ragghianti (1984, pp. 86–9).

The subject matter which is part of an important literary tradition (cf. *Arte della Caccia – Testi di falconeria, uccellagione e altre cacce*, ed. G. Innamorati, Milan, 1965, 2 Vols) is treated by Uccello with great autonomy and a freedom of invention unrivalled in contemporary painting; only the panel in the Musée des Augustins in Toulouse, formerly attributed to Pesellino (M. Laclotte, 1978, pp. 65–70) and now attributed to Giovanni di Francesco (E. Callmann, 1991, pp. 67–70), is comparable. In his life of Dello Delli, Vasari tells us that it was the fashion in Florence to have subjects of this type painted on household furniture. Uccello had also supplied *Hunts* on canvas for the Palazzo Medici. They came in the context of a cycle of the months, with a humanist slant (after the rediscovery of the *Astronomicon*, Book II, of Manilius, a poet of the Augustan period, when the practice of hunting was linked to the month of November: they cannot therefore have any connection with the Oxford panel), or of an amorous allegory, on the model of Boccaccio's *Hunt of Diana*. In the Medici milieu – Gozzoli's frescoes in the palace in the Via Larga are already indicative, even before Lorenzo's little poem on falconry, dating perhaps from 1476 – the chivalrous practice of falconry was regarded as the most distinctive mark of aristocratic life. The practice of hunting was, however, mentioned by Alberti in the *Della Famiglia* dialogues (Books III and IV) as a necessary complement to a humanist education. C. Lloyd (1977, pp. 172–5) recorded an interesting but improbable suggestion by E. Wind: that the *Hunt* was part of an astrological cycle consisting of twelve months. A. Padoa Rizzo (1991, p. 124) used it to support Gronau's and Parronchi's hypothesis (1974, p. 47) in favour of a direct COMMISSION from Count Federico, a hypothesis which used the inventories of the Palazzo Ducale of 1596 ('a boar hunt'), of 1599 ('an ancient hunt'), and of 1609 (with the improbable size, 'a span high'). All this ignores the more explicit entry in the 1631 inventory: 'a picture, a long panel, with paintings of hunting, one of a stag-hunt and the other of a boarhunt, in the middle there is a bridge' (F. Sangiorgi, *Documenti Urbinati: Inventari del Palazzo Ducale (1582–1631)*, Urbino, n. d. [1976], p. 272. The picture referred to cannot be the Oxford *Hunt*, unless we imagine that at least two-thirds of it have been lost (the board hunt and the bridge in the middle), which is hardly likely given the perspectival layout of the supposed 'fragment'. The description does, however, perfectly fit the painting in the Musée des Augustins. That panel was presumably sent to Urbino by Giovanni di Francesco's Florentine studio, for he does not appear to have had direct relations with the Montefeltro Court. These two Florentine *Hunts*, separated chronologically by about fifteen years, diverge even further in their narrative and spatial interpretation.

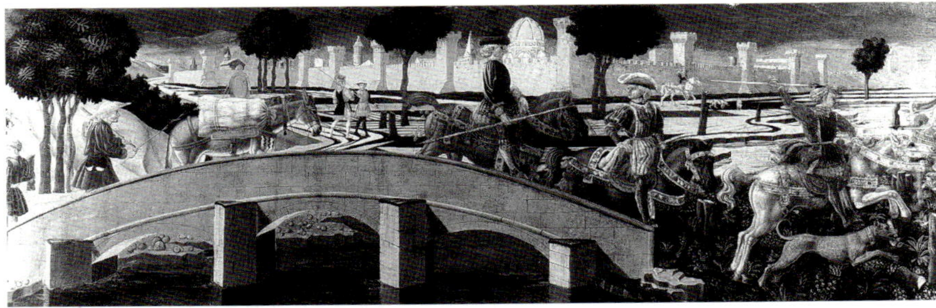

Giovanni di Francesco, *The Hunt*, Toulouse, Musée des Augustins.

The Oxford *Hunt* is a work of very high quality, of delicate, subtle execution, enriched with oil- and resin-based pigments. It seems inconceivable that it could have been the front of a *cassone* or a *spalliera*. That possibility is further ruled out by the extraordinarily fine condition of the painting, which is the best preserved of all Uccello's works. The perspectival construction, which is rigorous in spite of the apparent freedom of rhythm and movement, suggests that it was originally intended for a position about 1.5–2 m. from the ground, perhaps even lower, creating for the onlooker the illusion of participating in the action from horseback level. Here is an example of the refined, almost proto-Mannerist intellectuality of the elderly painter, who in this work accentuates the rigour of the composition without surrendering the immediacy of optic vision. It is the grand finale to an unrivalled journey through the laws of vision, a final act of confidence in the validity of his theory, at a time of reordering and reworking those preferences he had brought into play since his 'crisis decade' of 1430–40 (Longhi, 1956). Natural life and the energy principle coincided with the extreme perspective *ratio* of the wood. An X-ray taken in February 1979 showed that there was no preparatory drawing or perspectival grids; this confirms that Uccello had outgrown the method used for the fresco in San Martino alla Scala, where the perspectival grid had been drawn as a preliminary to the composition.

We can thus see to that point the elderly Uccello had absorbed the principles of vision so that they had become intuitive. Precise geometric construction and 'sweet perspective' allowed full freedom of movement and were by this time an intuitive feeling linked closely to pictorial invention. This is a free, fluid painting, both in the delicacy of the colouring and the few *pentimenti* (notably the red legs of the second figure on foot who is running with a lance on his shoulder). The 'nocturnal' or 'moonlit' tonality is due in great part to the tonal changes in the pigments, above all the greens, browns and blues which have grown darker, while the yellows and reds are well preserved. These reds, the 'scarlet clothes' mentioned in the Urbino documents, are the dominant colour. Perhaps Uccello took into account the different effects of the colours when shaded by foliage (following Alhazen's suggestion, which Ghiberti had adopted: in the darkness of the 'greenery', the reds are even more startling. Nature has been studied with a care that is reminiscent of Gothic (Zeri): the scene unfolds in an oak wood in summer (not autumn as in the Palazzo Schifanoia cycle in Ferrara). We can almost hear the cries of the beaters, along with the rhythmic 'swish' of the animals scattering through the wood. There is such a rich scale of effects that we almost forget the extreme spatial rigour of the forest, whose architectonic inspiration was noted by Ragghianti-Rossi (1984, p. 86, who proposed the Gothic dormitory at Santa Maria Novella as a model). Nature's regularity of nature, the harmony created between optic vision and scientific perspective, show that the painter had outgrown the polemics of the past, objections to the *costruzione legittima* of the 'mathematicians'. The debate on painting had been put aside: Uccello no longer had any desire to 'muse' over the anamorphic distortions and aberrations of 'composed' perspective, as he had in the Urbino predella. Here the indomitable Uccello shows that there is no contradiction between nature and theory, sentiment and rhythm, geometry and immediacy. The extraordinary freshness of invention on which he continued to draw, without freshness of invention on which he continued to draw, without relinquishing a rigorous system, not only confirms the great longevity of his inspiration, but also demonstrates in exemplary fashion the validity of his theory. Uccello's extraordinary farewell to the century, with its abundance of ideas, directions and themes, found no immediate echo in Pollaiuolo, Verrocchio, Baldovinetti or Gozzoli, who by 1470 had given the best of themselves. The Oxford *Hunt* is a moment of balance between complex and 'natural' culture; it is unique in Uccello's career and in the painting of his period. In this last work, there is a serene, ordered and ironic Socratic 'ingenuity' which appears to contradict that character of obsessive, hair-splitting, 'abstract', 'sophisticated' research, which 'wasted his time, wore him out, and filled his mind with difficult problems': an image Vasari has left us and that is so deeply embedded in the idea we have formed of the Florentine painter.

WORKS ATTRIBUTED TO UCCELLO

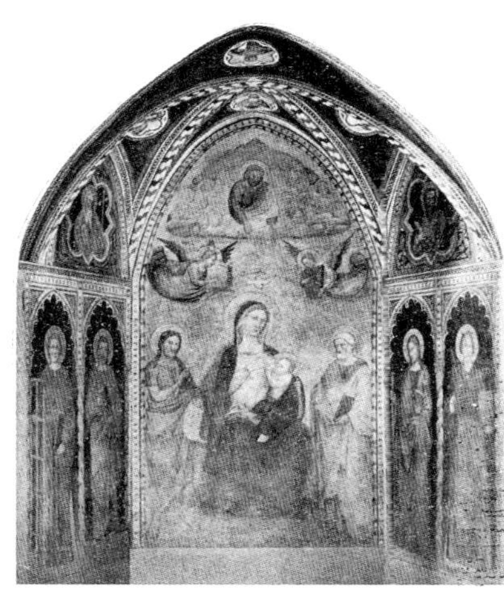

FRESCOES IN THE LIPPIE MACIA CHAPEL

Frescoes transferred to canvas.
Florence, Santa Maria Mater Dei a Lippi.
1416

On the pointed-arched wall at the end of the chapel are a Madonna and Child, accompanied by Saint John the Baptist and Saint Peter on either side with God the Father bestowing his blessing overhead. The side walls depict, on the left, the standing figures of Saint Laurence and Saint John the Evangelist (the identification is uncertain), surmounted by the bust of Saint Andrew in a medallion; on the right, Saint Stephen and Saint Philip, with, above, the bust of Saint Bartholomew in a Gothic polylobed medallion. In the vaulting are busts of the Evangelists in medallions. This is a traditional Gothic figurative ensemble and the name of Uccello is written in the inscription commemorating the restoration of 1716: 'ANNO DOMINI MCCCCXVI TABERNACULUM A PAULU UCCELLO DEPICTUM DINOTIUS ET LUCAS ALBERTUS DE LIPPIS RESTAURAVERUNT ANNO DOMINI MDCCXVI DIE VIII OCTOBRIS'. The fresco was dated 1416 by the eighteenth-century restorers, who probably eliminated the original inscription. The ATTRIBUTION to Uccello, which is disconcerting and not unanimously accepted, might have been derived from the artist's signature, now lost, or from a slip, or from a mistaken reading of the letters 'PUS. P. NELLI' in Gothic script. For stylistic reasons, the frescoes can be attributed to Pietro Nelli, a painter who was almost unknown in the eighteenth century. The early DATING (1416) raises the problem of Uccello's mysterious early career, probably in Starnina camp with its late Gothic experimentations, notwithstanding a number of opinions to the contrary (D. Gioseffi, 1958, p. 136: 'Any claims to a youthful period of Gothic initiation must be eliminated'). After the attribution to Uccello (*Kunsthistorische Gesellschaft*, 1895), G.

Carocci (1907, pp. 331–2) thought the frescoes bore similarities to Andrea Orca- gna's style, an idea corrected by R. van Marle (1928, III, p. 508, n. 1) who attributed them to Andrea's brother, Jacopo di Cione. When the frescoes were detached and the remarkable sinopias recovered, U. Procacci (1960, pp. 234–5) laid the problem of ATTRIBUTION to rest by suggesting that there were foundations for the reference to Uccello and stressed the superior quality of the sinopias in relation to the conventional execution of the fresco itself; he considered the numerous changes in the sinopie as a sign of the painter's 'youthful inexperience' (on the restoration: U. Baldini, 1957, p. 33). L. Berti (*Masaccio*, 1964, p. 76, n. 202) found late Gothic elements in the fresco which were similar to Starnina, and prudently maintained the attribution to Uccello K. Steinweg (in M. Boskovits, 1967, p. 59) proposed the Master of Santa Verdiana, a suggestion that Boskovits adopted (1967, pp. 3–60). L. Bellosi (1973, p. 192) proposed the name of Pietro Nelli (who died in 1419) with Boskovits's agreement (1975, p. 419) who moved the dating of the chapel to 1395–1400, because Nelli was quite old by 1416, while at the beginning of the century he had still been active and had decorated in fresco the refectory of the Bonifacio hospital in Florence.

A. Parronchi (1974, pp. 7–8) tackled the question by trying to attribute part of the fresco to Uccello: he saw two painters' hands at work: Uccello's and that of the Master of Santa Verdiana. Uccello would have painted the frescoes on the right wall (Saint Stephen and Saint Philip, and Saint Peter on the back wall, and especially the 'very beautiful' sinopias, on which the alterations would have been made in order to adjust the perspective; he saw it as a forerunner of the Carnesecchi altar at Santa Maria Maggiore. For R. Fremantle (1975, p. 613) the frescoes of the chapel were the work of an unknown Florentine artist, while D. Reggioli (*Lorenzo Ghiberti, 'materia e ragionamenti'*, 1978, pp. 101–4) put forward the hypothesis of a collaboration between the young Uccello and the elderly Nelli, emphasizing the stylistic similarities between the saints on the side walls and those in the stained-glass windows of the oculi on the façade of Santa Maria del Fiore, based on Ghiberti's cartoons (1412–15). In fact, these saints do have a Ghibertian 'modernism' when compared to the 'late Trecento' language of the back wall, which is closer to Orcagna than Gaddi and more receptive to Spinello than Starnina. The link with Uccello seems even more tenuous, but it could be that a young collaborator of Nelli was inspired in 1416 by the Duomo's windows. We have nothing at all to confirm that young Uccello, who had only just been registered as a Master in his own right, worked with Nelli. C. Volpe (1980, p. 24, n. 1) rejected Parronchi's hypothesis and confirmed the attribution to Pietro Nelli with influences from Spinello Aretino and the possibility of an intervention by Uccello. The fresco was finally restored to its original site, with some modifications. The family who commissioned the restoration in the eighteenth century had exercised their patronage on the chapel since 1470 (G. Carocci, 1906–7, I, p. 231): they had succeeded the Bartoli family, who had connections with the del Beccuto, who we know were indebted to Uccello in 1433–4. From this there arose an argument in favour of an attribution to Uccello that has recently been taken up again by A. Padoa Rizzo (1991, pp. 18–22, who has rejected the attribution to Nelli). The use of Roman capitals in the inscriptions ('ECCE AGNUS DEI') is not an argument in favour of Uccello, for this inscription probably dated from the restoration and bears no similarities to the inscriptions either on the *Hawkwood* or on the *Battle* in the Uffizi. Besides, no Florentine painter – not even Masaccio or Masolino – would have signed in 'humanist' lettering before the 1420s, even less so a young man like Uccello at the beginning of his career. As there are scarcely any reasons for doubting the date on the modern inscription (1416) it seems obvious that THE ATTRIBUTION TO UCCELLO IS NOT ACCEPTABLE. On the other hand, the iconographical precedent of the *Madonna del Latte* in the Museo di Santa Croce in Florence is plausible; though now almost indecipherable, we can still glean from it allusions to a devotion of Franciscan origin.

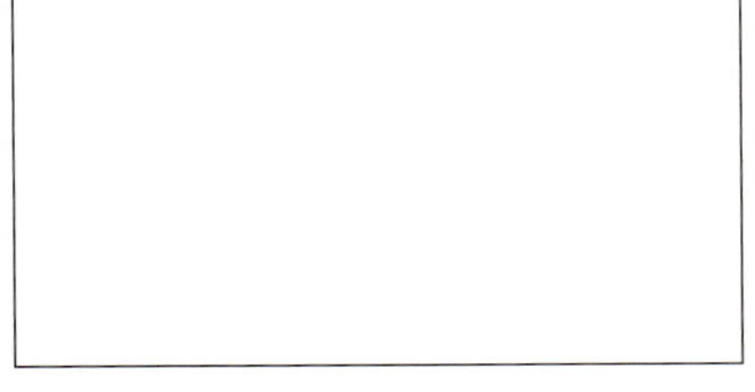

ALTAR FRONTAL OF SAINT COSMAS AND SAINT DAMIAN

Tempera on wood? (now lost).
Formerly Florence, Santa Maria del Carmine.
About 1420?

Vasari (1550, p. 254) briefly mentions this work along with paintings in the Palazzo Medici: 'At the Carmine, he painted the altar frontal of Saint Cosmas and Saint Damian for the chapel of Saint Jerome.' In the second edition, the passage has changed only slightly: 'After [the frescoes at San Miniato] he painted the altar frontal of Saint Cosmas and Saint Damian for the Pugliesi family's chapel of Saint Jerome'; he then moved on to the paintings in the Palazzo Medici (1568, I, p. 270). In G. Milanesi's view (Vasari-Milanesi, II, 1878, p. 208, n. 1.): 'The passage of time or the fire of 1771 caused their disappearance.' Vasari had no hesitation in placing the work in the chapel belonging to the Del Pugliese family, whose stories of Saint Jerome he had described in his *Vita* of Gherardo Starnina. In the *Vita* of Antonio Veneziano, Vasari had suggested that Starnina and Uccello had been followers of Antonio – a strange idea that he made no mention of in his biography of Uccello. There are many questions raised by this work. Was it destroyed in the fire at the Carmine in 1771? Did it really depict the doctor-saints and martyrs whose names it bore? If so, was it in the Del Pugliese family's chapel (dedicated to Saint Jerome) or in the Coletti family's chapel dedicated to the two saints? Was there a connection with the Medici patrons, as there was for Fra Angelico's panels, or was the mention of Saint Cosmas and Saint Damian enough for Vasari to make an immediate association with the paintings in the Palazzo Medici, mentioned just afterwards? Vasari, in the ecphrasis on Starnina's and Masaccio's frescoes, certainly had a good knowledge of the Carmine: could he have confused the siting of the painting? Above the altar in the del Pugliese chapel were a *Madonna and Child with Saints* by Gherardo Starnina, which later disappeared. The altar was damaged and moved at the beginning of the Seicento, in any case after Vasari's visits. In the first half of the seventeenth century the *Nota di pitture, sculture et fabbriche della città di Firenze*, published by Galletti (*Rivista Fiorentina*, 1, September 1908, p. 37) read: 'An altar frontal in the chapel of Saint Jerome, the work of Paolo Uccello', a pertinent and important note, clearly derived from Vasari and with no detail on the subject of the work. U. Procacci (1932, pp. 141–232) examined the problem of the fire at the Carmine and suggested an error on Vasari's part both in the attribution and subject matter (p. 198, n. 2), but he subsequently mentioned to A. Parronchi (1965, pp. 179–80, n. 21) that he had discovered documented proof with which he could identify the 'altar frontal of Saints Cosmas and Damian' with the Uffizi *Thebaïd*. The publication of the documents never followed, however. Parronchi (1966, pp. 45–7) resolutely attributed the *Thebaïd* to Uccello, though traditionally it had been attributed to Starnina; he tried to establish a link with the context of the *Scenes from the Life of Saint Jerome* by Gherardo Starnina (pp. 47–9). The link between the hermit saints and Saint Jerome comes from the fact that the text of their biography was attributed in ancient times to Saint Jerome himself. Technical and stylistic elements led Parronchi to date the work after 1423, and in order to corroborate the attribution to Uccello he gave a time limit of about 1431: this is a date which is too late and should be modified to 1420–25. Parronchi's hypothesis becomes less convincing in his attempt to explain how a *Thebaïd* – whose subject Vasari would have had little difficulty in identifying – could have had any connection with Saint Cosmas and Saint Damian, which forced Parronchi to admit (p. 51) the possible existence of other panels depicting the stories of the doctor-martyrs, which had later disappeared. J. Pope-Hennessy (1969, p. 178) firmly rejected Parronchi's suggestions. M. Salmi (1938, pp. 9, 101, 133 saw the altar frontal as an early work by Uccello (he opened his catalogue with it), having links with 'late Starnina'. The Uffizi *Thebaïd* is more influenced by late Starnina than Lorenzo Monaco (to whom M. Marangoni attributed it, 1931–2, p. 335). Perhaps R. Longhi (1940, pp. 173–4) was right in thinking it was by the young Fra Angelico rather than Uccello, while at the same time recognizing in it echoes of Masaccio.

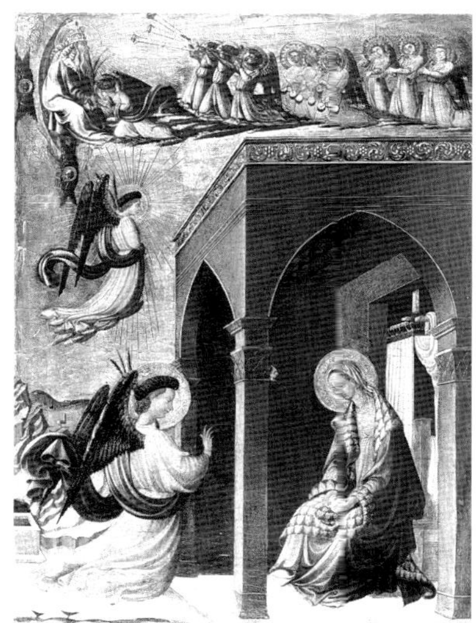

THE ANNUNCIATION

Tempera on wood, 64.6 × 47.5 cm.
Oxford, Ashmolean Museum, inv. no. A.80.
About 1420–25?

M. Salmi published this panel (1934–5, p. 177, ill. 9) with an attribution to Dello Delli. A. Parronchi (1974, p. 60) thought it had similarities to the Melbourne *Saint George* and attributed it to the young Baldovinetti. The panel's history has been put together by C. Lloyd (1977, p. 61), and more recently (C. Volpe, pp. 18 and 24, n. 19) suggested including the work in Uccello's catalogue, with a date of 1420, near in time to the del Beccuto lunette (see cat. no. 1) with which it shared 'the same purest quality lapis-lazuli, the same marvellously repeated rhythms in the roomy draperies, of an Iberian and Ghibertian type'. The pictorial language of the work is that of Florence *c.* 1420–23; the suggestion could be broadly acceptable, even if the absence of precise information on Uccello's activity before his departure for Venice (1425) makes this attribution somewhat doubtful. If the links with the del Beccuto lunette are perhaps excessive, the fresh Starninian language of the panel – which is relatively well-preserved – would fit in with what we can glean from Uccello's mysterious past. The link is even more obvious with the later Melbourne *Saint George*. Hypothetically, the two panels could mark the *before* and *after* of the artist's long stay in Venice. Recently, following on from Volpe, the possible connection with the lunette and the attribution to Uccello *c.* 1420 or before 1425 have been admitted by A. Angelini (1990, p. 73) and M. Sframeli (in *L'Età di Masaccio*, 1990, p. 94). For the history of ATTRIBUTIONS from the Sienese Ambrosi to Dello, we can consult the entry in C. Lloyd's catalogue (op. cit.) and: Berenson, 1932, p. 458; 1936, p. 393; J. Pope-Hennessy, *Sassetta*, London, 1939, pp. 202–3, n. 133; C. Volpe, 'Per Pietro di Giovanni d'Ambrogio', *Paragone-Arte*, 75, 1956, p. 55; and Lloyd, 1977, pp. 61–2, with a dating of 1420–30. The panel was cleaned in 1951. An eighteenth-century inscription in Italian on the back of the panel reads: 'Madonna with Angel in the ancient manner of Pesello Peselli n. 22'.

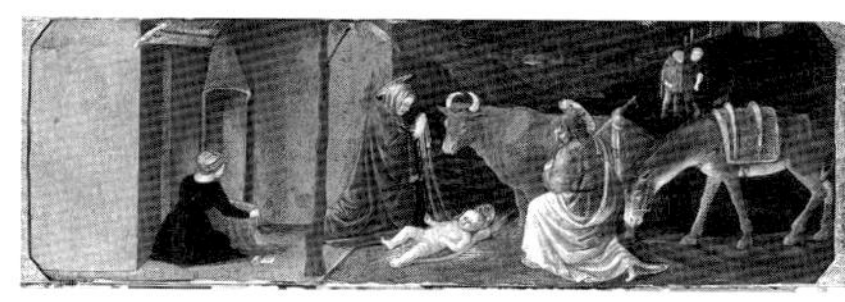

THE NATIVITY

Tempera on wood (central part of a predella), 21.6 × 65.7 cm.
London, National Gallery, inv. no. 1648.
About 1424–5

The painting reached its present location in 1922 as a gift from Sir Henry Howorth. C. Holmes (1922, p. 82) proposed attributing it to Andrea di Giusto (A. Parronchi, 1962/1964, p. 203, saw an echo in it of the lost left part of the *Assumption* polyptych [1437] of the Carnesecchi altar) and was anticipated in this by Langton Douglas (in Crowe-Cavalcaselle, 1911, IV, p. 64, n. 2). R. van Marle (1928, X, p. 306) pointed out its Masolinian character, while A. Schmarsow (1930–31, p. 1) rejected a Florentine origin for the work and proposed the (untenable) attribution to Boccati. M. Salmi thought at first (1932, pp. 130–31) that it had been painted by a follower of Masaccio influenced by Lippi; then (*Liburni Civitas*, 1938, p. 29) that it was by the Master of the Castello *Nativity*, an unknown follower of Domenico Veneziano (B. Berenson, 1963, I, p. 142, agreed with him). W. Stechow (1929–30, p. 125) was the first to suggest that the London panel was perhaps the central part of the predella of the Carnesecchi altar; Parronchi (1962; 1964, pp. 214–18) developed this suggestion and noticed a clear influence by Gentile, the 'Masolinian' atmosphere of the work, but also a composition formed of concentric circles which was typical neither of Masolino nor Masaccio (p. 216). He then suggested attributing the panel to Uccello, on the basis of the uncertain information given in Albertini's *Memoriale*: 'a panel by Masaccio: the predella and arch above are by Paolo Uccello'. M. Davies (1951, p. 272; 1961) thought it belonged to the 'school of Masaccio' and 'to a follower of Masaccio' in the National Gallery catalogue of 1973 (p. 418). Parronchi's hypothesis was accepted by L. Berti (1964, unnumbered; 1990, p. 152: 'it is a possiblity'). Parronchi's attribution to Uccello was considered as 'generally rejected' by L. Tongiorgi Tomasi (1971, p. 85). The reconstruction of the predella would be completed with *The Martyrdom of Saint Catherine* (now lost) after Andrea di Giusto, according to M. Salmi (1948, pp. 97–8 and 201–3) and with *The Martyrdom of Saint Catherine* (now lost) after Andrea di Giusto, according to M. Salmi (1948, pp. 97–8 and 201–3) and with *The Crime of Saint Julian* in the Musée Ingres at Montauban according to B. Berenson (1922–3, pp. 633, 636). U. Procacci rejected this reconstruction (*Masaccio*, 1956, p. 36): he proposed the version of the Museo Horne in Florence. Parronchi (1962, in 1964, p. 218) returned to Berenson's suggestion. The Carnesecchi panel, which Vasari (1568) confidently attributed to Masaccio, has had the benefit of a large bibliography (A. Tartuferi 1988, p. 202), which we prefer to pass over. The London panel could in fact have been part of the predella and it clearly reveals a strong Masolinian character – influenced by Gentile's Strozzi predella – as well as having echoes of Masaccio. Parronchi's hypothesis on the reconstruction of the altar is to be rejected in what it has to say on the Goldman *Annunciation*, while it can be prudently accepted for the predella. THE ATTRIBUTION OF THE PANEL TO UCCELLO IS DIFFICULT TO ACCEPT, for we must acknowledge a close adherence to the Masolino-Masaccio axis in his youthful work, before his time in Venice from 1425 to 1430. At that date, we are dealing with an Uccello who, rather than aligning himself with 'modernism', still tended towards Ghiberti's camp, and there are numerous pointers to this. On all the evidence, it is difficult to admit a connection between this panel and works such as the Oxford *Annunciation* or the Melbourne *Saint George*, recently attributed to the young Uccello on firmer grounds.

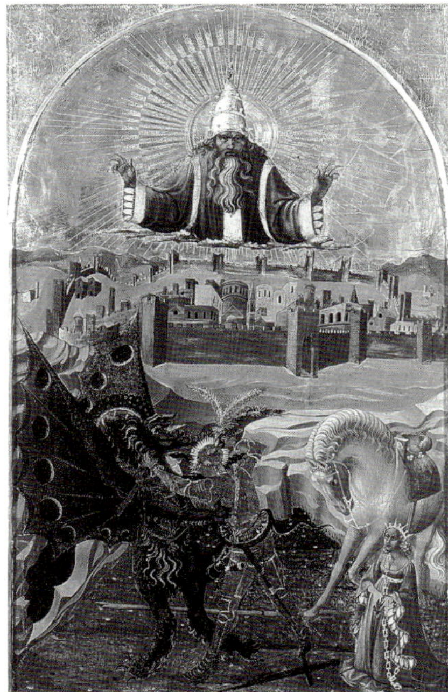

SAINT GEORGE AND DRAGON

Tempera on wood, 62.2 × 38.8 cm.
Melbourne, National Gallery of Victoria, inv. no. 2124/4.
About 1431

This remarkable panel, formerly in the National Gallery, Edinburgh, was published by R. van Marle (1928, IX, p. 544, ill. 342) with an attribution to Domenico di Bartolo: a doubtful suggestion which has been rejected ever since. R. Longhi (1928, p. 38) moved the work from a Sienese setting into a Florentine one, seeing it as by a 'direct follower of Paolo Uccello', with an imprecise dating but probably earlier than those he usually gave Uccello. B. Berenson (1932, p. 194) chose an unknown Florentine painter, shared between the Master of the Carrand Triptych (i.e. Giovanni di Francesco) and a refined follower of Domenico Veneziano known under the name of the Master of the Castello *Nativity*. G. Pudelko (1935, p. 128) proposed an unknown follower of Fra Angelico with referments to Uccello. People at that time were already noticing its very 'Uccellian' character and the influence of Fra Angelico before 1433 and the Linaioli tabernacle. A. Parronchi (1974, p. 60) included the panel in a group of works of 'Uccellian' character that he proposed attributing to the young Alesso Baldovinetti, thus attempting to resolve the old problem of the Karlsruhe Master. Baldovinetti's orientations, before he was influenced by Fra Angelico, Castagno and Domenico Veneziano, remain a mystery, but Parronchi's hypothesis is not convincing, especially as far as chronology is concerned: Baldovinetti was born in 1425 and the dating of the work would have to be pushed back to too late a period. The *Saint George* could have formed an ensemble with the Oxford *Annunciation* (U. Hoff, 1973, p. 84; C. Lloyd, 1977, p. 61). C. Volpe (1980, pp. 17–18) developed this suggestion, attributing his work to Uccello with influences by Fra Angelico and Sassetta during the 1430s and a consequent dating of *c.* 1430–31 – immediately after Uccello's return from Venice. The figure of God the father beaming out against a gold background was a northern motif brought back from the Venice area. More recently, A. Angelini (1990, p. 73) has accepted the attribution to Uccello, with a date of *c.* 1430–31.

We know too little of Uccello's youth to be able to give definitive answers, but THE PANEL CAN BE ATTRIBUTED TO HIM towards the beginning of 1431, at a time when he was little known in Florence (they asked for information on him from Venice in 1432) and when we can perceive a certain hesitancy in his painting, betrayed by the persistence of Gothic, but with a timid receptiveness to Fra Angelico. The Melbourne horse is undoubtedly a close relative of the one in the Quarate predella. The 'Bohemian' motif of gold rays around God the Father would be elevated to a principle of architectonic composition in the *Resurrection* window, while the town in the background reveals a complex spatial construction with differences in ground levels and vast perimeter walls. The attribution to Uccello is acceptable in spite of the lack of apparent consistency in relation to certain other works which have been attributed to him (the Lippi chapel, the del Beccuto lunette and the *Stories from Genesis* in the Chiostro Verde). The dating would be close to 1431, certainly before the Quarate predella and Prato cycle.

According to U. Hoff, this is a work of the Sienese school (*European Painting and Sculpture before the Eighteenth Century*, 1961, pp. 11–12, ill. 4); U. Hoff-M. Plant thought it was by Domenico di Bartolo (*National Gallery of Victoria, Painting, Drawing, Sculpture*, Melbourne, 1968, p. 38); A. Galbally by the Florentine Domenico di Michelino, *c.* 1440 (*The Collection of the National Gallery of Victoria*, Oxford, Auckland, New York, 1987, p. 103). The unusual abstract chromatic choice is remarkable, with the red fields and blue town: it anticipates the 'blue fields, towns of a red colour' in the San Miniato cycle, where the conjugation of colours is reversed.

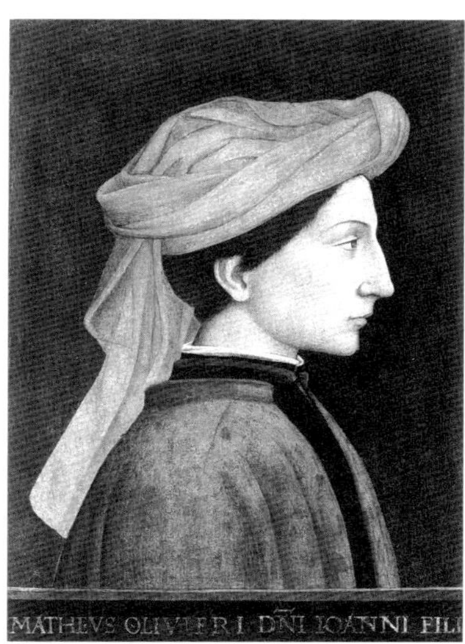

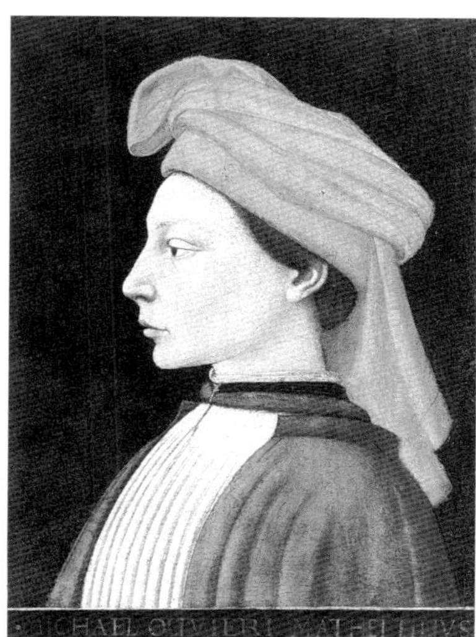

PORTRAIT OF MATTEO OLIVIERI

Tempera on wood, transferred to canvas, 47.6 × 33.7 cm.
Washington, National Gallery of Art (Mellon Collection).
About 1435–45

PORTRAIT OF MICHELE OLIVIERI

Tempera on wood, 48 × 33 cm.
Norfolk (Virginia), W. Chrysler Museum (before 1975, New York, John Rockefeller Collection).

These two portraits were attributed to Uccello by L. Venturi (1930, pp. 63–4) for whom the profile was to be 'one of Paolo's glories'. The attribution was taken up by G. Pudelko (1934, pp 249–50), R. Wedgwood Kennedy (1938, p. 132: late works), and W. Boeck (1939, p. 111: youthful works). Venturi thought they had been painted near the time of the *Flood*, *c.* 1433–4. B. Berenson (1932, p. 172) and M. Salmi (1938, p. 173) proposed Domenico Veneziano, an attribution welcomed with reservations by J. Pope-Hennessy (1969, pp. 149–51), while L. Tongiorgi Tomasi (1971, p. 87) included them among works generally attributed to Uccello. J. Lipman (1936, p. 64) suggested a follower of Uccello's, while E. Carli (1954; 1959, p. 69) proposed Veneziano, as did H. Wohl (1980, pp. 138–40, with bibliography) who dated it at 1440–45. R. Hatfield (1965, pp. 315 *et seq.* thought they were probably posthumous portraits. THE MOST CONVINCING ATTRIBUTION IS TO DOMENICO VENEZIANO, strongly influenced by Masaccio, who never attained such a high degree of influence with Uccello. The influence of the *Sagrà* and Brancacci chapel at the Carmine is obvious. The Norfolk portrait of Michele Olivieri has been drastically cleaned, but the other is in better condition (Wohl, 1980, p. 139). The chronology of the paintings is around the 1440s; the problem posed by the presence of Domenico Veneziano in Florence at an earlier date than the documented one of 1439 remains open. R. Longhi (1952, p. 33, n. 11) considers the two portraits to be copies after Domenico Veneziano.

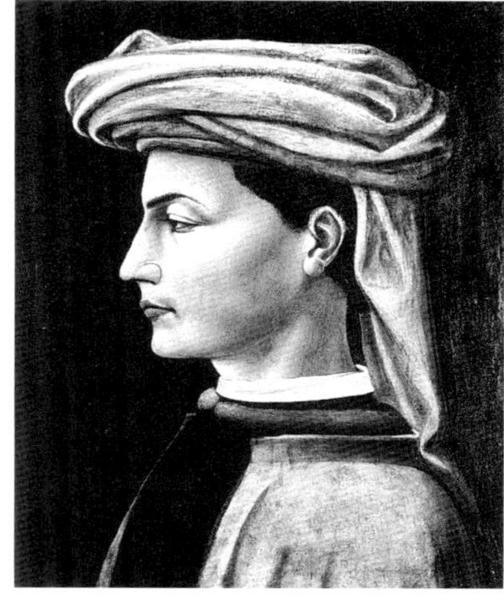

PORTRAIT OF A YOUNG MAN

Tempera on wood, 47 × 36 cm.
Chambéry, Musée des Beaux-Arts.
About 1435–40

Formerly in the Gariod collection, this painting reached its present location in 1850. It was attributed to Uccello by L. Venturi (1930, p. 63), who had adopted R. Longhi's attribution ('A portrait by Paolo Uccello', *Vita Artistica* 2, 1927, p. 45; *Piero della Francesca*, 1947, p. 89). G. Pudelko agreed (1934, p. 249, n. 26) and noticed large patches of repainting; he also thought the original shape of the head covering was bigger. M. Salmi (1938, p. 144) accepted the attribution to Uccello with reservations, while R. van Marle (1928, X, p. 240) followed Longhi's opinion. It was as a work by Uccello that the panel was shown at the *Quattro Maestri* exhibition in Florence (E. Micheletti, 1954, cat. no. 7) and also at the Paris exhibition *De Giotto à Bellini: les Primitifs italiens dans les Musées de Florence* (1956, cat. entry no. 122, ed. M. Laclotte). J. Lipman (1936, p. 101) pointed out that the inscription 'EN FIN FA TUTTO' (which echoed Machiavelli's 'the end justifies the means') had been added later. For M. Meiss ('Primitifs italiens à L'Orangerie', *Revue des Arts*, 6, 1956, p. 141), it was a sixteenth-century copy after Masaccio. E. Sindona (1957, p. 61) and L. Berti (1961, p. 304) veered towards an attribution to Uccello, while for B. Berenson (1932, p. 335) the panel was prudently likened to Masaccio, and for J. Lipman (op. cit.) to one of his followers. W. Boeck (1939, p. 120) and E. Carli (1954; 1959, pp. 28–9, 61) rejected the attribution to Uccello (Carli thought a follower of Domenico Veneziano), followed by J. Pope-Hennessy (1966, pp. 35–6; 1969, pp.

148–9). Parronchi admitted (1974, p. 94) the possibility that the two Olivieri portraits might be by Uccello, but excluded the other portraits from the catalogue, which he regrouped with the Boston portrait as being close to Masaccio. Far more than the previous two portraits, this remarkable portrait is one of the high points of the influence of Masaccio in Florentine painting after Masaccio's death, around the second half of the 1430s. Sufficient to voice SERIOUS DOUBTS ON THE ATTRIBUTION TO UCCELLO of this unidentified portrait.

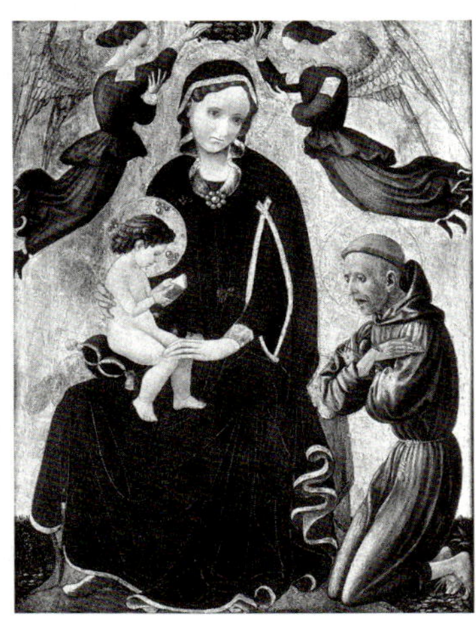

MADONNA AND CHILD WITH SAINT FRANCIS AND TWO ANGELS

Tempera on wood, 60.3 × 45.8 cm.
Allentown (Pennsylvania), The Allentown Art Museum (Kress Collection K 320).
About 1445–55

Purchased in 1935 in Florence, and originating in the Contini-Bonacossi Collection, this panel was attributed to Uccello by C. L. Ragghianti (1946, p. 75) and to the Quarate Master by M. Salmi (1950, p. 26). W. Suida (*Painting and Sculpture from the Kress Collection*, The National Gallery of Art, Washington, 1951, no. 10, p. 44) thought the work was by an unknown Florentine artist *c.* 1440, but admitted a possible attribution to Uccello. L. Berti (1961, p. 303) recognized Uccello as the artist and considered the work 'unusual, but of great refinment'. He established a link between the angels in the panel and the Virtues in Sassetta's *Mystic Marriage of Saint Francis*, in the Borgo San Sepolcro retable (1437–44). He felt that the image of the child reading was typically Florentine, 'rather like Andrea del Castagno'. Berti proposed a dating of *c.* 1450. J. Pope-Hennessy reported on the cleaning of the picture carried out in 1960 and rejected the attribution to Uccello in favour of the Karlsruhe Master. A. Parronchi (1974, p. 60) also rejected it, but in favour of the young Baldovinetti. L. Tongiorgi Tomasi (1971, p. 96) thought the authenticity of the work debatable and indicated that it was generally rejected by the critics. A history of the different attributions was established by F. R. Shapley (*Painting and Sculpture from the Kress Collection*, Allentown Art Museum, 1960, p. 48).

This is a Tuscan work of undeniable interest, created with more confidence than the Berlin, Raleigh and Florence *Madonnas* (Berti, 1961). It is reminiscent of Sienese painting and Uccello, but also of the singular Pratovecchio Master. The likeness is to a Uccello of an earlier period than the Madonnas mentioned above, which the similarity of the image of the kneeling saint to the one in the Karlsruhe *Adoration* confirms. The symmmetric angels in the sky are a Sienese-Flemish iconographical theme, rarely found in Florentine painting of the period. This is more of AN EXAMPLE OF THE SPREAD OF UCCELLIAN MODELS than the work of a direct follower of Uccello.

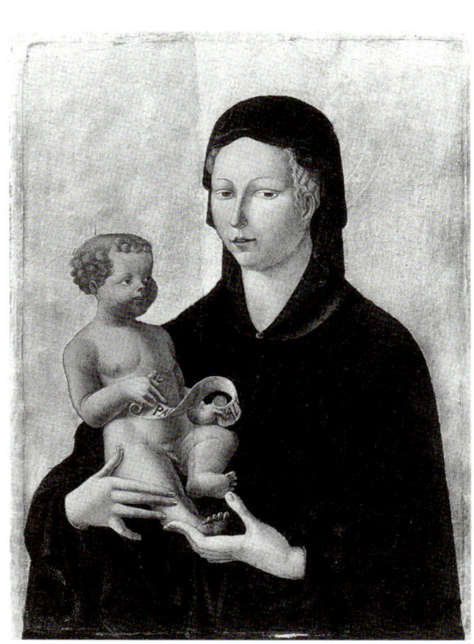

MADONNA AND CHILD

Tempera on wood, 60 × 42 cm.
Berlin, Bodemuseum, inv. no. 1470.
About 1450?

C. L. Ragghianti (1938, p. XXIV) was the first to attribute this work to Uccello, an opinion adopted by L. Berti (1961, p. 303) who dated it at *c.* 1443. J. Pope-Hennessy (1950; 1969, p. 171) noted affinities with the Raleigh Kress panel and attributed the two works to the Karlsruhe Master. For Ragghianti and Berti (who was following up an idea of M. Salmi, 1950), the two panels showed Uccello's close links with the Sienese art of Sassetta and Giovanni di Paolo. L. Tongiorgi Tomasi (1971, p. 91) noted that the Bode *Madonna* was generally attributed to Uccello, with a date of 1436–43, between the *Hawkwood* and the Duomo windows. A. Parronchi (1974, p. 60) rejected the attribution to Uccello in his attempt to establish the *corpus* of works by the young Alesso Baldovinetti. The problem of Baldovinetti's early career had not been resolved, but the information is important as far as the NON-ATTRIBUTION to Uccello. Here then is one of those rare Florentine works by the hand of an unknown master, which are proof of the spread of Uccello's style towards the middle of the century. The panel has been retouched, and the gilded background dates from its restoration.

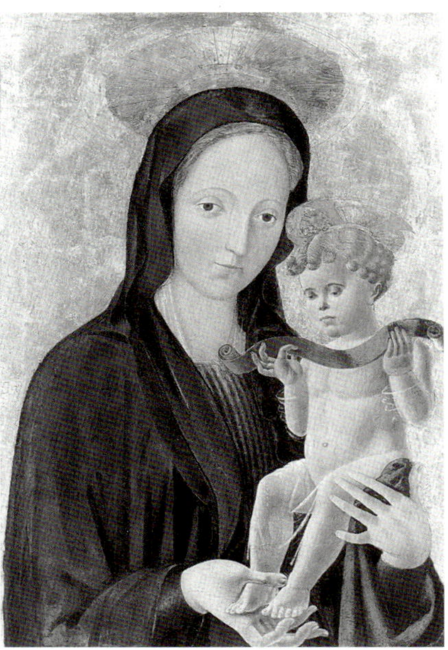

MADONNA AND CHILD

Tempera on wood, 58 × 41 cm.
Raleigh, North Carolina Museum of Art (Samuel H. Kress Collection), inv. no. K518.
About 1450?

This panel came from the Contini-Bonacossi Collection in Florence and was bought by Samuel Kress in 1938.

Formerly in the Chiesa Collection in Milan, it was purchased on the antiquarian market. We owe the attribution to Uccello to C. L. Ragghianti (1938, p. XXIV), who likened the work to the Bodemuseum *Madonna* and considered it a youthful work. In the National Gallery of Washington's catalogue (Perkins–Suida-Venturi, 1941, p. 201) the panel was linked to the frescoes of Uccello's circle at the Prato cathedral. In the catalogue of the Kress Collection (F. R. Shapley-W. Suida, Raleigh, 1960, p. 58), it was considered to be a work of Uccello's 'circle', while for Shapley (*Italian Paintings from the Samuel H. Kress Collection: Italian Schools XIII–XV Century*, London, 1966, pp. 101–2), it was 'attributed to Paolo Uccello'. L. Berti had in fact granted it to Uccello (1961, pp. 300, 303) after having shown it as an attributed work at the 1954 *Quattro Maestri* exhibition (ed. E. Micheletti, cat. no. 24). J. Pope-Hennessy 91950; 1969, pp. 168–9) attributed the panel, like the Berlin one, to the Karlsruhe Master, while Parronchi (1974, p. 60) rejected the Uccello hypothesis in favour of the early Baldovinetti. Effectively, the work, which is badly damaged, belongs to the same 'Uccellian' period of an UNKNOWN FOLLOWER *c.* 1450.

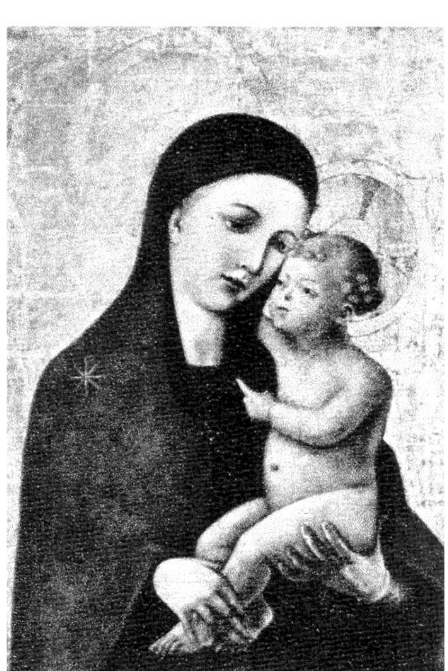

MADONNA AND CHILD

Tempera on wood.
Present location unknown (1961: Florence, Private Collection).
About 1452–6?

The work was mentioned by L. Berti (1961, pp. 298–309), who attributed it to Uccello after the Avane predella of 1452. It has been retouched, notably on the Madonna's face, and its state of conservation is mediocre (Berti, p 304, n. 1). L. Tongiorgi Tomasi (1971, p. 95) cited the work as being a recent attribution on which critics have yet to pronounce; it had been accepted into Uccello's catalogue by Parronchi (1963, col. 467) as 'a curious archaic exercise' compared with the Prato frescoes, and as an example of the 'small items' destined for private use which Vasari mentioned. Subsequently Parronchi (1974, p. 60) modified the attribution to the young Baldovinetti's advantage. The problem of the attribution has not been brought up again, because of the work's inaccessibility. It could be put with the Berlin and Raleigh panels, as a rare example of works by the school of Uccello in the 1450s and 1460s.

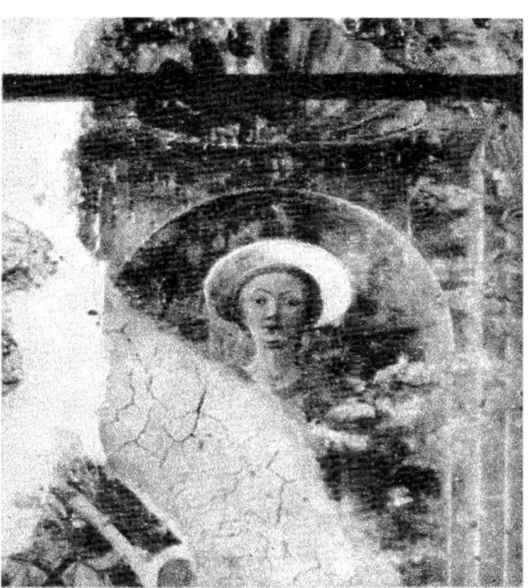

HEAD OF AN UNIDENTIFIED FEMALE SAINT

Fresco fragment.
Asolo, San Gottardo.
About 1450?

This is all that is left of a lifesize saint, in a niche painted in perspective in the Tuscan style. The foreshortened halo accentuates the experiment into spatial depth. The fragment was attributed to Uccello for the first time by G. Fiocco ('Un affresco di Paolo Uccello nel Veneto', *Bollettino d'arte*, 1923–4, p. 193; ibid., 1927, p. 35), followed by C. Volpe (156, p. 38). R. Longhi (1926, p. 132) rejected this possibility and attributed the Asolo fresco to Antonio Vivarini as being similar to the Parenzo *Madonna*. R. van Marle (1928, X, p. 250) thought it the work of a Venetian imitator of Uccello, a view taken by U. Procacci ('Gherardo Starnina', *Rivista d'Arte*, 17, 1935, p. 381) and by W. Boeck (1939, p. 119). Subsequently Fiocco (*Andrea Mantegna*, Novara, 1937, p. 197) mentioned the work as being by Uccello's school. The attribution to Uccello was resolutely rejected by J. Pope-Hennessy (1950; 1969, p. 174) and by E. Carli (1954; 1959, p. 70) who made it a work of the Venetian school. L. Coletti (*Pisanello*, Novara, 1953) proposed Veneziano, an hypothesis which was not followed up. E. Sindona (1957, p. 63) quoted the Asolo frescoes among works attributed to Uccello, as did L. Tongiorgi Tomasi (1971, p. 102) who however pointed out the rejection of the attribution by recent critics. M. Salmi (1938, p. 144) suggested an unknown Venetian sharing influences of Uccello and Filippo Lippi, while more recently H. Wohl (1980, p. 141) thought that the fresco was an apocryphal work by Veneziano and would be better imputed to an unknown Venetian influenced by Antonio Vivarini. We think THE ATTRIBUTION TO UCCELLO IS IMPOSSIBLE: the date of 1425–30 is too early (Uccello was in Venice). As Longhi had forecast, the Tuscan character derives more from Masolino's frescoes at Castiglione Olona; the dating of the fragment ought to be advanced to the middle of the century. With the new alliance between Florence and Milan, Venice closed its doors to Florentine artists; this makes any reference linked to Uccello's Paduan activity even more impossible.

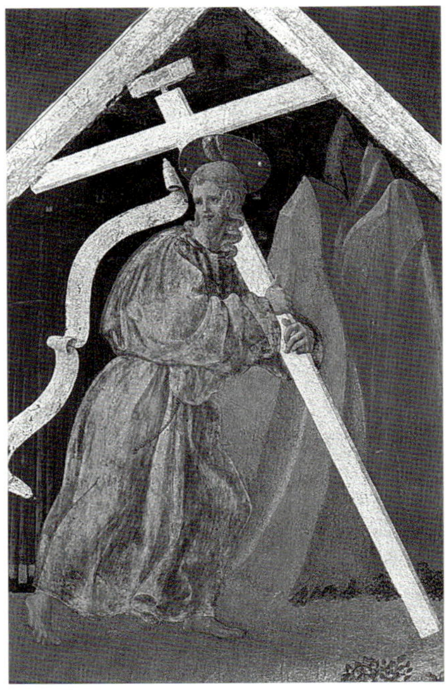

CHRIST BEARING THE CROSS

Tempera on wood, 53 × 34 cm.
Parma, Pinacoteca Stuard, inv. no. 10.
About 1450

This is one of the most problematic works in the whole of Uccello's oeuvre and though it may not benefit from a rich bibliography, its attribution and its dating are widely debated. The painting is not mentioned in the sources and no explicit reference in the documents of the period have any bearing on it. It is neither dated nor signed. It has undergone changes of format, expecially at the top and on the left-hand side. A part of the gold background at the top, still recorded in a ninteenth-century inventory, has disappeared. It must have been a small retable of unusual format, perhaps surrounded by a Gothic ornament (a flashback to Ghiberti's panels?). The long stylized cartouche, partly cut off on the lower left, bears an inscription drawn from the Gospels (Matthew, 16, 24): '(SI QVIS VULT POST ME VENIRE ABNEGET) SEMETIPSUM ET TOLLAT CRUCEM SVAM ET SEQV(ATVR)ME'.

The work was restored on the occasion of the *Mostra parmense di dipinti noti e ignoti* (held at Parma in 1948). It was part of the Florentine collection of the Marchese A. Tacoli Canacci (A. Talignani, 1986, p. 39), who had bought it on the local antiquarian market, as attribution to Andrea del Castagno. It was also mentioned in the inventories drawn up by the owner (A. Tacoli Canacci, *Catalogo ragionato dei pittori della scuola toscana, c.* 1791, no. 154; 1792, no. 105) and in the notes on the verso of the panel. The painting arrived in Parma *c.* 1805 in the collection of Duke Ferdinand of Bourbon (F. Zeri, 1971, pp. 12–14) where it was inventoried by G. B. Borghesi in 1834 (no. 135) as a work of the old Florentine school 'attributed to Andrea del Castagno'. The eighteenth-century inventories confirmed that the panel had a scalloped edge and Borghesi added that it had a background of gold. During its time in the private collection, alterations were made to modify its frame, which was removed at the time of the 1948 restoration. Its original provenance is unknown: there is a probably a connection with the widespread suppression of ecclesiastical institutions (1785–6) ordered by Leopold II, Grand Duke of Tuscany. Works of art which were involved passed into the hands of the Florentine Accademia, which decided on where they should be transferred (the verso of the panel bears the inscriptions '*Etruria pittrice*' and the seal of the Accademia). We are equally ignorant of the exact year Giuseppe Stuard, a collector from Parma, acquired the panel, though it should probably be dated between 1820 and 1830. Successive inventories (manuscript inventory, 1850, c. 16; exhibition at the pinacoteca, 1859; extract, 1891, no. 94; list, 1910, no. 28; list 1913, no. 176) attribute the work to Andrea del Castagno.

G. Copertini (1926, p. 21) thought it a work of the Tuscan Quattrocento school; B. Berenson attributed it to the Carrand Triptych Master/Giovanni di Francesco (1932, p. 342; 1936, p. 279; 1963, I, p. 88: with a landscape influenced by Domenico Veneziano and elements shared between Castagno and Pesellino), as did A. Santangelo (1934, p. 120). V. Giovannozzi (1934, p. 359) rejected this attribution in favour of the author of the Prato frescoes, followed by M. Salmi (1950, p. 26). Thus the bases were established for an attribution to Uccello, prudently proposed by E. Micheletti on the occasion of the *Quattro Maestri* exhibition (Florence, 1954, cat. no. 23, p. 58) and more closely argued by L. Berti (1961, p. 298). A. Parronchi (1963, col. 467): second half of Uccello's activity, like the whole Prato group. L. Tongiorgi Tomasi (1971, p. 95) and A. Angelini (1990, p. 82): has similarities to the Prato frescoes. J. Pope-Hennessy was in favour of an unknown follower of Uccello, the Karlsruhe Master (1950; 1969, p. 172: references to the Saint Jerome of the lower part of the Karlsruhe *Adoration*) as was J. Lauts (1966, pp. 187–8), while, at the time of the Parma exhibition, it was signalled as a work by Giovanni di Francesco (A. O. Quintavalle, 1948, p. 24). Among those who supported this attribution to Giovanni di Francesco (active from 1442, died 1459) were the proprietors of the former Stuard Collection (in its catalogue); the Congregazione di Carità di San Filippo Neri of Parma (inv. Congregazione, 1961, p. 17, 'attributed'); F. Cocconi (1962, p. 11, 'attributed'); L. V. Roncoroni (1967, p. 3); L. Farinelli-G. Godi-P. P. Mendogni (1981, p. 171 'attributed'); and, more confidently, G. Cirillo-G. Godi (1987, pp. 34–5, who considered the background as apocryphal and gave exhaustive data on the Stuard Collection). In the recent Florentine exhibition devoted to Giovanni di Francesco and his time (*Pittura di luce*, Casa Buonarroti, 1990) the panel was attributed to Uccello. A. Parronchi's hypothesis (1974, pp. 60–62) of an attribution to the young Baldovinetti has not been followed up: it is interesting on the question of Uccello's *alter ego*, but is not documented in authenticated works before Baldovinetti's intervention at Sant'Egidio in 1461.

The chronology is less controversal: it has been placed *c.* 1445 by those who attributed the work to the Prato Master; in the years from 1443 to 1445 by Tongiorgi Tomasi; in the final period of activity of Giovanni di Francesco (*c.* 1455–9) by Cirillo-Godi (1987, p. 35); and in the 1450s in Parronchi's hypothesis in favour of the young Baldovinetti. It is only early (1433–5) for Angelini (1990, p. 82) in relation to the Prato frescoes, before the crystalline atmosphere and blue sky introduced by Domenico Veneziano in 1439. In reality, it is difficult to place this panel with the Uccello of the 1430s. Its dating seems more likely *c.* 1450, with an archaic tendency which is justified by its being destined for a convent. The 'nocturnal' background is not apocryphal and it does not show crosses, but a very stylized thick wood of conifers whose colours have changed. It is a typically 'Uccellian' motif, but with a form of trees than can be found neither in the Quarate predella (right side) nor in the Oxford *Hunt*. It makes us think of the little retable attributed to Baldovinetti, currently in the Museo di San Marco in Florence (*Saint Antoninus in Adoration before the Crucifix*, Sala del Baldovinetti). The image of Christ, with alterations and its chiaroscuro flattened by cleaning, seems directly derived from the analogous scene on the plate cupboard of the Santissima Annunziata, painted by Fra Angelico *c.* 1449 and finished by Baldovinetti (*c.* 1450–1). We can then agree with the Baldovinetti hypothesis proposed by Parronchi, but there is no lack of problems: the simplified, non-stylized landscape in large crystals as in Alesso, the dryness of the details, the typically 'Uccellian' motifs in the nailed polished halo reflecting the top of Christ's skull and the 'dark forest', while the position of the cartouche in the manner of a strip cartoon, and the uncertain perspective of the cross make us think more of a close follower of Uccello. The wooded background, as in the Quarate predella and Oxford *Hunt*, is another important indicator in favour of a work by Uccello's circle. The introduction of one of Fra Angelico's subjects in a Uccellian atmosphere is to be noted, as are elements which are also reminiscent of Giovanni di Francesco, who at the beginning of the 1450s was influenced by Andrea del Castagno. The panel should therefore be ATTRIBUTED TO THE CIRCLE OF UCCELLO, *c.* 1451 (with serious doubts as to its autograph status); Uccello was still quite influential in Florence at that time. Among the young who followed his teaching attentively – as Giovanni di Francesco had done in the years around 1540 – we should certainly mention Baldovinetti, though it is possibly best to leave the reconstruction of his early years in abeyance. The author of this Parma panel, while repeating an image from the Santissima Annunziata cupboard in the brilliant nocturnal setting that Uccello cherished in his maturity, does not belong to Fra Angelico's milieu nor to Domenico Veneziano's but evolved in the double orbit of Uccello-Giovanni di Francesco. In 1453 these painters were at the head of the Guild of Saint Luke.

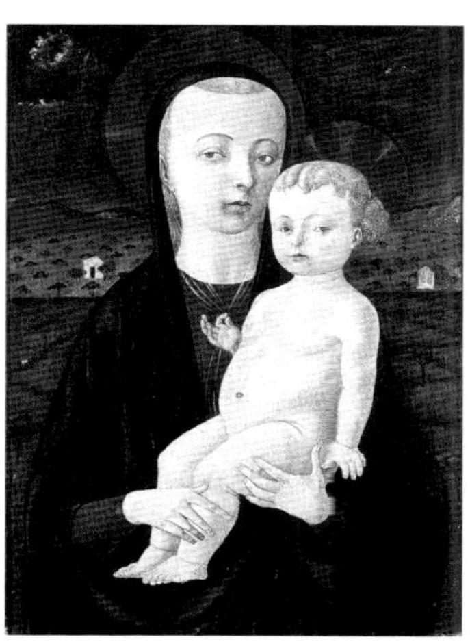

MADONNA AND CHILD (HYLAND MADONNA)

Tempera on wood, 47 × 34 cm.
Malibu, Paul Getty Museum (formerly Greenwich (Connecticut), T. H. Hyland Collection).
Early 1460s

This panel came from the Sestieri Collection in Rome, and before that from the Shine Collection in Dublin. It was shown at the *Quattro Maestri* exhibition in Florence (ed. E. Micheletti, 1954, cat. no. 24bis) and attributed to Uccello on the basis of opinions by Longhi, Toesca and Salmi. L. Berti adopted the attribution (1961, p. 304), thinking it a late work. A. Parronchi (1965, p. 178) proposed attributing it to the painter's daughter, Antonia di Paolo, a decision he also confirmed more recently (1974, pp. 65–6), while B. Berenson (1963, p. 87) proposed Giovanni di Francesco, and J. Pope-Hennessy (1969, p. 170) the Karlsruhe Master's later period. It is difficult to judge Parronchi's 'sentimental hypothesis'; the panel, painted at the beginning of the 1460s, is the work of a remarkable FOLLOWER OF UCCELLO'S LATE PERIOD, active between 1460 and 1470, aware of Sienese painting and capable of tackling the relationship between figure and landscape that was being propounded in Florence around 1460 by Baldovinetti. Since 1970 the work has been at the Getty Museum (B. Fredericksen, 1972, p. 13), but we have nevertheless retained the traditional name of 'Hyland *Madonna*'.

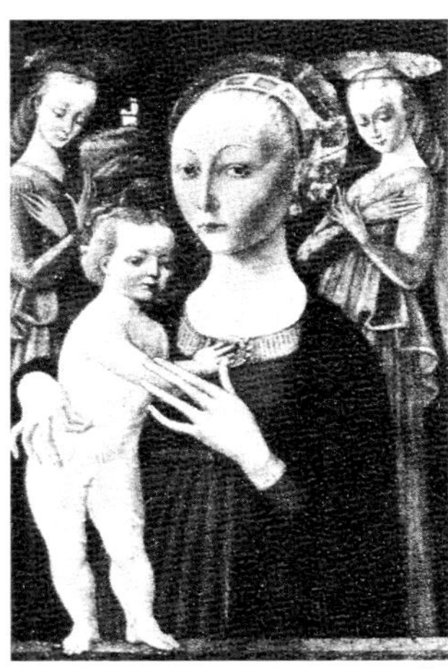

MADONNA AND CHILD WITH TWO ANGELS

Tempera on wood.
Present location unknown (formerly New York, Carl Hamilton Collection).
About 1470

This was published for the first time, with an attribution to Uccello, by R. van Marle ('Eine unbekannte Madonna von Paolo Uccello', *Pantheon*, 9, 1932, 176, pp. 76–80) and entered the Hamilton Collection in 1939. J. Pope-Hennessy was doubtful about its authenticity and rejected the attribution to Uccello; it was also rejected by E. Carli (1954; 1959, p. 70) but passed without comment by Sindona (1957). L. Berti (1961, p. 304) thought it a late work by Uccello: 'weakened to the point of caricature', with a style similar to Sienese painting of *c.* 1470. He stressed the vertical anamorphosis and the angels with folded arms whose fingers resembled 'insects' antennae'. J. Pope-Hennessy (1969, p. 170) judged it inseparable from the Hyland *Madonna*, which he attributed to the late activity of the Karlsruhe Master. A. Parronchi (1974, p. 66), on the other hand, separated it from the Hyland panel and proposed Donato di Paolo, the painter's son, instead of Sister Antonia. The hypothesis would seem difficult to support: every artistic trace of the Uccello children has been lost. This is a remarkable work, later than the Hyland *Madonna*, probably by the same ARTIST RELATED TO UCCELLO'S FINAL PERIOD; it is also close to works such as the Karlsruhe *Adoration* and to Baldovinetti in the 1460s and the Sienese. It is a rare example of the stylistic convergence of Florentine painting and the manner of the elderly Uccello, in a period which really belonged to the Pollaiuoli and Baldovinetti and saw Botticelli's official début, under the label of refined archaism.

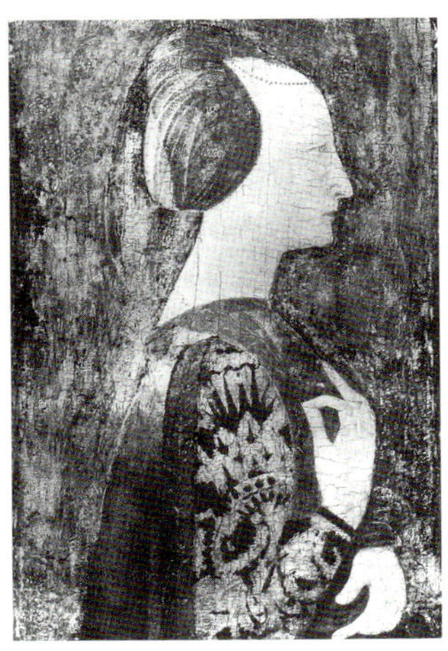

PORTRAIT OF A WOMAN

Tempera on wood, 57.5 × 38 cm.
New York, Private Collection (formerly Lehman Collection).
About 1470–5

This very badly damaged panel was until 1883 in the Toscanelli Collection in Florence, from where it moved to France, to the Aynard Collection in Lyons. In 1917, during the First World War, it was bought for the Lehman Collection, with an attribution to Piero della Francesca. This attribution must have gone back a long way, since there is an eighteenth-century inscription on the back which reads 'Portrait of Battista Sforza, wife of Federigo, Duke of Urbino, died 1473. By the hand of Piero della Francesca.' In the catalogue of his collection (*Catalogue of the Philip Lehman Collection*, New York, 1928), R. Lahman attempted to change the attribution in favour of Uccello, after the panel had been catalogued as Piero's work by the Toscanelli Collection (1883, no. 140) as well as the Aynard Collection (Paris, Petit Palais, 1913, no. 62). G. B. Cavalcaselle (Crowe-Cavalcaselle, ed., Hutton, 1909, III, p. 199) and B. Berenson (*Central Italian Painters of the Renaissance*, New York, 1909 [1896], 3rd edn) had already attributed it to Antoniazzo Romano. L. Venturi (1930, p. 64) confidently attributed it to Uccello, believing this to be a portrait of the Countess of Urbino, painted by Uccello in 1468. The following are in agreement over the attribution to Uccello: G. Pudelko (1934, p. 249, a later work); W. Boeck (1939, p. 121: an attributed work); E. Sindona (1957, p. 61: Uccello's final period); and L. Berti (1961, p. 304: *c.* 1465–9 but also, p. 309, n. 41, has similarities to the Prato frescoes, the second visitor in the *Birth of the Virgin*). O. Siren and M. Brockwell (*Catalogue of a Loan Exhibition of Italian Primitives at the Kleinberger Galleries*, New York, 1917, p. 57) and M. Salmi (1938, pp. 171–2) attributed the work to Domenico Veneziano, though with reservations. L. Mayer (1930, *Pantheon*, p. 113) to Uccello, while R. Offner (1933, p. 178) assigned it to the Master of the Castello *Nativity* (a painting which is now in the Uffizi, but was formerly in the Medici villa at Castello). Agreeing with Offner were J. Lipman (1936, pp. 114–18); B. Berenson (1963, p. 142); J. Pope-Hennessy (1950; 1960, p. 151); E. Carli (1954; 1959, p. 69) and H. Wohl (1980, p. 185). L. Tongiorgi Tomasi (1971, p. 102) quoted it among works attributed to Uccello. It was the only female portrait allowed by A. Parronchi (1974, pp. 49, 51) in Uccello's catalogue, an opinion shared by A. Padoa Rizzo (1983, p. 82). The largely unrestored portrait is in poor condition, but it reveals a remarkable atmospheric refinement that distinguishes it from the rest of the series quoted in connection with the Bache portrait (see the following entry). It probably came from Urbino, but it is not certain that it depicts Battista Sforza, Count Federico's wife, who died prematurely in childbirth. THE WORK IS CLOSER TO DOMENICO VENEZIANO THAN TO UCCELLO, but an attribution to that anonymous but remarkable follower of Domenico, the Master of the Castello *Nativity*, is the most likely.

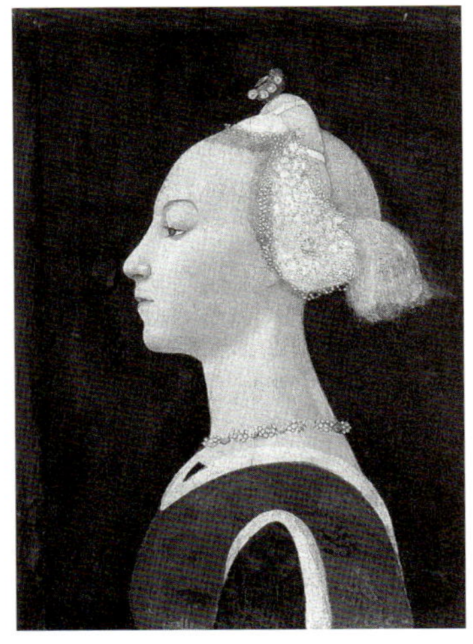

PORTRAIT OF A WOMAN

Tempera on wood (transferred to canvas), 39 × 26 cm.
New York, The Metropolitan Museum of Art, Jules S. Bache Collection, inv. no. 49.7.6.
About 1470–75

This came from the Holford Collection in London. According to O. Fischel (*Amtliche Berichte aus den Königlichen Preussischen Kunstsammlungen*, 41, 1920, p. 16) it is meant to depict Elisabetta di Montefeltro, wife of Roberto Malatesta. In the Holford Collection catalogue (1924) drawn up by B. Benson, and even in that of the Bache Collection (1929), the panel was atributed to Domenico Veneziano. The attribution to Uccello was first suggested by L. Venturi (1930, p. 64) followed by M. Marangoni (1931–2, p. 336), M. Salmi (1938, pp. 25, 142), E. Micheletti (*Quattro Maestri* exhibition catalogue, Florence, 1954, no. 17, as an attributed work), Salmi again (*Liburni Civitas*, 1938, pp. 38–40, 44), E. Sindona (1957, p. 40), E. Carli (1954; 1959, pp. 30–31, 55–6) and L. Berti (1961, p. 304). G. Pudelko (1935, *Pantheon*, p. 95) proposed 'his' Karlsruhe Master, an unsustainable attribution which has not been repeated. Others who favoured Uccello are W. Boeck (1939, p. 121, an attributed work), M. Pittaluga (1946, p. 14) and L. Malle ('Appunti albertiani in margine al Della Pittura', *Arte Lombarda*, 1965, p. 211 *et seq.*). R. Offner (1933, p. 178), J. Lipman (1936, pp. 11–24) and R. Wedgwood Kennedy (1938, p. 131), on the other hand, attributed the work to the Master of the Castello *Nativity*. They were followed by J. Pope-Hennessy (1950) and F. Zeri (1971). B. Berenson (1963, p. 62) suggested Domenico Veneziano, while H. Wohl (1980, p. 184) thought the portrait was an apocryphal work of Domenico's, a suggestion Pope-Hennessy (1969, p. 151) corrected in favour of an unknown Florentine painter. A. Parronchi (1974, p. 51) suggested the panel could have been part of the series of portraits of Count Federico da Montefeltro's eight daughters in the manner of Pollaiuolo, rejecting the attribution of the whole series to Uccello, except for the Lehman portrait. Wohl (op. cit.) thought it might be a Florentine copy after a portrait by Domenico Veneziano, *c.* 1460. The date ought rather to be placed after 1472, when Florence gave the splendid parade helmet by Pollaiuolo to Federico to commemorate his conquest of Volterra, marking his taste for the Baldovinetti-Pollaiuolo style. The panel was shown at the exhibition of the Burlington Fine Arts Club of 1910 as a work belonging to the Umbrian-Tuscan school (R. Fry, 1910). A similar critical fate and a similar history of attribution has meant that the Bache portrait has been grouped with a series of other portraits comprising individual paintings in the Johnson Collection in Philadelphia (inv. no. 24), Boston (Isabella Stewart Gardner Museum), Melbourne (National Gallery of Victoria) and London (National Gallery, inv. no. 758), this latter attributed by R. Fry (1910, p. 113) and R. Wedgwood Kennedy (1938, pp. 131–3) to Baldovinetti. So we have a series (whose formats today vary) that is stylistically homogeneous and recalls Pollaiuolo's work of the early 1470s, portraits probably painted after Uccello had left Urbino – where they undoubtedly originated – which differ markedly from the Lehman portrait and which have VERY LITTLE IN COMMON WITH UCCELLO. For bibliographical information see J. Pope-Hennessy (1969, pp. 149–51); L. Tongiorgi Tomasi (1971, pp. 98, 102; and H. Wohl (1980, pp. 181–6).

FIVE FAMOUS MEN (THE FATHERS OF PERSPECTIVE)

Tempera on wood, 42 × 210 cm.
Paris, Musée du Louvre, inv. no. 267/1272.
About 1500 and 1565

(Illustrated on p. 354).

At the bottom of the panel a later than fifteenth-century inscription lists the names, from left to right, of Giotto, Paolo Uccello, Donatello, Antonio Manetti and Filippo Brunelleschi. This identification is doubtful and has inconsistencies, in particular the fact that Uccello looks older than Brunelleschi and Donatello, who were in fact his elders. This panel is a pastiche which has taken the portraits from different earlier iconographical sources, scattered over a wide range of dates. Important differences in perspectival composition confirm that, in more than one case, we can unequivocally date it well into the Cinquecento. The two famous portraits of Francesco Giamberti and Giuliano Giamberti (Sangallo) by Piero di Cosimo (*c.* 1500–1505), now in the Rijksmuseum, Amsterdam, are an analogous case: there the posthumous portrait of Giuliano's father is in profile, an old-fashioned treatment when compared to Sangallo's very different, extraordinarily modern one.

Those panels, which probably made up a diptych, came from the Sangallo (subsequently Panciatichi-Ximenes) house in Borgo Pinti in Florence; the Louvre panel also came from there. Vasari, a close friend of Francesco da Sangallo, Giuliano's son, wrote: 'Although he was a man of abstraction, Paolo loved the virtue of inventiveness in his own fellow-craftsmen, and in order that they should be remembered for posterity, he painted the portraits of five outstanding men on a long panel that he kept at his house in their memory: one was Giotto the painter, for the luminous beginning of art; Filippo di ser Brunellesco, the second, for architecture; Donatello for sculpture, and himself, for perspective and animal painting; and for mathematics, Giovanni [*sic*] Manetti, his friend with whom he often conferred and argued over Euclid's theories' (1568, I, p. 273, in the *Vita di Paolo Uccello*), while, in the earlier edition (1550, pp. 290–91), where he attributes the painting to Masaccio, he wrote: 'He has shown who, after him, merited our recognition for progress in the arts, in five faces that he painted by way of a testament. Leaving them all, on a panel by his own hand, in Giuliano da San Gallo's house in Florence, the portraits which are extremely lifelike are these: Giotto, as founder of painting; Donato, for sculpture, Filippo Brunellesco, for architecture, and Paolo Uccello, for animals, and for Perspective. And finally Antonio Manetti, for being the most excellent Mathematician of his time.' Between the two editions therefore Vasari changed the attribution: he had obviously noticed that by attributing the panel to Masaccio, he had given him an impossible date, before 1428. The most important change, however, was that he altered the order of the identifications. Other similar examples to this panel are to be found, such as the triple portrait of the Gaddi in the Uffizi (possibly the work of Agnolo Gaddi), the quadruple one of Ghirlandaio in Munich (Gronau, 'Eine Deutsche Kopie nach Domenico Ghirlandaio im Münchner National Museum', in *Münchner Jahrbuch für Bildende Kunst*, I, 1906, pp. 109–12) or single portraits like the one of Donatello in the Museo Civico in Padua (inv. no. 422) published by Moschetti ('Un ritratto ignorato di Donatello' in *Bollettino del Museo Civico di Padova*, 11, 1908, pp. 174–7), the one of Giotto, formerly in the Pozzi Collection in London, or the multiple portrait of Giotto, Brunelleschi and Donatello accompanied by Raphael and Michelangelo in the Fitzwilliam Museum, Cambridge, attributed by Richter to Francesco Salviati (*The Mond Collection*, II, 1910, p. 477) (cf. J. Pope-Hennessy, 1969, p. 157).

The state of the panel, which has been extensively repainted, prevents any confident assessment and justifies the lively debate on the attribution and the uncertainties about the chronology. We are perhaps dealing here with a panel (it may have been a *spalliera* or an overdoor) commissioned by the Sangallo *c.* 1500 – in an attempt at a 'revival' of the *Famous Men (Uomini singhularii)* of Florentine art – probably from Filippino Lippi's studio, and used as part of the furniture which would have exposed it to deterioration and abrasions, thus rendering the 'restorations' necessary; one of them must have occurred between the two editions of the *Vite*. The painting provided the iconography for some of the portraits engraved by Coriolani for the second edition of the *Vite* dated 1568, which confirms Vasari's familiarity with the work and its owners, especially his 'great friend' (*amicissimo*) Francesco da Sangallo. It could be that the Sangallo commissioned this collage of the fathers of perspective (and perhaps originally Masaccio replaced Giotto, who was less pertinent in the context of the Quattrocento) in a sort of cultural self-promotion, more as cabinetmakers and masters of perspective and

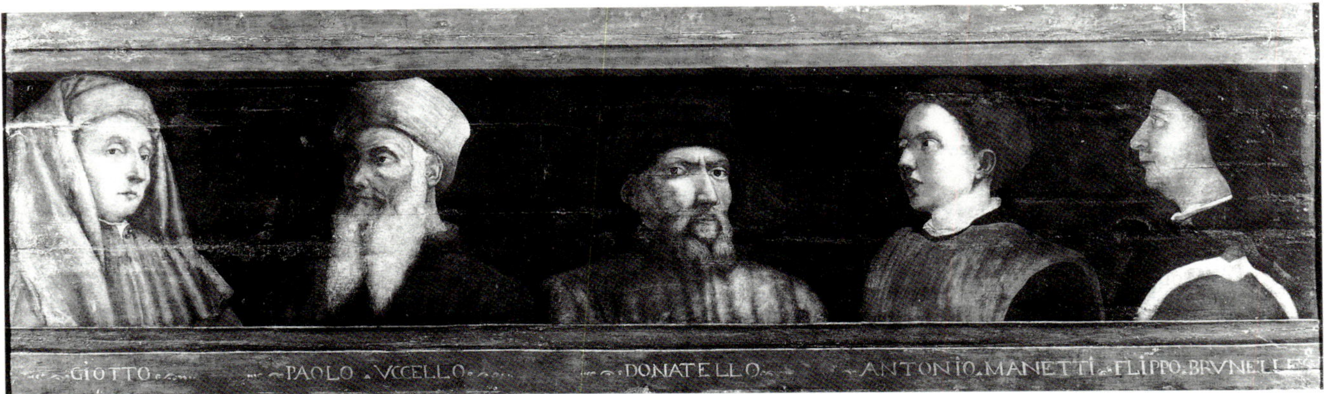

marquetry than as architects. The inscriptions and later restoration could have been ordered by Francesco da Sangallo, at Vasari's suggestion, in the 'academic' climate of the second half of the Cinquecento.

Uccello appears in the picture as one of the fathers of 'Brunelleschian' perspective, as a naturalist, a 'Euclidian' scholar, an animal and landscape painter of early figurative humanism, which was typically Vasarian. In this case, he was perhaps influenced by Vincenzo Borghini (in the second edition); a letter of 1565 exists from Borghini to Alessandro Allori offering solid proof of this cultural climate and Uccello's still lively renown in Florentine academic circles. In this letter (S. Bottari, *Racolta di lettere sulla pittura, scultura, architettura*, Rome, 1574, pp. 161–2) Borghini asks for a group portrait of Masaccio, Brunelleschi, Donatello, Ghiberti, Uccello and the two Lippi to decorate the burgeoning Florentine Accademia.

If the Louvre panel was a modified Quattrocento original, the firmly rooted reference to Uccello might at a pinch be conceivable, but the painting certainly has none of his 'characteristics, even as a copy' (C. L. Ragghianti, 1977, p. 106). Neither stylistic nor technical elements (the picture was painted in oil) favour Uccello. What is more, it would have to be dated, at the latest, at around 1470, which would not fit in with the 'revivalist' taste of the Sangallo household. We should have to imagine an earlier provenance for which there is no evidence, apart from Vasari's suspect information that Uccello created these portraits so that posterity would remember him. To this collection of conjectures must be added considerations on the uncertain iconography of the figures and the extremely doubtful hypothesis of Uccello as a portrait painter. Perhaps initially he did paint one of the five characters and, if Manetti, Brunelleschi and Donatello are excluded because they were not painters, Giotto for obvious chronological reasons, and Masaccio because for one reason or another all trace has been lost of his inclusion (and Vasari does not mention him), we could thus easily explain Vasari's correction: the attribution to Uccello as an alternative to Masaccio. As a hypothesis only, the original sequence could have been Manetti (?'Giotto'), Donatello ('Paolo Uccello'), Uccello ('Donatello'), Masaccio (?'Antonio Manetti', whom Vasari in 1550 calls 'Giovanni' Manetti), and 'Filippo Brunelleschi', stylistically the most old-fashioned, perhaps derived from Masaccio's frescoes in the Brancacci chapel (according to L. Berti's hypothesis, 1990, p. 35: I do not believe in a direct derivation, but rather in a series of interventions). It is more difficult to retain the frequently supported hypothesis that the portraits derived from Masaccio's famous *Sagrà* (*c.* 1424, now lost) as much by reason of the very Cinquecento style of some of the portraits, as because of the inexplicable fact (J. Pope-Hennessy, 1969, p. 156) that Vasari made no mention of it when he gave a careful description of Masaccio's fresco, quoting by name many who featured in it. It is probably through the historical bias of the picture and through its possible patrons that we can best tackle the problems raised by including this work in Uccello's catalogue. It was part of an important collection compiled by a great family of Florentine artists, the Sangallo, who belonged to the generation that followed Uccello's: a collection assembled after 1470. Apart from the ancient sculptures mentioned in Albertini's *Memoriale* (1510) and drawings, it included such masterpieces as the portraits quoted earlier of Giuliano and his father, Piero di Cosimo's *Cleopatra/Simonetta Vespucci*, the tondo of the *Madonna* from Botticelli's studio (National Gallery, London), possibly the *Madonna* by Botticelli's circle (formerly Ximenes and Benson) and a replica of the *Madonna and Child* of the San Barnaba retable by Botticelli, which probably arrived in the Ximenes Collection when the Panciatichi acquired the Sangallo *palazzetto* on Borgo Pinti.

After Vasari had mentioned the painting as being at the Sangallo's house, nothing further was heard of it until the nineteenth century when, with a provenance from the collection of Louis-Philippe, it passed to the Louvre in the 1847 Stevens sale. While rejecting this painting from Uccello's catalogue, it is interesting to run through its critical fortunes, as a significant example of the difficulties of attributing it to Uccello. The attribution to Uccello can be found in the Louvre catalogue of 1849 (F. Villot, I, 1849, no. 184), of 1913 (S. de Ricci, I, 1913, no. 1272) and 1926 (L. Hautecoeur, II, 1926, no. 1272). It is supported and its case argued by P. Schubring (1923, p. 105: the panel was repainted by Giuliano Bugiardini in the Cinquecento); R. van Marle (1928, X, p. 298); D. Colnaghi (1928, p. 265, but much repainted); P. Soupault (1929, p. 6: with Uccello's self-portrait; p. 19: he gives an idea of the Masters he knew at close hand; p. 21: Uccello sacrificed chronological truth and local colour for intensity of expression); B. Berenson (1932, p. 582; 1936, p. 500; 1963, p. 209); G. Pudelko (1934, *Early*, p. 233: the frame would be similar to that of the clock in the Duomo; 1935, 'Florentiner Porträts der Frührenaissance', *Pantheon* 15, 1935, p. 98); J. Lipman (1936, p. 101: Uccello's studio); M. Salmi (1938, pp. 147–8: a late work at all events, perhaps after a Flemish model); M. Wackernagel (1938; 1981 edn, p. 170: stressed the *sotto in su* foreshortenings and the three-quarter views); W. Boeck (1939, pp. 111–13: the work was meant to depict the inventors of perspective; Manetti would be the cabinet-maker Antonio Manetti-Ciaccheri and not the mathematician); M. Pittaluga (1946, p. 16: 'an eroded work of Paolo's'); E. Somaré (1946, p. 33; with the *Flood* one of the most significant works of his mature period, which is reminiscent of 'Masaccio's hand' and 'Donatello's nerve'); J. Pope-Hennessy (1950, pp. 150–4: undoubtedly painted in the Quattrocento, by someone familiar with Uccello's art, but later repainted); E. Carli (1954; 1959, pp. 60–61: the attribution to Uccello was 'probable' and Lanyi's (1944) hypothesis of the derivation of the portraits in the *Sagrà* at the Carmine should not be excluded); E. Sindona (1957, pp. 37–55, 60); D. Gioseffi (1958, p. 137: suggested reversing Uccello's and Donatello's 'title' and portraits because of the age of the faces); L. Berti (1961, p. 304); L. Tongiorgi Tomasi (1971, p. 96); C. L. Joost-Gaugier (1974, pp. 233–8: pointed out the resemblance between the presumed portrait of Uccello and the presumed Noah in the Chiostro Verde: doubts about this were expressed by E. Wakayama, 1982, p. 99). E. Battisti (1976, p. 17) thought it a work by Uccello's circle, while L. Berti (1964, n.p.) was flexible about the attribution but certain that it did contain a portrait of Uccello; subsequently (1990, p. 35) he suggested that the portrait of Brunelleschi derived from the one painted by Masaccio in the Brancacci chapel frescoes at the Carmine (a vague resemblance, a hypothesis which is acceptable only at one remove). W. Boeck (1931, pp. 143–7) suggested an early date and even thought of a collaboration between Masaccio and the young Paolo Uccello (in reality he was older), and consequently changed the sequence (1933, pp. 145–7), starting from the left, to: Uccello, Brunelleschi, Donatello, Manetti and Giotto. C. Shell's attempt (1961, p. 205) to attribute the panel to 'his' Master of the Trivulzio *Madonna* (Milan, Museo del Castello Sforzesco) was never followed up: somewhat unconvincingly he tried to group under one artists works by the young Lippi and the Prato Master. H. Beenken (1929, I, pp. 112–19) thought the panel had similarities to a painting from the school of Masaccio, a suggestion developed by J. Lanyi (1944, pp. 94–5) who pointed out the different formats of the figures and made the work an anonymous derivation from Masaccio. He also suggested that two of the characters could have been taken from Masaccio's *Sagrà* at the Carmine, and reordered the sequence (from left to right): Masaccio, Uccello (with doubts), Donatello, Manetti and Brunelleschi. A. Schmarsow (1930–31, p. 3) reached a similar conclusion: the work derived from the *Sagrà* or from a copy of the replica done by Masaccio and mentioned by Vasari as being 'in the house of Simon Corsi'. R. Longhi (1947, p. 157) agreed: the school of Masaccio, derived from the lost *Sagrà*; recently, the edition of Vasari edited by L. Bellosi and A. Rossi (Turin, 1986, p. 274, n. 24) also agreed.

J. Pope-Hennessy (1969, pp. 157–9) disagreed: according to him there were 'strong possibilities' that the painting was done at the end of the Quattrocento by a 'Uccellian' rather than a 'Masaccian' source and repainted in the following century; it was certainly not derived from the *Sagrà*, because Vasari, who knew and had described Masaccio's lost fresco, would have mentioned it. The attribution to Uccello, which had been prudently welcomed in the 1960 exhibition catalogue devoted to the reserve stock in the Louvre (*Exposition de 700 tableaux* [Réserve cat.], 1960, no. 60) had been rejected by: Crowe-Cavalcaselle (1864, ed Langton Douglas-De Nicola, VI, 1911, p. 119: a copy from the time of Pontormo [1494–1556], much repainted, modern inscriptions and links with the woodcuts of Vasari's *Vite*); Richter (1910, II, p. 477: might derive from the painters' guild portraits, as the one in Cambridge); E. Benkard (1927, pp. 47–9: an unknown painter of the Cinquecento); C. L. Ragghianti (1942; 1977, pp. 106–7: an anonymous copy from Pontormo's time, after a collection of portraits derived from the Quattrocento, probably from Masaccio's *Sagrà*); and P. D'Ancona (1959, p. 13, n. 3: perhaps by a follower or a 'late imitator of Uccello in the sixteenth century', but surely not by Uccello). In the new Louvre catalogue (1981, II, inv. no. 267, p. 257) the panel is labelled as an anonymous work of the Florentine school of the first half of the Cinquecento.

The debate on the work's chronology is equally fraught: Boeck (1931) announced a very early date of about 1425; those who credited it to the school of Masaccio gave it a date of later than 1428 (Beenken, 1929; Schmarsow, 1930–1; Lanyi, 1944; Longhi, 1947; for Beenken, *c.* 1426–8). It was moved to 1432 by Shell; between 1436 and 1443 by W. Boeck (1939, pp. 111–13); after 1440 by M. Wackernagel (1938/1981, p. 170); towards 1450 by Salmi (1938, pp. 34–5: among the oldest examples of portraits with a three-quarter view; he noted that Uccello appears older in it than his friend Donatello); followed by M. Pittaluga (1946, p. 16: 'around 1450'); D. Gioseffi (1958, p. 137); L. Berti (1961, p. 304, on the basis of Manetti's date of birth of 1423); and L. Tongiorgi Tomasi (1971, Fr. edn 1972, p. 96). It was later than 1450 for B. Berenson (1932; 1936; 1963) and J. Lipman (1936, p. 101: a late studio work); between 1450 and 1460 for E. Carli (1954; 1959, pp. 60–61); towards 1455 for E. Sindona (1957, p. 60); and it was thought to be a late work of Uccello, around 1460, by G. Pudelko (1935, *Pantheon*, p. 98). Pope-Hennessy (1969, p. 158) felt it was probably an original late Quattrocento work, repainted in the following century copying several models: he noticed that 'Giotto's' clothes dated from *c.* 1420.

The hypothesis proposed here is of a 'Vasarian' remodelling (more for the cultural climate than as a personal intervention) of a very damaged panel, formerly part of the interior decoration of the Sangallo's house, which they had commissioned *c.* 1500. Uccello's presence among the figures depicted, which led Vasari to his second attribution, could be explained by the celebration of the great Master of perspective in a milieu of cabinet makers: the Sangallo were sons of the cabinet maker Francesco Giamberti and pupils of the cabinet maker Francione (see S. Borsi *Maestri fiorentini nei cantieri romani del Quattrocento*, Rome, 1989, pp. 176–97). THE LOUVRE PANEL CANNOT BE INCLUDED IN THE CATALOGUE OF UCCELLO'S AUTOGRAPH WORKS. H. Saalman (in A. Manetti, *Life of Brunelleschi*, London, 1970, p. 19, n. 24) believed he had identified one of the portraits as that of Paolo dal Pozzo Toscanelli, a hypothesis which was rightly rejected by Parronchi (1974, p. 50): Vasari gave the famous mathematician a completely different posthumous portrait (Florence, Palazzo Vecchio, Sala di Cosimo; cf. Parronchi, 1974, p. 79, n. 107).

BIBLIOGRAPHY

The most important works are indicated by an asterisk (*)

SOURCES AND EARLY PUBLICATIONS

ALBERTI, L. B., *De Pictura*, ed. C. Grayson, Bari, 1980

ALBERTINI, F., *Memorial di molte statue et picture che sono nella inclita città di Florentia*, Florence, 1510; ed. A. Schmarsow, Heilbronn, 1886; ed. P. Murray, *Five Early Guides to Rome and Florence*, London, 1972

BALDINUCCI, *Notizie de' professori del disegno*, II, Florence, 1686; Florence, 1845, I

BARTOLOMEO DEL CORAZZA, *Diario fiorentino (1405–1439)*, ed. R. Gentile, Anzio, 1991

BIADI, L., *Notizie sulle antiche fabbriche di Firenze non terminate*, Florence, 1824

BOCCHI F., *Bellezze della città di Fiorenza*, Florence, 1591

——and CINELLI, G., *Le bellezze della città di Firenze*, Florence, 1677

BORGHINI, R., *Il Riposo*, Florence, 1584, 309–11

BOTTARI, S., *Raccolta di lettere sulla pittura, scultura ed architettura*, Rome, 1754

BRUNI ARETINO, Leonardo, *Humanistisch-Philosophischen Schriften*, ed. H. Baron, Leipzig, 1928; Wiesbaden, 1969

CARLIER, J., *Ristretto delle cose più notabili di Firenze*, Florence, 1689, 1698; 5th edn, Florence, 1745

CICOGNARA, L., *Storia della scultura*, VI, Prato, 1824

DEL MIGLIORE, F. L., *Firenze città nobilissima illustrata*, Florence, 1684; Sala Bolognese, 1976

FABRICZY, C. VON, *L'Anonimo Gaddiano*, Florence, 1893

FANTOZZI, F., *Nuova guida ovvero descrizione storico–artistico–critica della città e contorni di Firenze*, Florence, 1842; Sala Bolognese, 1979

FILARETE, *Trattato d'architettura*, ed. A. M. Finoli and L. Grassi, Milan, 1972, 235

FINESCHI, V., *Il Forestiero istruito in Santa Maria Novella di Firenze*, Florence, 1790

——and GIULIANI, G., *Il Forestiero istruito in Santa Maria Novella*, Florence, 1836

FREY, C., ed., *Il Codice Magliabechiano XVII, 17*, Berlin, 1892

——*Il Libro di Antonio Billi*, Berlin, 1892

GAYE, G., *Carteggio inedito d'artisti*, Florence, 1838

GHIBERTI, L., *I Commentari*, ed. O. Morisani, Naples, 1947

GILL, J., *The Council of Florence*, Cambridge, 1959

LANDINO, C., *La Comedia di Dante*, Florence, 1481

LANZI, L., *Storia pittorica della Italia*, Bassano del Grappa, 1789; Florence, 1834

MANETTI, A., *Vite di XIV uomini synghulary in Firenze dal MCCCC innanzi* (*c.* 1494–7); in *Operette istoriche*, ed. G. Milanesi, Florence, 1887; ed. P. Murray, in *The Burlington Magazine*, 99, 1957, 330–36

——*Vita di Filippo Brunelleschi*, ed. G. Tanturli and G. De Robertis, Florence, 1976; ed. H. Saalman, London, 1979

MARCHESE, V., *Memorie dei più insigni pittori, scultori e architetti domenicani*, Florence, 1854

MAZZEI, L., *Lettere di un notaio e un mercante del secolo XIV*, ed. C. Guasti, Florence, 1880

MECATTI, G. M., *Storia cronologica della città di Firenze*, Naples, 1755

MICHIEL, M. (Anonimo Morelliano), *Notizie d'opere di disegno*, ed. G. Frizzoni, Bologna, 1884

RICHA, G., *Notizie istoriche delle Chiese fiorentine*, Florence, 1755–62

SANTI, G., *Cronica rimata*, ed. Holtzinger, Stuttgart and Tübingen, 1897

VASARI, G., *Le Vite de' più eccellenti Architetti, Pittori, et Scultori italiani, da Cimabue insino a' tempi nostri*, 1st edn, Florence, 1550; 2nd edn, Florence, 1568

——*Le Vite de' più eccellenti pittori scultori e architettori nelle redazioni del 1550 e 1568*, ed. R. Bettarini and P. Barocchi, Florence, 1966–86

VASARI–MILANESI: *Le Vite de' più eccellenti pittori, scultori ed architettori scritte da Giorgio Vasari pittore aretino con nuove annotazioni e commenti di Gaetano Milanesi*, Florence, 1878

VERINO, U., *Libri tres de illustratione urbis Florentiae*, Florence, 1512; Paris, 1790

ON UCCELLO

[ALLENTOWN] *The Samuel Kress Memorial Collection of the Allentown Art Museum*, Allentown, Pa., 1960

ALPATON, M., 'A propos de la comparaison de deux œuvres de Paolo Uccello et de maître Denis', in *Scritti di storia dell'arte in onore di Roberto Salvini*, Florence, 1984, 325–8

AMES LEWIS, F., 'A Portrait of Leon Battista Alberti by Uccello?', in *The Burlington Magazine*, 116, 851, 1974, 103–4

ANGELINI, A., 'Paolo Uccello, il beato Jacopone da Todi e la datazione degli affreschi di Prato', in *Prospettiva*, 61, 1991, 49–53

APA, M., 'Paolo Uccello e Beato Angelico', in *Arte moderna e contemporanea*, Rome, 1983, 70–3

ARASSE, D., *Les Primitifs italiens*, Geneva 1986, 192–203

ARGAN, G. C., 'Paolo Uccello', in G. C. Argan and J. Lassaigne, *De Van Eyck à Botticelli*, Geneva, 1955

ARONBERG LAVIN, M., 'The altar of Corpus Domini in Urbino: Paolo Uccello, Joos van Ghent, Piero della Francesca', in *The Art Bulletin*, 49, 1967, 1–24

BACIANI, A., 'Paolo Uccello, Domenico Veneziano, Piero della Francesca e gli affreschi del Duomo di Prato', in *Archivio Storico Pratese*, 12, 1934, 97–102

BALDINI U., 'Restauri di dipinti fiorentini in occasione della Mostra di quattro maestri del Rinascimento', in *Bollettino d'arte*, 39, 1954, 226–40

——'L'orologio di Paolo Uccello nel Duomo di Firenze', in *Commentari*, 21, 1970, 1/2, 44–50

——'L'Orologio di Paolo Uccello' in *La Nazione*, 24 Dec. 1973, 3

——'Così l'orologio di Paolo Uccello', in *La Nazione*, 4 Jan. 1974, 3

——and BERTI, L., *Mostra di affreschi staccati* (exh. cat.), Florence, 1957

BECK, J., 'Paolo Uccello and the Paris St George', 1465. Unpublished documents: 1452, 1465, 1474, in *Gazette des Beaux-Arts*, 93, 1320, 1979, 1–5

——'Uccello's apprenticeship with Ghiberti', in *The Burlington Magazine*, 122, 933, 1980, 837

BERNINI, D., 'Una "pittura solennissima" per Federico da Montefeltro', in *Studi in onore di Giulio Carlo Argan*, I, Rome, 1984, 127–35

*BERTI, L., 'Una nuova Madonna e degli appunti su un grande maestro', in *Pantheon*, 12, 1961, 298–309

——*Paolo Uccello*, Milan, 1964

——, GURRIERI, F. AND LEONARDI, C., *La basilica di San Miniato al Monte di Firenze*, Florence, 1988

*BOCCIA, L. G., 'Le armature di Paolo Uccello' in *L'Arte*, 3, 11/12, 1970, 54–91

BOECK, W., 'Ein Frühwerke von Paolo Uccello', in *Pantheon*, 8, 1931, 276–81

——'Die "Erfinder" der Perspektive', in *Repertorium für Kunstwissenschaft*, 52, 1931, 145ff.

——'Uccello-Studien' in *Zeitschrift für Kunstgeschichte*, 2, 1933, 249–75

——'Drawings by Paolo Uccello', in *Old Master Drawings*, 8, 29, 1933, 1–3

*——*Paolo Uccello. Der Florentiner Meister und sein Werk*, Berlin, 1939

BORGHERO, G., *Collezione Thyssen-Bornemisza*, Milan, 1986

*BORSOOK, E., 'L'Hawkwood d'Uccello et la Vie de Fabius Maximus de Plutarque. Evolution d'un projet de cénotaphe', in *Revue de l'art*, 55, 1982, 44–51

BOSKOVITS, M., 'Due secoli di pittura murale a Prato', in *Arte Illustrata*, 1970, 38ff.

BOTTICELLI, G. and GIOVANNONI, S., 'L'orologio di Paolo Uccello nel Duomo fiorentino', in *Critica d'arte*, n.s., 44, 166–8, 1979, 177–81

BRION, M., 'Paolo Uccello', in *L'Art vivant*, 13, 1925, 7–9

BROMMELLE, N. S., 'St. George and the Dragon, painting cleaned at the National Gallery', in *National Gallery of London. Museums Journal*, 1959, 95–7

CAMPANI, E. G., 'Uccello's Story of Noah in the Chiostro Verde', in *The Burlington Magazine*, 17, 1910, 203–10

CANUTI, F., *Paolo Uccello in Urbino*, Urbania, 1954

CARLI, E., *Tutta la pittura di Paolo Uccello*, Milan, 1954; 1959

CARRÀ, C., 'Paolo Uccello costruttore', in *La Voce*, 30 Sept. 1916; in *Pittura metafisica*, Milan, 1945 and in *Tutti gli scritti*, Milan, 1978, 72–9

CAVIGGIOLI, A., 'Una fronte di cassone di Paolo Uccello', in *Arte figurativa*, 2, 1, 1954, 28ff.

CLARK, K., 'Paolo Uccello and abstract painting', in *Art of Humanism*, London, 1983, 43–77

CORTI, G. and HARTT, F., 'New Documents concerning Donatello and Andrea della Robbia, Desiderio, Mino, Uccello, Pollaiuolo, Filippo Lippi and others', in *The Art Bulletin*, 44, 1962, 154–67

CRISTIANI TESTI, M. L., 'Panoramica a volo d'Uccello. La battaglia di San Romano', in *Critica d'arte*, 46, 175–7, 1981, 3–47

D'ANCONA, P., *Paolo Uccello*, Milan, 1959

DAVIES, M., 'Uccello's "St. George" in London', in *The Burlington Magazine*, 101, 1959, 303–16

DEGENHART, B. and SCHMITT, A., 'Uccello. Wiederherstellung einer Zeichnung', in *Albertina Studien*, 1, 1963, 101–17

DEL BRAVO, C., 'Cosimo il Vecchio, Lorenzo e alcuni dipinti', in *Gli Uffizi. Quattro secoli di una Galleria*, Florence, 1983, I, 201–6

DE MARCHI, A., 'Note alla *Vita di Paulo Uccello*', in G. Vasari, *Le Vite de' più eccellenti architetti, pittori, et scultori italiani, da Cimabue insino a' tempi nostri*, ed. L. Bellosi and A. Rossi, intro. G. Previtali, Turin, 1986

DE WITT, A., *La Pietà di Paolo Uccello affresco che trovasi nella casa di Baldaccio d'Anghiari n. 24 di via Romana*, Florence, 1886

[DUBLIN] *Centenary Exhibition of the National Gallery of Ireland*, Dublin, 1964

EISLER, C., 'A portrait of Leon Battista Alberti', in *The Burlington Magazine*, 116, 858, 1974, 529–30

EVEN, Y., 'Paolo Uccello's John Hawkwood: reflections of a collaboration between Agnolo Gaddi and Giuliano Pesello', in *Sources*, 4, 4, 1985, 6–8

FAISON, G. L., review of W. Boeck, *Paolo Uccello*, in *The Art Bulletin*, 22, 1940, 282–4

FIOCCO, G., 'Un affresco di Paolo Uccello nel Veneto', in *Bollettino d'arte*, 17, 1923–4, 93–6

——'Il rinnovamento toscano dell'arte del mosaico a Venezia', in *Dedalo*, 6, 1925–6, 109–18

——'I Giganti di Paolo Uccello', in *Rivista d'arte*, 17, 1935 385–404

FONTANA, W., 'Affreschi di Paolo Uccello nel Palazzo Ducale di Urbino', in *Federico di Montefeltro. Lo stato, le arti, la cultura. Le arti*, Rome, 1986, 131–49

FRANCASTEL, P., 'Un Mystère parisien illustré par Uccello', in *Revue Archéologique*, 39, 1952, 180–91

FRY, R., 'The Umbrian Exhibition at the Burlington Fine Arts Club', in *The Burlington Magazine*, 16, 1909, 267–76

——'Three Pictures in the Jacquemart-André Collection', in *The Burlington Magazine*, 25, 1914, 79–85

GALBALLY, A., *The Collections of the National Gallery of Victoria*, Oxford, Auckland and New York, 1987

GAMBA, C., 'Di alcuni quadri di Paolo Uccello e della sua scuola', in *Rivista d'arte*, 6, 1909, 19–30

——'La Mostra del Tesoro di Firenze sacra', in *Bollettino d'arte*, 27, 1933–4, 145–63 (and exh. cat., Florence, 1933)

GEBHARDT, V., *Paolo Uccellos 'Schlacht von San Romano'. Ein Beitrag zur Kunst der Medici in Florenz* (diss., Bochum Univ.), Frankfurt, Berne and New York, 1991

GIOVANNOZZI, V., 'Note su Giovanni di Francesco', in *Rivista d'arte*, 16, 1934, 337–65

GRADY, J. O., 'An Uccello Enigma', in *Gazette des Beaux-Arts*, 105, 1985, 99–103

GRIFFITHS, G., 'The political significance of Uccello's Battle of San Romano', in *Journal of the Warburg and Courtauld Institutes*, 51, 1978, 313–16

GRONAU, G., 'Zu Paolo Uccello', in *Repertorium für Kunstwissenschaft*, 25, 1902, 318

——'Zu Paolo Uccellos Schlachtenbildern', in *Pantheon*, 9, 1932, 176

GUZZI, V., 'Affreschi di Paolo Uccello', in *Civiltà*, 6, 1941, 17–18

HENDY, P., *Some Italian Renaissance Pictures in the Thyssen Bornemisza Collection*, Zurich, 1964

HOFF, U. and PLANT, M., *National Gallery of Victoria. Painting, Drawing, Sculpture*, Melbourne, 1968

HORNE H. P., 'The Battle-piece by Paolo Uccello in the National Gallery', in *The Monthly Review*, 114

JOOST-GAUGIER, C. L., 'Uccello's "Uccello": a visual Signature', in *Gazette des Beaux-Arts*, 6, 84, 1974, 233–8

——'Un'eco veneziana nell'opera di Paolo Uccello?', in *Arte illustrata*, 7, 59, 1974, 350–52

*KEMP, M. and MASSING, A., 'Paolo Uccello's "Hunt in the Forest" in the Ashmolean Museum, Oxford', in *The Burlington Magazine*, March 1991, 164–78

KERN, C., "Der Mazochio des Paolo Uccello', in *Jahrbuch der Königlichen und Kaiserlichen Preussischen Kunstsammlungen*, 26, 1915, 513–38

LANYI, J., 'The Louvre Portrait of Five Florentines', in *The Burlington Magazine*, 84, 1944, 87–95

LAUTS, J., *Meisterwerke der Kunsthalle Karlsruhe*, Karlsruhe, 1957

——*Katalog Alte Meister*, Staatliche Kunsthalle Karlsruhe, I, 1966, 186–8

LIPMAN, J., 'The Florentine Profile in the Quattrocento', in *The Art Bulletin*, 18, 1936, 54–102

LLOYD, C., *A Catalogue of the Earlier Italian Paintings*, Oxford, 1977

*LOESER, C., 'Paolo Uccello', in *Repertorium für Kunstwissenschaft*, 1898, 83–94

[LONDON] National Gallery, *Conservation Report 1962–64*, London, 1964

LONGHI, R., 'Lettera pittorica a Giuseppe Fiocco', in *Vita artistica*, 1, 1926, 127–39

——'Un ritratto di Paolo Uccello', in *Vita artistica*, 2, 1927

——'Ricerche su Giovanni di Francesco', in *Pinacotheca*, 3, 1928, 34–8; in *Opere complete*, IV, Florence, 1968, 21–36

MALKIEL-JIRMOUNSKY, M., 'Une nouvelle prédelle de Paolo Uccello', in *Gazette des Beaux-Arts*, 2, 1932, 64

MALQUORI, A., in *Bernardo di Chiaravalle nell'arte italiana dal XIV al XVIII secolo*, ed. L. Dal Prà (exh. cat., Florence, 1990) Milan, 1990, 128–30

MARANGONI, M., 'Osservazioni sull'Acuto di Paolo Uccello', in *L'Arte*, 22, 1919, 37–42

——'Gli, affreschi di Paolo Uccello a San Miniato al Monte a Firenze', in *Rivista d'arte*, 12, 1930, 403–17

——'Una predella di Paolo Uccello', in *Dedalo*, 12, 1932, 329–47

MARCHINI, G., *Il Duomo di Prato*, Milan, 1957

*——*Due secoli di pittura murale a Prato. Mostra di affreschi, sinopie e graffiti dei secoli XIV e XV*, Prato, 1969

——'Una meravigliosa avventura tra arte e religiosità', in *Progress*, 49–50, 1984, 38–43

MARIN, L., 'Architecture et représentation: Paolo Uccello au Chiostro Verde de Santa Maria Novella à Florence', in *Symboles de la Renaissance*, III, Paris, 1990, 115–36

MAYER, A. L., 'Die Ausstellung der Sammlung "Schloss Rohoncz" in der Neuen Pinakothek, München', in *Pantheon*, 6, 1930, 297–322

MEISS, M., 'The original position of Uccello's John Hawkwood', in *The Art Bulletin*, 52, 3, 1970, 231

MELONI TRKULJA, S., 'Vicende ignorate della "Battaglia di San Romano", in *Paragone. Arte*, 26, 309, 1975, 108–11

MICHELETTI, E., 'Paolo Uccello', in *Quattro Maestri del primo Rinascimento* (exh. cat.), Florence, 1954, 21–76

——*Paolo Uccello*, Novara, 1956

MITTIG, H. E., 'Uccellos Hawkwood-Fresko: Platz und Wirkung', in *Mitteilungen des Kunsthistorischen Instituts in Florenz*, 14, 1969, 235–9

MODE, R. L., 'Masolino, Uccello and the Orsini "Uomini Famosi", in *The Burlington Magazine*, 114, 831, 1972, 368–78

MOLTESCA, *Paolo Uccello*, Copenhagen, 1924

MURARO, M., 'L'esperienza veneziana di Paolo Uccello', in *Atti del XVIII Congresso Internazionale di storia dell'arte*, Venice, 1955, 197–9

OERTEL, R., 'Wandmalerei und Zeichnung in Italien', in *Mitteilungen des Kunsthistorischen Instituts in Florenz*, 5, 1937–40, 303–6 (216–313)

OFFNER, R., 'The Mostra del tesoro di Firenze sacra', in *The Burlington Magazine*, II (Oct. 1933; I: Aug. 1933), 63, 1933, 166–78

PAATZ, W., 'Una Natività di Paolo Uccello e alcune considerazioni sull'arte del Maestro', in *Rivista d'arte*, 16, 1934, 111–48

PADOA RIZZO, A., 'La predella di Paolo Uccello', in *Urbino e le Marche prima e dopo Raffaello* (exh. cat., Urbino, 1983), Florence, 1983, 79–88

——*Paolo Uccello*, Florence, 1991

——'Recensione alla mostra "L'Età di Masaccio"', in *Antichità viva*, 29, 5, 1990, 56–9

PAOLIERI, A., *Paolo Uccello, Domenico Veneziano, Andrea del Castagno*, Florence, 1991

[PARIS] *Exposition de 700 tableaux de toutes les écoles antérieures à 1800 tirés des réserves du Département des Peintures*, Musée du Louvre, Paris, 1960

——*Catalogue sommaire illustré des peintures du musée du Louvre. II. Italie, Espagne, Allemagne, Grande-Bretagne et divers*, ed. A. Brejon de Lavergnée and D. Thiébaut, Paris, 1981

PARKER, R. A., 'Paolo Uccello, a precursor of modern Art', in *International Studio*, 89, 1928, 21ff.

*PARRONCHI, A., 'Le fonti di Paolo Uccello: i "Perspettivi passati". 1–2. I filosofi', in *Paragone. Arte*, 89, 1957, 3–32; 95, 1957, 3–33

——'Cammello per camaleonte', in *Paragone. Arte*, 13, 153, 1962, 64–7

——'Paolo o Piero?', in *Studi di storia dell'arte dedicati a Roberto Longhi. Arte antica e moderna*, 1961, 13/16, 138–47; and in *Studi*, 1964, 533–48

——'Una Nunziatina di Paolo Uccello. Ricostruzione della Cappella Carnesecchi', in *Studi urbinati*, 36, 1962, 1–38; and in *Studi*, 1964, 182–225

——'Paolo Uccello', *Enciclopedia Universale dell'Arte* (EUA), X, Venice and Rome, 1963, col. 463–71

——'Il San Tommaso di Mercato Vecchio', in *La Nazione*, 13 May 1963, 3

——'La "sfera dell'ore"', in *La Nazione*, 12 Dec. 1964, 3

*——*Studi su la 'dolce' prospettiva*, Milan, 1964

——'Ornitologia uccellesca', in *La Nazione*, 1 Feb. 1964, 3

——'Due note para-uccellesche', in *Arte antica e moderna*, 30, 1965, 169–80

——'Il "dossale di San Cosimo e Damiano"', in *Arte antica e moderna*, 1966, 45–57

——'Vergine contadina', in *La Nazione*, 2 Oct. 1970, 3

——'Una data per le Battaglie', in *La Nazione*, 9 Dec. 1972, 3

——'Gli Evangelisti dell'Orologio', in *La Nazione*, 2 Feb. 1974, 3

*——*Paolo Uccello*, Bologna, 1974

——'Paolo Uccello nel Chiostro Verde', in *Santa Maria Novella. La basilica, il convento, i chiostri monumentali*, Florence, 1981, 135–41

——'Paolo Uccello segnalato per la prospettiva e animali', in *Michelangelo*, 34, 1981, 25–34

PHILIPS, C., 'The Hunt by Paolo Uccello in Oxford', in *The Burlington Magazine*, 34, 1919, 215

PITTALUGA, M., *Paolo Uccello*, Rome, 1946

POGGI, G., *Il Duomo di Firenze*, Berlin, 1909, 142–7

*——'Paolo Uccello e l'orologio di Santa Maria del Fiore', in *Miscellanea di studi di storia dell'arte in onore di Igino Benvenuto Supino*, Florence, 1933, 323–36

*POPE-HENNESSY, J., *The Complete Work of Paolo Uccello*, London, 1950; 2nd edn. 1969, repr. 1980

PROCACCI, U., 'Paolo Uccello', in *Affreschi da Firenze* (exh. cat.), Florence, 1971, n. 33

——*Sinopie e affreschi*, Florence, 1960

PUDELKO, G., 'The Early Works of Paolo Uccello', in *The Art Bulletin*, 16, 1934, 231–59

*——'Der Meister der Anbetung in Karlsruhe, ein Schuler Paolo Uccellos', in *Festschrift zum 70. Geburtstag von Adolf Goldschmidt*, Berlin, 1935, 123–30

——'Paolo Uccello peintre lunaire', in *Minotaure*, 7, 1935, 33–41

——'The Minor Masters of the Chiostro Verde', in *The Art Bulletin*, 17, 1935, 71–89

——'An Unknown Holy Virgin Panel by Paolo Uccello', in *Art in America*, 24, 1936, 127–34

——'Paolo Uccello, in U. Thieme and F. Becker, *Allgemeines Künstlerlexikon*, 33, Leipzig, 1939, 523–7

RAGGHIANTI, C. L., 'Casa Vitaliani', in *Critica d'arte*, 2, 4, 1937, 236–50

——'Argomenti lippeschi e uccelleschi', in *Miscellanea minore di storia dell'arte*, Bari, 1946

——and ROSSI, C. A., 'Paolo Uccello Caccia di Oxford', in *Critica d'arte*, ser. IV, 49, 1, 1984, 86–9

RAVA, C. E., 'La mostra di quattro maestri del Primo Rinascimento a Firenze. Paolo Uccello, Domenico Veneziano, Piero della Francesca, Andrea del Castagno', in *Prospettive*, 3, 1954–6, 63–72 and 89–90

ROSSI, P. A., 'Il calice di Paolo Uccello', in *Critica d'arte*, 44, 166–8, 1979, 35–46

——'La Madonna di Dublino', in *Critica d'arte*, 51, 2, 1986, 40–50

*SAALMAN, H., 'Paolo Uccello at San Miniato', in *The Burlington Magazine*, 106, 1964, 558–63

SALMI, M., 'Paolo Uccello, Domenico Veneziano, Piero della Francesca e gli affreschi del Duomo di Prato', in *Bollettino d'arte*, 28, 1934, 1–27

*——*Paolo Uccello, Andrea del Castagno, Domenico Veneziano*, Rome, 1936; Milan, 1938

*——'Riflessioni su Paolo Uccello', in *Commentari*, 1, 1950, 22–33; and in *Parvae favillae*, Florence, 1989, 125–37

——'Per Paolo Uccello', in *Studies in Late Medieval and Renaissance Painting in Honor of Millard Meiss*, I, New York, 1977, 373–6

SCATASSA, E., 'Chiesa del Corpus Domini in Urbino', in *Repertorium für Kunstwissenschaft*, 25, 1902, 438–46

SCHEFER, J. L., *Le Déluge, la Peste. Paolo Uccello*, Paris, 1976

SCHLOSSER, J. von, *Künstlerprobleme der Frührenaissance. II. Paolo Uccello*, Vienna, 1933, 33–43

SCHMITT, A., 'Paolo Uccellos Entwurf für das Reiterbild des Hawkwood', in *Mitteilungen des Kunsthistorischen Instituts in Florenz*, 3, 1, 1957–9, 125–30

SCHWOB, M., *Vies imaginaires*, Paris, 1896

SEIDEL, C., 'Paolo Uccello', in *Arte e Storia*, April 1913, 97–102

SERRA, L., 'Mostra del Tesoro di Firenze sacra', in *Bollettino d'arte*, 27, 1, 1933, 37–48

*SINDONA, E., *Paolo Uccello*, Milan, 1957

——'Gotico e Rinascimento. Pisanello, Paolo Uccello e il pittore dell'Adorazione', in *Fede e Arte*, 7, 1960, 172f.

——'Una conferma uccellesca', in *L'Arte*, 3, 9, 1970, 66–107 (with perspective analyses by P. A. Rossi, 105–6)

——'Introduzione alla poetica di Paolo Uccello. Relazioni tra prospettiva e pensiero teorico', in *L'Arte*, 17, 1972, 4–100

SKERL DEL CONTE, S., 'Una tesi di laurea sul Maestro del 1419 e Paolo Uccello', in *Arte in Friuli. Arte a Trieste*, 3, 1979, 175–84

SOMARÉ, E., 'Repertorio critico dell'opera di Paolo Uccello', in *L'Esame*, 5, 1933, 10–34

——*Paolo Uccello*, Milan, 1946

SOUPAULT, P., *Paolo Uccello*, Paris, 1929

STARN R. and PARTRIDGE, L., 'Representing war in the Renaissance: the Shield of Paolo Uccello', in *Representations*, 5, 1984, 33–65

TONGIORGI TOMASI, L., *L'Opera completa di Paolo Uccello*, Milan, 1971

VAN MARLE, R., 'Eine Kreuzigung von Paolo Uccello', in *Pantheon*, 1, 1928, 242

——'I quadri italiani della raccolta del Castello Rohoncz', in *Dedalo*, 11, 1930–31, 1372

VENTURI, L., 'Paolo Uccello', in *L'Arte*, 33, 1930, 52–87

VERGANI, M., 'Bologna: affresco di Paolo Uccello', in *Arte cristiana*, 68, 1980, 324

*VOLPE, C., 'Paolo Uccello a Bologna', in *Paragone. Arte*, 31, 365, 1980, 3–28

WACKERNAGEL, M., 'Paolo Uccello', in *Pantheon*, 27–8, 1941, 102–10

WAKAYAMA, E. M. L., 'Per la datazione delle storie di Noè di Paolo Uccello: un'ipotesi di lettura', in *Arte lombarda*, 61, 1, 1982, 93–106

ZERI, F., 'Major and Minor Italian Artists at Dublin', in *Apollo*, 99, 1974, 88ff.

ON QUATTROCENTO ART

ALAZARD, J., *Le portrait florentin*, Paris, 1924

AMES LEWIS, F., *The Chronology of Domenico Veneziano*, University of London diss., Courtauld Institute, London, 1968

——'Domenico Veneziano and the Medici', in *Jahrbuch der Berliner Museen*, 21, 1979, 67–90

ANGELINI, A., *Disegni italiani del tempo di Donatello* (exh. cat.), Florence, 1986

ANTAL, F., 'Studien zur Gotik im Quattrocento', in *Jahrbuch der Preussischen Kunstsammlungen*, 46, 1925, 8–14

ARGAN, G. C., *Storia dell'arte italiana*, II, Florence, 1968; new edn 1988

Arte lombarda tra Gotico e Rinascimento (exh. cat.), Milan, 1988

BACOU, R. and BEAN, J., *Dessins florentins de la collection de Filippo Baldinucci* (exh. cat.), Paris, 1958

BALDANZI, *Della chiesa cattedrale di Prato*, Prato, 1846

BATTISTI, E., *Filippo Brunelleschi*, Milan, 1976; English edn *Brunelleschi*, London and New York, 1981

BAXANDALL, M., *Giotto and the Orators*, Oxford, 1971

——*Painting and Experience in Fifteenth Century Italy*, Oxford, 1972

BELLINI, F., *I disegni antichi degli Uffizi: i tempi di Ghiberti*, intro. L. Bellosi, Florence, 1978

BELLOSI, L., 'Intorno ad Andrea del Castagno', in *Paragone. Arte*, 211, 1967, 3–18

——'Due note per la pittura fiorentina del secondo Trecento, in *Mitteilungen des Kunsthistorischen Instituts in Florenz*, 17, 1973, 179–94

——'Giovanni di Piamonte e gli affreschi di Piero ad Arezzo', in *Prospettiva*, 50, 1987, 15–35

BENKARD, E., *Das Selbstbildnis*, Berlin, 1927

BENSON, R., *The Holford Collection*, London, 1924

BERENSON, B., *The Florentine Painters of the Renaissance. With an Index to their Works*, New York, 1896; London, 1907

——*The Drawings of the Florentine Painters*, London, 1803; Chicago, 1938

——'Una predella di Masolino nel Museo Ingres di Montauban', in *Dedalo*, 1922–3, 633–5

——*Italian Pictures of the Renaissance*, Oxford, 1932

——'Quadri senza casa. II. Il Quattrocento fiorentino', in *Dedalo*, 12, 1932, 512–41

——*Italian Pictures of the Renaissance: Florentine School*, London, 1963

BERTI, L., 'Domenico Veneziano', in *Enciclopedia Universale dell'Arte* (EUA), IV, Venice and Rome, 1958, 398–404

——*Andrea del Castagno*, Florence, 1966

——, ed., *Frescoes from Florence* (exh. cat.), London, 1970

—— and BALDINI, U., *Seconda mostra di affreschi staccati* (exh. cat.), Florence, 1958

——, NATALI, A. and PAOLUCCI, A., *L'Età di Masaccio* (exh. cat. Florence, 1990), Milan, 1990

BOCCIA, L. G., 'Materiali iconografici sull'armamento quattrocentesco d'ambiente toscano', in *Antichità viva*, 1987, 2, 37–53

BOMBE, W., 'Zur Kommunion der Aposteln von Josse van Gent in Urbino', in *Zeitschrift für Bildenden Kunst*, 65, 1931, 68ff.

BORSOOK, E., *The Mural Painters of Tuscany*, London, 1960; Oxford, 1980

BOSKOVITS, M., 'Der Meister der Santa Verdiana', in *Mitteilungen des Kunsthistorischen Instituts in Florenz*, 13, 1967, 31–60

——'Su Don Silvestro, Don Simone e la "scuola degli Angeli"', in *Paragone. Arte*, 265, 1972, 35–61

——*Pittura fiorentina alla vigilia del Rinascimento*, Florence, 1975

——'Fra Filippo Lippi, i Carmelitani e il Rinascimento', in *Arte cristiana*, 1986, 715, 235–52

Brandi, C., *Disegno della pittura italiana*, Turin, 1980

Brockwell, M. and Siren, O., *Catalogue of Italian Primitives*, New York, 1917

Bulst, W. A., 'Die ursprüngliche innere Aufteilung des Palazzo Medici in Florenz', in *Mitteilungen des Kunsthistorischen Instituts in Florenz*, 14, 1970, 390–91

——'Uso e trasformazione del palazzo mediceo fino ai Riccardi, in *Il Palazzo Medici Riccardi di Firenze*, Florence, 1990, 98–124

Burckhardt, J., *Il Cicerone*, Basel, 1855; Florence, 1952

Buscaroli, R., *La pittura romagnola del Quattrocento*, Florence, 1931

Callmann, E., *The Thebaid in Tuscan Painting in the Fourteenth and Fifteenth Century*, diss., Columbia Univ., New York, 1956

——'A Quattrocento Jigsaw Puzzle', in *The Burlington Magazine*, 99, 1957, 149–55

——*Apollonio di Giovanni*, Oxford, 1974

——'Apollonio di Giovanni and Painting for the Early Renaissance Room', in *Antichità Viva*, 27, 3–4, 1988, 5–18

——'Lo sport aristocratico della caccia: una spalliera per Federico da Montefeltro', in *Bollettino d'arte*, 65, Jan. 1991, 67–70

Calzini, E., *Urbino e i suoi monumenti*, Rocca San Casciano, 1897

——*La Galleria annessa all'Istituto di Belle Arti di Urbino*, Urbino, 1901

Carl, D., 'La Casa Vecchia dei Medici e il suo giardino', in *Il Palazzo Medici Riccardi di Firenze*, Florence, 1990, 38–43

Carrà, C., 'Piero della Francesca', in *L'Ambrosiano*, 5 Sept. 1927; and in *Tutti gli scritti*, Milan, 1978, 378–82

Castelli, P., 'Ghiberti e gli Umanisti', in *Lorenzo Ghiberti "materia e ragionamenti"* (exh. cat.), Florence, 1978, 512–48

Chastel, A., *Art et Humanisme à Florence au temps de Laurent le Magnifique*, Paris, 1959

——*Italie, 1460–1500, Renaissance méridionale*, Paris, 1965

——*Fables, Formes, Figures*, Paris, 1978

——*Chronique de la peinture italienne à la Renaissance 1280–1580*, Fribourg, 1983; English edn, Ithaca, N.Y., 1984

Christiansen, K., *Gentile da Fabriano*, Ithaca, N.Y., 1982

——'New Light on the Early Work of Filippo Lippi', in *Apollo*, 122, 285, 1985, 338–43

Clark, K., 'Leon Battista Alberti on Painting', in *Proceedings of the British Academy*, XXX, London, 1944

Cocconi, F., 'Giuseppe Stuard e la sua Pinacoteca', in *Parma nel mondo*, 1, 5 (June), 1962

Cohn, W., 'Maestri sconosciuti del Quattrocento fiorentino. Stefano d'Antonio', in *Bollettino d'arte*, 44, 1959, 61—8

Cole, B., *Agnolo Gaddi*, Oxford, 1977

Cole, D. E., 'Fra Angelico: a new chronology for the 1420s', in *Zeitschrift für Kunstgeschichte*, 43, 4, 1980, 360–81

Coletti, L., *Pisanello*, Milan, 1953

——*Pittura veneta del Quattrocento*, Novara, 1953

Colnaghi, D. E., *A Dictionary of Florentine Painters from the 13th to the 17th centuries*, London, 1928, 264–5; repr. Florence, 1986

Colvin, H. M., *Florentine Picture Chronicle*, London, 1898

Condorelli, A., 'Precisazioni su Dello Delli e su Nicola Fiorentino', in *Commentari*, 19, 1968, 197–211

Congregazione di San Filippo Neri, *La Pinacoteca Stuard di Parma*, Milan, 1961

Conti, A., ed., *Sul restauro*, Turin, 1988, 74ff. (Introduction)

Copertini, G., *La Pinacoteca Stuard di Parma*, Parma, 1926

Covi, D., *The Inscription in Fifteenth Century Florentine Painting*, New York and London, 1986

Crowe, J. A. and Cavalcaselle, G. B., *A New History of Painting in Italy*, London, 1864

Dalli Regoli, G., *Lorenzo di Credi*, Milan, 1966

Dal Poggetto, P., *The Great Age of Fresco. Giotto to Pontormo* (exh. cat.), Florence, 1968

Dal Prà, L., 'L'immagine di Bernardo nell'arte italiana', in *Bernardo Cistercense* (Atti del XXVI convegno storico internazionale, Todi, 1989), Spoleto, 1990, 345–76

——, ed., *Bernardo di Chiaravalle nell'arte italiana dal XIV al XVIII secolo* (exh. cat., Florence, 1990), Milan, 1990

Dami, L., 'Giovanni di Paolo miniatore e i paesisti senesi', in *Dedalo*, 1923–4, 269ff.

D'Amico, R., *Conoscenza e conservazione* (exh. cat.), Bologna, 1981, 51–61

Davies, M., *National Gallery Catalogues. Early Italian Schools*, London, 1951; 2nd edn, 1961

Degenhart, B., *Italienische Zeichnungen des Frühen 15. Jahrhundert*, Basel, 1949

——and Schmitt, A., *Corpus der Italienischen Zeichnungen 1300–1450*, I, Süd und Mittelitalien, 2, Berlin, 1968

Delaborde, H., *Les Maîtres florentins au XVe siècle. 30 dessins de la collection de M. Thiers*, Paris, 1889–90

Del Bravo, C., 'Etica o poesia, e mecenatismo: Cosimo il Vecchio, Lorenzo, e alcuni dipinti', in *Gli Uffizi. Quattro secoli di una galleria* (conference proceedings, Florence, 1982), ed. P. Barocchi and G. Ragionieri, I. Florence, 1983

Donato, M. M., 'Gli eroi romani tra storia ed exemplum. I primi cicli umanistici di Uomini Famosi', in *Memoria dell'antico nell'arte italiana*, ed. S. Settis, II, Turin, 1985, 97–152

Doren, G., *Le Arti fiorentine*, Florence, 1940

Ede, H. S., *Florentine Drawings of the Quattrocento*, London, 1926

Eisenberg, M., *Lorenzo Monaco*, Princeton, 1989

Eluard, P., *Anthologie des écrits sur l'Art*, III, Paris, 1954

Ettlinger, L. D., *Antonio and Piero Pollaiuolo*, Oxford, 1978

Farinelli, L., Godi, G. and Mendogni, P. P., *Guida di Parma*, Parma, 1981

Fengler-Knapp, C., *Lorenzo Ghiberti's second Commentary*, Univ. of Michigan diss., Ann Arbor, 1974

Ferrara, M. and Quinterio, F., *Michelozzo di Bartolomeo*, Florence, 1984

Fiocco, G., *L'Arte di Andrea Mantegna*, Bologna, 1927

——'Risposta a Roberto Longhi', in *Vita artistica*, 1, 1926, 144–7

——'Dello Delli scultore', in *Rivista d'arte*, 11, 1929, 25–42

——'Filippo Lippi a Padova', in *Rivista d'arte*, 18, 1936, 25–44

——'Il mito di Dello Delli', in *Arte in Europa. Scritti di storia dell'arte in onore di E. Arslan*, Milan, 1966, 341–9

Fortuna, A. M., *Andrea del Castagno*, Florence, 1957

——'Alcune note su Andrea del Castagno', in *L'Arte*, 57, 1958, 345–55

Fossi, G., *Filippo Lippi*, Florence, 1989

Fossi Todorow, M., *I disegni di Pisanello e della sua cerchia* (exh. cat.), Florence, 1966

Francastel, P., *Peinture et Société. Naissance et destruction d'un espace plastique. De la Renaissance au Cubisme*, Lyon, 1951; new edn, Paris, 1977

Fredericksen, G., *Giovanni di Francesco and the Master of Pratovecchio*, Malibu, 1974

Fremantle, R., *Florentine Gothic Painters*, London, 1975

Frey, C., *Vasari*, Munich, 1911

Fry, R., 'On a Profile Portrait by Baldovinetti', in *The Burlington Magazine*, 18, 1910, 311–12

——'The Art of Florence', in *Vision and Design*, London, 1920

Gamba, G., 'Induzioni sullo Starnina', in *Rivista d'arte*, 14, 1932, 55–74

Gandi, G., *Le Arti Maggiori e Minori in Firenze*, Florence, 1929

Goldsmith Phillips, J., *Early Florentine Designers and Engravers*, Cambridge, Mass., 1955

Gombrich, E., 'The Early Medici as Patrons of Art' (1960), in *Norm and Form. Studies in the Art of Renaissance*, London, 1966

Goukowski, M., 'A representation of the profanation of the Host: a puzzling painting in the Hermitage and its possible author', in *The Art Bulletin*, 51, 1969, 170–73

Gronau, G., 'In margine a Francesco Pesellino', in *Rivista d'arte*, 20, 1938, 123–46

Guthmann, J., *Die Landschaftsmalerei der toskanisch–umbrischen Kunst von Giotto bis Raffael*, Leipzig, 1902

Haines, M., *La Sacrestia delle Messe nel Duomo di Firenze*, Florence, 1983

Hartt, F., 'The earliest Works of Andrea del Castagno', in *The Art Bulletin*, 41, 1959, 159–81 and 227–36

——'Art and Freedom in Quattrocento Florence', in *Essays in Memory of Karl Lehmann*, New York, 1964, 114–31

——*A History of Italian Renaissance Art*, 2nd edn, London, 1971

——, Gorti, G. and Kennedy, C., *The Chapel of the Cardinal of Portugal at San Miniato al Monte in Florence*, Philadelphia, 1964

Hatfield, R., 'The "Compagnia de' Magi"', in *Journal of the Warburg and Courtauld Institutes*, 33, 1970, 107–61

——'Some unknown Descriptions of the Medici Palace in 1459', in *The Art Bulletin*, 52, 1970, 232–49

Hautecoeur, L., *Musée National du Louvre. Catalogue des peintures exposées dans les galeries. II. Ecole italienne et école espagnole*, Paris, 1926

Heydenreich, L. H., *Eclosion de la Renaissance. Italie 1400–1460*, Paris, 1972

Hoff, U., *European Painting and Sculpture before 1800*, Melbourne, 1973

Holmes, C., 'Recent Additions to the National Gallery', in *The Burlington Magazine*, 1922, 76–87

——*The National Gallery. Italian Schools*, London, 1935

Horne, H. P., '*Andrea del Castagno*', in *The Burlington Magazine*, 7, 1905, 222–33

Hyman, I., *Fifteenth Century Florentine Studies: the Palazzo Medici and a Ledger for San Lorenzo*, diss., New York, 1968

Improta, M. C., 'La pittura su tavola dell'Angelico e del Quattrocento', in *La chiesa e il convento di San Marco a Firenze*, II, Florence, 1990, 67–114

Janke, S., 'The Vision of St Bernard: a Study in Florentine Iconography', in *Hortus imaginum. Essays in Western Art*, ed. R. Engass and M. Stokstad, Lawrence, 1974, 45–50

Jones, R., 'Palla Strozzi e la sagrestia di Santa Trinita', in *Rivista d'arte*, 37, 1, 1984, 9–106

Kaftal, G., *Iconography of the Saints in Tuscan Painting*, Florence, 1952

Kennedy, R. W., *Alesso Baldovinetti. A Critical and Historical Study*, New Haven and London, 1938

Krautheimer, R. and Krautheimer-Hess, T., *Lorenzo Ghiberti*, Princeton, N.J., 1956; repr. 1970 and 1982

Kurth, W., *Die Darstellung des Nackten in dem Quattrocento von Florenz*, Berlin, 1912, 61

Laclotte, M., *De Giotto à Bellini* (exh. cat.), Paris, 1956

——*Musée du Louvre. Peintures*, Paris, 1970

——'Une "Chasse" du Quattrocento florentin', in *Revue de l'art*, 40–41, 1978, 65–70

Leporini, H., *Die Stilentwicklung des Handzeichnung, XIV–XVIII Jahrhundert*, Vienna, 1925

Lipman, J., 'Three Profile Portraits by the Master of the Castello Nativity', in *Art in America*, 24, 3, 1936, 127–34

Lisner, M., *Die Sängerkanzel des Luca della Robbia*, Freiburg im Breisgau, 1955

——*Luca della Robbia: Die Sängerkanzel*, Stuttgart, 1960

Longhi, R., 'Piero dei Franceschi e lo sviluppo della pittura veneziana' (1914), in *Scritti giovanili*, Florence, 1956, 61–106

——'Un frammento della pala di Domenico Veneziano per Santa Lucia de' Magnoli', in *L'arte*, 28, 1925, 31–5; and in *Opere complete. II. Saggi e ricerche (1925–1928)*, Florence, 1967, 3–8

——*Piero della Francesca*, Rome 1927; and in *Opere complete III. Piero della Francesca*, Florence, 1963, 3–152, 171–85 and 207–17; and *Note aggiunte alla seconda ed.*, Florence, 1942

——'Fatti di Masolino e Masaccio', in *Critica d'arte*, 23, 1940, 145–91; and in *Opere complete, VIII*, 1, Florence, 1975, 3–65

——'Il Maestro di Pratovecchio', in *Paragone. Arte*, 35, 1952, 10–37; and in *Opere complete, VIII*, 1, Florence, 1975, 99–122

——'Una "Madonna" fiorentina del decennio di crisi 1430–40', in *Paragone. Arte*, 187, 1965, 56ff.

MARCHINI, G., *Le vetrate italiane*, Milan, 1956
——*Filippo Lippi*, Milan, 1975
——'Ghiberti pittore di vetrate', in *Ghiberti e la sua arte nella Firenze del '3–400*, Florence, 1979
——'Le vetrate', in *Antichità viva*, 2, 1987, 8–13
MARIN, L., *Opacité de la peinture*, Paris and Florence, 1989
MARQUAND, A., 'Two Windows in Santa Maria del Fiore at Florence', in *American Journal of Archaeology*, 2, 1900, 192–203
MATHER, R. G., 'Documents mostly new relating to Florentine Painters and Sculptors of the Fifteenth Century', in *The Art Bulletin*, 30, 1948, 62–4
MAYER, A. L., 'Die Sammlung Philip Lehman', in *Pantheon*, 5, 1930, 111–18
——'Die Sammlung Jules Bache in New York', in *Pantheon*, 6, 1930, 537–44
MEDER, J., *Die Handzeichung, ihre Techuik und Entwicklung*, 1919
MEISS, M., *Painting in Florence and Siena after the Black Death*, Princeton, 1951
——*The Great Age of Fresco: Discoveries, Recoveries and Survivals*, London and New York, 1970
MESNIL, J., *Masaccio et les débuts de la Renaissance*, The Hague, 1927
MODE, R. L., 'Cristo morto, SS. Francesco, Chiara e Gerolamo', in *The Burlington Magazine*, 114, 837, 1972, suppl., ill. XVI
MOSCHINI, V., *Gli affreschi del Mantegna agli Eremitani di Padova*, Bergamo, 1944
MÜNTZ, E., *Les Collections des Médicis au XVe siècle*, Paris, 1888
——*Histoire de l'art pendant la Renaissance*, I, Paris, 1889
MURARO, M., *Nuova guida di Venezia e delle sue isole*, Florence, 1953
——'The Statues of the Venetian Arti and the Mosaics in the Mascoli Chapel', in *The Art Bulletin*, 43, 1961, 263–73
MURRAY, L. and MURRAY, P., *The Art of the Renaissance*, London and New York, 1963

NEERMAN, G., 'Giusto di Gand: la "Comunione degli Apostoli"', in *Urbino e le Marche prima e dopo Raffaello*, ed. M. G. Ciardi Dupré and P. Dal Poggetto (exh. cat., Urbino, 1983), Florence, 1983, 84–6

OERTEL, R., 'Die Frühwerke des Masaccio', in *Marburger Jahrbuch für Kunstwissenschaft*, 7, 1933, 289
——*Fra Filippo Lippi*, Vienna, 1942
OFFNER, R., 'Un pannello di Masolino a san Giuliano a Settimo', in *Dedalo*, 3, 1922–3, 636–41
——*Studies in Florentine Painting*, New York, 1927
ORLANDI, S., 'Il Beato Angelico. Note cronologiche', in *Rivista d'arte*, 29, 1954, 161–97
——*'Necrologio' di Santa Maria Novella*, Florence, 1955
——*Beato Angelico*, Florence, 1964

PACCAGNINI, G., *Pisanello e il ciclo cavalleresco di Mantova*, Venice, 1972, 231–40
——, ed., *Pisanello alla corte dei Gonzaga*, Milan, 1972
PADOA, A., 'Benozzo ante 1450', in *Commentari*, 20, 1969, 52–62
PADOA RIZZO, A., 'L'Adorazione dei Magi di Gentile da Fabriano per Palla Strozzi', in *La chiesa di Santa Trinita a Firenze*, Florence, 1987, 115–17
PAOLUCCI, A., *Il Museo della Collegiata di Sant'Andrea in Empoli*, Florence, 1985
——'Firenze 1400–1420: la stagione delle "attitudini" e degli "affetti"', in *L'Età di Masaccio* (exh. cat., Florence, 1990), Milan, 1990, 19–32
PARRONCHI, A., 'Rinascimento agro', in *La Nazione*, 6 June 1965, 3
——'Beata', in *La Nazione*, 31 Dec. 1971, 3
PATCH, T., *Le porte di San Giovanni di Firenze*, Florence, 1774
PINI, C., *La scrittura di artisti ialiani*, Florence, 1869–74, I, n. 47
PITTALUGA, M., 'Note sulla bottega di Filippo Lippi', in *L'Arte*, 44, 1941, 20–37
——*Filippo Lippi*, Florence, 1949
Pittura di luce, ed. L. Bellosi, with contributions by A. Angelini, A. De Marchi *et al.* (exh. cat., Florence, 1990), Milan, 1990
Pittura sensese: see *Sienese Painting*
POPE-HENNESSY, J., *Sassetta*, London, 1939
——*Fra Angelico*, London, 1952; 2nd edn, Ithaca, N.Y., 1974
——*The Portrait in the Renaissance*, New York, 1966 and London, 1967
——'The Interaction of Painting and Sculpture in Florence in the Fifteenth Century', in *Journal of the Royal Society of Arts*, London, May 1969, 406–24
——*Luca della Robbia*, Oxford, 1980
POPHAM, A. E., *Italian Drawings exhibited at the Royal Academy*, London, 1931
PRINZ, W., 'Vasaris Sammlung von Künstlerbildnissen', in *Mitteilungen des Kunsthistorischen Instituts in Florenz*, 12, 1966, 71–6
PROCACCI, U., 'L'incendio della Chiesa del Carmine del 1771', in *Rivista d'arte*, 14, 1932, 141–232
——'Sulla cronologia delle opere di Masaccio e di Masolino tra il 1425 e il 1428', in *Rivista d'arte*, 28, 1953, 3ff.
——*La tecnica degli affreschi antichi e il loro distacco e restauro*, Florence, 1958
——'Di Jacopo d'Antonio e delle Compagnie di pittori del Corso degli Adimari nel XV secolo', in *Rivista d'arte*, 35, 1960, 3–70
——*The Great Age of Fresco, Giotto to Pontormo*, The Metropolitan Museum of Art, New York, 1968
PUDELKO, G., 'Studien über Domenico Veneziano', in *Mitteilungen des Kunsthistorischen Instituts in Florenz*, 4, 1932–4, 145–200
——'Florentiner Porträts der Frührenaissance', in *Pantheon*, 15, 1934, 92–8
——'Per la datazione delle opere di Fra Filippo Lippi', in *Rivista d'arte*, 18, 1936, 45–76

Quattro Maestri del primo Rinascimento, ed. E. Micheletti, intro. M. Salmi (exh. cat.), Florence, 1954
QUINTAVALLE, A. O., *Mostra parmense di disegni noti e ignoti dal XIV al XVIII secolo* (exh. cat.), Parma, 1948

RAGGHIANTI, C., 'Intorno a Filippo Lippi', in *Critica d'arte*, 3, 1938, 22–5

RAGGHIANTI, C. L., *Filippo Brunelleschi. Un uomo, un universo*, Florence, 1977
——and DALLI REGOLI, G., *Firenze 1470–1480. Disegni dal modello*, Pisa, 1975
RIGONI, E., 'Notizie di scultori toscani a Padova nella prima metà del Quattrocento', in *Archivio Veneto*, 6, 1929 (reviewed by G. Fiocco in *Rivista d'arte*, 12, 1930, 151ff.)
RONCORONI, L. V., 'La Galleria Stuard', in *Gazzetta di Parma*, 26, May 1967, 3
ROSINI, G., *Storia della pittura italiana*, II, Pisa, 1849
RUDA, J., *Filippo Lippi Studies*, New York and London, 1982
RUSSEL SALE, J., 'Palla Strozzi and Lorenzo Ghiberti', in *Mitteilungen des Kunsthistorischen Instituts in Florenz*, 22, 1978, 355–8
RUSSO, D., *Saint Jérôme en Italie. Etude d'iconographie et de spiritualité (XIIIe–XVe siècle)*, Paris and Rome, 1987, 218

SAALMAN, H. and MATTOX, P., 'The First Medici Palace', in *Journal of the Society of Architectural Historians*, 44, 1965, 329–45
SACCARDO, P., *Les Mosaïques de Saint-Marc à Venise*, Venice, 1896
SALMI, M., 'La giovinezza di Fra Filippo Lippi', in *Rivista d'arte*, 18, 1936, 1–24
——'La Madonna dantesca del Museo di Livorno e il Maestro della Natività di Castello', in *Liburni Civitas*, 11, 1938, 217–56
——'Lorenzo Ghiberti e la pittura', in *Scritti di storia dell'arte in onore di Lionello Venturi*, Rome, 1956, 223–37; and in *Parvae favillae. Scritti di storia dell'arte dal tardo antico al barocco*, Florence, 1989, 327–31
——'Aspetti del primo Rinascimento: Firenze, Venezia e Padova', in *Rinascimento*, 2, 1962, 77–87; and in *Parvae favillae*, Florence, 1989, 25–33
——'Commento al coro del San Francesco di Sansepolcro', in *Commentari*, 23, 1972, 351–65
SALVINI, R., 'The frescoes in the "altana" of the Rucellai Palace', in *Giovanni Rucellai e il suo Zibaldone. II. A Florentine Patrician and his Palace*, London, 1981 (*Studies of the Warburg Institute*, 24, 2), 241–52
SANDBERG VAVALÀ, E., *Uffizi Studies*, Florence, 1948
SANTANGELO, A., *Inventario degli oggetti d'arte d'Italia. Provincia di Parma*, Rome, 1934
SANTI, B., 'Pittura "minore" in Santa Trinita: da Bicci di Lorenzo a Neri di Bicci', in *La chiesa di Santa Trinita a Firenze*, Florence, 1987, 132–41
SAXL, F., *Catalogue of Astrological and Mythological Illustrated Manuscripts*, London, 1953, 279–81
SCALINI, M., 'The Weapons of Lorenzo de' Medici', in *Arts, arms and armour. An International Anthology*, ed. R. Held, Chiasso, 1979–80, I (1979)
SCHAEFER, E., *Das Florentiner Bildnis*, Munich, 1904
SCHLOSSER, J. von, *Leben und Meinungen des Florentinischen Bildners Lorenzo Ghiberti*, Munich, 1941
SCHMARSOW, A., *Kunsthistorische Gesellschaft für Photographische Publikationen*, Leipzig, 1900
——'Domenico Veneziano', in *L'Arte*, 15, 1912, 9–20 and 81–97
SCHUBRING, P., *Cassoni. Truhen und Truhenbilder der italienischen Frührenaissance*, Leipzig, 1915; 2nd edn, Leipzig, 1923
SCHULZ, A. M., *The Sculpture of Bernardo Rossellino and his Workshop*, Princeton, 1977
——*Niccolò di Giovanni Fiorentino and Venetian Sculpture of the Early Renaissance*, New York, 1978
SCIOLLA, G. C., *Letteratura artistica dell'età dell'umanesimo*, Turin, 1982
SELVATICO, P., *Storia estetico-critica delle arti del disegno*, II, Venice, 1852–6
SEROUX D'AGINCOURT, *Histoire de l'Art*, Paris, 1823
SEYMOUR DE RICCI, *Description raisonnée des peintures du Louvre. I. Italie et Espagne*, Paris, 1913
SHAPLEY, R. F., *Catalogue of Italian Paintings. I. National Gallery of Washington*, Washington, D.C., 1979
SHELL, C., 'The Early Style of fra Filippo Lippi and the Prato Master', in *The Art Bulletin*, 43, 1961, 197–209
——'Francesco d'Antonio and Masaccio', in *The Art Bulletin*, 47, 1965, 465–9
SHELLER, R. W., 'Uomini famosi', in *Bulletin van het Rijksmuseum*, 10, 1962, 56–67
Sienese Painting of the Renaissance (exh. cat.), New York, 1988
SIRAISI, N. G., *Arts and Sciences at Padua*, Toronto, 1973
SIRÉN, O., *Dessins et tableaux de la Renaissance italienne de la Collection de Suède*, Stockholm, 1902
——'Di alcuni pittori fiorentini che subirono l'influenza di Lorenzo Monaco', in *L'Arte*, 7, 1904, 342ff.
——*Don Lorenzo Monaco*, Strasbourg, 1905
——and BROCKWELL, M., *Catalogue of a Loan Exhibition of Italian Primitives in Aid of the American War Relief*, New York, 1917
STECHOW, W., 'Zum Masolino-Masaccio Problem', in *Zeitschrift für bildende Kunst*, 63, 1929–30, 125–7
STERLING, C., *La Collection Lehmann de New York*, Paris, 1957
STIX, A. and FRÖLICH-BUM, L., *Albertina Katalog*, Vienna, 1932

TALIGNANI, A., 'La collezione di dipinti toscani del marchese Alfonso Tacoli Canacci', in *Parma nell'arte*, 2, 1986, 39
TESTI, L., *Storia della pittura veneziana*, II, Bergamo, 1916
TOESCA, I., 'Gli "Uomini famosi" della Biblioteca Cockerell', in *Paragone. Arte*, 25, 1952, 16–20
——'Di nuovo sulla "Cronaca Cockerell"', in *Paragone. Arte*, 21, 1, 1970, 63
TOESCA, P., *La pittura e la miniatura in Lombardia*, Milan, 1912
TRIONFI HONORATI, M., 'A proposito del "lettuccio"', in *Antichità viva*, 3, 1981, 39–47

VAN MARLE, R., *The Development of the Italian Schools of Painting*, The Hague, 1928, IX, X; repr. New York, 1970
VAN STRAELEN, H., *Studien zur Florentiner Glasgemälde*, Münster, 1938
VAN WAADENOIJEN, J., 'A proposal for Starnina: exit the Maestro del Bambino Vispo?', in *The Burlington Magazine*, 116, 1974, 82–91
VARESE, R., 'Una postilla per l'Oratorio di San Giovanni Battista in Urbino', in *Notizie da Palazzo Albani*, 10, 1, 1981, 13–14

VENTURI, A., 'Il "Libro di Giusto"', in *Le Gallerie Nazionali Italiane*, 4, 1899, 345–78, and 5, 1902, 391–426
——*Storia dell'arte italiana*, VII, I, Turin, 1910, 332–45
——'Una risorta casa del Rinascimento italiano', in *L'arte*, 17, 1914, 64
——'Lorenzo Ghiberti', in *L'Arte*, 26, 1923, 233–45
——*Pitture italiane in America*, Milan, 1931
VILLOT, F., *Notice des tableaux exposés dans les Galeries du Musée National du Louvre, 1re partie, Ecoles d'Italie et d'Espagne*, Paris, 1849
VOLPE, C., 'Per Pietro di Giovanni d'Ambrogio', in *Paragone. Arte*, 7, 75, 1956, 51–5
——'In margine a un Filippo Lippi', in *Paragone. Arte*, 7, 83, 1956, 38–45
——'Tre vetrate ferraresi e il Rinascimento a Bologna', in *Arte antica e moderna*, 1958, 23–37

WACKERNAGEL, M., *Der Lebensraum des Künstler der florentinischen Renaissance*, Leipzig, 1938; English edn *The World of the Florentine Renaissance Artist*, ed. A. Luchs, Princeton, 1981
WEISBACH, W., *Francesco Pesellino und die Romantik der Renaissance*, Berlin, 1901
WEIZSÄCKER, H., 'Das Pferd in der Kunst des Quattrocento', in *Jahrbuch der Königlichen und Kaiserlichen Kunstsammlungen*, 7, 1836, 45–167
WITTING, F., 'Forschungen', in *Kunstchronik*, 21, 1910, 495
WOHL, H., *The Paintings of Domenico Veneziano*, Oxford, 1980

ZERI, F., 'Ricerche sul Sassetta: la Pala dell'Arte della Lana (1423–26)', in *Quaderni di Emblema*, 2, 1973, 22–34
——*Italian Paintings in the Walters Art Gallery of Baltimore*, Baltimore, 1976
——, ed., *La pittura in Italia. Il Quattrocento*, I, Milan, 1987
——*La percezione visiva dell'Italia e degli Italiani*, Turin, 1976; 2nd edn, Turin, 1989

ON OPTICS AND PERSPECTIVE

ALESSIO, F., 'Per uno studio sull'Ottica del Trecento', in *Studi Medievali*, 2, Spoleto, 1961, 444–504

BAEUMKER, C., 'Witelo, ein Philosoph und Naturforscher des XIII. Jahrhunderts', in *Beiträge zur Geschichte der Philosophie des Mittelalters*, III, 2, Münster, 1908
BERGDOLT, K., *Der dritte Kommentar Lorenzo Ghibertis. Naturwissenschaften und Medizin in der Kunsttheorie der Frührenaissance*, Weinheim, 1988
BLOOM, K., 'Lorenzo Ghiberti's Space in Relief: Method and Theory', in *The Art Bulletin*, 51, 1969, 164–9
BOSKOVITS, M., 'Quello ch'e dipintori oggi dicono prospettiva. Contributions to the 15th Century Art Theory', in *Acta Historiae Artium Accademiae Scientiarum Hungaricae*, 8, 1962, 241–60, and 9, 1963, 139–62
BUNIM, M. S., *Space in Medieval Painting and the Forerunners of Perspective*, New York, 1940

CHASTEL, A., 'Les apories de la perspective au Quattrocento', in M. Dalai Emiliani, 'Perspective', 1972 (see below), 45–62

DALAI EMILIANI, M., 'Perspective', in *Encyclopaedia Universalis*, XIII, Paris, 1972
——'La question de la perspective', intro. to E. Panofsky, *La perspective comme forme symbolique*, Paris, 1975, 7–35
——, ed., *La prospettiva rinascimentale. Codificazioni e trasgressioni*, Florence, 1980
DAMISCH, H., *L'origine de la perspective*, Paris, 1987

EDGERTON, S. Y., Jr, 'Alberti's Perspective: a new discovery and a new evaluation', in *The Art Bulletin*, 48, 3–4, 1966, 367–78
——*The Renaissance Discovery of Linear Perspective*, New York, 1975
ELKINS, J., 'Piero della Francesca and the Renaissance Proof of Linear Perspective', in *The Art Bulletin*, 69, 1987, 220–30
——'Did Leonardo develop a Theory of Curvilinear Perspective', in *Journal of the Warburg and Courtauld Institutes*, 51, 1988, 190–96
EUCLID, *Die Elemente*, ed. C. Thaer, Darmstadt, 1980

FEDERICI VESCOVINI, C., 'Problemi di fisica aristotelica in un maestro del XIV secolo, Biagio Pelacani da Parma', in *Rivista di Filosofia*, 51, 1960, 181ff., 201ff.
——'Le questioni di "perspectiva" di Biagio Pelacani', in *Rinascimento*, 12, 1961, 163ff.
——'Contributo per la storia della fortuna di Alhazen in Italia: il volgarizzamento del Ms. Vat. 4505 ed il "Commentario Terzo" del Ghiberti', in *Rinascimento*, 5, 1965, 17–49
——*Studi sulla Prospettiva Medievale*, Turin, 1965
——'La prospettiva del Brunelleschi Alhazen e Biagio Pelacani a Firenze', in *Filippo Brunelleschi. La sua opera e il suo tempo* (conference proceedings, Florence, 1977), Florence, 1980, 333–48
——'Il problema delle fonti ottiche medievali del "Commentario Terzo" di Lorenzo Ghiberti', in *Lorenzo Ghiberti nel suo tempo* (conference proceedings, Florence, 1978), II, Florence, 1980, 349–87

GAGE, J., 'Ghiberti's third Commentary and its Background', in *Apollo*, 95, 1972, 346ff.
GIOSEFFI, D., *Perspectiva Artificialis. Per la storia della prospettiva. Spigolature e appunti*, Trieste, 1957
——'Complementi di prospettiva 2.', in *Critica d'arte*, 25–6, 1958, 102–49
GIOSEFFI, D., 'Il Terzo Commentario e il pensiero prospettico', in *Lorenzo Ghiberti nel suo tempo* (conference proceedings, Florence, 1978), II, Florence, 1980, 389–405
GIOVI, G., *L'ottica di Claudio Tolomeo*, Turin, 1885

HAEFELI-TILL, D., *Constantinus Africanus, Liber de oculis*, diss., Zurich Univ., 1977
HOPPE, E., *Geschichte der Optik*, Leipzig, 1926
HYMAN, I., *Brunelleschi in Perspective*, Englewood Cliffs, N.J., 1974

KEMP, M., 'Science, Non-science and Nonsense: the Interpretation of Brunelleschi's Perspective', in *Art History*, 1, 1978, 134–41
——*The Science of Art. Optical themes in Western Art from Brunelleschi to Seurat*, New Haven and London, 1990, 36–40
KERN, G. J., 'Die Anfänge der zentral-perspektivischen Konstruktion in der italienischen Malerei des 14. Jahrhunderts', in *Mitteilungen des Kunsthistorischen Instituts in Florenz*, 2, 1912, 58–64
——'Die Entdeckung der Fluchtpunktes', in *Kunstgeschichtliche Gesellschaft*, Berlin, Sitzungbericht 1938, 14ff.
KLEIN, R., 'Pomponius Gauricus on Perspective', in *The Art Bulletin*, 43, 1961, 211–30
——'Etudes sur la perspective à la Renaissance 1956–1963', in *Bibliothèque d'Humanisme et Renaissance*, 25, 3, 1963, 577–87; and in *La Forme et l'intelligible*, Paris, 1970

LEMOINE, J. G., 'Brunelleschi et Ptolémée. Les origines géographiques de la "boîte d'optique"', in *Gazette des Beaux-Arts*, 51, 1958, 281–96
LINDBERG, D. C., 'Roger Bacon's Theory of the Rainbow: Progress or Regress', in *Isis*, 57, 1966, 235–48
——'Alhazen's Theory of Vision and its Receptions in the West', in *Isis*, 58, 1967, 321–41
——*John Peckham and the Science of Optics*, Madison and Milwaukee, 1970
——*A Catalogue of Medieval and Renaissance Manuscripts*, Toronto, 1975
——*Theories of Vision from Al-Kindi to Kepler*, Chicago, 1976

MALTESE, C., 'Ghiberti teorico: i problemi ottico-prospettici', in *Lorenzo Ghiberti nel suo tempo* (conference proceedings, Florence, 1978), II, Florence, 1980, 407–19

NICCO FASOLA, G., 'Svolgimento del pensiero prospettico nei trattati da Euclide a Piero', in *Le Arti*, 4, 1942–3, 59–71

OERTEL, R., 'Perspective and Imagination', in *Studies in Western Art: Acts of the Twentieth International Congress of the History of Art*, II, Princeton, 1963, 146–59

PARRONCHI, A., 'Le misure dell' "occhio" secondo il Ghiberti', in *Paragone. Arte*, 12, 133, 1961, 24–37; and in *Studi*, 1964, 313–48
——'Il "punctum dolens" della costruzione legittima', in *Paragone. Arte*, 145, 1962, 58–72
PECKAM, J., *Perspectiva communis*, Venice, 1504; ed. Keulen, 1593
PIERO DELLA FRANCESCA, *De Prospectiva Pingendi*, ed. G. Nicco Fasola, Florence, 1942
——*Trattato d'abaco*, ed. G. Arrighi, Pisa, 1970
La pittura in Italia. Il Quattrocento, ed. F. Zeri, I (with contributions by M. Lucco, F. Petrucci *et al.*), Milan, 1987
PRANTL, K., *Aristoteles, Physik*, Leipzig, 1854; repr. 1978

RISNER, F., *Opticae Thesaurus Alhazeni Arabis libri septem, eiusdem Liber de Crepusculis et Nubium Ascensionibus. Item Vitellionis Thuringopoloni Libri X*, Basel, 1572; New York, 1972

ROLFES, E., *Aristoteles, Parva Naturalia*, Leipzig, 1924
RONCHI, V., *Storia della luce*, Bologna, 1952
——*L'ottica scienza della visione*, Bologna, 1955
ROSS, W. D., *Aristoteles, Physica*, Oxford, 1950
——*Aristoteles, De anima*, Oxford, 1963

SCHWARTZ, H., 'The Mirror in Art', in *The Art Quarterly*, 15, 1952, 96–118
SIEGEL, R. E., *Galen on Sense Perception*, New York, 1970
SIMON, G., *Le Regard, l'être et l'apparence dans l'optique de l'Antiquité*, Paris, 1988

TEA, E., 'Witelo, prospettico del secolo XIII', in *L'Arte*, 30, 1927, 3–30
TEN DOESSCHATE, G., 'Over de Bronnen van de Derde Commentaar van Lorenzo Ghiberti', in *Tijdschrift voor Geschiedenes*, 47, 1932, 432–8
——*De Derde Commentaar van Lorenzo Ghiberti in verband met de mildeleeuwsche Optiek*, Utrecht, 1940

VAGNETTI, L., *De naturali et artificiali perspectiva*, Florence, 1979
——'Ghiberti prospettico', in *Lorenzo Ghiberti nel suo tempo* (conference proceedings, Florence, 1978), Florence, 1980, 421–34
VAN VEEN, H., 'Leon Battista Alberti and a Passage from Ghiberti's Commentaries', in *Lorenzo Ghiberti nel suo tempo* (conference proceedings, Florence, 1978), II, Florence, 1980, 343–8
VER EECKE, P., *Euclide. L'optique et la catoptrique*, Paris and Bruges, 1938

WHITE, J., 'Developments in Renaissance Perspective', in *Journal of the Warburg and Courtauld Institutes*, 12, 1949, 58–79
——*The Birth and Rebirth of Pictorial Space*, London, 1957; 1972
WIND, E., 'The Revival of Origen', in *Studies in Art and Literature for Belle Da Costa-Greene*, 1954, 412–24
WITTKOWER, R. and ARGAN, G. C., *Perspective et histoire au Quattrocento*, Paris, 1990
WOLFF, G., 'Mathematik und Malerei', in *Mathematica Bibliotheca*, 20–21, 1916

ZERVAS, D. FINIELLO, *Systems of Design and Proportion used by Ghiberti, Donatello and Michelozzo in their large-scale Sculpture-Architectural Ensembles between 1412 and 1434*, diss., Baltimore, 1976

ON FLORENCE

La Badia Fiorentina, Florence, 1982
BONSANTI, G., *La Galleria dell'Accademia di Firenze. Guida e catalogo completo*, Florence, 1987, 42 and 88

CAROCCI, G., *I dintorni di Firenze*, Florence, 1907
CECCHI, C. in, *Il centro di Firenze restituito*, ed. M. Sframeli, Florence, 1989

DAMI, L., 'La basilica di San Miniato al Monte', in *Bollettino d'arte*, 9, 1915, 217–44
DAMIANI, G., *San Niccolò Oltrarno*, Florence, 1982

GOTTI, A., *Le Gallerie di Firenze*, Florence, 1872
GURRIERI, F., 'La facciata di San Bartolomeo, ultima fatica di Michelozzo', in *La Nazione*, Florence, 6 Aug. 1969, 3
——'Il chiostro di S. Miniato al Monte', in Berti, Gurrieri and Leonardi, 1988 (above, p. 355)

LUNARDI, R., *Arte e storia in Santa Maria Novella*, Florence, 1983

MACK, C. R., 'The Building Program of the Cloister of S. Miniato', in *The Burlington Magazine*, 115, 1973, 447–8
MEONI, L., 'La chiesa di San Felice in Piazza a Firenze all'epoca del granducato mediceo', in *Annali della Fondazione di Studi di Storia dell'Arte Roberto Longhi*, 2, Pisa, 1989

NOCIONI, T. A., *La Basilica di Santa Trinita a Firenze*, Florence, 1980

ORLANDI, S. and GROSSI, I. P., *Santa Maria Novella e i suoi Chiostri Monumentali*, Florence, 1930

PAATZ, W. and PAATZ, E., *Die Kirchen von Florenz*, Frankfurt, 1940; 1952

ULLMAN, B. L. and STADTER, M. A., *The Public Library of Florence*, Padua, 1972

WOOD BROWN, J., *The Dominican Church of Santa Maria Novella at Florence: a Historical, Architectural and Artistic Study*, Edinburgh, 1902

GENERAL HISTORY

CALZOLAI, C. C., 'Il "Libro dei Morti" di Santa Maria Novella (1290–1436)', in *Memorie Domenicane*, n.s., 11, 1980, 15–218

DINI TRAVERSARI, A., *Ambrogio Traversari e i suoi tempi*, Florence, 1942

MALLETT, M., *Mercenaries and their Masters: Warfare in Renaissance Italy*, Totowa, N.J., 1974, 181–6

ORLANDI, S., 'Il Concilio Fiorentino e la residenza dei Papi in S. Maria Novella', in *Memorie domenicane*, 80, 1963, 2–3

SOMIGLI, C., 'Traversari, Ambrogio', in *Enciclopedia Cattolica*, XIII, 1954, col. 453–4
——*Un amico dei Greci: Ambrogio Traversari*, Arezzo, 1964
STINGER, C. L., *Humanism and the Church Fathers. Ambrogio Traversari (1386–1439) and Christian Antiquity in the Italian Renaissance*, New York, 1977

INDEX

Page numbers in *italics* refer to illustrations

PHOTO CREDITS

(a = above, b = below, c = centre, l = left, r = right)

THE ALLENTOWN ART MUSEUM: 348 l
AUTHOR'S ARCHIVES: 51 a, 58, 62 l, 87, 95 l, 107, 109 r, 116 l, 121 r, 123–4, 128, 130, 132, 135, 155 b, 197, 293, 295, 303, 307 b, 309, 317, 331, 334–5
BERLIN, BODEMUSEUM: 348 c
BREMEN, KUNSTHALLE: 74 r
CHAMBÉRY, MUSÉE DES BEAUX-ARTS: 347 ar
THE CLEVELAND MUSEUM OF ART: 70 l
DUBLIN, NATIONAL GALLERY OF IRELAND: 237, 314
FLORENCE, ALINARI: 47
FLORENCE, ANDREA BAZZECCHI: 60, 62 r, 109 l
FLORENCE, CASA BUONARROTI: 85
FLORENCE, SCALA: 4, 50, 51 b, 52 b, 53, 56, 69, 71–3, 74 l, 76, 77 r, 79 a, 81 l, 82, 84, 90–1, 95 r, 96–7, 101 r, 102, 110, 118–19, 120, 121 l, 144, 159, 161 a and b, 162 al, ar, cl and cr, 164 cl, cr and br, 165–8, 176, 180, 183 a, 184–6, 189–94, 204–5, 207, 209–11, 213, 226, 238–41, 245–7, 250–1, 253–5, 260–5, 296–7, 302, 306, 318–20, 330, 336, 339
KARLSRUHE, STAATLICHE KUNSTHALLE: 232–4
LILLE, MUSÉE DES BEAUX-ARTS: 88
LONDON, NATIONAL GALLERY: 48 r, 49 b, 66–7, 215, 217, 219–23, 257 b, 258, 331, 345 r
MADRID, THYSSEN-BORNEMISZA COLLECTION: 243, 333
MALIBU, J. PAUL GETTY MUSEUM: 351 l
MELBOURNE, NATIONAL GALLERY: 346
NAPLES, FRANCESCO TANASI: 54, 59, 61, 64, 68 l, 93, 104, 111, 113, 115, 125, 133–4, 155 a, 164 ar, 174, 179, 183 b, 198–9, 200–3, 312, 325
NEW YORK, THE METROPOLITAN MUSEUM OF ART: 352 r
NORFOLK, VA., CHRYSLER MUSEUM: 347 bl
OXFORD, ASHMOLEAN MUSEUM: 269–74, 341, 345 l
PARIS, BIBLIOTHÈQUE NATIONALE: 63 l, 136, 148, 323 b and r
PARIS, GIRAUDON: 48 l, 49 a, 63 r, 79 b, 81 r, 86, 92, 129, 143 b, 147 b, 323 al(b), 342
PARIS, MUSÉE JACQUEMART-ANDRÉ: 164 al and bl, 257 a
PARIS, RÉUNION DES MUSÉES NATIONAUX: 138, 145, 161 c, 162 bl and br, 224–5, 227, 229, 354
PHILADELPHIA MUSEUM OF ART: 52 a
RALEIGH, NORTH CAROLINA MUSEUM: 348 r
WASHINGTON, D.C., THE NATIONAL GALLERY OF ART: 347 al

The drawings on pp. 142 and 143 are by Dominique Chieux.